TREASURES OF INDIA

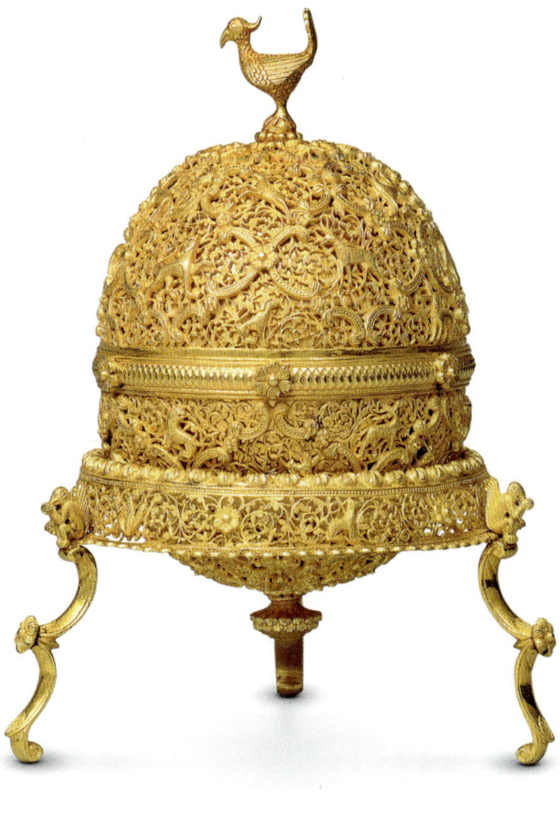

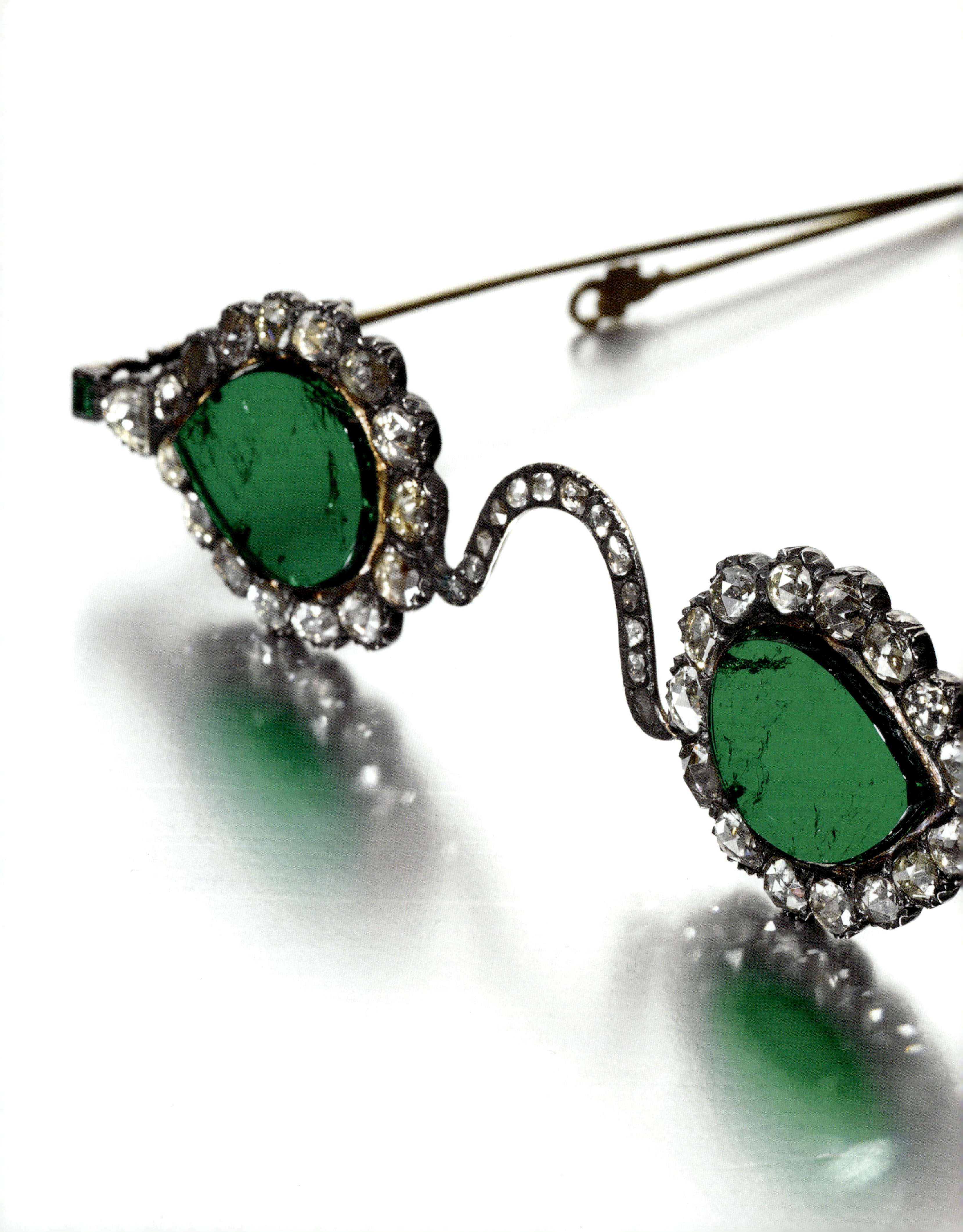

TREASURES OF INDIA

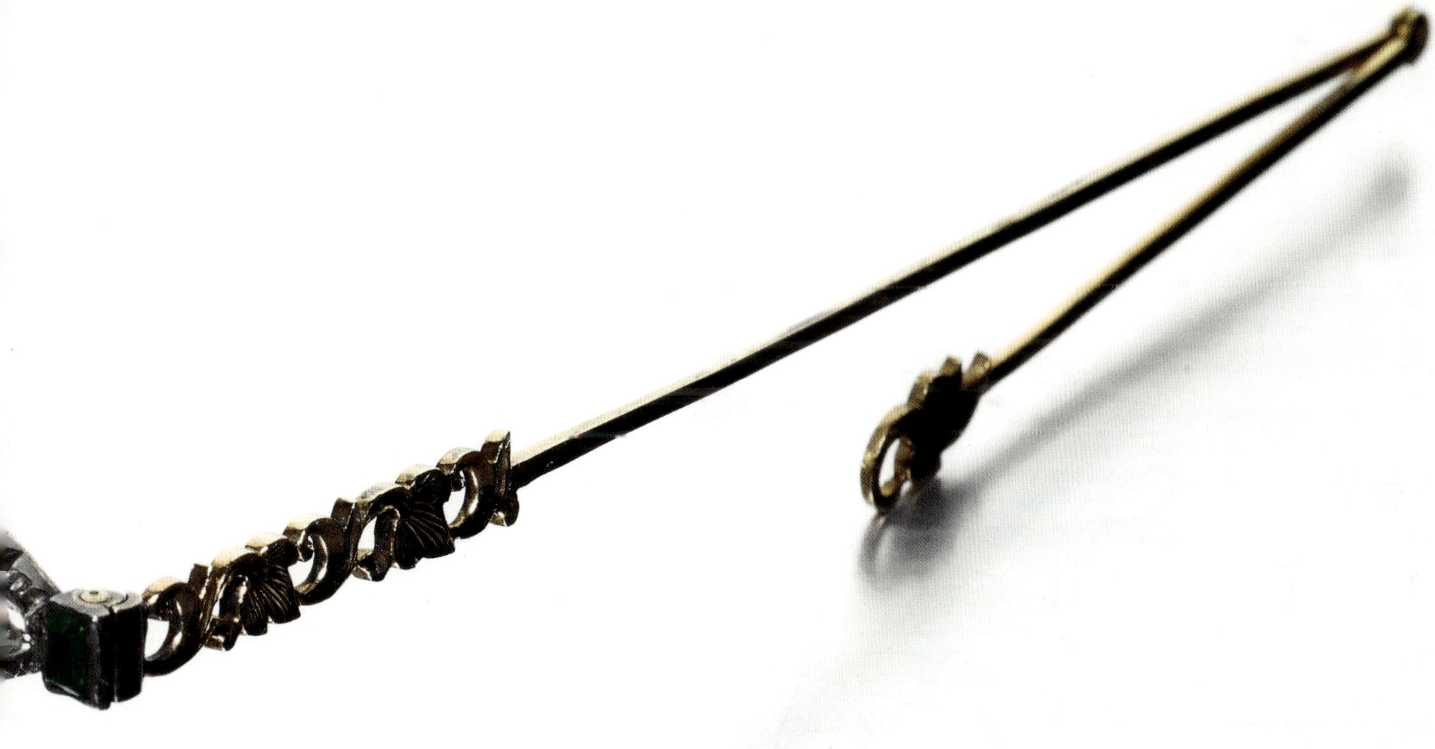

DK

DK | Penguin Random House

Editorial Team Nayan Keshan, Avanika
Senior Art Editor Devika Awasthi
Art Editor Priyal Mote
Jacket Designer Bhavika Mathur
Assistant Picture Researchers Mamta Panwar, Shubhdeep Kaur
Senior Picture Researcher Sumedha Chopra
DTP Designers Vijay Kandwal, Umesh Singh Rawat
DTP Coordinator Tarun Sharma
Pre-Production Manager Balwant Singh
Production Manager Pankaj Sharma
Picture Research Manager Taiyaba Khatoon
Managing Editor Chitra Subramanyam
Managing Art Editor Neha Ahuja Chowdhry
Managing Director, India Aparna Sharma

Consultant Ranjana Sengupta
Writers and Researchers Arushi Mathur, Madhavi Singh, Ankita Vinayak

First published in India in 2023 by
Dorling Kindersley Publishing Private Limited,
208, Ansal's Laxmi Deep
Laxmi Nagar District Centre
New Delhi 110092, India

10 9 8 7 6 5 4 3 2 1
001–334510–Jul/2023

A CIP catalogue record for this book is available from The British Library.

ISBN: 978-81-9556-591-7

Printed and bound in China

For the curious
www.dk.com

MIX
Paper | Supporting responsible forestry
FSC www.fsc.org
FSC™ C018179

This book was made with Forest Stewardship Council™ certified paper – one small step in DK's commitment to a sustainable future.
For more information go to www.dk.com/our-green-pledge

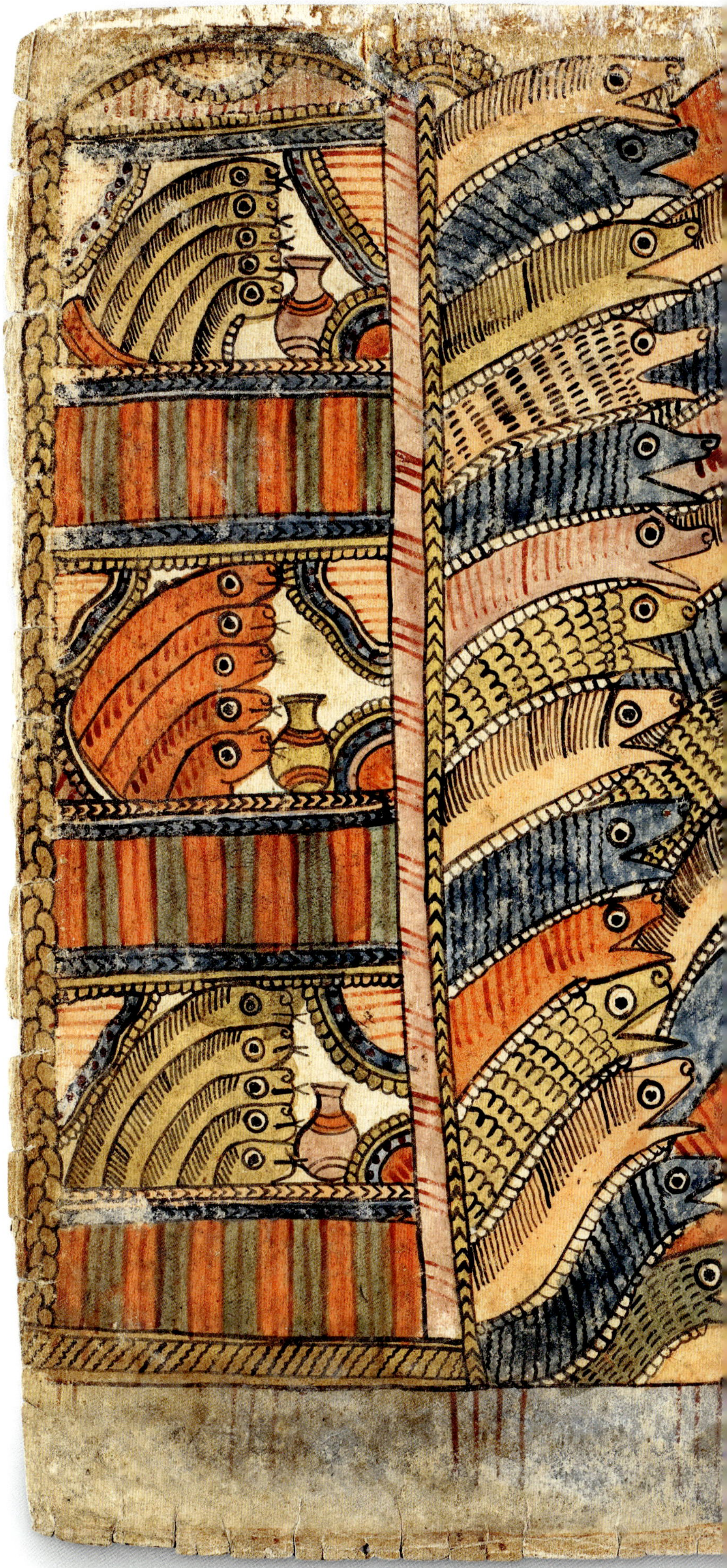

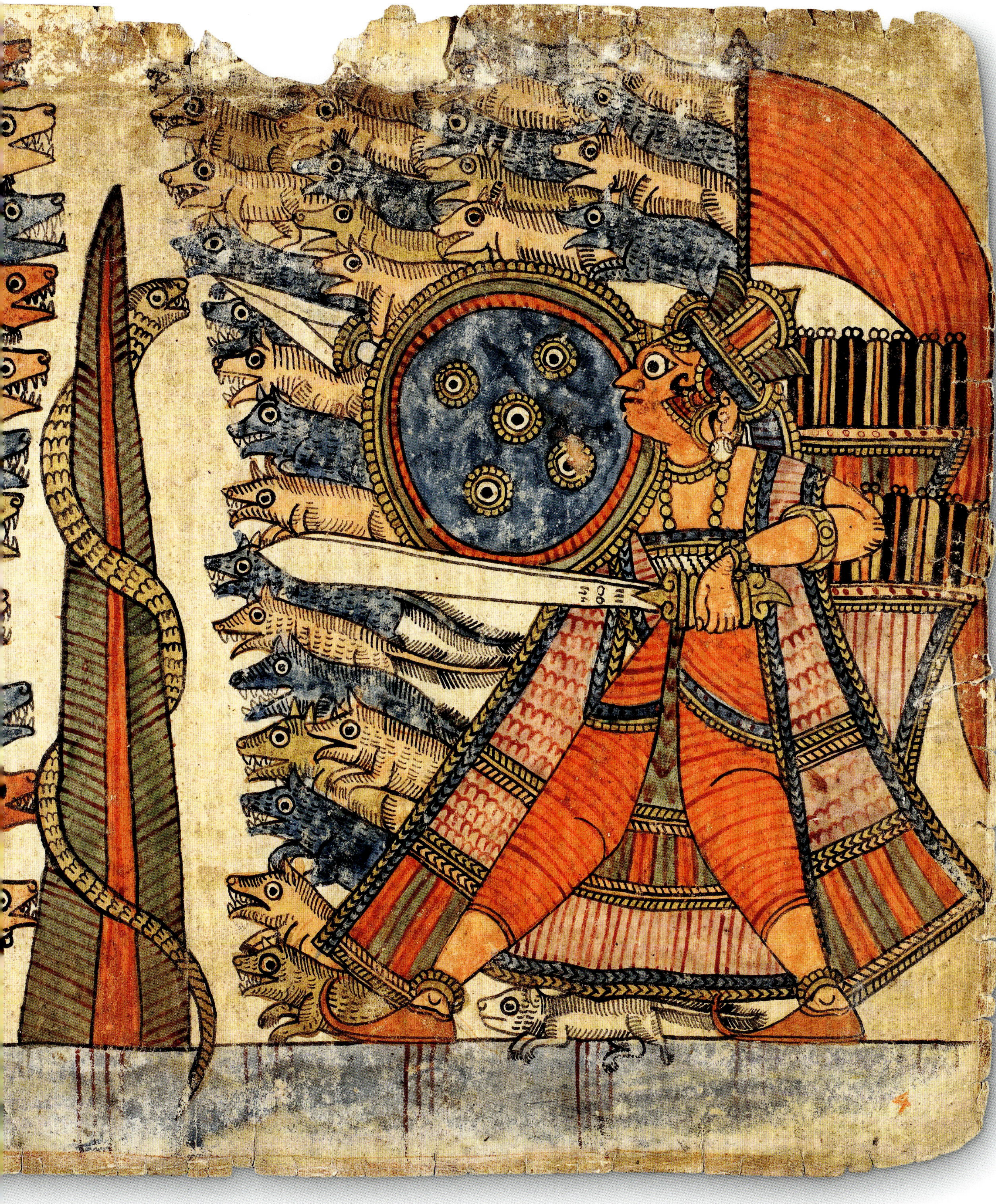

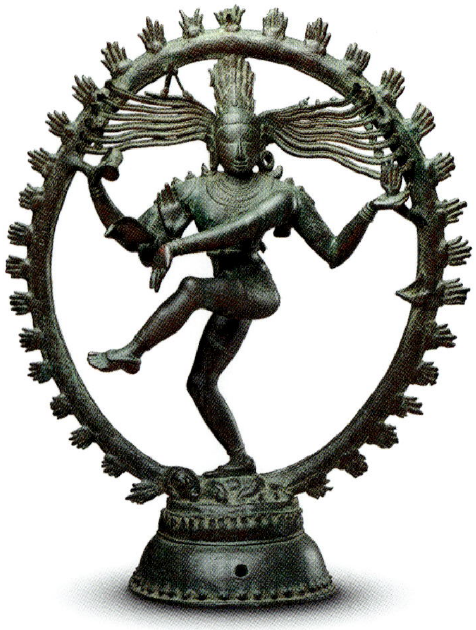
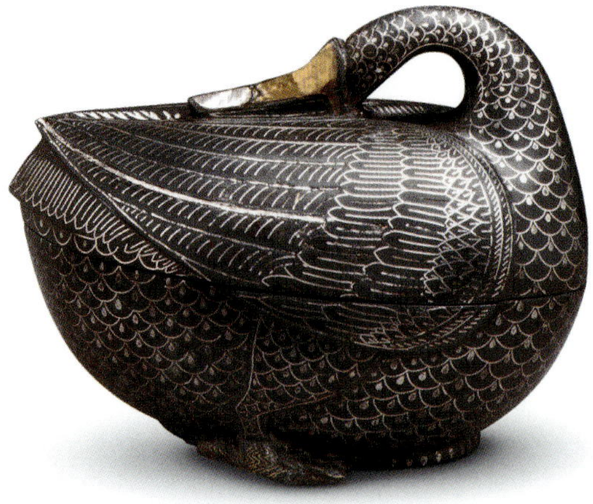
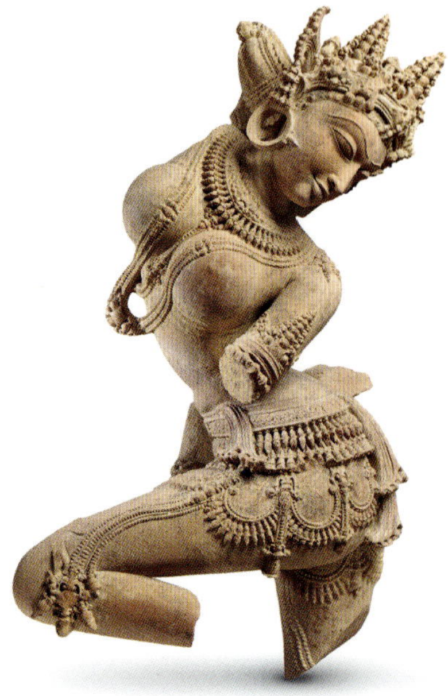

CONTENTS

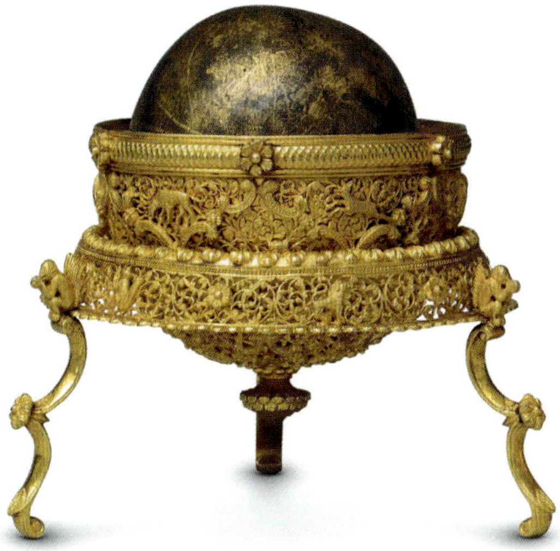
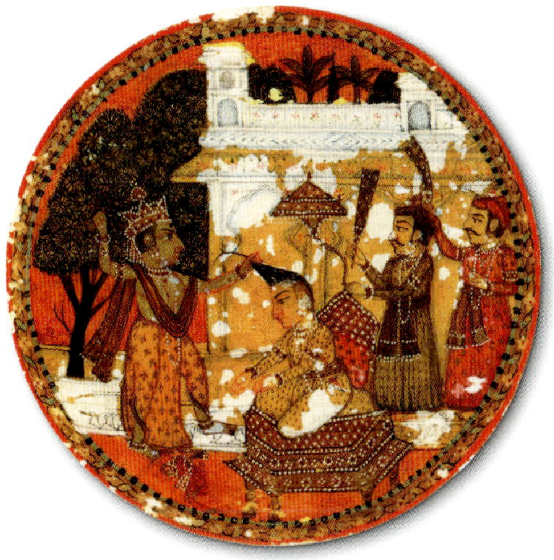
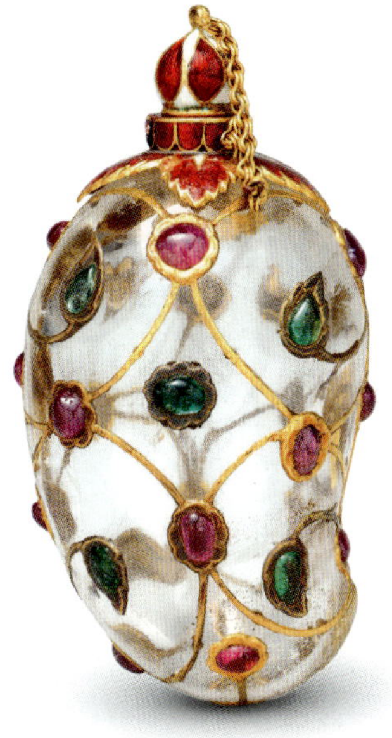

Prehistory–7th century CE

ANCIENT INDIA

The dawn of human civilization brought with it a time of exploration and discovery, and heralded an age of growth. The rock shelters at Bhimbetka, the early signs of hunting and gathering, the development of communities, the birth of religious thought, the formation of systems of leadership, and the early advancements in architecture and art, all exemplified ancient India and the circulation of ideas during this period.

EMERGENCE OF CIVILIZATION

From ancient humans to early societies

Ancient cave paintings, shards of pottery, jewellery, statues, and epics that continue to be studied and revered, illustrate not just the emergence and evolution of civilizations but also the transition from early settlements to urban centres that took place over the course of a million years.

The earliest history of the Indian subcontinent begins millions of years ago, when the giant supercontinent Pangaea broke off from the southern part, Gondwanaland, and moved northwards. It finally collided with Laurasia, the Asian mainland, about 50 million years ago. The edges of the Asian landmass bore the impact to form the Himalayas, the youngest and the tallest mountains on earth.

THE FIRST PEOPLES

The earliest people in the subcontinent lived a nomadic lifestyle in small groups and used stone tools. Evidence of this has been found across India with the excavation of Palaeolithic sites in the Shivalik and Vindhya mountain ranges, as well as in modern-day Rajasthan, Gujarat, Delhi, and northern Karnataka. The rock paintings and engravings of Bhimbetka and the Daraki-Chattan caves in Madhya Pradesh provide a glimpse into the lives of the people who inhabited these sites.

Changes in climate, flora, and fauna as well as living patterns map the transition to the Neolithic Age. Evidence from Madhya Pradesh and Rajasthan dating back to c. 4500 BCE indicates the emergence of permanent settlements, domesticated animals, cultivation, and the use of fire. The invention of the wheel transformed life; it was used for pottery, transport, and spinning of yarn.

c. 300 MYA Pangaea supercontinent

c. 200 MYA Gondwana splits from Pangaea

c. 3.8–2 MYA Earliest evidence of use of stone tools

c. 1.5 MYA Earliest human-made tools in South Asia

c. 130,000 YA Tools become more refined

c. 75,000 YA Modern humans first appear in India

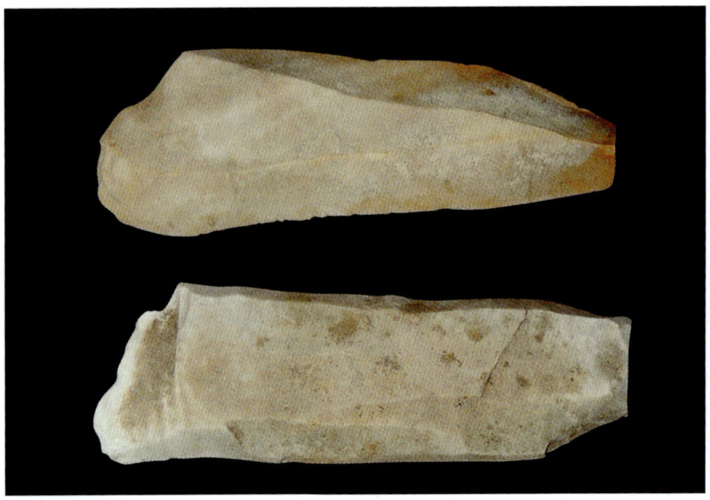

These flint stones from south India, dating to the Upper Palaeolithic period, were one of the many types of implements used to make smaller stone tools and start fires.

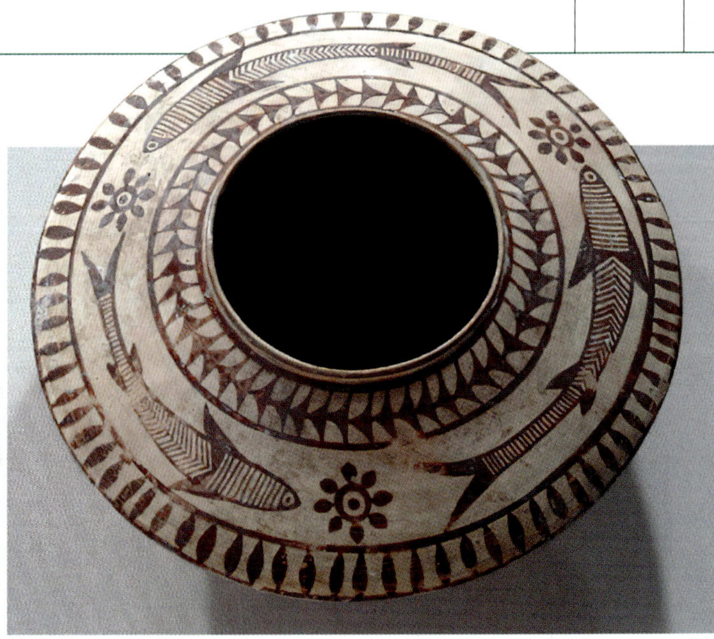

This pot, painted with geometric, floral, and animal motifs, gives evidence to the earliest urban settlements developed in South Asia, from the edge of the Indus plain, at Mehrgarh in the 7th millennium BCE.

The first signs of the use of wheel in India date to c. 3000–2500 BCE. The earliest known communities that used the wheel have been found in Balochistan (in modern-day Pakistan), with similar communities appearing shortly after in the Gangetic plain and the Deccan plateau.

The last of the three periods of the Stone Age, the Neolithic period or New Stone Age saw communities initiate an epoch which eventually culminated around 500 BCE, when the pre-formation of urbanization and civilization was completed. Gradually, the Stone Age matured into the use of metals, ushering in the Bronze Age, and civilization, as we recognize it today.

BEGINNINGS ON THE INDUS

In the early 1920s, archaeological excavations in the Punjab and Sindh region revealed the remains of a highly developed urban culture, which date back to 3000–1750 BCE and existed around the same time as the civilizations of Egypt, China, and Mesopotamia. Known as the Indus Valley Civilization or the Harappan Culture, so named after the Indus River and the first site that was discovered respectively, was made of large and small cities with impressive towns, markets, and houses. More than a thousand urban cultures dotted the northern subcontinent. Mohenjo Daro and Harappa were the first and the biggest settlements of the Indus Valley

c. 34,000–24,000 YA Settlements shift from cave dwellings to primitive huts

c. 7000 BCE Earliest urbanism in Balochistan

c. 6000 BCE Humans domesticate animals and hunt wild ones

c. 4000 BCE Potter's wheel imported from West Asia and pottery flourishes

c. 3000 BCE Cultivation of rice, mainly in the Gangetic valley, begins

c. 2600 BCE First great cities of the Indus Valley Civilization emerge

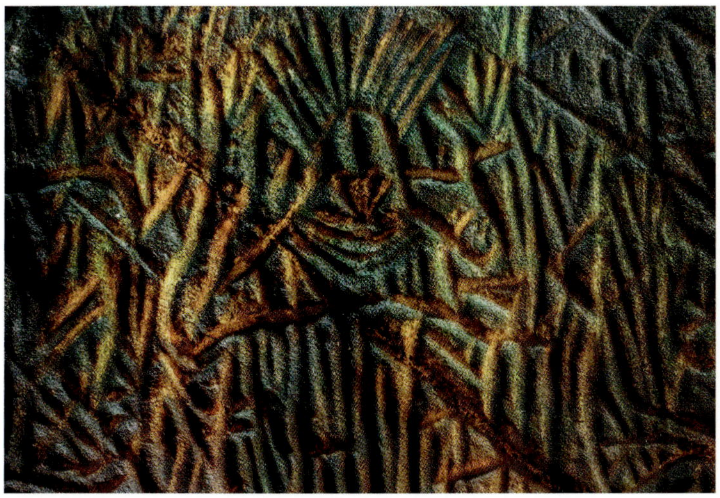

Petroglyph from a large prehistoric rock shelter at Edakkal in Kerala. These engravings or carvings are believed to date back to the Stone Age.

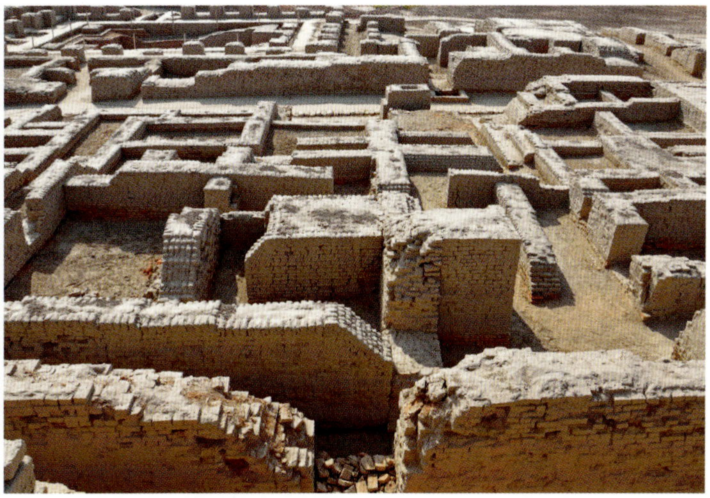

Ruins of the residential quarter of Mohenjo Daro, built on a grid pattern with main streets parallelly divided into neat rectangular blocks. These show that the city was carefully planned.

Civilization. Other important sites include Kalibangan in Rajasthan, Ropar in Haryana, Lothal and Dholavira in Gujarat, and Lurewala and Ganeriwala in Cholistan (in modern-day Pakistan).

The Indus Valley Civilization was distinguished by its system of town planning. Both Harappa and Mohenjo Daro had a citadel, a walled, high, mud-brick site with structures such as a public bath, a granary, and an assembly hall, which was probably inhabited by the ruling classes. A walled residential area (Lower Town) below the citadel was occupied by the common people. Brick houses were laid out in a grid pattern with right-angled streets and lanes. Each house had several rooms, a courtyard, bathrooms, and drains; some even had wells to draw water from. The bricks, sun-dried or baked, were standardized in a 1:2:4 ratio. All were orderly and symmetrical, expressing the emphasis given to uniformity for the civilization.

Historians have pieced together a vibrant picture of Harappan society and culture through archaeological evidence. Some assert that there may have been a strong, central rule and the rulers were either religious priests, kings, or merchants. However, the absence of supporting religious structures rejects this notion. They were a trading people with goods being exchanged within their territory as well as over long distances, such as Afghanistan, Iran, and Iraq. Goods were transported using ox carts, donkeys, and boats. Harappan crafts were advanced and ceramics, jewellery, tools, and toys were made for export. They produced pottery in grey and buff, or red and black. The Harappans, it is believed, wore clothes made of cotton and wool and adorned themselves with jewellery made of beads, silver, gold, shell, and terracotta. Fertility and female figures featured heavily in Harappan religious practices and they cremated or buried their dead. People hunted wild animals and domesticated livestock as well as kept dogs and cats as pets.

What became of the Harappans is shrouded in mystery. By 2000 BCE, a 600-year-long decline started and many settlements were abandoned, but not destroyed, as people moved eastwards and southwards to form newer settlements.

Historians have posited many theories around the decline of the Indus Valley Civilization. Some connect it to an Aryan invasion from the north, an event that carries little archaeological credibility. Another idea blamed drastic climate change, especially the recurrent flooding of the area around Mohenjo Daro, but the climate conditions seem to have changed much before

c. 2600–1000 BCE Indus script

c. 2600–600 BCE Chalcolithic cultures emerge in the subcontinent

c. 2500–1500 BCE Copper Hoard Culture of Indo-Gangetic plain

c. 2450–2220 BCE Earliest signs of cotton weaving and silk spinning in South Asia

c. 2000 BCE onwards Wide use of black-and-red ware

c. 2000–1500 BCE Migrations of Indo-European speakers into India

c. 2000–500 BCE Composition and compilation of the Vedic corpus

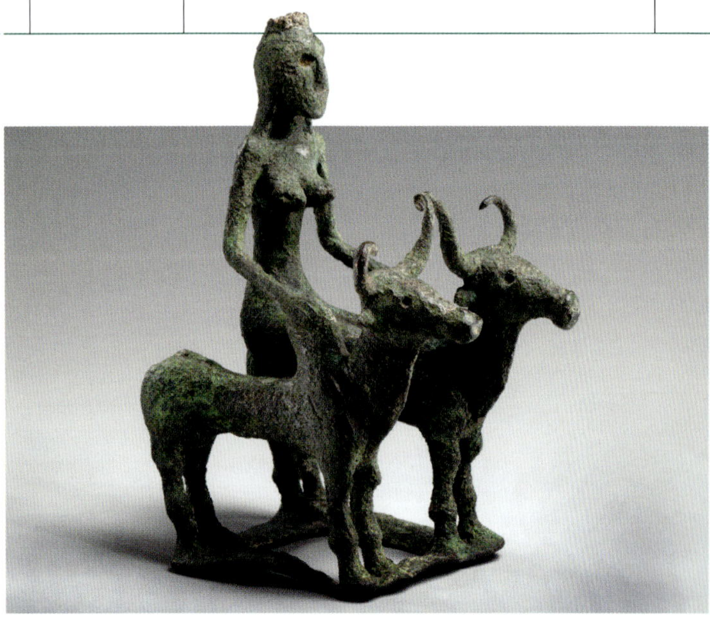

This figure of a woman riding two bulls from the late Indus Valley Civilization belongs to the early Bronze Age. It evidences the use of domesticated animals and points to farming practices in Harappa.

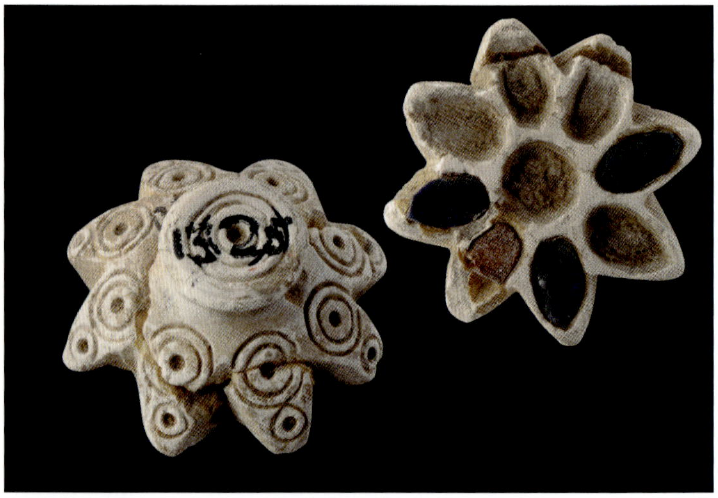

A star-shaped ear ornament from the Indus Valley, featuring coloured inlays on one side and concentric circles on the other. Such jewellery points to the earliest ornamentation needs.

the abandonment. Perhaps, it is fair to suggest that a combination of reasons determined the decline of the Harappan cities. Since the civilization was spread over a large area, it is possible that there may not have been a single cause and the particulars could have varied over different regions.

THE AGE OF THE VEDAS

By 1500 BCE, cities may have disappeared from the Indus plains, but rural settlements sprung up in the Indus and the Gangetic plains. There are no ruined cities, monuments, or stone inscriptions; however, some tools, broken pots, and extant texts, such as the Vedas, offer an insight into their lives. Historians combine these sources to reconstruct aspects of what is known as the Vedic age.

The word *veda* means to know and the Vedas consist of four kinds of compositions - the *Samhitas* (collections of verses), the *Brahmanas* (exegeses of the rituals), the *Aranyakas* (forest treatises), and the *Upanishads* (philosophical discourses) which were in prose and in verse. It is believed that a group of people known as the Aryans who migrated from Central Asia composed the Vedas. They spoke a version of the Indo-European languages and came from a mixed pastoral and agricultural economy. While the Rig Vedic religion worshipped nature gods, such as Indra, the god of thunder, or Agni, the god of fire, the deities of the later Vedic period were more complex, including Brahma, Vishnu, and Shiva. The Vedas make no mention of any religious idols or temples, and no physical evidence has been found either.

The Vedic society was based on a caste system, which initially formed around occupations, but soon became hereditary and rigid. At the apex were the *brahmins* or priests, followed by the *kshatriyas* (rulers or warriors), the *vaishyas* (farmers and traders), and *shudras* (servants and labourers). Each tribe or group of tribes had a territory for agricultural cultivation. Iron and copper implements were used and non-agricultural occupations, such as carpenters, potters, and metalsmiths, existed as well.

As the Aryan people and Vedic culture moved across the Indian subcontinent, intermingling with local religious practices, a pantheistic, vibrant religion and society emerged. About 3000 years ago, the epics, the Ramayana and the Mahabharata were composed, which remain an extremely important part of Vedic culture.

c. 1900 BCE Decline of the Indus Valley Civilization

c. 1800–1000 BCE Clearing of forests for agriculture by the Aryans

c. 1700 BCE Existence of the horse and Bactrian camel in Balochistan

c. 1000 BCE Neolithic cultures in various parts of the subcontinent

c. 1000–300 BCE Iron Age culture in southern India

c. 700 BCE Earliest of the *Upanishads* orally compiled.

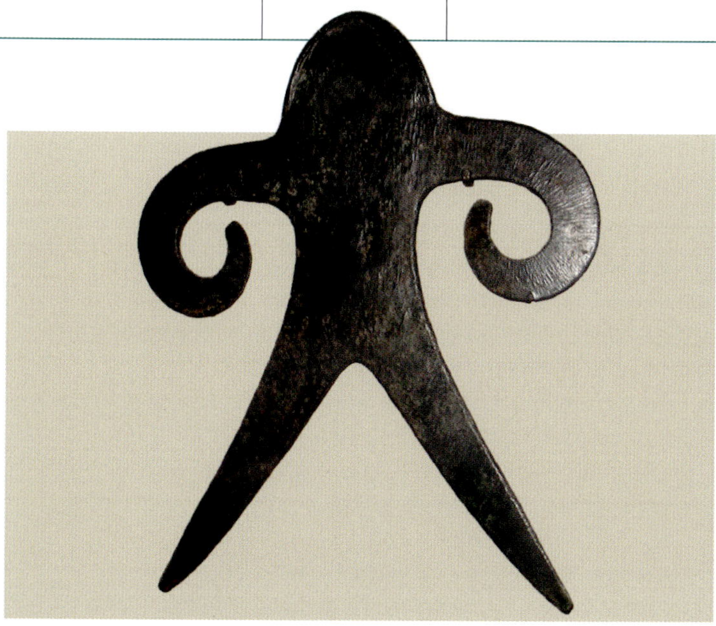

An anthropomorph copper tool, dating back to c.1000 BCE, from the Copper Hoard Culture, or the period that followed the Harappan Civilization.

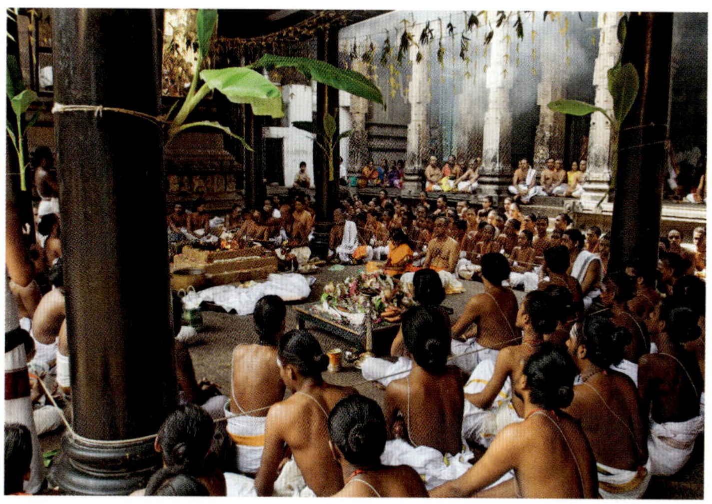

A continued Vedic practice, a *yagna* or a ritual being performed in front of a sacred fire, accompanied with the chanting by a head priest and his disciples.

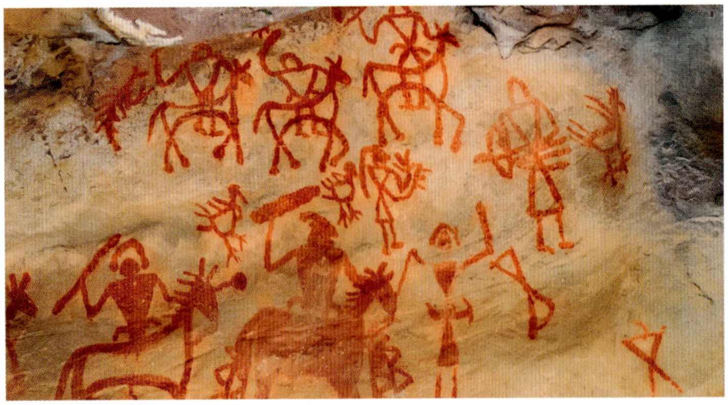

Painting of a hunting scene from one of the nearly 700 caves at Bhimbetka depicting male and female figures with domesticated animals and weapons.

Era 10,000–2000 BCE | **Medium** Natural pigments

BHIMBETKA CAVE PAINTINGS

Chronicles of the evolution of humans

Deep in the jungles of central India, the weathered sandstone rocks of the Vindhyachal range provide a glimpse into the lives and the changing times of the hunter-gatherers of the Stone Age that it sheltered. Over five of the more than 700 rock shelters around Bhimbetka contain paintings of remarkable narrative vitality.

The earliest paintings introduce a time when the jungle was dominant. The nomadic hunter-gatherers had a deep understanding of the wildlife surrounding them and the paintings reflect this, not only in anatomical accuracy but in the capturing of movement and mood. Animals such as lions and monkeys are shown individually and in groups, grazing, hunting, or being hunted. Other scenes detail how flowers and fruits were picked. In a poignant scene, a family mourns over a child, while another captures the joyful stamping of feet as dancers circle a drummer.

A TURNING POINT

The transitional period towards a sedentary civilization produced fewer paintings that were not as detailed. Hunter-gatherer groups had begun to settle and change. The human figure drawings were larger and made with more precision in contrast to the stick-figure representation in earlier paintings. Domestic animals were demonstrated grazing placidly under the protective eye of humans, while wild animals were not as prolific.

Later paintings, dated to the historical period of India, are even more human-centric, depicting riders on caparisoned elephants and horses, processions, battle scenes, archers, and soldiers armed with shield, sword, and dagger. Clothing is detailed and male and female figures are differentiated; gods, goddesses, and religious motifs such as the *trishul* (trident) can be seen. Wildlife does not intrude at all. The style and expressive fluidity of the earlier art, rooted in an immediate connect with its subject, could be observed to have been transformed.

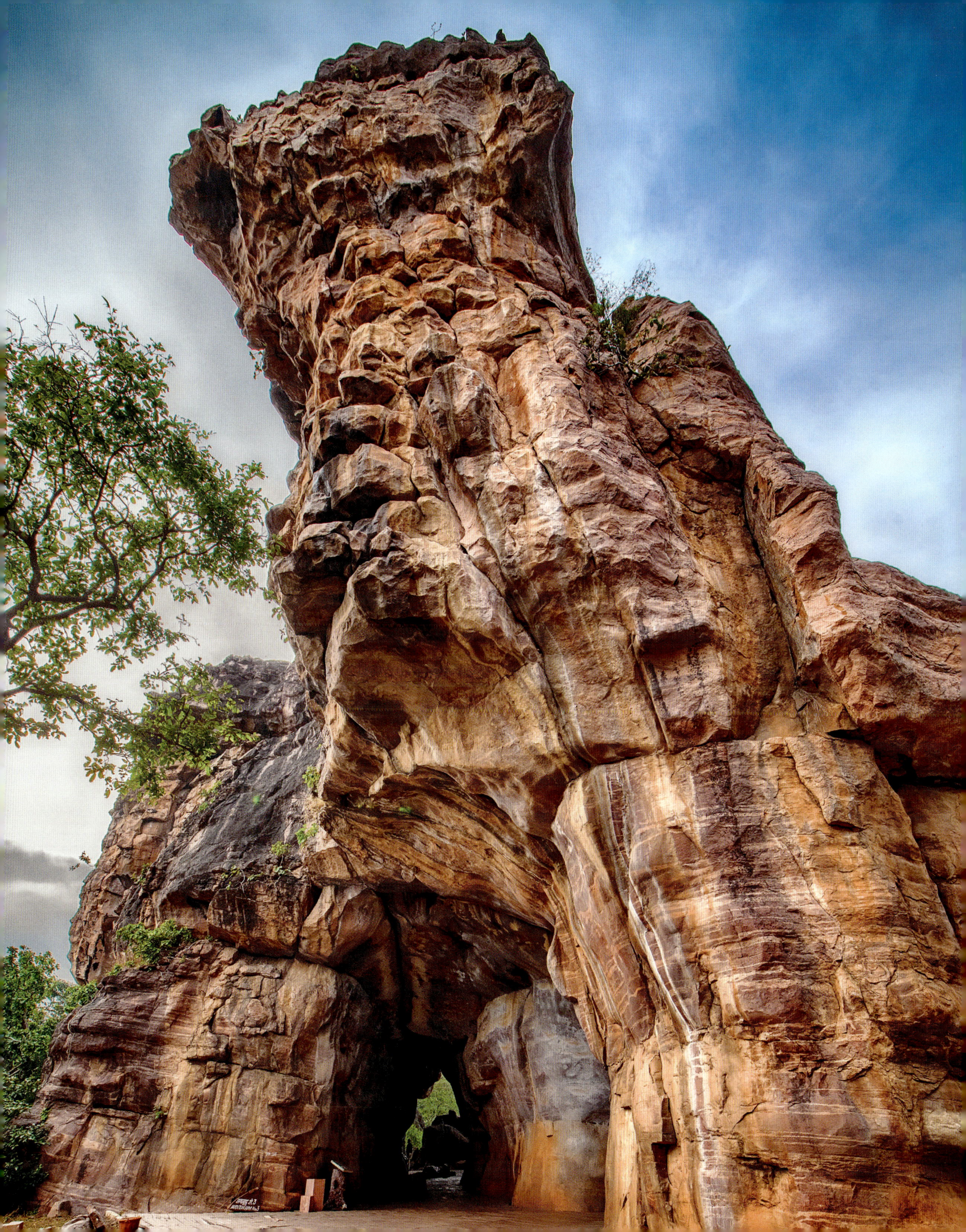

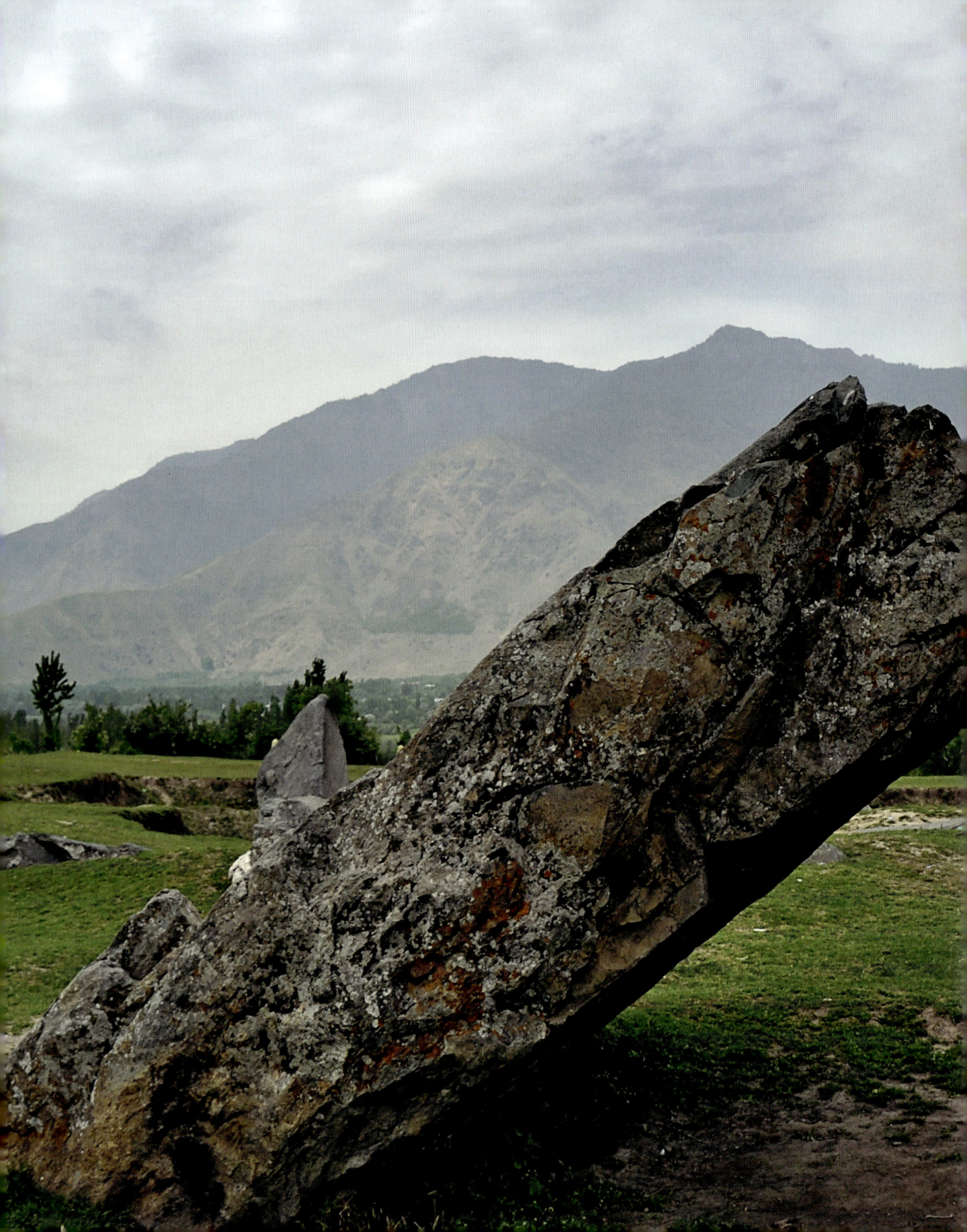

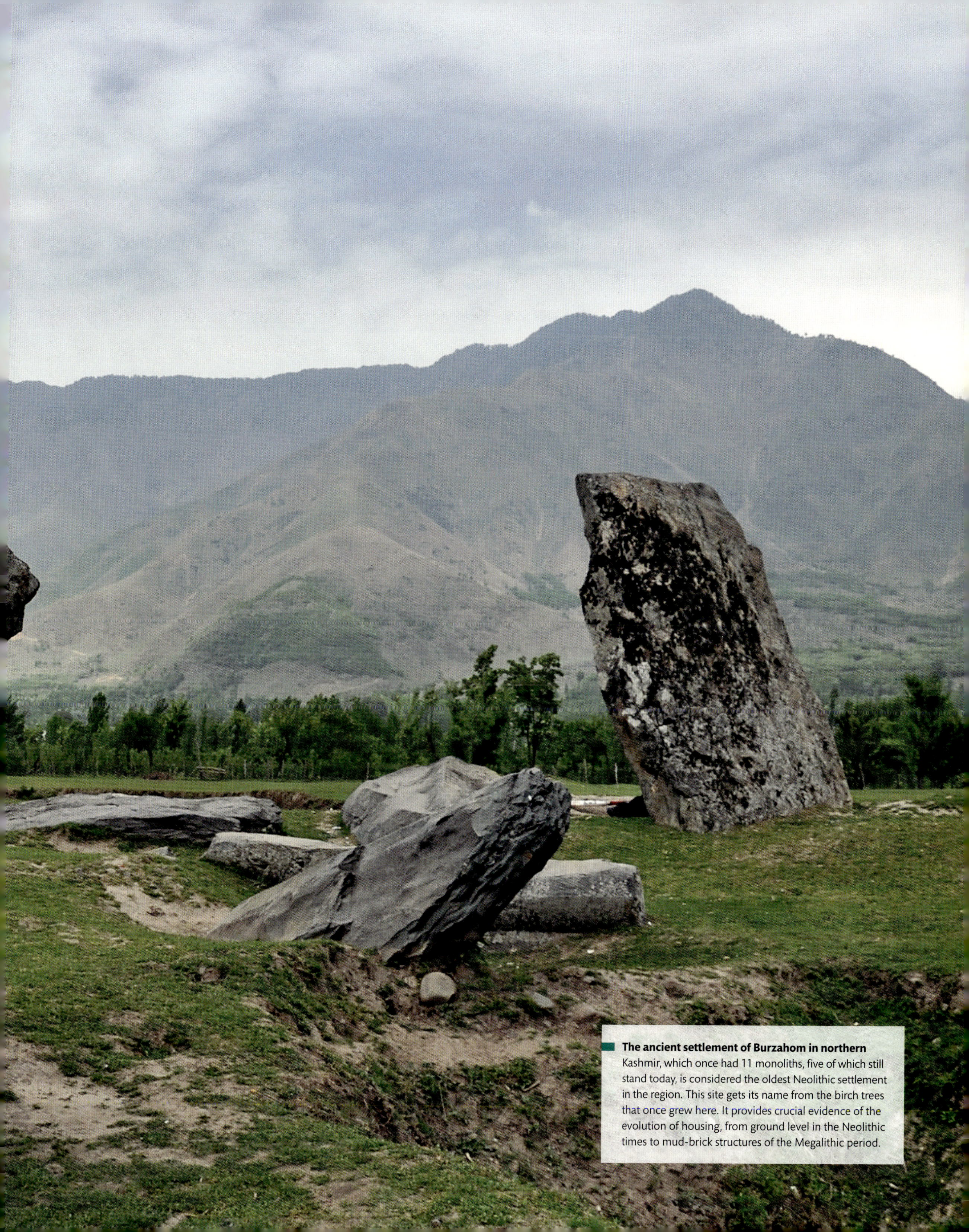

The ancient settlement of Burzahom in northern Kashmir, which once had 11 monoliths, five of which still stand today, is considered the oldest Neolithic settlement in the region. This site gets its name from the birch trees that once grew here. It provides crucial evidence of the evolution of housing, from ground level in the Neolithic times to mud-brick structures of the Megalithic period.

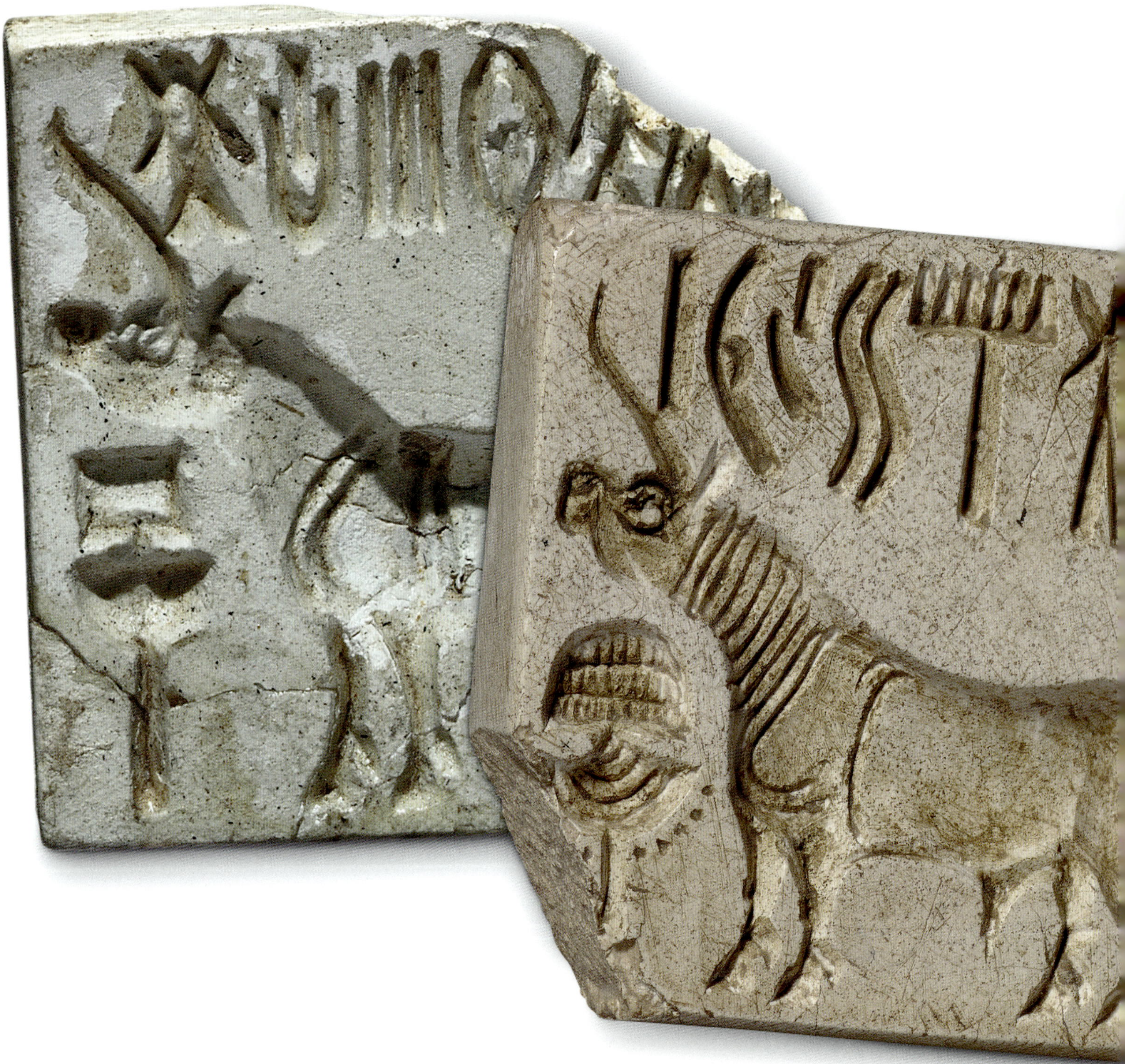

Some of the best known Indus Valley artefacts are the seals. Small, flat, usually ¾ to 1½-inch rectangles, they depict a variety of animal, human, as well as composite figures, and often carry an inscription. They were made of steatite or faience and were probably used to stamp wet clay and seal packages with rope. Sack imprints on the rear indicate that they may have sealed bundles of cotton textiles and other exported merchandise.

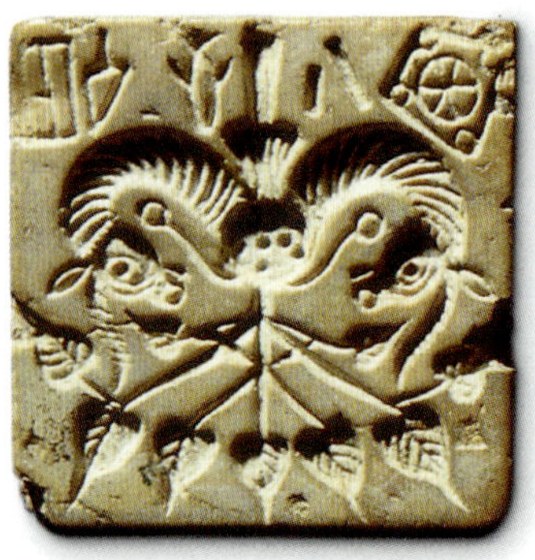

◄ **Sacred tree and the unicorn**
This seal from Mohenjo Daro, depicts a pipal tree *(Ficus religiosa)*, presumably venerated by the Indus people, flanked by two unicorns.

Era c. 3300–1700 BCE | **Medium** Steatite | **Dimension** 3.5 × 3.6 cm (1.3 × 1.4 in)

UNICORN SEAL

Simple yet powerful representations of a mythological animal

Among the most prolific artefacts from the Indus Valley Civilization are seals. Over 2,000 have been unearthed, a majority of which feature a single-horned bovid – popularly known as the unicorn. These seals intrigue archaeologists, who believe they may be key to understanding the social structure of the ancient civilization.

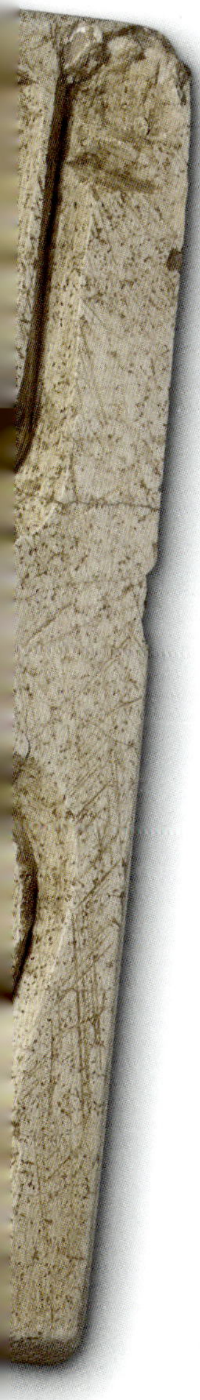

The focus of the unicorn seal is the powerful, elongated body and beautifully arched neck of a creature, identified by the single horn that curves out of its forehead as a unicorn. The tail ends in a bushy tuft and the strong, slender legs have bovine hooves. Additional folds, natural or indicative of a collar or a blanket, cover the neck and shoulders. The object in front of the animal has been identified as a ritual offering stand, with what looks like a bowl with a circular cylinder placed above it. An inscription, which is yet to be deciphered, runs across the top of the seal.

MANY AND MORE

Within this broad template, there are stylistic variations that are common to seals found at a particular site: the shape of the horn and whether it appears smooth, spiral, or ringed, the shape of the ears and eyes, the number and placement of incisions that mark the folds on the neck and shoulder, the form of the altar-like object. It is these that archaeologists look to for clues on the ancient civilization.

The remarkable uniformity of the unicorn seal, over time as well as locations where they have been found, suggests a standardization, indicating control over production despite the vast landscape the civilization covered. This means that the Indus Valley townships were connected to each other through a well-developed transportation system, enabling a free flow of art and trade. This also means that the seals were an important symbol of authority or standard. The variations could mean that there were different centres or artisans allowed to produce the seals, or different levels of authorization, and perhaps different elites who used them.

This is supported by the fact that the variations in style and detail are not random but can be divided into groups. These groups rise in number over different periods of the civilization and tell a story of a dynamic, vibrant society.

◄ **Originally found in the cities of the Indus Valley,** such seals and countless others can now be seen in museums across the world, including National Museum in Delhi, India.

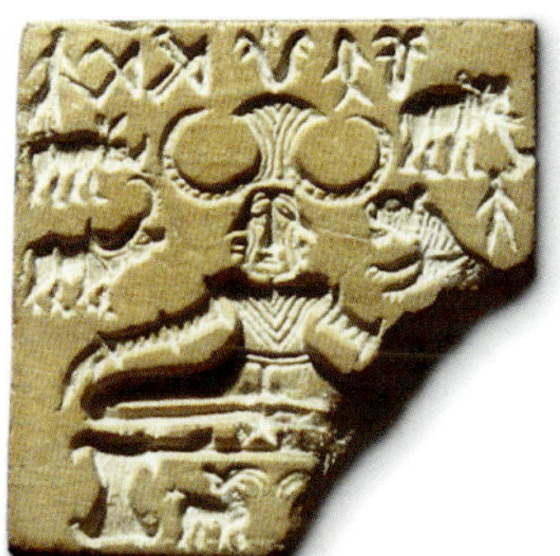

◄ **Proto-Shiva seal**
This seal from Mohenjo Daro depicts a three-faced deity in a yogic position, adorning a trident headdress, surrounded by a bull, rhino, elephant, and tiger. It has been suggested by historians that he is a precursor of the Hindu god, Shiva.

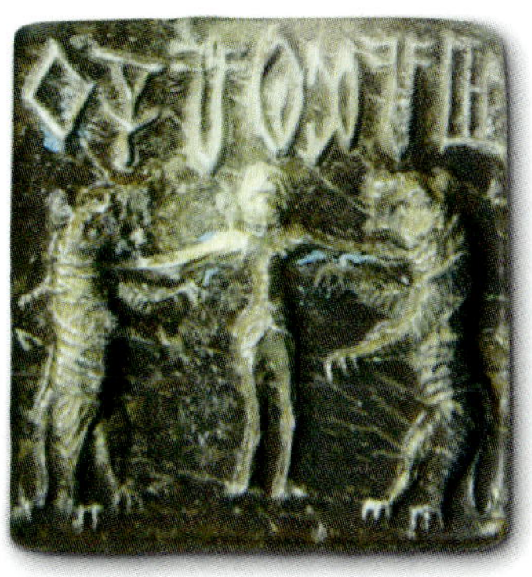

◄ **Mythological scene**
Some seals depict a deity in the centre, a female one perhaps, wrestling two tigers, as seen here in this seal from Mohenjo Daro, while others feature a half-tiger, half-goddess composite figure.

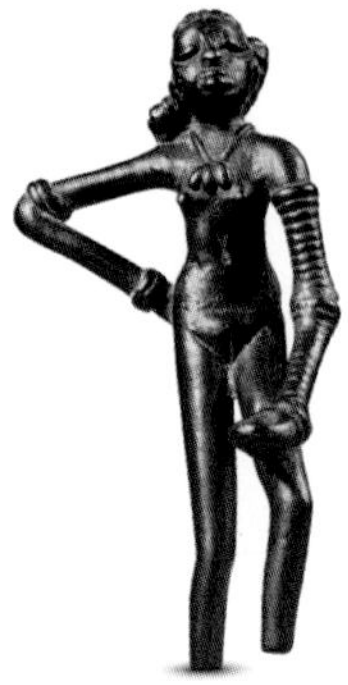

Era c. 2500 BCE | **Medium** Bronze | **Height** 10.8 cm (4 in)

DANCING GIRL

A vivacious symbol of a glorious civilization

Small enough to fit in the palm of a hand, utterly confident and not without a touch of impudence, the Dancing Girl is often referred to by archaeologists as the most captivating piece of art from an Indus Valley site.

She is young, probably no more than 15, and though her face still shows a trace of fat, her body is long and slim. Her right hand is adorned with an armband and four bangles; her left hand is ringed with 25 bangles all the way from shoulder to wrist. She stands nude, totally relaxed, self-possessed, with her head slightly bent back, knees flexed, and one arm on a hip, in the pose of a dancing girl, which gives the statuette its name. Her chin is slightly raised with a slight smile on her lips.

SOPHISTICATED MODELLING

Found in a house at the archaeological site of Mohenjo Daro, in present-day Pakistan, during the 1926 excavations, this is one of the two works of figurative art in bronze from Indus Valley that is realistically posed. The statuette is significant in the sophistication of creation. It reveals the civilization's technical achievements and intricate knowledge and understanding of metallurgy, metal blending, and casting. The use of metal was unusual for this object, as most of the many figurines from Indus Valley sites were made of fired clay. The lost-wax process, which is how the Dancing Girl was made, required the artist to create a detailed wax model of the sculpture. This model was then covered with a clay coating and fired. As the wax melted and drained away through holes left specifically for that purpose, a hollow mould was left into which molten metal was poured. Once cool, the clay was chipped away for the solid metal statue to be revealed and finished.

IS SHE DANCING?

There is no real evidence that she is dancing; nothing to indicate that she was an entertainer other than the skill of the craftsman. And even though the figure has lost her feet due to damage, the distinct sense of her arrested movement cannot be denied.

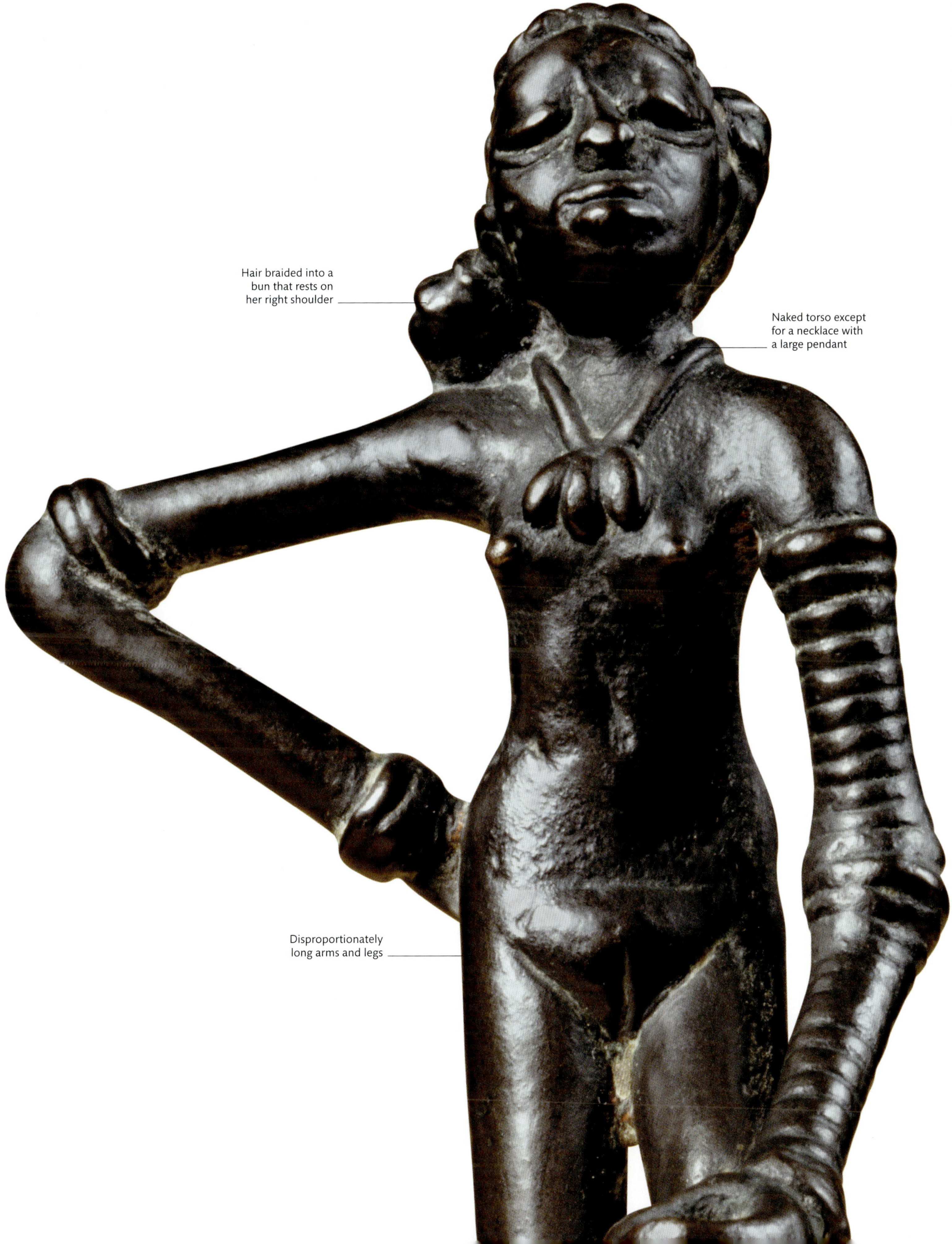
Hair braided into a bun that rests on her right shoulder
Naked torso except for a necklace with a large pendant
Disproportionately long arms and legs

c.3300–1700 BCE

HARAPPAN CULTURE MATERIALS

Excavations of the cities of Indus Valley have yielded considerable evidence of aesthetic activity. The pottery, statues, and architecture provide insights into the lives, minds, and beliefs of the inhabitants.

The Harappan Culture points to an outstanding application of different materials and methods in the production of objects. The cities had long, straight roads, an excellent drainage system, soak pits for sewage disposal, and demarcated residential areas. The conformity in layouts speaks of a degree of standardization maintained over, what were in ancient times, significant distances. This insight is underlined by the perfect ratio, 4:2:1, of the baked bricks used in construction, as well as the uniform system of weights and measures. Hexahedron weights for measuring mass ensured fair exchange in the marketplace of a bustling economy.

Standardization over distance also implies a well-developed system of transport and communication. The oxcarts – terracotta toys clearly detail their design – may well have been the first wheeled transport ever to be used. In addition to facilitating interaction, they would have transported raw material: gold from what is now Rajasthan, fuchsite from Karnataka, amethyst from Maharashtra, turquoise and lapis lazuli from Iran, and jade from Central Asia.

"The cities were centres for the production of crafted items that were traded both overland and across the seas."

– Romila Thapar, *The Penguin History of Early India*, 2002

A TREASURE TROVE OF INNOVATION

Evidence suggests that new techniques in metallurgy evolved; copper, bronze, lead, and tin were produced and used to make tools and implements. Gold and silver were less frequently used, gold was mostly utilized in small ornaments such as beads and pendants. Ornaments, beads, and combs in a range of materials such as faience, shell, ivory, pearl and, of particular beauty, carnelian, have been excavated. Lapis lazuli, turquoise, and alabaster were imported from present-day Iran and Afghanistan; jade came from China. Pottery was mass produced but of fine quality, expertly thrown on the wheel and then fired. A number of artefacts in faience, as well as handmade terracotta figurines, ornaments, and toys – ox carts, cattle that nod their heads, monkeys that scramble up a string – were unearthed.

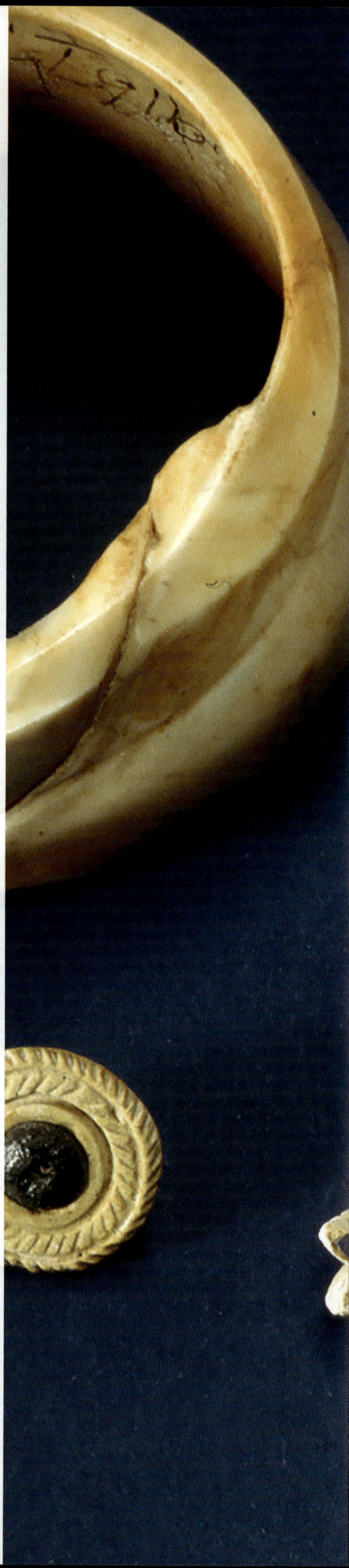

► **Different ornaments from the Indus** Valley displayed at the National Museum in New Delhi, including bangles of shell and faience.

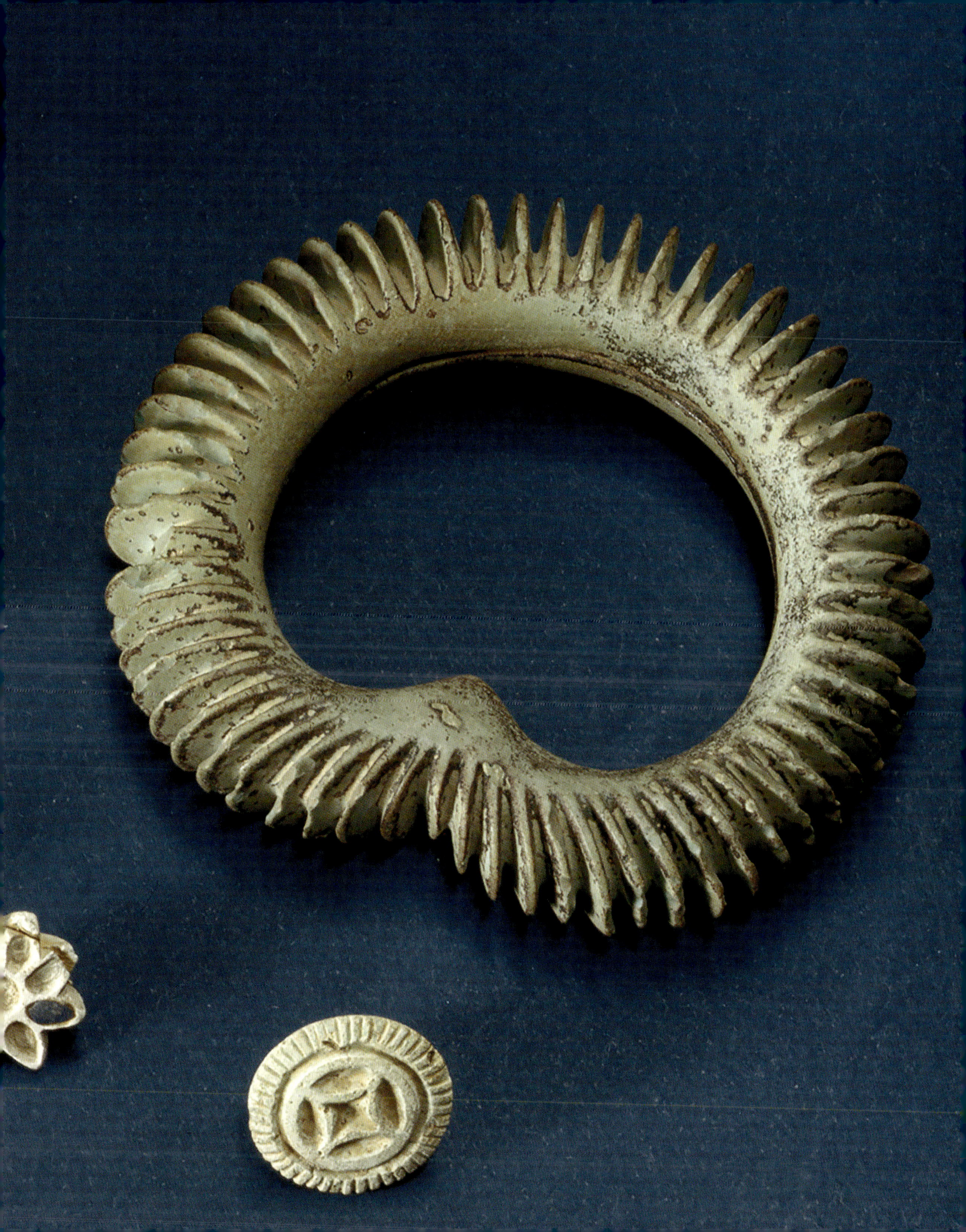

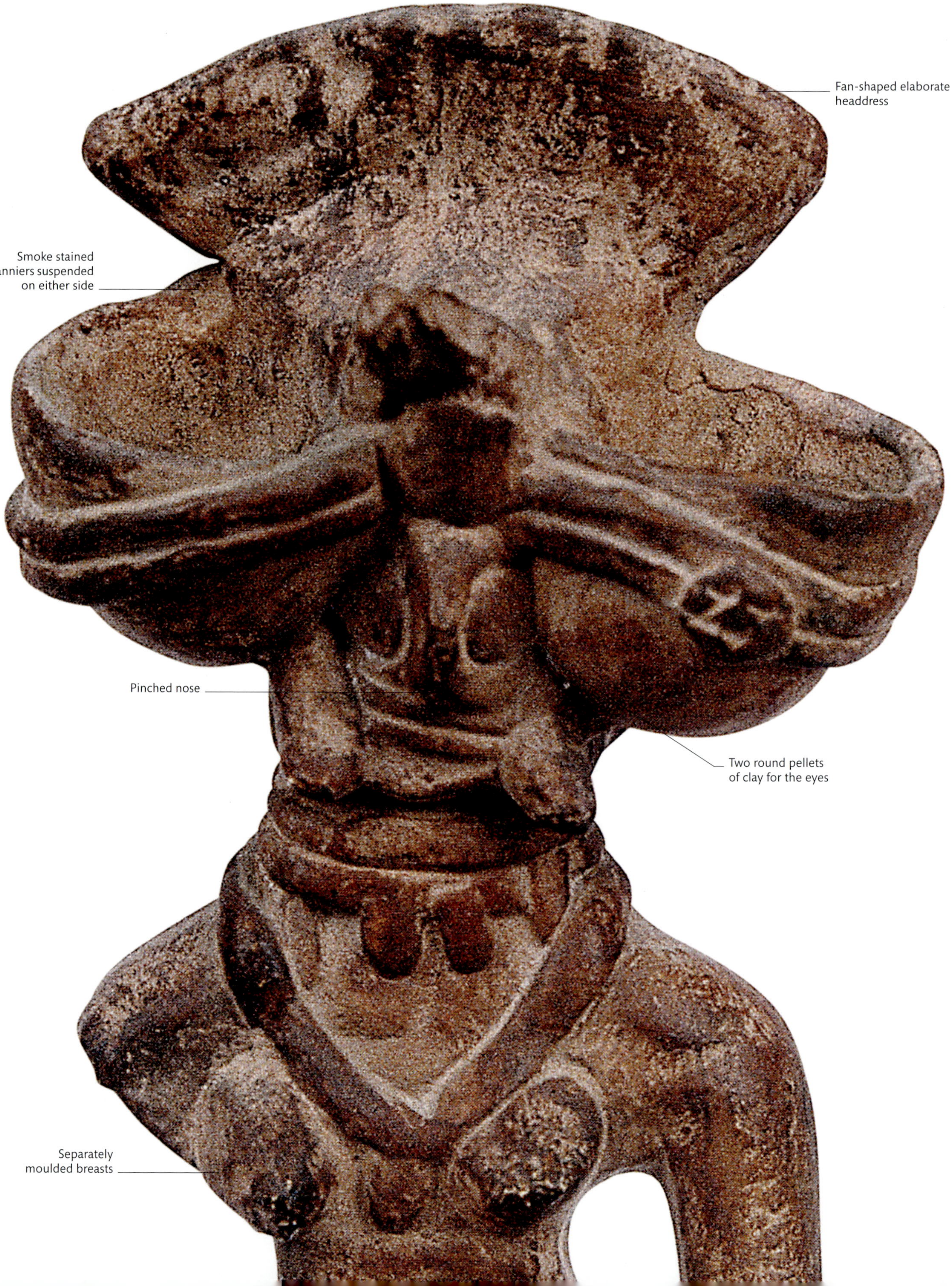
Fan-shaped elaborate headdress
Smoke stained panniers suspended on either side
Pinched nose
Two round pellets of clay for the eyes
Separately moulded breasts

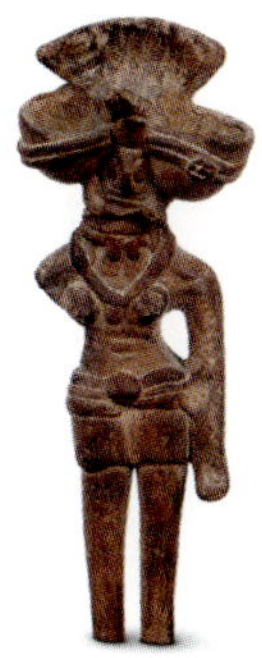

Era 2700–2100 BCE | **Medium** Terracotta | **Dimension** 230 × 85 cm (90.6 × 33.5 in)

MOTHER GODDESS

Ancient female religious figure from Mohenjo Daro

The earliest signs of feminine worship in the Indian subcontinent are seen in the Indus Valley Civilization, when archeological excavations yielded many female figurines. Believed to have religious relevance, the most prominent among these is the mother goddess.

The slim female figurine, such as the one on the left, is among the most distinguished type of terracotta figurines from the Indus Valley Civilization found during archeological excavations. Displayed in the National Museum, New Delhi, this figurine is often understood to be the central figure of the Harappan religion.

It has a short kilt around the waist, which is heavily ornamented with a belt that has three strands and a circular clasp. The figurine has a deep navel and doesn't appear to have any clothes above the waist, but the upper segment is adorned with several rows of necklaces, including a choker with many pendants. One particular necklace is longer than the others and it sits between her breasts, which are separately moulded and attached to the body. It is possible that the conical object on the forehead could be another type of ornament. This figurine has a forward-projecting face with prominent eyes and thick lips. The handiwork is rudimentary with the technique of pellets of clay applied to create eyes, breasts, and ornaments.

Although badly broken, the headdress is elaborate. While some figurines may have flowers on either side, others, such as this one, have cup-like attachments. The cups of the fan-shaped pannier headdress in this figurine were found to contain black residue. The black residue suggests that these sculptures were of religious significance since the cups may have been used to burn oil or some sort of incense.

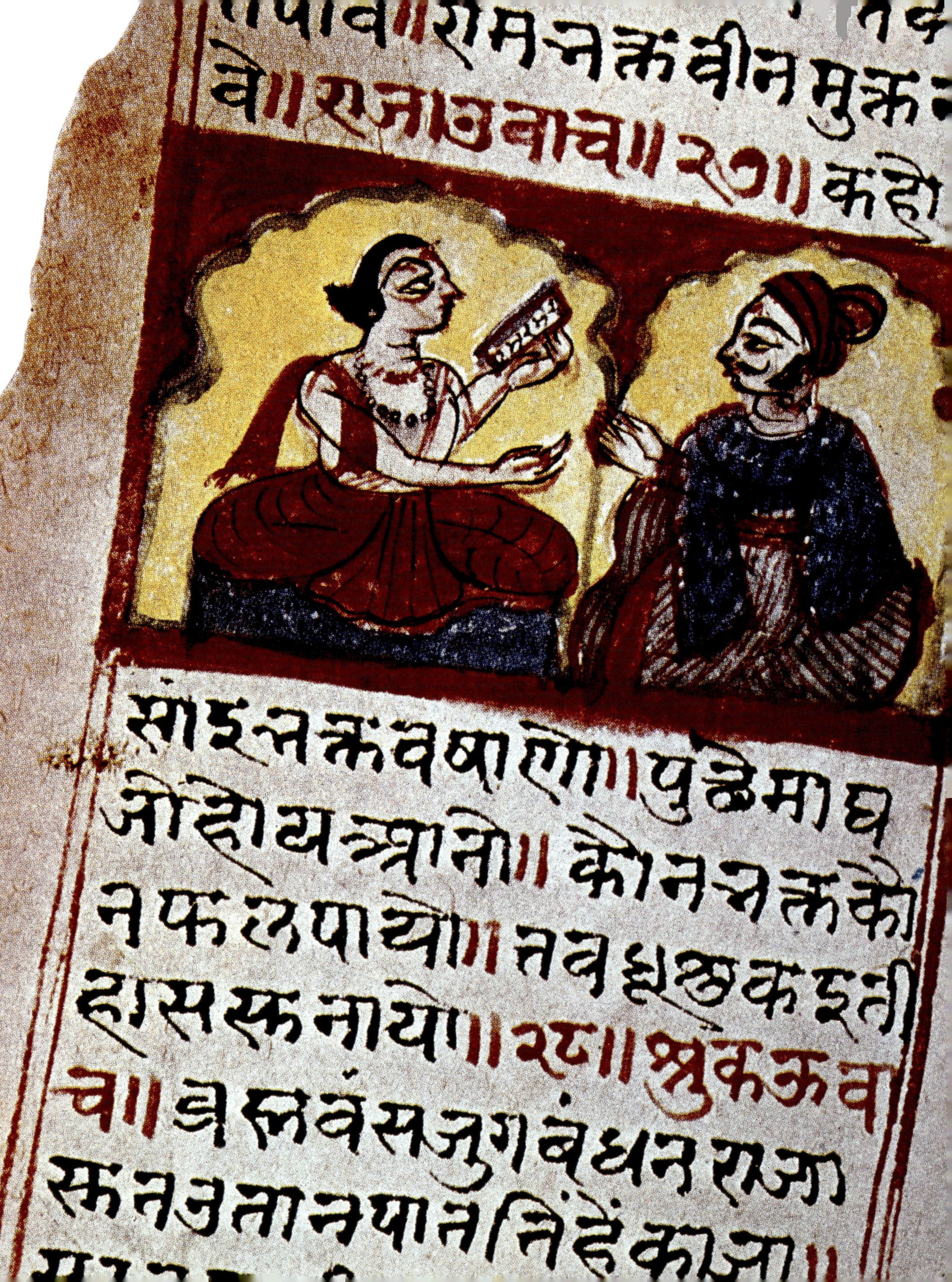

Era c. 1500 BCE

RIG VEDA

An ancient repository of wisdom

The Rig Veda encapsulates the beginnings of philosophical enquiry in India – into nothingness; into thought and its power to create; into existence; into life and its myriad forms; into death and renewal. It is one of the four sacred canonical Hindu texts.

The oldest and most important of all Vedas, the Rig Veda (see pp. 26–27) provides the basis for the entire expanse of Vedic corpus. It comprises ten books, a total of 1,028 hymns made up of 10,600 individual verses, and must have been composed over a long period. Most of the hymns are in books 2 to 7, each of which is attributed to a particular family of sages. These 'family' books are believed to be older than the others.

SACRED KNOWLEDGE

True to the *sruti* (heard) tradition, the Rig Veda was passed down orally for centuries before being written down. The earliest manuscripts used perishable materials, often birch bark and palm leaves. Consequently, the oldest surviving manuscript only dates to about 1040 CE. In 2007, recognizing the significance of the Rig Veda to the cultures of South and South-east Asia, 30 manuscripts, the oldest from 1464, were included in UNESCO's Memory of the World Register, which seeks to preserve the documentary heritage of the world.

The hymns address different deities, including Agni, the god of fire; Vayu, the god of wind; Indra, the ruler of heaven; Soma, the moon; Varuna, the guardian of the cosmic order; and his counterpart Mitra who represented integrity, friendship, harmony and maintained order in the human world. Questions about the meaning of personal existence, the world and man's place in it, are beautifully integrated into the text. In addition to its religious and philosophical importance, the Rig Veda is an invaluable academic resource. For instance, two complete hymns are dedicated to a horse; Indra's chariot is described as drawn by seven white horses. However, there is no evidence of horses in the subcontinent until about 2000 BCE; the animal is not among the many that feature in artefacts found in the Harappan civilization. This helps to date Vedic culture in the subcontinent to the late-, or even post-Harappan era.

◄ **An illustrated page from an** undated manuscript of the Rig Veda, as printed in an academic text in 2002.

c. 1500 BCE–300 CE

VEDAS AND EPICS

The core of Hindu thought, philosophy, and practices is an assortment of texts that have informed it over the centuries. They provide a complex matrix to study the religion in all its glory and diversity.

In the Hindu tradition, the oldest, and for some, the most sacred body of texts are the Vedas – the Rig Veda, the Yajur Veda, the Sama Veda, and the Atharva Veda. They are a collection of hymns and chants, dating back to c. 1500–500 BCE. Their intonation is believed to replicate the sounds of the universe, and the tonal variation and syllabic emphasis was critical. First conceptualized by ancient sages deep in meditation, their oral expression resulted in the awareness and knowledge of existence. The word Veda is derived from the root *vid*, which means 'to know'. These are heard texts, or *srutis*, that as oral encapsulations of creation had to be enunciated with precision. The transmission of the Veda, therefore, continued orally for centuries.

"There was neither death nor immortality then. There was not distinction of day or night. That alone breathed windless by its own power. Other than that there was not anything else."

– Creation Hymn, Rig Veda, 10:129

ETERNAL STORIES THAT GUIDE READERS

The next set of texts that appeared are the epics – the Ramayana and the Mahabharata. The composition of the Mahabharata can be placed between the 4th century BCE and 4th century CE, and the Ramayana between the 5th–4th centuries BCE and 3rd century CE. Bardic in origin, the epics narrate the stories of royalty. While the Ramayana traces Prince Ram's exile and journey to rescue his wife Sita from the demon king Ravana, the Mahabharata tells the tale of an armed conflict between two groups of cousins, the Pandavas and the Kauravas. Both texts are understood to be *smritis*, or narratives with essential plots and characters, which were recalled by holy men and are accepted as human in origin. They interpret the philosophy of the *sruti* texts for people, using situations and choices to illustrate *dharma* (guides for behaviour). Eventually, they gained as much religious importance as the Vedas. As such there is no one original, but multiple layers added to over generations as well as alternate re-tellings. The Puranas are also examples of *smriti* texts. Each act as a guide for worshippers of specific deities, and helped to popularize and expand the reach of Hinduism.

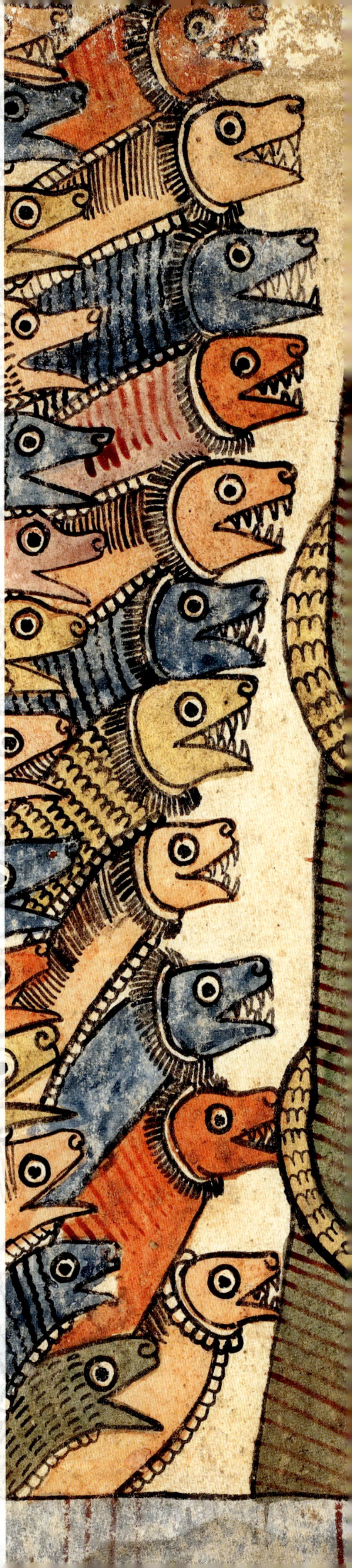

► **Folio from a Mahabharata manuscript made in** Paithan, in the western state of Maharashtra, c. 1850. It shows Babhruvahana, a prince from the epic, fighting an army of serpents.

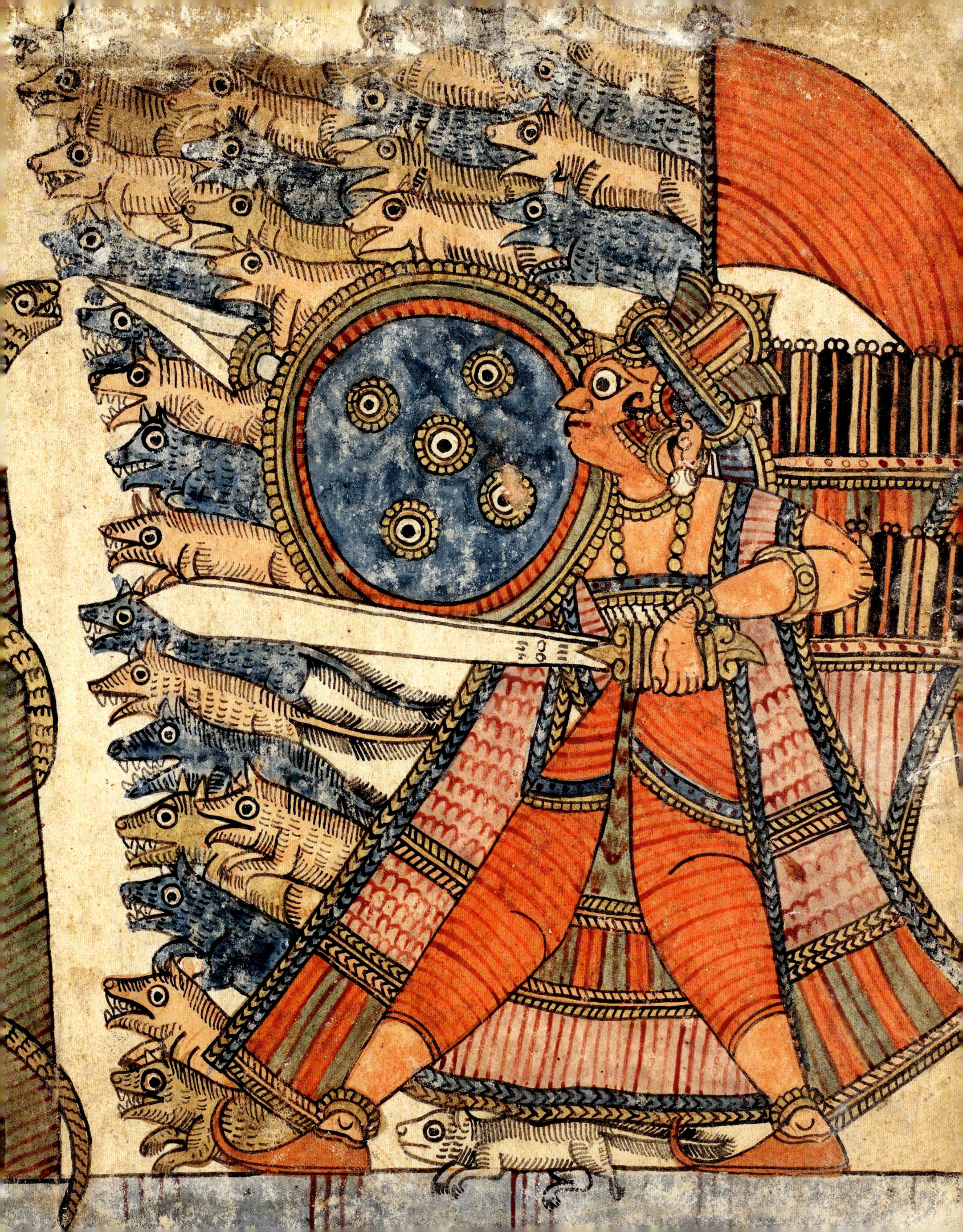

Era 6th century CE | **Medium** Sandstone | **Dimension** 10.3 × 10.3 cm (4 × 4 in)

LAJJA GAURI

An ancient symbol of fertility

This striking sandstone sculpture of the Goddess reportedly originates from Seoni, Madhya Pradesh. A popular iconography in Hindu goddess worship is the lotus-headed Lajja Gauri, the Fertility Goddess, often identified as Parvati (Shiva's consort).

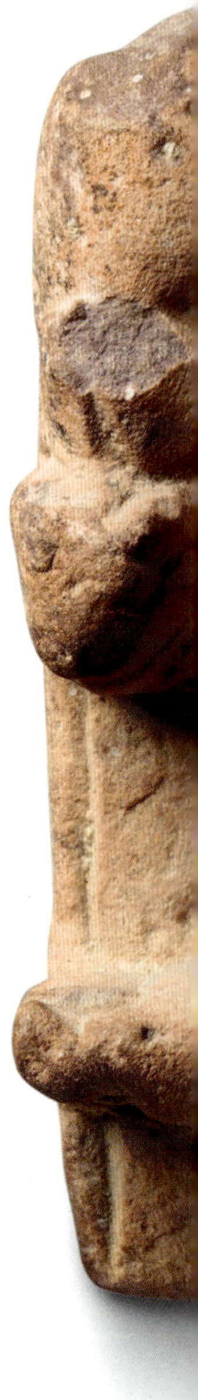

Indian iconography is replete with examples of the female body as a site for manifesting life-affirming forces. However, none stands out more strongly than the image of Lajja Gauri. Hailed as the elemental force of all life, the striking fertility figure is represented with a female torso in *malasana* or a squatting position that implies birthing. In place of her head is a giant lotus flower in full bloom, a symbol that frequently appears in Hindu mythology as the cosmic womb, carrying the potential for future generations and signifying the cyclic renewal of life or reincarnation.

A STRIKING ICON

This form of Lajja Gauri can be traced back to the Harappan Culture, which witnessed significant production between the 2nd and 11th centuries, especially in central India and the Deccan as well as parts of present-day Pakistan. Although there are no surviving texts to explain her form or origins, Lajja Gauri's genealogy has been established by scholars through symbols such as *purna kumbha* or *kalash*, a brimming pot used in worship as a sign of plenty, and the *srivatsa*, an Indic mark of auspiciousness that usually takes the shape of a triangle or flower. Lajja in Sanskrit translates as shame and Gauri is an epithet of the goddess Parvati. Lajja Gauri can thus be understood as Gauri, the Goddess of Modesty. It is believed that the sculpture would have been used by tribal communities to invoke the goddess at the time of important life events such as marriage, childbirth, or the start of new ventures. The deity's association with fecundity and prosperity is also evident in the discovery of Lajja Gauri icons near sources of water, which may be seen as acts of propitiation for agricultural abundance.

By the 6th century, the image of Lajja Gauri had moved on from being restricted to village cults, and made its way into temples, including those in royal complexes. Its proliferation was also carried out notably by aristocratic female patrons such as the Andhra Ikshvaku queens, belonging to a dynasty dating to 3rd and 4th centuries CE, who commissioned Lajja Gauri idols and cave images.

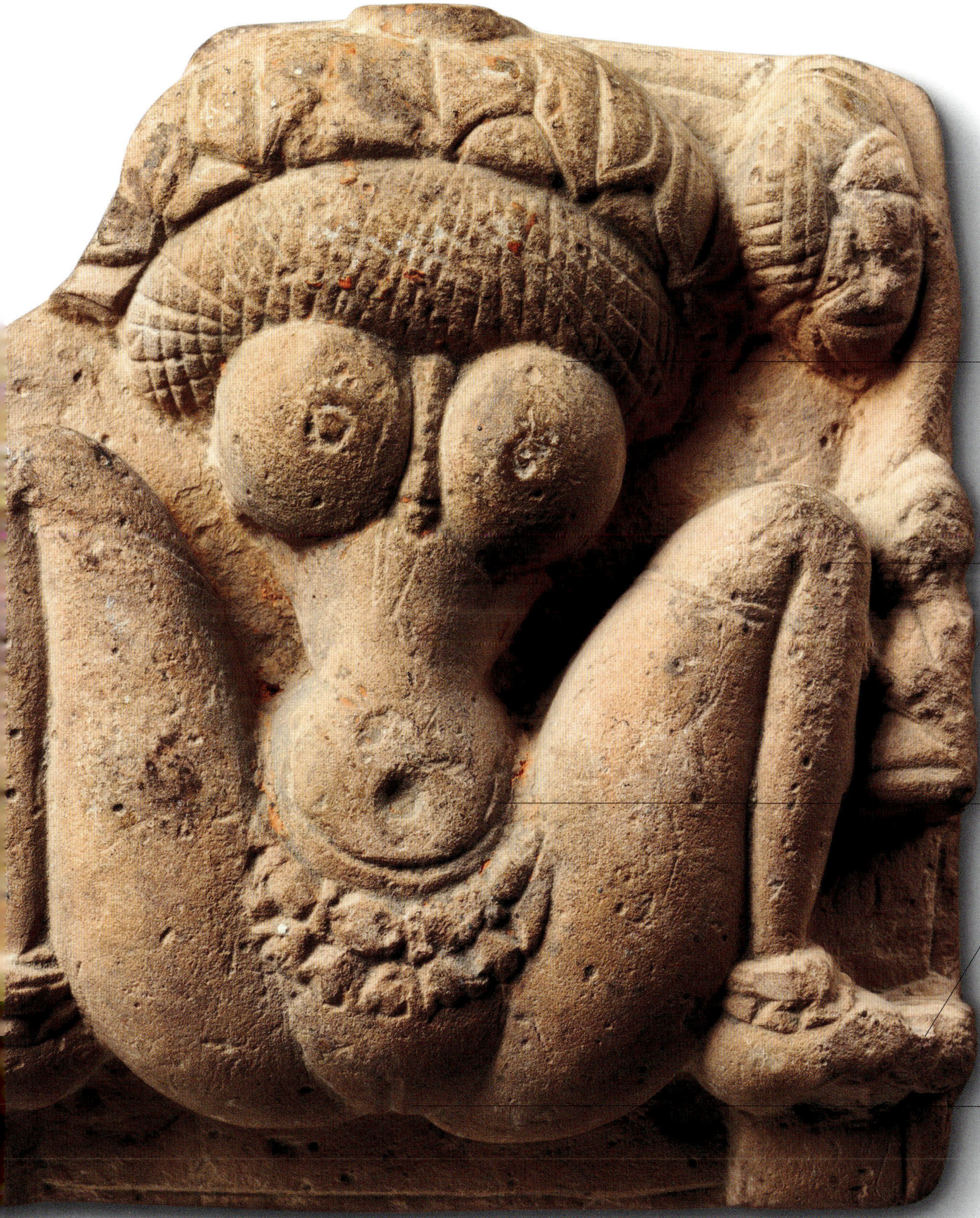

The goddess's procreative power is reinforced with the depiction of a heavy bosom.

Spread-out legs drawn up laterally and bent at the knees symbolize a birthing position.

Waist belt and anklets enhance her grace and reaffirm her femininity.

The soles of the feet are turned upwards, with it appearing as though there is a contraction of the toes as in the struggle of a body preparing for parturition.

Although the goddess's belly is not depicted as swollen to connote pregnancy, sexual fecundity is made explicit with the exposed genitals.

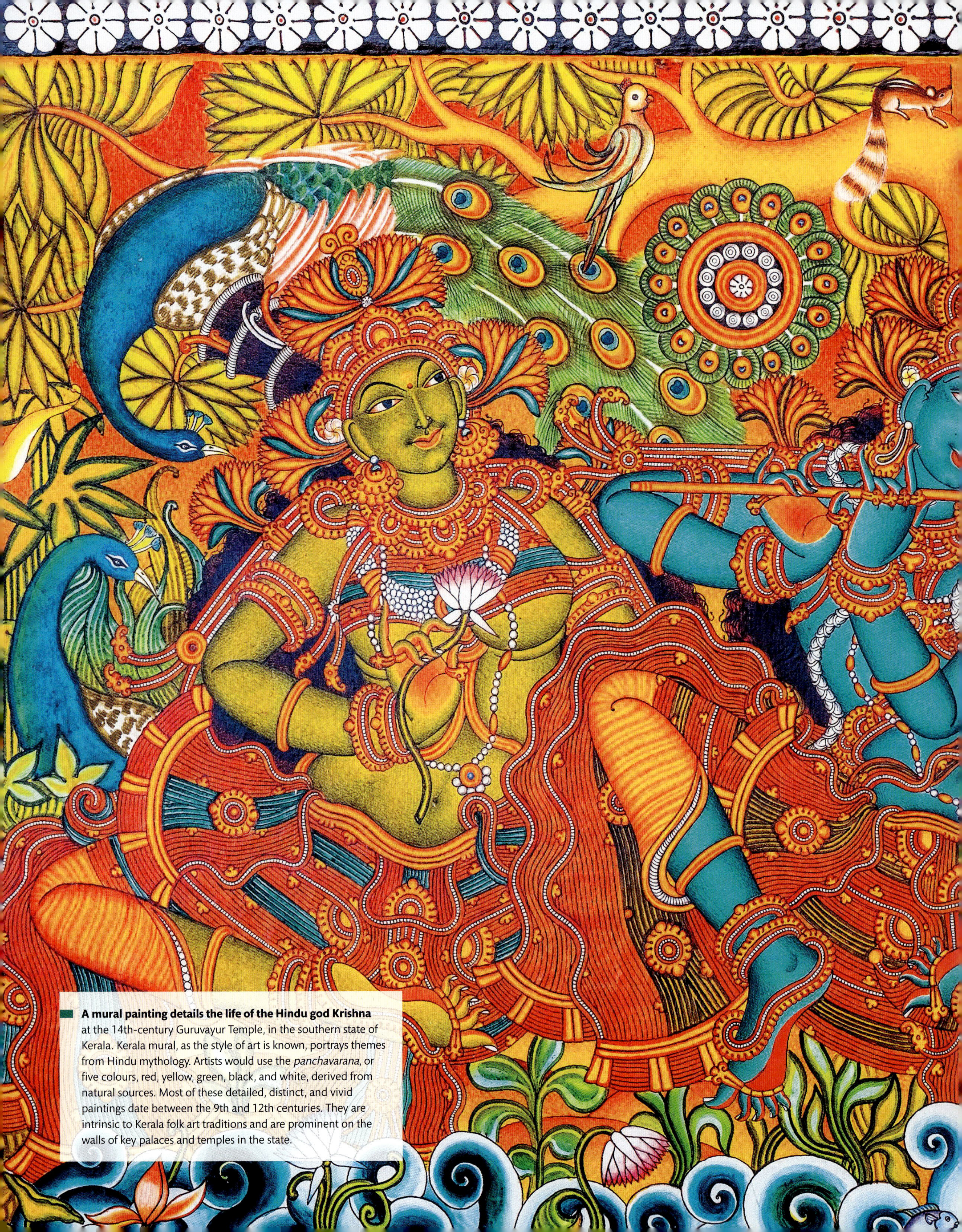

A mural painting details the life of the Hindu god Krishna at the 14th-century Guruvayur Temple, in the southern state of Kerala. Kerala mural, as the style of art is known, portrays themes from Hindu mythology. Artists would use the *panchavarana*, or five colours, red, yellow, green, black, and white, derived from natural sources. Most of these detailed, distinct, and vivid paintings date between the 9th and 12th centuries. They are intrinsic to Kerala folk art traditions and are prominent on the walls of key palaces and temples in the state.

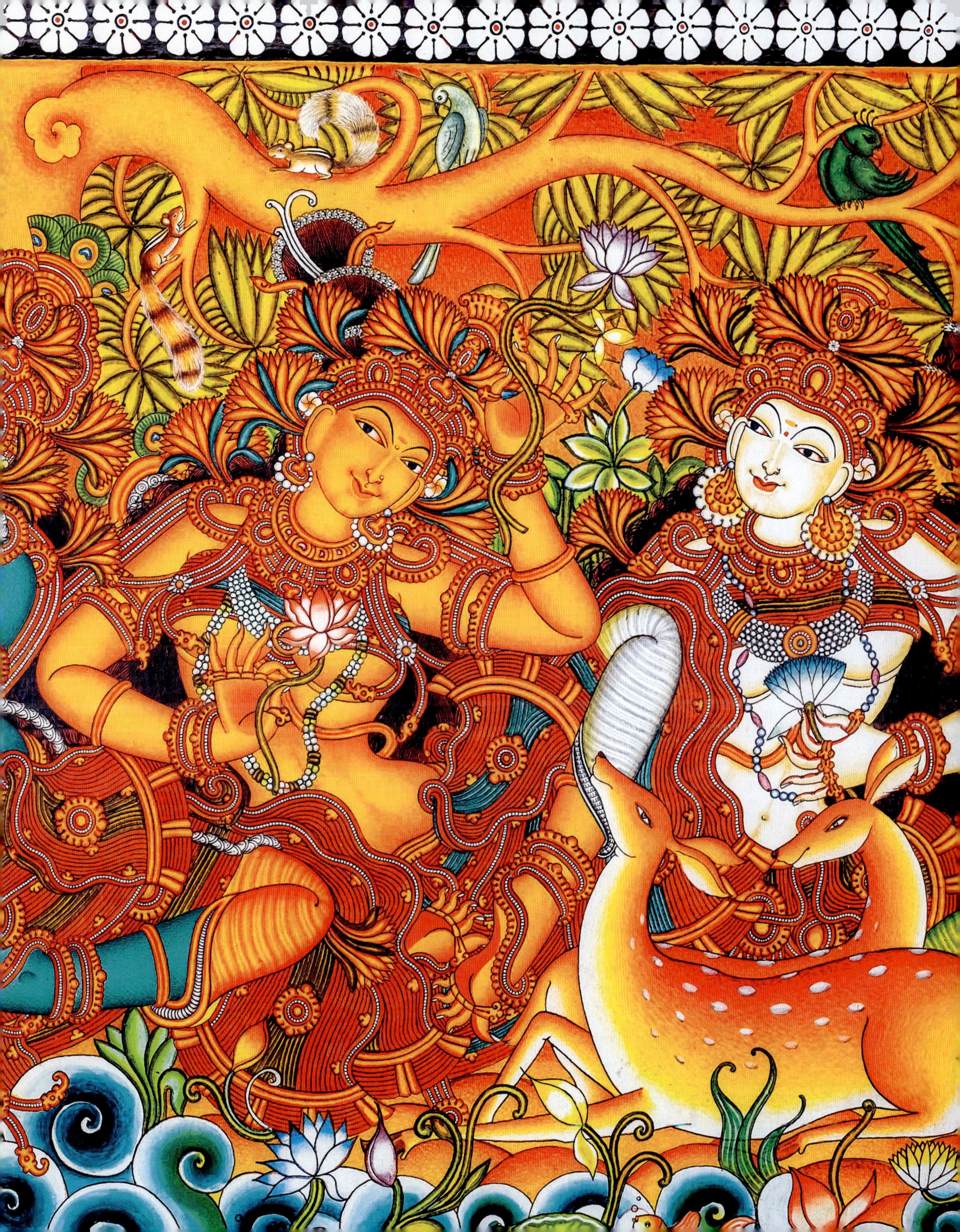

A DYNASTY FORMS

Shifting dynasties and the establishment of the first empire

Popular belief may hold that northern India's historical period began around 600 BCE, but a longer historical continuum spanned several centuries, saw the rise of centres of power, and witnessed the evolution of art and literature, from elaborate structures to political treatises.

The planned communities of the Harappan Civilization and the age of the Vedas gave way to a new period, as state polities and communities began to emerge in the 6th and 5th centuries BCE, in the region extending from Gandhara in the north-west to Anga in the east. Buddhist and Jain writings list 16 states (*mahajanapadas*) that were active in the early 6th century BCE. The term also referred to a territory, which included both urban and rural villages, and their residents. It is probable that there were other lesser states and chiefdoms. There were two types of states within the *mahajanapadas:* monarchies (*rajyas*) and non-monarchies (*ganas* or *sanghas*). Some historians say that they could have been oligarchies, where a small group controlled the state and its subjects. An aristocracy of the most influential families held power, instead of their being a single hereditary monarch. In the 6th century BCE, the kingdoms of Magadha, Kosala, Vatsa, and Avanti were the most powerful states, and often interacted with one another through trade, social relations, and even military conflict.

RISE OF MAGADHA

Of these kingdoms, the state of Magadha was perhaps the most powerful, and emerged as one of the most significant kingdoms in the era that followed. It had vast stretches of lush land ideal

c. 600 BCE Formation of the 16 *mahajanapadas* (states or kingdoms)

c. 599 BCE Birth of Mahavira, the founder of Jainism

c. 563 BCE Birth of Siddhartha Gautama (Buddha), founder of Buddhism

c. 538 BCE Cyrus the Great conquers parts of Pakistan

c. 500 BCE Earliest written records in the Brahmi script

c. 500 BCE Birth of Classical Sanskrit, and the end of the Vedic period

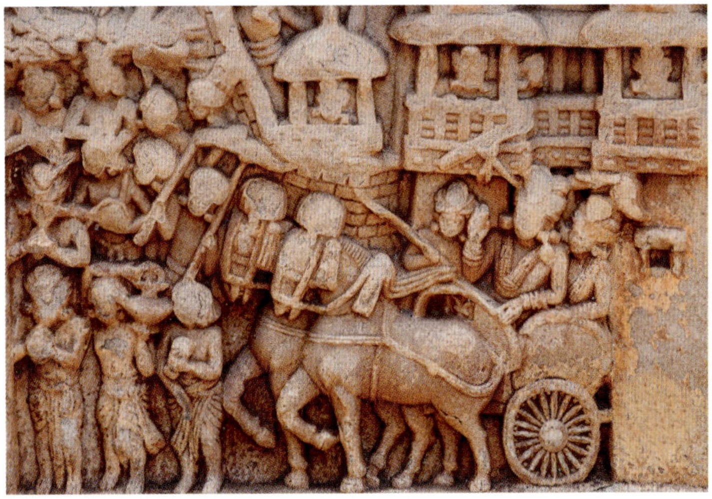

Panel on a pillar at the east gateway at the Sanchi Stupa depicting a royal procession with King Bimbisara, who was the founder of the Haryanka dynasty, and one of the great kings of Magadha.

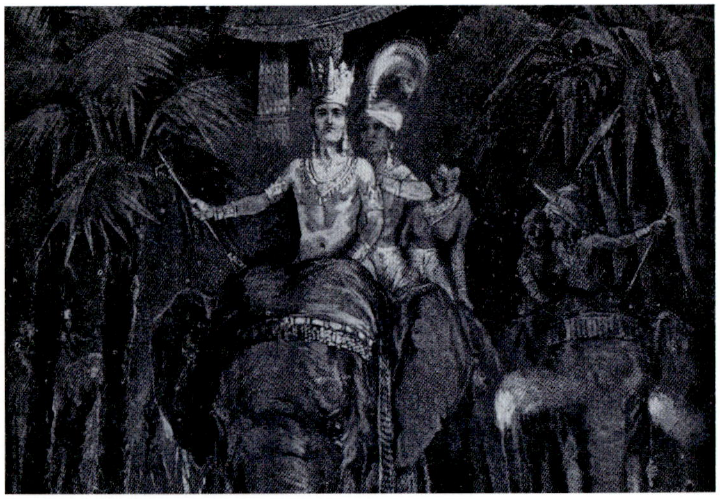

A folio from *Hutchinson's Story of the Nations* showing the Magadha king Ajatashatru atop an elephant on his way to meet the Buddha. The story depicted dates back to 495 BCE.

for growing wet rice, along with control over the iron ore fields in the south of Bihar, a state now in eastern India. It also developed a pluralistic society. The region itself was first mentioned in the Atharva Veda, the last of the four Vedas (see pp. 26–27). The kingdom also finds mention in Jain and Buddhist texts, as well as in Hindu epics, the Ramayana and the Mahabharata (see pp. 26–27).

Historians believe that the kingdom was ruled by many dynasties, the Brihadratha and Pradyota dynasties (682–544 BCE) being two of the first among them. More is known about the Haryanka dynasty founded by Bimbisara. The Magadha chief Bimbisara is often considered the catalyst for the state's steady ascent to political dominance. According to Jain literature, including *Uttara Dhyayana Sutra*, he was a devotee of the tirthankara (teacher) Mahavira. However, according to Buddhist sources, he was a disciple of the Buddha. The Magadha region included the areas around Patna and Gaya in present-day Bihar. It extended as far south as the Chota Nagpur plateau, which covers much of the present-day state of Jharkand. In the east, it was separated from the ancient kingdom of Anga by the river Champa. Five hills surrounded its first capital at Rajagriha, and the city walls served as one of the earliest examples of fortification in ancient India. In the 5th century BCE, Pataliputra (Patna) became the new capital of Magadha.

c. 544–413 BCE Pradyota and Haryanka dynasties rule the Magadha region

c. 333 BCE Alexander the Great defeats Darius III and establishes the Macedonian Empire

c. 326 BCE Battle of the Hydaspes River

c. 326 BCE Alexander the Great defeats Ambhi, the king of Taxila

c. 321 BCE Chandragupta Maurya establishes the Mauryan Empire

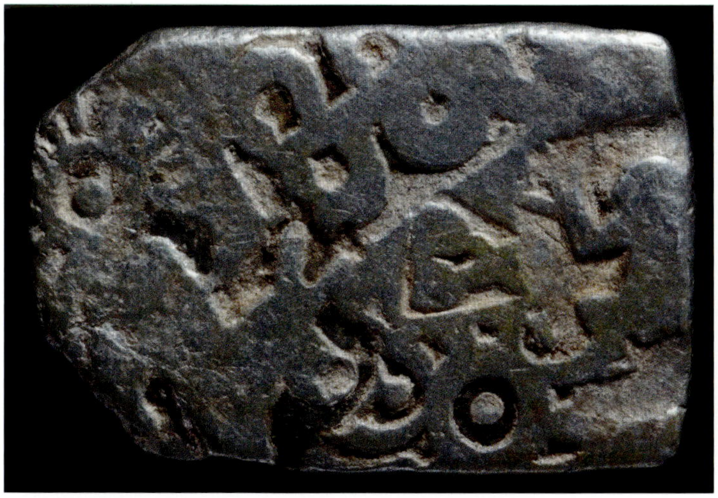

A coin from the Magadha kingdom, c.600–321 BCE made from the precious metal, silver. It bears inscriptions that possibly relay its value.

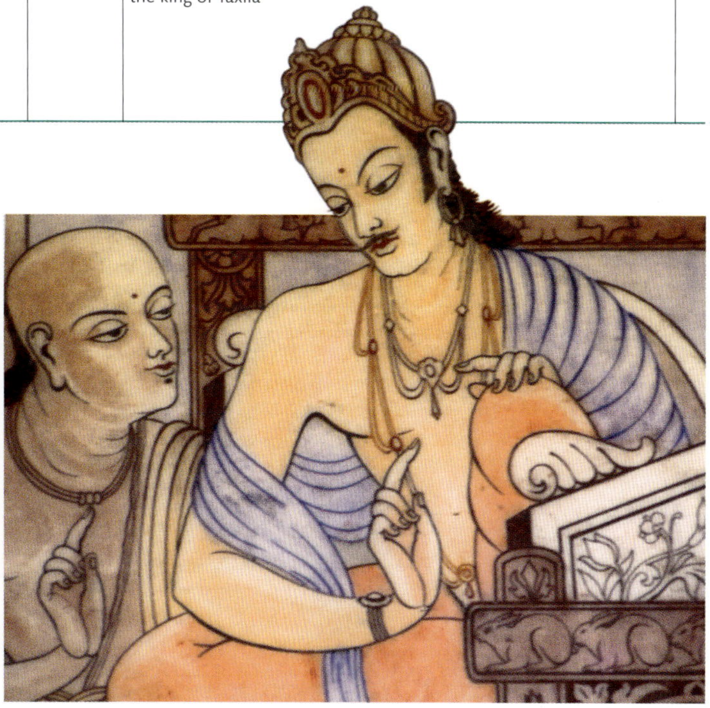

A painting from the Dinodia collection depicting the first Mauryan king Chandragupta, with Chanakya, his royal advisor and teacher, and a revered scholar.

PERSIAN INFLUENCE

The Persian Empire reached the subcontinent's north-west in the 6th century BCE. The city of Kapisha, located south-east of the Hindu Kush mountains, was destroyed by a military expedition under command of Achaemenid monarch Kurush or Cyrus (558–529 BCE). According to Greek historian Herodotus, India constituted the 20th and the most successful satrapy (province) of the Persian Empire. Aside from the political influences, the introduction of the Kharosthi script, derived from Aramaic, was the most pronounced and direct Persian influence in India.

NEW BELIEFS AND FAITHS

The 6th century BCE also saw a rise in popular discontent with the rigid, more ritualistic ideals of the Brahmanas. As a result, other religious movements slowly emerged, including Buddhism and Jainism, which evolved into well-organized and popular faiths.

The Pali canon describes the Buddha as a man, albeit a remarkable one, whose body bore the 32 marks of a *mahapurusha* (great man). He is the Tathagata, the one who has broken free from the cycle of rebirth and death. There is some uncertainty about when he lived, and different texts provide insight into his life. The *Sutta* and *Vinaya Pitakas* are early hagiographies, but later literature from the 1st century CE, such the *Lalitavistara*, *Mahavastu*, *Buddhacharita*, and *Nidanakatha* give more details.

The Buddha founded the *sangha*, an organization of ascetics, and spent more than 40 years travelling and preaching his philosophy. Buddhist legends say he lived till the age of 80, and died in Kusinara (identifiable with modern Kasia in Uttar Pradesh).

In comparison, it is difficult to pinpoint the exact age of the Jain doctrine, but it is significantly older than the Buddhist one. Because it is believed that the Buddha and Mahavira lived at the same time, both belief systems share similarities, such as the rejection of Vedic authority, non-theistic doctrine, emphasis on renunciation and human effort as a means of achieving salvation, and the establishment of a monastic order for both men and women.

THE FIRST SUBCONTINENTAL EMPIRE

Between 324 and 187 BCE, an empire arose that covered more than half of the subcontinent and lasted about 137 years. This was the Mauryan Empire, and Chandragupta and Bindusara were its first two kings. The *Arthashastra of Kautilya* and *Indica of Megasthenes* are of particular significance as textual sources of Mauryan history.

c. 300–400 BCE Kalidasa composes poetry and plays

c. 300 BCE Greek ambassador Megasthenes sent to the Mauryan Empire

c. 273 BCE Ashoka takes over the Mauryan Empire

c. 266 BCE Ashoka conquers most of South Asia, Afghanistan, and Iran

c. 265 BCE The Battle of Kalinga takes place

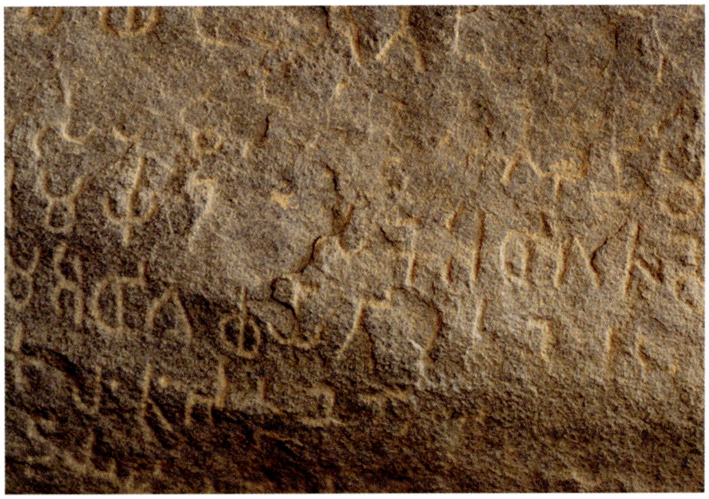

A rock edict of Ashoka recovered in 1915 at the archaeological site of Maski, in the city of Raichur in Karnataka, a state in southern India shows inscriptions in stone.

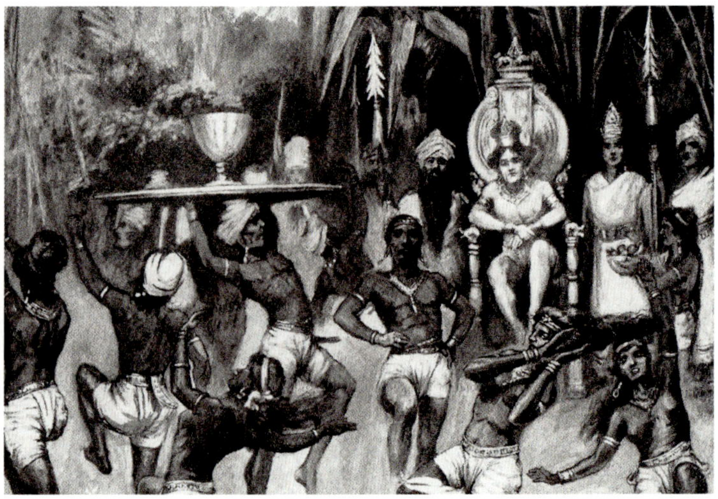

A print by Richard B. Ogle depicting an envoy of Emperor Ashoka declaring the end of the Kalinga War (261 BCE), which turned the warrior king into a peaceful ruler.

Chandragupta Maurya, who defeated the Nanda rulers in 321 or 324 BCE, laid the foundation for the Mauryan Empire. He might have initially made a name for himself in Punjab before making his way east until he took over the Magadha area. The only clear mention of Chandragupta is in Rudradaman's Junagarh inscription from the 2nd century CE. Many locations in the Shravana Belgola highlands have 'Chandra' as their last name. Jain sources indicate that the saint Bhadrabahu and Chandragupta were related. He was succeeded by his son Bindusara, who ruled between 297 and 273 BCE.

ASHOKA, A RULER BEYOND HIS TIMES

Little was known about Ashoka, the third Mauryan ruler, until 1837, when James Princep translated a Brahmi inscription that mentioned a ruler termed *Devanampiya* and *Piyadasi* ('beloved of the gods' and 'one who looks on auspiciousness'). The *Dipavamsa* and *Mahavamsa* texts also called him by these epithets. In the next few decades, versions of the Minor Rock Edict I, which included his given name, Ashoka, were discovered at several archaeological sites across the subcontinent, first at Maski and then at Udegolam, Nittur, and Gujarra. The vast distribution of Ashoka's inscriptions suggests the extent of the Mauryan Empire.

His association with Buddhism and his pacifist rule, both of which are declared in Buddhist literature and in his own inscriptions, are the reasons for Ashoka's popularity. He is regarded by Buddhist tradition as an excellent king and a devout Buddhist. Ashoka is credited with redistributing the Buddha's relics and placing them in stupas in all significant cities. According to legend, he constructed 84,000 stupas and viharas. He is also said to have made pilgrimages to all the significant locations associated with the Buddha's life and placed markers for the benefit of future travellers. A large number of Ashoka's edicts carry inscriptions which explain Dhamma (the Prakrit form of dharma) and its rules.

This display of architecture, and other forms of Mauryan art, expressed political and religious realities, and many of the surviving works, particularly courtly art, were created under the patronage of the rulers (especially Ashoka). However, there is also art related to the daily lives and pursuits of common people in the form of stone sculptures, terracotta figurines, and ring and disc stones.

Of the later kings, only Dasharatha is known to have produced inscriptions. Only Puranic, Buddhist, and Jain accounts are available for some of the others. However, as the first subcontinental empire, the Mauryan Empire set a precedent for all future empires.

265 BCE Emperor Ashoka embraces Buddhism

232 BCE The death of King Ashoka

232 BCE Dasaratha is crowned the next Mauryan king

c. 200 BCE Construction of earliest stupas at Amravati

c. 200 BCE Earliest rock-cut caves at Ajanta excavated

c. 200 BCE Earliest Tamil literature is written

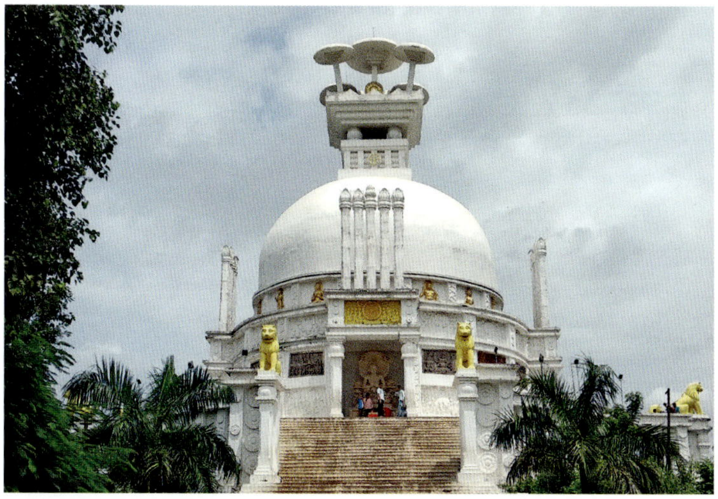

The Shanti Stupa, or mound of peace, was built at the site of the Kalinga War as a symbol of the Emperor's commitment to peace. The area contains many edicts from Ashoka's time.

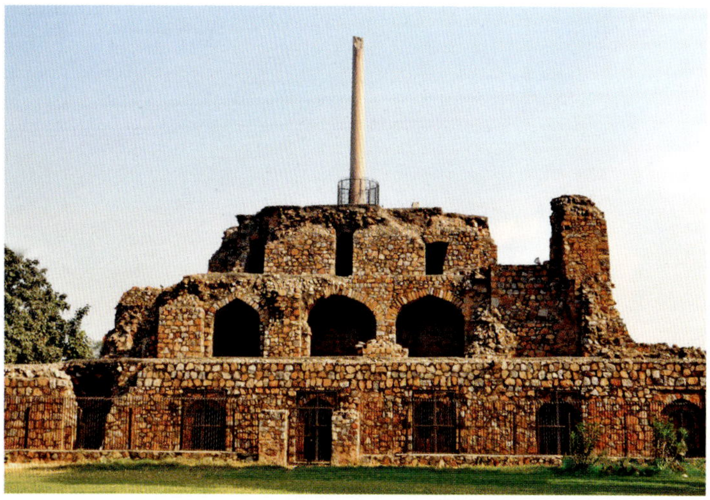

The Ashokan pillar in Delhi is located atop ruins from Feroze Shah's rule. It contains inscriptions in Brahmi bearing the teachings of the king. It is one of many such pillars in New Delhi.

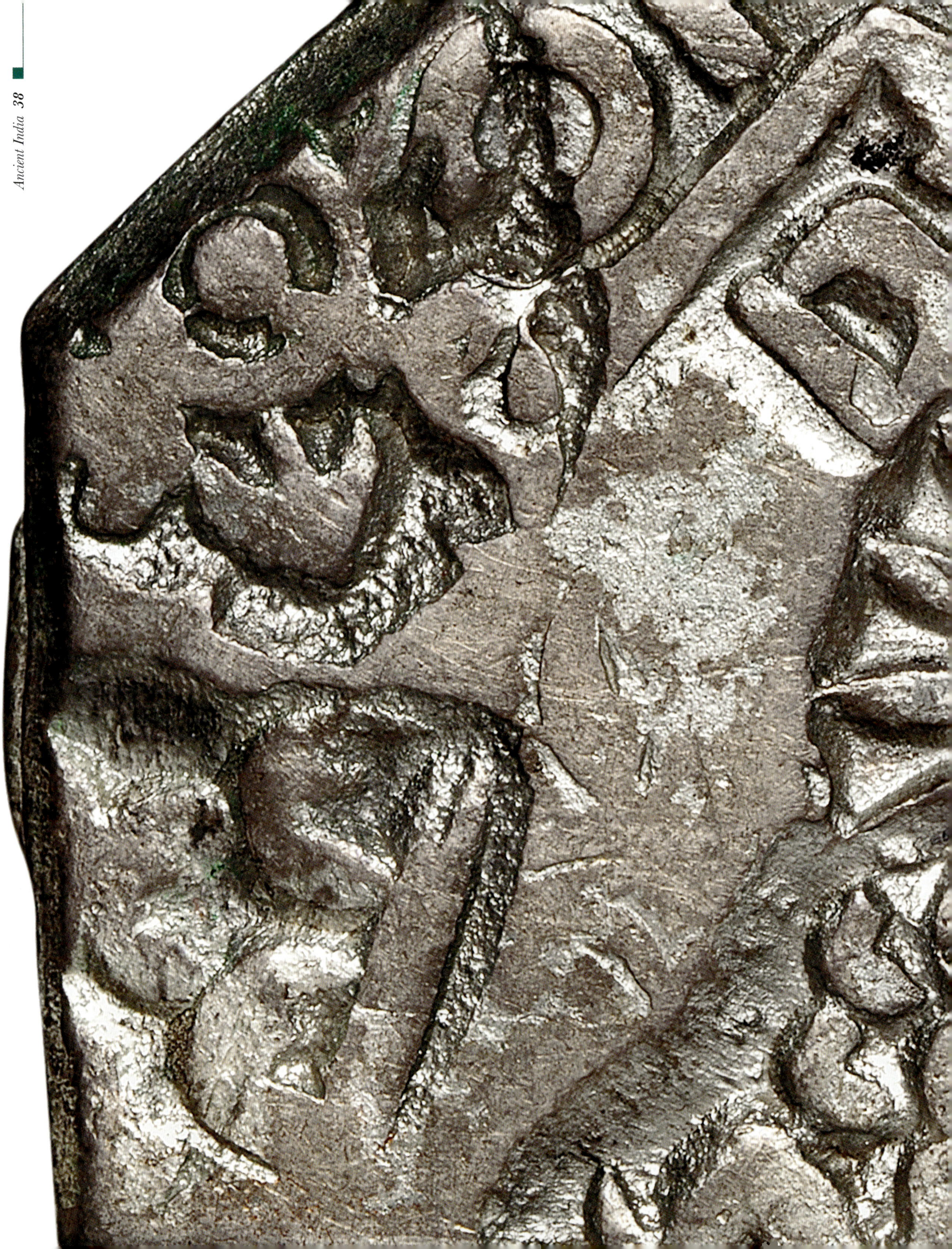

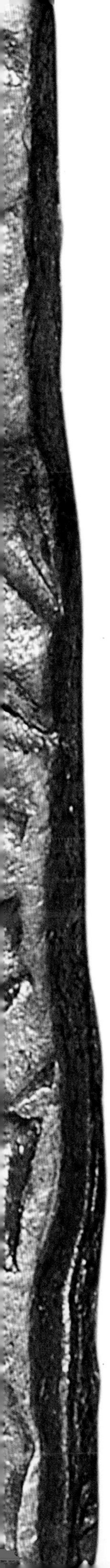

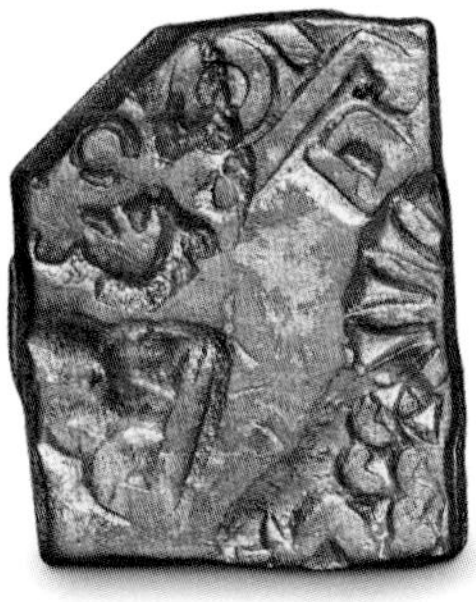

Era 4th century BCE | **Medium** Silver | **Dimension** 1.4 × 1.2 cm (0.5 × 0.4 in)

PUNCH-MARKED COINS

The origins of metal currency in India

The history of coinage in the Indian subcontinent can be traced to the first appearance of punch-marked coins in silver and copper. They signalled a distinct shift from a barter economy to a more formal system of trade.

Pieces of silver and copper with deep impressions, usually symbols, including hills, trees, animals, and crescents became the oft-used currency from 4th century BCE. These punch-marked coins, termed so because of the way the symbols had been impressed into the metal, symbolized a transition from the barter system to a new form of formal trade. The deep impressions attested to the purity of the metal, as they could be seen all the way through.

Sheets of metal were cut into rectangular, square, or round shapes to produce these coins. Some were formed from moulded metal globules. Then, symbols were stamped onto the coins using a die or a punch, creating a distinctive emblem. Not always uniform, these coins were occasionally snipped at the corners to regulate their weight.

◀ **This rectangular silver coin is from** the Mauryan period. It bears no inscriptions but is punch-marked with a variety of motifs, including trees, animals, and natural elements.

COINS GAIN CURRENCY

The oldest known metallic coins (silver and copper) in the subcontinent date back to the 6th century BCE. In the Mauryan era, punch-marked silver coins featuring peacocks and crescent hills constituted the imperial currency. Cast and die-struck coins of varying metals were also in use. The uniformity of currency facilitated wider market exchange. Around 500 BCE, punch-marked coins were circulated in the regions of modern-day eastern Uttar Pradesh and Bihar. New urban centres emerged, including Kaushambi, Kusinagar, Varanasi, Rajgir, and Pataliputra. These cities were bustling with artisans and merchants who utilized coins for the first time.

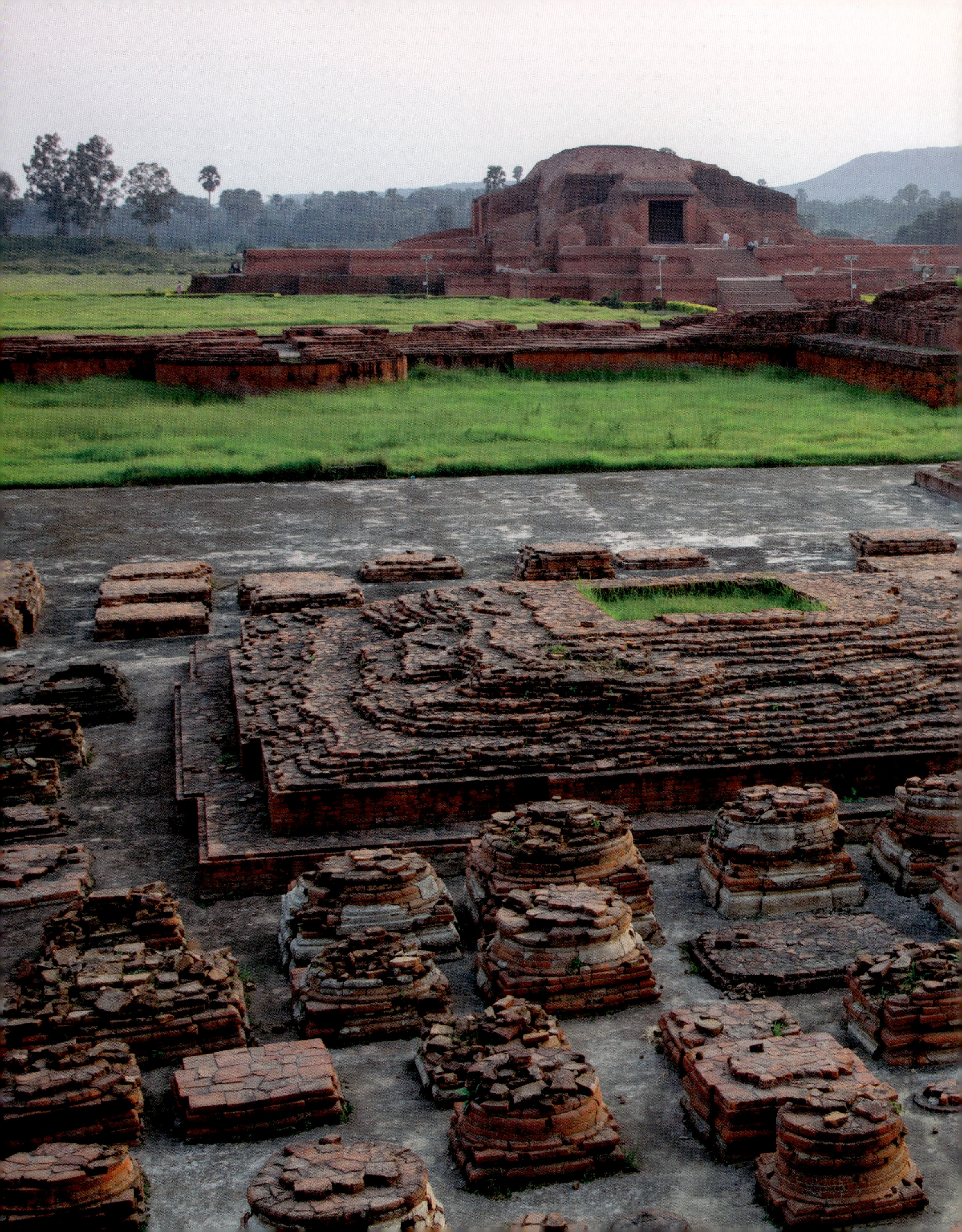

ANCIENT UNIVERSITIES

An individual's moral, physical, spiritual, and intellectual development was of utmost importance from the Vedic period. Centres of learning flourished, inviting students and travellers from across the Indian subcontinent, and the world.

Some of the region's most influential spaces in ancient times were universities which disseminated Buddhist and Brahmanical teachings. One of the three important Buddhist centres of learning in ancient India was Nalanda in the east, which educated students from 427 to 1197 CE. Another centre was the university at Valabhi in the west that flourished between 600 and 1400 CE, while the third was Vikramshila in the east, established in the 8th or early 9th century CE. On the banks of river Indus in the north, between the 10th century BCE and the 5th century CE, was Taxila, a Buddhist and Brahmanical university. Education obtained at these universities did not necessarily lead to a specific profession for students. Instead, they were encouraged to pursue knowledge for its own sake. It was common for students to spend 10–12 years away from their homes at a monastic centre (*vihara*) or the teacher's abode (*gurukul*), where they would serve and learn from him.

"The outstanding feature of the oldest Indian education … is its orality."

– Hartmut Scharfe, *Education in Ancient India*, 2018

AN ANCIENT TRADITION OF LEARNING

While higher education at these institutions was largely free and students did not have to pay tuition fees on a compulsory basis, as teaching was believed to be a sacred pursuit, it was not accessible to everyone. The tradition of *guru dakshina* (repaying the teacher) was prevalent, which could be in the form of a token of gratitude such as a turban, garment, or even a pair of sandals. Historians believe that the universities' operations and administration were financed by contemporary rulers as well as merchants and other upper-caste society members.

There were no strict rules dictating the length of a course. Students usually stayed at the universities until the time that the teacher felt they had achieved the expected level of learning. Since teaching was focused on experiential learning, formal examinations were never conducted. The entire tradition of these universities was dependent on the belief that knowledge was its own reward, and using it for personal gain was sacrilegious.

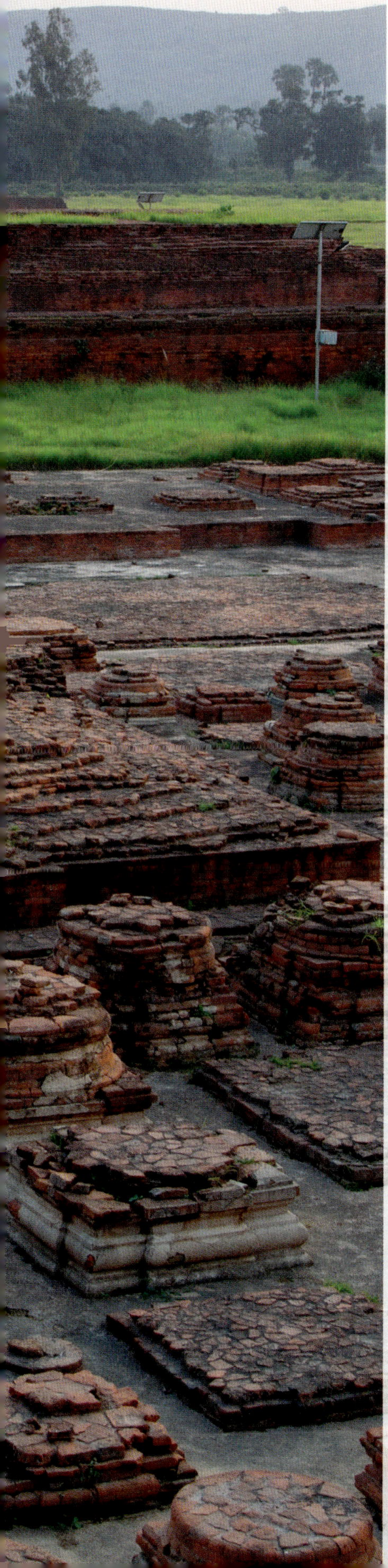

◀ **Ruins of Vikramshila, a Buddhist centre of learning** in the eastern Indian state of Bihar. It was established by Dharampala, a king of the Pala dynasty between the 8th and 9th centuries CE.

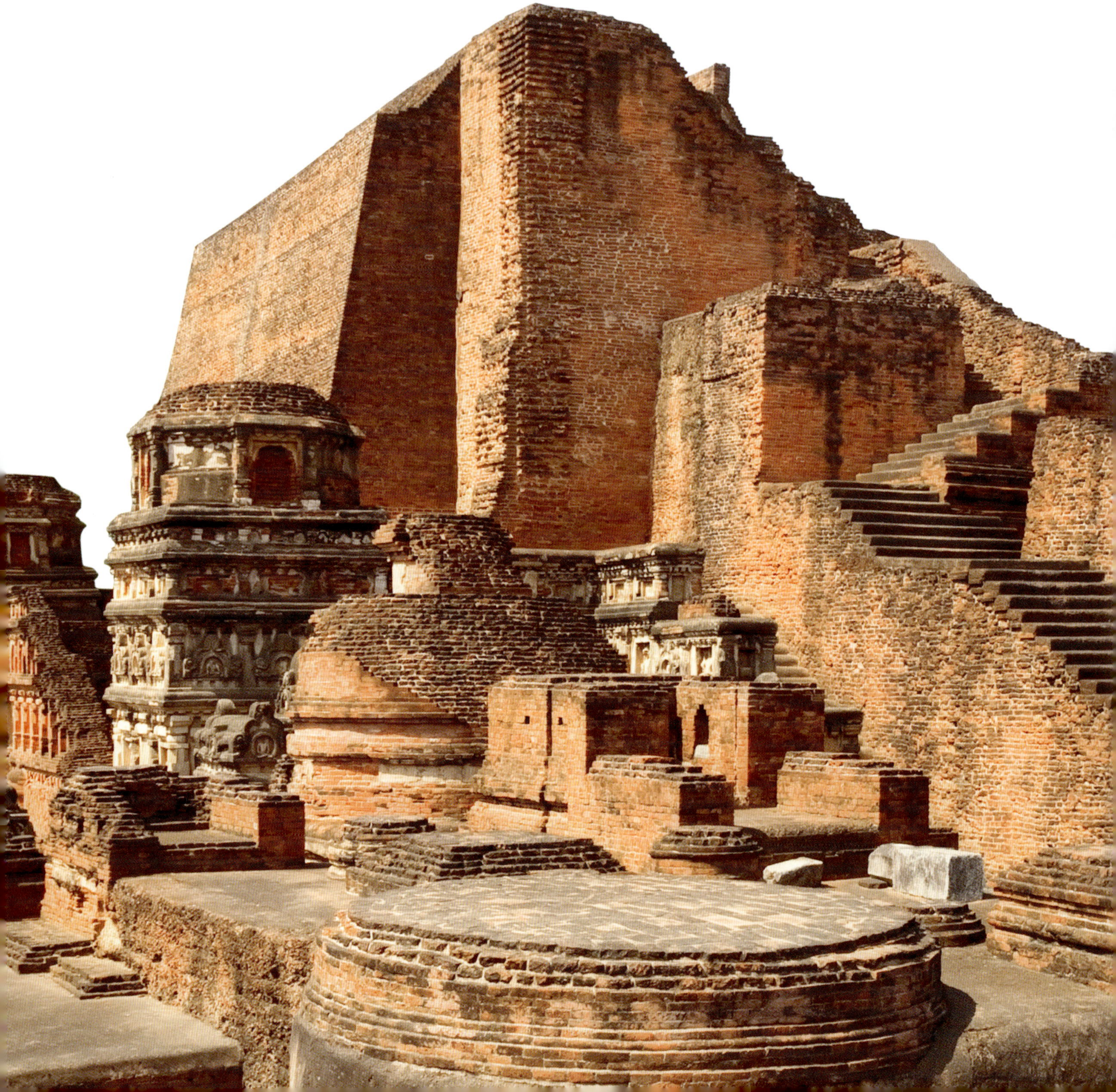

Era 5th century CE | **Medium** Brick | **Area** 12 ha (30 acres)

NALANDA UNIVERSITY

The foremost centre of Buddhist monastic learning

Once the most prestigious centre of learning in Asia, Nalanda University was founded at the birthplace of Buddha's disciple Sariputra in ancient Magadha. It flourished under the Gupta Empire as a monastic and educational institution.

From 427 to 1197 CE, Nalanda, located in ancient Magadha, in what is now Bihar in the east, was a hallowed hub for learning. It is believed that a group of 500 merchants bought the land for the university and presented it to the Buddha, who is said to have preached at the site for several years. Others assert that it was set up by Kumaragupta I of the Gupta Empire in the 5th century CE. Later kings, including Harshavardhana, a 7th-century ruler of Kannauj, were also patrons of the university. Students and monks at the centre would rely upon this royal patronage for survival.

◄ **The excavated remains of Temple No. 3,** one of the oldest structures in the complex of the Nalanda university, offer a glimpse of its former glory.

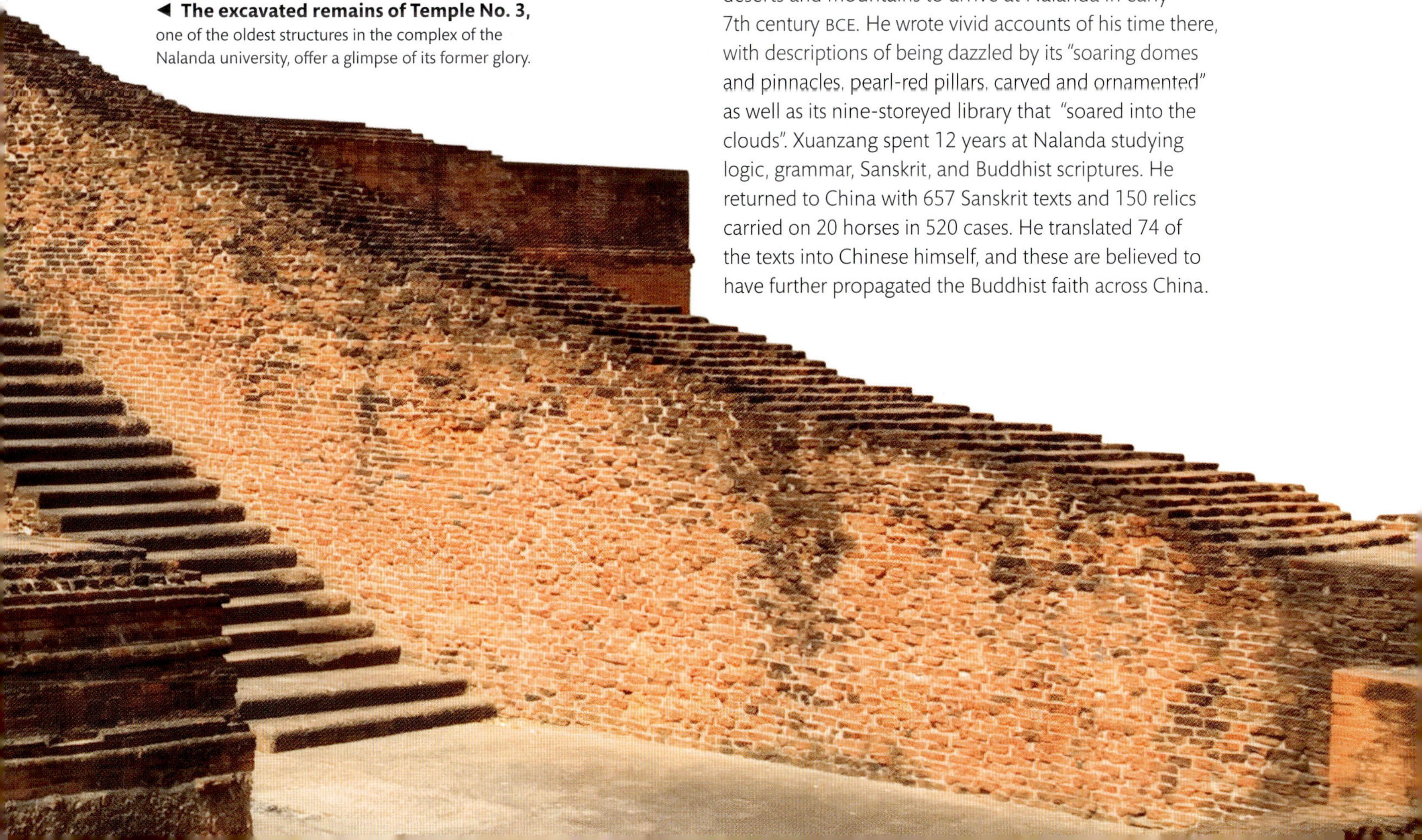

At its peak, Nalanda hosted more than 10,000 students from lands as far as present-day South Korea, Japan, Indonesia, China, Iran, Greece, and Mongolia. Monks at the university taught a variety of subjects, including literature, psychology, law, astrology, astronomy, mathematics, economics, history, and medical science. To aid learning, the complex also had an impressive library which had an enviable collection of more than nine million manuscripts on various topics.

FOREIGN IMPRESSIONS

One of the university's most famous students was the scholar monk Xuanzang from China, who braved harsh deserts and mountains to arrive at Nalanda in early 7th century BCE. He wrote vivid accounts of his time there, with descriptions of being dazzled by its "soaring domes and pinnacles, pearl-red pillars, carved and ornamented" as well as its nine-storeyed library that "soared into the clouds". Xuanzang spent 12 years at Nalanda studying logic, grammar, Sanskrit, and Buddhist scriptures. He returned to China with 657 Sanskrit texts and 150 relics carried on 20 horses in 520 cases. He translated 74 of the texts into Chinese himself, and these are believed to have further propagated the Buddhist faith across China.

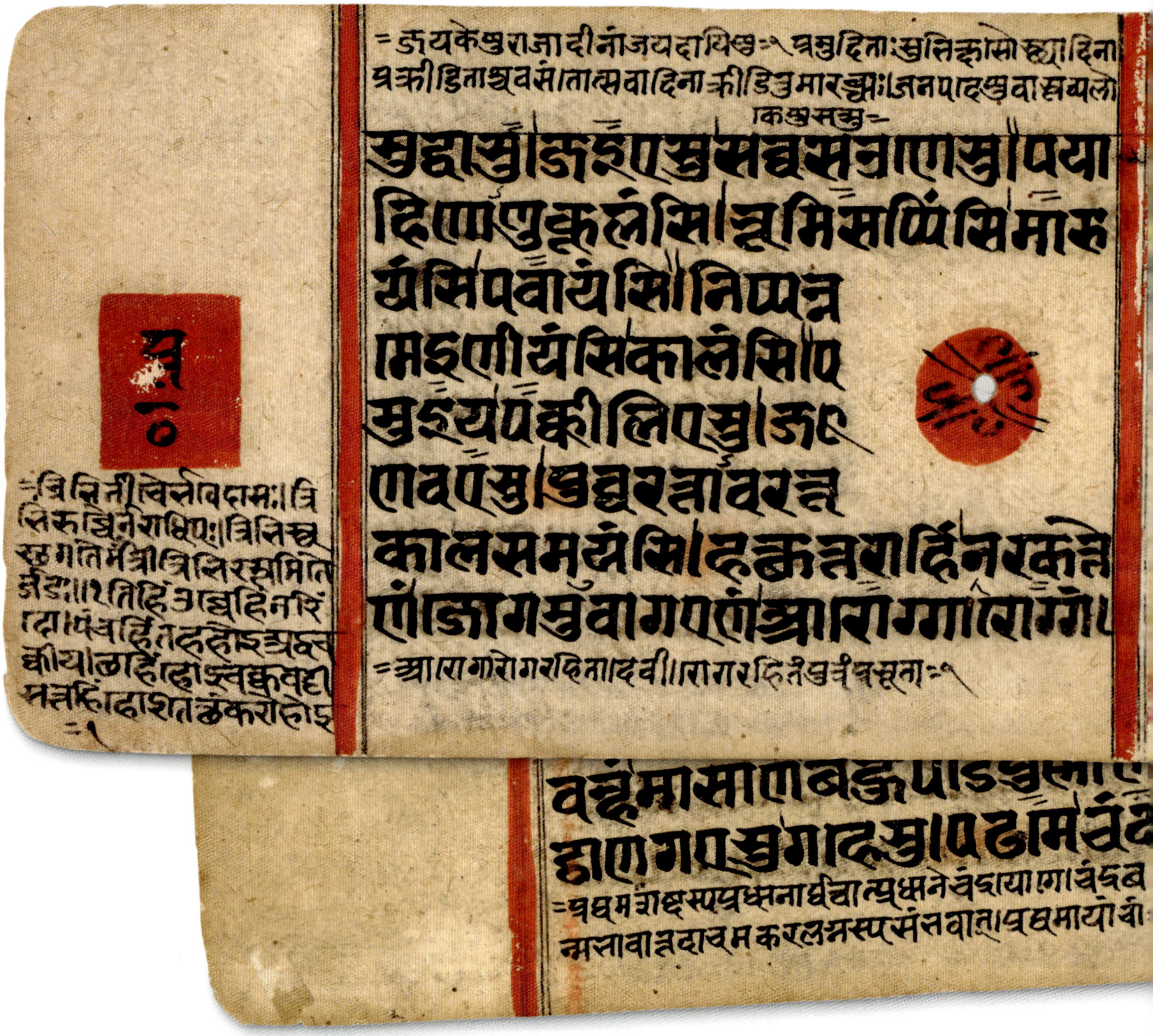

Era 4th century BCE | **Medium** Gum tempera, ink, and gold on paper | **Dimension** 9.4 × 28.4 cm (3.7 × 11.1 in)

KALPASUTRA

A window into an ascetic religion

The *Kalpasutra*, or the Book of Rituals, is one of the two principal texts of Shvetambara Jainism. It is the earliest known biographical account of Vardhaman Mahavira, the 24th tirthankara and founder of Jainism.

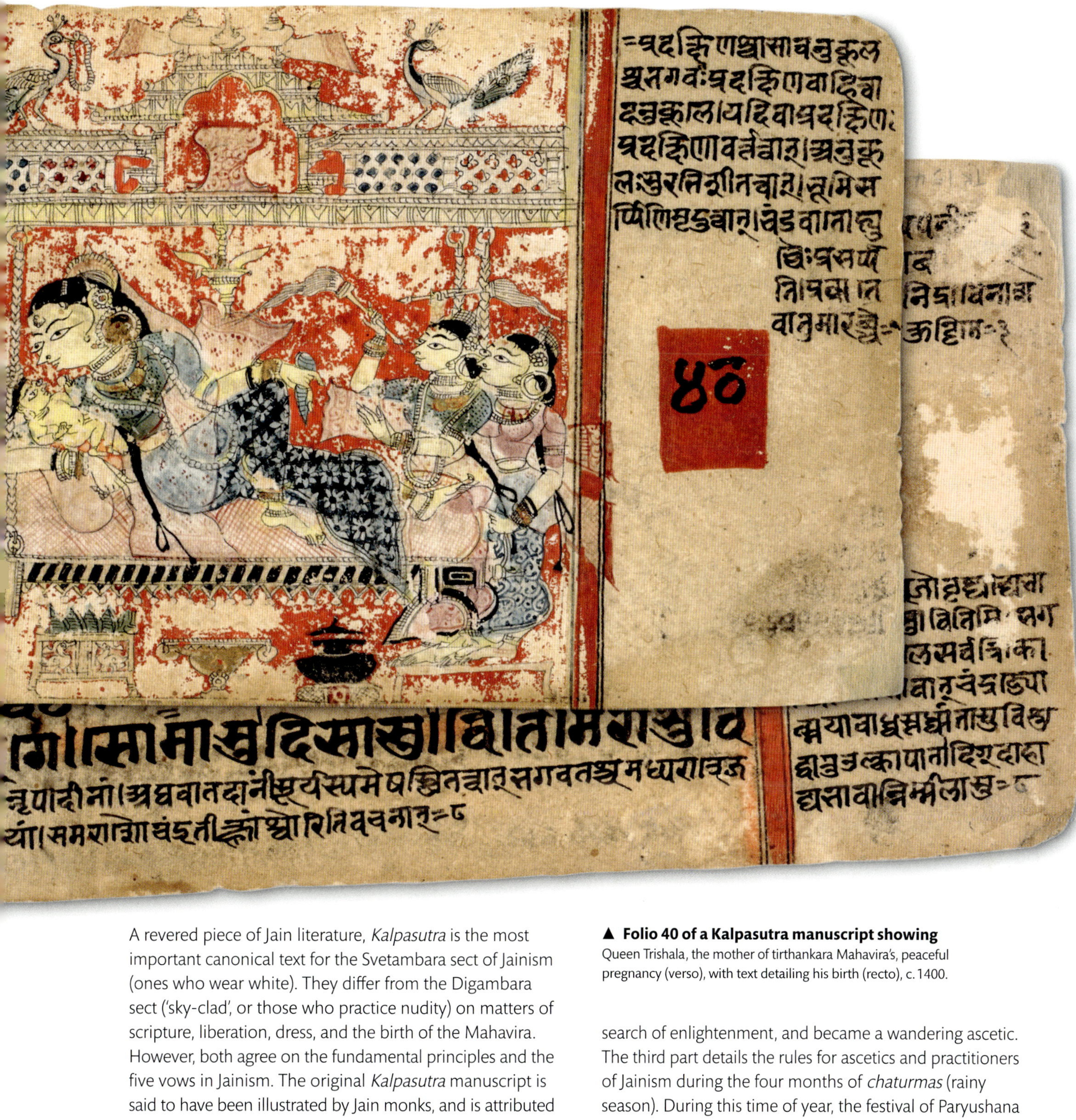

▲ Folio 40 of a Kalpasutra manuscript showing
Queen Trishala, the mother of tirthankara Mahavira's, peaceful pregnancy (verso), with text detailing his birth (recto), c. 1400.

A revered piece of Jain literature, *Kalpasutra* is the most important canonical text for the Svetambara sect of Jainism (ones who wear white). They differ from the Digambara sect ('sky-clad', or those who practice nudity) on matters of scripture, liberation, dress, and the birth of the Mahavira. However, both agree on the fundamental principles and the five vows in Jainism. The original *Kalpasutra* manuscript is said to have been illustrated by Jain monks, and is attributed to Bhadrabahu, the spiritual teacher of the Mauryan emperor Chandragupta. Featuring Sanskrit prose, the text is divided into three parts. The first section narrates the lives of the 24 *jinas* (victors) or tirthankaras, the Jain spiritual teachers who lead souls across the ocean of rebirth, or *samsara*, to spiritual freedom. The second part describes the life of the Mahavira, the 24th tirthankara, who was a contemporary of the Buddha. According to the text, the Mahavira was born a prince who renounced the world in search of enlightenment, and became a wandering ascetic. The third part details the rules for ascetics and practitioners of Jainism during the four months of *chaturmas* (rainy season). During this time of year, the festival of Paryushana is celebrated and the *Kalpasutra* is traditionally recited.

A CONTINUED TRADITION

During the 5th century CE, the act of reciting the sacred *Kalpasutra* in a group setting started. Still in practice today, this custom necessitated the availability of multiple copies of the text. As a result, the *Kalpasutra* is the most widely reproduced Jain text and its copies are preserved in large numbers in Jain libraries known as *bhandaras*.

Era 3rd century BCE | **Medium** Brick and sandstone | **Dimension** 40 × 16.5 m (131 × 55 ft)

SANCHI STUPA

A timeless ode to the Buddha

The Buddha is said to have never visited Sanchi. Yet, the monuments here, the most significant of which is the Great Stupa, are among the oldest examples of aniconic art and free-standing structures that document the history of Buddhism.

Erected to house the ashes and relics of Buddha's closest disciples, the Great Stupa in Sanchi, Madhya Pradesh, is a well-preserved example of ancient Buddhist architecture in India. It stands on a flat-topped hill within a monastic complex, which features monasteries and several other stupas. It was built by Mauryan emperor Ashoka, who converted to Buddhism after regretting the carnage of battles fought to extend his empire in 3rd century BCE.

A PERENNIAL SYMBOL OF PIETY

Buddhist devotees who came to pay homage at the Great Stupa, a hemispherical solid mound, would have walked around the structure in a clockwise direction, reciting prayers and worshipping sacred images placed against the base of the mound, in a ritual known as *pradakshina*. This practice held cosmic significance, as the stupa's design was meant to replicate the hemispherical shape of the universe. Another school of thought believes the shape symbolizes the upturned alms bowl of a Buddhist monk or an umbrella of protection for followers of the Buddhist dharma. Emperor Ashoka initially only commissioned a monolithic pillar and a small stupa made of brick, which form the core of the Great Stupa. About two centuries after its construction, the stupa was patronized by merchants from the nearby ancient city of Vidisha, who added sandstone railings and portals to the structure. Temples, gateways, and monasteries continued to be built here until the 7th century CE.

1. The majestic Great Stupa seen with the *torana*, or the ornamental, arched gateway. **2.** The finial, a three-tiered stone parasol, symbolizing the layers of heaven, rising above a square railing *(harmika)*. **3.** One of the four life-sized sandstone images of the Buddha on the ground-level path, added in the 5th century. **4.** One of the two staircases leading pilgrims to the high circular drum meant for circumambulation. **5.** Majestic lions standing as emblems of royal authority on a south *torana* pillar. **6.** A bas-relief depicting the Buddha as a tree being worshipped by devotees. **7.** The north *torana* consisting of two square pillars and three architraves with scrolled ends, crowned by tridents symbolizing the Buddha and his teachings.

1

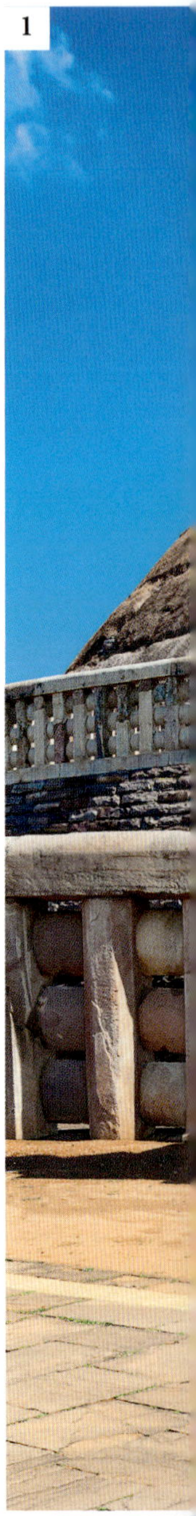

2

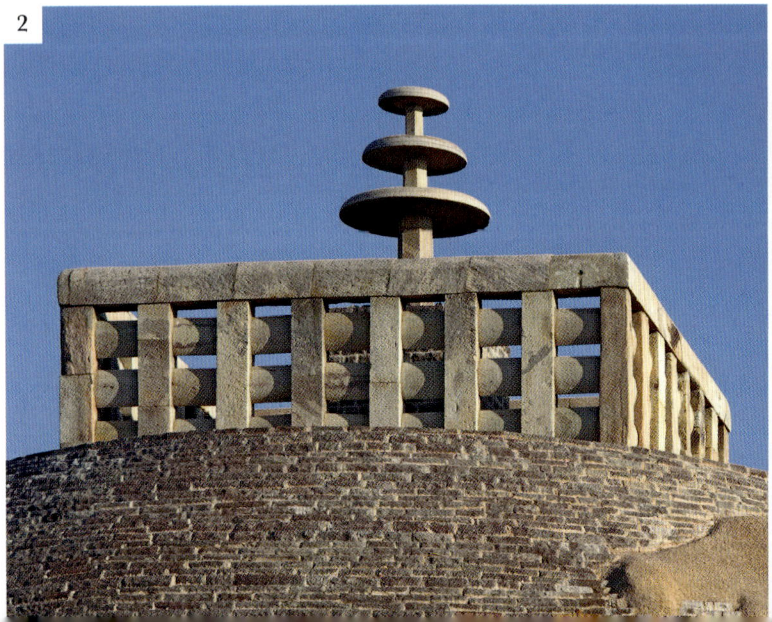

3

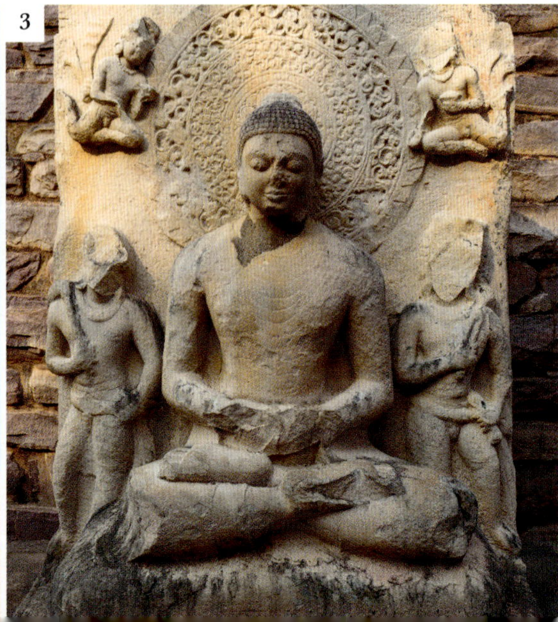

4

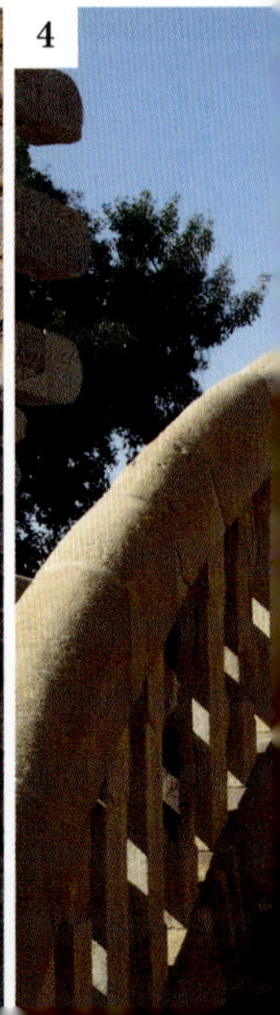

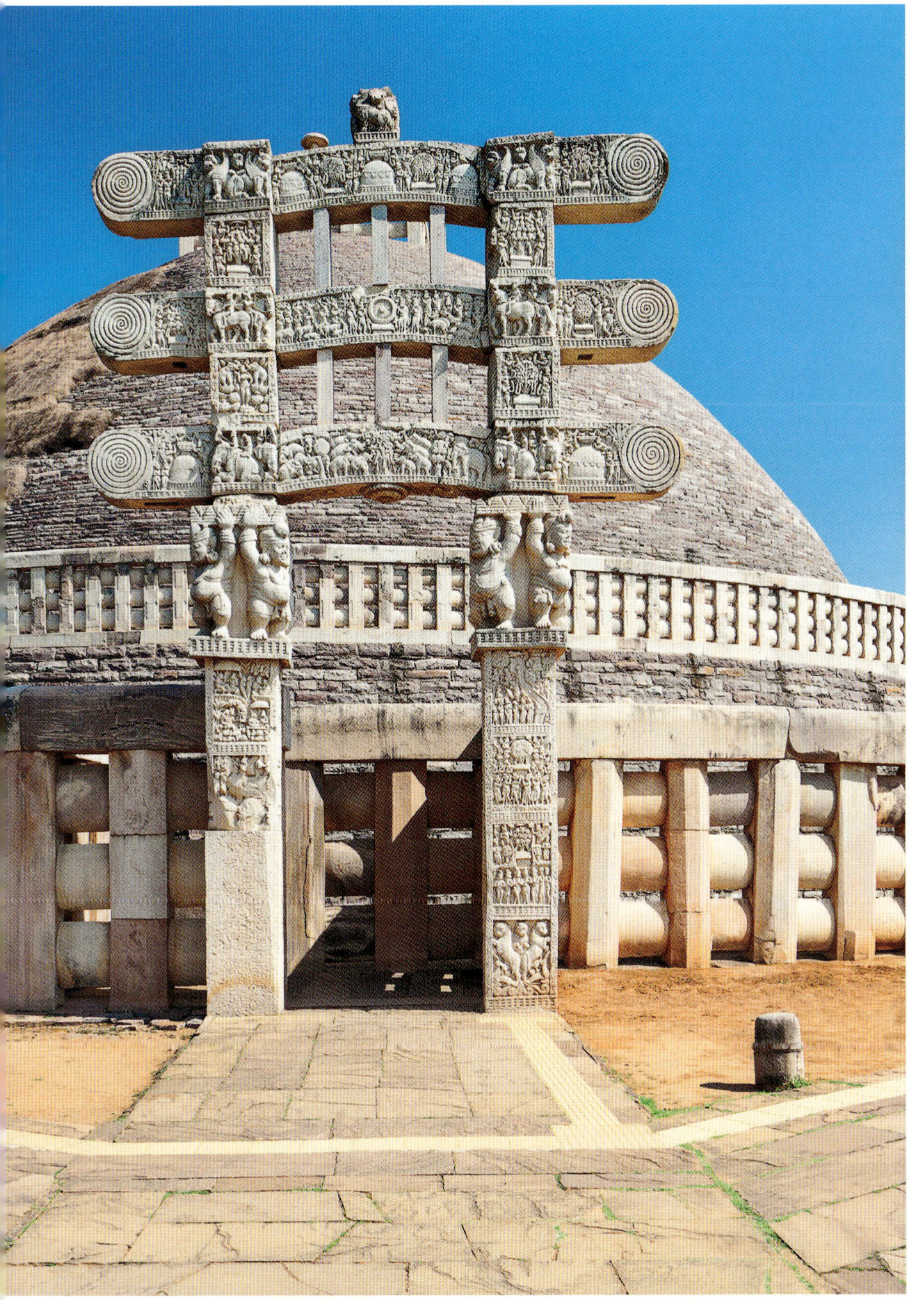

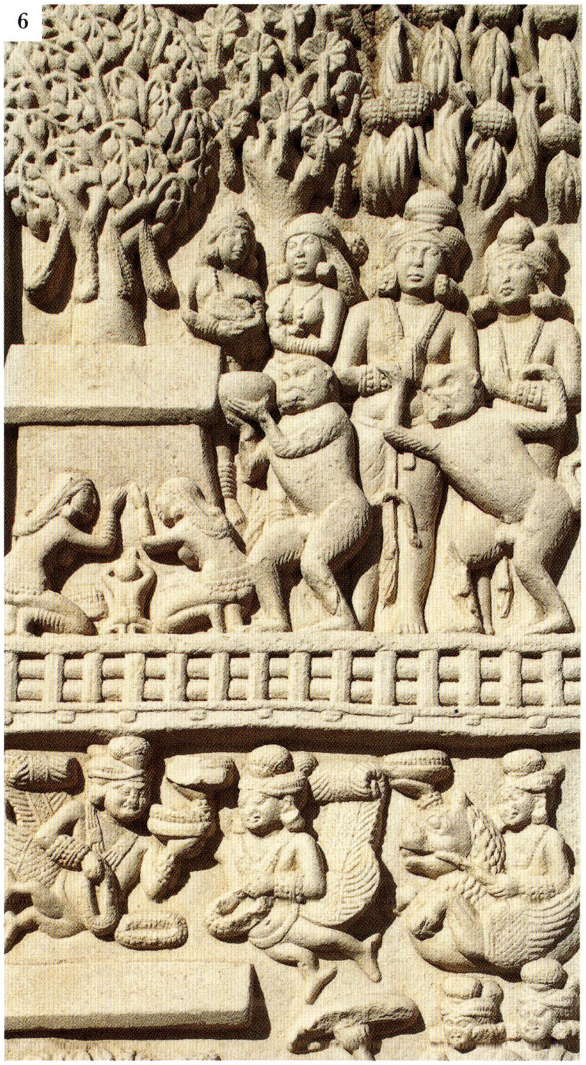

6

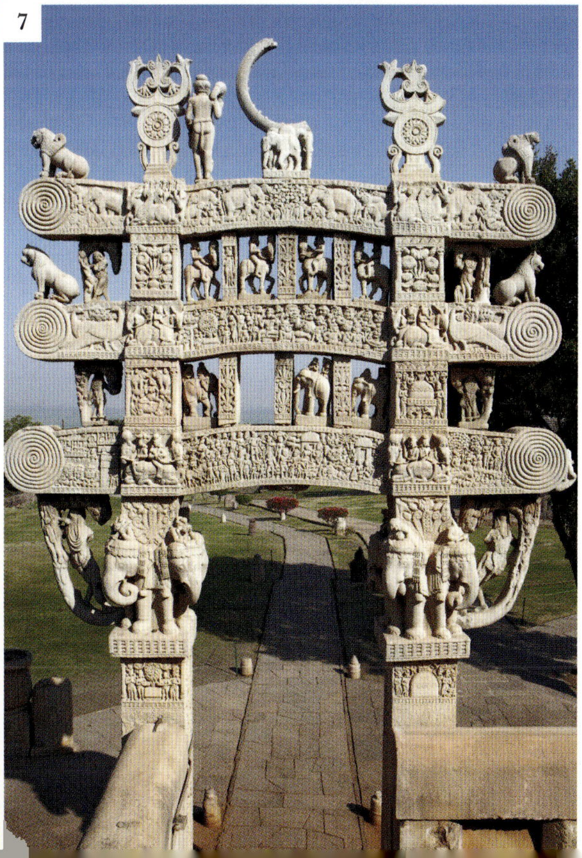

7

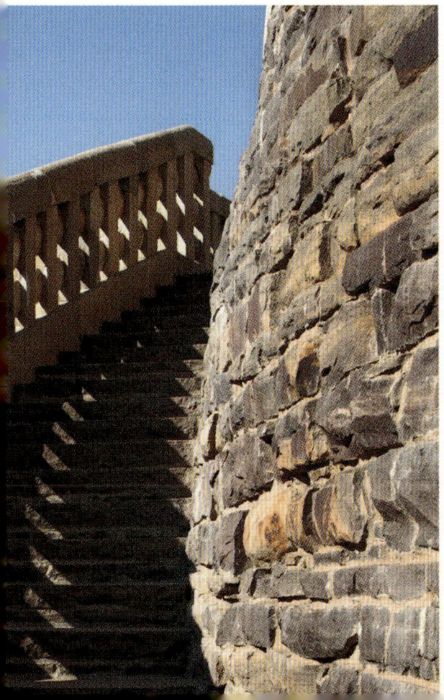

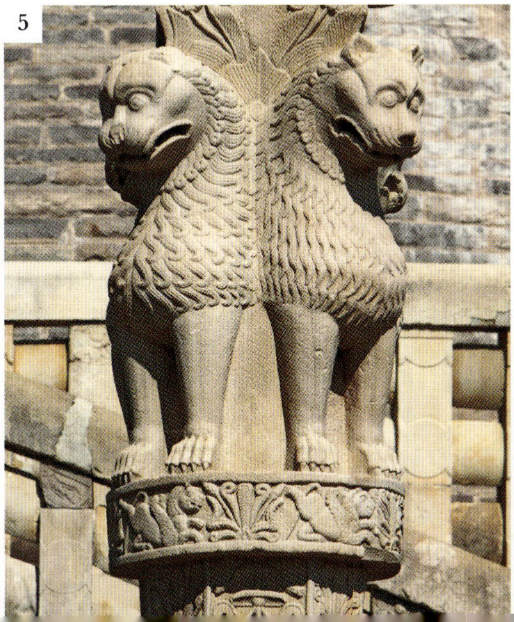

5

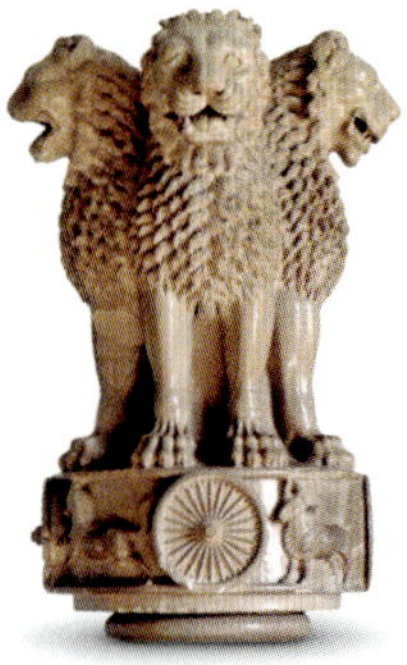

Era 2nd century BCE | **Medium** Sandstone | **Dimension** 2.1 × 0.86 m (7 × 2.8 ft)

LION CAPITAL

The legacy of India's first Buddhist rule

Now a national emblem, visible on Indian currency and official documents, the Lion Capital of Ashoka is a sculpture that dates to the Mauryan Empire. It features four Asiatic lions seated back to back on an ornamented base.

Originally set upon a column erected by the Mauryan emperor Ashoka in Sarnath in northern India in c. 250 BCE, the Lion Capital is now displayed at the Sarnath Museum near Varanasi in the state of Uttar Pradesh, not far from its excavation site. It features striking embellishments, the most iconic of which are the four Asiatic lions mounted on a circular abacus. The lions are believed to symbolize power, courage, pride, and confidence. However, some Buddhist interpretations suggest that they signify the four directions in which the Buddha delivered his message. Yet another interpretation associates the lions with the reign and influence of Ashoka in the four cardinal directions.

ROYAL ORDER

During Ashoka's reign, pillars such as this one were placed throughout the Mauryan empire. These impressive examples of architecture were either positioned along the roads or in city centres. It is believed that they served as a kind of public address system: they were inscribed with proclamations or edicts from the ruler, which were then disseminated throughout the territory. In addition,

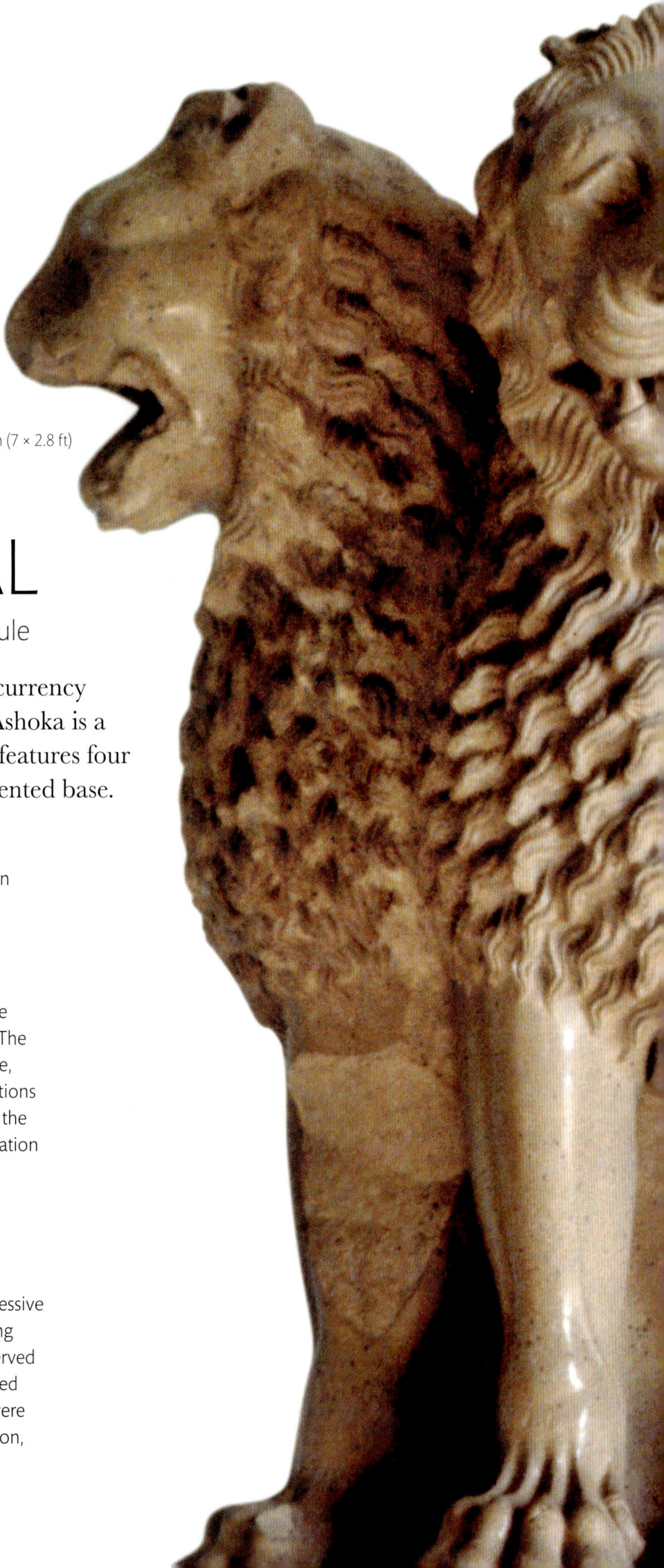

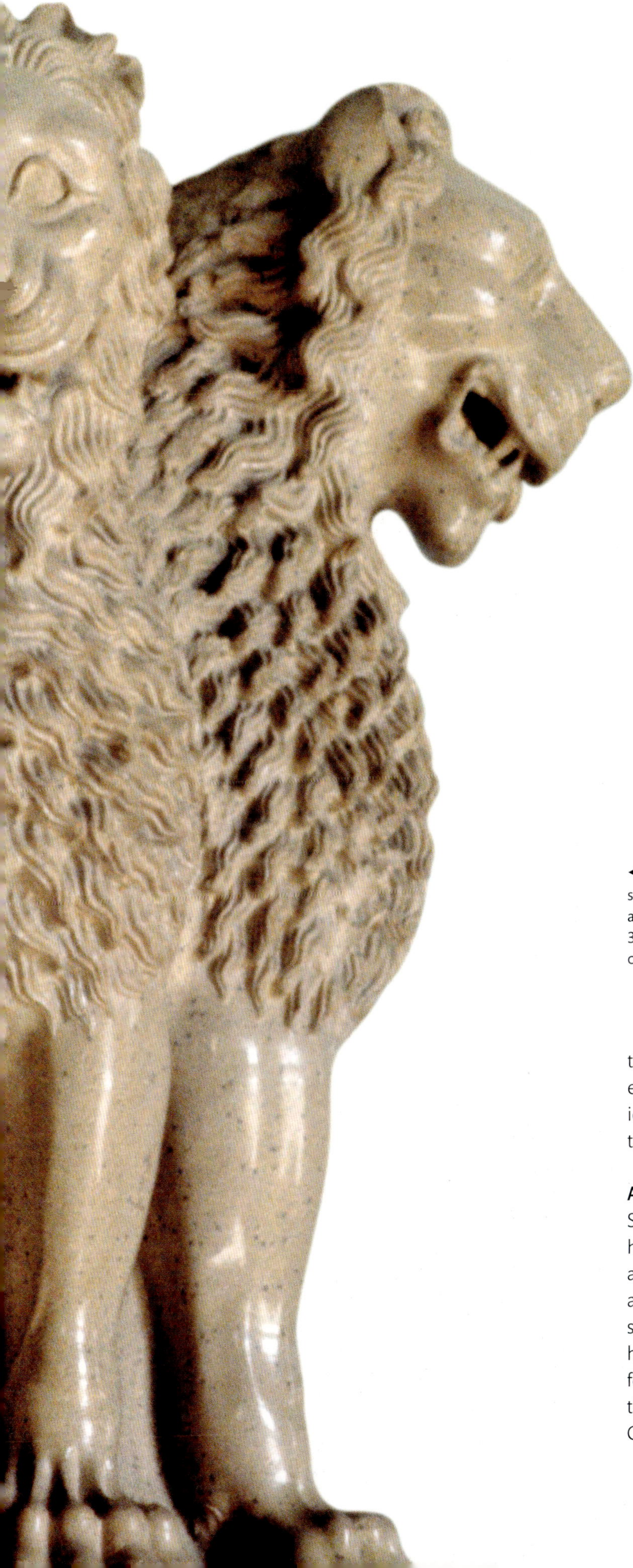

◄ **Four Asiatic lions are depicted as** seated atop a base with the Ashoka Chakra, a Buddhist motif, perhaps created in the 3rd century BCE. It, as well as other animal-form capitals were once set upon inscribed pillars.

the *dharmachakra* or the Buddhist 'wheel of law' embedded on the pillars possibly sought to recall the idea of the Chakravartin, 'the holder of the wheel' or the solar symbol of divine knowledge and authority.

A LASTING LEGACY

Separated from its base pillar and lying buried for several hundred years, the Lion Capital was excavated in 1904 at Sarnath, an important site in Buddhism. It was adapted as the national emblem of independent India in 1950, signifying an acknowledgement of modern India's ancient heritage, cultural traditions, and core values. It now features prominently on all official documents and is the official seal of the President of India and the Central and several state governments.

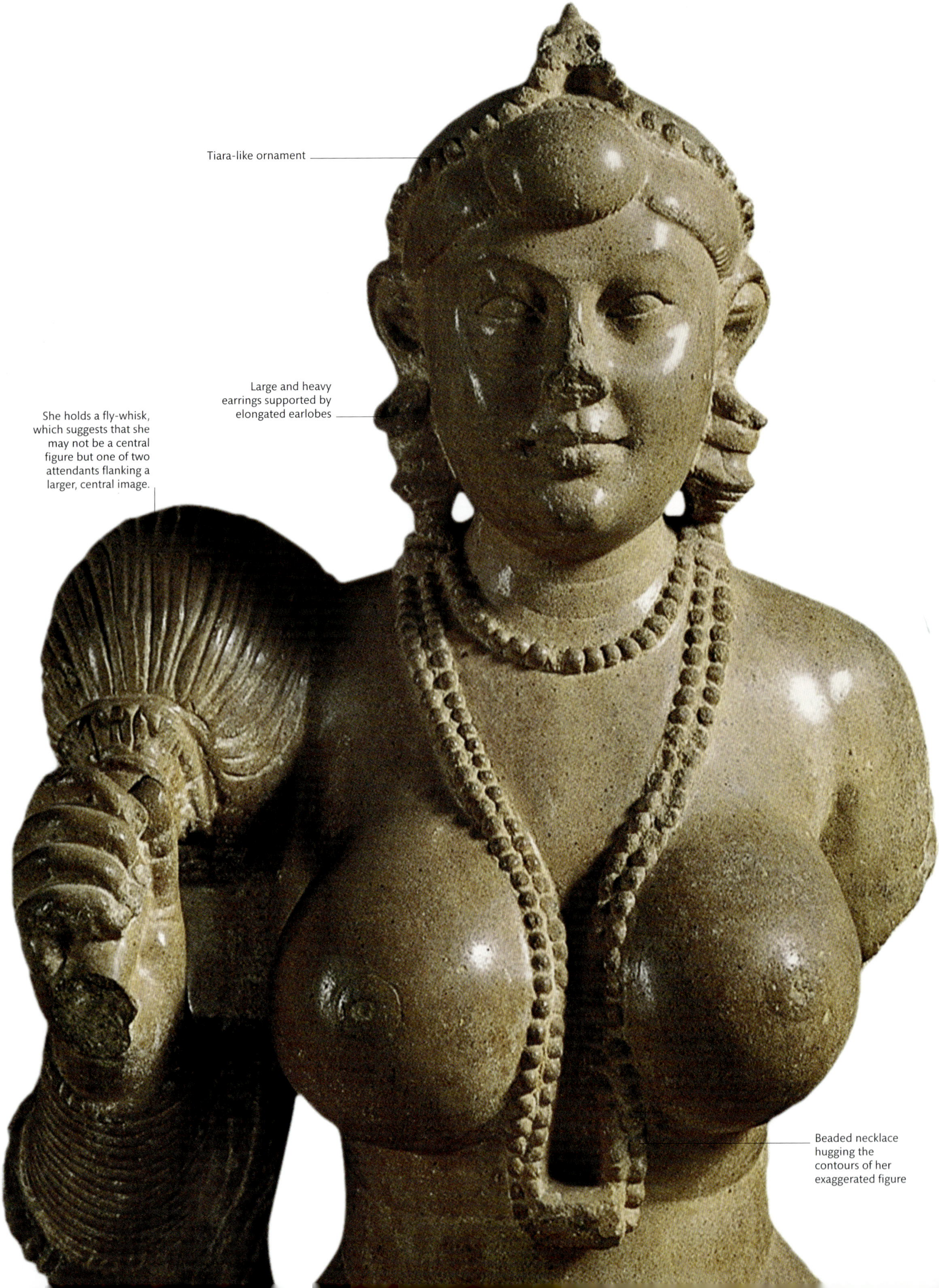
Tiara-like ornament
Large and heavy earrings supported by elongated earlobes
She holds a fly-whisk, which suggests that she may not be a central figure but one of two attendants flanking a larger, central image.
Beaded necklace hugging the contours of her exaggerated figure

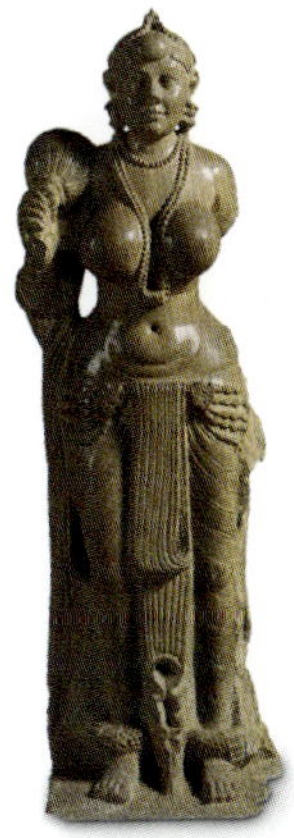

Era 4th century BCE | **Medium** Chunar Sandstone | **Height** 1.5 m (5.2 ft)

YAKSHI OF DIDARGANJ

A deity shrouded in mystery

Serendipitously discovered in 1917 on the banks of river Ganga by local washermen in Bihar, this polished sculpture of a female figure has been hailed as one of the finest examples of Mauryan art.

Made of burnished Chunar sandstone, featuring intricate modelling and voluptuous nude anatomy, the Didarganj Yakshi strongly recalls the *surasundaris* (young maidens) depicted on the walls of the Khajuraho temples (see pp. 128–129) built nearly a thousand years later. The sculpture is now attributed to the Mauryan era; however, its origins, representational style, and iconographic identification have long stirred debate among historians.

A GUARDIAN OR A DEITY?

Before it was acquired by colonial-era archaeologists and moved to the Patna Museum, in Bihar, the figure was briefly worshipped by the local community of Didarganj that discovered it. At the time, they were told that the statue represented a guardian spirit rather than a deity, and therefore was not meant to be worshipped.

◀ **The life-sized figure stoops** slightly forward instead of standing upright, with its weight carried largely on the left leg.

However, this explanation was widely disputed, as the statue was popularly seen as a yakshi, a tutelary deity typically placed on the walls or entrances of temples. The interpretation depends on whether the fly-whisk she is seen holding can be considered a symbol of an attendant's subservience or that of a deity's glory. Other features, including its large size, polished surface, and intricate carving of jewellery and clothing, support the latter idea, indicating that she may have been of great importance.

DECODING THE FIGURE

The Didarganj Yakshi's prominent breasts and wide hips have also been the subject of much discussion. One theory views the yakshi's sensuous form as being part of a spiritual aesthetic in which eroticism is viewed as artistic expression. Others have posited that the statue's sexualized features represent fertility and motherhood, though these interpretations do not quite align with the guardian duties or the symbolism of a yakshi. It is now believed that this statue was intended to be an idealized version of the female form, rather than a conscious representation.

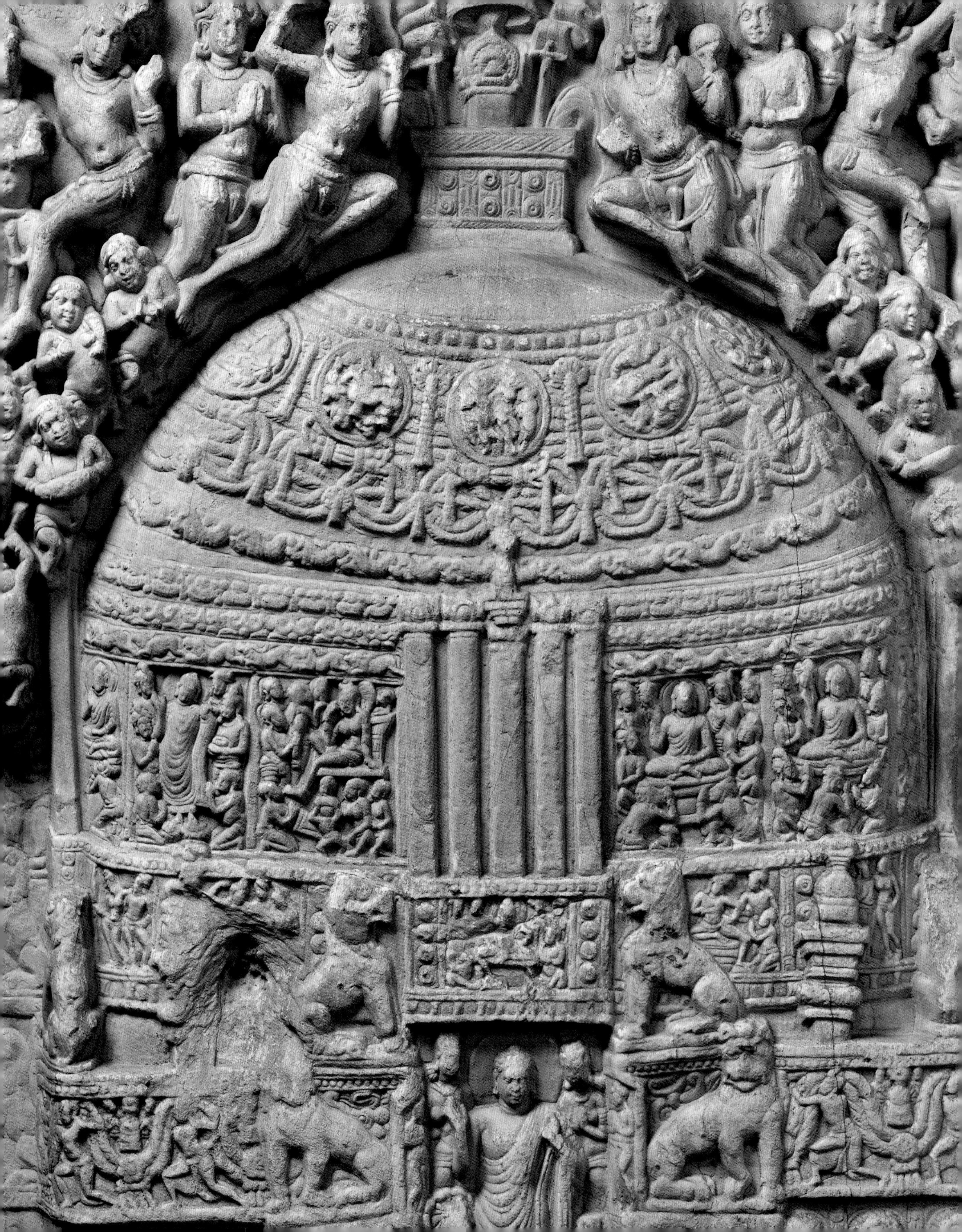

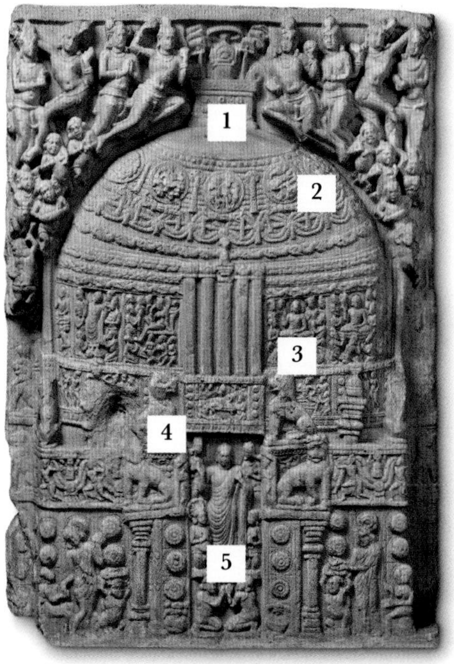

1. Yakshas, some playing musical instruments, keeping a watchful eye on the domed structure of the shrine. **2.** Carved medallions depicts Prince Siddhartha on horseback, leaving his life of luxury behind. **3.** A scene showing the Buddha delivering his first sermon after gaining enlightenment. **4.** Lions, symbols of protection and power, face all four directions and guard the gateway to the shrine. **5.** The statue of the Buddha, flanked by devotees who clasp their hands in reverence.

Era 2nd century CE | **Medium** Limestone | **Height** 124.4 cm (48.9 in)

AMRAVATI STUPA RELIEF

The lost splendour of the Satavahanas

Perhaps one of the grandest of Buddhist stupas, located in Amravati, now in the southern Indian state of Andhra Pradesh, was built under the patronage of the Satavahanas, who ruled the central Deccan region for nearly half a millennium.

Very little remains of the Mahachaitya, or the Great Stupa at Amaravati, constructed in 200 CE as a brick-cored shrine near Dhanyakataka, the capital of the later Satavahanas. It was considered the largest of the Deccan stupas.

The Amravati stupa was once an earthen mound, about 45 m (147 ft) in diameter and more than 30 m (98 ft) in height, including its supporting drum and capping finial, clad in the local white limestone. It was surrounded by an exuberantly carved high railing and cross pieces, as well as lofty entrance gateways standing at the cardinal points.

In the following centuries, it received major additions in the form of carved facings and railings, but was abandoned after the 14th century. In 1796, a British officer began excavating the site. However, most of the limestone portions had been pillaged by corrupt landowners who viewed the abundant marble as a source for plaster and proceeded to reduce it in lime kilns. Today, pieces of the stupa – reliefs and decorative plaques – are preserved in museums in Chennai and the United Kingdom.

FRAGMENTS OF THE STUPA

This relief is a drum panel depicting the stupa itself and incorporating a compact composition of animated figures in fluid postures. Each figure is not only animated internally, but the surfaces' fluidity is reminiscent of water-worn pebbles and further enhances the action. It features an image of the Buddha in human form – the style of carving aligns with the last phase of Satavahana patronage at the site, by which time, anthropomorphic depictions of the Buddha had become popular. In addition, the details of this relief give us an idea of what the stupa would have looked like in its heyday.

A CARVED MASTERPIECE

Intricate sculptures depicting various scenes from the life of the Buddha were discovered inside the stupa. Posts and railings show ornate lotus medallions, friezes of garlands carried by dwarfs, and tales from the Buddha's life illustrated with vivid scenes of crowds, horse riders, and courtiers.

CONSOLIDATION

An age of empires

Five centuries of chaos and change followed the decline of the Mauryan Empire, the rise of several kingdoms, and the forging of a sprawling empire. Each kingdom left its mark, whether it was the impressive rock-cut caves of Ajanta, or evocative sculptures such as the headless statue of Kanishka.

The decline of the Muaryans left the subcontinent in a state of flux. Many new states, unable to capture the expansive realm of the Mauryans, emerged with constantly changing kings and boundaries.

THE SHUNGAS AND OTHERS

A 7th-century court poet, Banabhatta's seminal *Harshacharita* tells us that the termination of the Mauryan reign was orchestrated in a dramatic fashion by an assassination. The last Mauryan ruler, Brihadratha, was killed by his military commander Pushyamitra, while the king inspected his troops. Pushyamitra founded the Shunga dynasty around 185 BCE, which encompassed only a portion of the erstwhile Mauryan Empire. During this period, architectural monuments, and many art forms, including terracotta images and stone sculptures flourished. However, stability eluded the Shungas, thanks to the emergence of other kingdoms in the Deccan as well as the onslaught from Central Asia by the Graeco-Bactrians and the remnants from Alexander's old army, now under independent kings who sought to rule more powerful states. This involved the Shungas in wars in which they were not always victorious. The Puranas refer to the Graeco-Bactrians or the Indo-Greeks as Yavanas (though this term was loosely applied to all foreigners from the West). Historians suggest that Pushyamitra

c. 187 BCE Fall of the Mauryan Empire

185 BCE Establishment of the Sunga dynasty

165–145 BCE Indo-Greek king Menander or Milinda reigns

83–73 BCE Reign of the last Shunga ruler, Devabhuti

80 BCE Establishment of the Indo-Scythian kingdom

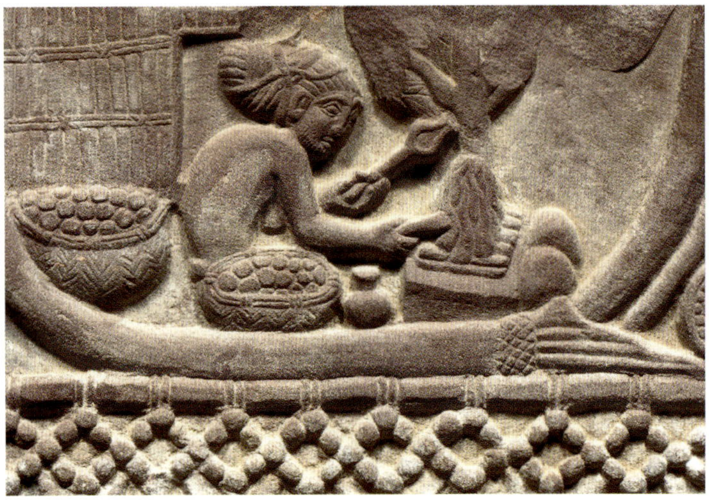

These sculptures, depicting scenes from the Buddha's past lives, belong to a coping railing that was added to the Barhut Stupa, in Madhya Pradesh, during the rule of the Shunga dynasty, c. 150 BCE.

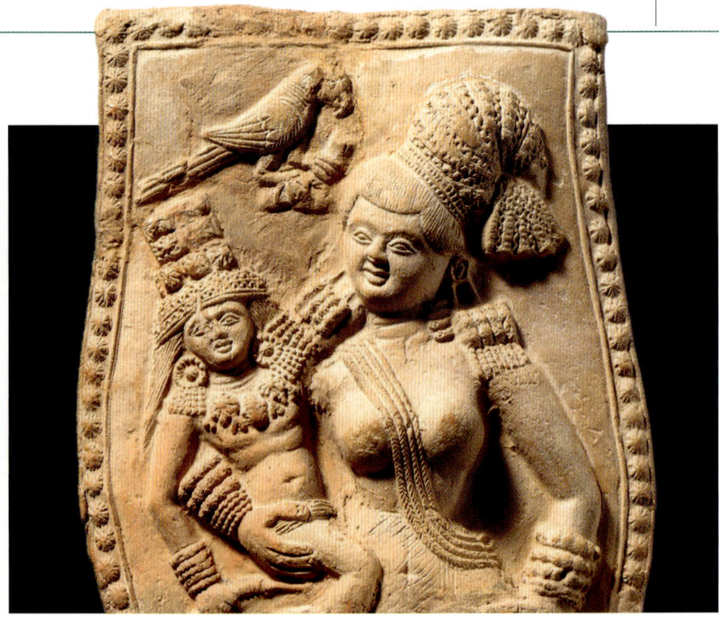

A terracotta panel from the Shunga dynasty, c. 1st century BCE, showing a yakshi or nature spirit holding a crowned child. A visiting parrot perches near her head.

launched a series of campaigns against them, including blocking them from conquering Pataliputra, the capital. After 112 years of unstable reign, the Shungas were overthrown by Vasudeva Kanva, who founded the Kanva dynasty that ruled the area around Magadha, rather uneventfully, and ended around 28 BCE due to the rise of the Satavahanas in the south.

THE SATAVAHANAS

Around the 1st century CE, southern India witnessed the rise of the Satavahanas in the western Deccan region. In time, the kingdom expanded to include modern-day Andhra Pradesh and Maharashtra. Though precise dates for its rule are unavailable, inscriptions document the order of succession of their rulers. Simuka, the founder of the kingdom who started as a Mauryan feudatory, was succeeded by his brother Kanha, who was instrumental in expanding the empire as far as Nashik in the west. The most famous king was Gautamiputra Satakarni, who revived the Satavahana power and defeated the Sakas, Pahlavas, and Yavanas.

The Satavahana rule was marked by the rise of territory consolidation and urbanization. Political structures and chains of command were more visible now than in the preceding Mauryan period. New traditions of governance such as joint

72–28 BCE Emergence of the Kanva dynasty

68 CE Establishment of the Kushana Empire by Kujula Kadphises

70–60 CE Satakarni I expands the Satavahana Empire

78 CE Gautamiputra Satakarni takes over the Satvahana Empire

165–194 CE Rule of Yajna Sri Satakarni, one of the later Satavahana kings

130–140 CE Vashishthputra Pulumayi succeeds Gautamiputra

c. 100–500 CE Gandharan art flourishes

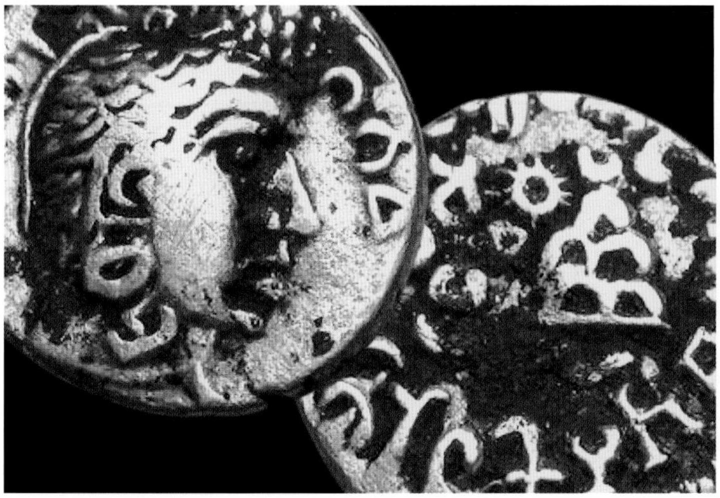

Silver coinage of Gautamiputra Satakarni, ruler of the Satavahanas, marked by his portrait on one side and the symbols of the dynasty as well as the sun and moon on the other side.

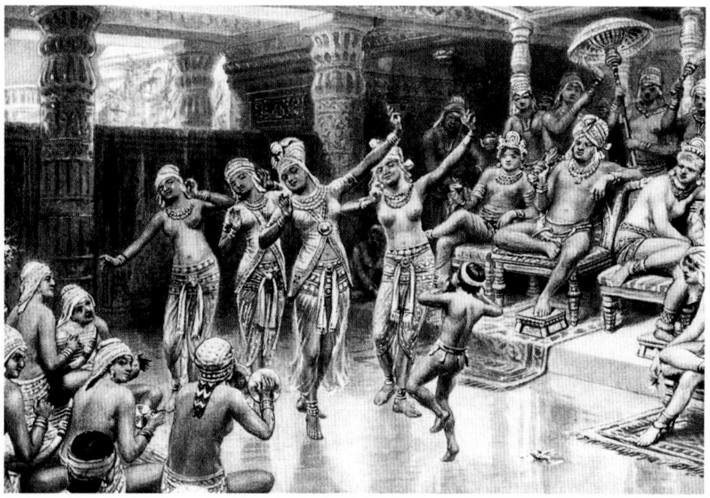

The 19th century artist Ambrose Dudley's impression of Gautamiputra Satakarni celebrating a significant victory. During his reign, the Satavahana Empire is said to have reached its peak.

rule and a system of subordinate rulers emerged. Trade flourished under the Satavahanas. The western and the eastern coasts had several active ports and many market towns. Even though the Satavahana rulers were Hindus, Buddhism grew under their rule. The empire disintegrated by the 3rd century CE into smaller kingdoms.

THE KUSHANAS

Around the time the Satavahanas were gaining prominence in southern India, certain developments were taking place far away in Central Asia. In the 1st century CE, the Kushanas emerged as an influential kingdom in the north-west of the subcontinent. The first ruler of the Kushana dynasty was Kujula Kadphises. However, the empire reached its apogee under Kanishka who came to the throne in 78 CE and greatly expanded their territory. He reigned over an area that straddled eastern parts of Xinjiang in China, Uzbekistan, and Afghanistan in Central Asia, and northern India up to Maharashtra and Madhya Pradesh. The political unification of these regions facilitated trade. Kanishka was a great patron of Buddhism, and supported monasteries and scholars. However, the most important development was that a new form of Buddhism emerged during this period. Unlike the earlier form which came to be known as Hinayana Buddhism, the Mahayana beliefs elevated the Buddha to godhood, and his images were made. The idea of a bodhisattva, a being who existed only to help others, and other Buddhist deities developed. These developments are said to have taken place due to close contact with foreign cultures and new changes in economy. This also influenced a new style of art, Gandhara art, which produced the first anthropomorphic representations of the Buddha unlike the aniconic ones earlier.

The Kushanas survived for a few hundred years after Kanishka and dissolved in the 4th century CE. This does not mean that there was a political vacuum – minor kingdoms and new rulers were constantly emerging and political boundaries shifting. At this time, the Guptas came up as a new centralizing power in 320 CE.

THE GUPTA AGE

The first Gupta monarch took the name of the first Mauryan emperor – Chandragupta. With his accession, the dynasty came into its own as he transformed the region from a simple principality to a veritable empire. Chandragupta I married into the powerful Lichchhavi dynasty, formerly a *gana-sangha* (non-monarchy) of

c. 100–500 CE Buddhism split into Mahayana and Hinayana

127–147 CE Kanishka rules the Kushanas

240 CE Sri Gupta establishes a feudatory

319–334 CE Chandragupta I founds the Gupta Empire

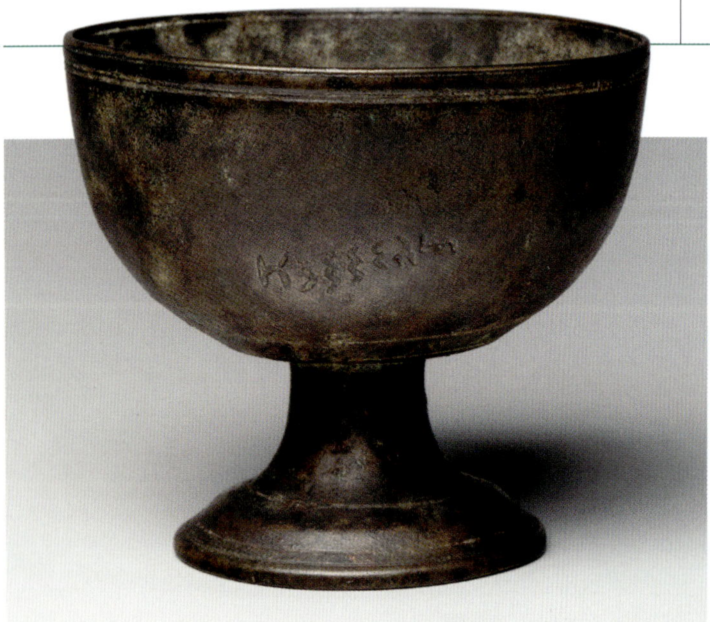

A bronze chalice from the Kushan or early Gupta period, dating to 2nd–4th centuries CE. The inscription on the body of the cup is in the Kharosthi language, which was used by the Kushanas.

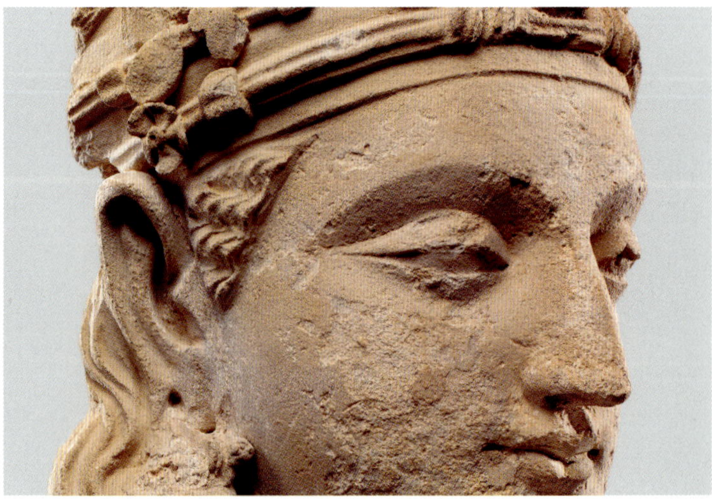

This sculptural head of a bodhisattva comes from a structure that would have stood near a stupa. The bodhisattvas emerged under Mahayana Buddhism during the Kushana dynasty.

Vaishali, now in north Bihar. His empire spanned the Gangetic heartland, and he adopted the title *maharaja-adhiraja* (the great king of kings). Samudragupta succeeded his father around 335 CE. Often portrayed as the ideal king, he expanded his empire to include the region from Rajasthan to Bengal. Samudragupta also maintained a significant navy and sea trade thrived. Several neighbouring eastern and southern kingdoms, including Sinhala (Sri Lanka), paid tribute to him. Later descendants who succeeded Samudragupta were Chandragupta II, who further expanded the empire, and Kumaragupta I, whose reign focused heavily on art and culture, taking the Gupta Empire to new heights. By 510 CE, the empire had mostly crumbled due to frequent invasions by the Huns, a nomadic tribe from Central Asia, and minor kingdoms appeared.

THE GUPTA WAY

In contrast to the Mauryan state, which maintained a rigid control over governance and was deeply involved at all levels of polity, the Guptas devolved power into the hands of the nobility and conquered kings were left to rule in largely feudal systems. The state received a large portion of its income from agriculture and other sources included mining, taxes on trade, and conquests. Products like fabrics, gems, and spices were traded with foreign merchants and crafts such as metalworking became highly developed. Chinese traveller Faxian notes that poeple in the empire were well off and lightly taxed. In terms of cultural advancements, the Gupta era is often called the classical age, mostly because there was a profusion of arts, architecture, and science, and it was a time of intellectual curiosity and new ideas.

The Gupta rule marked a resurgence of Hinduism with several key developments: the trinity of Shiva, Vishnu, and Brahma were followed widely and local deities were absorbed into the Vedic pantheon. Buddhism and Jainism continued to be financially supported. This was an important period in the history of temple architecture. The Mahabodhi Temple in Bodhgaya, Bihar, and the Dashavatara Temple in Deogarh, Odisha, are two renowned types of large-scale temples that are temples characteristic of Gupta architecture. Gupta sculptures were intricate and depicted Hindu, Buddhist, and Jain deities in stone or terracotta. Religious and cultural texts such as the Hindu epics Ramayana and Mahabharata, some of the Puranas, the Bhagavad Gita, and the Panchatantra were written down at this time - earlier, they were passed on orally, and Sanskrit, an ancient language was revived.

335–375 CE Reign of Samudragupta

375–414 CE Chandragupta II succeeds Samudragupta

400–411 CE Chinese traveller Faxian travels to India

c. 4th–5th century CE Mahabharata and Ramayana penned

414–455 CE Kumaragupta I succeeds Chandragupta II

c. 400 CE Vatsyayana's *Kama Sutra* composed

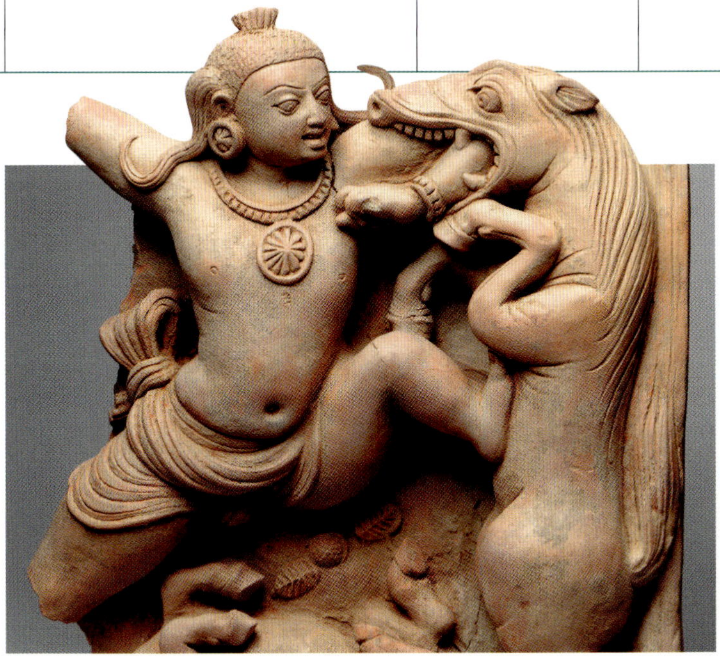

A terracotta sculpture depicting Lord Krishna slaying demon Keshi, who appeared in the guise of a horse. This panel from the Gupta period would have been used to decorate temples of the time.

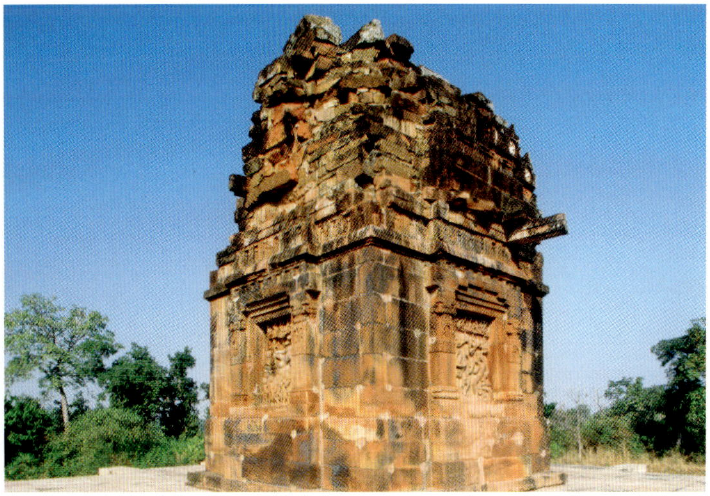

One of the earliest Hindu stone temples, the Dashavatar Temple in Deogarh, Uttar Pradesh was constructed during the reign of the Guptas in the typical temple architectural style of the period.

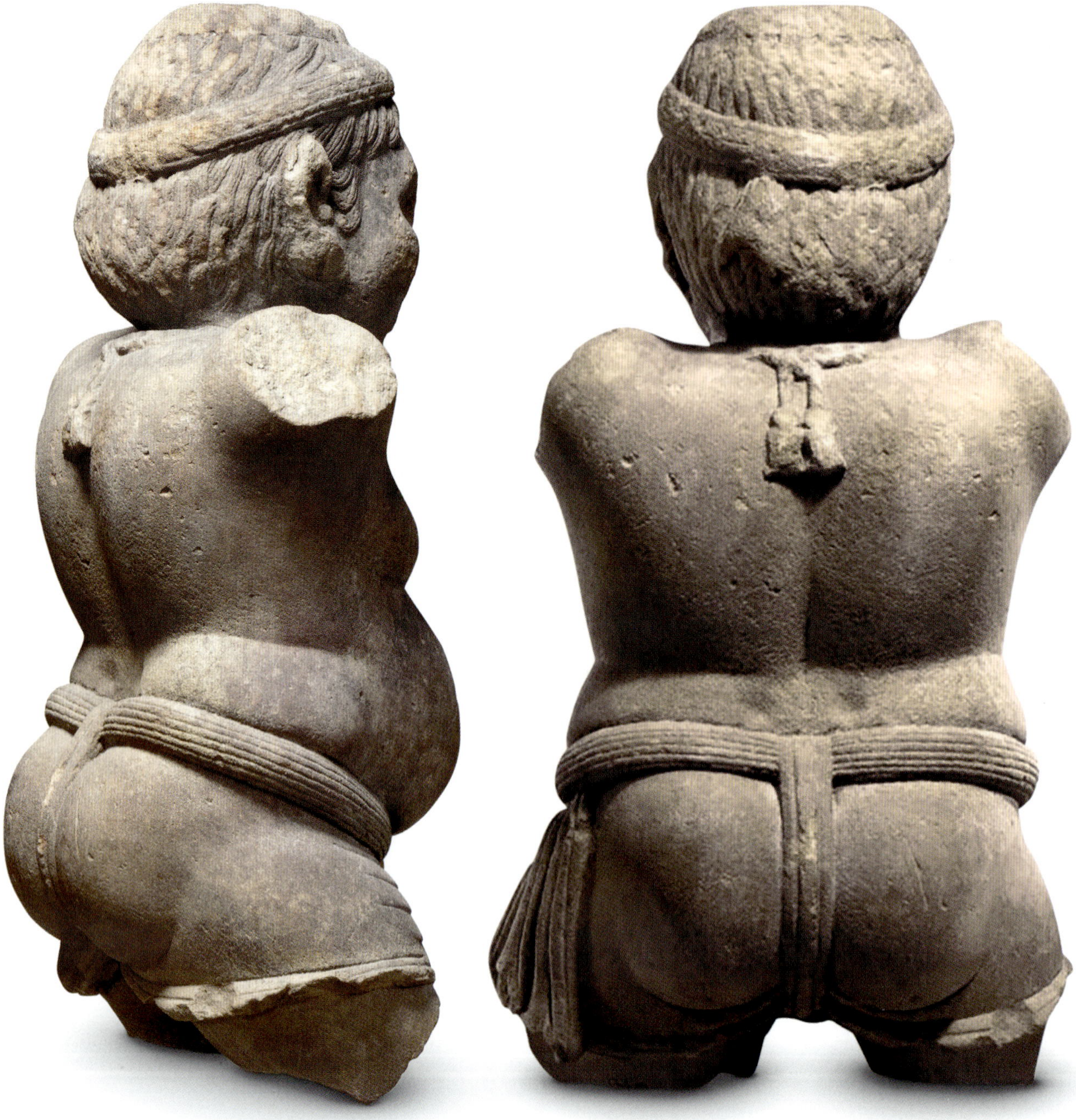

Era 2nd–1st centuries BCE | **Medium** Sandstone | **Height** 89 cm (35 in)

POTBELLIED YAKSHA

Guardian of the riches

Dwarf-like with a pendulous stomach, the evocative statue of a yaksha bears all the mysterious aura of the male nature spirits or demigods from Hindu and Buddhist mythology.

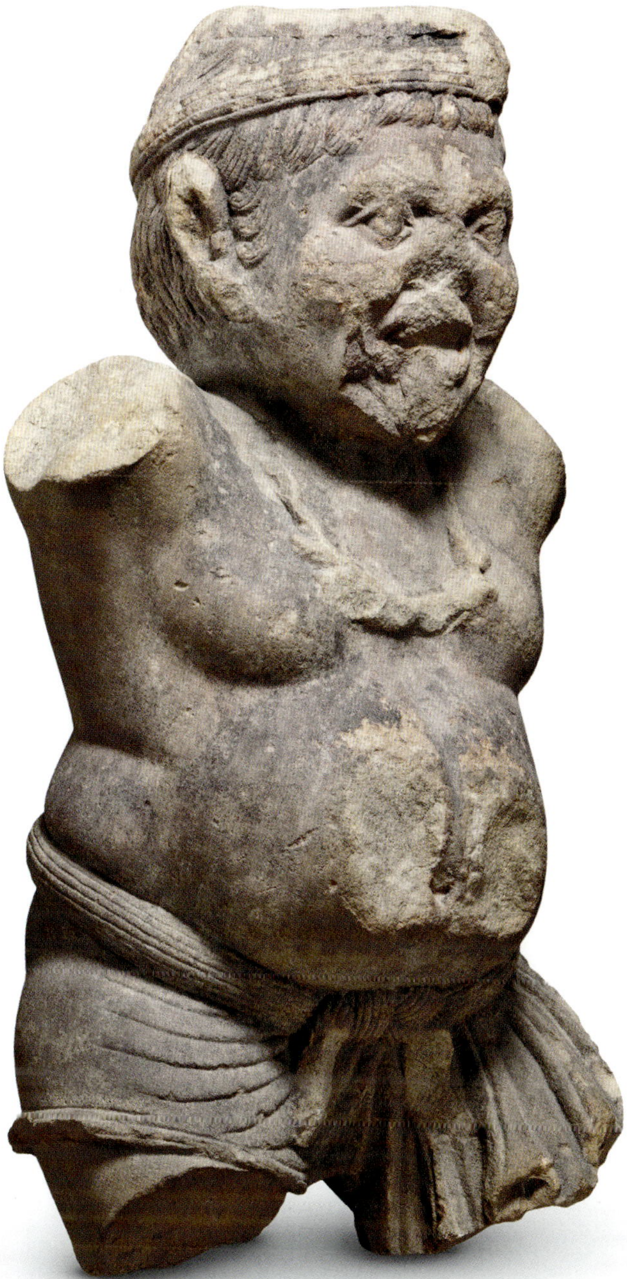

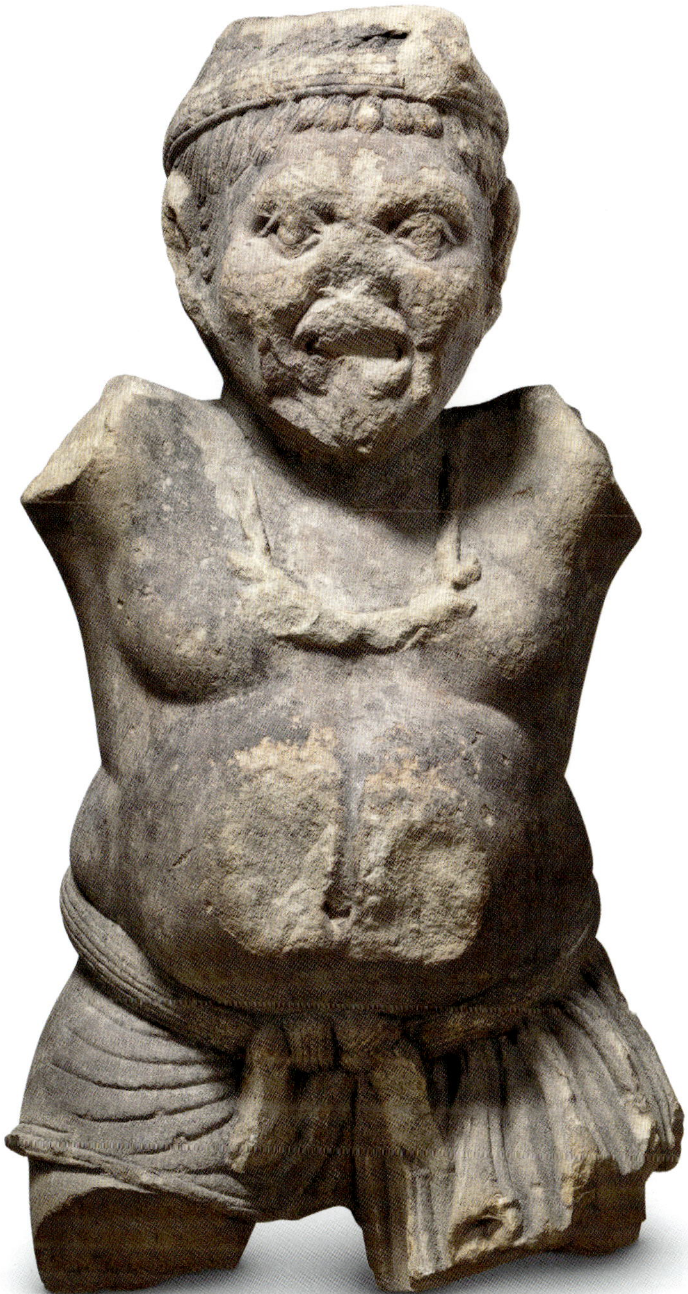

▲ **The yaksha's colossal** rotund belly is his most defining characteristic. Ravages of time have robbed many of his features, including his hands.

The exact identity of this sculpture of a potbellied yaksha from the Shunga dynasty is unknown. Some archeologists, however, identify him as a carrier or *bharavahaka* yaksha. They believe that its raised arms once supported a bowl on his head. Perhaps, he was meant to be a guardian or an attendant installed at the entrance of a stupa, the bowl used to collect donations from devotees.

The statue bears a torque, a headband, and a short garment secured with a thick, knotted sash at the waist. A series of folds accumulated at the left hip accentuate the heaviness of the cloth.

GUARDIANS OF THE RICHES

Yakshas, much like this one, along with their female counterparts, the yakshis, are a popular theme across ancient Indian arts, literature, and architecture. Their earliest mention can be traced to the *Jaiminiya Upanishad Brahmana*, where the term is used to refer to a mysterious being. However, by the time of the epics such as the Ramayana, they were considered spirits who were similar, yet superior, to ghosts and demons. The Buddhist Jataka tales portray them as savage and cannibalistic, known for their insatiable sexuality and greed. They reformed their ways after converting to Buddhism.

Over time, yakshas were worshipped as protectors of nature's bounty and were associated with wealth and abundance. The Mauryan and post-Mauryan periods saw them featured on many architectural elements.

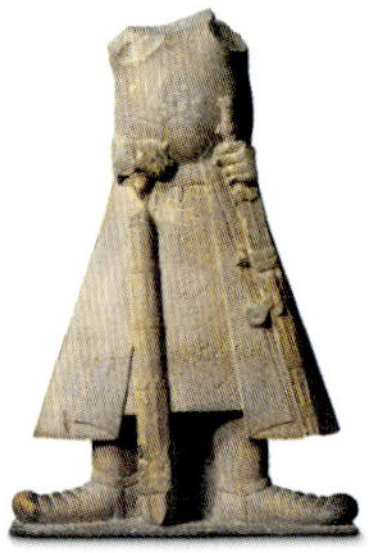

Era 1st–2nd century CE | **Medium** Sandstone | **Height** 1.85 m (6 ft)

STATUE OF KANISHKA

Figure of power and imperial legitimacy

Carved from red and white spotted sandstone, this headless statue of Kanishka, a powerful ruler of the Kushana dynasty, is notable for revealing the influences of the Kushanas' Central Asian nomadic ancestors.

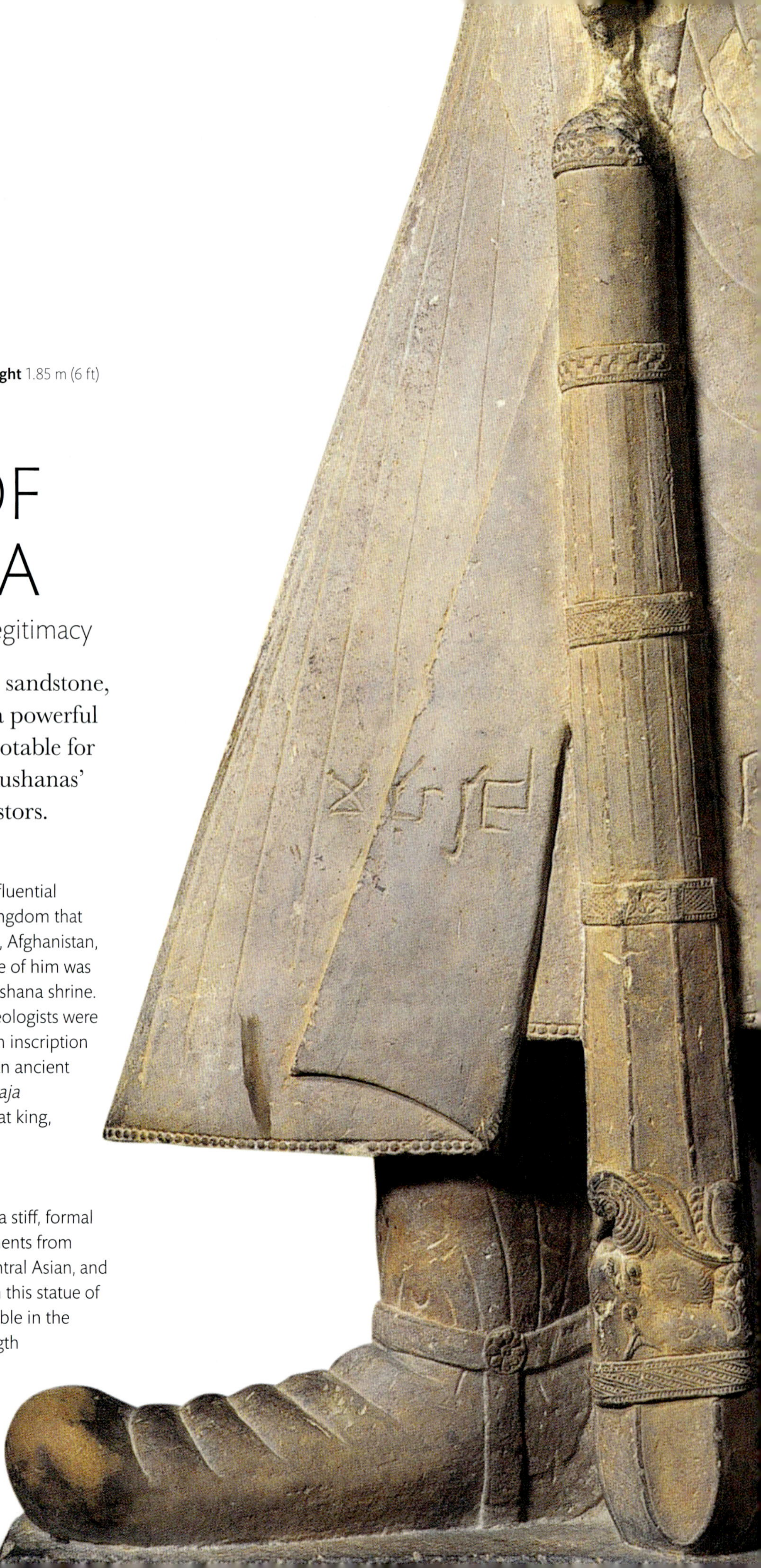

Kanishka was among the most powerful and influential emperors of the Kushana Empire, a syncretic kingdom that included the present-day regions of Uzbekistan, Afghanistan, Pakistan, and northern India. This life-size statue of him was excavated near Mathura at the site of Mat, a Kushana shrine. Although the statue was found headless, archaeologists were able to identify whom it represented through an inscription at the base of the statue. Written in Kharosthi, an ancient script from north-western India, it reads *Maharaja rajatiraja devaputra Kanishka*, meaning "the great king, the king of kings, the son of God, Kanishka".

A SYMBOL OF MIGHT

Kushana artwork has been identified as having a stiff, formal style with front-facing figures. It combines elements from various cultures including Classical, Iranian, Central Asian, and Indian in a unique style that clearly manifests in this statue of Kanishka. Central Asian influences are most visible in the statue's heavy clothing, including the ankle-length kaftan and thick boots, that seem impractical for the hot climate of Mathura, in modern-day Uttar Pradesh. Kanishka is also depicted with regal poise and grandeur, with his attire

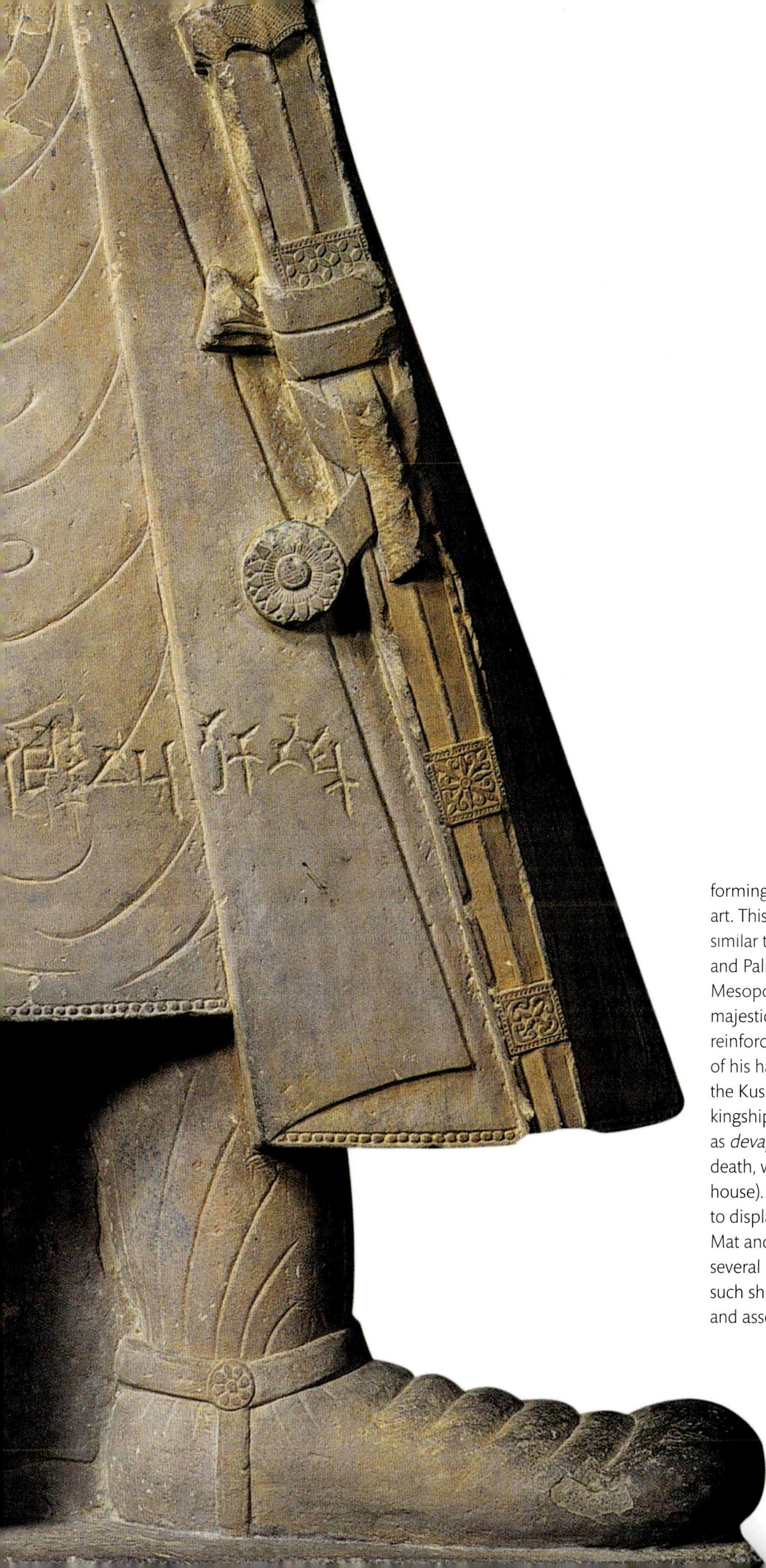

forming an angular silhouette – a hallmark of Kushana art. This monumental, rigid, and frontal imagery style is similar to that found in Parthian art from Dura Europos and Palmyra in present-day Syria, and Hatra in Upper Mesopotamia, Iraq. An impression of authority and majestic dignity also emanates from the statue, reinforced by the sword and club he holds in each of his hands. More than anything, the statue reflects the Kushana political system, which associated kingship with divinity. Kushana kings were referred to as *devaputra* (the son of God) and were deified after death, with their statues placed in a *devakula* (God's house). That Kushana kings commissioned galleries to display their portrait statues, as seen in both the Mat and Surkh Kotal shrines, has been noted by several historians. It is also believed that building such shrines served to legitimize their royal lineage and assert their divine right to kingship and power.

◄ **The statue of Kanishka is sculpted** from the front, though its arms and head have been lost to time. It is displayed at the Government Museum, Mathura in northern India.

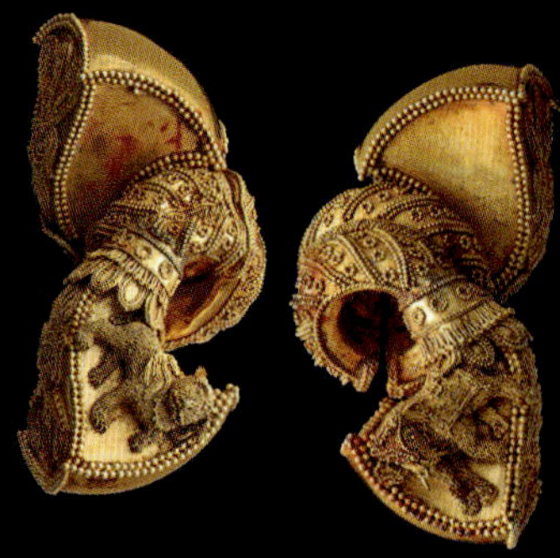

Era c. 1st century BCE | **Medium** Gold | **Length** 4 cm (1.5 in)

GOLD EARRINGS

Relics that embody the splendour of ancient Indian craftsmanship

Rare in having survived the ravages of time, this heavily embellished pair of gold earrings dates from the Satavahana dynasty and sheds light on the impeccable gold artistry in the region at the time.

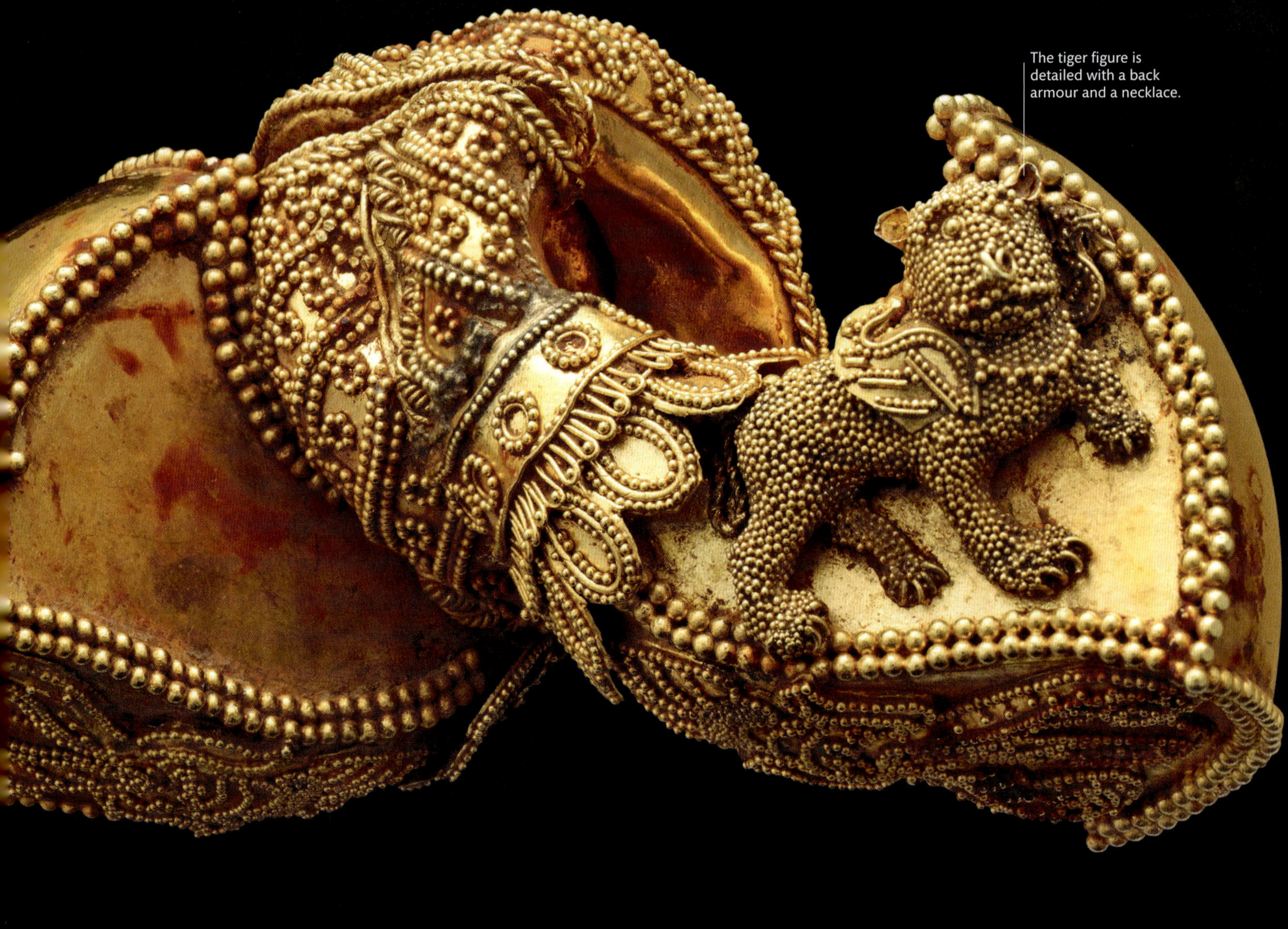

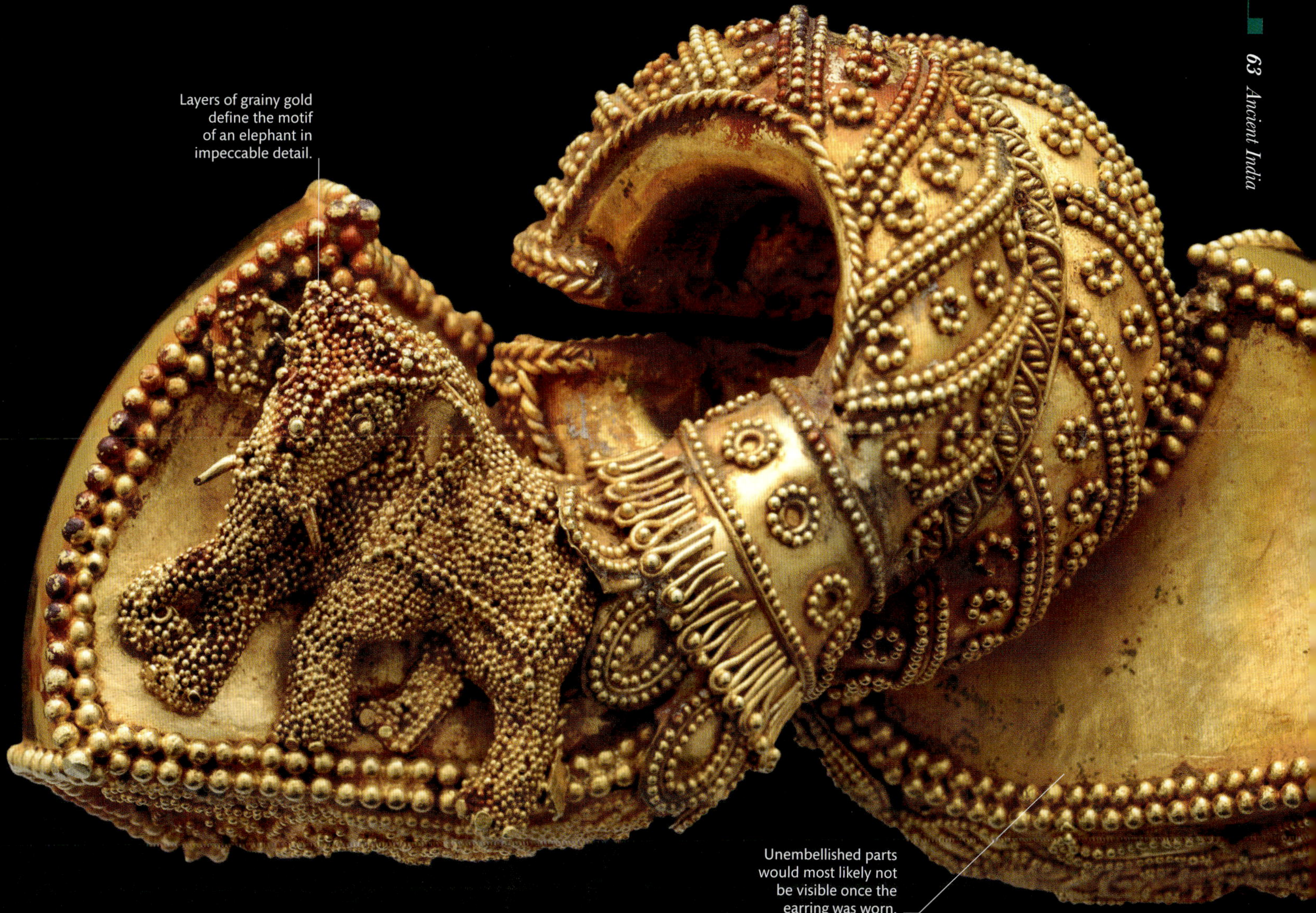

Few pieces of jewellery as exquisite as these gold earrings exist today. Although splendid ornaments of this kind feature heavily in early stone sculptures and terracotta plaques of regal and divine figures, indicating that they were worn customarily in the region, only a handful artefacts of such fine craftsmanship have actually been found. This was perhaps because, according to several historians, jewellery of the time was not passed down, but rather melted down to prevent the transfer of the owner's karma (a Hindu belief that one's actions affect the future).

DETAILED ADORNMENT

Given the earrings' size, weight, material worth, expert craftsmanship, and royal emblems embossed in the design, it is fair to conclude that they would have been made as royal commissions. Each earring features a combination of clusters and rows of beads, a winged lion, an elephant, and two vases filled with vegetation. The design is composed of two rectangular shapes that resemble buds, which extend outwards from a central tendril. The elephant and lion are made of repoussé gold and are intricately detailed using granules, snippets of wire and sheet, and are individually crafted with hammered pieces of gold. The two earrings are not completely identical; both feature a traditional early Indian design of a vase with three palmettes on the bottom, but the pattern of the fronds is different on each earring. To wear the earrings, one would have had to slip them through a stretched earlobe from the back. When worn, the lion would have faced the wearer's cheek and the elephant would have been seen on the outside.

Interestingly, a similar pair of earrings, nearly identical in size and shape, adorn the Chakravartin statue found on a relief from the stupa at Jaggayyapeta, in present-day Andhra Pradesh. These gold earrings, therefore, serve as tangible evidence of the jewellery depicted in Satavahana sculptures being based on real-life examples.

◀ **These ornaments were worn** by male and female members of the aristocracy as well as seen sculpted on statues of semi-divine figures.

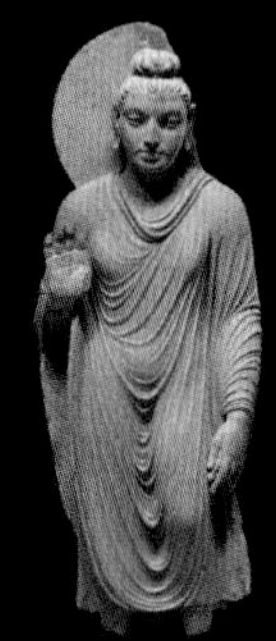

Era 1st–3rd centuries CE | **Medium** Grey-blue schist | **Height** 119.7 cm (47.1 in)

STANDING BUDDHA

The divine takes human form

Unique expressions of the confluence of Hellenistic, Persian, and Kushan cultures, the Gandharan Buddha sculptures are the earliest known anthropomorphic depictions of the Buddha. They are noteworthy for their syncretic visual vocabulary.

Gandharan Buddhas, such as the Standing Buddha, were noticeably Indian (or Mauryan, rather) in their sensuousness, but featured influences that were absorbed from the rules of Macedonians, Graeco-Bactrians (Hellenists), Sakas, and Indo-Parthians. This sculpture has its origins in the Kushan Empire of Gandhara, an important crossroads along the Silk Route. One of the 16 *mahajanapadas*, or ancient kingdom-states from northern India, Gandhara is known for its cosmopolitan culture and artistic styles which emerged as a consequence of several waves of conquest.

SURROUNDING INFLUENCES

Immediately apparent in this statue is the fact that the Buddha is portrayed wearing a garment resembling a Roman toga, with the folds of drapery carved with the same precision and detail that are typical of Roman sculptures from the same era. The pose is also more European in style; the Buddha stands upright on a small plinth rather than being seated or in an active pose, which is more common in Indian art. The figure also has a hint of the *contrapposto* (counterpoise) pose found in classical Greek statues, with weight on the right foot and the other leg slightly bent, though in this case it is not as pronounced

The head of the Gandharan Buddha is where the syncretic Graeco-Indian art is most evident. The halo, commonly used in Greek art to denote holiness, surrounds the head. In addition, the top-knot of curly hair is reminiscent of Greek portrayals of the god Apollo in which his wavy hair was similarly styled.

ANICONIC TO ANTHROPOMORPHIC

The Gandharan Buddhas reveal a marked shift from the preceding traditions in Buddhist art, wherein, for several centuries, explicit representations of the Buddha were avoided. The Buddha was only alluded to in images such as an empty throne, a riderless horse, a footprint, or the Bodhi tree under which he attained enlightenment. He was also represented by more abstract signs and symbols, including the 24-spoked wheel or *dharmachakra* that symbolized his teachings.

► **The Standing Buddha carving sculpted** from schist in 150–200 CE in the region of Gandhara, in modern-day Pakistan. It is now housed in the Cleveland Museum of Art, USA.

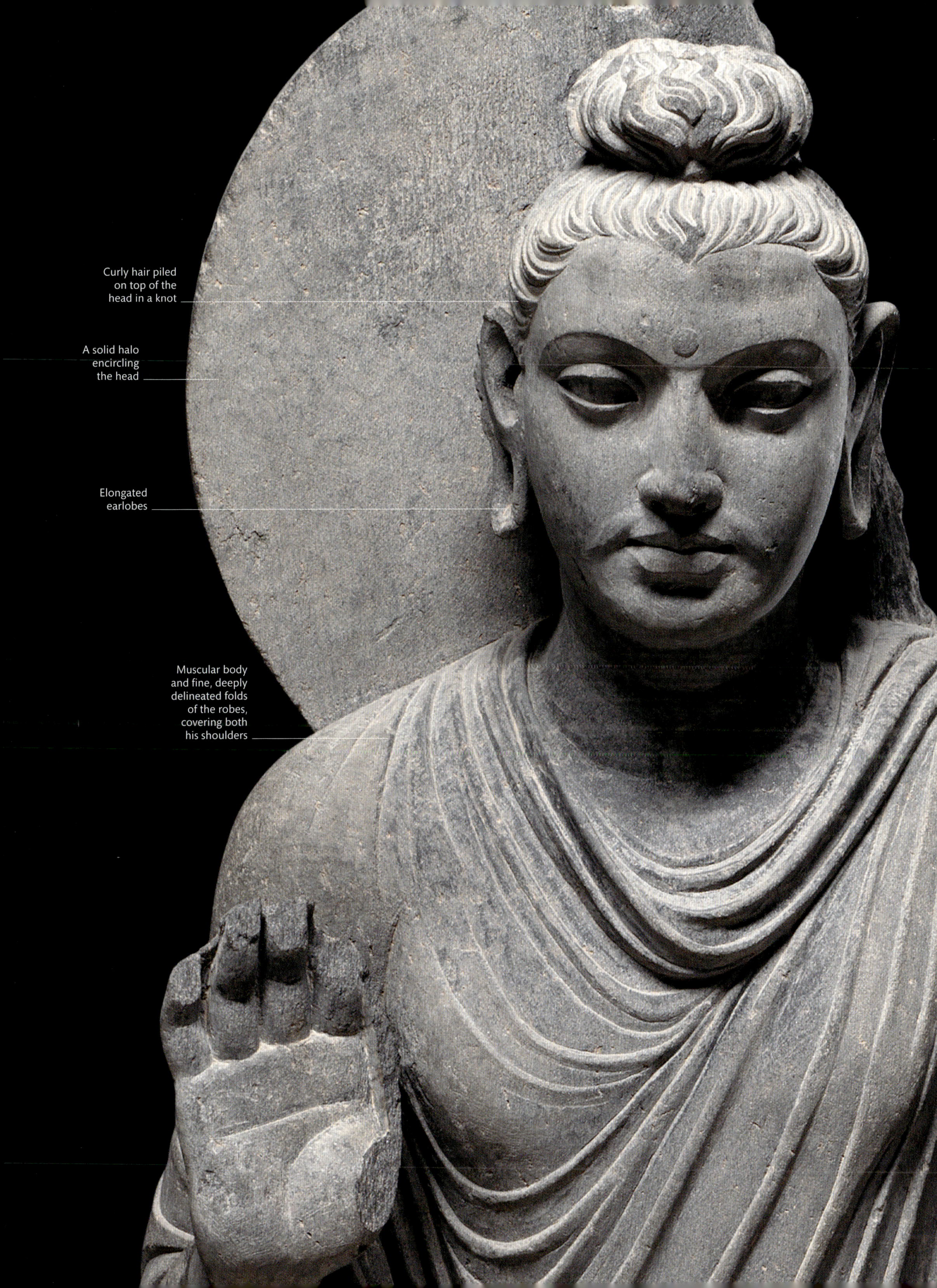
Curly hair piled on top of the head in a knot
A solid halo encircling the head
Elongated earlobes
Muscular body and fine, deeply delineated folds of the robes, covering both his shoulders

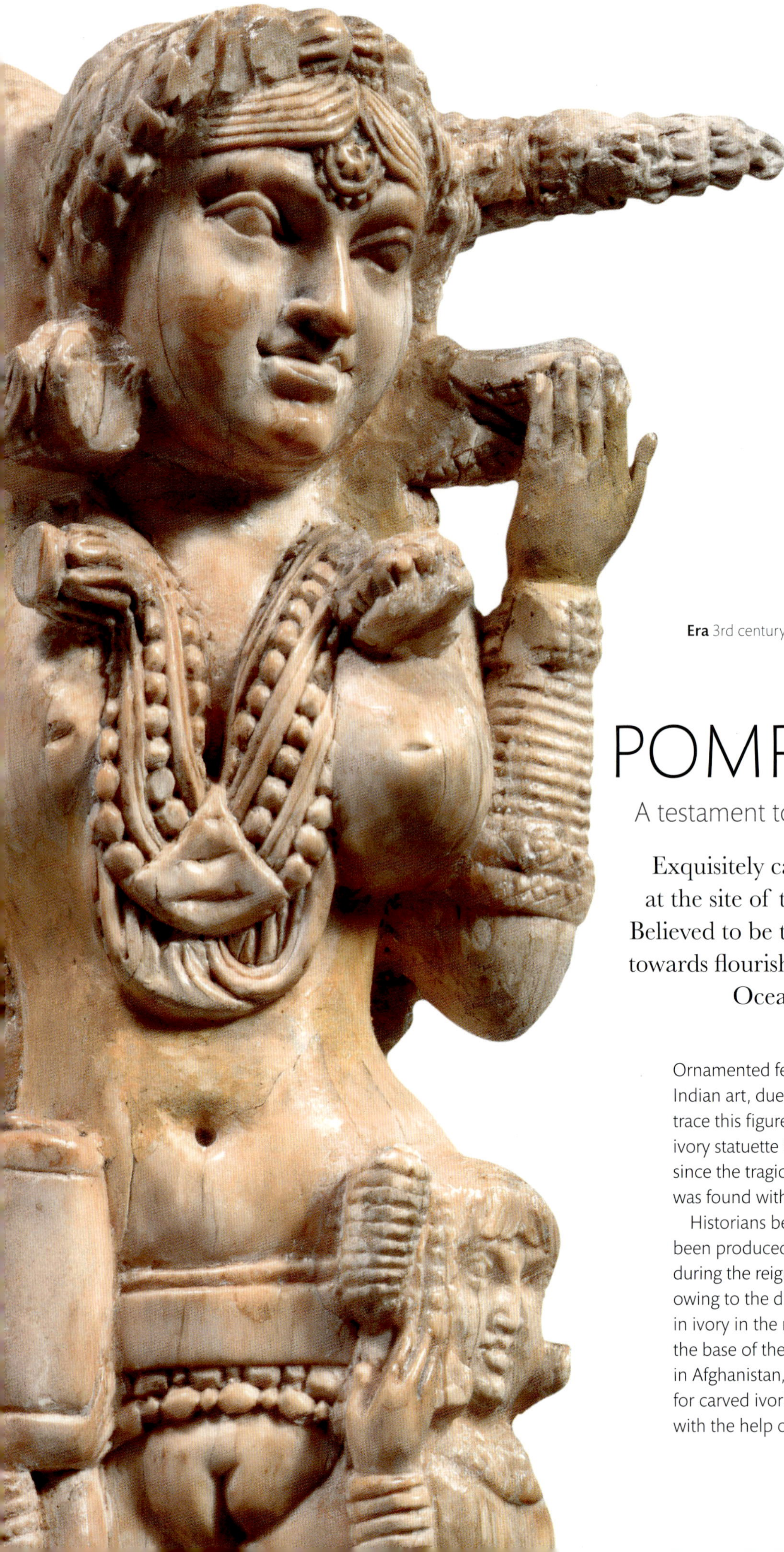

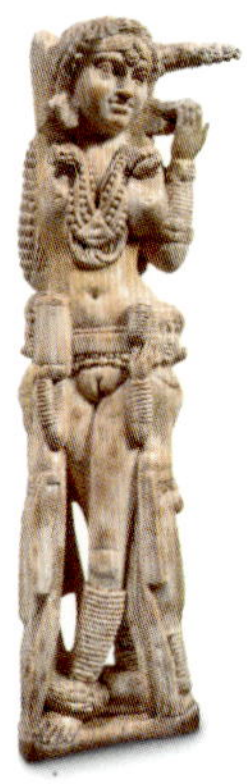

Era 3rd century BCE | **Medium** Ivory | **Height** 24.5 cm (9.6 in)

POMPEII LAKSHMI

A testament to Indo-Mediterranean confluence

Exquisitely carved, this statuette was discovered at the site of the ancient Roman city of Pompeii. Believed to be the Hindu goddess Lakshmi, it points towards flourishing trade networks across the Indian Ocean and Mediterranean Sea.

Ornamented female figures appear frequently in ancient Indian art, due to which it was easy for archeologists to trace this figure to the Indian subcontinent. Reputedly, this ivory statuette had remained buried under volcanic ash since the tragic eruption of Mount Vesuvius in 79 CE and was found within the ruins of a residence in Pompeii.

Historians believe that the Pompeii Lakshmi would have been produced in Bhokardan, in present-day Maharashtra, during the reign of the Satavahana dynasty (see pp. 54–57), owing to the discovery of many similar figurines carved in ivory in the region. However, a Kharosthi inscription at the base of the statuette suggests a link to Begram, now in Afghanistan, which was once a major production centre for carved ivories. Scenes of women adorning themselves with the help of female attendants also appear commonly

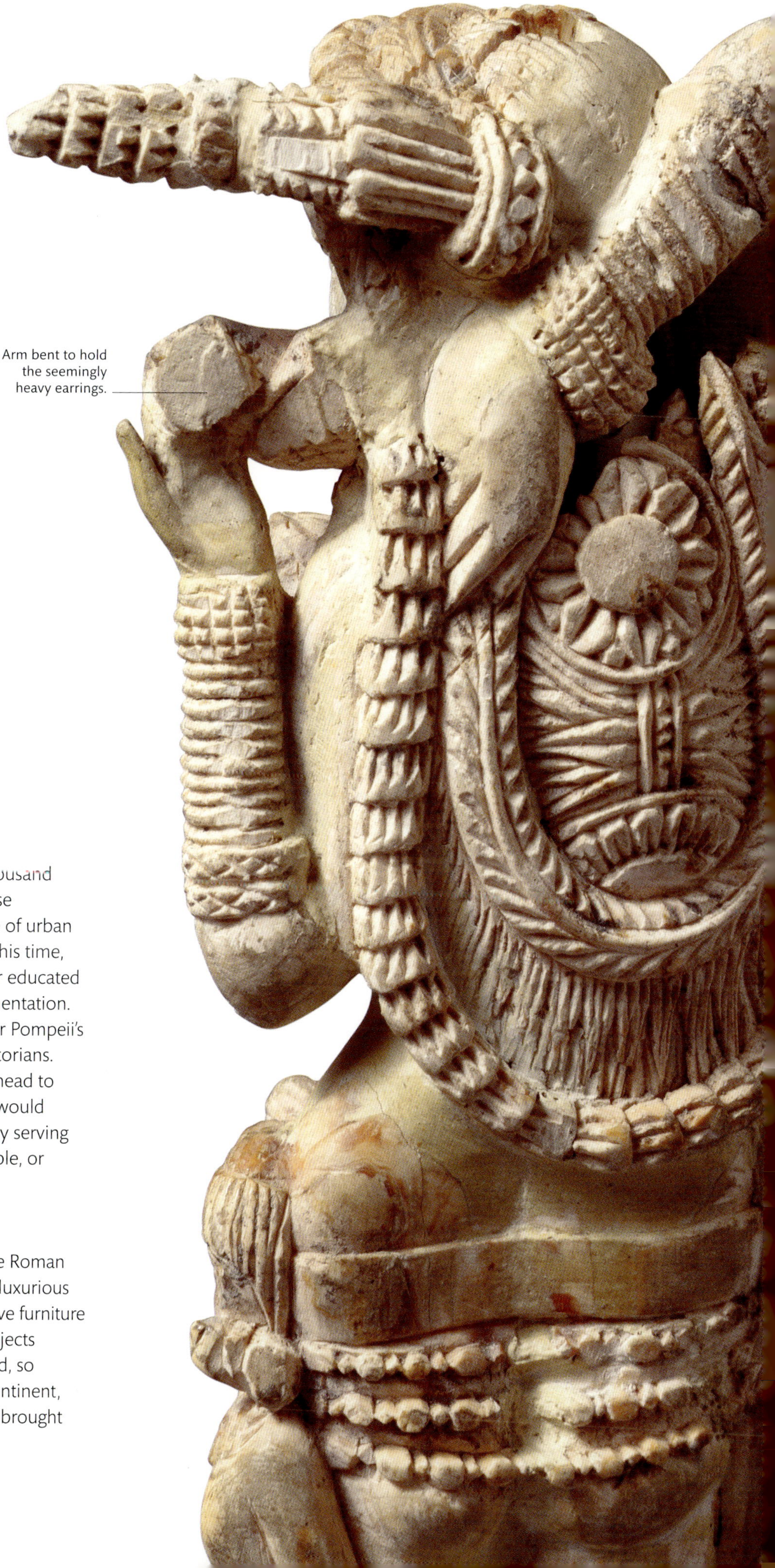

► **Although appearing to be naked,** the figure is clothed below the waist in a sheer garment, adorned with heavy bangles, anklets, a necklace, and a belt around the waist.

in the Begram hoard – a collection of over a thousand ivory artefacts dating to the 1st century CE. These representations of beauty coincide with the rise of urban centres starting in the 3rd century BCE. During this time, it was considered a socially prescribed norm for educated members of the urban elite to engage in ornamentation. The purpose or the significance of this statue for Pompeii's residents is often a matter of debate among historians. It features a hole drilled through its body from head to waist, leading archeologists to conclude that it would have been a fragment of a larger object, possibly serving as a mirror handle, one of the legs of a small table, or even as a support for a standing tray or dish.

A STATUS SYMBOL

It was considered prestigious for members of the Roman elite to be seen as collectors and consumers of luxurious items, and patrons often commissioned expensive furniture and figurines made of imported ivory. Exotic objects imported from Asia or Africa were highly desired, so owning a figurine produced in the Indian subcontinent, such as the Pompeii Lakshmi, would have likely brought a great deal of prestige to its owner.

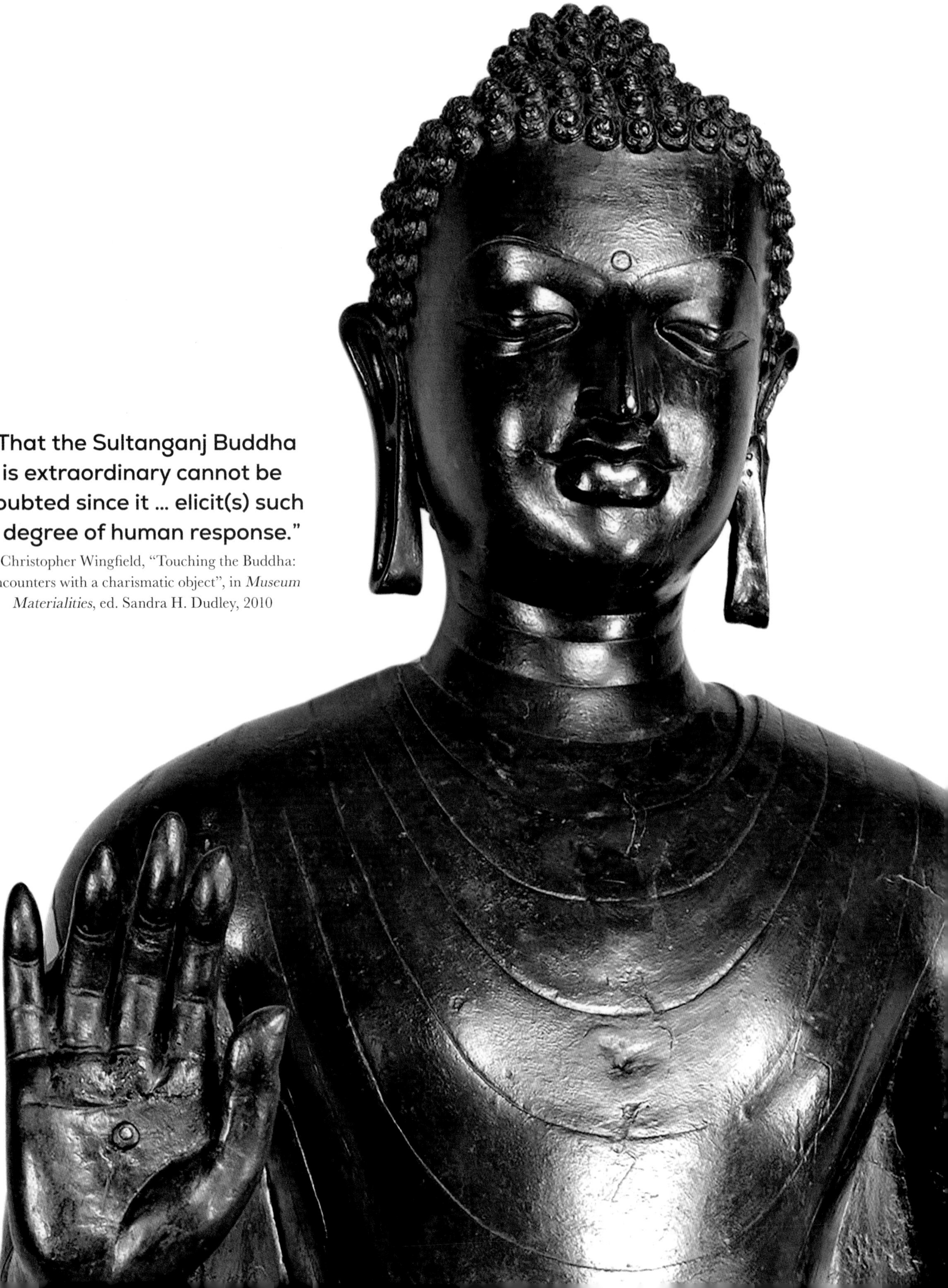

"That the Sultanganj Buddha is extraordinary cannot be doubted since it … elicit(s) such a degree of human response."

– Christopher Wingfield, "Touching the Buddha: Encounters with a charismatic object", in *Museum Materialities*, ed. Sandra H. Dudley, 2010

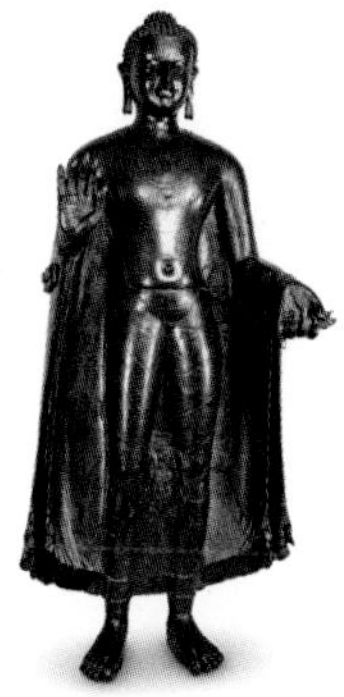

Era 6th–8th centuries CE | **Medium** Copper | **Height** 2 m (6.5 ft)

SULTANGANJ BUDDHA

Early medieval cast metal sculpture

The largest known complete metal sculpture from the Gupta period, the Sultanganj Buddha remained buried for nearly 700 years until a British railway engineer unearthed it in 1861.

This copper statue, cast using the lost-wax process (see p. 20), may have remained undiscovered for centuries had it not been found at a construction site of the East Indian Railway in Sultanganj, Bihar in 1861. The statue lay buried upside down in a cavity, located in close proximity to a seemingly defaced stone bodhisattva as well as several Buddhist mounds. Its state led to speculation of it being hidden away for safekeeping against a series of attacks by rival kingdoms on religious sites in the area, or at least to hide it in order to preserve it.

A CHARISMATIC FIGURE

The sculpture shares several attributes with the Buddha figures seen at Sarnath and Mathura, including a fleshy torso, stiff and smooth legs, accentuated kneecaps, and right hand in a fear-dispelling gesture or *abhaya mudra*. The treatment of the transparent monastic robe *(sangathi)* lies somewhere between the Mathura style, in which the folds of the robe were clearly depicted with stringed courses, and that of Sarnath, where there are none. Here, the maker has simply indicated the folds with faint, incised curves in the smooth surface. The dignity of the Buddha has been heightened by the fall of the robe, which in its sweeping lines also enhances the impression of movement created by the posture that is slightly off balance. Other characteristics such as the sharply defined facial features have led scholars to believe that the statue was created in Nalanda or Bodhgaya, located in Bihar, representing an eastern variation of the Gupta style.

Soon after its discovery, the Sultanganj Buddha was acquired by Samuel Thornton, owner of a brass foundry and former mayor of Birmingham, who paid to have the statue shipped to the city in the United Kingdom. As an industrial hub where most of the metal for the new Indian railway was being fabricated into rails and carriages, Birmingham would have seen the end of this striking copper icon. Fortunately, the statue escaped the melting furnace and was acquired instead by the Birmingham Museum and Art Gallery in 1864, where it has been housed and displayed till date, for over a century and a half.

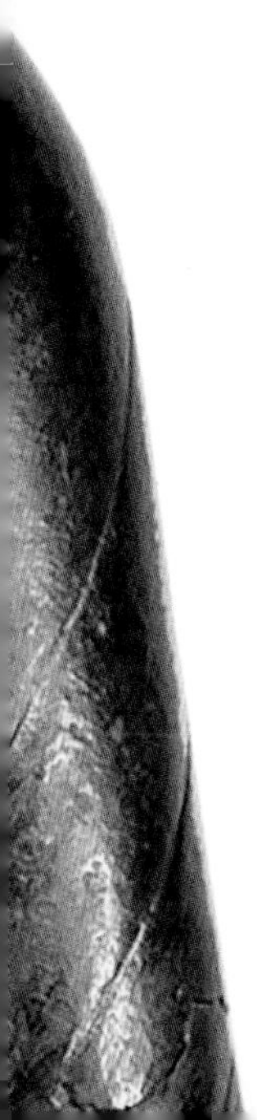

◀ **A closer look at the colossal** statue of the Sultanganj Buddha. It depicts the divine figure as he was visualized during the Gupta period, when the faith was well established in India.

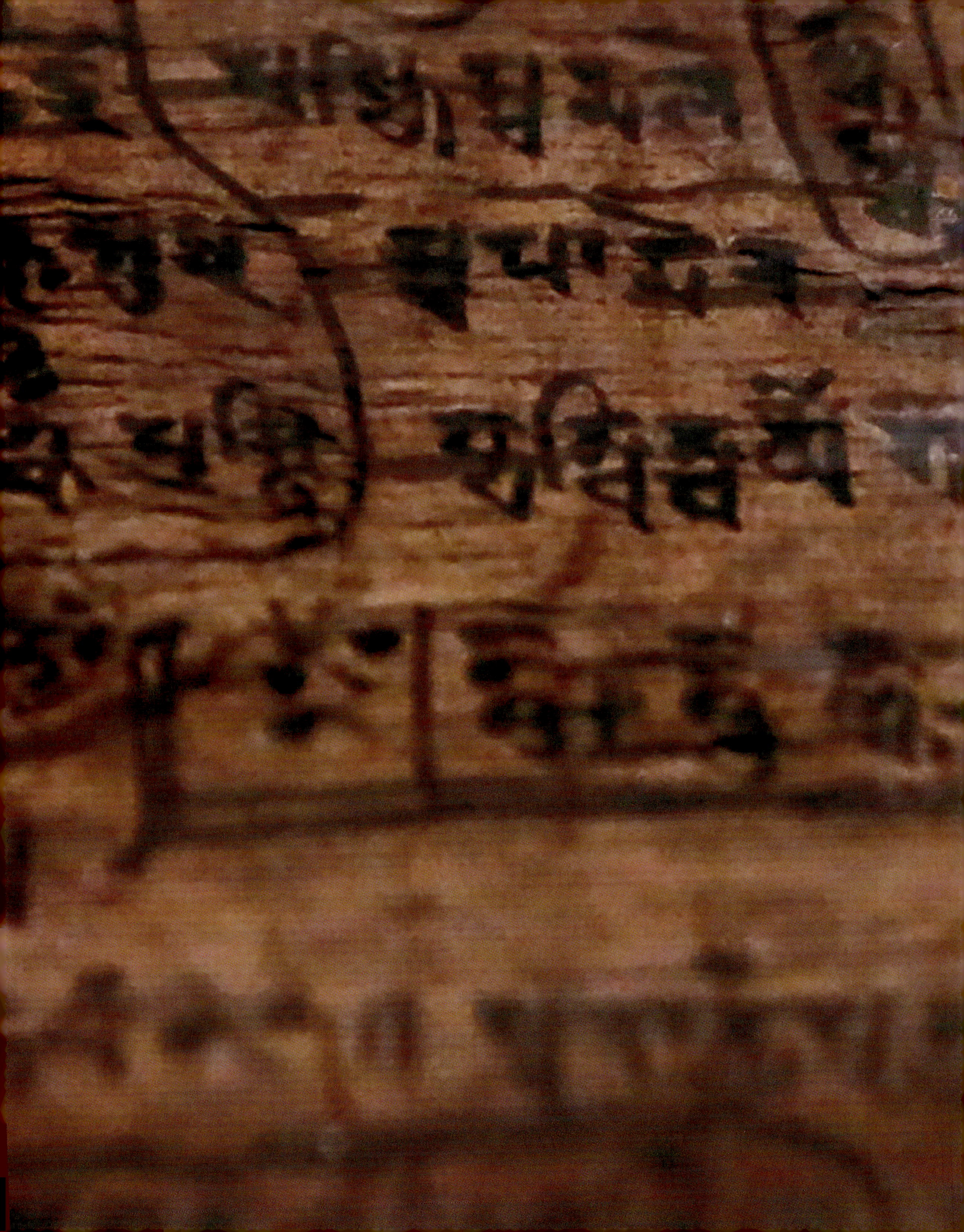

Era 3rd–4th centuries CE | **Medium** Birch bark | **Dimension** 14.5 × 8.9 cm (5.7 × 3.5 in)

BHAKSHALI MANUSCRIPT

The origin of nothing

The Bhakshali manuscript is the oldest Indian mathematical text. Inscribed in birch bark, it contains the earliest known textual mention of one of the greatest conceptual breakthroughs in mathematics – zero.

Even before India's most notable mathematicians Aryabhata I (c. 476–550 CE) and Brahmagupta (c. 598–668 CE) made use of zero as a number in their works, the revolutionary mathematical concept found mention in the Bhakshali manuscript, dating to 3rd–4th centuries CE. Found buried by a local farmer in 1881, in Bhakshali in present-day Pakistan, the manuscript contains practical arithmetic exercises and elements of what could be called proto-algebra. It is written in a version of Sanskrit and is believed to have been a training manual or document used by merchants conducting trade along the Silk Road. Zero does not feature as a number in its own right in the manuscript, revealing that at the time it had not yet developed as a distinct value. Instead, signified by a dot, it serves as a placeholder to indicate orders of magnitude in a number system – for instance, denoting 10s, 100s, and 1000s. The manuscript also includes a problem to which the answer is zero, but the answer is left blank in the document.

◀ **The Bhakshali manuscript** tells us of the origins of the numeral zero in the subcontinent. Seen here is a part of a parchment from it.

SOMETHING FOR NOTHING

Though ancient Indians were not the only ones to use a placeholder to imply nothingness or the absence of something (the ancient Mayans and Babylonians were known to use a double wedge or a shell shape for the same purpose), the Bhakshali manuscript's zero holds major historical significance. This is firstly because the dot that represents the zero here evolved to have a hollow centre, becoming the symbol we recognize as zero today. Secondly, it was only in India that the symbol grew into a standalone numeral that could be used for mathematical operations such as addition, subtraction, and multiplication. Although division using zero was more challenging, it led to the birth of an entirely new branch of mathematics as mathematicians grappled with the concept of infinity.

Why zero happened to emerge and flourish in the subcontinent has been theorized and debated. It is said that it was rooted in local religious beliefs and echoed the Buddhist sentiment of *sunyata*, which refers to a void.

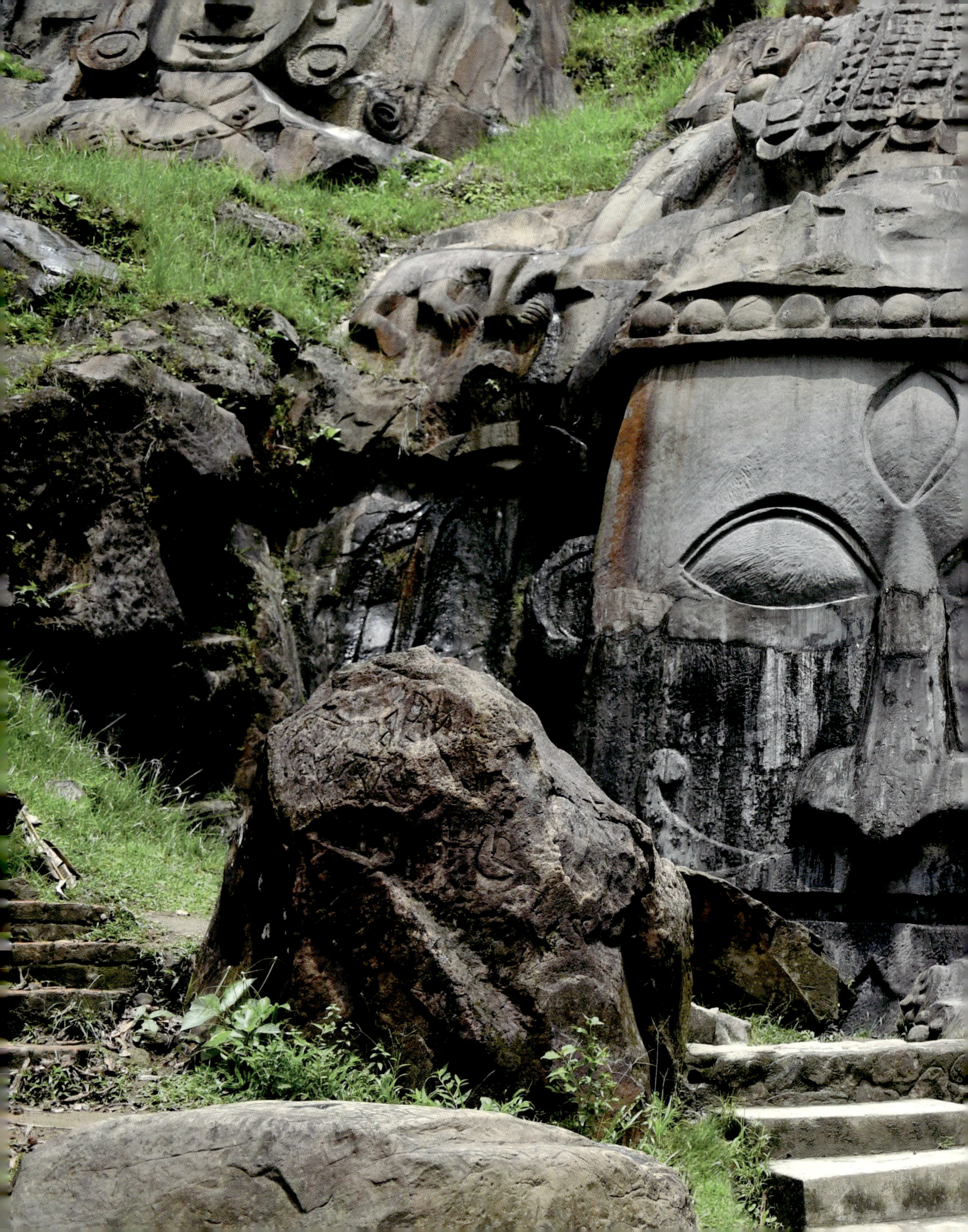

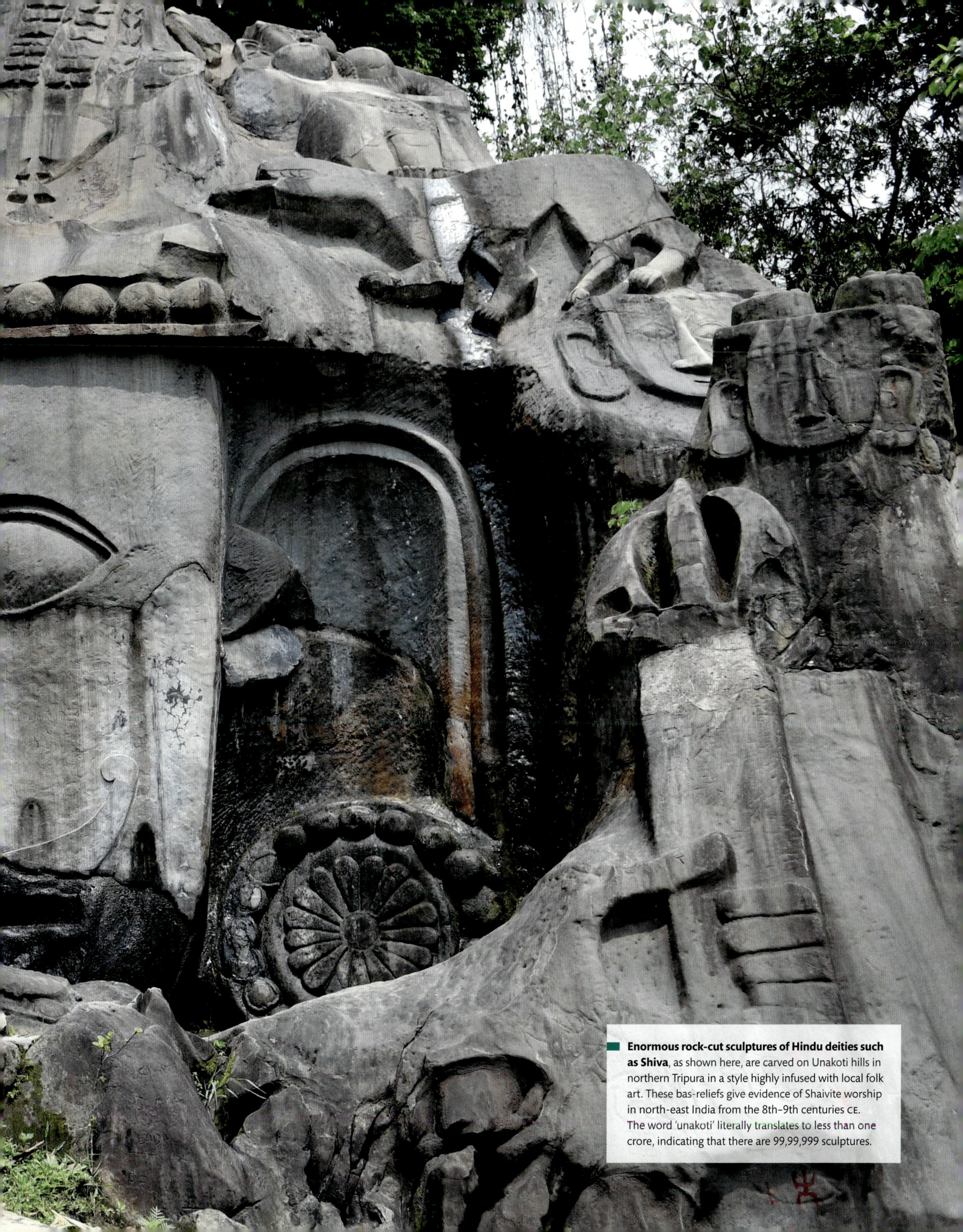

Enormous rock-cut sculptures of Hindu deities such as Shiva, as shown here, are carved on Unakoti hills in northern Tripura in a style highly infused with local folk art. These bas-reliefs give evidence of Shaivite worship in north-east India from the 8th–9th centuries CE. The word 'unakoti' literally translates to less than one crore, indicating that there are 99,99,999 sculptures.

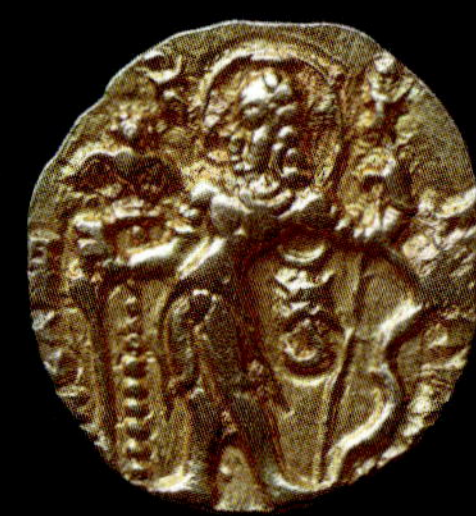

Era 5th century CE | **Medium** gold | **Diameter** 2 cm (0.08 in)

GOLD COINS OF THE GUPTAS

Symbol of economic prosperity

The coins from the Gupta period were much more than a reflection of abundance. They represented the cultural and economic opulence of an empire that drew its success from trade with the Romans.

The emperor Kumaragupta I stands in an archer pose wielding a bow and arrow on a gold coin from the Gupta period. His powerful stance emphasizes his status as a heroic leader and warrior king. Part of the king's name, 'Kumara', is itself an alternative name for the god of war, Skanda, also known as Kartikeya. The coin designs take this association further. Much like this coin, the gold coinage from the Gupta period was uniform in size and weight and displayed the figure and name of the issuer.

Considered to be among the finest in ancient India, the gold coins from the Gupta period were renowned for their artistic merit, diversity, and originality.

The weight and spectacular engravings on coins of this period ranging from animals such as horses and peacocks, and the likenesses of goddesses and of the king, tell us about the unprecedented prosperity the region saw owing to its volume of trade with the Roman Empire.

PEAK OF AFFLUENCE

The Guptas, a ruling dynasty in ancient India, were known for producing a large number of gold coins, referred to as *dinara* in their inscriptions. So called after the Roman *denarius aureus*, the gold *dinaras* reflected India's trade relations with Rome and the import of gold bullion. During the Gupta reign, the economy reached the pinnacle of its wealth. It was a time of unprecedented progress, a culmination of the growing cultural and scientific expansion that had been witnessed in the previous centuries.

The impact of this affluence was felt most in the urban areas of the empire, where individuals began to live in comfort, devoting their time to various refinements of life. A Gupta city, according to Kalidasa in *Shakuntala*, was "sunk in pleasures". It catered to every indulgence – for the hedonists, there were restaurants and taverns, brothels, and gambling dens; and for the cultured, there were literary gatherings, music, dance, literature, art, and theatre.

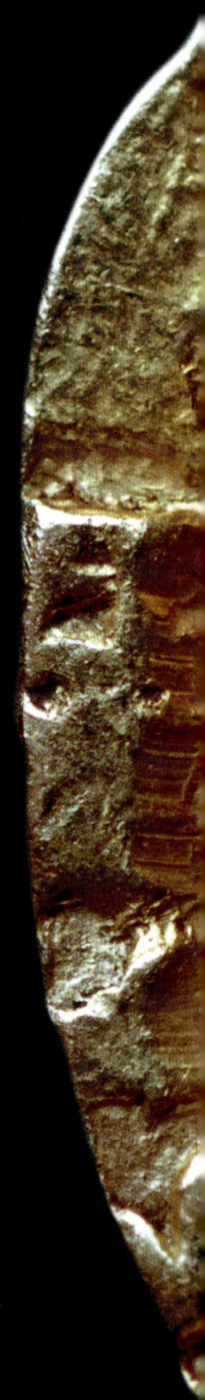

▶ **This gold coin from the Gupta period** depicts the king Kumaragupta I as an archer, c. 415–455 CE. Beautifully detailed with intricate motifs, it was donated by a private collection to the Metropolitan Museum of Art in 1990

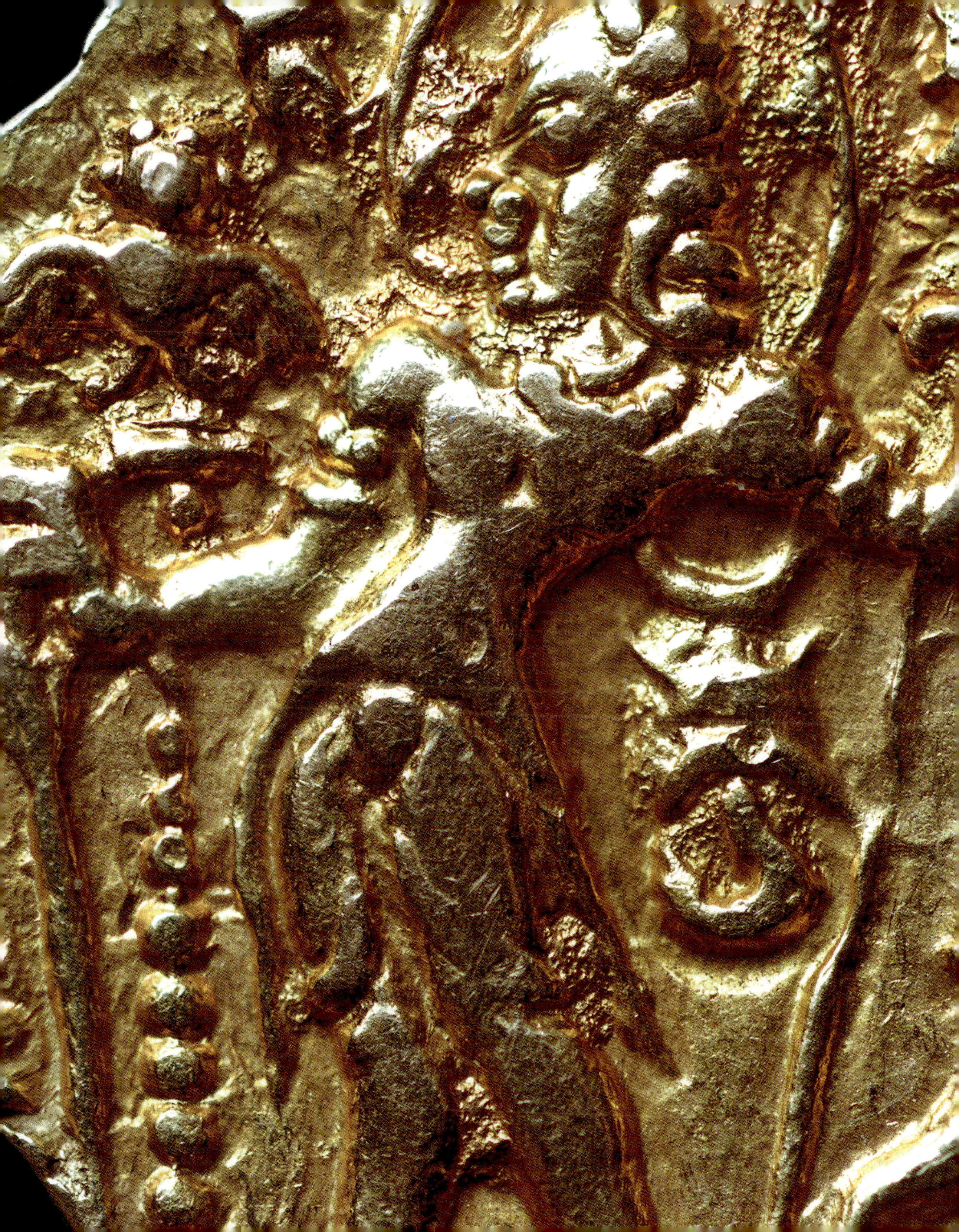

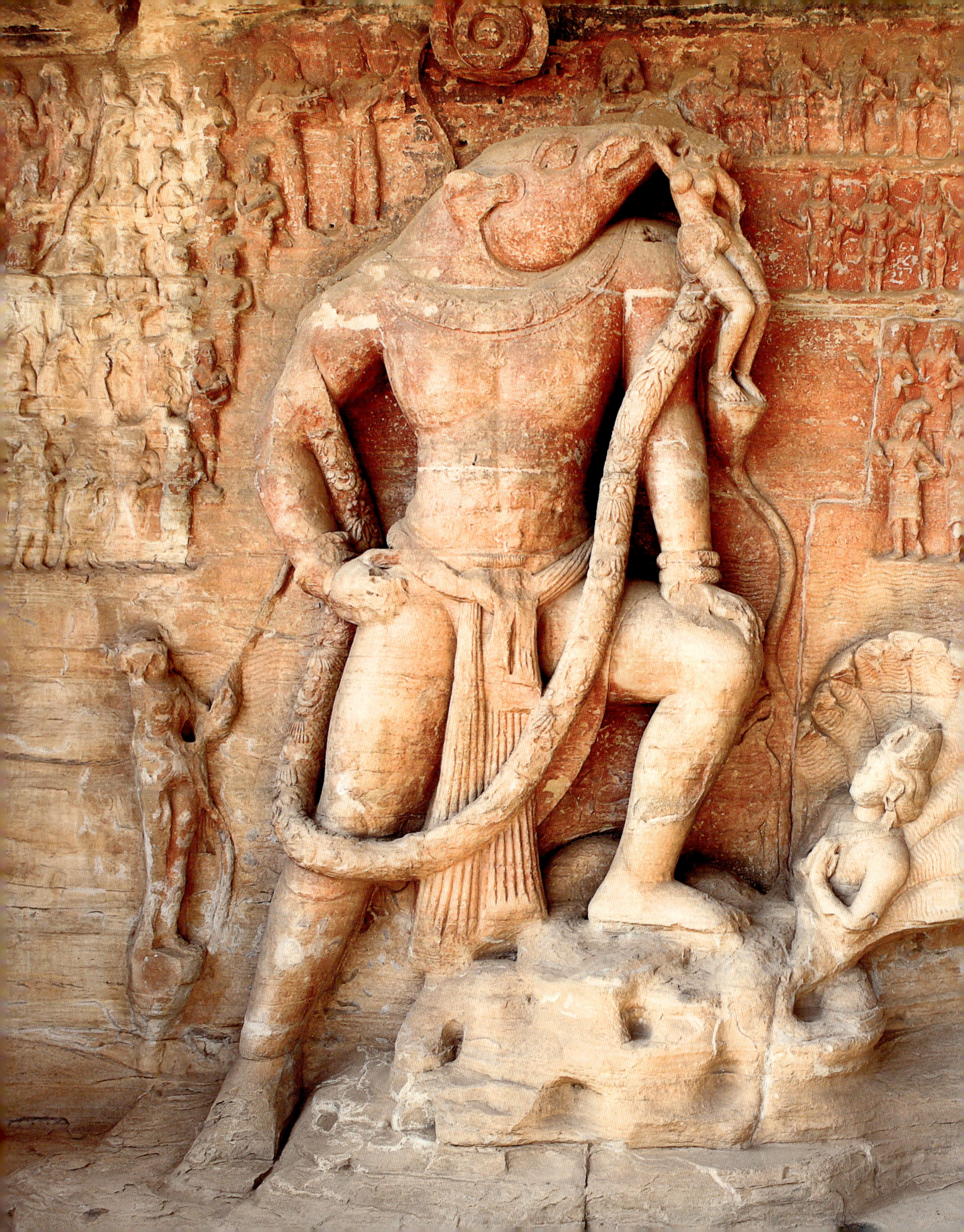

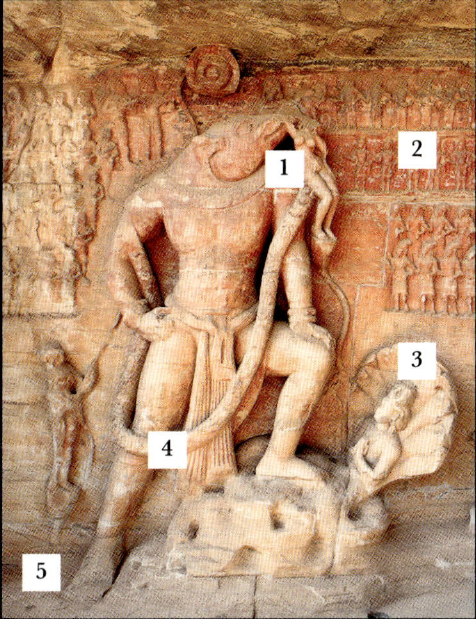

1. Varaha lifts the earth goddess effortlessly, hooked to his tusk and perched slightly on his left shoulder. **2.** The figure is flanked on both sides by sages and celestial beings, carrying water pots, who bear witness to his greatness. **3.** The multi-hooded serpent king's coils are trapped under Varaha's left foot and he has his hands folded in salutation. **4.** The Varaha figure dons a pleated garment around his waist and a long, thick garland, a hallmark of Vishnu, graces his body. **5.** Wavy lines represent the cosmic ocean.

Era 4th–5th centuries CE | **Medium** Sandstone | **Dimension** 7 × 4 m (22 × 13 ft)

VARAHA, UDAYGIRI

The great cosmic rescuer

The Udayagiri caves, in Madhya Pradesh, were important ritual centres for the Gupta dynasty. Here, Chandragupta II commissioned a sizable sculpture of Varaha, which covers the myth in outranked scale.

One among the several striking reliefs found in Udayagiri Cave no. 5 is the sculpture of Varaha, an incarnation or avatar of the Hindu deity Vishnu, in the form of a man-boar.

The sculpture portrays an oft-told mythological story that has its origins in the *Vishnu Purana*, a sacred text of the Vishnu-worshipping branch of Hinduism. The giant carving of the partly anthropomorphic form of Varaha dominates the scene. He stands tall and proud; resting his right hand on his hip while the other rests on his bent knee. He is shown rising out of the cosmic waters, once churned by gods and demons in search of the elixir of immortality, with the earth goddess in the form of a maiden suspended from his tusks. The king of the serpents who tried to pull the goddess into the depths of the ocean is caught beneath his left foot in a great show of power and strength. Row upon row of gods and saints who have come to witness the cosmic event are depicted on either side of the figure. Their small size emphasizes the colossal Varaha.

ICONOGRAPHY AND PATRONAGE

The medieval period in the subcontinent saw a notable proliferation of this mythological scene, depicted through sculptures commissioned by royal patrons. An inscription found near the Udayagiri sculpture suggests that it was built by the Gupta emperor Chandragupta II, who was not only an ardent believer of Vishnu but also visualized himself and his victory over political rivals in the relief.

The Guptas are known to have been the foremost patrons of art and architecture and several images of Vishnu, Shiva, and other Hindu gods materialized for the first time during their reign. This is not to say that the Guptas invented religious patronage. However, their rule did herald the rise of kings and courtiers as a significant class of patrons, whereas earlier only groups of lay people were the sponsors. It was also during their rule that dressed stone masonry emerged, marking a huge step in the evolution of construction techniques. The 20 rock-cut caves of Udayagiri are testament to this development.

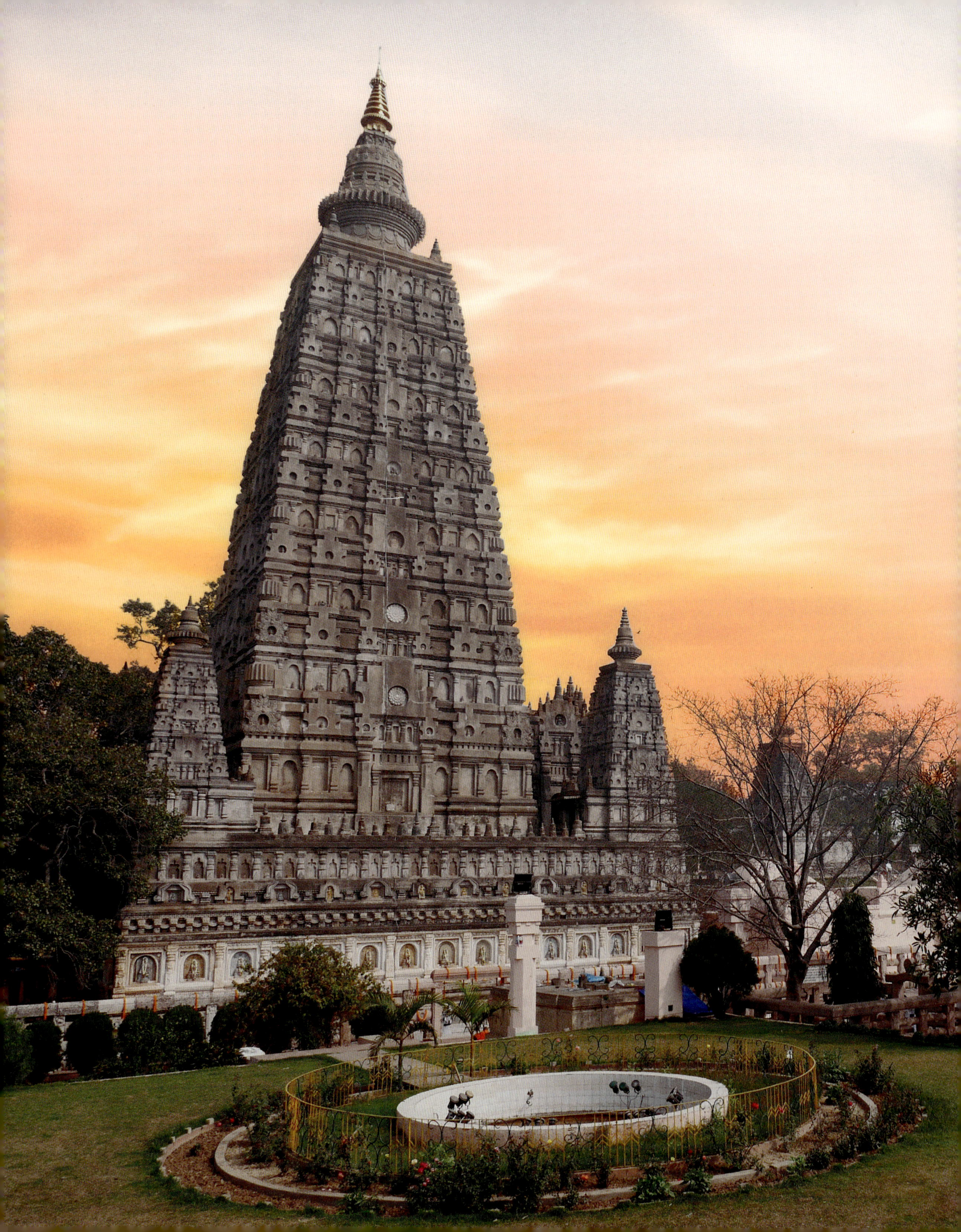

Era 3rd century BCE | **Medium** Brick | **Height** 55 m (180 ft)

MAHABODHI TEMPLE

Seat of the Buddha's enlightenment

After seven weeks of meditation and contemplation on the causes of human suffering, Prince Siddhartha found his answers and became the Buddha – the Enlightened One – here. Since then, this temple has become one of the four pilgrimage sites for Buddhists.

The Mahabodhi Temple, with its soaring spire, was built over the ruins of a circular stupa that was first constructed by the Mauryan king Ashoka in 260 BCE. The complex includes a total of seven sites related to the Buddha, of which the sacred Bodhi Tree *(Ficus religioso)* is the principal attraction, encased in an original sandstone railing installed by the emperor. Though not the exact one under which the Buddha gained enlightenment, the tree here is believed to be a direct descendant of the Buddha's tree. According to historical accounts, Ashoka's son Mahinda took a sapling to Sri Lanka on one of his proselytizing missions in 236 BCE. There, the tree flourished and was brought back to the complex to be re-planted after the original tree died.

A TEMPLE BY THE TREE

The main gateway is from the east, leading down a flight of steps through a small hall into the sanctum where a gilded statue of the Buddha sits in the *bhumisparsh mudra* (one finger pointing to earth). Votive stupas, shrines, innumerable statues of the Buddha, bodhisattvas, and trees are all later additions by rulers and devotees. They adorn various parts of the complex associated with events that recall the seven-week period before and after the Enlightenment. A black stone in the inner courtyard is engraved with the Buddha's footprints, while the Ratnachakrama (Jewel Walk), marking his steps with 18 carved lotuses, is where he walked and meditated during his third week.

The complex has seen many additions and renovations through the centuries. However, the main edifice, restored during the age of the Guptas (5th–6th centuries CE) remains essentially unchanged in design and is remarkable as one of the earliest examples of brick architecture in India as towered brick temples became fashionable. The complex fell into disrepair between the 13th and 19th centuries, but was later restored by monks and pilgrims.

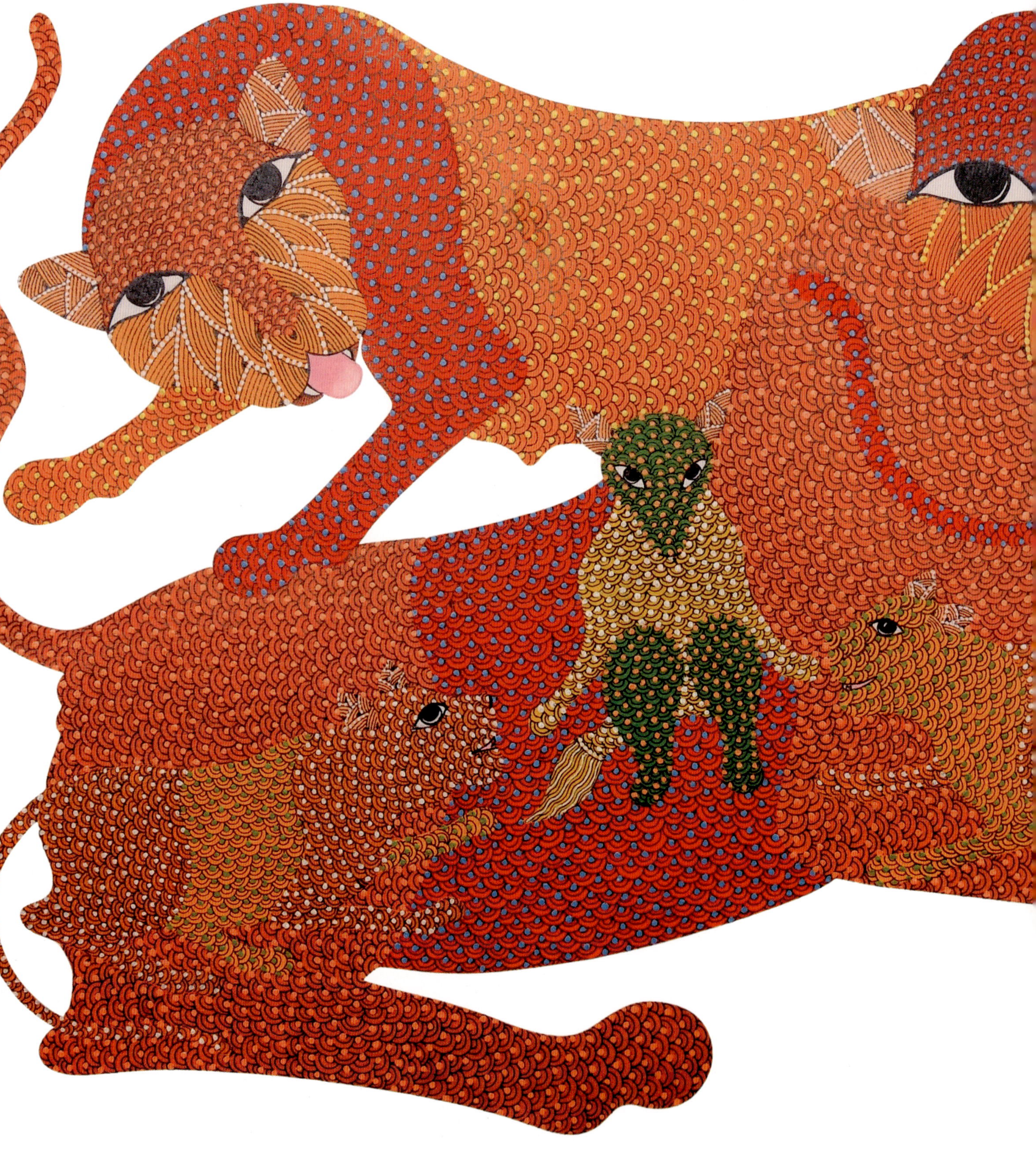

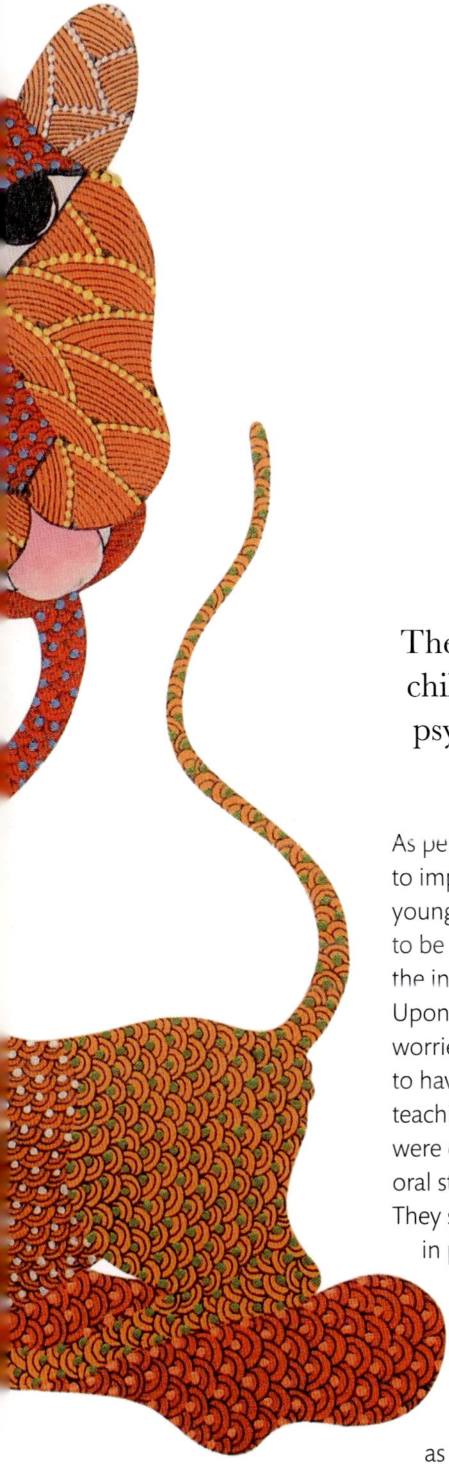

Era 100 BCE–500 CE

PANCHATANTRA

Interconnected fables that impart worldly wisdom

The Panchatantra may appear to be a collection of anthropomorphic stories for children, but it is much more. It delves into subjects such as philosophy, politics, psychology, and astronomy, and guides the reader towards an ideal way of life.

As per the text, the earliest stories were composed to impart *niti*, the art of intelligent living, to three young princes in a city called Mahilaropya, believed to be in the south, by an ageing scholar, identified in the introductory narration as Pundit Vishnu Sharma. Upon being called to court by the king who was worried for his sons' education, the teacher is said to have devised these stories as an unconventional teaching aid. Though, not all stories in the collection were composed by him. Many can be traced to the oral storytelling traditions from the Vedic period. They speak of skills and values no less relevant in present day, and continue to be taught and circulated.

THE FIVE BOOKS

'*Panchatantra*' means five principles, and these are unveiled through fables compiled as five books. The first, which forms a little less than half the collection, is the *Mitra-bheda*, or the breaking of friendships. It teaches discernment, giving insight into the fragility of human relationships and how susceptible they are to wily manipulation. The second, *Mitra-samprapti*, highlights the importance of forging friendships. The third book, *Kakolukiyam*, deals with war and peace. With traditional enemies, the crows and the owls, as protagonists, it teaches strategy. The last two books are short, and speak of the importance of anticipating consequences. The fables in *Labdhapranasam*, the fourth book, show how easily gain can turn into loss, while the last, *Apariksitakarakam*, draws attention to the importance of inquiry, consideration, and patience over actions made in haste.

LASTING INFLUENCE

The first known translation of the Sanskrit compilation is in Middle Persian, or Pahlavi, done by a Persian physician in the 6th century. A Syriac version drawn from this translation, followed by one in Arabic were done. In the 11th century a Greek version became known, on which retellings in Latin and various Slavic languages were based. However, most European versions are rooted in the 12th century Hebrew retelling by a man, identified as Rabbi Joel.

◀ **This 2013 painting, by artist** Venkataraman Singh Shyam, depicts a Panchatantra fable of a lioness and a jackal in the Indian folk art style of Gond from Madhya Pradesh. It is currently housed in Crafts Museum, New Delhi.

Era 2nd century BCE–650 CE | **Medium** Basalt | **Area** 8,242 ha (20,366 acres)

AJANTA CAVE PAINTINGS

Buddhist tales brought to life

The Jataka frescoes of Ajanta are iconic, the caves' walls, ceilings, and columns entirely devoted to a stunning visual narration of the lives and incarnations of the Buddha. Their exuberance and vitality is a celebration of Buddhist religious art.

High on the side of a horseshoe-shaped cliff in Maharashtra lie the Ajanta Caves. This complex of 30 rock-cut caves, chiselled out of vertical cliffs, contains the finest surviving examples of ancient Indian painting. The architectural forms of *vihara* (monasteries) and *chaityagriha* (prayer hall), the archetype of Buddhist art, were excavated out of these caves. They are usually square-shaped and have vaulted ceilings, the colonnades dividing the prayer halls into central walkways that lead to the apsidal and side aisles around the apse. The *viharas* have cell dwellings circling a central congregational hall.

INSIDE THE ANCIENT CAVES

The fresco in Cave 10, which has an inscription dating it to the 2nd century BCE, is widely recognized as the oldest example of this artistic technique in India. Though damaged and fragmented, the scenes it depicts have lost none of their luminescence. The graceful fluidity of its lines is still imbued with a realism that must have set the standard for all the artists who followed. The six caves (8, 9, 10, 12, 13, 15A) built in the first phase are simpler, more austere, in keeping with the prevalent Theravada practice of Buddhism. That the idolatrous Mahayana Buddhism had gained dominance by time the second phase (400–650 CE) of excavations were undertaken is apparent from the lush beauty and abundance of the sculptures and frescoes in the later caves. They are characterized by ornately carved façades and interiors, as well as figurative depictions of the Buddha and bodhisattvas.

1. A fresco in Cave 17 depicting the Jataka tale of the 'Simhala Avadana', the coming of a prince. **2.** Avalokiteshwara, also identified as Vajrapani, is the most venerated bodhisattva in the Mahayana pantheon, and can be seen to the right of the antechamber doorway. **3.** This detail of jewelled *apsaras* (celestial maidens) is part of a larger mural. **4.** A scene from Sankhapala Jataka portraying an ascetic giving sermon to the Naga king Sankhapala and hunters dragging him. **5.** The Miracle in Sravasti, seen on the antechamber's right wall, depicts the legend of the Buddha multiplying himself a thousand-fold. **6.** Padmapani (lotus-holder), the bodhisattva of compassion, can be seen on the wall to the left of the antechamber doorway. **7.** Panel of paintings showing the life cycle of the Buddha. **8.** Palace women from the Vidura Pandita Jataka depicted in Cave 2.

4

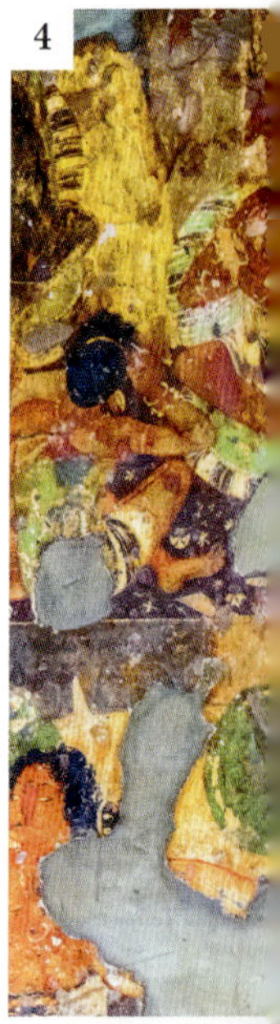

5

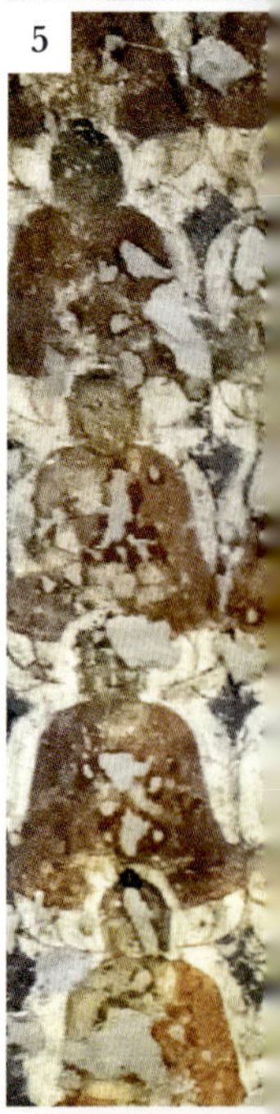

1

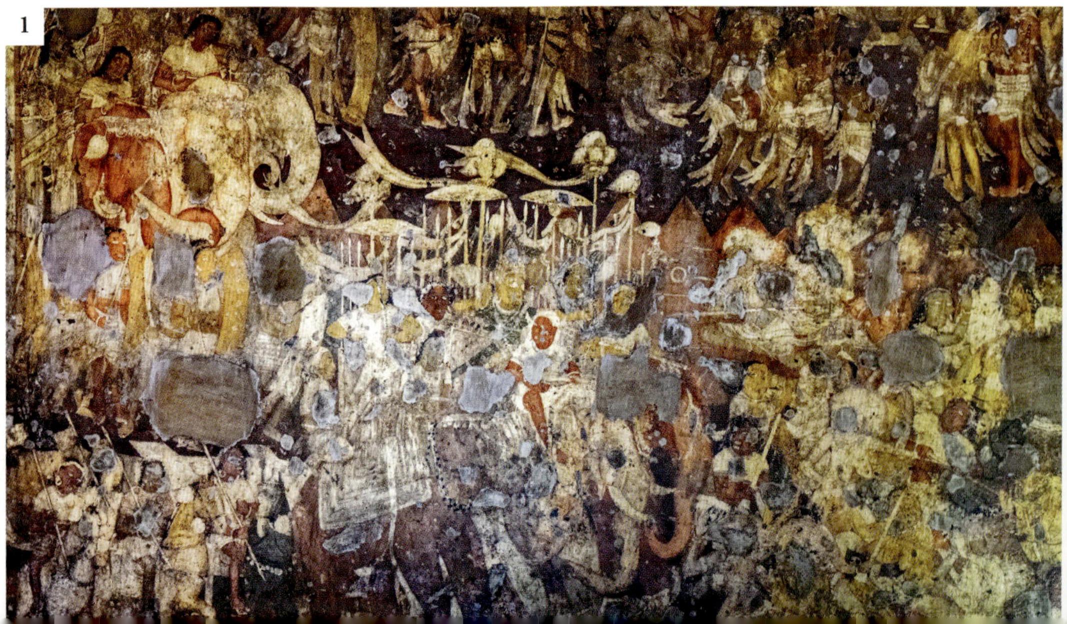

2

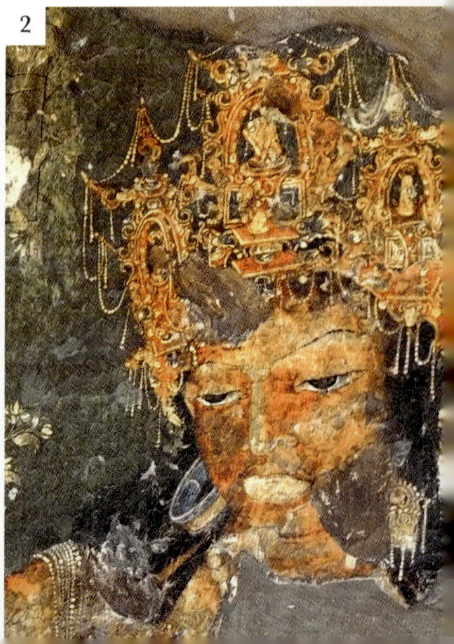

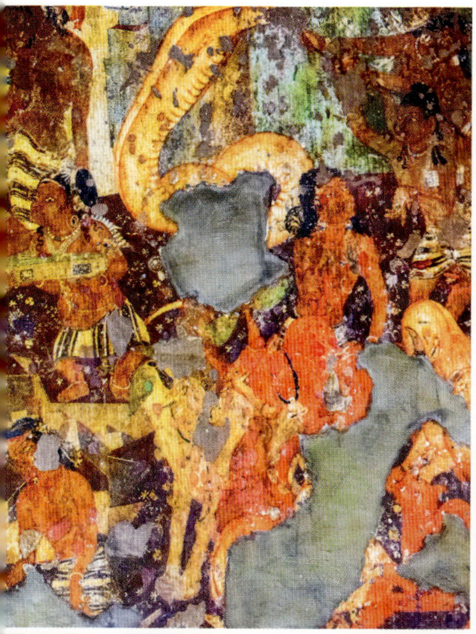

6

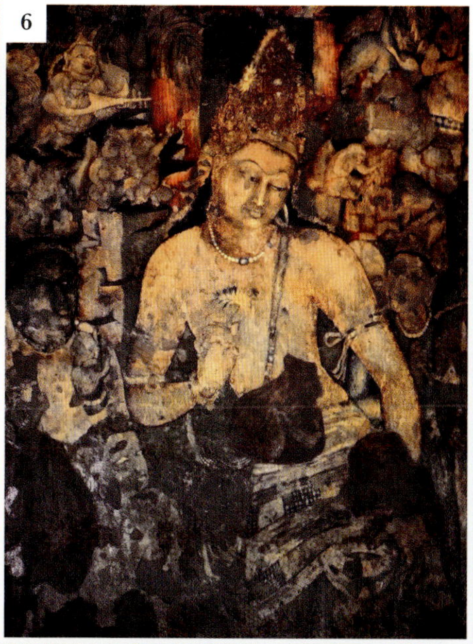

7

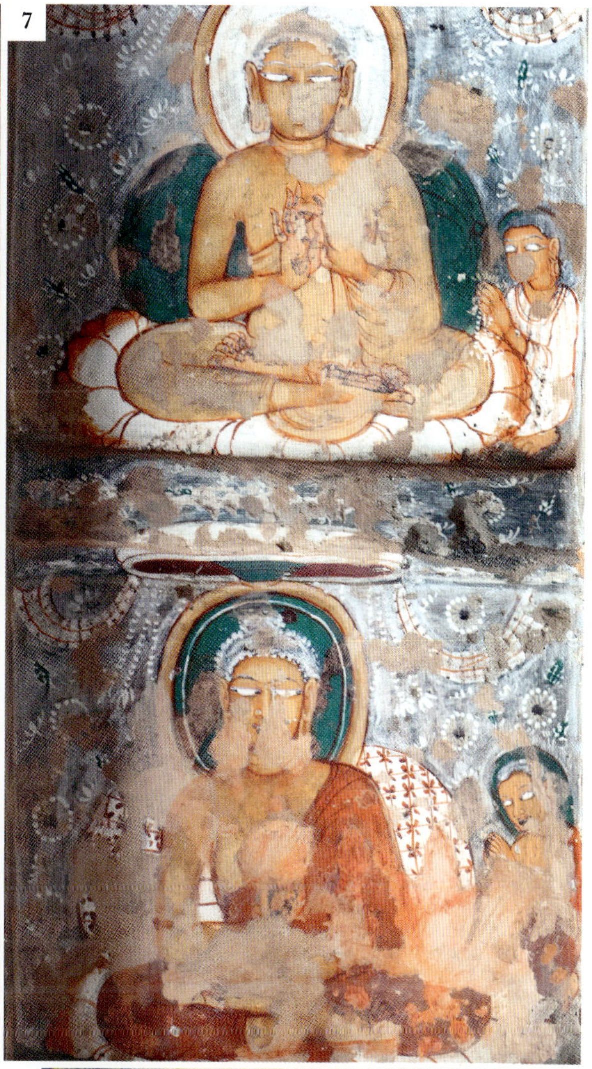

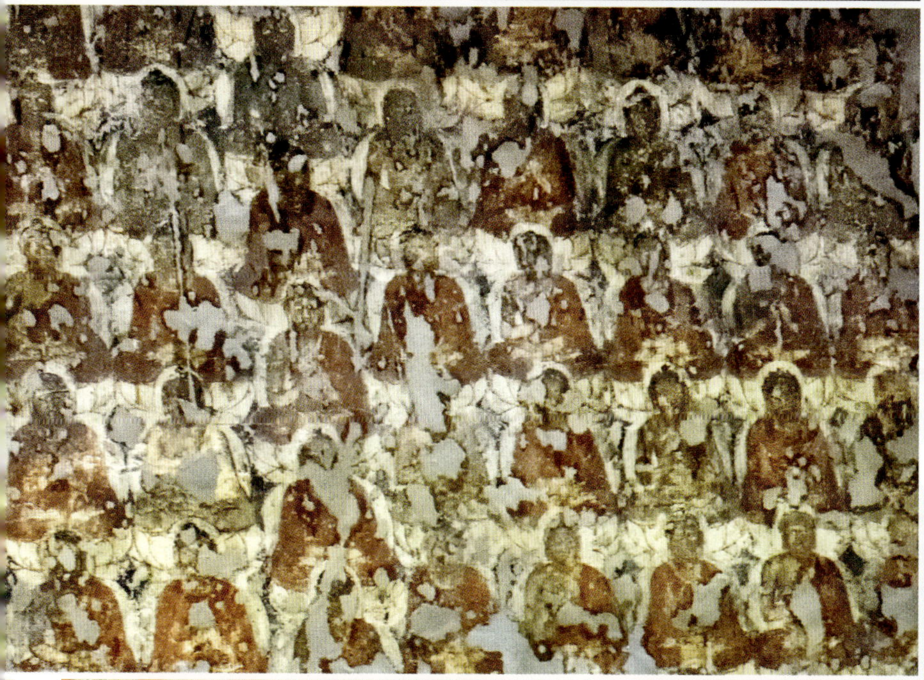

3

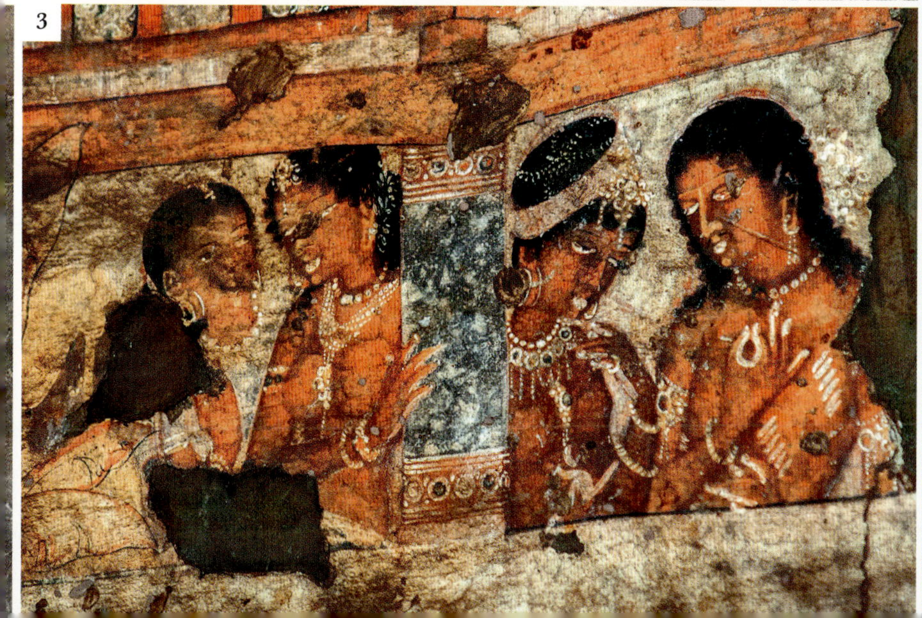

8

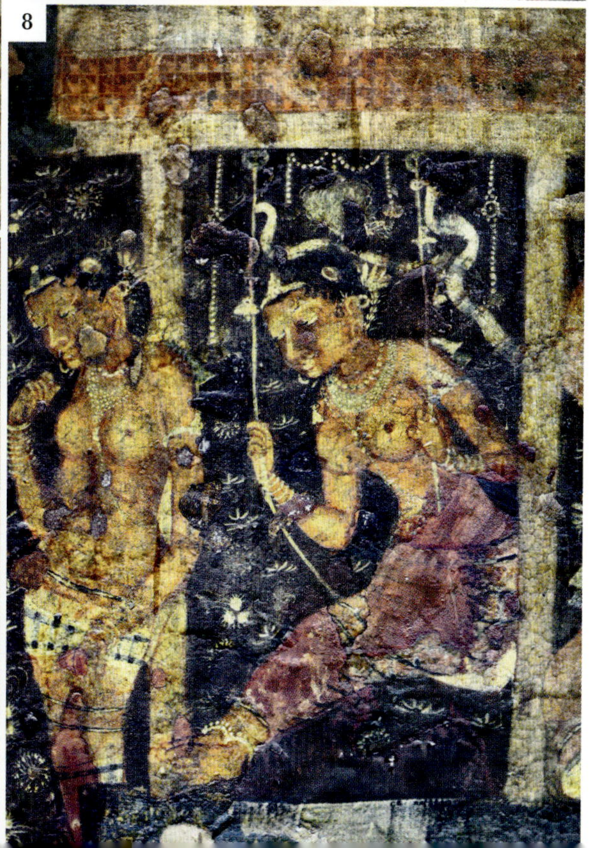

Era 2nd–3rd centuries BCE | **Medium** Paint on paper

KAMA SUTRA

The philosophy and theory of love and sexuality

One of the oldest extant Indian texts, the *Kama Sutra* is a compendium on the achievement of *kama* (pleasure), an essential goal every human being should be able to attain in a well-rounded, fulfilling life. It also provides rare insights into an affluent ancient society.

Far from being an erotic text, the *Kama Sutra* is dry and instructional in its tone. Attributed to Vatsyayana Mallanaga, a 2nd or 3rd century philosopher and author, it is likely distilled from many other ancient texts that have not survived. A large part of the book is devoted to a treatise on the philosophical and theoretical aspects of love, what instigates desire, how is it sustained, and when is desire good or bad. It was written as a manual for young, wealthy men on how to live well. As such, it is better viewed in context of the urbane, courtly culture that developed under the prosperous Gupta Empire, and thus paints a vivid portrait of the lifestyle of the wealthy.

MATTERS OF CONSIDERATION

From instructions on how to build a house to how the *nagaraka* (man about town) should manage a household, and his social obligations, deepen bonds between family and friends, the *Kama Sutra* covers a wide range of topics. It elaborates on the arts he should be proficient in to be socially attractive and how he should approach potential female partners. Other chapters are devoted to courtship, the duties and privileges of a wife, remarriage, adultery, relations with courtesans, homosexuality, as well as a list of ways to increase physical attractiveness, and taking care of sexual organs. The *Kama Sutra* is also a textbook on sexuality – the sophistication reflected in it came to be echoed in art and sculpture of the period and of many centuries thereafter. Over time, as ideas of morality changed, the text fell into obscurity.

Western translations of the book appeared in the 19th century and they seemed to focus solely on the erotic and the intimate elements, producing a skewed, inaccurate, and misleading version. They became wildly popular and were gradually accepted as a definitive translation in the West, which transformed this ancient treatise into just a book of exotic sex positions.

► **A Rajput miniature painting depicting two** lovers in an embrace. This gouache illustration from the *Kama Sutra* was possibly created in Mewar, c. 1795.

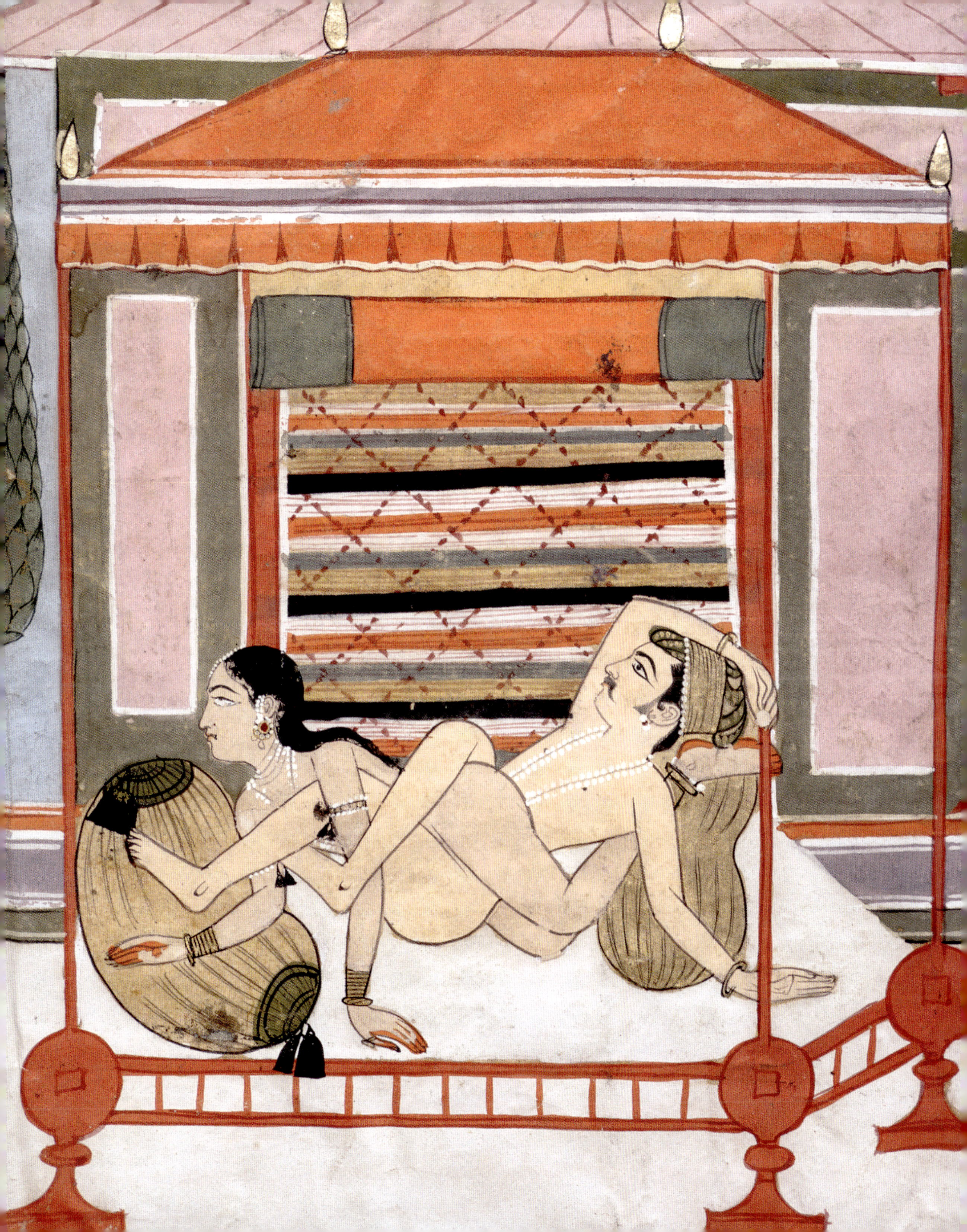

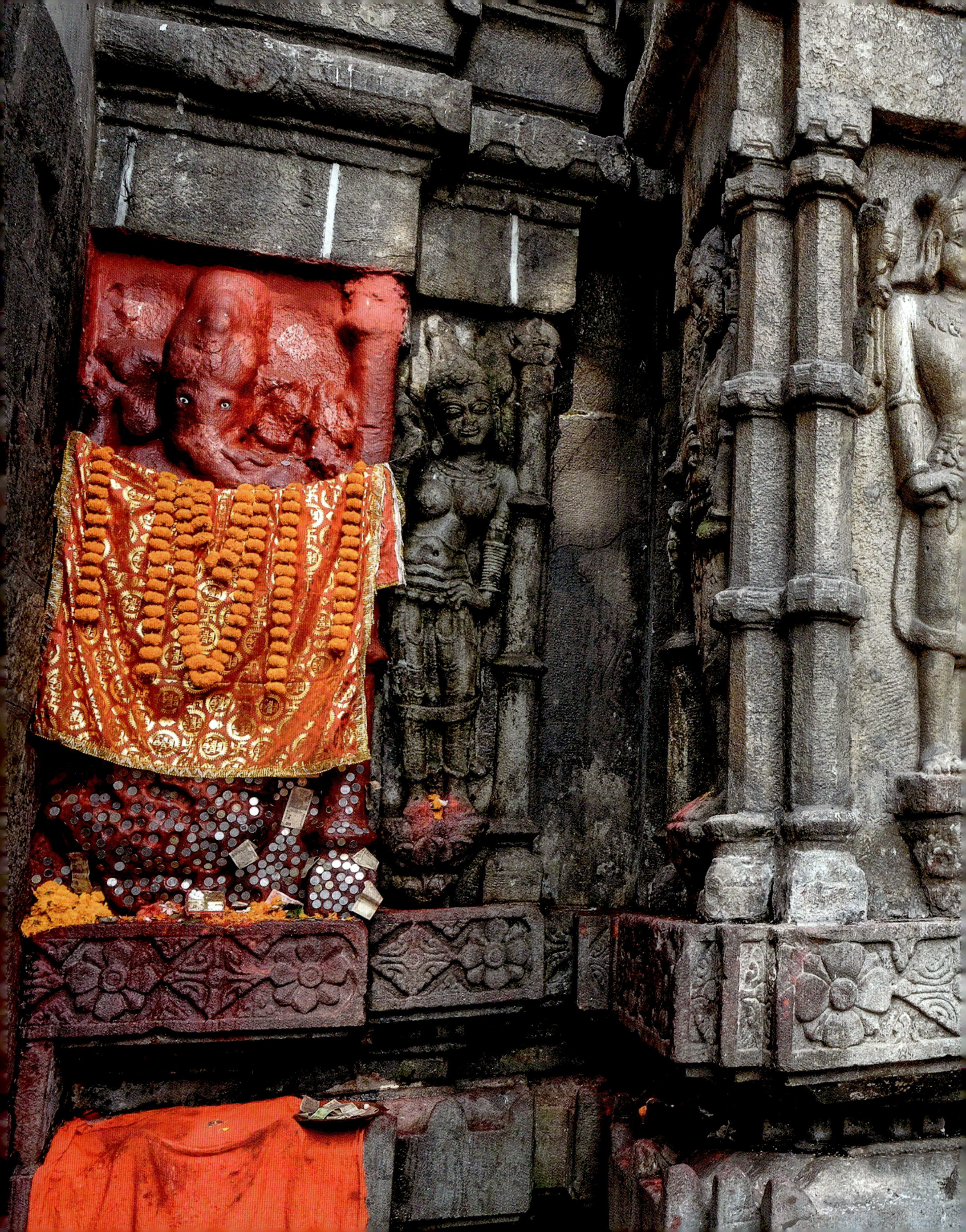

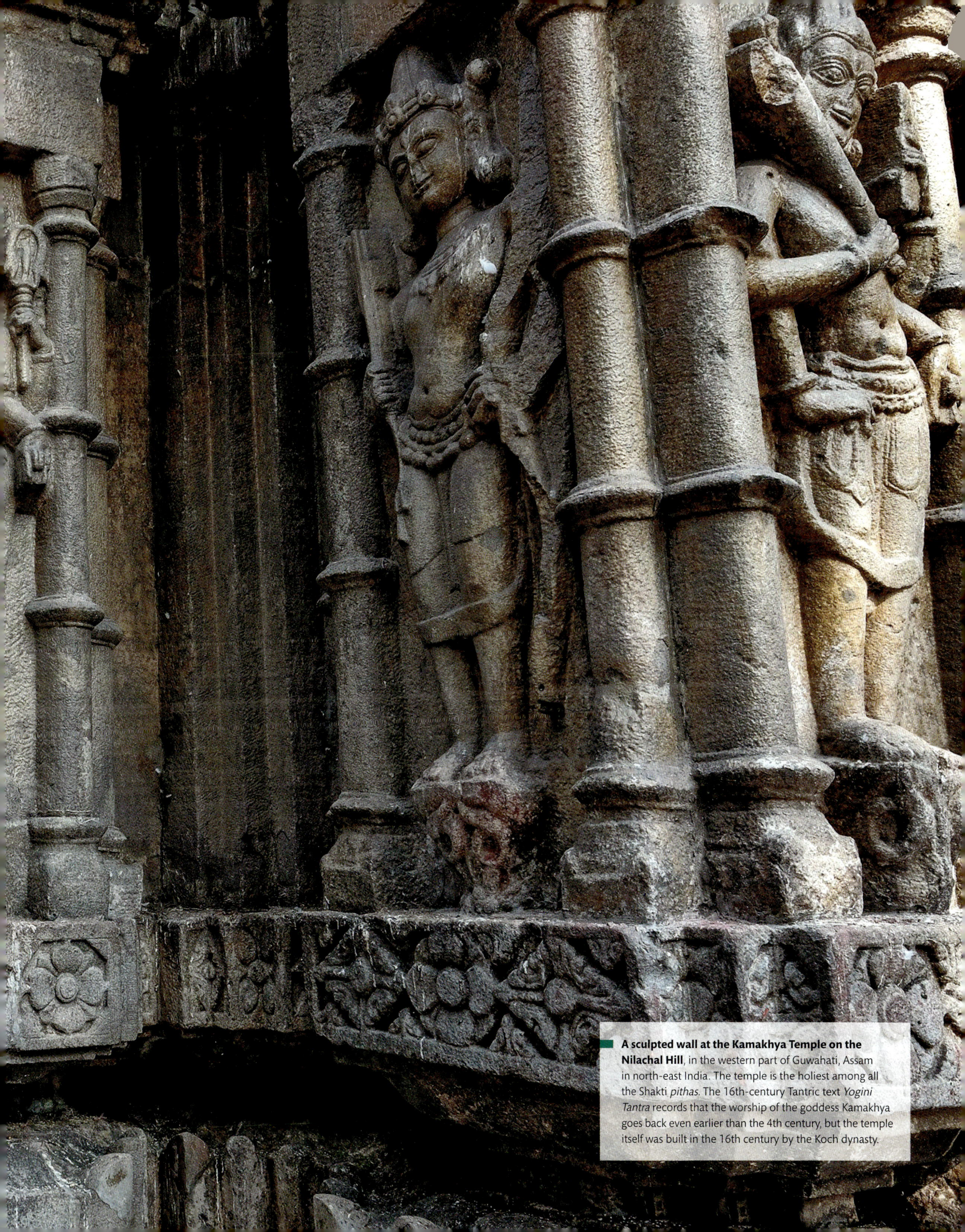

A sculpted wall at the Kamakhya Temple on the Nilachal Hill, in the western part of Guwahati, Assam in north-east India. The temple is the holiest among all the Shakti *pithas*. The 16th-century Tantric text *Yogini Tantra* records that the worship of the goddess Kamakhya goes back even earlier than the 4th century, but the temple itself was built in the 16th century by the Koch dynasty.

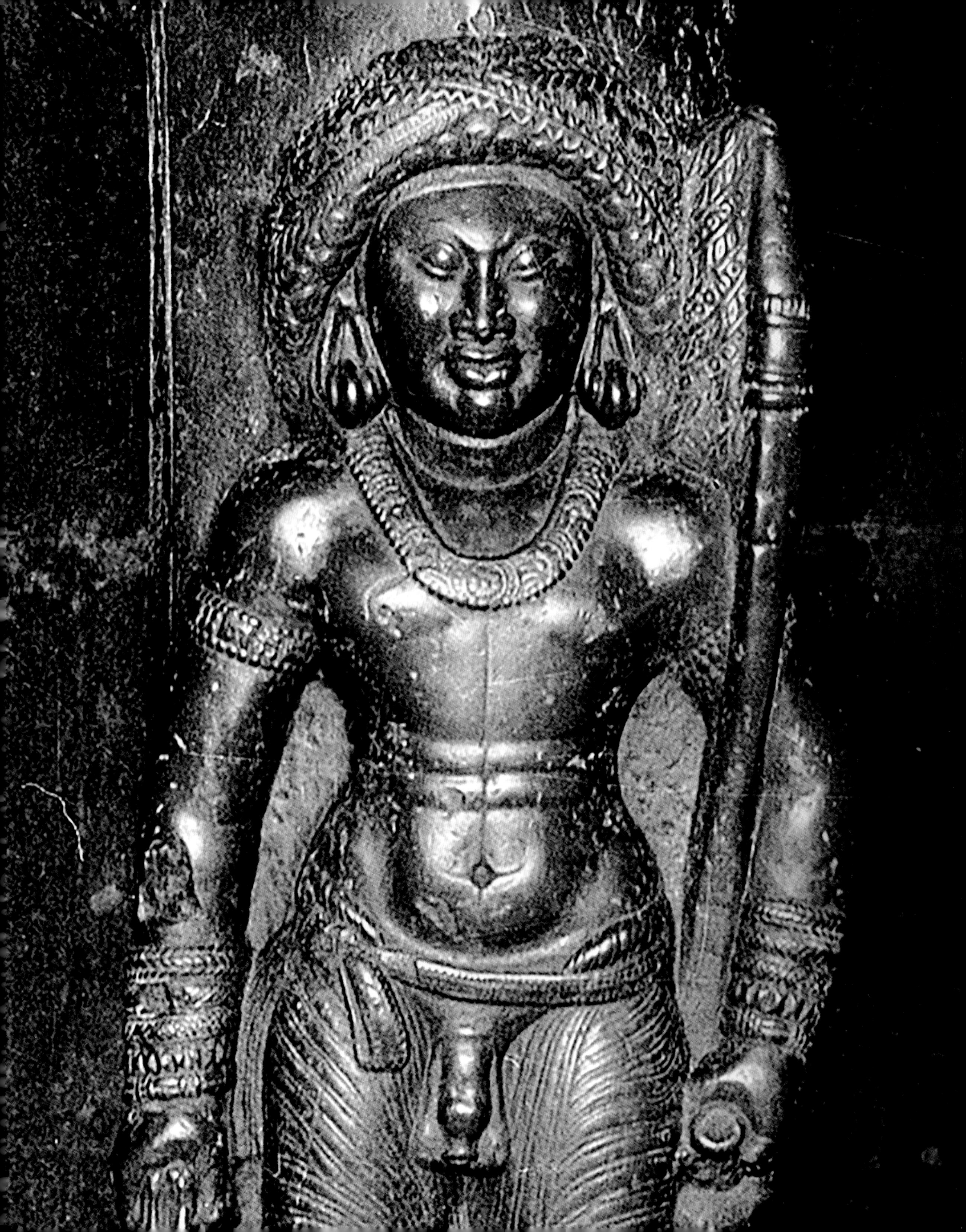

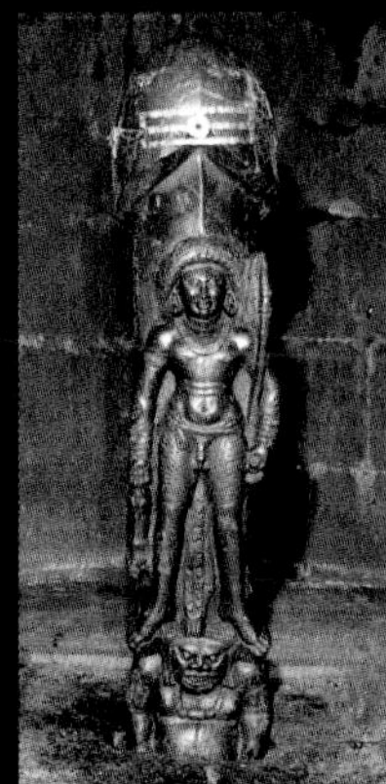

Era 3rd–1st centuries BCE | **Medium** Reddish igneous rock | **Height** 1.5 m (5 ft)

GUDIMALLAM LINGAM

Tracing the origins of Shiva worship

Carved from a single rock, the life-sized Gudimallam Lingam from Andhra Pradesh boasts a 2,200-year old history as the longest continuously worshipped statue of Lord Shiva in the world.

An air of mystery surrounds the Gudimallam Lingam; no other object similar to it has ever been found in the nearby area, or even in southern India. Installed in the apsidal sanctum sanctorum *(garbhagriha)* of the Parasurameswara Swamy Temple in Gudimallam, Andhra Pradesh, the statue is attributed to the Satavahana dynasty and stands as one of the earliest surviving images of the Hindu deity Shiva.

A NATURALISTIC REPRESENTATION

The statue depicts Shiva in human form in anatomical detail, standing in front of a phallus, on the shoulders of a crouching dwarf believed to be one of the *yakshas* (nature spirits) he tamed or one of his *ganas* (irreverent followers). Shiva is shown holding a water pot in one hand while an axe rests on his shoulder. In his other hand, he holds the body of a small antelope, which recalls one of his epithets, 'Pasupati' or the Lord of the Animals. This imagery has been remarked upon by archaeologists in connection with seals from the Indus Valley (see p. 19) that feature a 'proto-Shiva' figure surrounded by wild animals. Gudimallam Lingam is significant not only because of its ancient origins but also because of the physical attributes of Shiva depicted. What also stands out is the placement of the idol in a rectangular enclosure, a feature commonly found in early Buddhist sites. This suggests that Shiva worship during the 2nd and 1st centuries BCE may have incorporated elements that were more common among non-Shaivite groups.

Another notable aspect of the statue is that, unlike other *lingams* that came up later, it is not placed within a *yoni*, the vulva-shaped symbol of female power. Instead, it is simply inserted between two circular stone elements. In most depictions of Shiva, the *yoni* is often carved from the same piece of stone as the *lingam* and serves as a base for it. The Gudimallam statue's deviation from this norm thus suggests that the depiction of the *lingam* rising from the *yoni* is perhaps a later development.

7th–19th centuries CE

MEDIEVAL INDIA

The period from 7th century CE to 19th century CE was one of transformation and revival. Military and civil powers emerged across the subcontinent, dynasties rose and declined, even as foreign rulers tried to establish a stronghold over the resource-rich Indian subcontinent. A symphony of thought emerged through this turbulence, spearheading an exchange of cultural ideas, art, and philosophies, that led to a cultural coalescence that lasts to this day.

POCKETS OF POWER

Medieval polities and continuous conflicts

Between the 7th and the 13th centuries CE, several sizeable kingdoms with ill-defined boundaries emerged throughout the subcontinent. Whether it was the Delhi Sultanate in the north or the Chola kingdom in the south, each had its own discernible style of architecture and sculpture.

The centuries that followed the breakdown of the Gupta Empire witnessed the emergence of several contemporary kingdoms, all vying for power. To the north-west of Delhi, the Pushyabhuti dynasty rose to prominence under Harshavardhana, or Harsha, which spanned modern Punjab to Bihar and Odisha but he did not succeed in making inroads into the Deccan. The prosperous empire had a self-sufficient economy with no heavy taxation.

Harsha was also probably the first important Indian monarch to have a biography, written by his friend Banabhatta. The *Harshacharita* provided a chronological account of major events in his kingdom.

THE THREE EMPIRES

The kingdom fell apart after Harsha's death in the 7th century, breaking into smaller kingdoms that fought over the capital city of Kannauj, considered a symbol of sovereignty, for the next 500 years. These states included the Pala kingdom, which dominated eastern India till the middle of the 9th century; the Gurjara-Pratihara kingdom, which ruled in western India and the upper Gangetic valley till the middle of the 10th century, and the Rashtrakuta kingdom, which ruled over the Deccan and had territories in north and south India at various times. The tripartite conflict between the Palas, Gurjara-Pratiharas, and Rashtrakutas

606 CE The Pushyabhuti dynasty's king Harshavardhana comes to power

c. 640 CE Biography of Harsha, *Harshacharita*, by Banabhatta

c. 753 CE Emergence of the Rashtrakutas in the Deccan

760 CE Palas come to power in eastern India

c. 770 CE Dharampala, the second Pala king rises to prominence

c. 783 CE Gurjara-Pratihara dynasty founded

c. 600–800 CE Emergence of Tamil saint poets

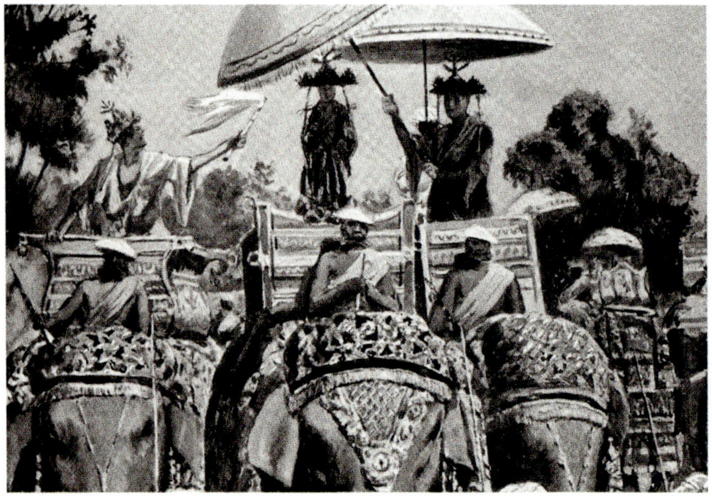

A 1915 painting visualizing Emperor Harsha paying homage to an image of Buddha on a state occasion. This event was documented by Xuanzang, a Chinese traveller in the subcontinent.

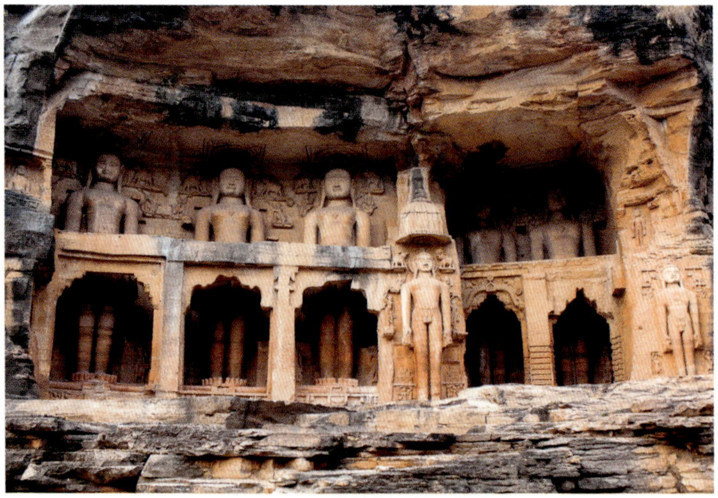

An excellent example of Maru-Gurjara architecture, which developed during the Gurjara-Pratihara dynasty. The Siddhanchal caves in Madhya Pradesh feature a row of sculptures depicting meditating *jinas* or teachers.

was one of the most notable aspects of the political history of the period. Although they fought amongst themselves for control over resources, their rule provided stable living conditions over large areas, extended agriculture, and encouraged the arts, including temple building. The Palas were a wealthy kingdom due to profitable trade with south-east Asia, as their seaports were natural stopping points for traders between the Far East and the West. They were also great patrons of Buddhist learning. It was Dharampala who revived the famous Nalanda university in modern Bihar. He also founded Vikramshila, a university second only to Nalanda in fame. The Gurjara-Pratiharas were patrons of learning and literature and embellished Kannauj with many fine buildings and temples. Of the three, the Rashtrakuta kingdom was not only the one that lasted the longest, but was also the most powerful. It acted as a bridge between north and south India in economic as well as in cultural matters.

SOUTHERN EMPIRES

During the 6th and 8th centuries, many sizeable kingdoms gained importance in the southern part of the Indian subcontinent. Among them were the Pallavas and the Pandyas who ruled present-day Tamil Nadu, the Cheras of modern Kerala, and

850 CE Thanjavur of Pandyas captured by Vijayalaya Chola

c. 973 CE Foundation of the Western Chalukya Empire

985–1014 CE Reign of Rajaraja, ruler of the Cholas dynasty

1000–1025 CE Invasions in north India by Mahmud of Ghazni

1014–1044 CE Reign of Rajendra Chola

1020–1030 CE Moroccan traveller Al-Beruni visits the subcontinent

1022 CE Chola conquest of the Gangetic valley and defeat of the Palas

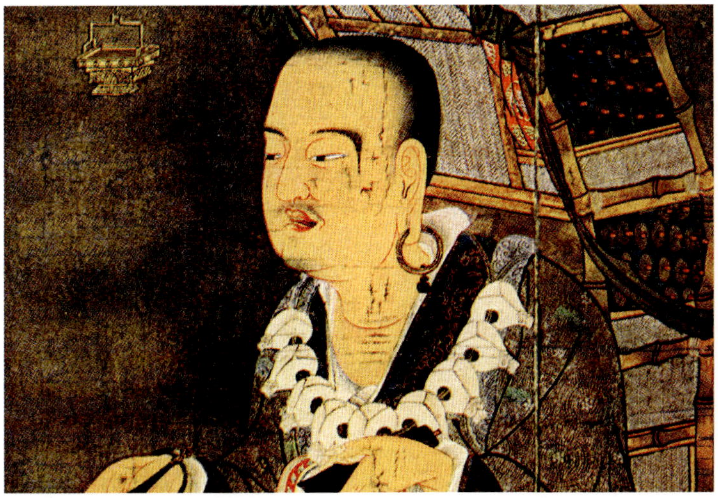

A 14th-century portrait of Xuanzang, a Chinese traveller who came to India in mid-7th century on a religious mission. His travelogues serve as records of several Indian kings and dynasties.

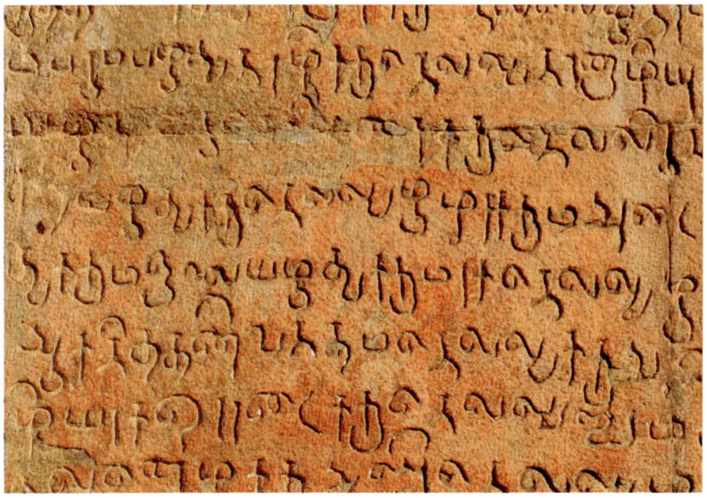

These inscriptions on the walls of the Brihadiswara Temple are part of a tradition started by the Chola emperors, wherein they etched important public documents or records on temple walls.

the Chalukyas who ruled Maharashtra and parts of the Deccan. The Chalukyas controlled a large portion of the Deccan through three interrelated dynasties: the Chalukyas of Badami, the Eastern Chalukyas of Vengi, and the Western Chalukyas of Kalyani.

The founder of the Chalukya dynasty, Pulakeshin I, started out as a minor tribal chief who served the Kadamba kingdom of Karnataka and then swiftly seized power. Within a few generations, the Chalukyas were seen as a mighty kingdom. Pulakeshin II became the next ruler to leave a profound impact, as not only did he expand territory, he also built diplomatic relations with Persia. Contemporary Chinese traveller Xuanzang described him as a "man of far-sighted resource and astuteness who extends kindness to all". Further south, in the 6th century, the Pallavas and the Pandyas rose to prominence.

Among them, the most important of the Pallava rulers was Mahendravarman I, a great patron of Tamil literature and music, and rock-cut temples, such as the ones seen in Mamallapuram, Tamil Nadu. The Pallavas faced constant threat from the Pandyas, who ruled from their capital at Madurai, as the latter vied for more territory in the region.

THE RISE OF THE CHOLAS

The rivalry for more land between the Chalukyas, the Pandyas, and the Pallavas lasted about 300 years. During this time, the Chola kingdom emerged, relatively smaller, that also paid tribute to its neighbours, the Pandyas and the Pallavas. The Cholas, grew in power over time, bringing under their control a large part of the Indian peninsula and dominating the political history of the far south from the mid-9th century onwards.

The greatest among them was Rajaraja (985–1014) and his son Rajendra I (1014–1044) who took the empire to dizzying heights. They amassed territories up to Sumatra and parts of the Malay Peninsula with the help of a strong navy and extended their reign from the western to the eastern coast of India. Both rulers followed a tradition of commemorating their victories by commissioning Shiva and Vishnu temples at chosen places. They also adopted the practice of inscribing the walls of these temples with historical narratives of their victories.

The Chola temples were rich and intricately carved; some continue to be in use even today. Notably, the age of the Cholas was a period of great development for trade, commerce, art, and literature. Prominent court poets, such as Kamban, produced

1076 CE Eastern Ganga dynasty rises to power in Odisha

1106 CE Vishnuvardhana takes over the Hoysala dynasty

1175 CE Muhammad Ghuri's conquest of the Punjab region

1189 CE Yadavas of Devagiri emerge

1191 CE First Battle of Tarain and Prithviraj Chauhan's victory over Muhammad Ghuri

1192 CE Second Battle of Tarain and Muhammad Ghuri's victory over Prithviraj Chauhan

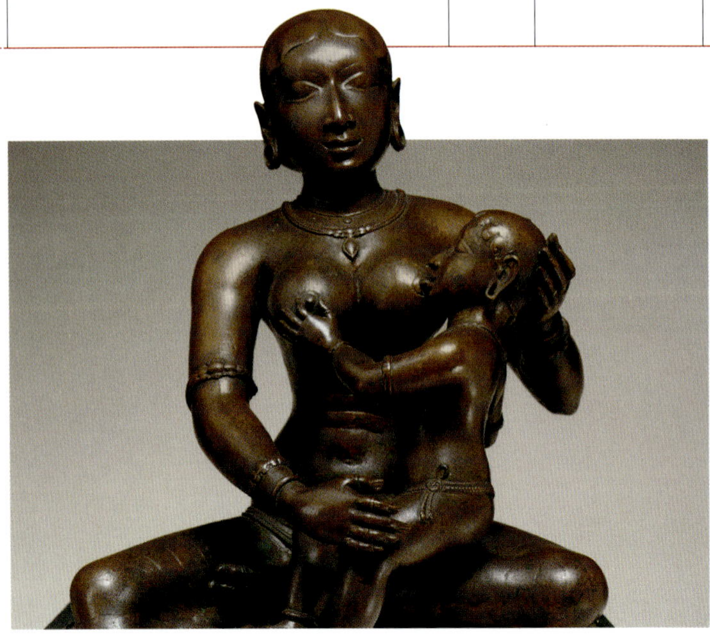

A bronze sculpture from the Chola dynasty, this figure depicts the Hindu lord Krishna as a baby, being nursed by his foster mother, Yashoda. These sculptures were crucial aspects of temple worship.

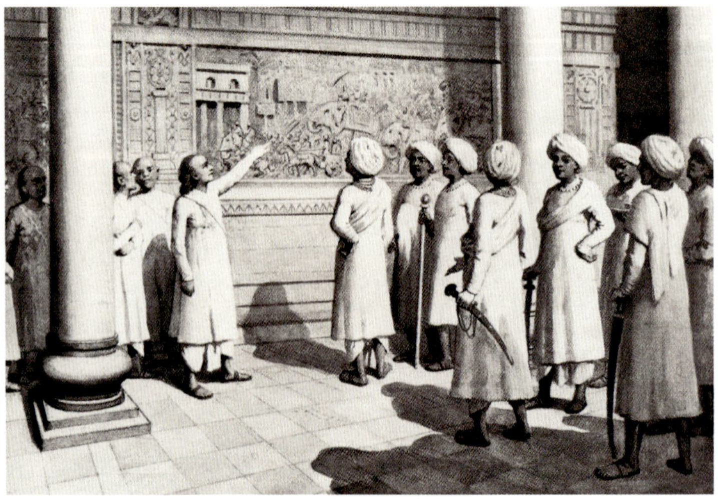

A 1915 painting depicting Emperor Rajaraja Chola inspecting the elaborate bas-reliefs documenting his military victories at the Brihadiswara Temple in Thanjavur.

masterpieces including retellings of the ancient Hindu epics Mahabharata and Ramayana in the Dravidian languages of Tamil, Kannada, and Telugu.

The Chola Empire flourished during the 12th century but declined at the beginning of the following century. The disintegration of the empire led to the emergence of the smaller Hoysala, Kakatiya, and Yadava dynasties as well as a resurgence of the Pandyas.

NORTH-WEST INVASIONS

From the 11th–12th centuries onwards, northern India saw times of great strife and power struggle, as well as invasions, especially from Central Asia.

By this time, the Turkic tribes were expanding eastwards into the Indian subcontinent. The first invasion came from Mahmud, the ruler of Ghazni in Afghanistan, and the second burst of raids from Muhammad Ghuri, of Ghur, in modern-day Afghanistan. Ghuri's victory at the second battle of Tarain marked the beginning of Islamic rule in India and, subsequently, the Delhi Sultanate.

The Delhi sultans not only survived the political upheavals, but also went on to conquer and annex most of the Indian subcontinent in the 14th century. It is during this time that Delhi, a largely insignificant, small city, was transformed into a powerful state capital – a position it would continuously hold in the centuries that followed.

THE DELHI SULTANATE

Ghuri entrusted the rule over the newly conquered territories in the Indian subcontinent to his general Qutbuddin Aibak, who had played an important part in the invasions. Starting with Aibak, a series of dynasties ruled from Delhi, known as the Delhi Sultanate.

Aibak, who established the Mamluk dynasty in the 13th century, began conquering territories to expand the sultanate, until his sudden death during a game of polo. His general and son-in-law, Iltutmish, succeeded the throne. Historians suggest that the Delhi Sultanate's paramountcy became evident during this time as Iltutmish led a series of military campaigns that significantly expanded its territories. The subsequent rulers had no major impact and there was a period of political uncertainty, until the emergence of Ghiyasuddin Balban, the second sultan of Delhi.

Balban squashed many rebellions, introduced new practices in court, reorganized the army, and built defensive military forts. Historical records indicate that trade and agriculture

1193 CE Ghuri captures Delhi

1202 CE Conquest of Bihar and Bengal by Bakhtiyar Khilji, military general of Ghuri

1206 CE Death of Muhammad Ghuri

1206 CE Qutbuddin Aibak establishes the Mamluk dynasty, the first to rule the Delhi Sultanate

1211 CE Iltutmish takes control of the Mamluk dynasty

1216 CE Pandyas of Madurai emerge in southern India

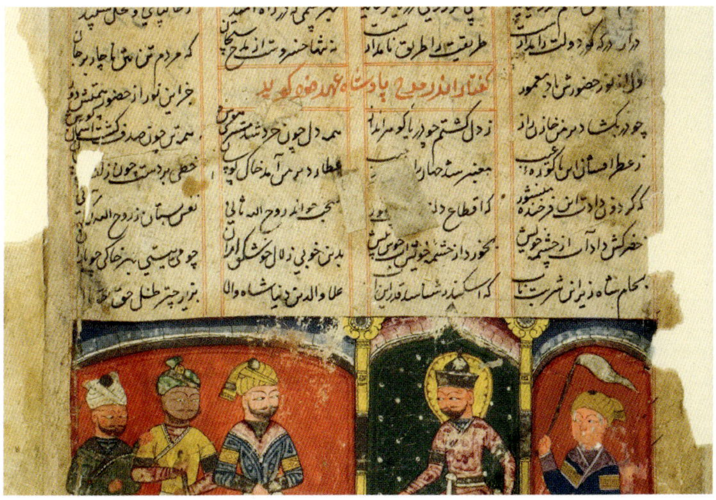

This illuminated folio from *Khamsa-e-Khusro* contains the Delhi Sultanate court poet Amir Khusro's verses as well as a dedication to Alauddin Khilji of the Khilji dynasty.

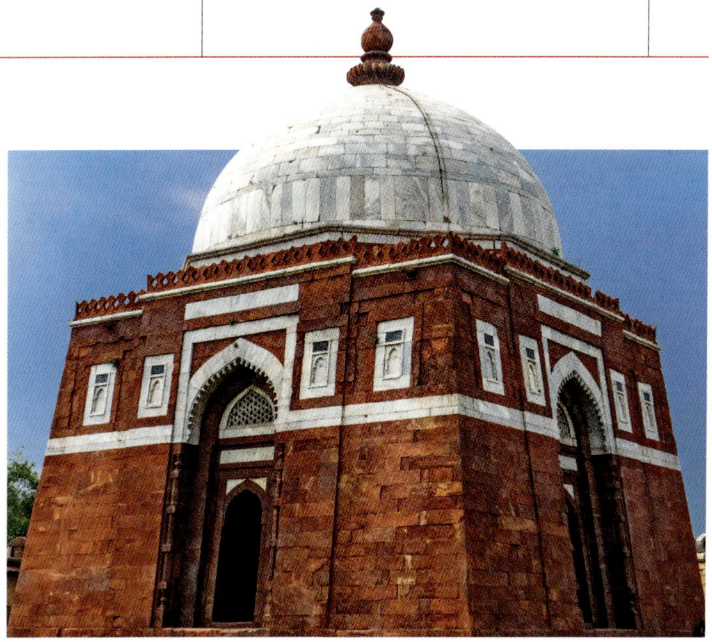

The tomb of Ghiyasuddin Tughlaq, the founder of the Delhi Sultanate's Tughlaq dynasty. An early example of Indo-Islamic architecture, it was built in 1325 with red sandstone and white marble.

improved during his reign. His demise led to Jalaluddin Khilji's reign in the late 13th century and the short-lived Khilji dynasty. Jalaluddin's nephew Alauddin Khilji usurped the throne shortly afterwards, marking the beginning of a 20-year-long reign with ceaseless military activity. Ibn Battuta, a Moroccan traveller who spent time in Delhi, noted that people considered Alauddin's rule as prosperous. His death, however, led to the decline of the Khiljis. Later, one of the sultan's senior lieutenants, Ghazi Malik, announced himself as the sultan Ghiyasuddin Tughlaq and set up a new dynasty of the Delhi Sultanate.

Perhaps one of the most significant dynasties of the Delhi Sultanate, the Tughlaqs saw several important leaders. Among them, Ghiyasuddin and Muhammad bin Tughlaq governed an empire that spanned practically the entire subcontinent. The third sultan, Feroz Shah Tughlaq, had a larger empire than the Khiljis, but it was similar in influence. He had the reputation of being a kind and merciful ruler and his reign was characterized by justice, kindness, prosperity, and security.

The end came in the form of an invasion by Timur from Uzbekistan at the end of the 14th century. His troops sacked Delhi for several days leading to devastating bloodshed and loss of property. From this wreckage emerged the pitifully small Sayyid dynasty, followed closely by the Lodhis, who were the last ruling dynasty of the Delhi Sultanate. They reconquered parts of present-day Punjab and Uttar Pradesh, built many public structures, and founded the city of Agra.

During the Delhi Sultanate, architecture was a hotbed of new trends: mosques and tombs were built with arches and huge domes. Trade flourished especially with regions like the Persian Gulf and South-east Asia. Silk, cotton, spices, and precious stones were exported. Writers wrote in regional languages as well as Persian; Amir Khusro wrote verse in Hindi and Hindavi (Urdu) and Ziauddin Barani, a historian, who wrote in Persian. The sultans even established workshops *(karkhanas)*, where specialized luxury items were produced for royal use, including brassware, glassware, paintings, and carpets.

THE VIJAYANAGARA AND BAHMANI KINGDOMS

The Delhi Sultanate did not remain restricted to the northern region. It extended its political frontier into the Deccan and spread the influence of Persian culture. A series of rebellions

1221 CE Mongol invasions in India by Chengiz Khan

1266 CE Reign of Ghiyasuddin Balban

1288 CE Marco Polo, Venetian traveller, comes to India

1290 CE Khilji dynasty established

1296 CE Alauddin Khilji assumes throne

1309 CE Khilji dynasty's Malik Kafur's expedition to south India

1320 CE Emergence of the Tughlaq dynasty

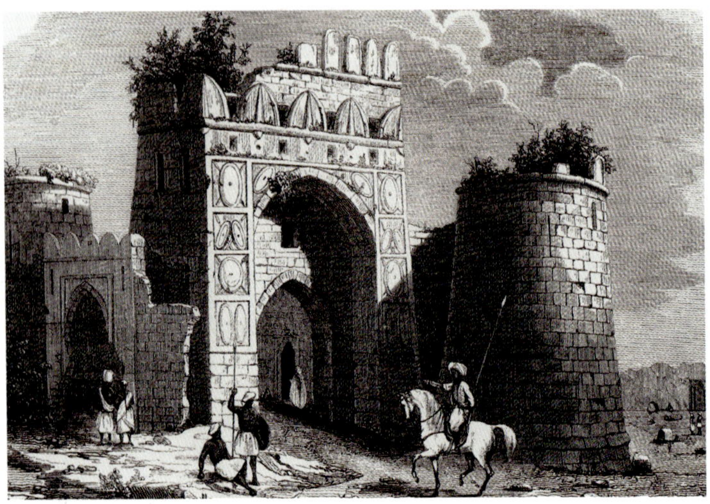

A wood engraving by French artist Ernest Breton from 1846 portraying the ruined entrance of Feroz Shah Kotla, a fortress built by Feroz Shah Tughlaq in c. 1354.

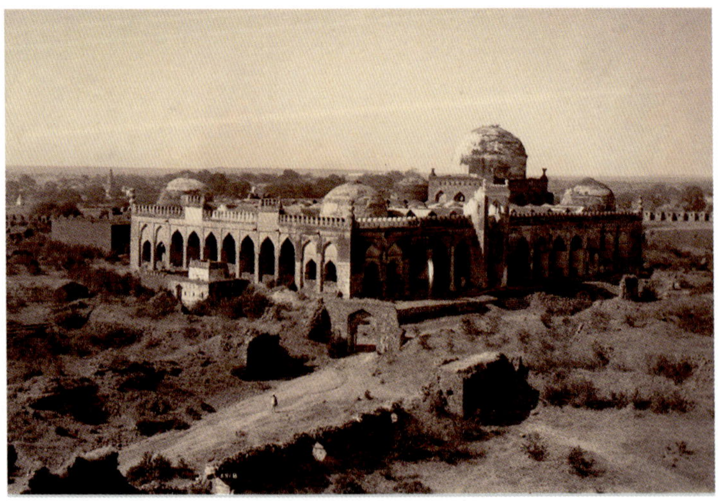

A late 19th-century photograph of the Jami Masjid in Gulbarga, taken by Lala Deen Dayal. The mosque was erected by Alauddin Hasan Bahmani Shah, the founder of the Bahmani dynasty.

and the declaration of independence by groups and individuals followed, lead to the establishment of two Deccan kingdoms: the Vijayanagara Empire and the Bahmani Sultanate.

The founders of the Vijayanagar Empire, Harihara and Bukka were feudatories who became ministers in the kingdom of Kampili, in modern Karnataka. When Muhammad Tughlaq overran Kampili for sheltering a Muslim rebel, the two brothers were imprisoned, converted to Islam, and appointed to subdue the rebellions there. The governor of Madurai had already declared his independence, and the Hoysala rulers of Mysore and Warangal were attempting to do the same. Following suit, Harihara and Bukka abandoned their new sultan and their new faith.

Instead, they established their capital at Vijayanagara, in modern-day Karnataka. The city also lent its name to the formidable empire. Harihara's coronation is said to have taken place in the mid-14th century. The empire's rising power brought it into conflict with many powers in the south and north. The sultans of Madurai and the Hoysala ruler of Mysore in the south were its main rivals and the conflict lasted nearly four decades. To the north, Vijayanagara faced a challenging rival in the Bahmani kingdom. It was established in 1347 by Alauddin Hasan, an Afghan adventurer who rose through the ranks. Following his coronation, he took the name Alauddin Hasan Bahman Shah. The Vijayanagara rulers and the Bahmani sultans' interests clashed in three distinct areas: the Tungabhadra doab (the area between two rivers), the Krishna–Godavari delta, and the Marathwada country. Military conflicts between the Vijayanagara and the Bahmani kingdom were almost a regular feature and lasted as long as these kingdoms did. This period was distinguished by the accomplishments of Vijayanagara's greatest ruler, Krishnadevaraya. Over time, the Bahmani power declined, and they disintegrated into five smaller kingdoms, collectively known as the Deccan sultanates: the Nizam-Shahis of Ahmadnagar; the Adil Shahis of Bijapur; the Imad Shahis of Berar, the Qutb Shahis of Golconda, and the Barid Shahis of Bidar. Though they were rivals, the Deccan sultanates allied with each other against the Vijayanagara Empire in the mid-16th century, permanently weakening it in the Battle of Talikota. Notably, this alliance destroyed the city of Vijayanagara, and many important temples, such as the Vitthala Temple in Hampi, were razed to the ground.

1327 CE Transfer of capital from Delhi to Daulatabad

1334 CE Ibn Battuta comes to Delhi Sultanate's courts

1336 CE Foundation of Vijayanagara Empire

1345 CE Establishment of Bahmani Kingdom

1489 CE Bahmani kingdom breaks up into five Deccan Sultanates

1565 CE Fall of the Vijayanagara Empire

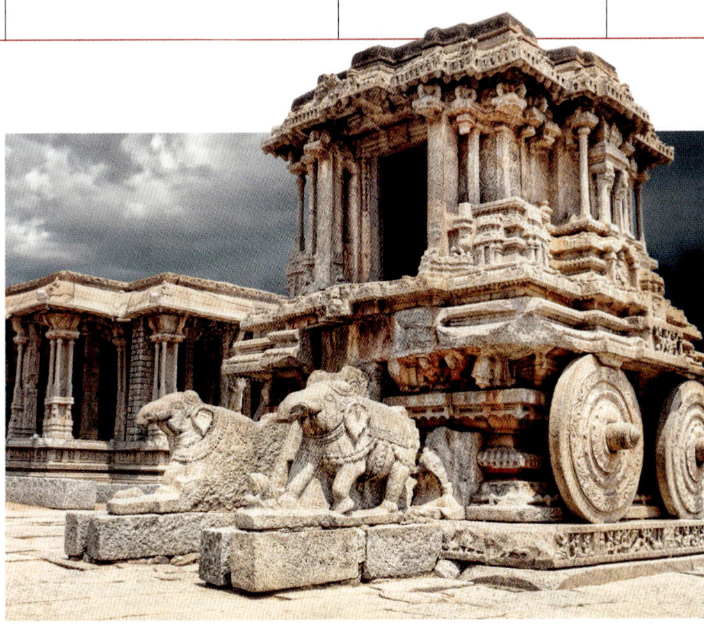

This exquisitely carved stone chariot or *ratha* is in Hampi, Karnataka. It is a shrine dedicated to Garuda, Lord Vishnu's escort, inside the Vitthala Temple complex built during the Vijayanagara Empire.

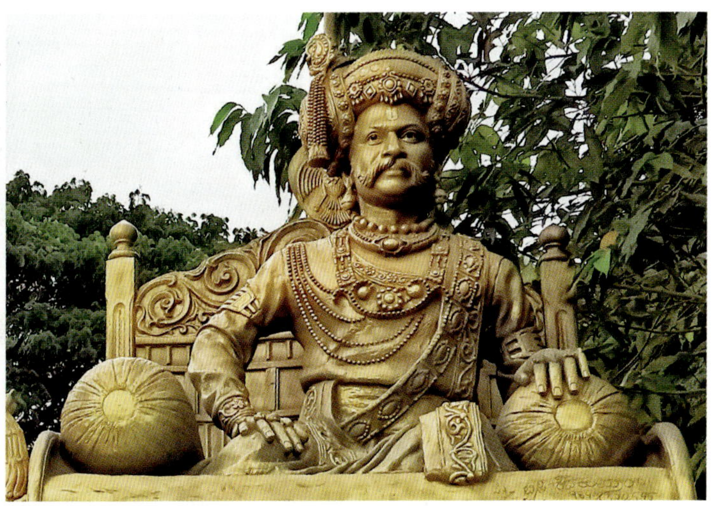

A statue of Vijayanagara empire's formidable ruler Krishnadeveraya. Presiding over the empire at its zenith, he made significant efforts in expanding and consolidating it.

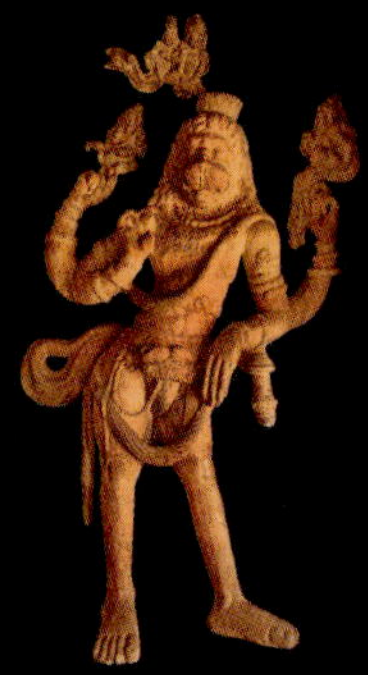

Era c. 578–579 CE | **Medium** Sandstone | **Height** Cave: 4.6 m (15 ft)

NARASIMHA OF BADAMI

A composite of man and beast

Carved into the sandstone cliff at the Badami cave temples, in the southern state of Karnataka, is the half-man, half-lion avatar of Vishnu, the Preserver. He is believed to have vanquished evil and restored harmony on earth.

The four rock-cut temples in the caves at Badami, in south-east Karnataka, date back to the 6th century, when the city was the capital of the Chalukya kingdom. Cut into the soft sandstone escarpment rising above a man-made lake in this rocky tableland of the Deccan, they exemplify some of India's greatest sculptures in situ. Three of the caves are Brahmanical, while the fourth is Jain.

The caves are among the earliest examples of Hindu temple architecture. Each features entrance columns, a verandah, and a hall leading into the *garbhagriha* (inner sanctum). The third cave, called Cave 3, is the largest and highest on the cliff. It is also the only one that can be precisely dated – an inscription records its creation as a shrine in 578 CE. It is exquisitely detailed with large sculptural reliefs and other decorative elements. At least five of the reliefs depict aspects of Lord Vishnu. Narasimha, standing tall, with claws and the face of a lion and the body of a man, dominates a niche on the wall on the right of the *mukh mandapa* (entrance verandah).

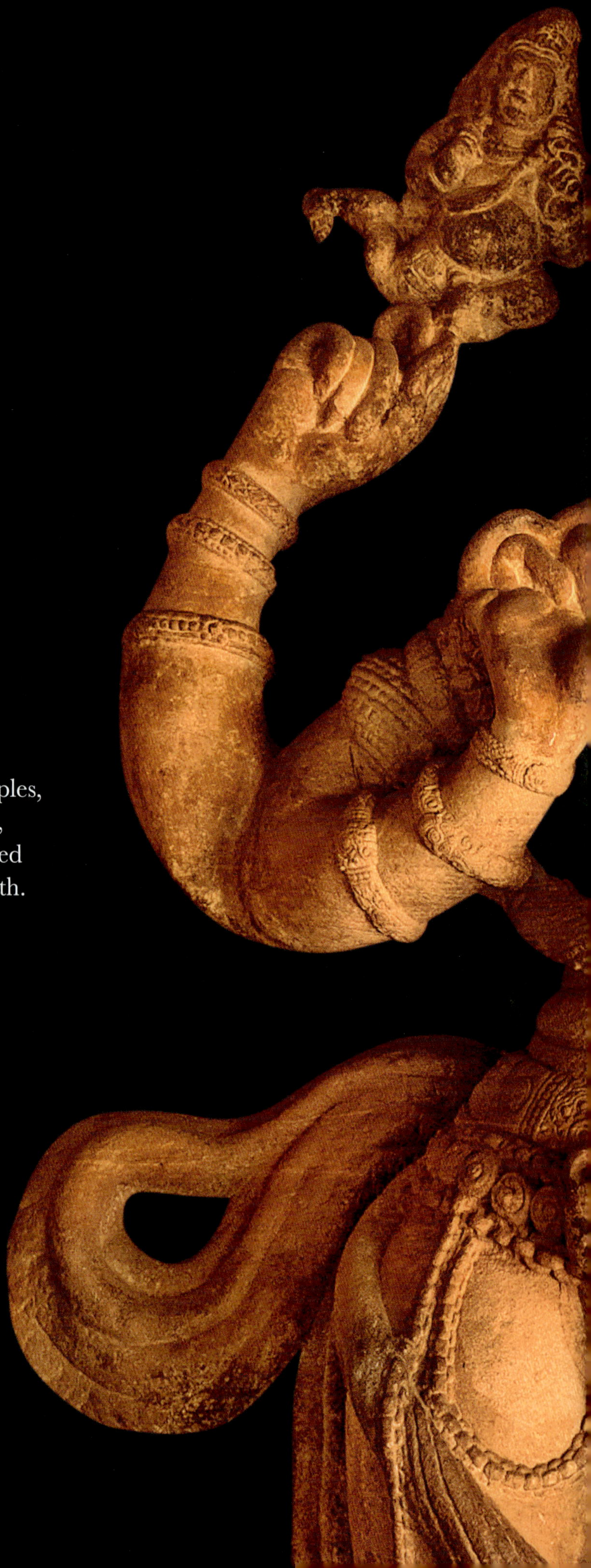

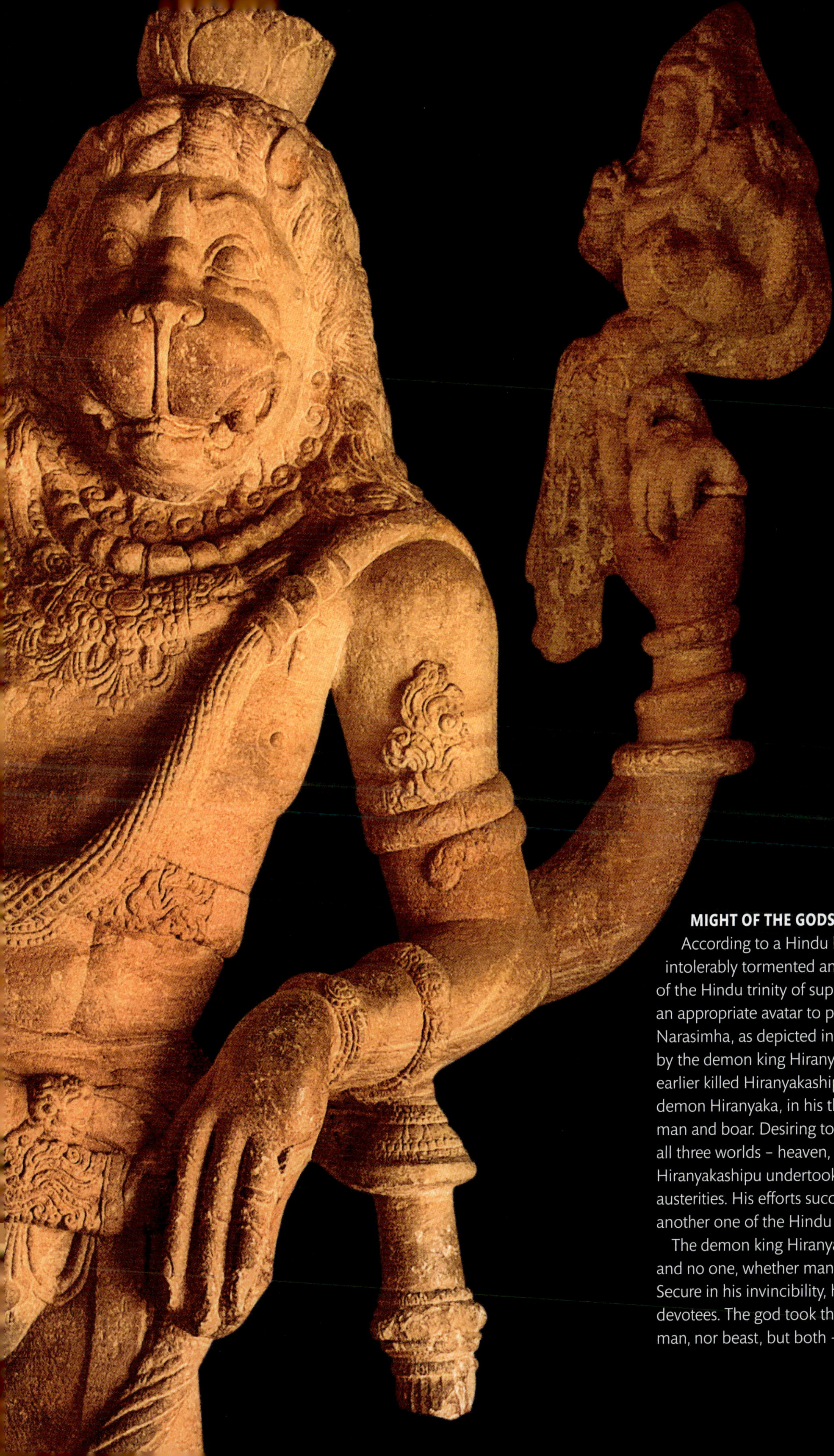

MIGHT OF THE GODS

According to a Hindu legend, whenever the earth is intolerably tormented and distressed, Lord Vishnu, one of the Hindu trinity of supreme divinity, is said to assume an appropriate avatar to protect it. His fourth avatar Narasimha, as depicted in the cave, was necessitated by the demon king Hiranyakashipu. Lord Vishnu had earlier killed Hiranyakashipu's younger brother, the demon Hiranyaka, in his third avatar as a composite of man and boar. Desiring to avenge his brother and rule all three worlds – heaven, earth, and the netherworld – Hiranyakashipu undertook severe penance and immense austerities. His efforts succeeded in pleasing Lord Brahma, another one of the Hindu trinity, who granted him a boon.

The demon king Hiranyakashipu asked that nothing and no one, whether man or animal, be able to kill him. Secure in his invincibility, he then tyrannized Lord Vishnu's devotees. The god took the form of Narasimha – neither man, nor beast, but both – to destroy him.

Era 6th–9th centuries CE | **Medium** Basalt | **Area** 2 km (1.2 miles)

ELLORA CAVES

Rock-cut cave temples and monasteries

Scooped out of basalt cliffs are a series of monasteries and temples set in one of the biggest complexes of rock-cut temples in India. Representing Hinduism, Buddhism, and Jainism, the Ellora Caves, in Maharashtra, lend credence to the coexistence of religious beliefs.

The 34 caves of the Ellora complex are spread over a distance of more than 2 km (1.2 miles). The oldest of these are the 12 Buddhist *viharas* (monasteries) and *chaityas* (prayer halls), dating from 5th to the 7th centuries CE, which were made for Buddhist monks to live and meditate in. The range of Buddhist deities sculpted on to these caves reflect the Mahayana Buddhist philosophy of the time.

ETERNAL SHRINES

While the Buddhist caves were cut horizontally into the rock, the 17 Hindu temples constructed between the 7th and 10th centuries CE were carved vertically, demonstrating amazing creative and structural innovation. It is an 84-m (276 ft) drop into the 47-m (154 ft) wide courtyard of the spectacular Kailashanatha. The free-standing, multi-storeyed temple was inspired by Mount Kailash, the abode of the Hindu deity Shiva and his wife Parvati, and is carved out of a single rock. It took 100 years to build and required the removal of 85,000 cu m (3,000,000 cu ft) of rock. In contrast, the five Jain temples are smaller, reflective of the asceticism of the philosophy, but no less appealing in ornamentation. The sculptures are detailed and intricate, and though the paintings have degraded, the fragments that remain are rich and skilfully executed. The entire complex was created over 6th to 7th centuries, spanning a range of beliefs and philosophy. The unbroken, harmonious rhythm of artistic and architectural development and expression is remarkable - as are the insights into the socio-cultural environment of the time.

1. A panoramic view of the two-storeyed, rock-cut gateway, or *gopuram*, leading into the Kailashanatha Temple. **2.** Multi-level monastery cells with adorning figures. **3.** The Carpenter's Cave, or Vishwakarma, is named after the celestial carpenter and is dominated by the figure of a seated Teaching Buddha, carved in front of a votive stupa. **4.** Detailed carvings on the outside walls of the Kailashanatha Temple. **5.** A flight of stairs to the first level of Cave 15, or Dashavatara Cave. **6.** The Kailashanatha Temple's courtyard flanked by a pillar as well as panels depicting scenes from the epic Ramayana. **7.** A carving from Cave 29, Dhuma Lena, depicting a scene from the Ramayana in which Ravana shook Mount Kailasha. **8.** A statue of the Jain goddess Ambika, worshipped for prosperity, sitting beneath a fruit-laden tree in Cave 32.

1

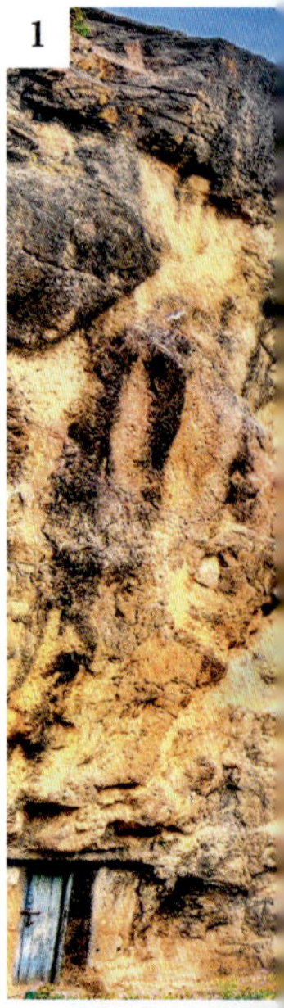

2

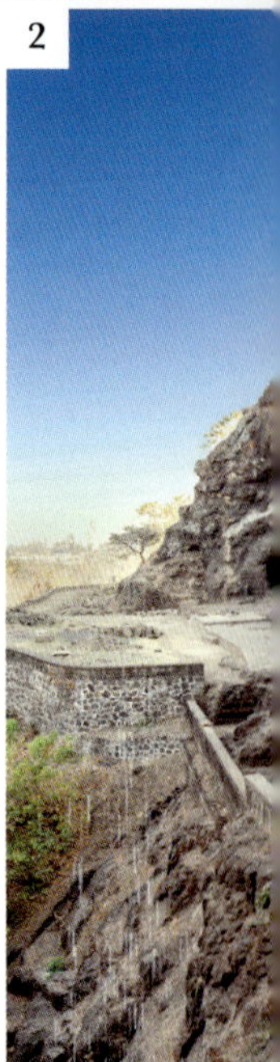

5

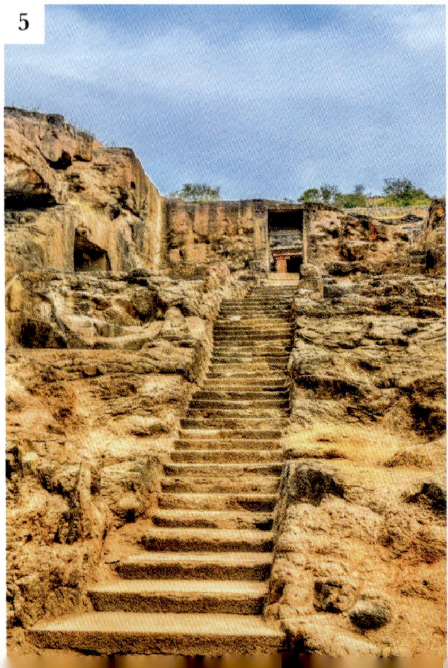

6

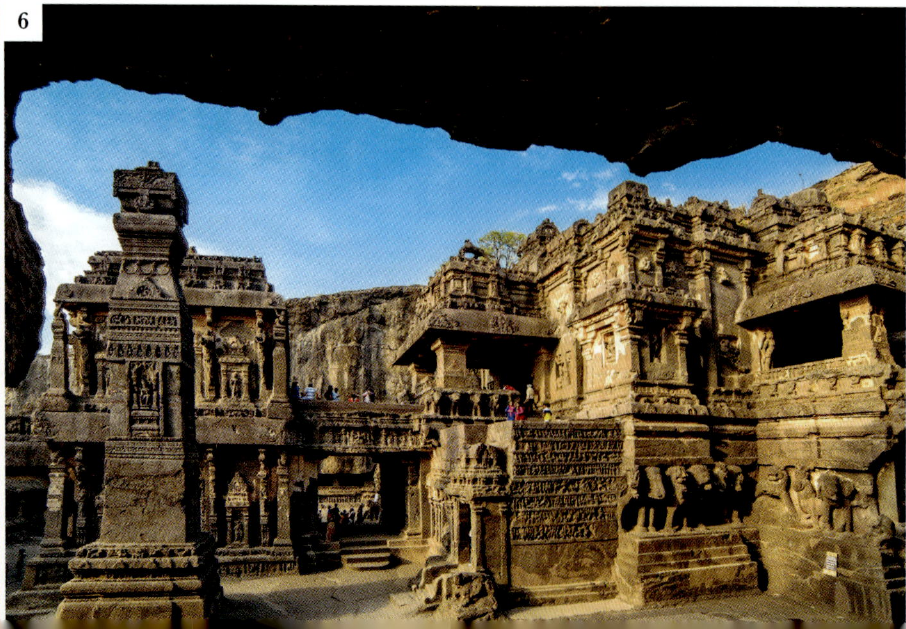

7

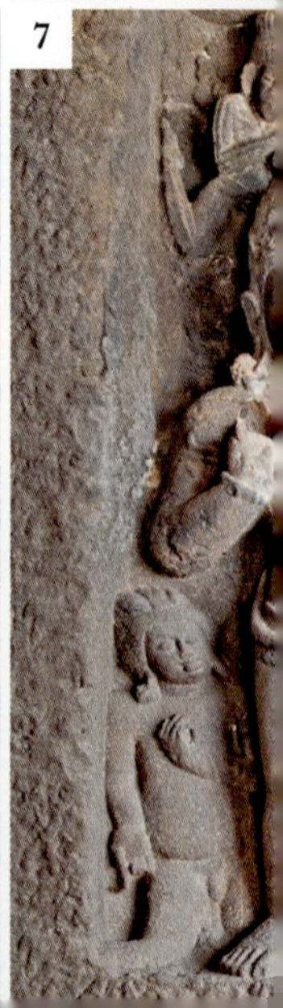

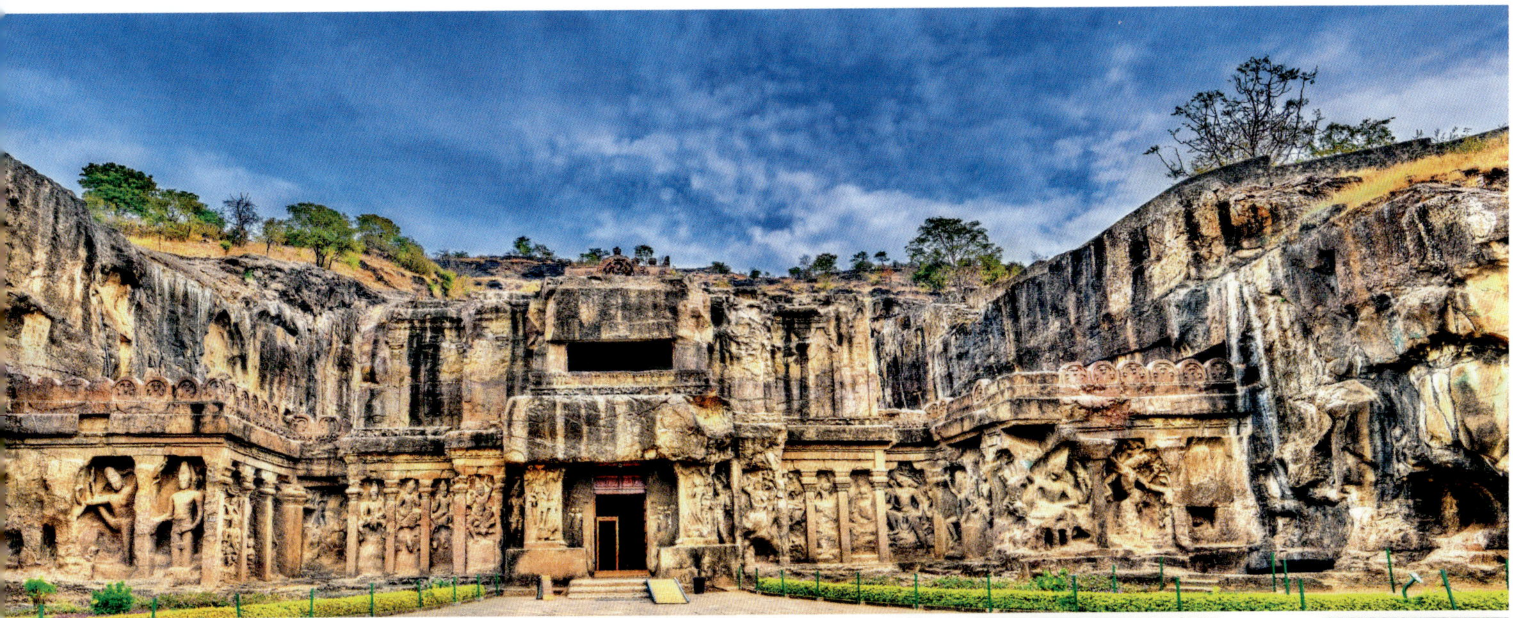

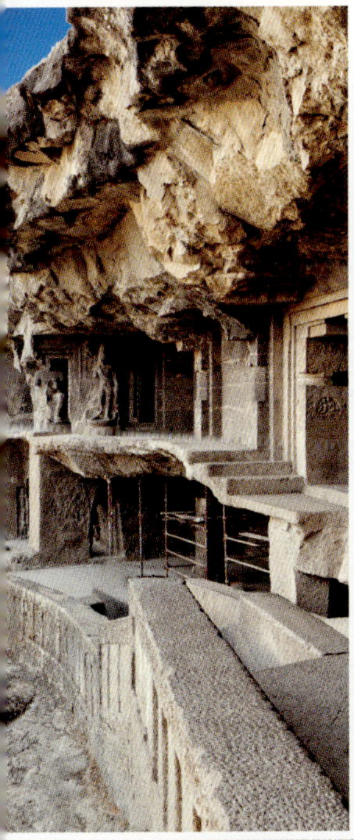

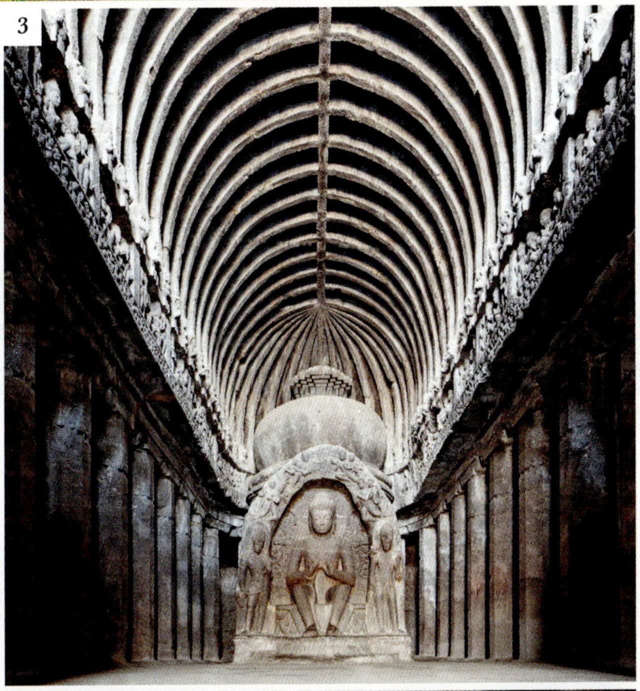

3

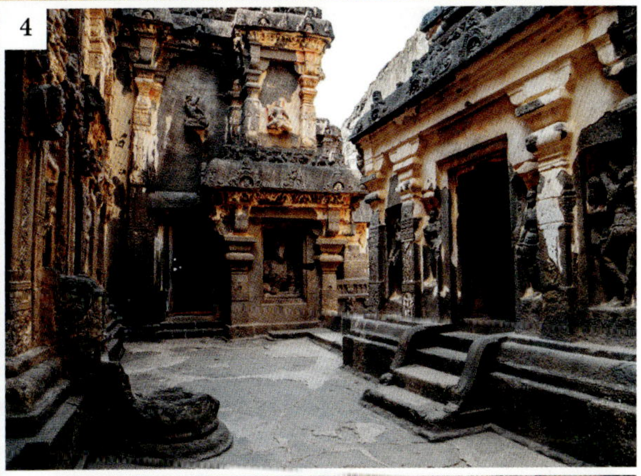

4

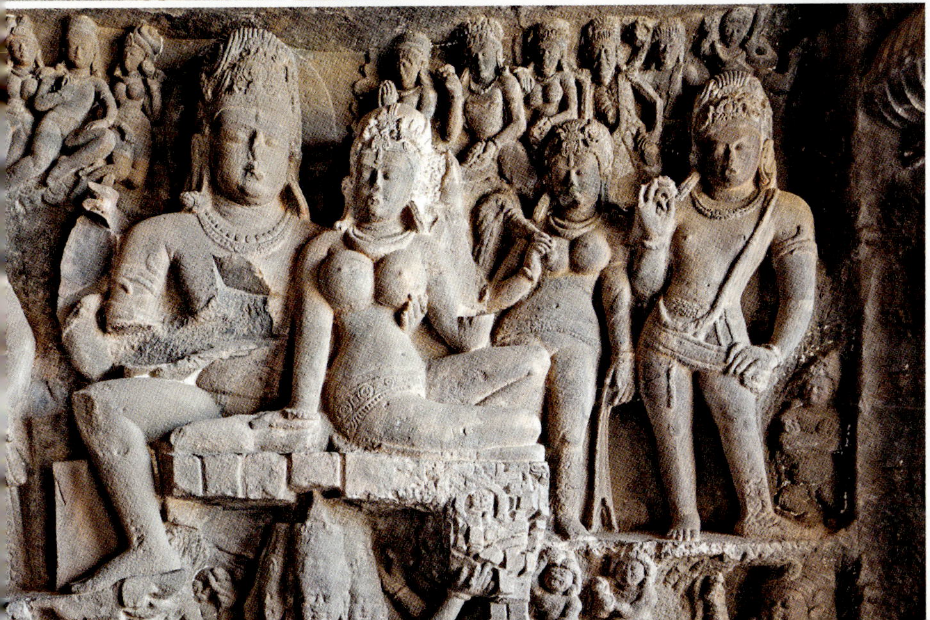

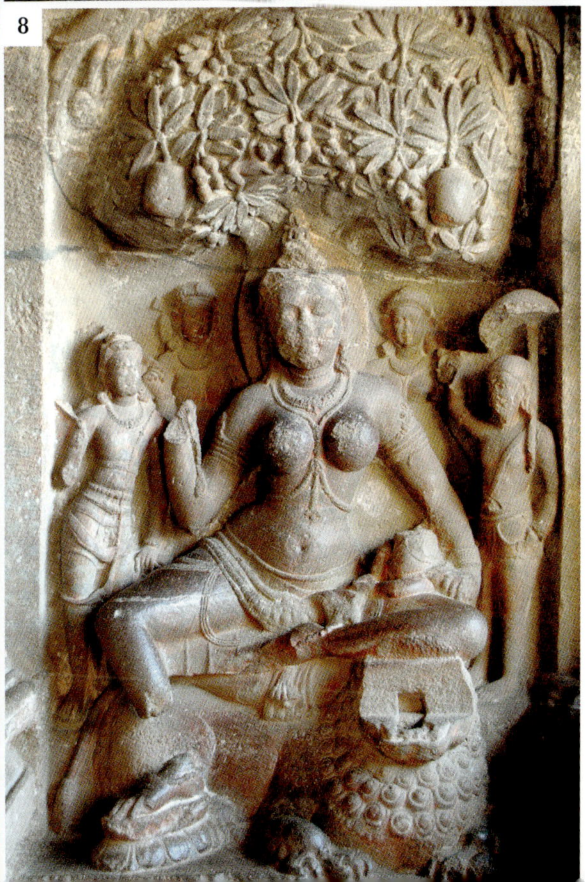

8

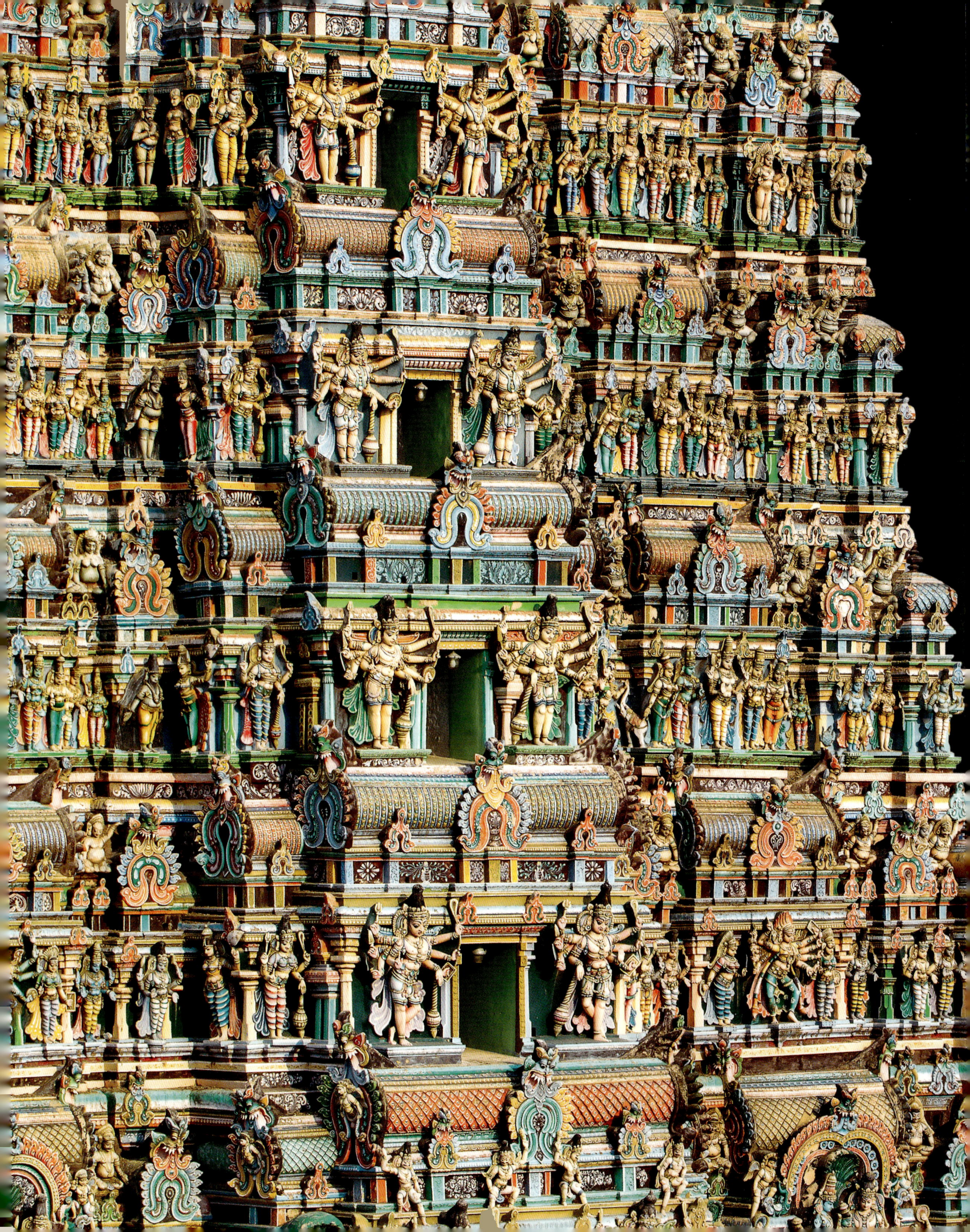

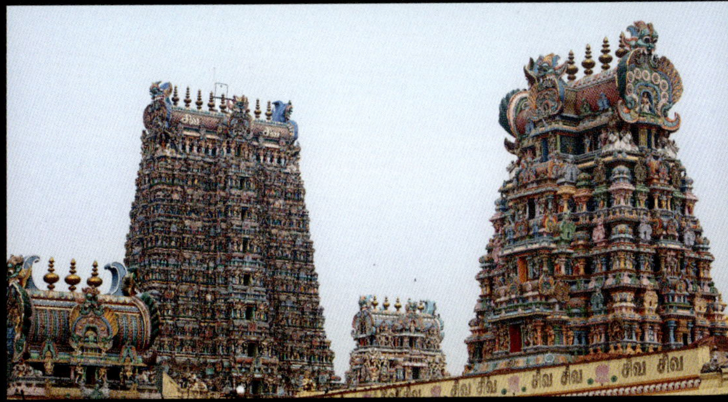

Exquisite gold finial on the façade of the Meenakshi Sundereshwara Temple built by the Pandya dynasty of Madurai in the southern state of Tamil Nadu.

Era 7th century CE | **Medium** granite and limestone | **Elevation** 144 m (472 ft)

MEENAKSHI SUNDERESHWAR TEMPLE

The pinnacle of south Indian temple architecture

One of the oldest and most important temples in India, the Meenakshi Amman Temple, as it is also known, celebrates the spot where Shiva, as the handsome Sundareshwara, wed Parvati in the form of Meenakshi, the 'one with beautiful eyes'.

Madurai finds mention in early Tamil texts from the 6th century, which speak of it as a temple town and a gathering place (*sangam*) of scholars. The temple complex as it stands today, however, is attributed to the Nayaka rulers who made Madurai their capital between the 16th and 18th centuries.

ARCHITECTURAL SPLENDOUR

Spread over 14 acres (5.6 ha), the temple follows the ancient architectural rules of Vastu Shastra in layout and plan, and is a prime example of the Vesara style of temples found in southern India. A succession of *mandapas* (pavilions) and courtyards lead to the square sanctuaries of the deites, Sundaraeshwara and Meenakshi, housed in individual enclosures that are surrounded by colonnades. A gold finial tops each sanctuary. The *porthamarai kulam*, or golden lotus pond, for ritual bathing occupies the south end of the complex. The sanctuaries are protected by three walled enclosures, each of which has four *gopurams*, or gateways, increasing in height as they go further away from the centre.

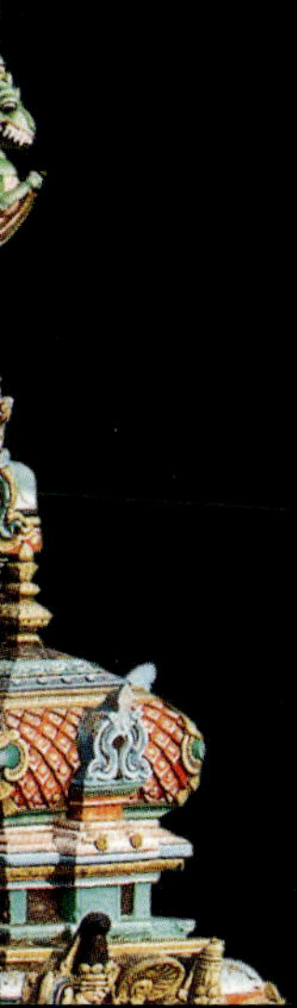

Multi-coloured stucco sculptures, rich in mythological references, rise up to the sky with an exuberant display of gods and goddesses, their consorts, and attendants. The temple has 14 *gopurams*. The four at the cardinal points on the outer boundary are over 50-m (164-ft) tall. The southern gateway rises to almost 52 m (170 ft), with over 1,500 sculptures that are repaired and painted every 12 years.

PRAYING TO THE GODDESS

The temple has a shrine to Vishnu – here, he is depicted as Meenakshi's brother – which brings together different strands of Shaivite (belief in Shiva being the central deity), Vaishnavite (worship of Vishnu as the prime god), and Shakti (worship of the Goddess) traditions of south India. It also enshrines Ganesha, as well as Lakshmi, Saraswati, and other aspects of the Mother Goddess, but the main deity of the temple is Meenakshi. She is the one to whom devotees offer prayers, even before approaching her consort, Sundareshwara.

Era 7th century CE | **Medium** Granite | **Dimension** 15 × 30 m (49 ft × 98 ft)

DESCENT OF THE GANGES

A king's reassurance etched in stone for a millennium

Deities, spirits, humans, and animals surround an ascetic offering austerities to the Hindu god Shiva, appealing for a boon, on this tall bas-relief carving near the coast in Mamallapuram, or Mahabalipuram, in south-east India.

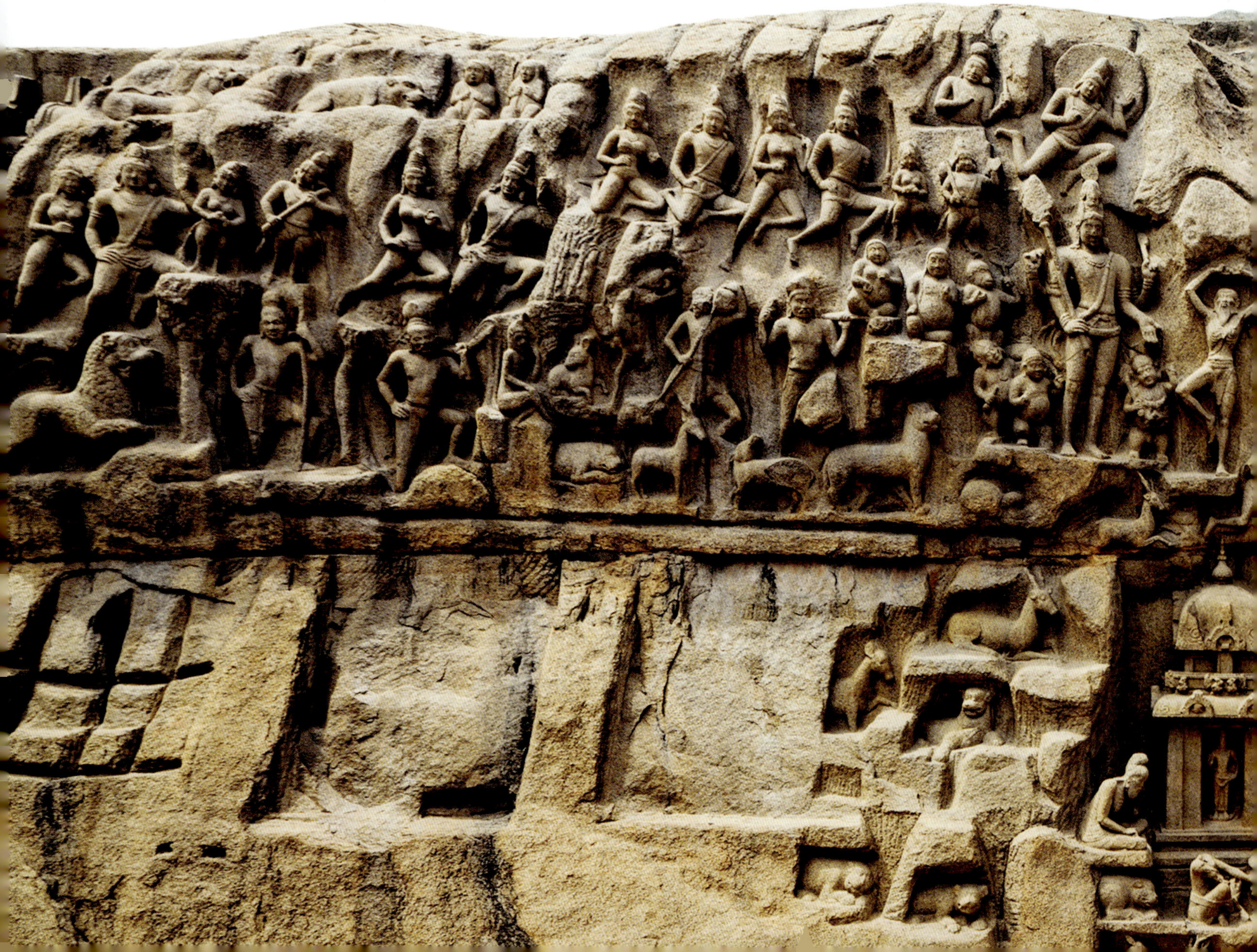

Located amid the Group of Monuments at Mahabalipuram, a UNESCO World Heritage Site, in the south-eastern state of Tamil Nadu, is an extraordinary artistic achievement in stone. The huge carving is one of many great open-air reliefs and cave temples created over two generations.

Known as the Descent of Ganges, this bas relief brings to life the mythical story of the holy river's arrival from the heavens through the tresses of the Hindu deity Shiva. He is one of the largest figures here. The ascetic imploring him to bring the Ganges to earth looms nearly as large. The river itself 'descends' down a natural cleft in the rock as many creatures look on. Another interpretation, Arjuna's Penance, sees Arjun, a character in the Hindu epic Mahabharata (see pp. 26), in place of the ascetic, praying for a boon.

▼ Carving of the Hindu legend Descent of the Ganges where a hollow channel marks the path through which water, perhaps during the monsoon season, would flow down the boulder.

EXAMPLE OF GREAT ARTISANSHIP

The Descent of the Ganges was possibly carved at the time of the rule of the Pallava king Narasimha Varman I (c. 630 CE) to celebrate a victory over the ruler of another prevalent dynasty, the Chalukya king Pulakesin II.

Here, the granite becomes fluid under the skilled chisels of the artisans. Stories from the Panchatantra (see pp. 80–81) come alive through the detailed figures: life-size and life-like elephants appear to be walking down to the river for a drink of water. The many calves gambolling, secure and protected, around their massive legs could be an allusion to the aegis of the mighty Pallavas. There is a gentle humour and lightness to the relief as well, as in the figure of a cat standing on one leg, akin to depictions of holy men, surrounded by mice. Its multi-layered storytelling is perhaps indicative of the benevolence of Pallava rule.

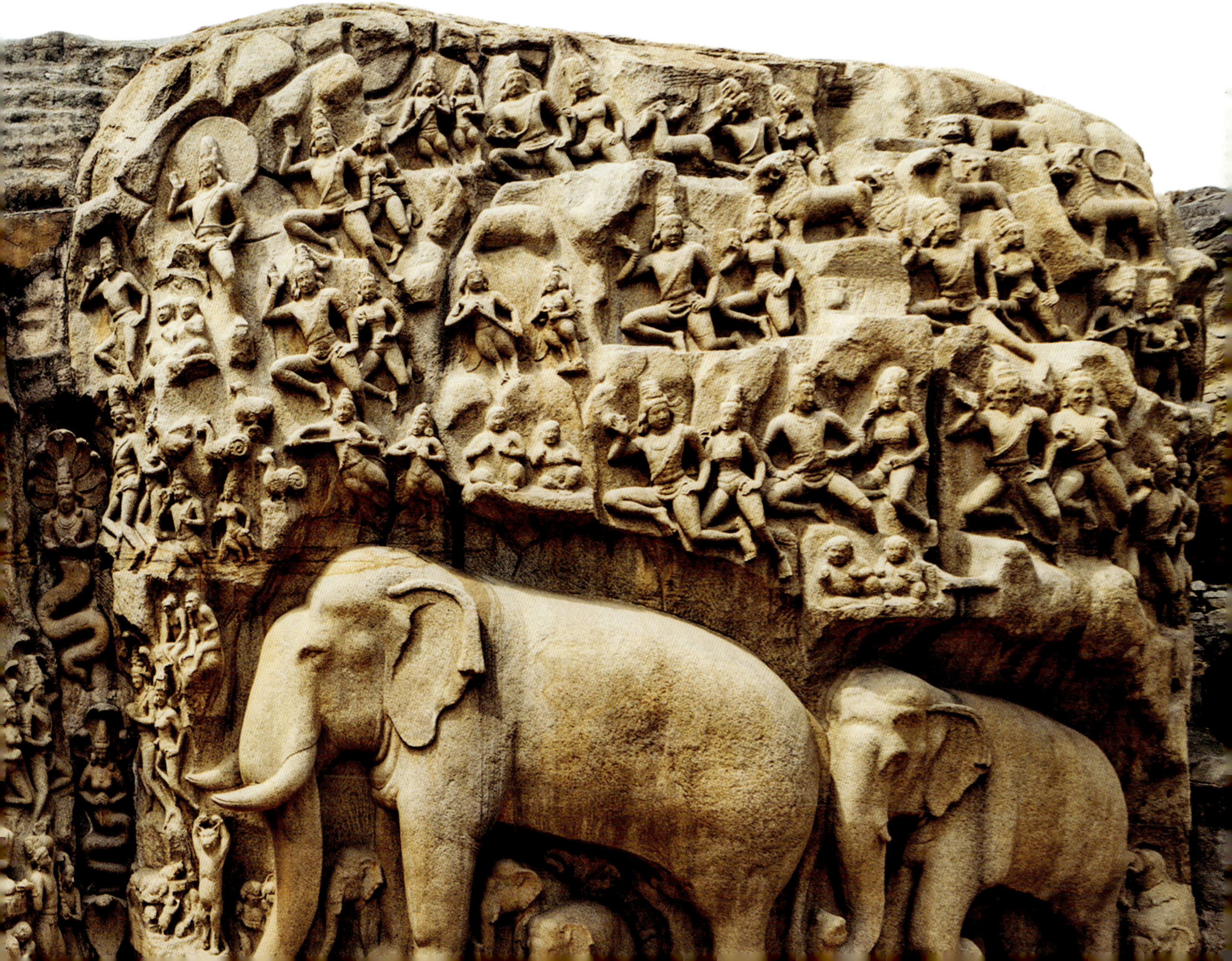

Era 8th century CE | **Medium** Limestone, lime mortar | **Area** 67 × 43 m (220 × 142 ft)

MARTAND SUN TEMPLE

A formidable edifice with mysterious origins

In the northern region of Kashmir's Anantnag district stand the ruins of one of the few surviving temples to the sun god in India. The remaining structure of the Martand Sun Temple conveys Hellenistic influence on Indian architecture.

Dedicated to the Hindu deity Martand, the Sanskrit name for the sun god Surya, is this imposing temple located in the north of the Indian subcontinent. The temple features three distinct chambers - the *mandapa* (pavilion), *garbhagriha* (shrine room), and *antarala* (connecting chamber between the two).

The temple is built on top of a plateau and offers expansive views of the Kashmir valley below. Its pillars feature detailed carvings and the complex alludes to remarkable structures, now in ruins. Although its architecture clearly embodies a unique Kashmiri style, there are Graeco-Roman, Buddhist-Gandharan, and north Indian styles referenced in its carvings, sculptures, and spire.

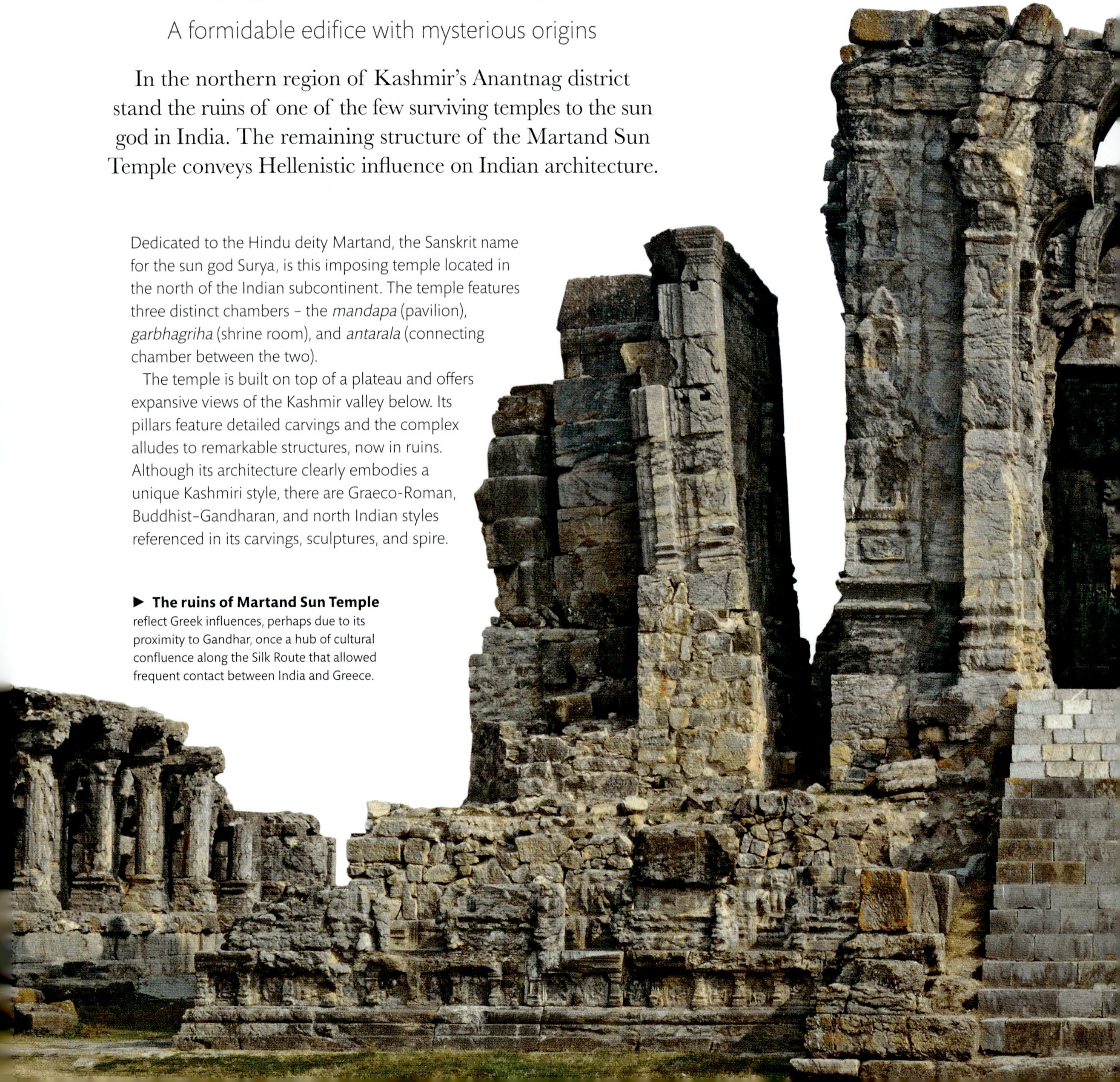

► **The ruins of Martand Sun Temple** reflect Greek influences, perhaps due to its proximity to Gandhar, once a hub of cultural confluence along the Silk Route that allowed frequent contact between India and Greece.

> **"The temple at Martand is a building of average size, but throughout a feeling of large scale is consistently maintained, as there is nothing small of sparing in its composition."**
>
> – Percy Brown, *Indian Architecture (Buddhist and Hindu Period)*, 1900

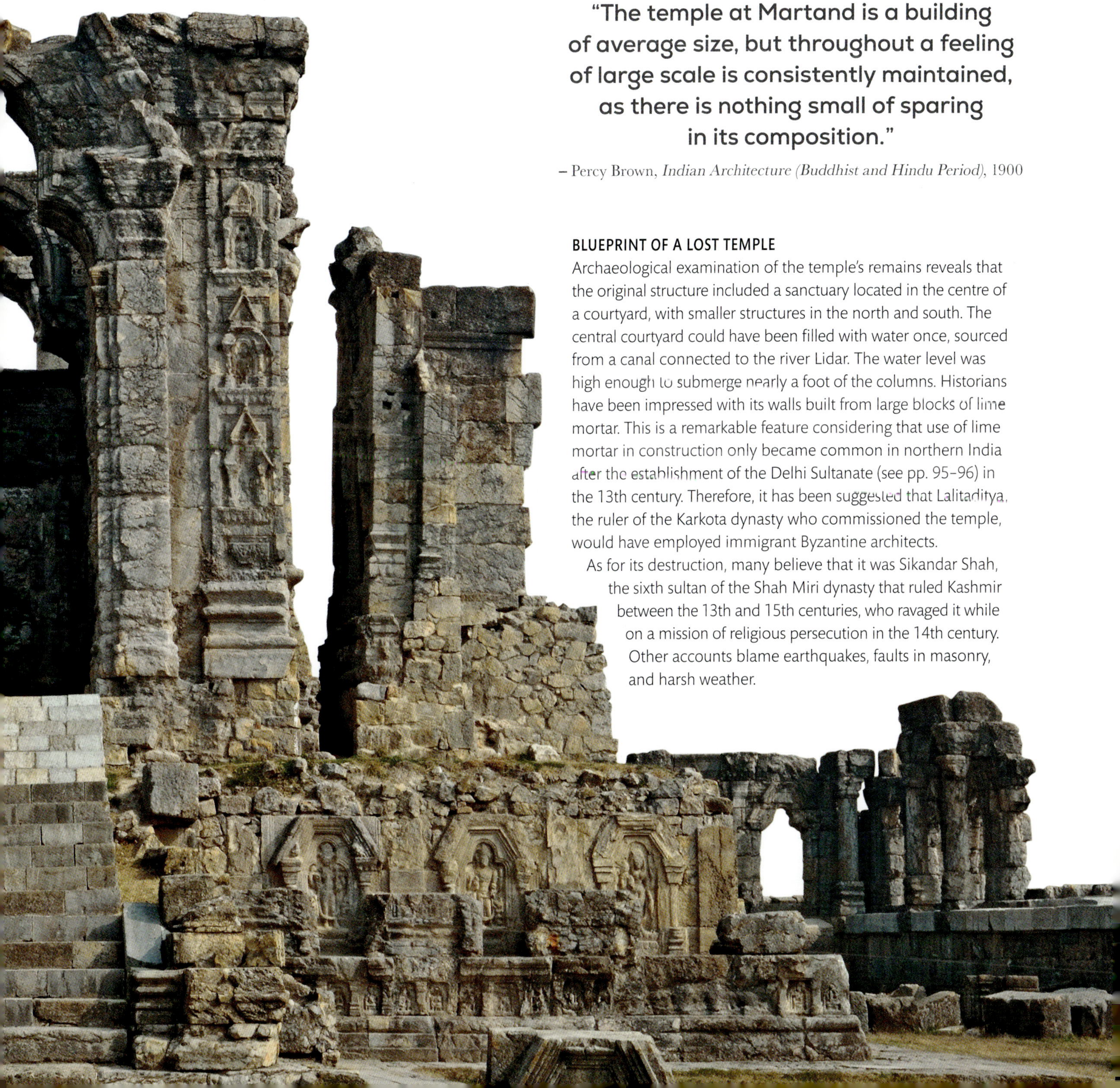

BLUEPRINT OF A LOST TEMPLE

Archaeological examination of the temple's remains reveals that the original structure included a sanctuary located in the centre of a courtyard, with smaller structures in the north and south. The central courtyard could have been filled with water once, sourced from a canal connected to the river Lidar. The water level was high enough to submerge nearly a foot of the columns. Historians have been impressed with its walls built from large blocks of lime mortar. This is a remarkable feature considering that use of lime mortar in construction only became common in northern India after the establishment of the Delhi Sultanate (see pp. 95–96) in the 13th century. Therefore, it has been suggested that Lalitaditya, the ruler of the Karkota dynasty who commissioned the temple, would have employed immigrant Byzantine architects.

As for its destruction, many believe that it was Sikandar Shah, the sixth sultan of the Shah Miri dynasty that ruled Kashmir between the 13th and 15th centuries, who ravaged it while on a mission of religious persecution in the 14th century. Other accounts blame earthquakes, faults in masonry, and harsh weather.

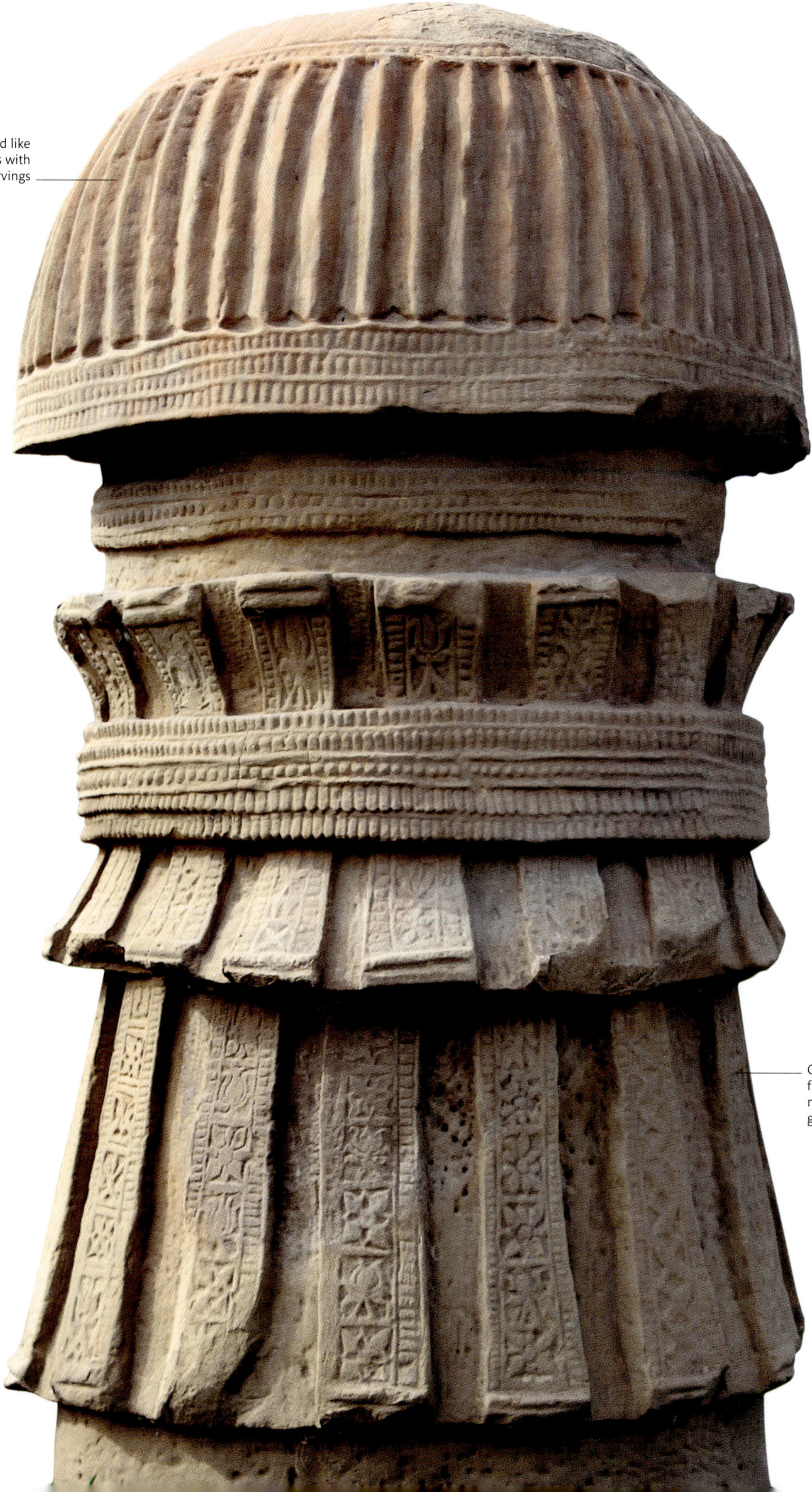
Domes shaped like inverted cups with geometrical carvings
Carved designs feature floral and animal motifs, and some geometrical patterns

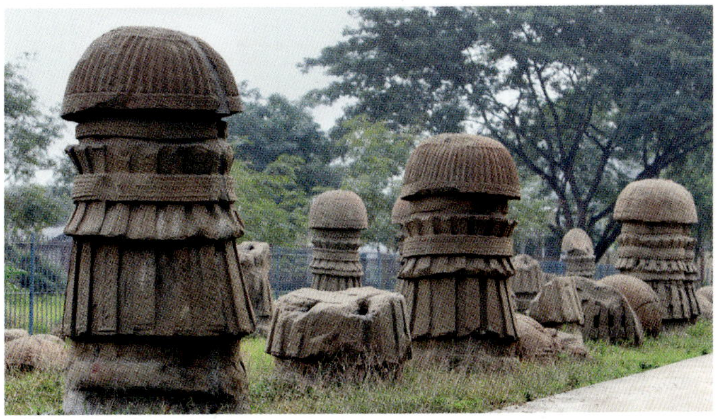

A series of monolithic pillars at Kachari Rajbari. Some of these still stand in all their glory but others have crumbled.

Era 10th–13th centuries CE | **Medium** Sandstone | **Height** 2.4 m (8 ft)

MONOLITHS OF KACHARI RAJBARI

Enigmatic stone monuments

The ruins of Kachari Rajbari in Nagaland feature fascinating mushroom-shaped, domed stone pillars, representative of one of the oldest kingdoms in the region. The exact nature or purpose of these pillars remain a mystery.

The pillars stand in three clusters, numbering hundreds. No two are precisely alike in their minor ornamentation, however, all are of one general form. They are large semi-circular tops with concentric, foliated carvings on the shaft. Though they vary in height, the pillars are largely 2.5–3.5 m (8–12 ft) tall. Found in Dimapur, Nagaland, in the north-eastern region of India, these monoliths serve as a reminder of the Kachari kingdom's enduring legacy in the state.

A PIECE OF A PUZZLE

The purpose of these ancient structures remains shrouded in mystery. One theory suggests that the pillars may have served as phallic symbols representing fertility. It is believed that the area was once inhabited by followers of the Hindu god of destruction, Shiva, and the kings commissioned these pillars as a symbol of their devotion to the deity during a time of crisis. It is possible, too, that the pillars were votive offerings for the Buddhist faith and the area may have served as a stop for Buddhist monks travelling to and from South-east Asia, through Bihar and Bengal. Another explanation posits that this is a burial ground for prominent Kachari figures and that the pillars are memorial stones. Due to the domes, they are also referred to as gigantic chessmen, implying that a game similar to chess was played with them.

Whatever their purpose, it seems that these structures were important to the Dimasa Kachari dynasty, which ruled the Dhansiri Valley from the 10th century CE. They reigned for almost ten centuries. Though they were briefly disrupted in the 13th century CE, the kingdom essentially lasted until British annexation in 1832.

◀ **One of the pillars from the ruins of** Kachari Rajbari in Dimapur, Nagaland. The unusual shape has led to many theories behind its real purpose.

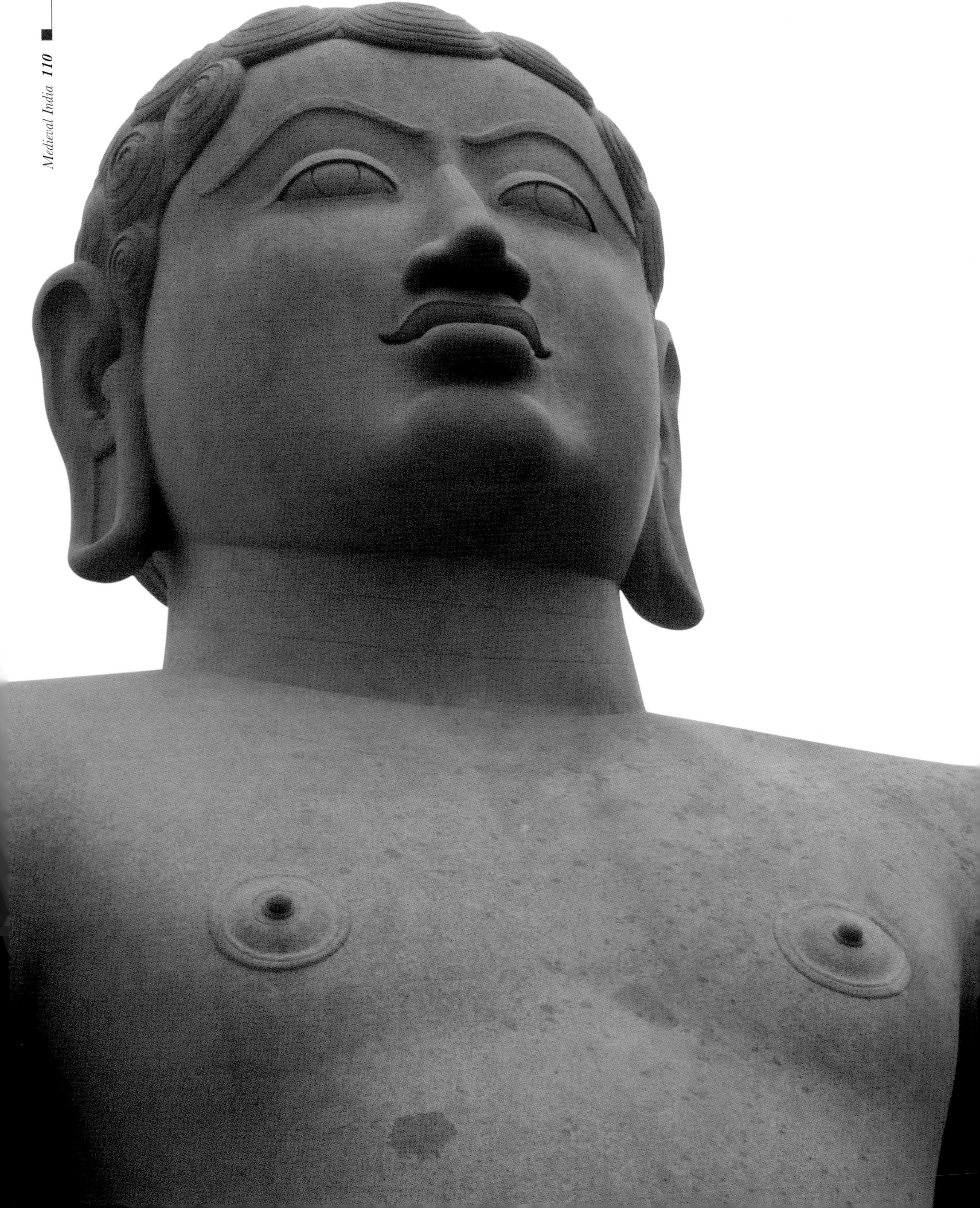

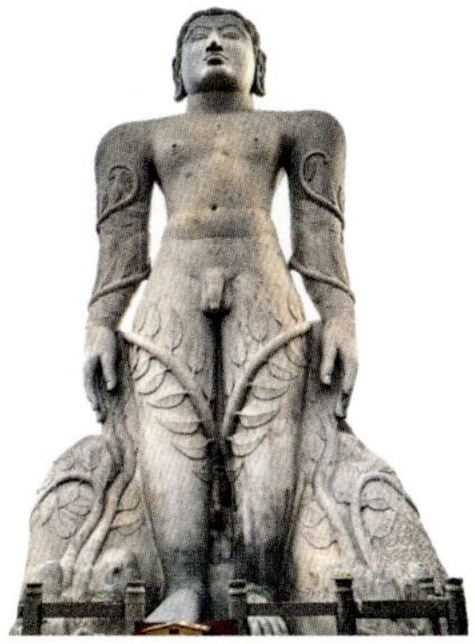

Era c. 980 CE | **Medium** Gneiss | **Height** 17.7 m (957 ft)

GOMATESHWARA

A beacon of hope, strength, and absolute harmony with the infinite

Visible from afar, the solemn figure of the Jain saint Gomateshwara stands tall atop the Indragiri hill in the southern Indian state of Karnataka. His serene visage reflects the inner peace that comes from the renunciation of the world.

The tall monolithic statue of the meditating Jain saint Gomateshwara stands at Sravanabelgola in southern India's Karnataka. It was consecrated in 981 CE by Chavundaraya, a commander in the service of the Ganga king Rajamalla IV, as an act of atonement, which is detailed in an inscription engraved at the base of the statue. Flowering creepers wind their way upwards to reach the shoulders of the giant figure. The unclothed body, long ears and graceful, heavy-lidded eyes gazing unblinkingly into the far distance are all indicative of an Digambara Jain ascetic. Carved from a single block of gneiss, it is one of the largest free-standing sculptures in the world. A flight of 700 stairs leads up to its location on the summit of the 143-m (469 ft) high Indragiri hill.

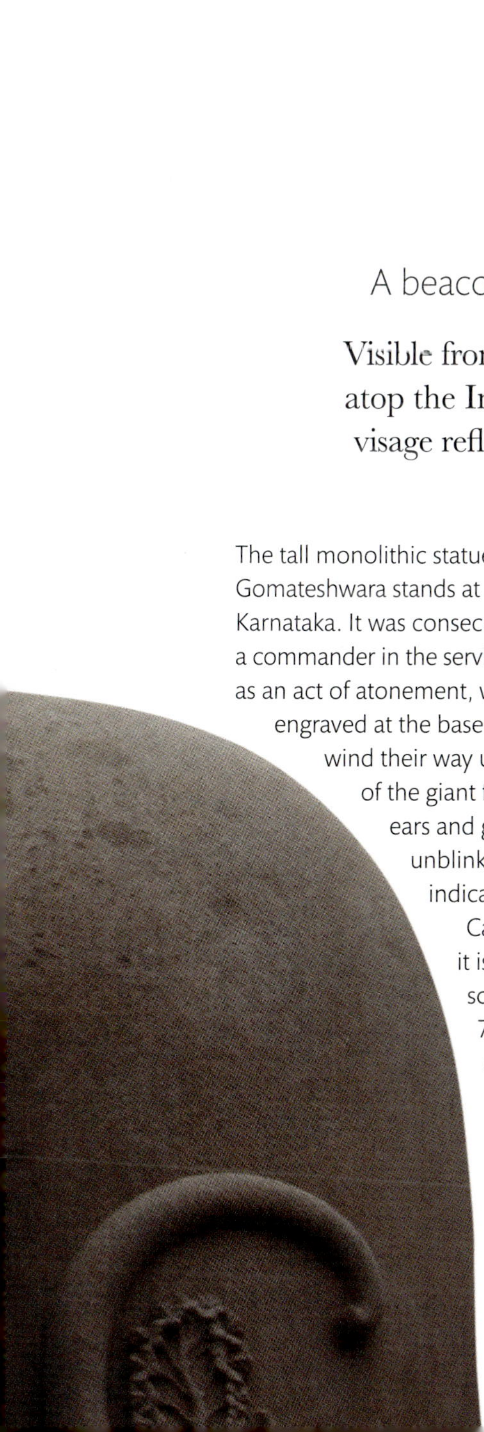

◀ **One of the world's tallest** monolithic statues, the Jain ascetic Gomateshwara's rock figure stands high on a hill in Karnataka.

A PILGRIMAGE SITE

The statue is an important pilgrimage for Jains, particularly during Mahamastakabhisheka (grand anointing) celebrated at Sravanabelgola every 12 years. Lakhs of devotees congregate to watch the gigantic statue being ceremonially bathed in holy water and anointed with libations of milk, curd, and ghee, as well as turmeric, sandalwood, and saffron paste.

WARRIOR AND ASCETIC

Gomateshwara, also known as Bahubali, was born to the first tirthankara (ford-maker, or enlightened being), Rishabhanatha. Legend has it that Bahubali fought mighty duels with his brother Bharata to retain his patrimony, from which he emerged victorious, but disillusioned. Consequently, Bahubali renounced all worldly possessions and became an ascetic of the Digambara (sky-clad) sect of Jains. He began to meditate in *kayotsarga* (standing pose), completely impervious to anthills that rose around him, or the vines that grew along his limbs. The story goes that he remained immobile for a year, until he achieved *kevala gyana*, or omniscience, considered to be the highest degree of wisdom, and eventual salvation.

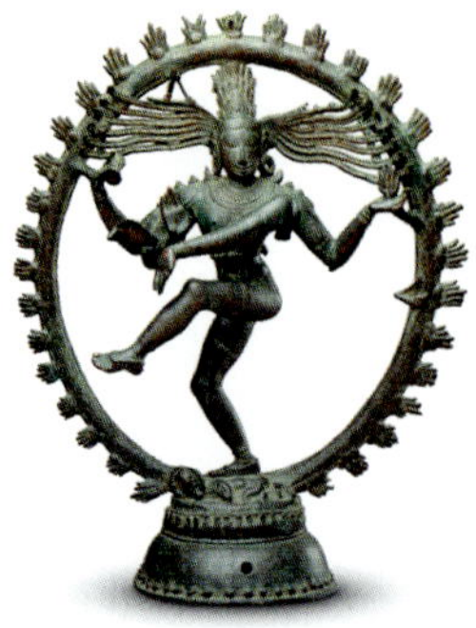

Era 9th–11th centuries CE | **Medium** Bronze (copper alloy) | **Height** 68.3 cm (26.8 ft)

NATARAJA

The lord of dance

The Nataraja beautifully embodies myth, symbolism, movement, and mysticism. Though it has appeared in the form of sculpture from the ancient period, its present, easily recognizable form evolved under the Chola dynasty.

Represented as the Lord of the Dance, whirling within a ring of fire, hair flying with the energy of the dance, Lord Shiva manifests in his role as the destroyer of the universe, and the redeemer of all of humankind from the perils of illusion and ignorance in this fine statue dating to the Chola dynasty (9th–13th centuries).

THE COSMIC DANCER

Nataraja's upper right hand holds a drum (*damaru)* that made the first sound of creation. His upper left hand holds the fire that will destroy the universe. With his lower right hand, he makes the *abhaya mudra* gesture that allays fear. The dwarf-like figure under his right foot represents *apasmara purusha*, or illusion, which leads mankind astray. The front left hand, pointing to his raised left foot, signifies refuge for the troubled soul. Entangled in his flying locks is the river goddess Ganga, while a snake is coiled around Shiva's head. This Nataraja sculpture is famous for its delicate detailing, perfect proportions, and graceful sensuousness of form, as well as its spiritual significance. The sculpture encapsulates the technical sophistication, artistic skill, and the advanced prevailing aesthetic of the time. Shiva as Nataraja was deeply revered by the rulers of the Chola dynasty, and the temple bronzes of this period are among the finest examples of Chola craftsmanship. They embody the belief that the inner beauty of enshrined figures is reflected in their external splendour.

Sculptures such as this were made for worship, from an alloy of copper, tin, lead, silver, and gold called *pancha loha* ('five iron'), using the lost-wax technique – also used by craftsmen of the Indus Valley Civilization (see pp. 10–13). They were *chalabhcra* (moving) and would have been carried in a procession in *rathas* (vehicle) around the temple complex, sometimes even to surrounding settlements, stopping every now and then to bless devotees. So prevalent were such sculptures that almost every Shiva temple in the south of India included a bronze Nataraja.

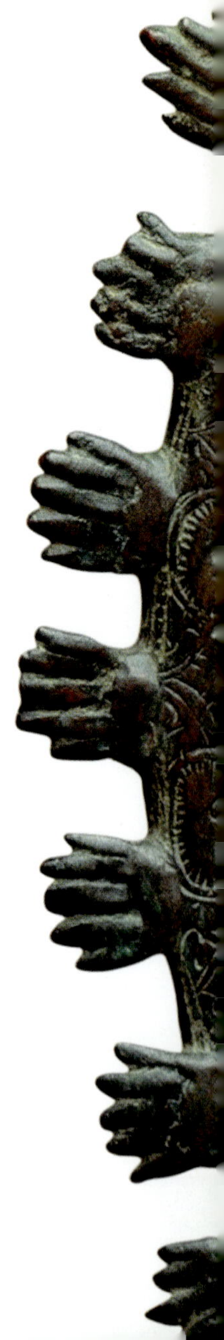

▶ **This bronze sculpture of the Nataraja** figure, located at the The Metropolitan Museum of Art, USA, embodies the Chola artists' mastery of form and expression, for which they were famous.

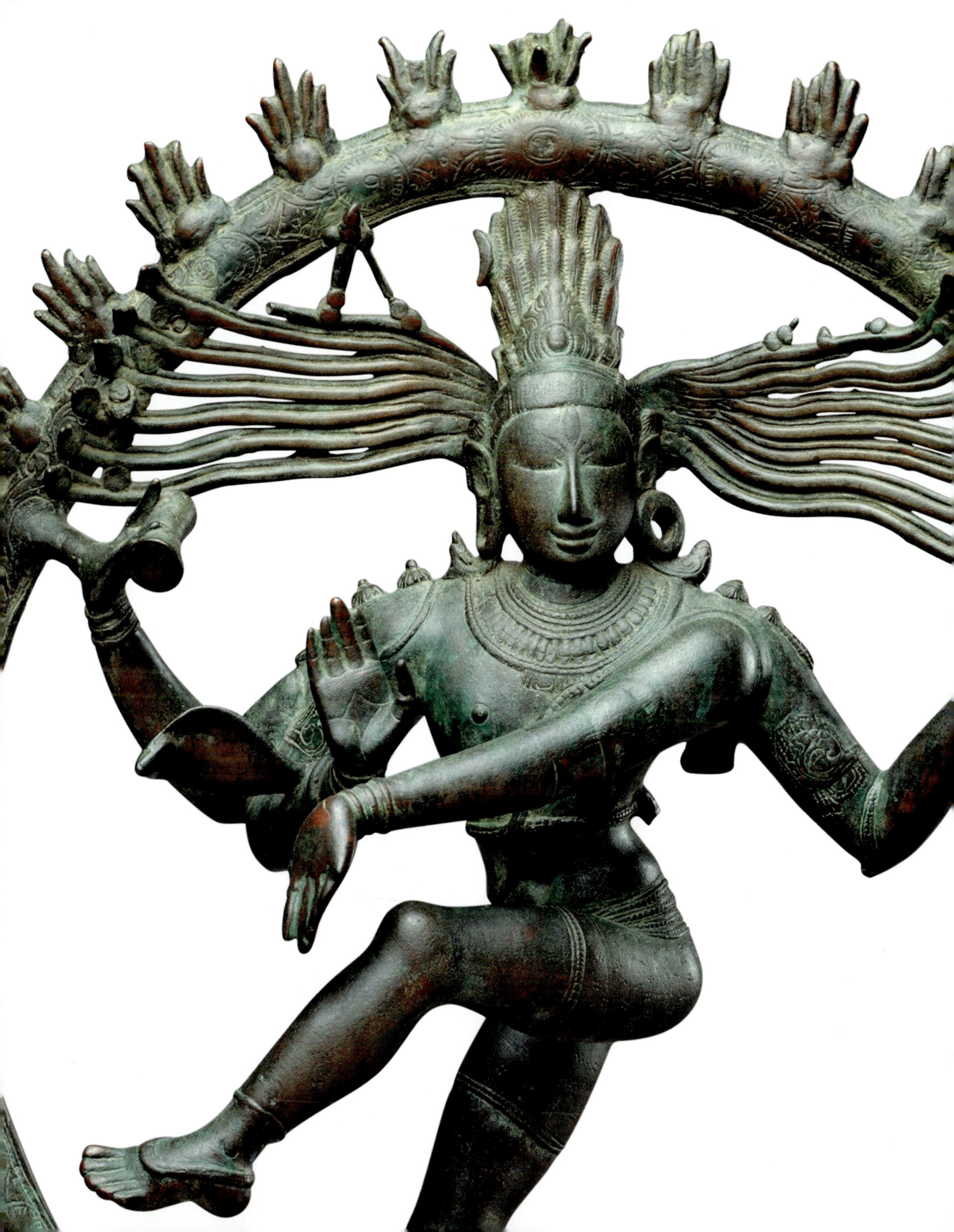

7th–16th centuries CE

TEMPLE ARCHITECTURE

A representation of philosophy, art, beliefs, values, and a way of life, the architecture of Hindu temples has evolved over 2,000 years.

The earliest of temples were focused around fire – around an open-air altar or mostly made from perishable materials such as wood and clay. The revival of Hinduism under the Guptas after the 3rd century CE saw Hindu deities making an appearance in early rock-cut temples (notably the cave temples at Udaigiri, Odisha, from the 5th century CE). Harmony is at the heart of Indian temple architecture, prescribed by the precise sacred geometry laid down as the *vastupurusha mandala* – the miniature configuration of the structure and order of the universe. At the centre is the windowless *garbhagriha* (sanctum) where the deity resides. There are variations in the façade.

The most prominent feature of the Nagara (northern) temples is the *shikhara* that covers the sanctum. The tall, curved roof is capped by a circular disc, a small pot and a finial. Dravidian (southern) temples are distinguished by the elaborate pyramidal *gopurams* (gateways) that punctuate their enclosing walls.

"The temple is the most characteristic artistic expression of Hinduism, providing a focus for both social and spiritual life of the community it serves."

– George Michell, *The Hindu Temple: An Introduction to Its Meaning and Forms*, 1988

THE EVOLUTION OF TEMPLES

Over time the temple complex grew bigger with the addition of pillared halls, porticoes, structural elaboration, and artistic ornamentation. Early use of wood and terracotta gave way to stone and the rock-hewn drama of the shore temples at Mamallapuram in southern India followed. The period between the 6th and 8th centuries CE saw the creation of magnificent rock architecture, such as the Kailasa Temple at Ellora, Maharashtra, and Aihole in Badami, Karnataka.

Later temples, free-standing, built in stone that was sometimes transported over great distances – Srirangam, Brihadeeshwara, Khajuraho, Bhubaneshwar, Sohagpur – all follow the movement toward increasing elaboration and ornamentation. North or south, as new dynasties rose and consolidated their rule, stability and prosperity was marked by dazzling expressions in art and architecture – with the temple, as the centre of intellectual and artistic life.

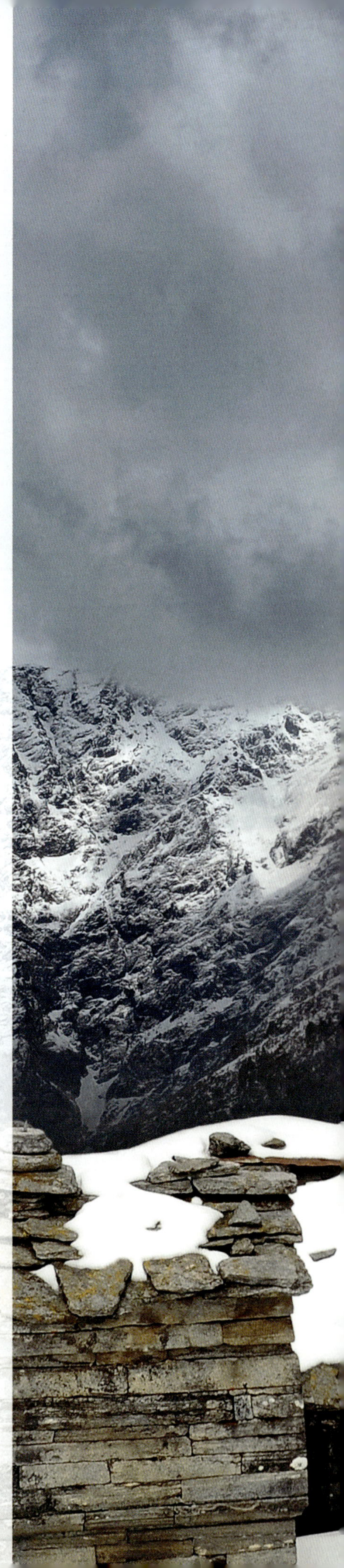

► **Located at an altitude of 3,690 m (12,106 ft),** Tungnath, or the 'lord of the peaks', is the highest Shiva temple. It lies in Rudraprayag district, in the state of Uttarakhand. The temple structure is a great example of the Himalayan architecture style of northern India.

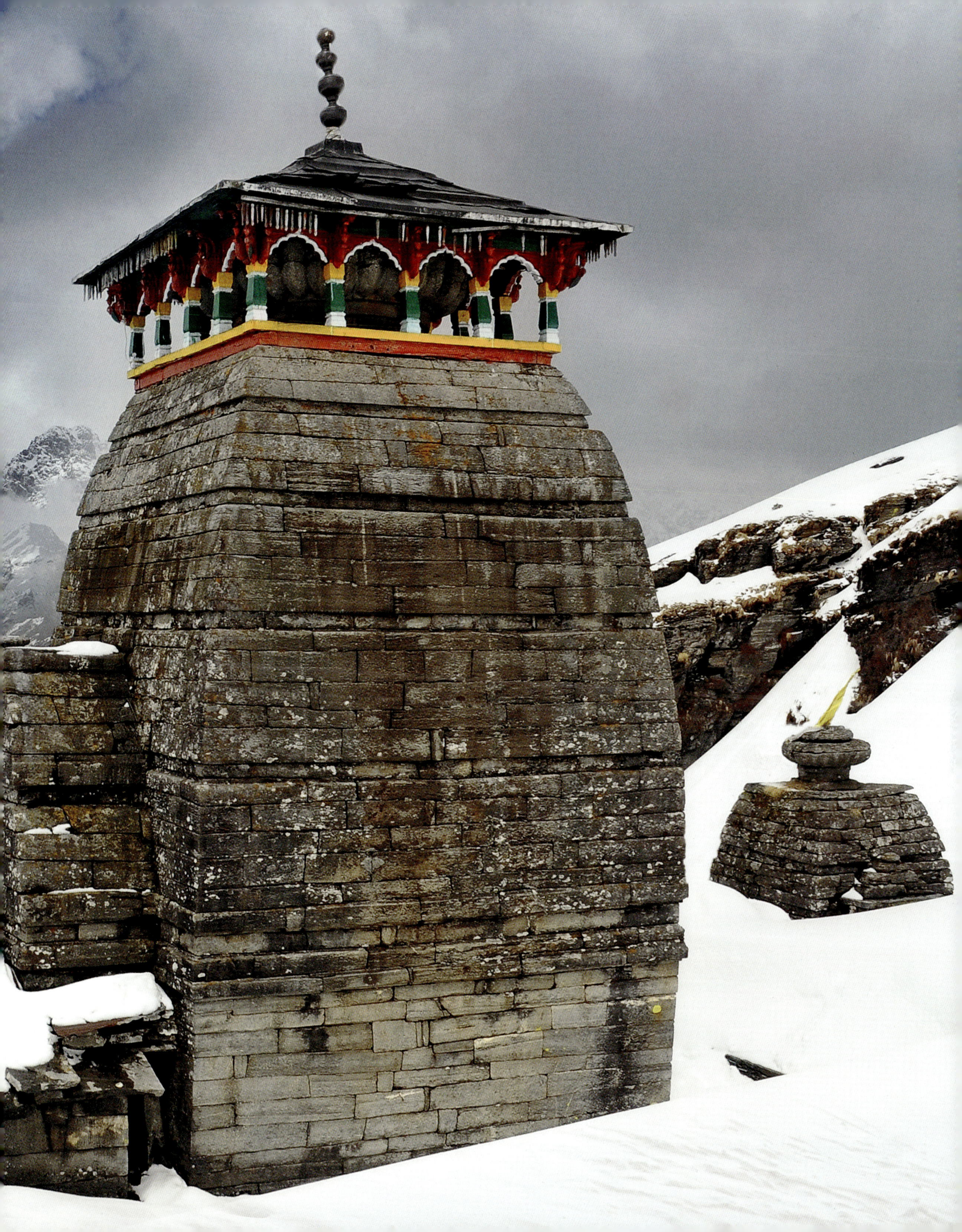

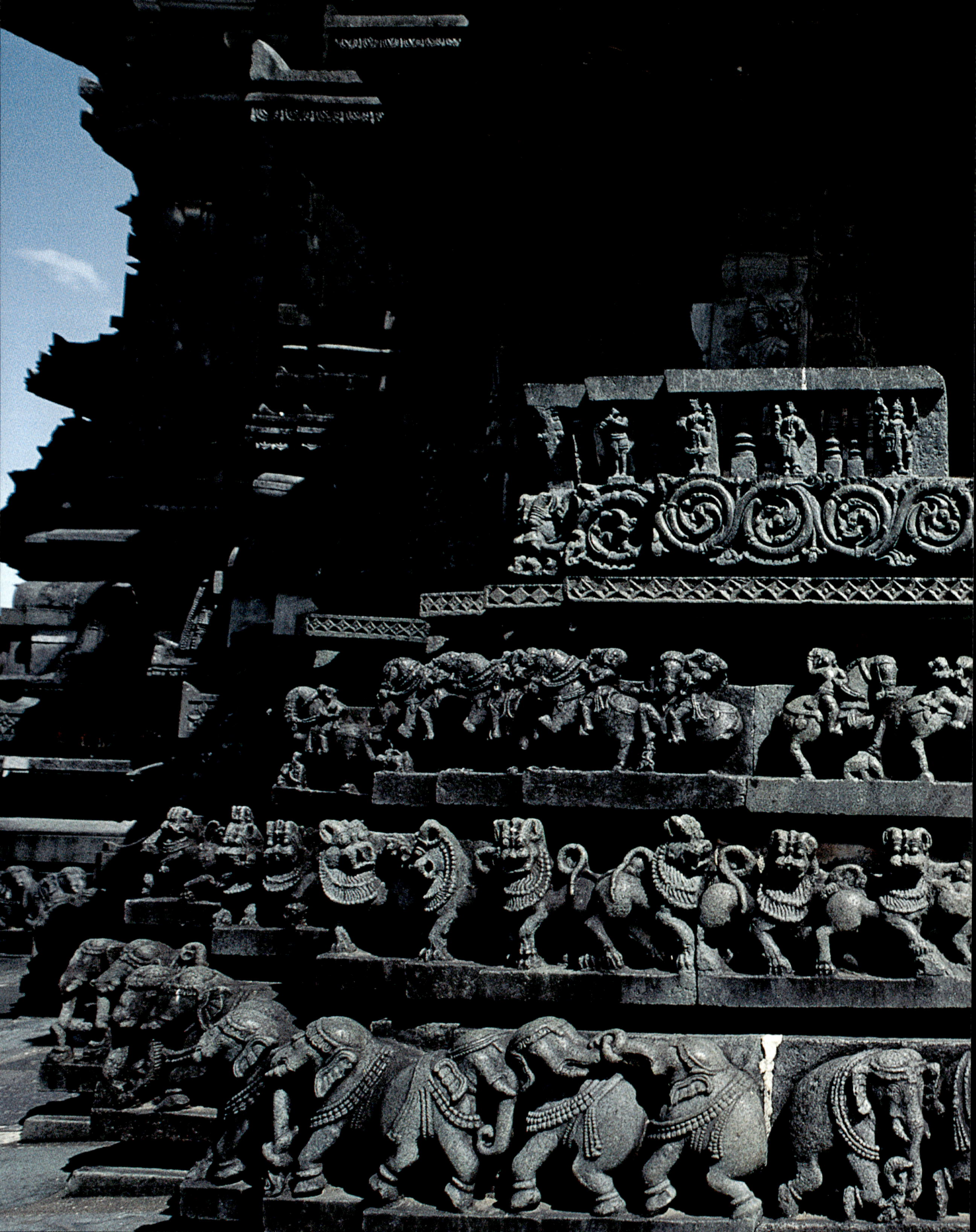

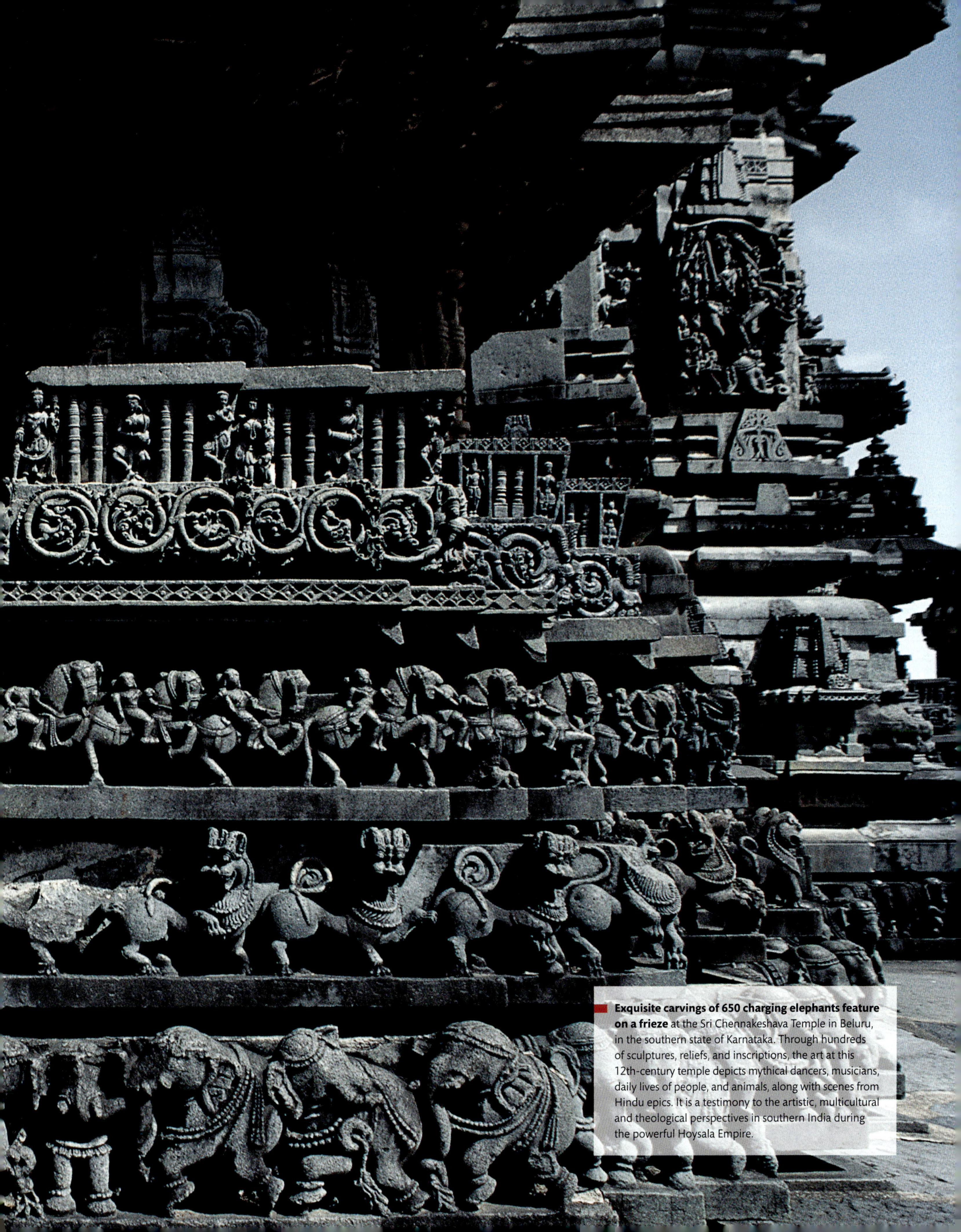

Exquisite carvings of 650 charging elephants feature on a frieze at the Sri Chennakeshava Temple in Beluru, in the southern state of Karnataka. Through hundreds of sculptures, reliefs, and inscriptions, the art at this 12th-century temple depicts mythical dancers, musicians, daily lives of people, and animals, along with scenes from Hindu epics. It is a testimony to the artistic, multicultural and theological perspectives in southern India during the powerful Hoysala Empire.

Era 11th century CE | **Medium** Granite | **Area** 21.7 ha (53.7 acres)

BRIHADISWARA TEMPLE

A great, living Chola temple

A UNESCO World Heritage Site, this temple is a living testimony to the glory of the Chola Empire. Built on a massive scale, it was the largest in the Indian subcontinent at the time and established the standard for a new phase of grandiose design.

The Brihadiswara Temple in Thanjavur, Tamil Nadu was commissioned by the Chola king Rajaraja I (985–1081) as a shrine to Lord Shiva as well as a symbol of power and wealth. Dedicated to Shiva, the patron deity of the Cholas, the complex features a giant Nandi bull statue, his sacred mount, carved out of a single piece of granite and seated on a high plinth. It occupies the first of three halls *(mandapas)* leading to the sanctum sanctorum *(garbhagriha)* where a huge stone *lingam* is the focus of worship. It is so big that a second-floor gallery had to be built to enable the priests to anoint and decorate it. Equally breathtaking is the entrance tower *(gopuram)* opening into a sea of expansive, stone-laid courtyards surrounded by magnificent stone walls.

The majestic pyramidal spire rises 13 storeys to a height of nearly 70 m (230 ft). It is capped by a monolithic dome stone. Exquisite sculptures and engravings cover all surfaces, and beneath the later veneer of Maratha paintings around the sanctum, frescoes have been uncovered. Inscriptions at the basement give details of the Cholas' achievements in art, governance, and military conquests.

THE GREAT, LIVING CHOLA TEMPLES

The Chola emperors sponsored three temple complexes in and around Thanjavur, the capital of their empire. Sharing the same name, the smaller Brihadiswara Temple in Gangaikonda Cholapuram, built in 1035, has a more curvilinear tower but still in the same pyramid-like style. The smallest but most lavishly carved out of the three temples, the Airavateswara, completed in 1166 at Darasuram, includes a chariot and horses sculpted into its entrance hall.

1. The 16-storeyed *vimana* or main tower of the temple, which dominates the Thanjavur complex. **2.** Detail of a bright mural adorning the ceiling of the Nandi *mandapam* (hall). **3.** The colossal Nandi statue. **4.** *Rajarajan thiruvasal,* the gateway opening into the inner courtyard. **5.** Brihadiswara Temple at Gangaikonda with the Nandi bull statue facing its sactum. **6.** The Airavateswara Temple at Darasura characterized by a smaller spire.

1

2

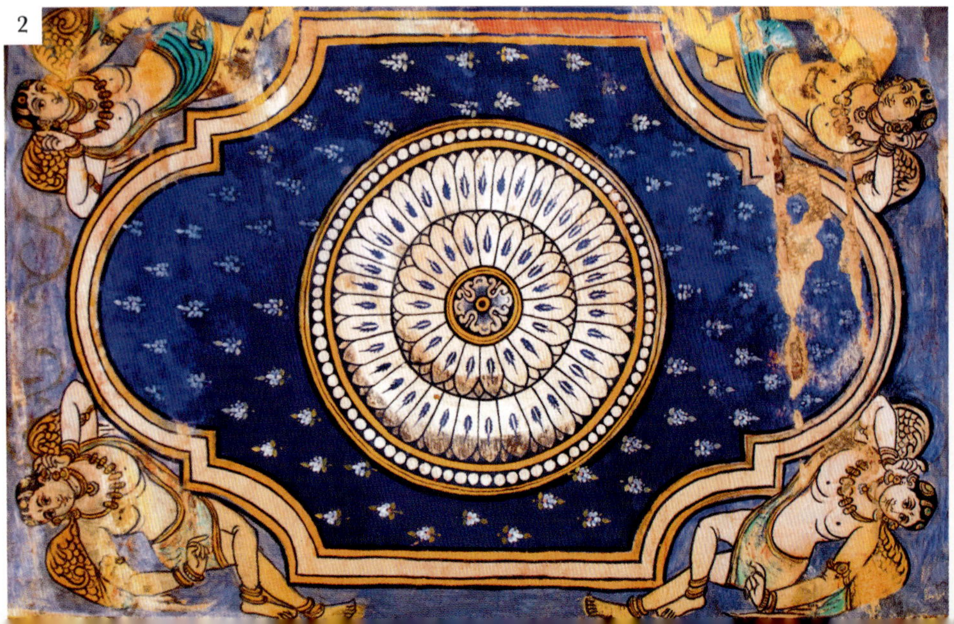

3

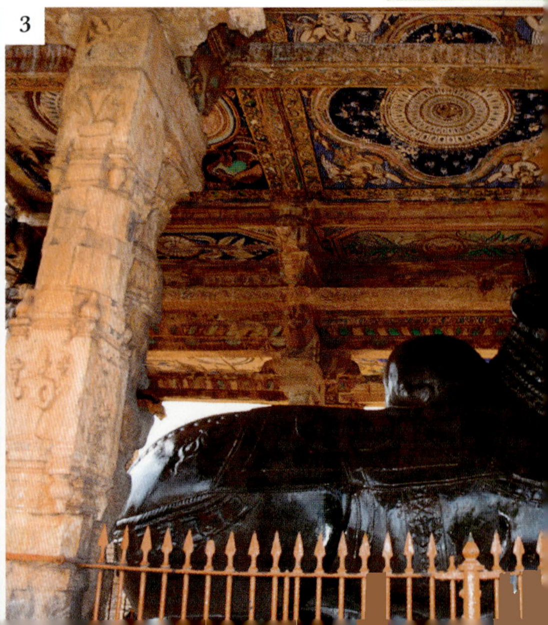

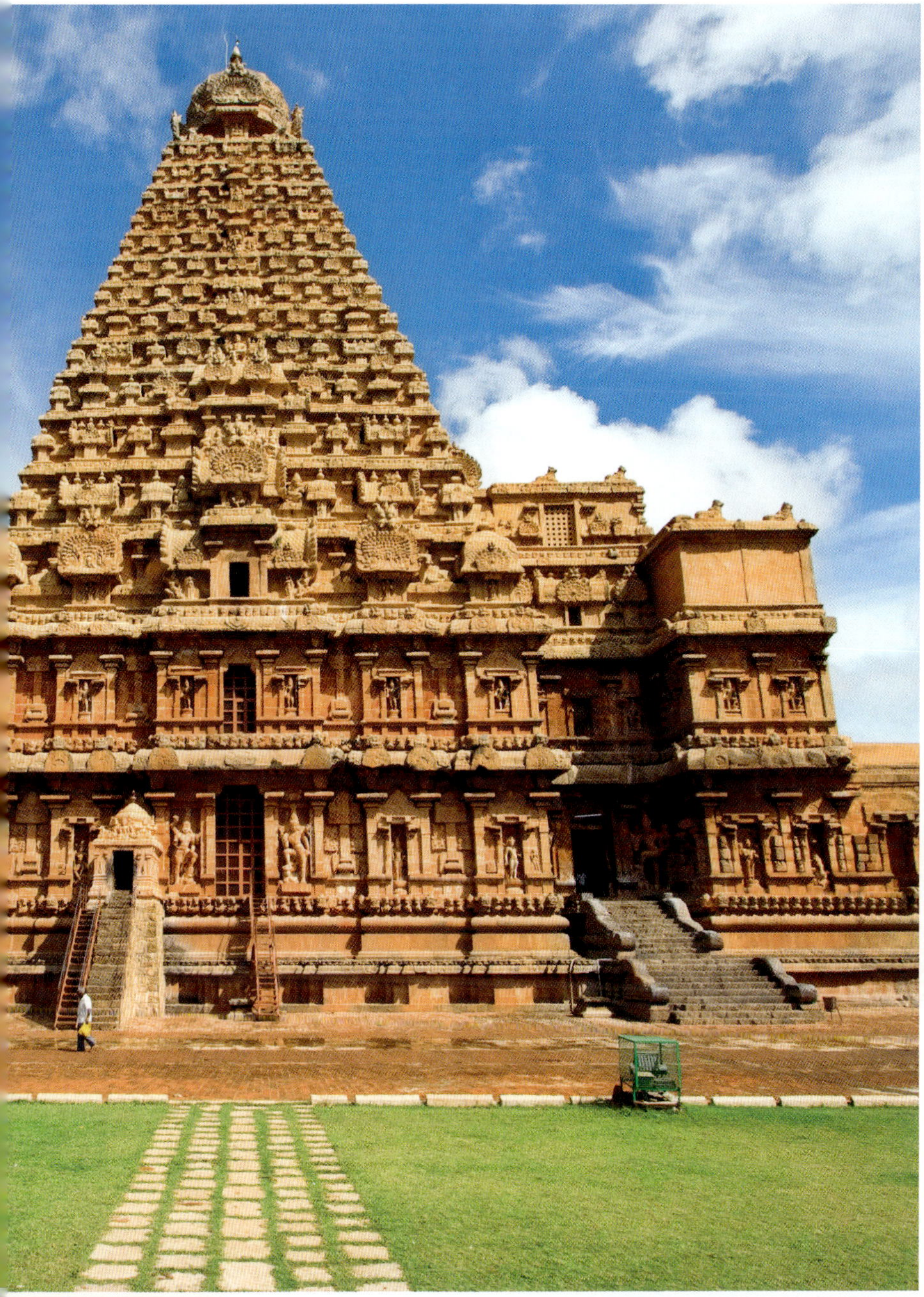

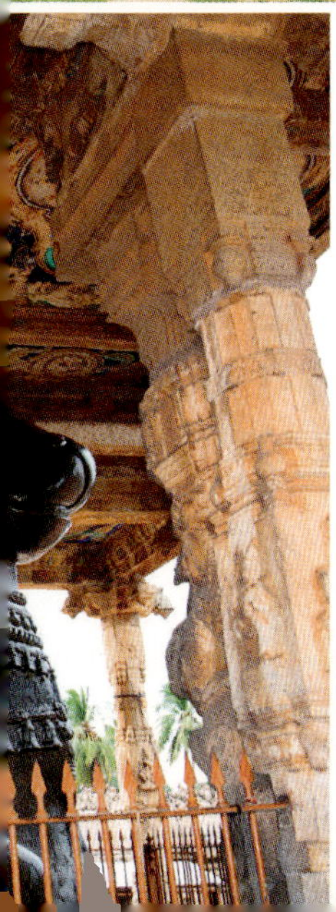

4

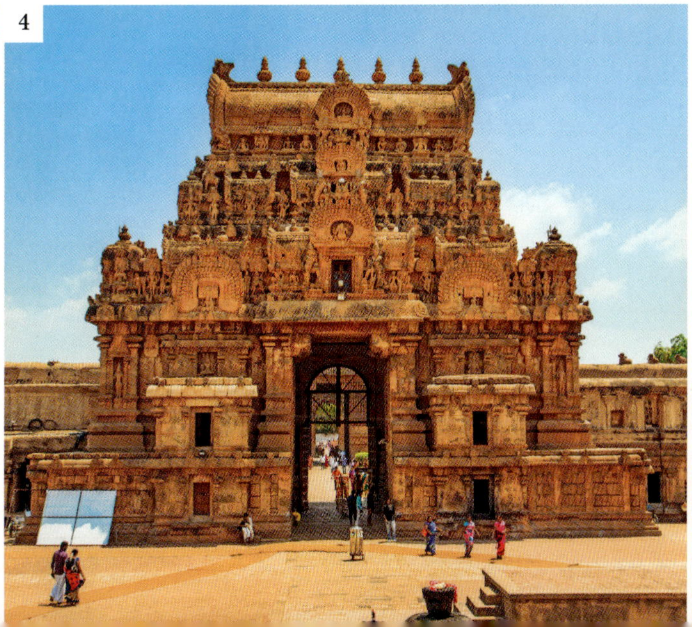

OTHER LIVING CHOLA TEMPLES

5

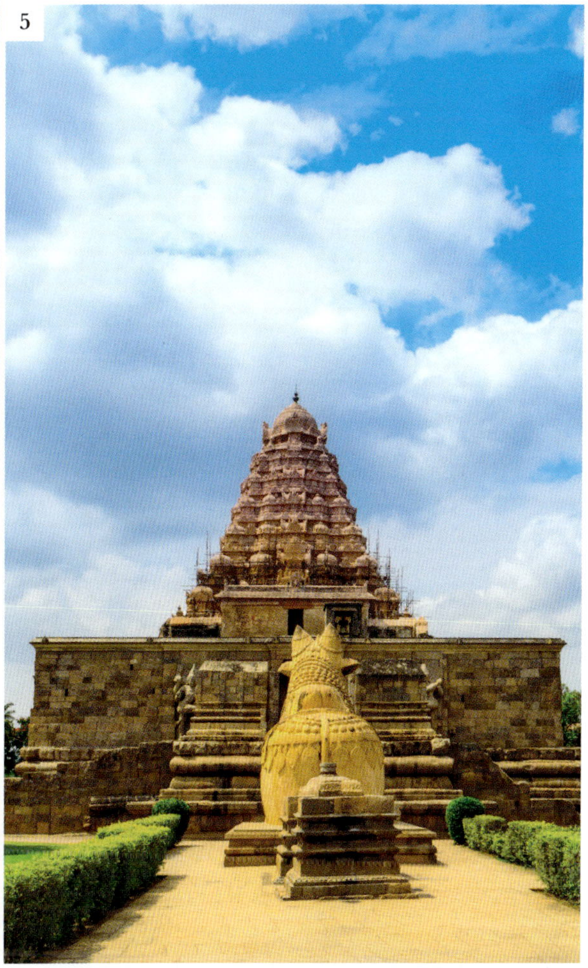

6

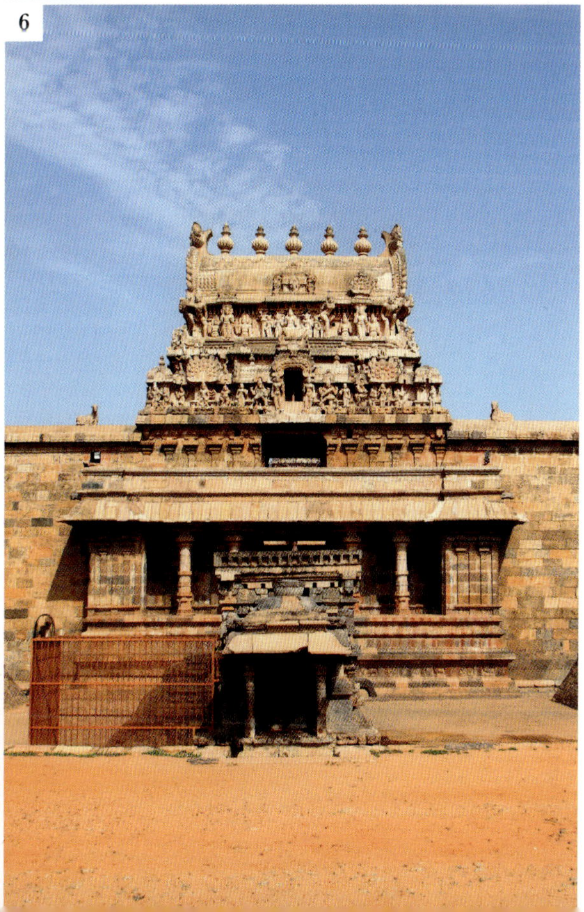

c. 300 BCE–600 CE

SANGAM LITERATURE

Predominantly poetry characterized by brevity, directness, and secular content, Sangam literature is the earliest accessible Tamil literature and one of the main sources of documentation of the early history of Tamil Nadu.

Among the earliest examples of writing in the Tamil language and historically known as the poetry of the noble ones, Sangam literature provides an insight into early Tamil culture. Literally meaning association, 'sangam' was an assembly or gathering of Tamil poets, most probably held under royal patronage. It is believed that there had been three such literary conclaves, held in Madurai. All that is certain, however, is that the literature produced at these assemblies was compiled during 300–600 CE. Written on palm leaf, the original manuscripts either perished or were destroyed after being copied on paper by later generations of scholars. These copies were then discovered in monastic libraries in the late 19th century CE.

"At parting / his arms twined with mine / he gave me inviolable guarantees / that he would live in my heart / without parting."

– "Kuruntokai 36" by Paranar, translated by A.K. Ramanujan

CLASSIFICATION AND MAJOR WORKS

The corpus includes 18 major and 18 minor collections much later collated as two anthologies – *Ettutokai* (The Eight Collections) and *Pattuppattu* (The Ten Songs). These are ascribed to 473 poets, of whom about 30 were women. Included in the corpus is the *Tolkappiyam*, a book of grammar, possibly the earliest surviving work essential for understanding the linguistic nuances of the Sangam poetry. Two main themes define the text – *akam* or interior, in which aspects of love predominate the theme, and fewer *puram* or exterior, where heroism, war and public life are primary. A reflection of the daily life and culture of the time, the verses also tell of the period's trade, craftsmen, and farmers, as well as the taxation system, the judiciary, and the army. The singularly secular nature of these writings makes them devoid of the complex mythical allusions that are dominant in most Indian art forms. Devotional poetry emerged in later Tamil literature. Among the poets, it is Karaikkal Ammaiyar from 6th century CE, one of three women Nayannar saints, who is distinctive for her single-minded adoration of Shiva. In one of her works is a verse where she implores her lord to strip her of her beauty and transform her into a ghoul so she would not distract him.

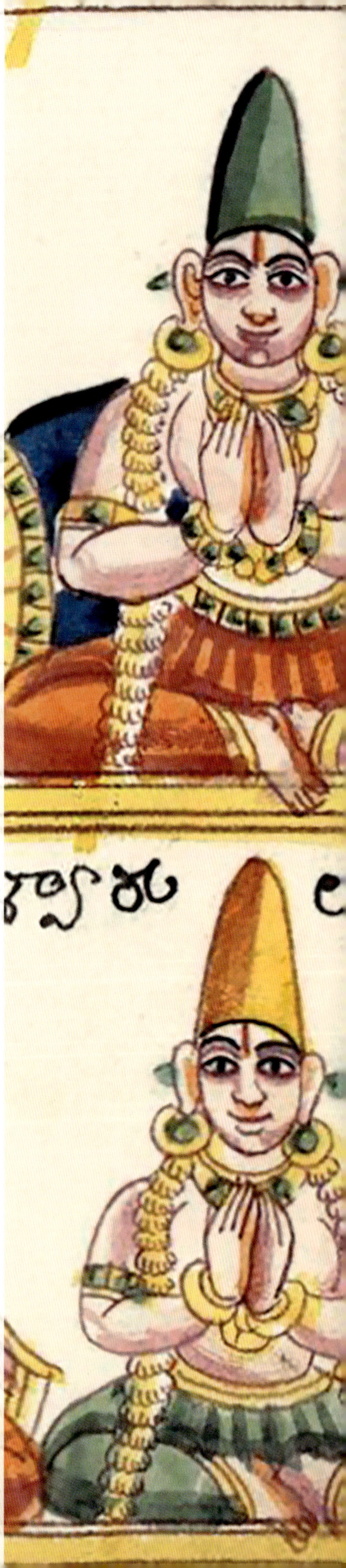

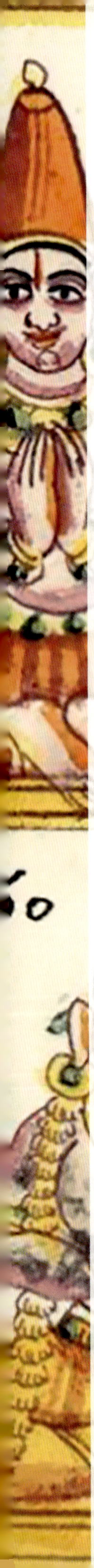

► **A mid-19th century gouache painting** on paper from Tiruchirappalli, Tamil Nadu, depicts ten *alvars* (Vaishnavite saints) in two rows, seated in identical posture.

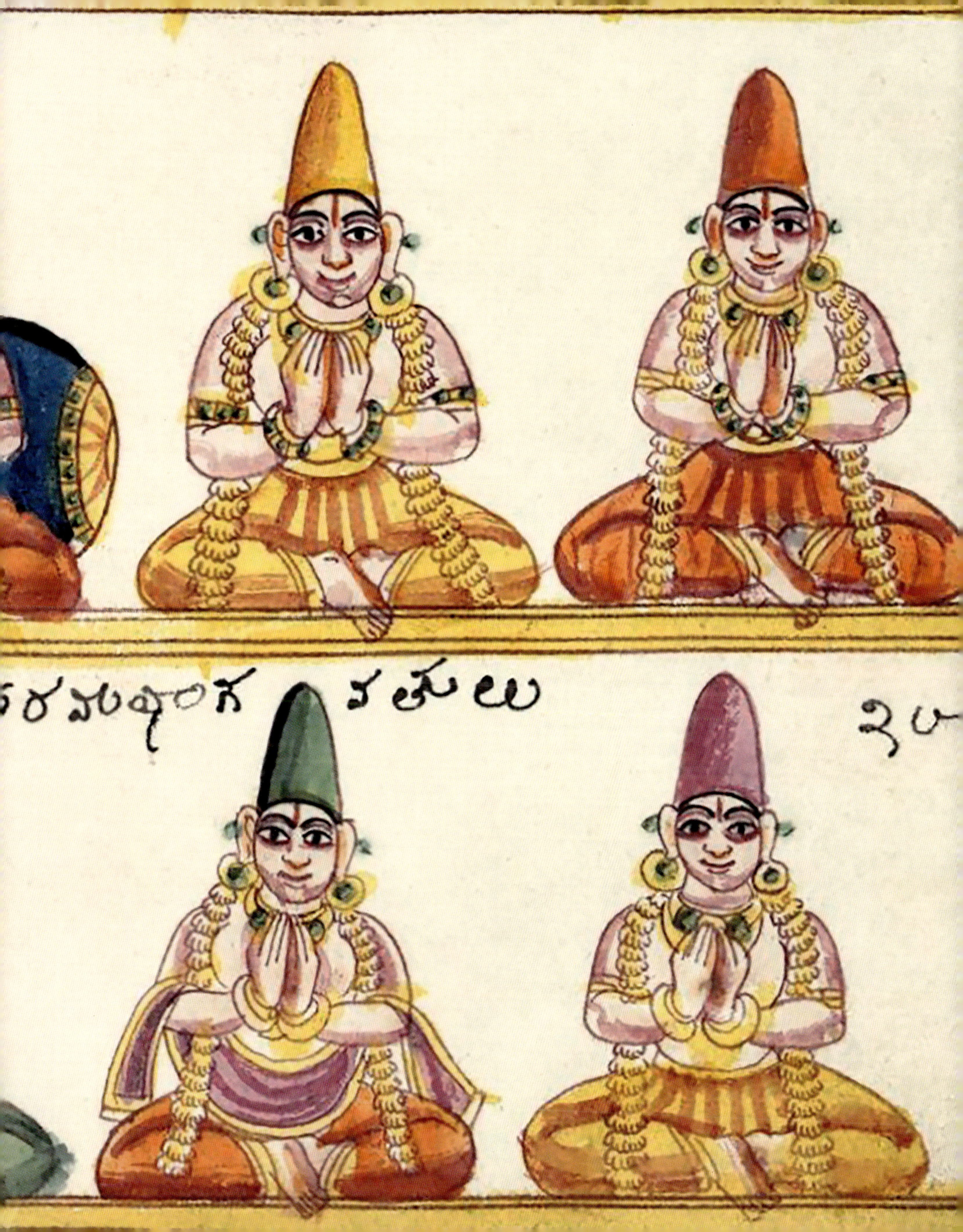
రవత్యాంగ వతులు

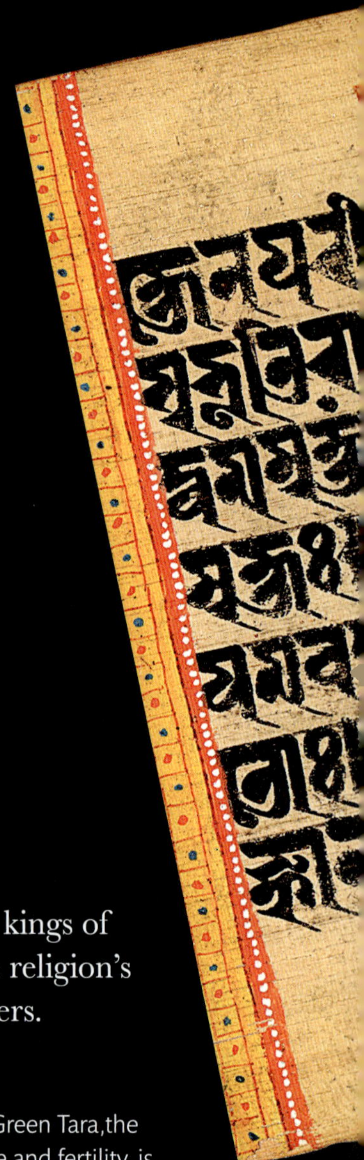

Era 8th–12th centuries CE | **Medium** Talipot palm leaf | **Dimension** 50 × 7 cm (20 × 3 in)

PALA PAINTINGS

Illustrating the sublime grace of the sacred

Incredibly detailed and richly coloured, the paintings patronized by the Pala kings of eastern India were created as part of Buddhist manuscripts that explained the religion's beliefs and myths, and became objects of great veneration for its followers.

The Pala kings (750–1151 CE) were generous patrons of Buddhist monasteries and universities and their rule is notable for the creation of illustrated Buddhist manuscripts, particularly in the reign of Mahipala I (913–944 CE). These manuscripts were made from the leaves of the talipot palm, each horizontal leaf panel measuring about 50 cm (20 in) in length and 7cm (3 in) in width. The panels were strung together by a cord secured through holes. Scribes, usually monks, used reed pens dipped in black ink to write on the prepared leaves. From the 10th century onwards, these manuscripts were illuminated with fine paintings in jewel tones using mineral and vegetable paints, and even gilded with gold leaf later. Painted wooden covers protected the finished manuscript, or *pothi*.

DEPICTIONS OF PHILOSOPHY

The *Astasahasrika Prajnaparamita* (Perfection of Wisdom in Eight Thousand Lines) is the most-seen illustrated version of the Mahayana Buddhist scripture. Some scenes from the Buddha's life are depicted, but the majority of artworks represent different Buddhist deities and bodhisattvas, such as Prajnaparamita, Avalokiteshwara, Manjushri, and Tara. An illustration of the Green Tara,the female bodhisattva associated with courage and fertility, is a part of the manuscript (see right). She is shown holding a blue lotus and has two female attendants, one with a thunderbolt (*vajra*) in her hand, and the other, Mahakali, holding a flaying knife and a skullcup (*kapala*).

IMBIBING FAITH

Thousands of manuscripts were copied and stored in the Buddhist monastic university libraries at Nalanda, Somapura, Vikramshila, and Jagaddala, in the central and eastern parts of the Indian subcontinent. These folios acquired a sacral character and became objects of great veneration. The public veneration (*jnana puja*) and recitation of texts, and the display of the manuscript itself, became an important part of Buddhist ritual, showing the followers' faith.

► **The two folios belong to the** early 12th century manuscript, *Ashtasahasrika Prajnaparamita*. The first presents the bodhisattva Avalokiteshwara in the form of Shadakshari Lokeshvara (top), and the second, the Green Tara (bottom).

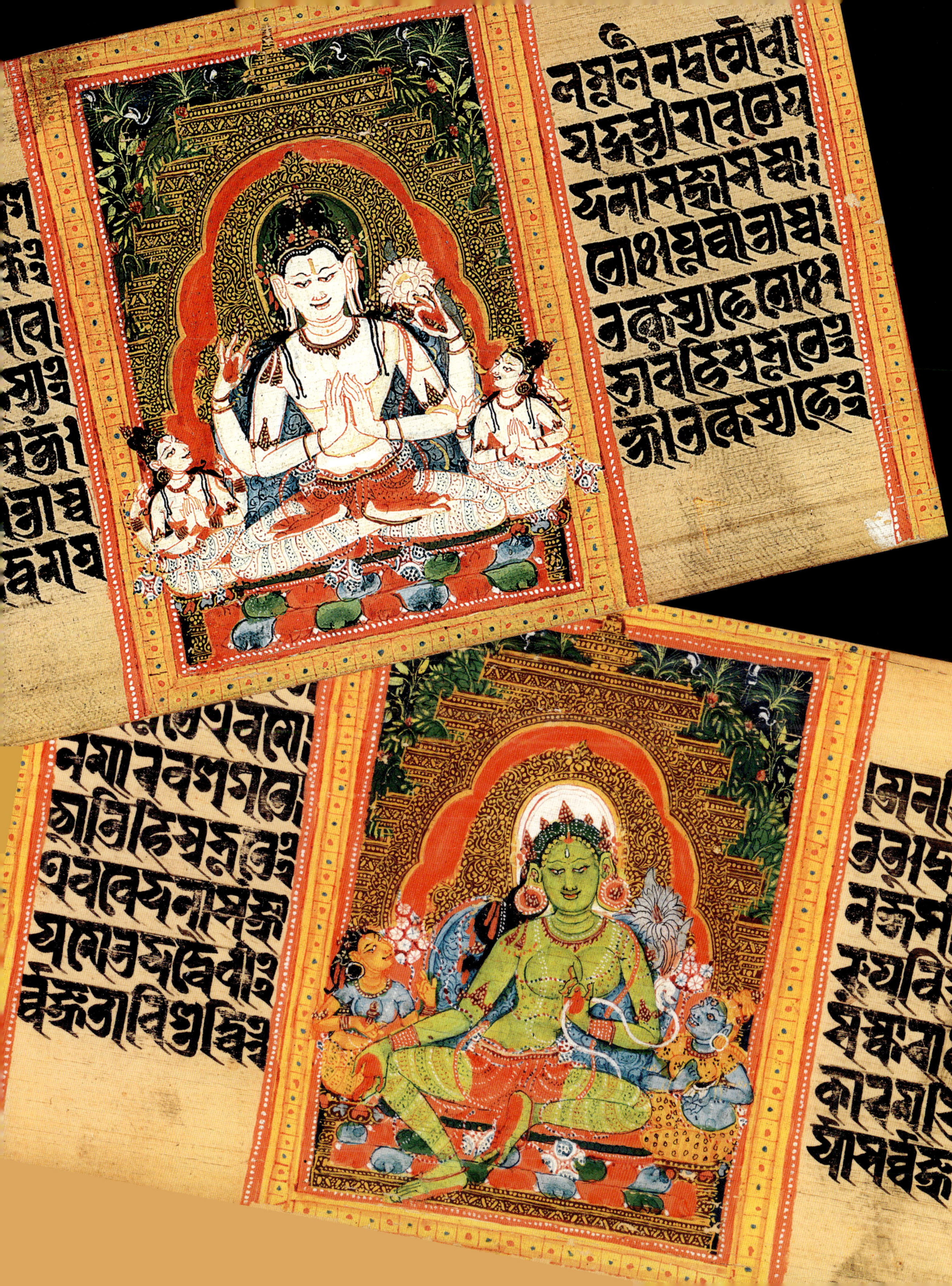

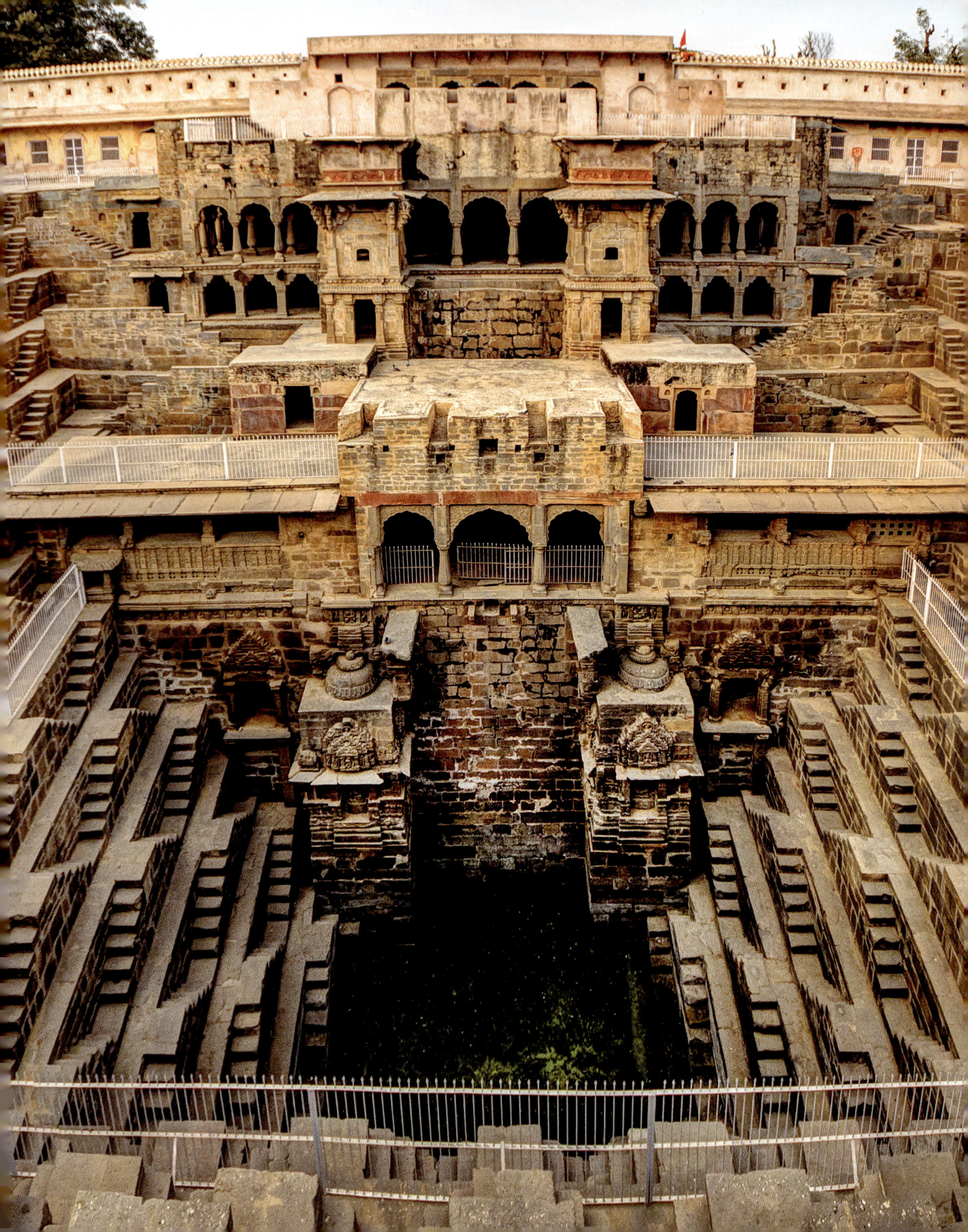

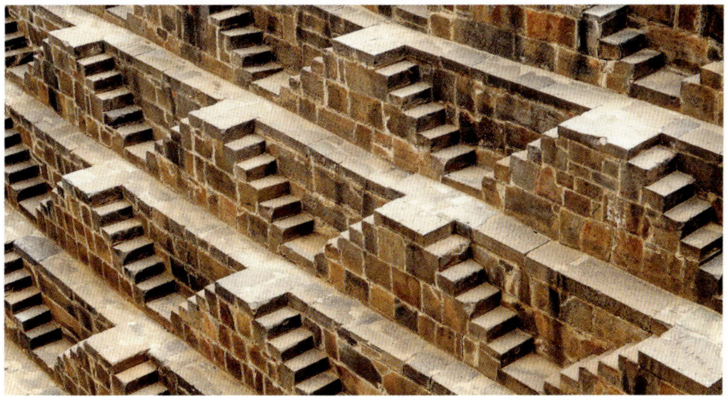

Era 9th century CE | **Medium** Volcanic stones | **Depth** 20 m (64 ft)

CHAND BAORI

A magical descent in search of water

The precise geometry of this stepwell, one of the largest and deepest in India, is mesmerizing. At any time of the day, the optical illusion created by the play of light and shadow is both disorienting and fascinating.

Although there is little written evidence surrounding the construction of Chand Baori, it is believed to have been built by Chand Raja of the Pratihara dynasty (6th–10th centuries). The striking stepwell is about 20-m (64-ft) deep. The 3,500 steps leading down to the water along three sides criss-cross vertiginously in perfect symmetry. On the fourth side is a three-storeyed pavilion for the royal family, with galleries and balconies decorated with beautifully crafted sculptures. The larger complex also features shaded walkways that are dotted with the ruins and remains of some of the internal structure, which provide a glimpse into the intricate stonework that adorned the stepwell. Adjoining the *baori* is the Harshat Mata Temple, which was built between the 7th and 8th centuries, but was later damaged by invaders.

◀ **This ancient stepwell with 3,500** steps is located in Abhaneri, a village in the western state of Rajasthan. It was constructed c. 800–900 CE.

STRUCTURES OF REST AND RESPITE

Stepwells, or *baoris,* were popular resting spots along trade and caravan routes for travelling merchants and their animals. While essentially utilitarian, their functionality extended beyond that. In the arid regions of north-western India (present-day Gujarat and Rajasthan) the *baoris* evolved into highly complex structures, each different and unique from the other. Within the stepwell structure, around the large opening for water, ledges were built that could be accessed by orchestrated flights of stairs. These levels housed galleries, chambers, halls, and temples and the cool, below-ground depths of the *baoris* became ideal spaces for social gatherings.

Unique to the subcontinent, the stepwells were first built in the 3rd century CE to ensure year-round access to water for communities. Their construction was considered a meritorious act, and several thousand stepwells, both extensive and simple, existed in the cities, towns, and villages of this region. Modernization and the falling water table resulted in neglect over the years, but these stepwells are once again being revived and restored in the present day for their value as efficient water management systems.

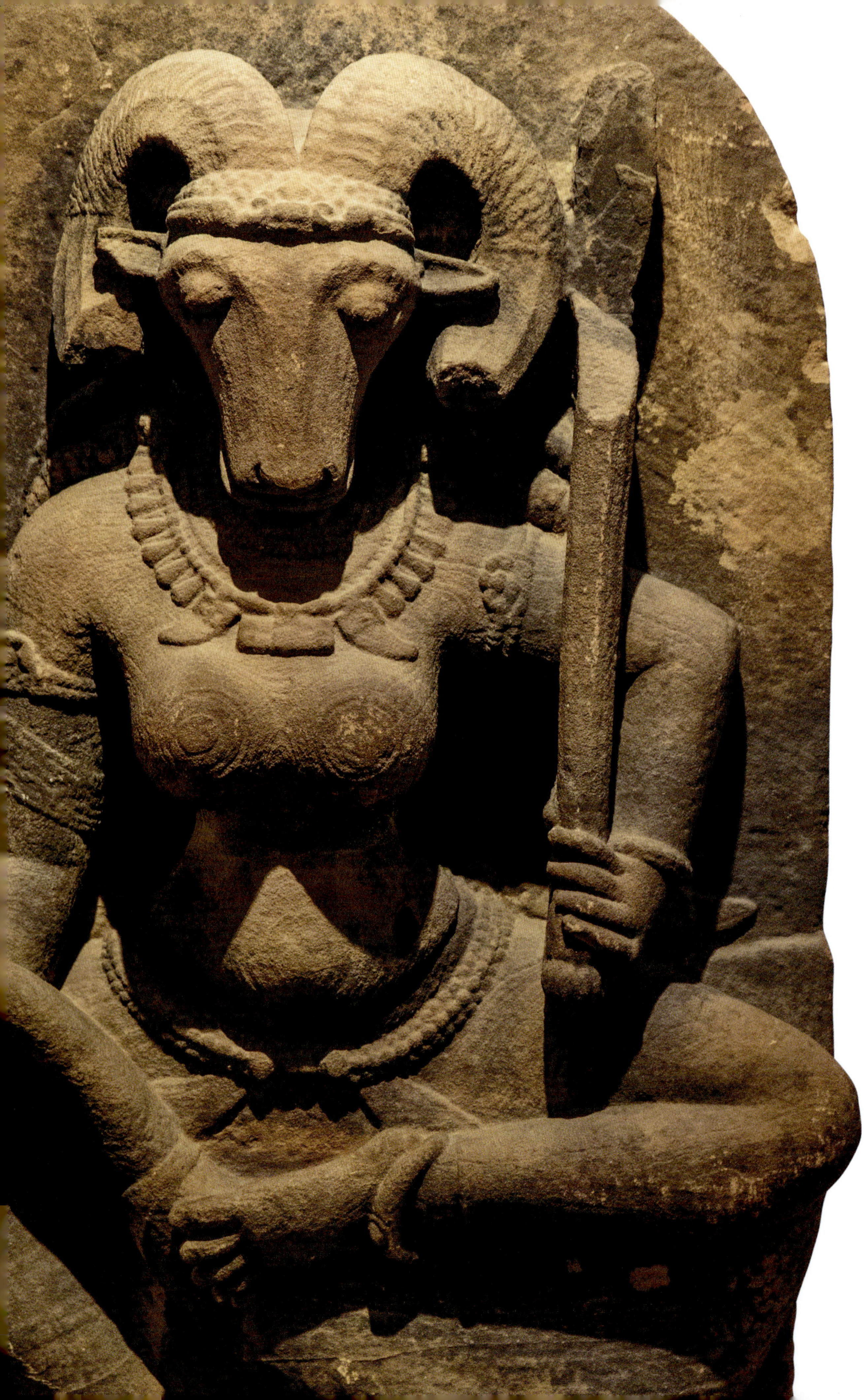

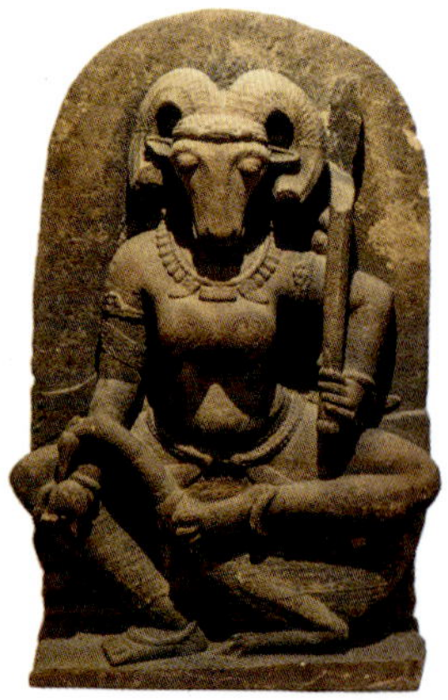

▲ **One of the most famous** yogini sculptures, this buffalo-headed sandstone figure is from the 10th–11th centuries.

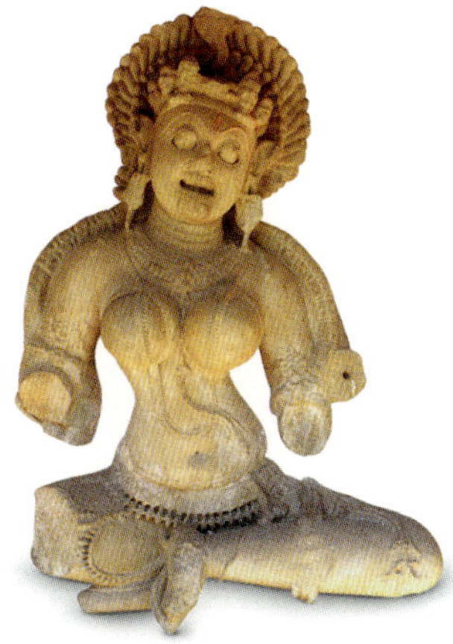

▲ **Antakari Yogini**
Sitting with an open mouth, this c. 9th century Yogini from Bhedagat, Madhya Pradesh, was known as a death giver.

Era 10th–11th centuries CE | **Medium** Sandstone | **Height** 1.32 m (4.3 ft)

YOGINI VRISHANANA

The buffalo-headed goddess

This sculpture, which remained missing for decades after being stolen from a village temple, belongs to the Yogini cult that emerged in the early medieval era in India.

This buffalo-headed goddess graced a temple near the village of Lokhari, Uttar Pradesh, along with 19 other large yogini sculptures in stone. However, it was stolen in the 1980s and taken to France, until its return to the nation in 2013.

Devoid of decorations such as details of her throne or attendant figures, this statue is modelled minimally. She is seated with one leg folded against a base and the other firmly on the ground. In her right hand, which rests lightly on her thigh, she holds a fruit, as a swan, possibly her mount or *vahana*, pecks at it. In her other hand, she holds a club. She has large, rounded breasts and stomach. Covered in ornaments, her expression suggests she may be in meditation. However, the special fascination lies in the fact that unlike most yogini statues, several of the Lohari figures such as this one, had animal heads.

ICONOGRAPHY

Yoginis are rarely spoken of in the singular: they are worshipped as group divinities. Unlike other goddesses, they bear no relationships as consorts, and appear to be independent of male deities. In their material form, yoginis are large, life-sized, seated or standing images. These alluring and magnificent sculptures in stone, mostly full-bodied and voluptuous with dissimilar expressions - calm or frightening - are found in the select open-air temples dedicated to them across certain parts of central and northern India. There is no uniformity in the iconography and each group appears to have a separate identity. Occasionally, a group may have their names inscribed on the pedestals.

THE YOGINI CULT

During the early medieval period, a slew of goddess images, known as yoginis, appeared across India. A legend states that Goddess Durga fought a demon king, Raktabija, whose spilt blood produced thousands of demons. She then released 64 yoginis (celestial beings) who consumed each drop before it could touch the ground. Within Indian culture, the term "yogini" is broadly defined, and the lines between deities and women are frequently blurred. It refers to sorceresses, demons, or attendants. Some village cults associate them with village deities, who are invoked during rituals pertaining to fertility, marriages, snake bites, or diseases.

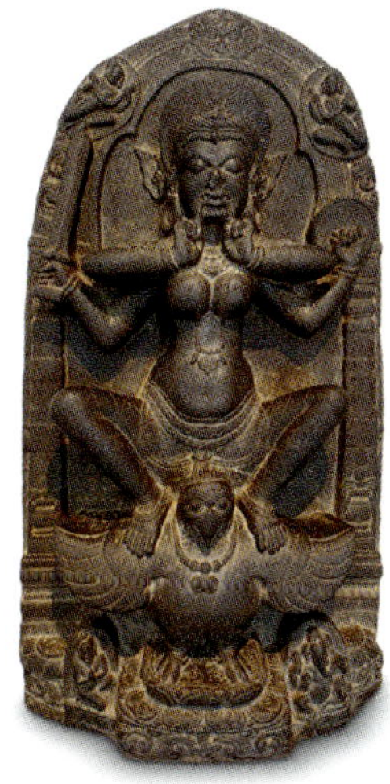

▲ **Shri Vaishnavi Yogini**
From Eastern India, c. 11th–12th centuries, this yogini figure had a bird mount.

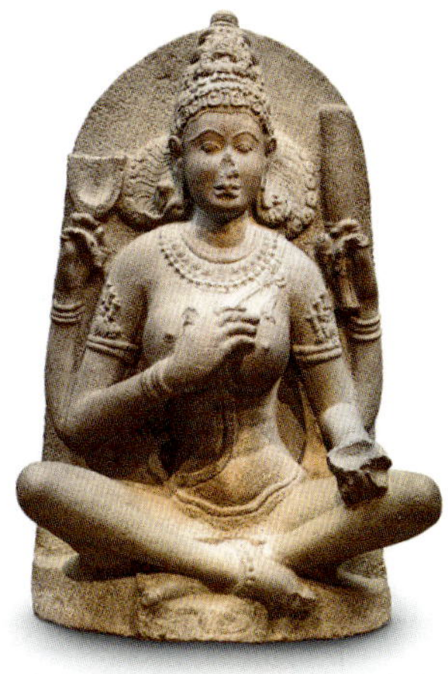

▲ **Winnow-bearing Yogini**
This c. 10th century figure with four hands from Tamil Nadu can be seen holding a winnow in her left hand. Another hand holds a head of corn and a cup.

Era c. 950–1050 CE | **Medium** Hard sandstone | **Area** 6 sq km (2.3 sq miles)

KHAJURAHO TEMPLES

An architectural celebration of a rich cultural past

The ebullient glory of form and ornamentation commemorates both the power and cultural aesthetics of the Chandelas, as well as their commitment to the patronage of art and architecture in their kingdom.

Only 22 of the 85 Hindu and Jain temples that dotted the ancient capital at Khajuraho (in present-day Madhya Pradesh) have survived the ravages of time. Located in the heart of the verdant wilderness of central India, they showcase the apogee of the Nagara style of north Indian temple architecture. With just a few early exceptions, the temples are constructed of hard, river sandstone, in strict accord with the principles of architecture (*vastushilpa*) as laid down in the ancient text, Vastu Shastra. True to the Nagara style, they are defined by the high plinth on which the entrance hall (*mandapa*) leading to sanctum (*garbhagriha*) sits and the tower (*shikhara*) that rises above - the tallest, where there is more than one, always marking the *garbhagriha*.

FINESSE AND FORM

The structure is highlighted by a delightful profusion of sculptural ornamentation that has become synonymous with Khajuraho. There are thousands of statues and artworks depicting gods, goddesses, teachers and disciples, dancers, musicians, amorous couples, and mythical creatures, all engaged in everyday activities reflecting the four essential goals of life - *dharma* (duty), *artha* (wealth), *kama* (desire), and *moksha* (liberation). The Kandarya Mahadeva Temple within the complex is alone decorated with over 870 figures. Only about 10 per cent of the depictions in the complex are sexual or erotic; however, there is a sensuousness in the sculptures that the craftsmen achieved that sensitively captures the intangible expression of human emotion. In the subtlety of facial expression, fluidity of limbs, beautifully modelled bodies, delicate folds of garments, and intricate detailing of ornaments, there is a vibrancy that makes the temples shimmer with life even today.

1. Intricate details from bas-reliefs showing erotic scenes at a temple; **2.** A high-relief carving from a temple showing a couple in an embrace; **3.** Courtyard and façade of a well-preserved temple at Khajuraho; **4.** Erotic sculptures depicting attributes of *kama* (desire) line the exterior walls at many of the temples; **5.** Stone carving of Vishnu and Laxmi at the Parsvanath temple in the Khajuraho complex; **6.** Statue of a horse in a temple compound; **7.** Wall carvings of sensuous celestial maidens and gods that show the finery of their garments and weapons

3

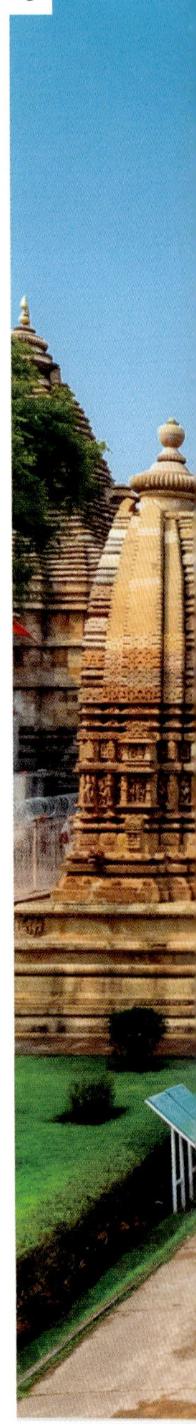

1

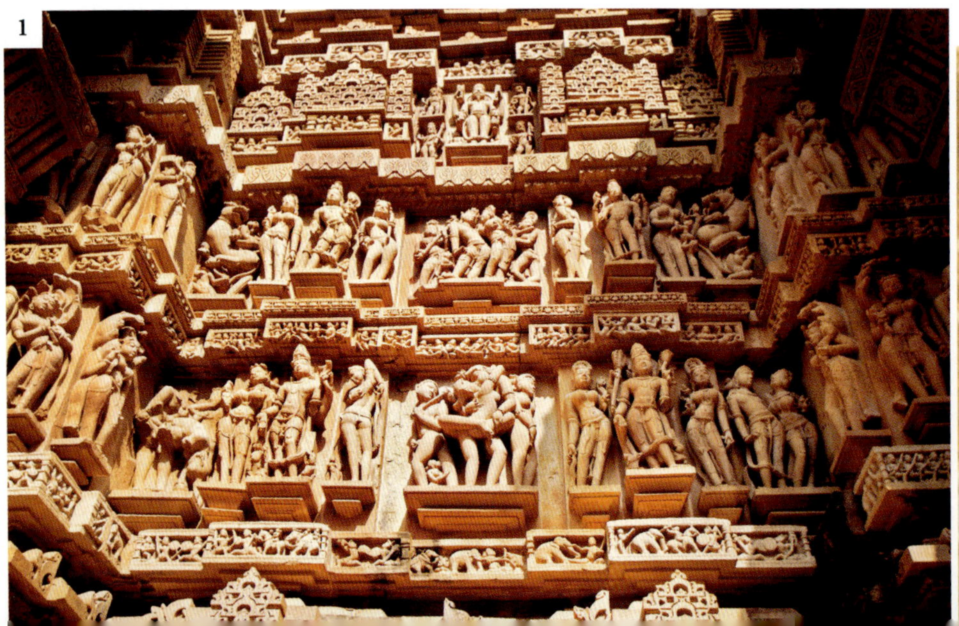

2

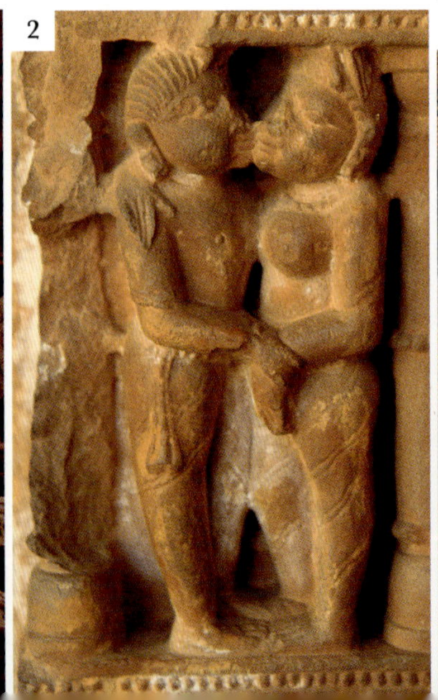

4

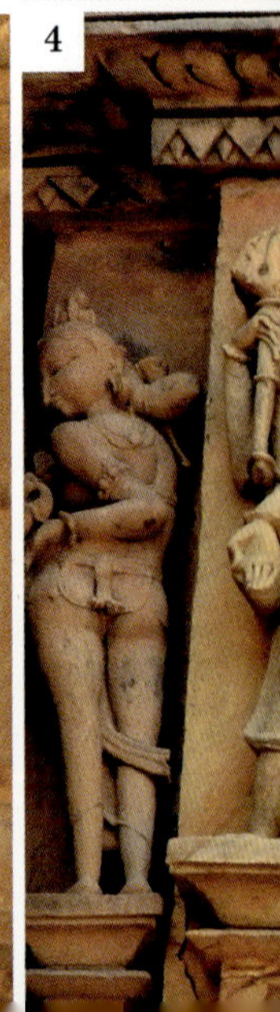

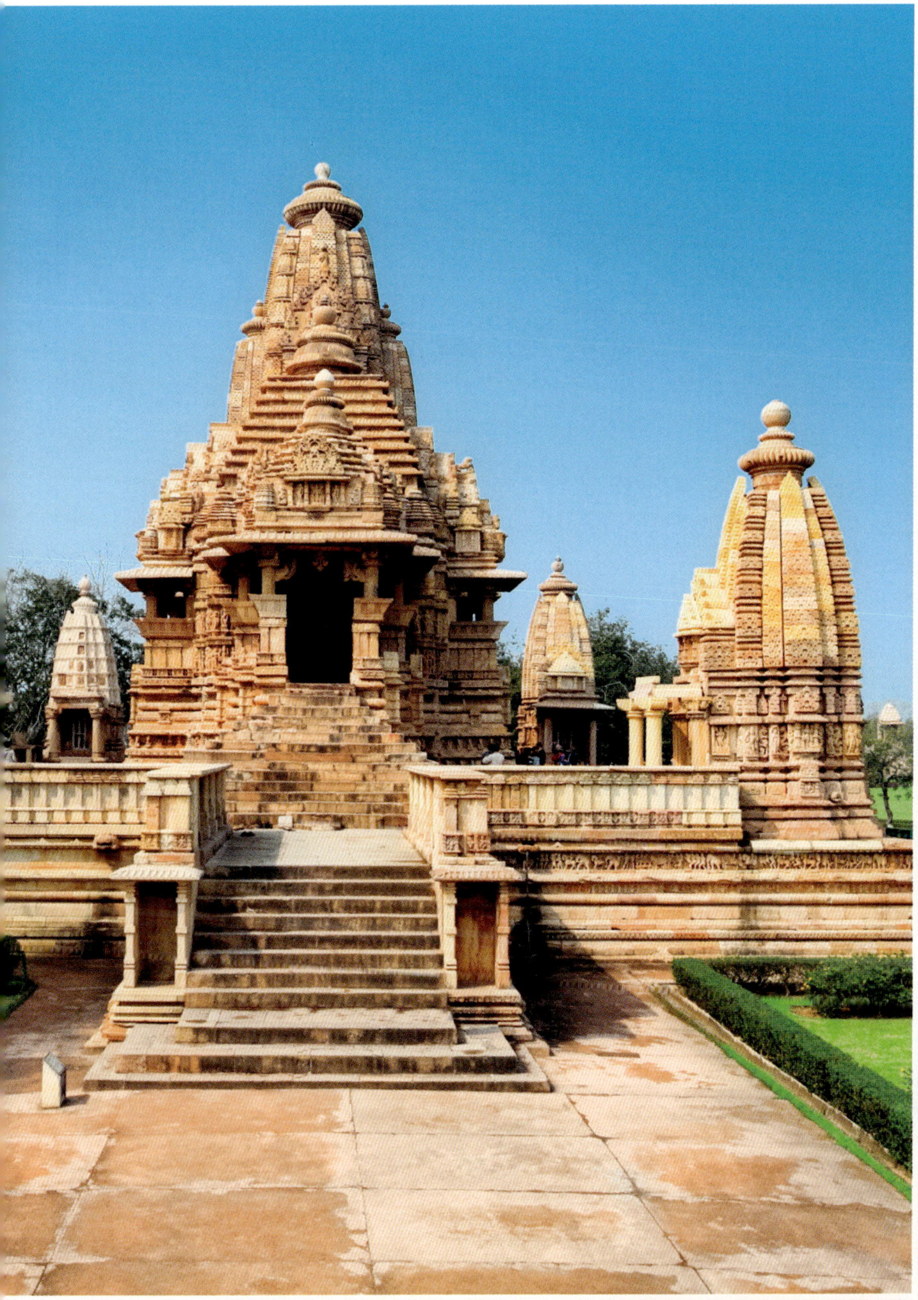

5

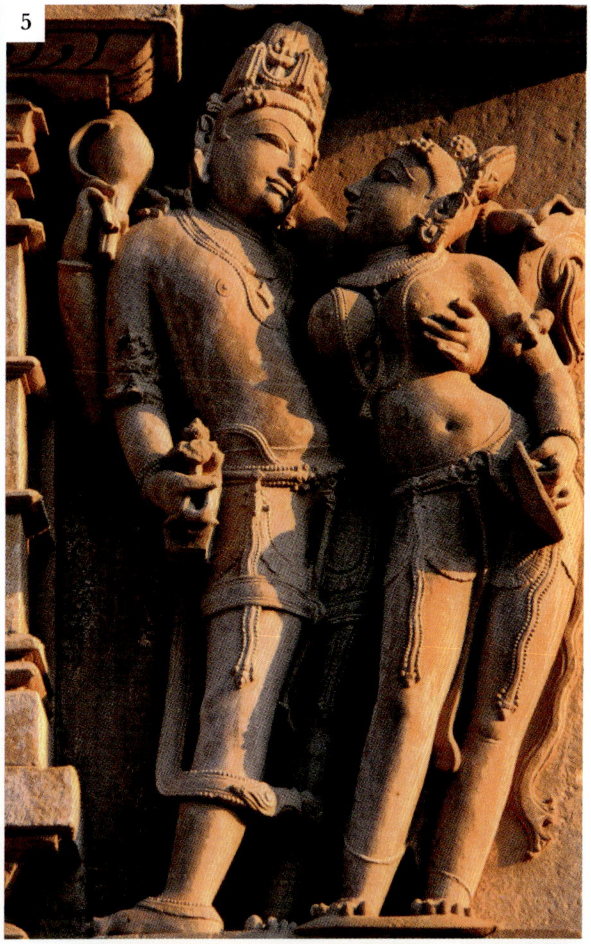

6

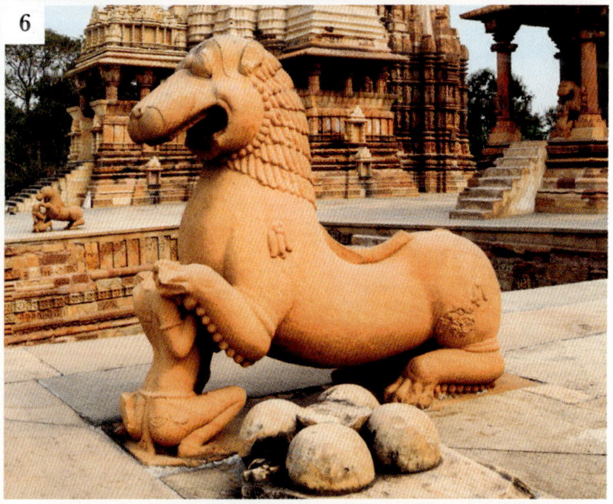

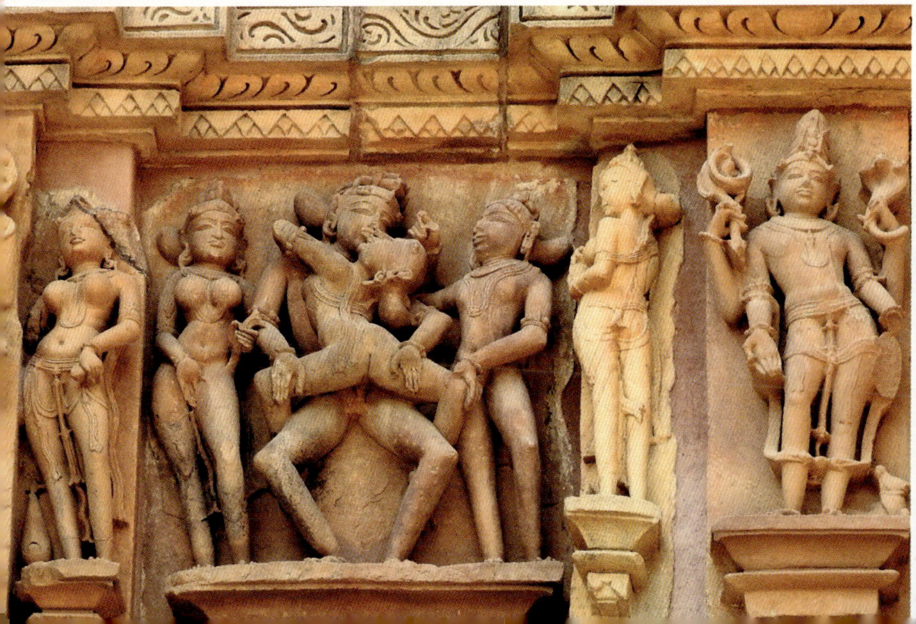

7

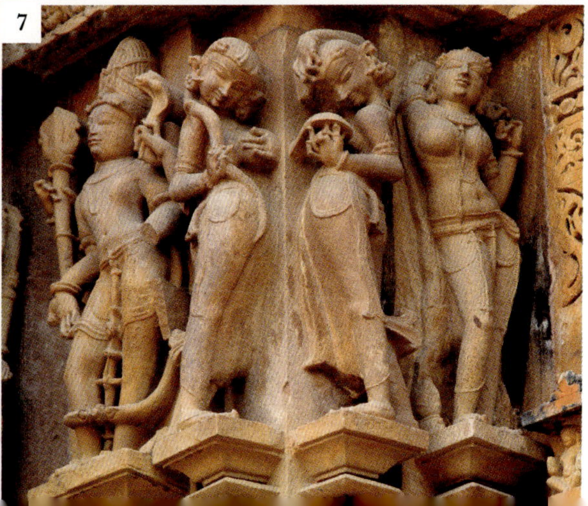

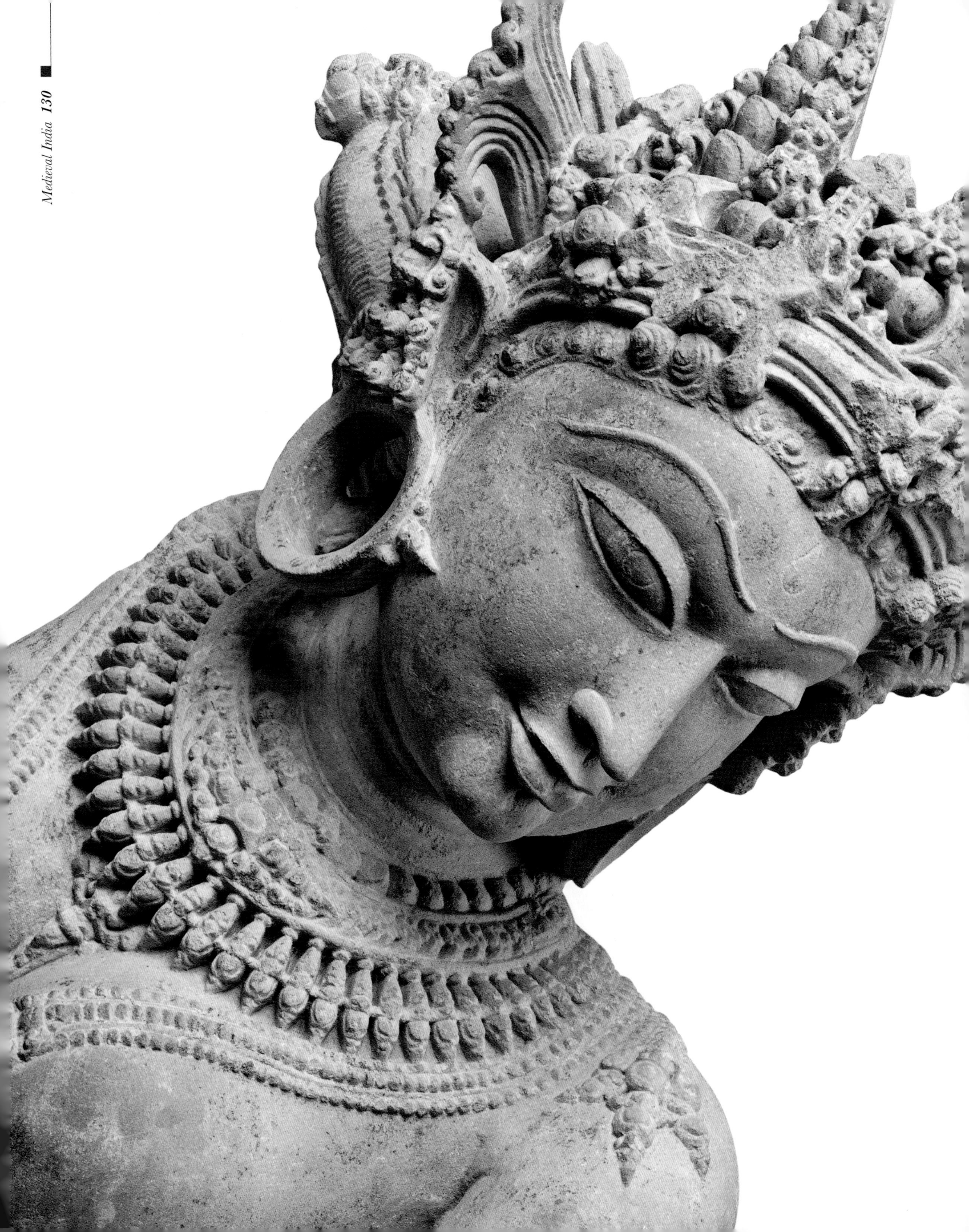

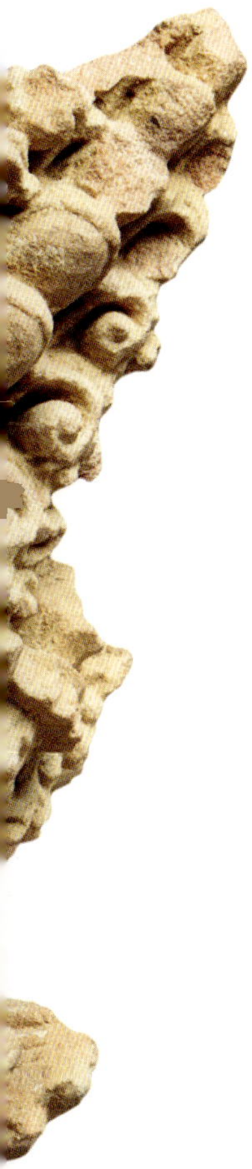

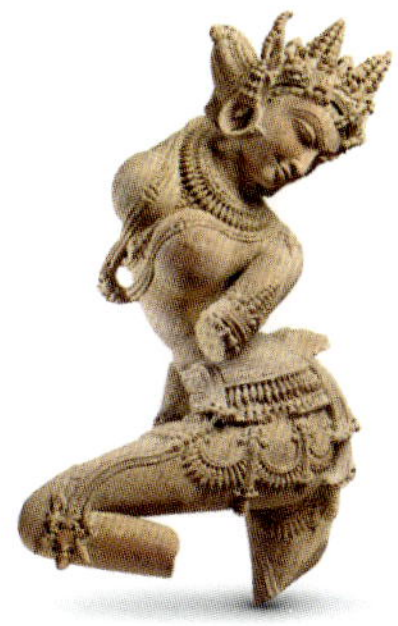

Era c. 11 century CE | **Medium** Sandstone | **Height** 88.3 cm (34.7 in)

CELESTIAL DANCER

Remarkable depiction of a divine danseuse

This sandstone carving of a dancer was probably located in a temple niche built by the Chandela rulers in Madhya Pradesh in central India. It exquisitely captures the fluidity of movement of a celestial being in a solid material.

As in the heavens, so also on earth, the celestial court was replete with musicians, dancers, and a full assembly of gods and goddesses. This sculpture of a dancer reflects one such *apsara*, or the celestial maiden whose *tribhanga* or triple-bend pose is a popular stance indicative of graceful movement in classical dance. In a perfectly timed step that captures the essence of her movement, she pirouettes animatedly as she lifts her leg, twists her torso, and turns her head to gaze backwards. It was prescribed as such in the *Natya Shastra*, an ancient dramatic arts treatise, and became a popular trope in classical Indian art and dance forms. The celebrant is heavily bejewelled, the detail of each ornament carved with loving precision. She is shown to wear an elaborate crowned headdress set with precious stones and numerous flowers. Her smile carries a touch of flirtatious delight, and the confidence that her beauty and grace will please the audience. The sculpture eloquently reflects the artisans' skills in rendering movement in stone.

◀ **Adorned only with** jewellery, this exuberant dancer is captivating and her grace is enhanced by the chiselled precision of each sensual detail.

EXEMPLAR OF DELICATE CHANDELA ART

The Chandelas were prodigious builders and their rule saw the pinnacle of the Nagara (north Indian) style of temple architecture, characterized by towering, stepped, and indented exteriors, reminiscent of the mountainous abode of the presiding deity. The most spectacular example of this that survives to this day can be found in the temples at Khajuraho (see pp. 128–129). The sculpted panels in temple complexes pulsate with life and energy, particularly the figures of the *apsaras*, portrayed singing, dancing, playing games, or adorning themselves.

The aesthetics of the Chandela sculptures follow the prescribed artistic canons of form and beauty. These sculptures are renowned for the full-breasted, slim-waisted female figures, with sharply defined noses, heavy-lidded eyes, slim and defined eyebrows, round cheeks, and full lips. They are heavily ornamented, with each piece of jewellery clearly detailed.

Era 1250 CE | **Medium** Chlorite, laterite, and khondalite stone | **Area** 10.62 ha (26.2 acres)

KONARK SUN TEMPLE

The sun god's chariot

Set on the sandy shores of the Bay of Bengal, the temple at Konark is an awe-inspiring monument and a UNESCO World Heritage Site. It is also one of the greatest examples of the culmination of the Kalingan (Odisha) style of temple architecture.

Conceptualized as a chariot drawn by seven horses, the magnificent Konark Temple is one of a handful temples built in the praise of Surya, the sun god. It is set on the eastern coast of present-day Odisha, at a spot believed to be the most auspicious place to welcome the first rays of the Sun as they touch the shore. The north and south sides of the high plinth on which the temple sits are 12 pairs of intricately carved wheels, 3.5 m (12 ft) in diameter. The entire composition is said to represent the passing of time based on the Hindu lunar calendar -the seven horses are the days of the month and the 12 wheels are the months of the year. The wheels also function as sundials, accurate to within a minute.

GLORIOUS TEMPLE

Built by the Eastern Ganga dynasty's king Narasimhadeva I in the 13th century, its scale and conception evidence the strength and stability of the Gangas as well as their value systems. Over time corrosive sea winds and structural instability have damaged the structure. Fortunately, the main assembly hall or *jagmohan* was restored in its entirety after being unearthed in the 20th century. The walls, the pillars, and the entire plinth area of the temple are embellished with a rich array of figures and scenes from the lives of both commoners and royalty. Sun was worshipped in the form of three images made in colour contrasting stone, each placed to catch the sun at dawn, noon and dusk. However, only the pedestal of the main image in the sanctum remains now.

1. One of the 12 pairs of wheels from the chariot of the Sun god, on each side of the *jagmohan* platform. **2.** One of the two statues of roaring lions standing guard at the steps leading to the dance pavilion. **3.** To the south of the temple, this battle horse, carved with its bridle, harness, and saddle in fine detail, tramples an enemy soldier. **4.** Flight of steps leading to the platform on which the dance pavilion stands, with the main temple visible in the background. **5.** Dancers and celestial musicians depicted on the outer walls of the temple. **6.** Statue of the sun god, astride his horse, in a niche on the south wall.

4

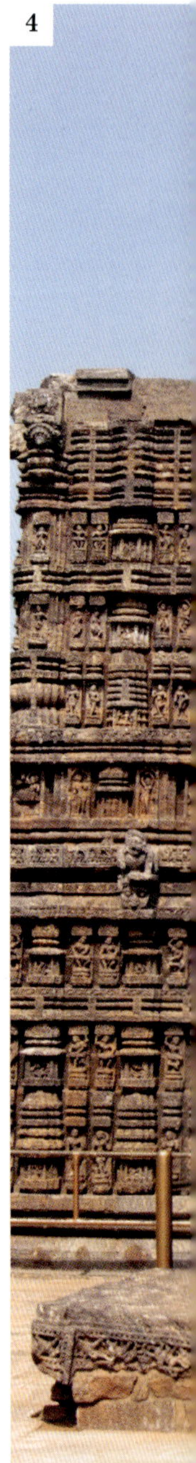

1

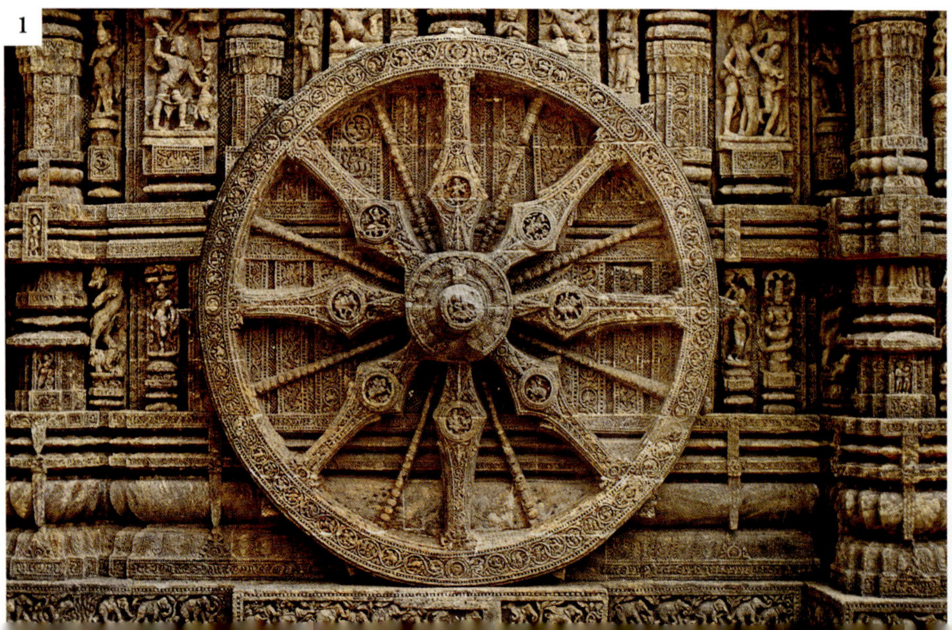

2

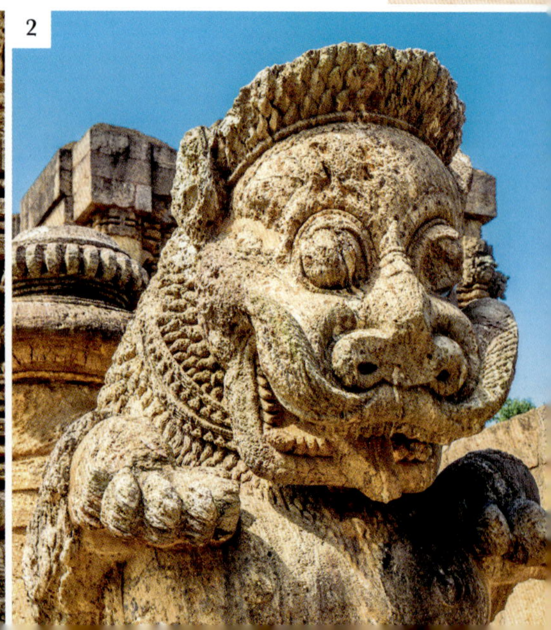

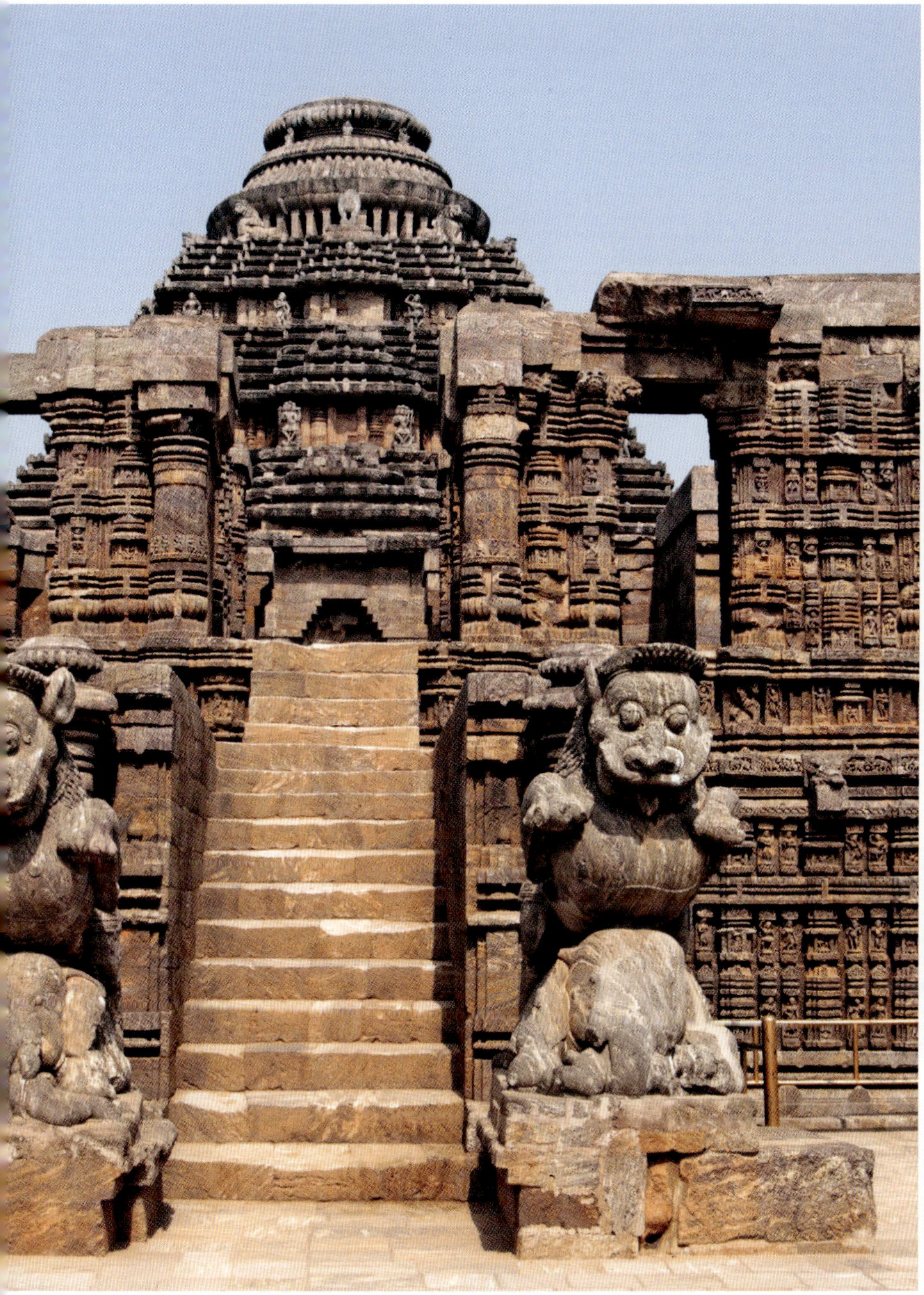

5

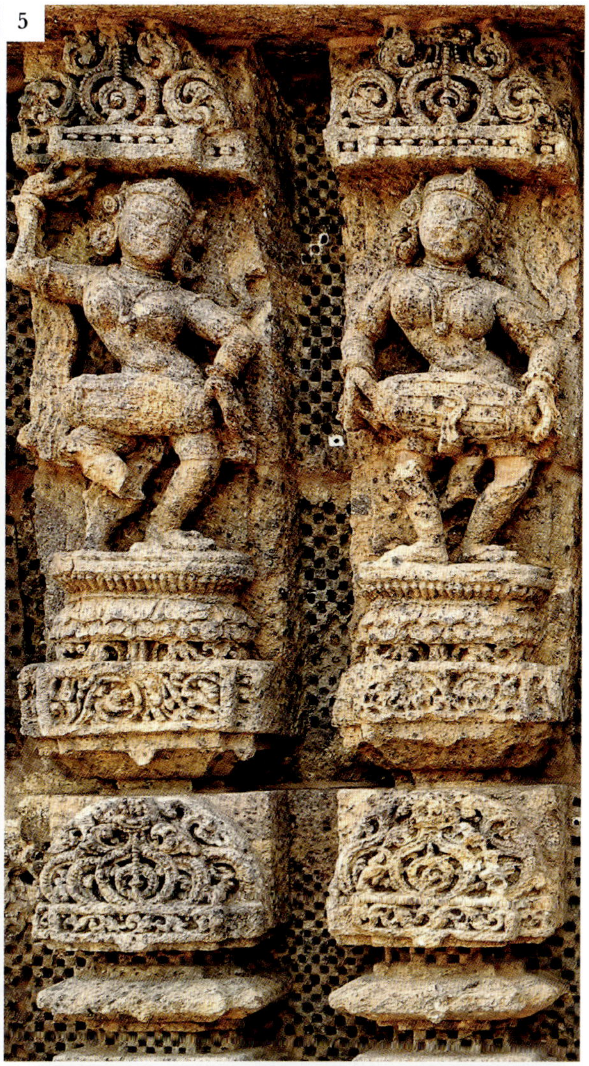

6

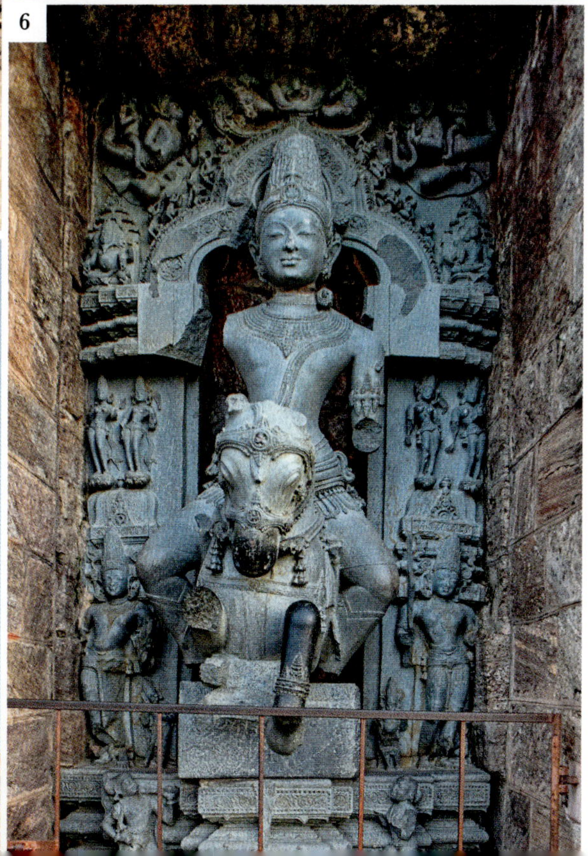

3

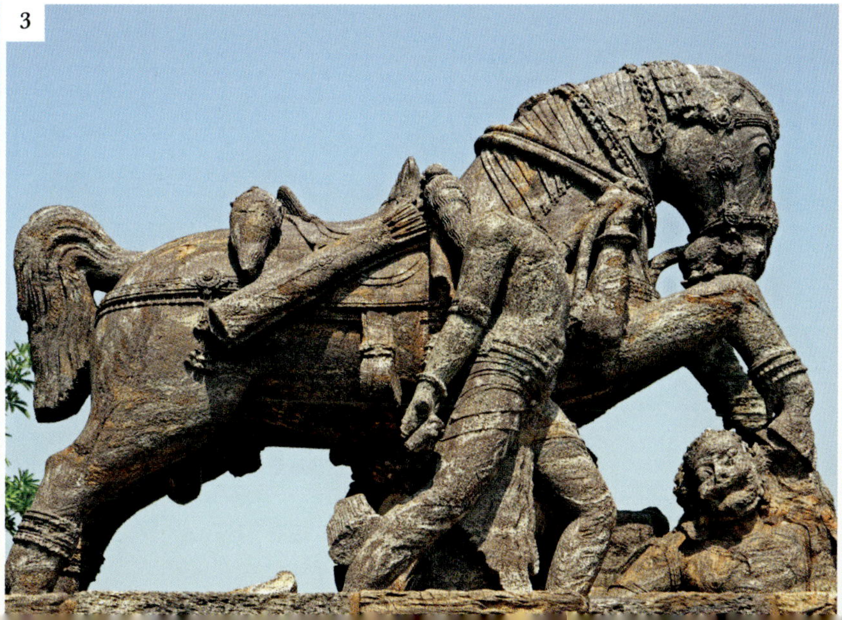

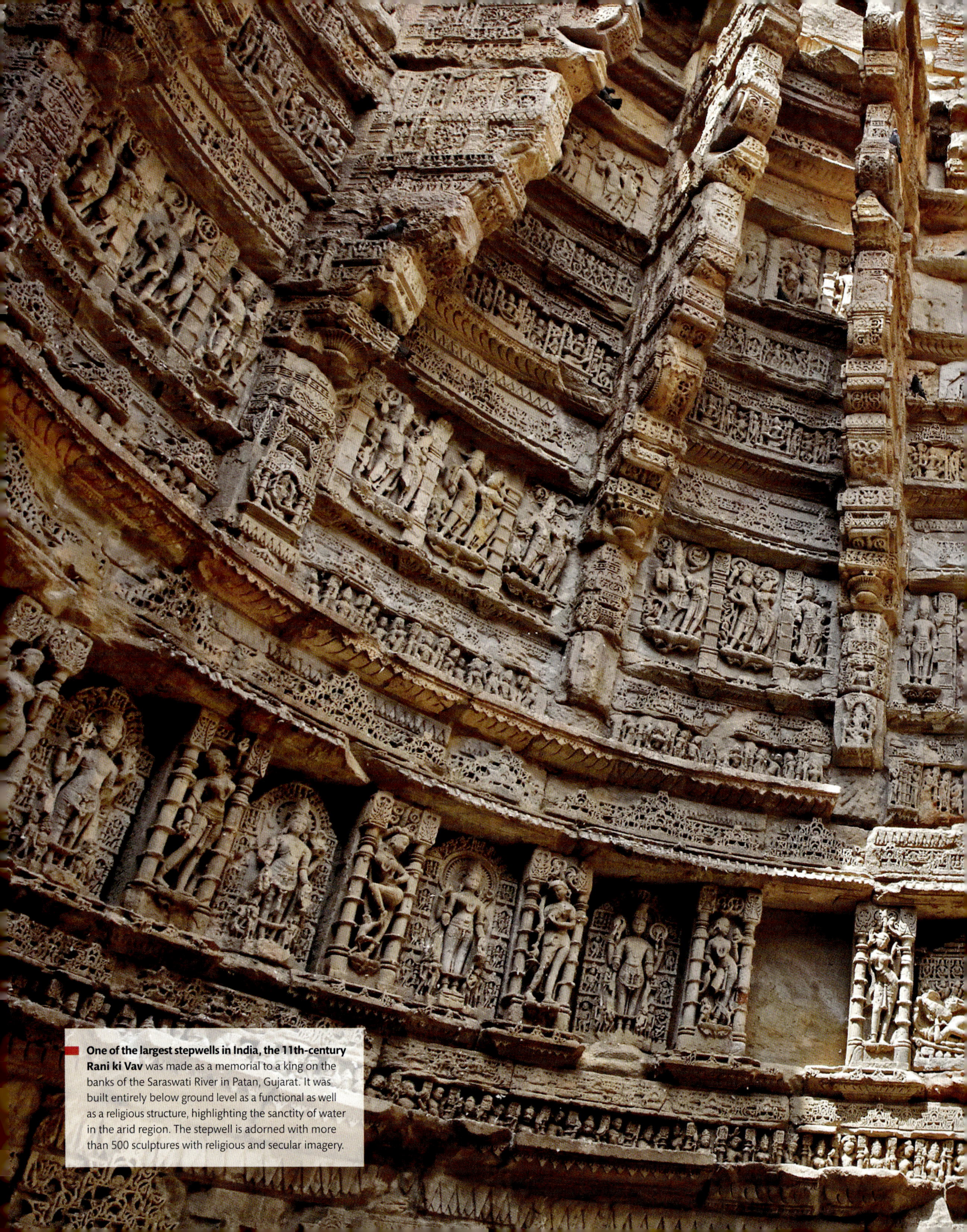

One of the largest stepwells in India, the 11th-century Rani ki Vav was made as a memorial to a king on the banks of the Saraswati River in Patan, Gujarat. It was built entirely below ground level as a functional as well as a religious structure, highlighting the sanctity of water in the arid region. The stepwell is adorned with more than 500 sculptures with religious and secular imagery.

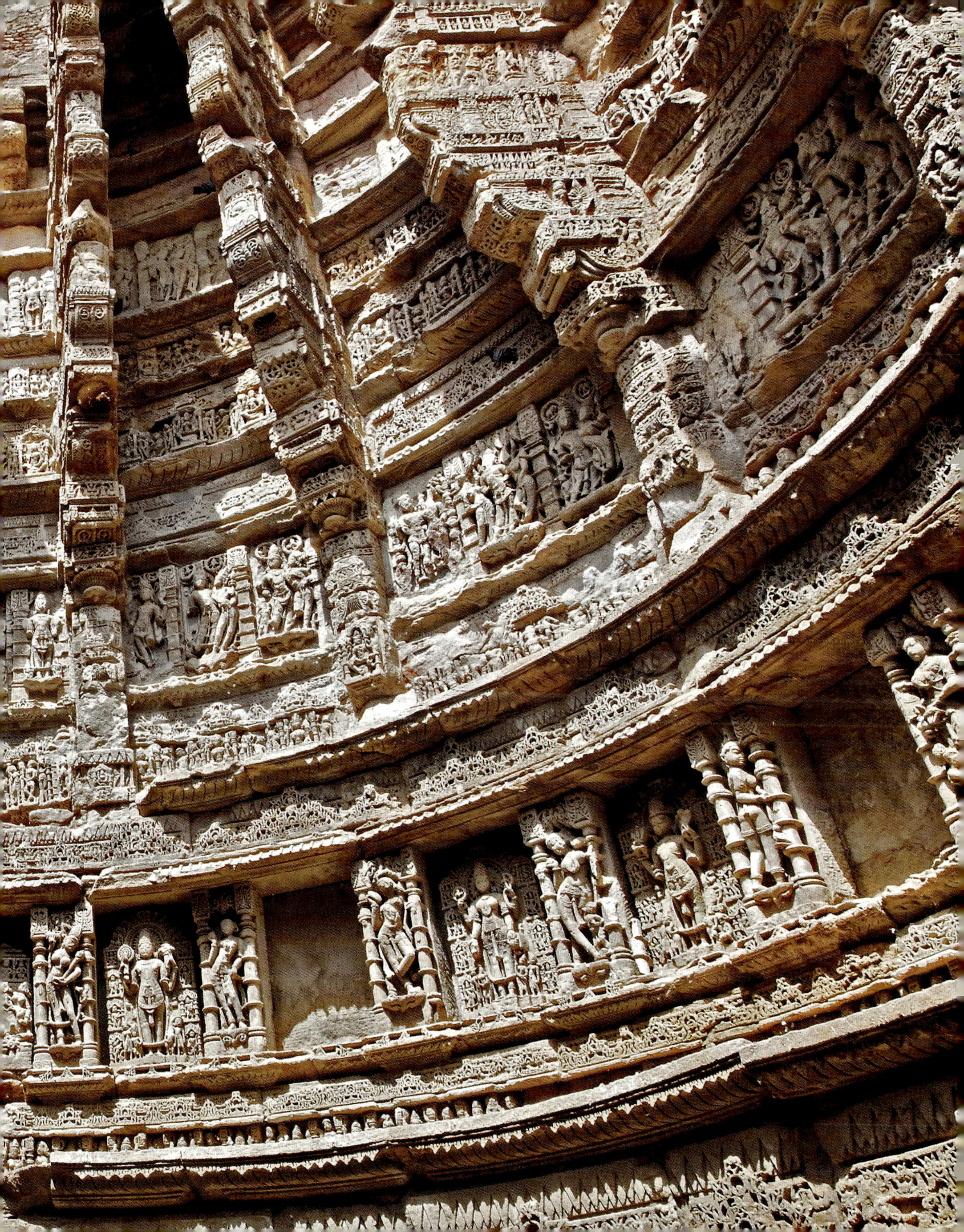

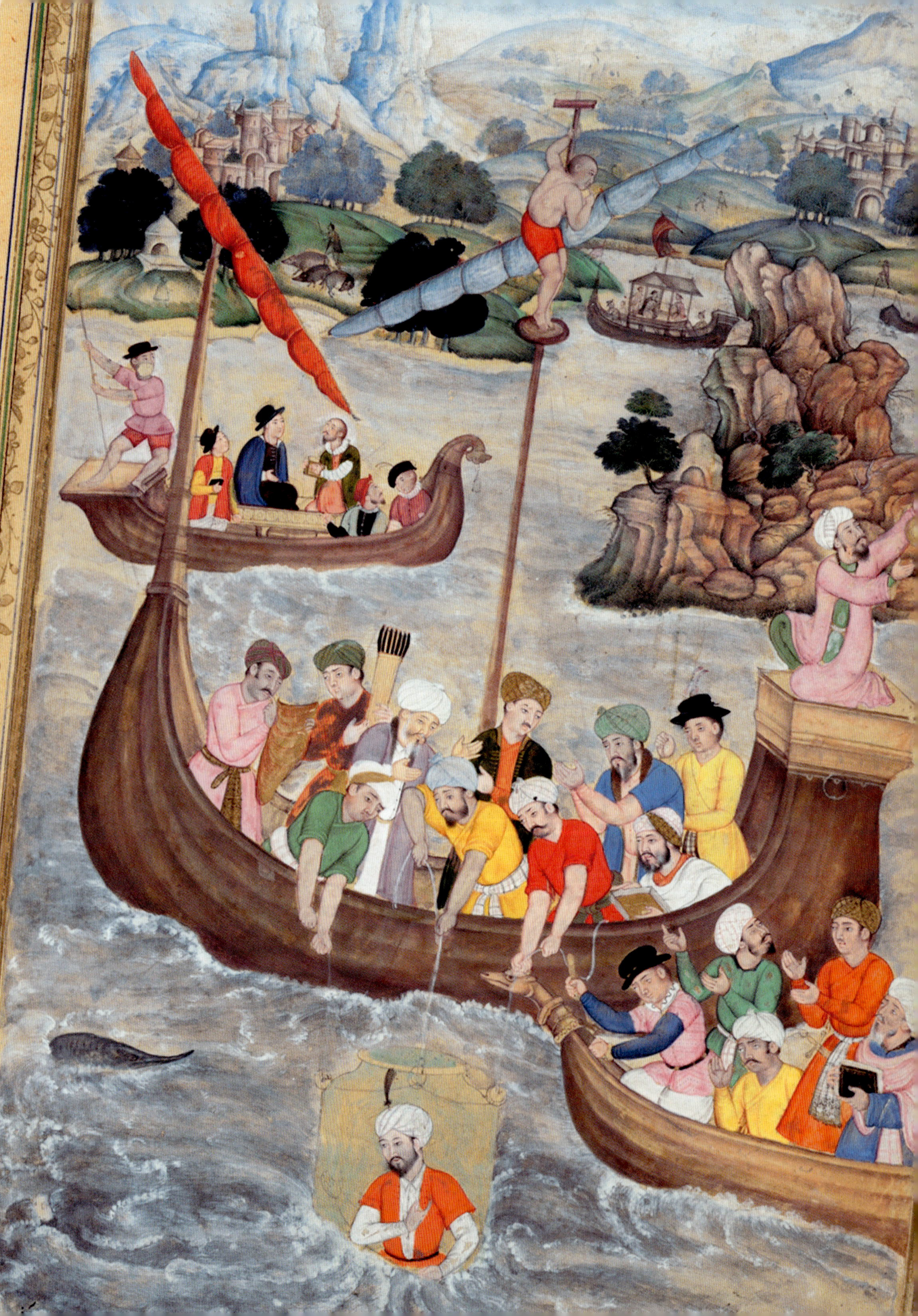

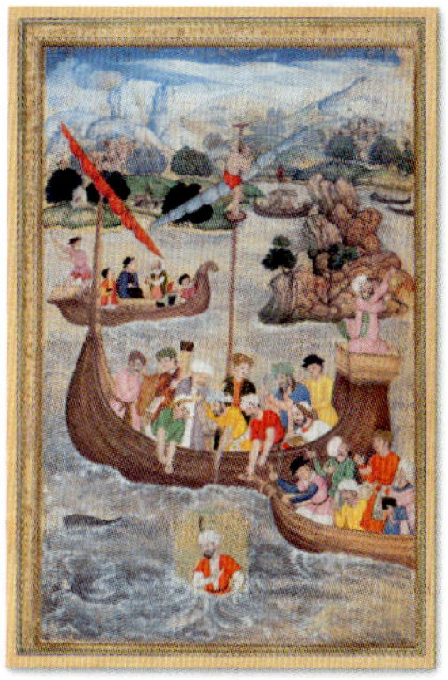

Era 12th century CE | **Medium** Ink and watercolour on paper | **Dimension** 19.7 × 12.7 cm (7.7 × 5 in)

KHAMSA-E-KHUSRO

Narrative poems of the past

The anthology by Amir Khusro, one of the most prolific Sufi poets of the Delhi Sultanate, is a collection of quintet, or five-stanza, poems. Modelled after a celebrated Persian poet's literary form, the khamsa initiated a long tradition of narrative poems in the subcontinent.

Around the late 12th century, the *qasida* and *gazal* forms of poetic expression had begun to flower in Indo-Persian court literature under the patronage of the Delhi sultans (see pp. 92–97). No poet had attempted to write narrative poetry at such a large scale. It was around this time that Amir Khusro, having previously made innovative efforts to express contemporary historical events in narrative verse, assumed the khamsa project. The original khamsa called *Panj Ganj* (Five Treasures), composed by Persian mystic and poet Nizami Ganjavi, had already caught the fancy of scholars and court poets and garnered considerable acclaim. Khusro's composition sought to not only pay homage to Nizami, but also produce a body of literature that aligned with his cultural milieu. What resulted was verse that contained a flavour of Persia, but infused with the Indian literary and folk traditions of storytelling.

◀ **A folio from a copy of the Khamsa** prepared for Mughal emperor Akbar and illustrated by the late 16th-century painter Mukunda, depicting Alexander the Great. He was shown by Khusro as an adventurer, being lowered into the sea in a bell-shaped diving glass, where the ruler is visited by an angel who foretells his death.

ADOPTING A FORM

Khusro's khamsa, though overlapping with Nizami's style, makes notable departures from it. The five poems follow the same metre as Nizami's *mathnawi* form, but their titles are cleverly modified so as to be reminiscent of, yet be distinct from the original ones. Each poem is dedicated to Delhi's patron saint Nizamuddin Auliya and the Sultanate ruler Alauddin Khilji, which tells us of the influence the Chishti Sufis (disciples of Moinuddin Chishti, a Sufi mystic) had on society and literature. In the style of Nizami, references to Khusro's own family members are peppered throughout the verses, offering insights into his personal life. His narrative also replaces Nizami's mature, spiritual tone with a fast-paced, light-hearted one laden with wordplay and double entendre, often punning on Persian words that have Hindi homonyms.

It appears that Khusro was highly conscious of the fact that his work would inevitably be compared to that of his Persian predecessor. He thus mentions Nizami by name in each of his poems, acknowledging the source of his inspiration and making statements about the practice of literary imitation. Although he playfully complains about Nizami having consumed the fine wine from the goblet of the stories, leaving nothing but the excess for other poets, his verse has been said to reflect confidence and a unique voice.

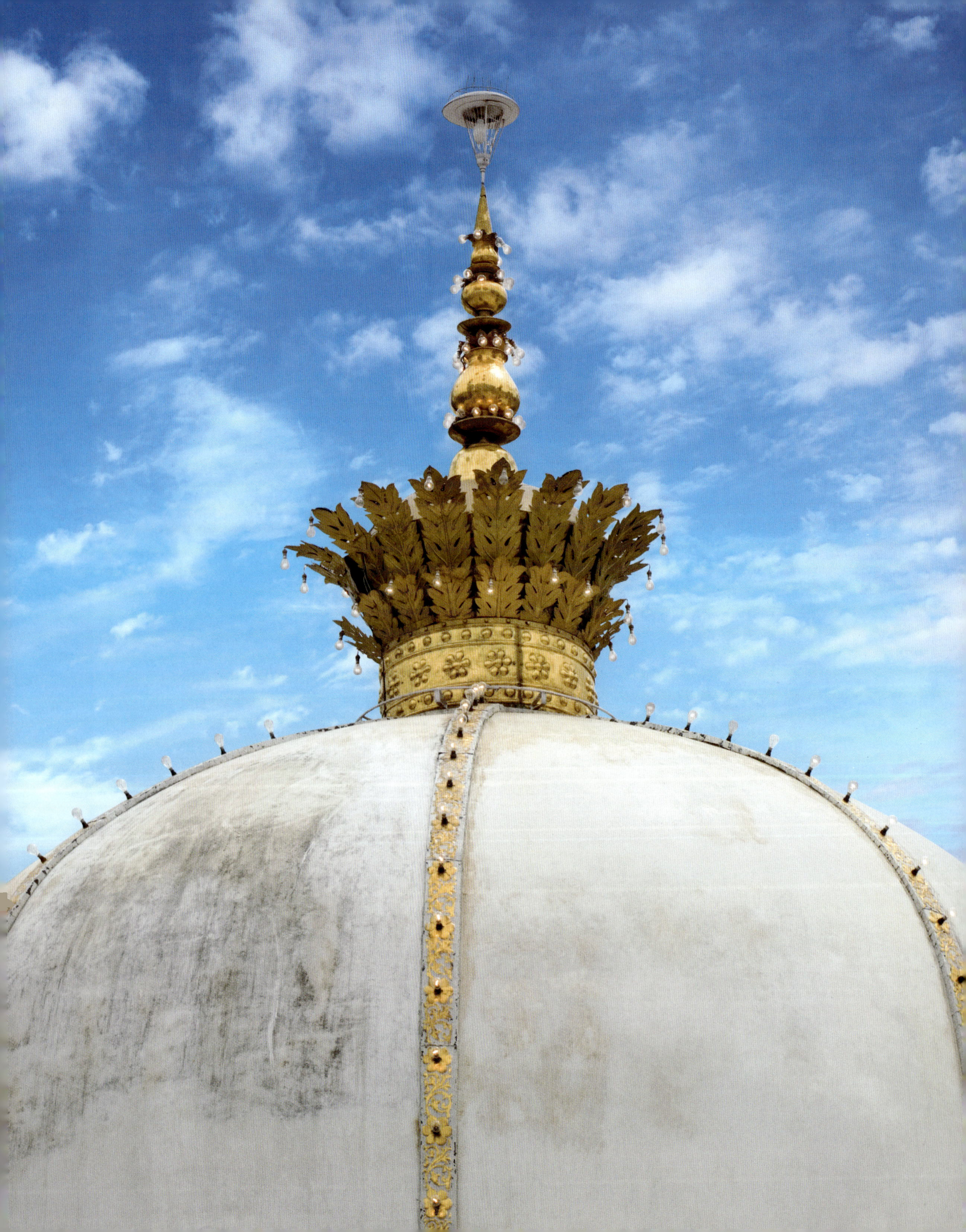

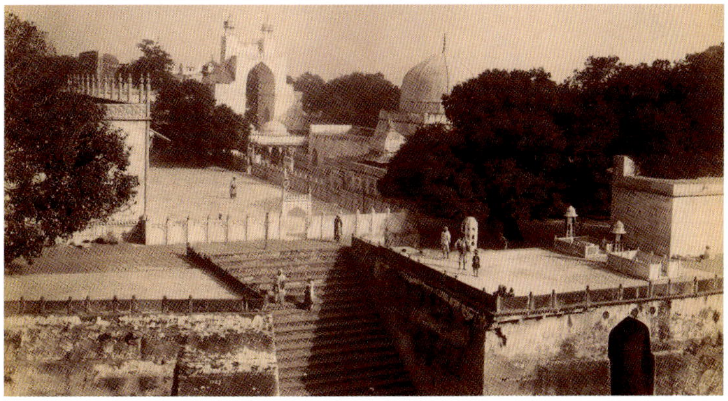

A photograph from late 19th–early 20th centuries showing the white dome and entry gates of the Dargah Sharif.

Era 12th century CE | **Medium** marble, brick, and sandstone

DARGAH SHARIF

The heart of Sufism in India

A revered pilgrim centre in Ajmer, Rajasthan, the Dargah Sharif contains the tomb of the Sufi saint Khwaja Moinuddin Chishti (1143–1236), and is one of the holy sites in the country that draws people of all faiths seeking favours and blessings.

Khwaja Moinuddin Chishti came to India from Persia in the 11th century and laid the foundation of the Chishti Order, a school within Sufism - a mystical Islamic belief and practice - in the Indian subcontinent. The Dargah Sharif is a prominent symbol of the proliferation of Sufism that took place in medieval India, especially during the Delhi Sultanate. An unorthodox, Islamic, mystic order, Sufism rejected the elaborate rituals and codes of behaviour laid down by Muslim priests. It focused instead on the pursuit of spiritual union with God through practises such as meditative music and dance.

◄ **This 17th-century white** dome, with the apex plated in gold, was constructed by Emperor Shah Jahan. It is one of the many additions made by Mughal rulers to the structure.

A DIVINE CENTRE

The focal point of the complex is the tomb of Chishti, which was initiated during the saint's lifetime by Iltutmish, the third ruler of the Delhi Sultanate, and completed three centuries later by the Mughal emperor Humayun. The tomb is now crowned with a marble dome, surrounded by a silver fence and a marble lattice screen. The shrine also features two courtyards, the Nizam Gate donated by the Nizam of Hyderabad, and the Akbari Mosque erected by the Mughal emperor Shah Jahan. Beyond this lies the Buland Darwaza, upon which the Urs flag is raised annually in a major event to mark Chishti's death anniversary rituals. The shrine is also well known for its *qawwali* performances. Dating back to medieval times, *qawwali* is a style of Sufi devotional songs that are sung intensely to lead listeners into a state of religious ecstasy and celebrate the power of divine love.

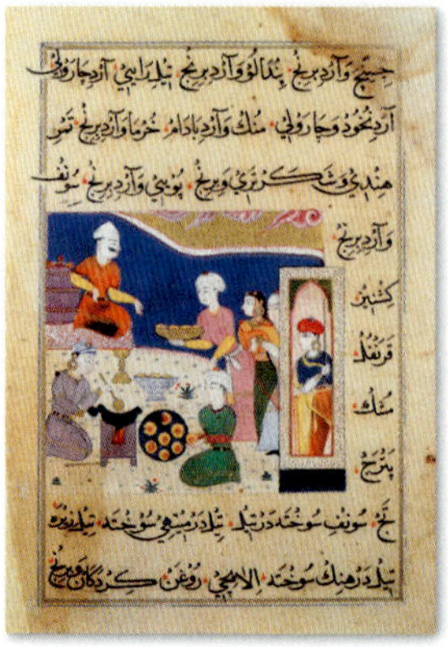

Era 16th century CE | **Medium** Watercolour

NIMATNAMA-I-NASIRUDDIN-SHAHI

A royal treasure trove of recipes

The only surviving copy of the *Nimatnama-i-Nasiruddin-Shahi*, a beautifully illustrated cookbook from the Malwa Sultanate, is written in the Persian Naskh script. It is an important source in the study of miniature painting and Indo–Persian syncretism.

Eloquently written, this recipe book, whose name literally translates to "Nasir Shah's Book of Delights", was composed for the Sultan of Malwa, Ghiyasuddin Khilji who ruled the northern and central parts of the Indian subcontinent in the 15th century. It was only completed between 1495 and 1505, during the reign of his son Nasiruddin Shah. Within its pages, 50 illustrations showcase a fusion of Persian and Indian styles, including the pre-Mughal *Chaurapanchasika* style of painting. The influence of the Persian 'Turkman' style from Shiraz is most visible in the early miniatures. As the manuscript progresses, the illustrations become more Indianized, particularly in terms of costume, architecture, and the representation of faces in full profile, as opposed to the more common half-profile of Persian painting.

FROM FOOD TO FINE SMELLS

The *Nimatnama* covers foods, aphrodisiacs, perfumery, and remedies for illnesses, and includes everything from ten ways to prepare the famous, fried savoury snack *samosa,* to the benefits of betel chewing. A list of ingredients features in the manuscript, including plant-based materials like gum, resin, and fruits, and more exotic items such as bamboo and the "perfumed shell of freshwater mollusc". The perfumery section lays detailed emphasis on making *ittar* (essential oil) and *abir* (perfumed paste). Advice on matters of royal life such as hunting - "don't leave without a picture of your beloved, camphor to have rubbed into your feet, your best sparrow hawk, and a cheetah or two" - can also be found within the pages. It is noteworthy that nearly five centuries on, many of the recipes are still being used.

► **Folio from the *Nimatnama-i Nasiruddin-Shahi*** depicting the preparation of *samosas*, as noted in the text, along with detailed instructions, including a reminder: "don't forget to add saffron, fried aubergines, and ginger".

آرد نخود و چارولی • منك و آرد بادام • خرما و آرد برنج • تمر

هندی و شکرتری و برنج • پوسیی و آرد برنج • سونف

و آرد برنج •

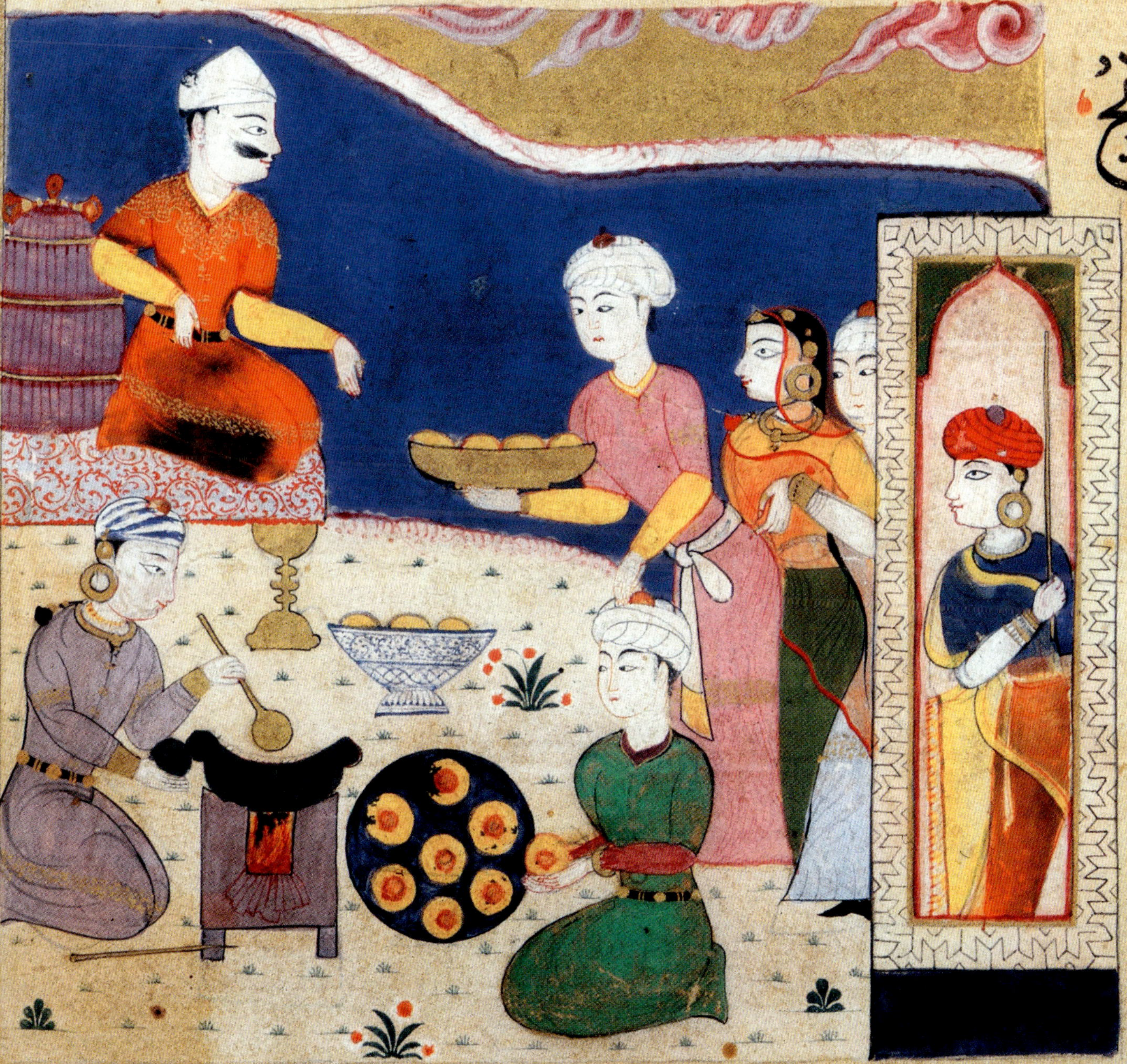

کشنیز •

قرنفل •

مشك •

پترج •

تج • سونف سوخته در تیل • تیل در میتهی سوخته • تیل زیره

Era 12th–13th centuries CE | **Medium** Minar: sandstone, marble | **Height** Minar: 73 m (240 ft)

QUTUB MINAR COMPLEX

A symbol of victory gracing New Delhi's skyline

The crowning architectural achievement of the Delhi Sultanate and one of the city's most spectacular sites, the Qutub Minar complex houses a number of historical buildings, including the imposing victory tower and the city's oldest mosque.

The Qutub Minar complex is nestled in the heart of Qila Rai Pithora, the first of the fabled cities that made up Delhi. Although called a 'complex', it was not planned in a cohesive way. Various rulers added structures to it over the centuries following the conquest of northern India.

THE TOWERING MINAR

The most striking structure within the complex is the Qutub Minar itself, a five-storeyed, 73-m (240-ft) sandstone and marble minaret believed to have been built as a symbol of victory and to celebrate the establishment of the Delhi Sultanate (see pp. 92–97). The building of the tower cannot be attributed to a single ruler. Its construction was begun by Qutbuddin Aibak in the year 1199, but he died in 1210 after only the first storey had been built. Iltutmish, Aibak's son-in-law, added three more storeys to it, and Feroz Shah Tughlaq added the fourth and fifth storeys in 1368 after a lightning strike knocked off the top. Archaeologists speculate that the tower might have also served as a look-out and as a place for the muezzin's call to prayer.

OTHER STRUCTURES

Subsequent rulers of Delhi, including the Tughlaqs, Khiljis, and the British added structures to the complex. One of these is Delhi's oldest mosque, the Quwwat-ul-Islam (Might of Islam) built between 1192 and 1198 by Qutbuddin Aibak, which features a spectacular sandstone screen. It is a fusion of decorative Hindu panels from the temples, and Islamic domes and arches. Another significant addition to the complex is the Alai Darwaza, a gateway erected in 1311 by Alauddin Khilji, which established a new Islamic architectural style, marked by arches and panels carved with verses from the holy book, the Qur'an.

1. The towering, five-storeyed Qutub Minar, after which the complex is named; **2.** Intricate carvings adorn the walls of Iltutmish's tomb situated within the complex; **3.** Verses from the Qur'an carved into the red sandstone walls in the Qutub Minar complex; **4.** Alai Darwaza, constructed in the early 14th century; **5.** Ruins of a second tower within the complex; **6.** Ruins at the entrance of the Quwwat-ul-Islam, with the Iron Pillar, dating to the 4th century, just beyond; **7.** An intricately decorated wall in the Qutub Minar complex, featuring carvings of text from the holy book, Qur'an

1

2

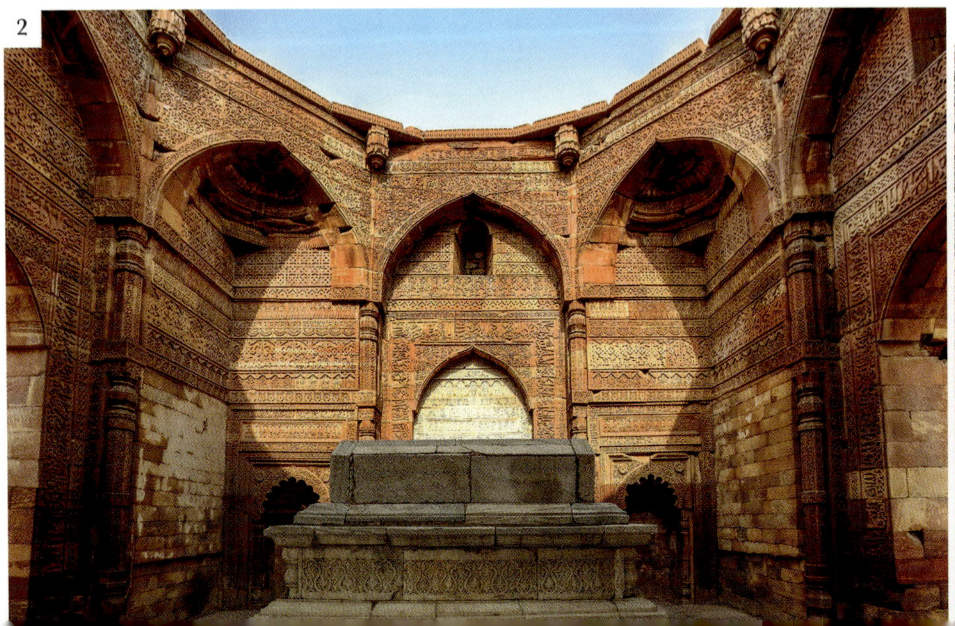

3

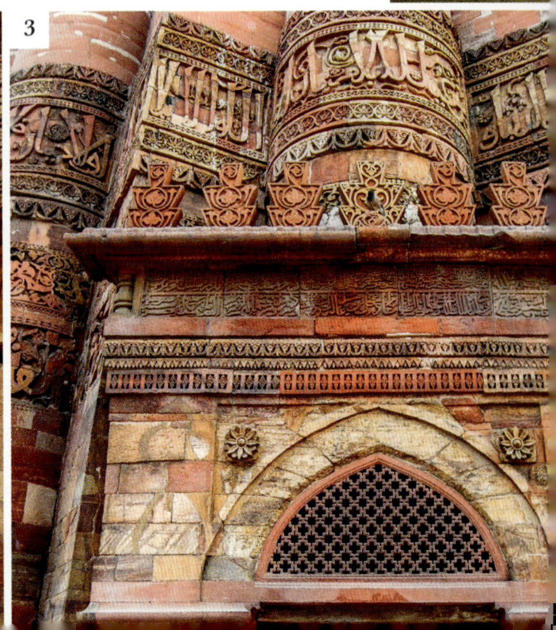

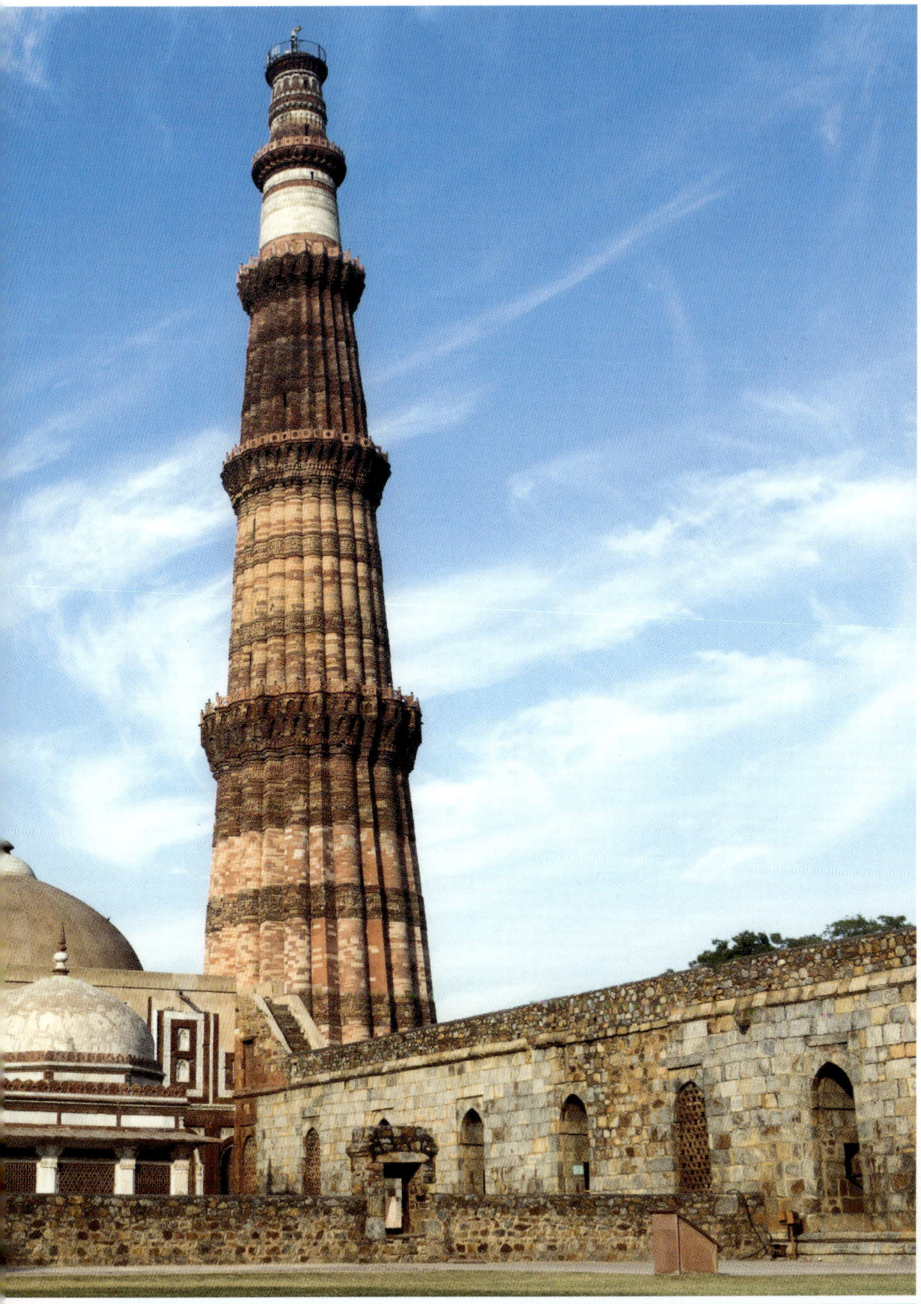

5

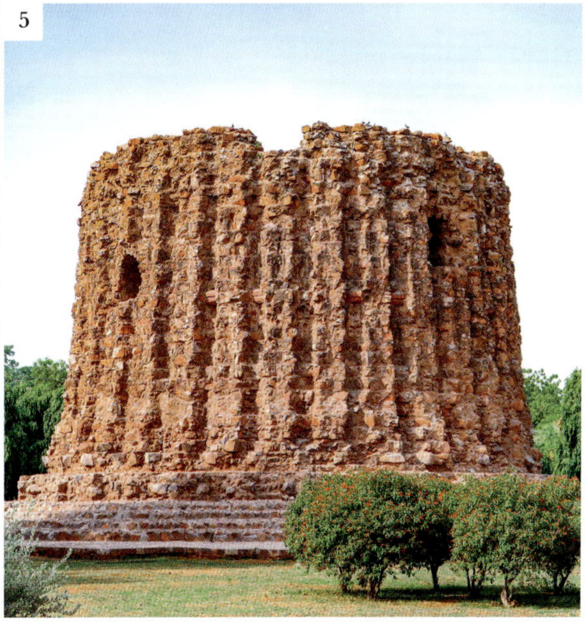

6

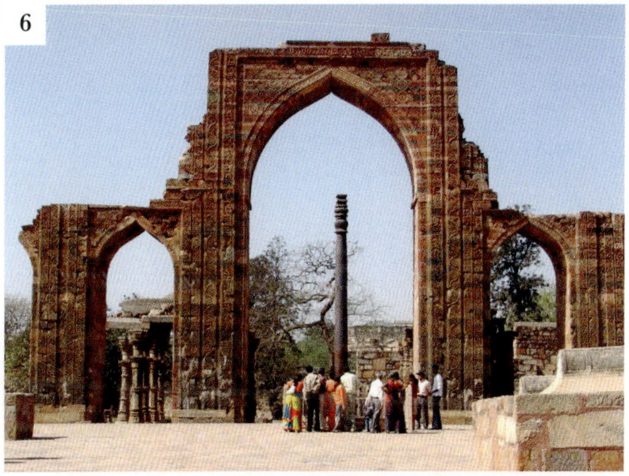

7

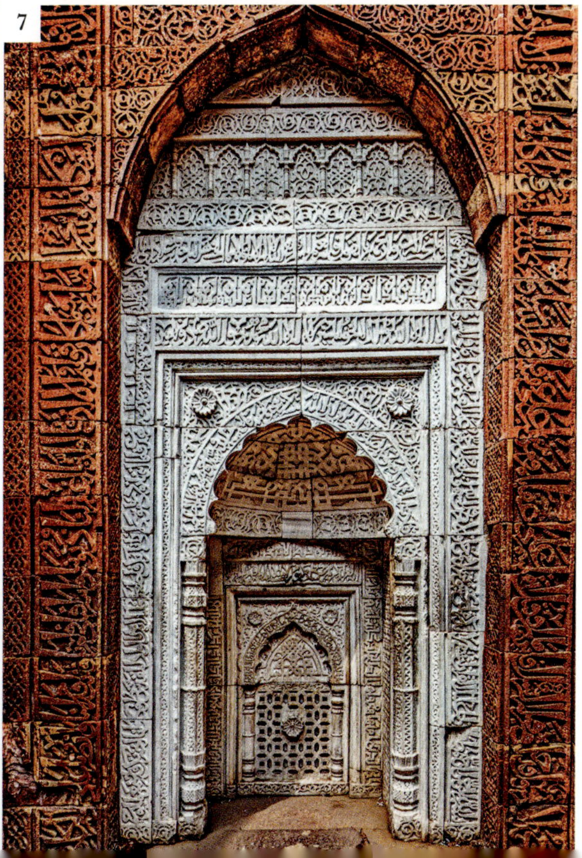

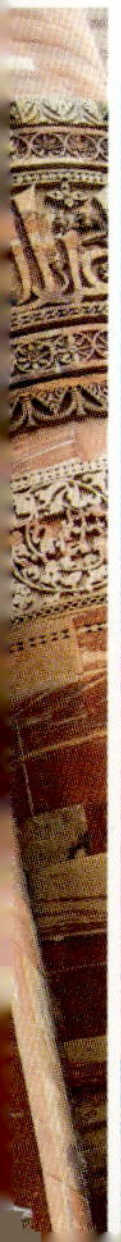

4

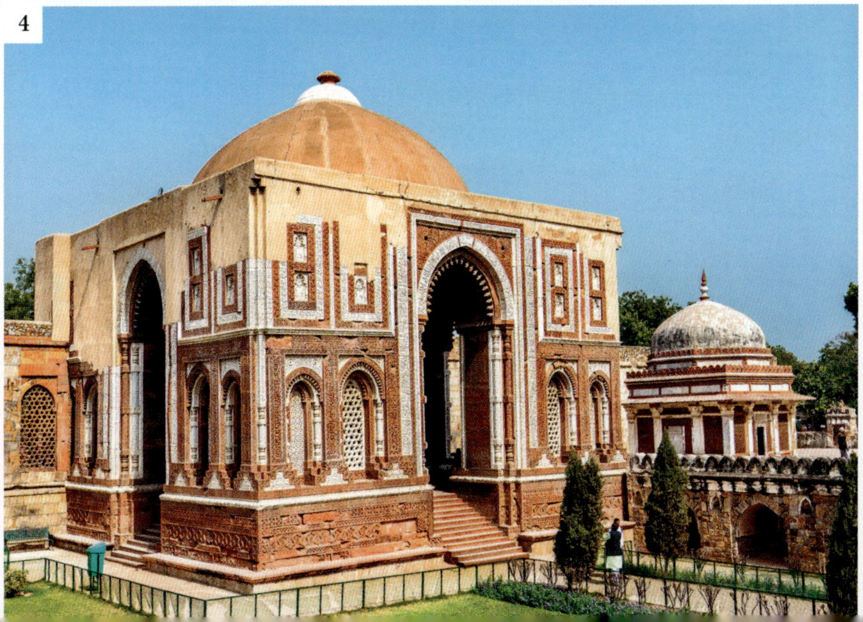

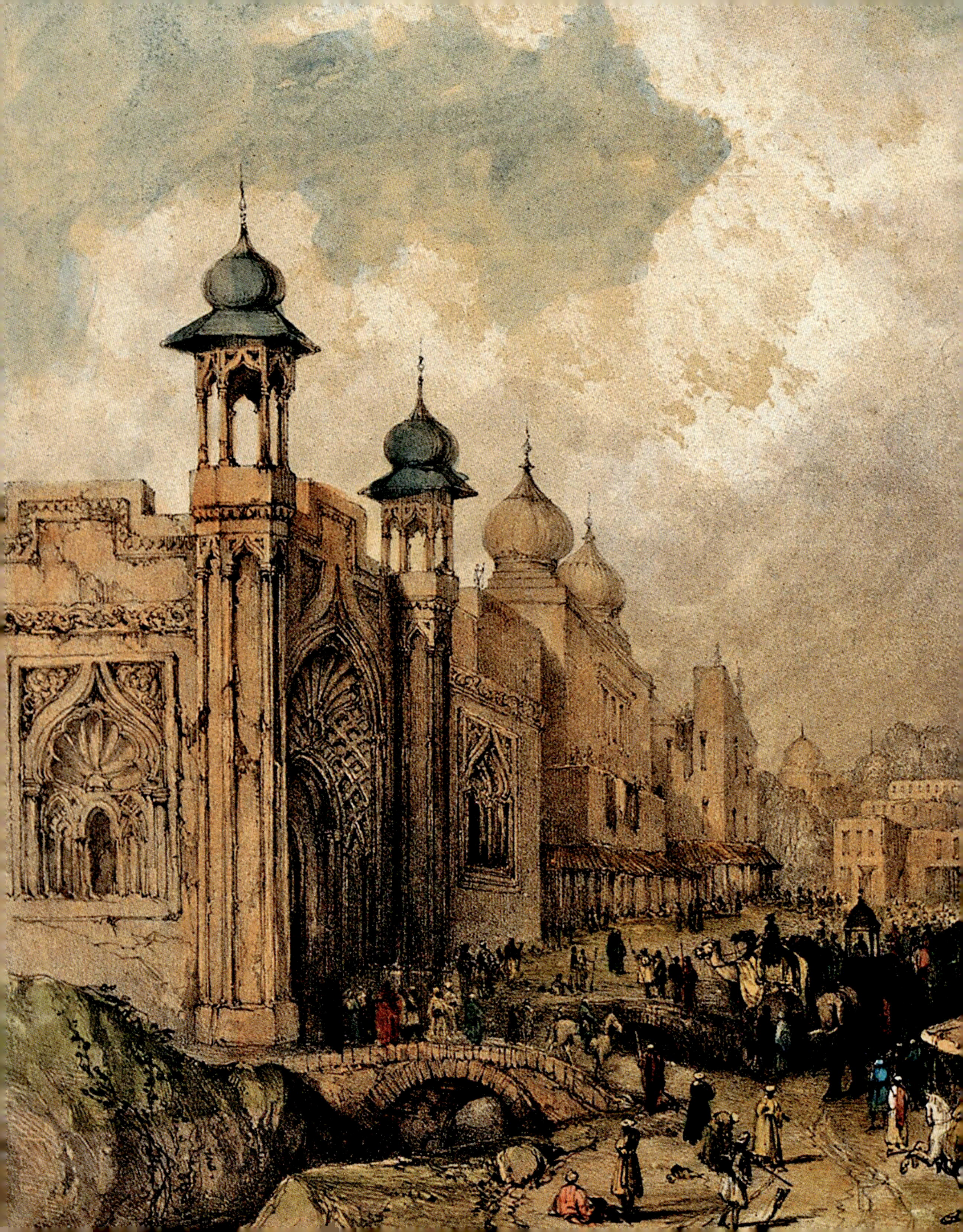

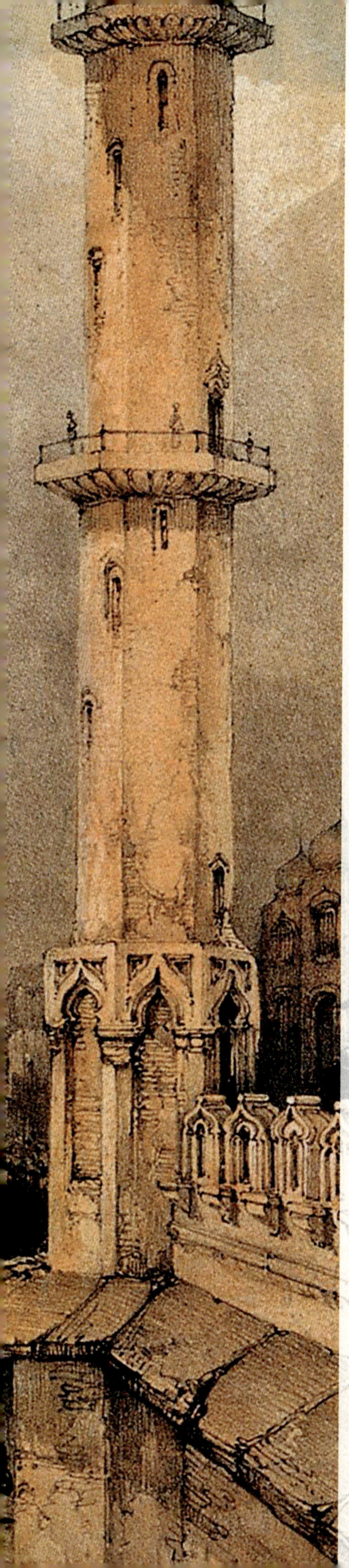

c. 1st century BCE *onwards*

DELHI

The epicentre of political power in the Indian subcontinent for most of the last millennium, Delhi has witnessed the rise and fall of capital cities and been a fabled centre of art and architecture.

For centuries, Delhi has been a place where history and culture have intertwined. The city even finds mention in the ancient Indian epic Mahabharata as Indraprastha, the capital city built by the Pandavas. Excavations suggest that the area has been inhabited since c. 1000 BCE, though the first reference to Delhi doesn't appear until the 1st century BCE, when a local chieftain, Dhilu, is said to have named the settlement he built there after himself.

A CANVAS FOR THE EMPIRES

Delhi was established as a strategic political stronghold in the 12th century CE when it came under the rule of the Turkic ruler Muhammad Ghuri in a decisive battle that paved the way for Central Asian armies to conquer the Indian subcontinent. Over the next three centuries, capitals of successive dynasties known as the Delhi Sultanate, including the Khiljis, Mamluks, Tughlaqs, Sayyids, and Lodhis (see pp. 92–97), were built in Delhi. They remain immortalized in the many surviving and ruined forts, battlements, and tombs that are sprinkled across the city.

The Delhi Sultanate was followed by the Mughal Empire in 1526. Under the Mughals, who were great patrons of the arts as well as inveterate builders of opulent palaces and monuments, Delhi reached its zenith as an Indo-Islamic cultural centre. Shah Jahan, the fifth Mughal emperor, commissioned the construction of the brand new city Shahjahanabad, today known as Old Delhi, on the river Yamuna. His masterpiece metropolis served as the city's administrative core, featuring the massive Red Fort, the commercial heart of Chandni Chowk, and the city's main mosque, the Jama Masjid. In the 18th century, however, the Mughal grip on the city weakened with repeated incursions from the Maratha Empire from western India and Afghan invaders from the north-west frontier.

Throughout the ages, in spite of its many rulers, Delhi has continued to be a cultural hub where arts and literature flourished in royal courts.

**"I asked my soul: what is Delhi?
She replied: the world is the body and Delhi its life."**

– Mirza Asadullah Khan Ghalib (Translated by Khushwant Singh in *Delhi: A Novel*, 1990)

◄ **A late 19th-century print capturing** the markets of Chandni Chowk, framed by the golden domes of the Sunehri Masjid.

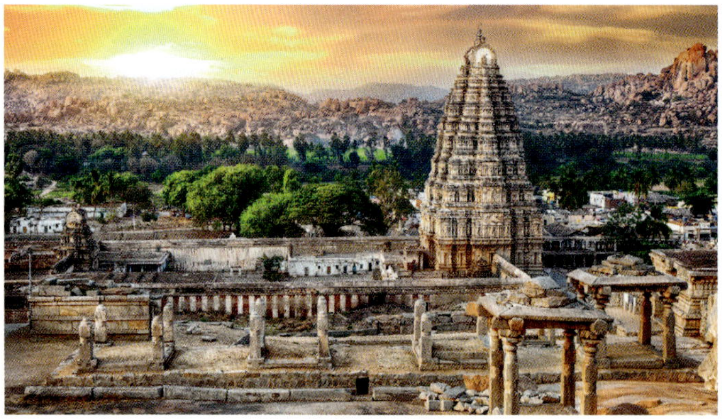

Virupaksha Temple, located amid the ruins of the historical town, Hampi, in the southern state of Karnataka, is dedicated to one form of Lord Shiva.

Era 8th century CE | **Medium** Stone slabs and bricks | **Height** Gopuram: 49 m (160 ft)

VIRUPAKSHA TEMPLE

A Dravidian masterpiece dedicated to Shiva

The Virupaksha Temple in Hampi, in central-eastern Karnataka, is an architectural gem of the Vijayanagara Empire. Built in the Dravidian style, it is known for its towering *gopurams*, intricate carvings, and ornate sculptures.

Virupaksha Temple, the main shrine in Hampi, is one of the oldest and most important structures in the region. It has an imposing elevation and its main *gopuram* (tower), which stands at a height of 49 m (160 ft), is adorned with intricate carvings of scenes from Hindu mythology that feature the deities Virupaksha (Shiva), Pampa Devi (Parvati), Rama, and Sita, among others. There are several shrines dedicated to different gods and goddesses within the complex, including Lokeshwara (Ganesha), the son of Virupaksha and Pampa Devi. The temple also houses a number of smaller shrines. In the centre is a single-storey ornate *ranga mandapa* (temple hall) built in c. 1510 CE to celebrate the coronation of the Vijaynagara Empire's eminent ruler, Krishnadevaraya.

JEWEL OF THE VIJAYANAGARA EMPIRE

A masterpiece of medieval architecture, the temple stands within the Group of Monuments at Hampi, a UNESCO World Heritage Site. The area is fittingly called the largest open-air museum in the world, and it has colossal granite statues and carvings that rub shoulders with the ornate pillars, pavilions, and gateways of its large temple complexes. Originally it had a few small, 7th-century shrines, but many additions were made over the years.

Situated amid a splendid setting of massive boulders and craggy hills, with the river Tungabhadra on one side, Hampi was once the capital of the Vijayanagara Empire, which was founded in 1336 against the backdrop of Central Asian invasions (see pp. 92–97). From the accounts of Portuguese, Italian, and Persian visitors, it seems that as the kingdom grew into a formidable power. It traded with many countries and became famous for its art and culture. As Fernao Nuniz, a Portuguese traveller, described in 1535, Hampi was as "large as Rome and very beautiful to the sight". The empire flourished for 200 years but it collapsed in 1565, after the battle at Talikota between the monarch of Vijaynagara and a league of sultans from nearby states. After being defeated, Vijayanagara broke up into small fiefdoms ruled by the Nayaka dynasty.

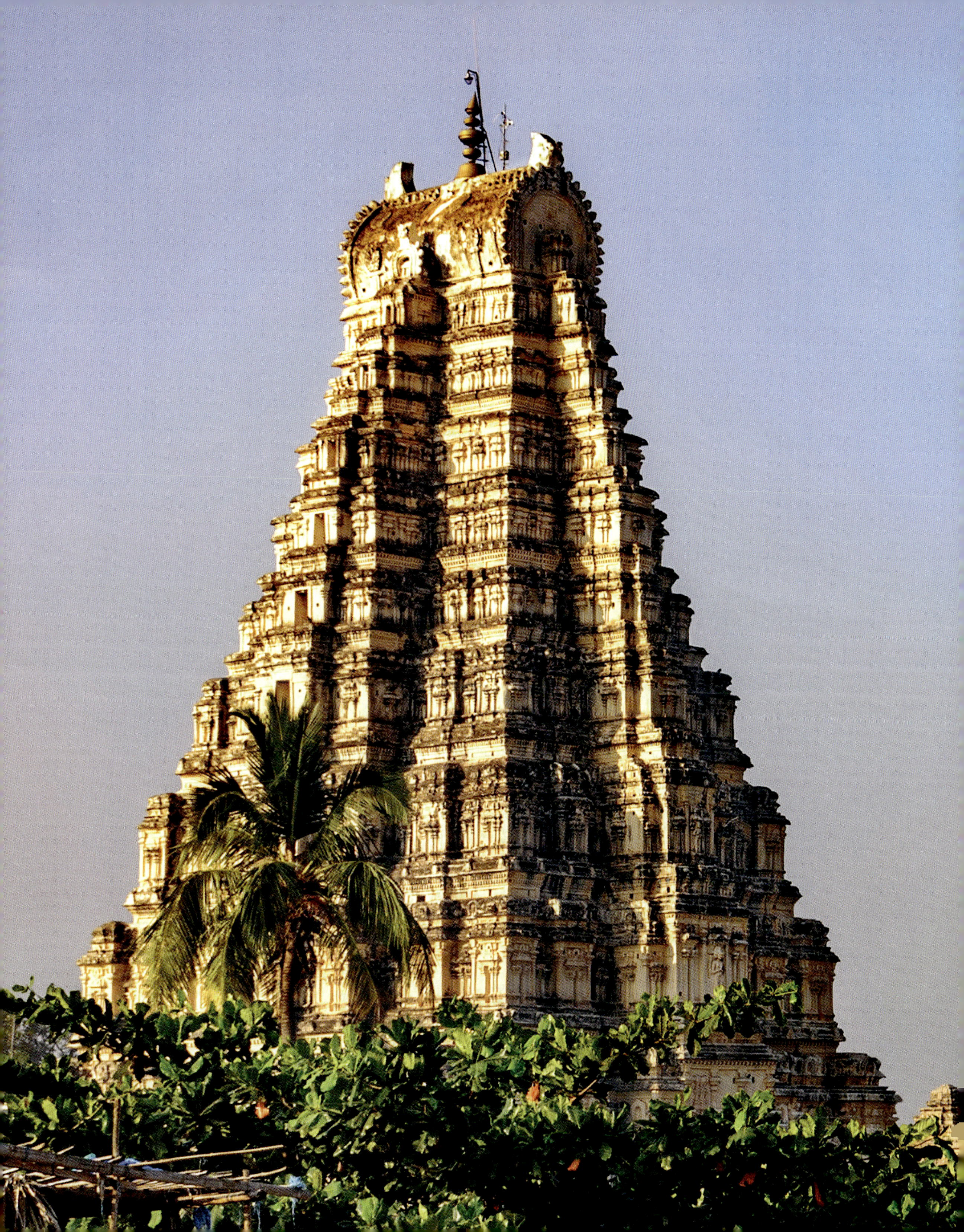

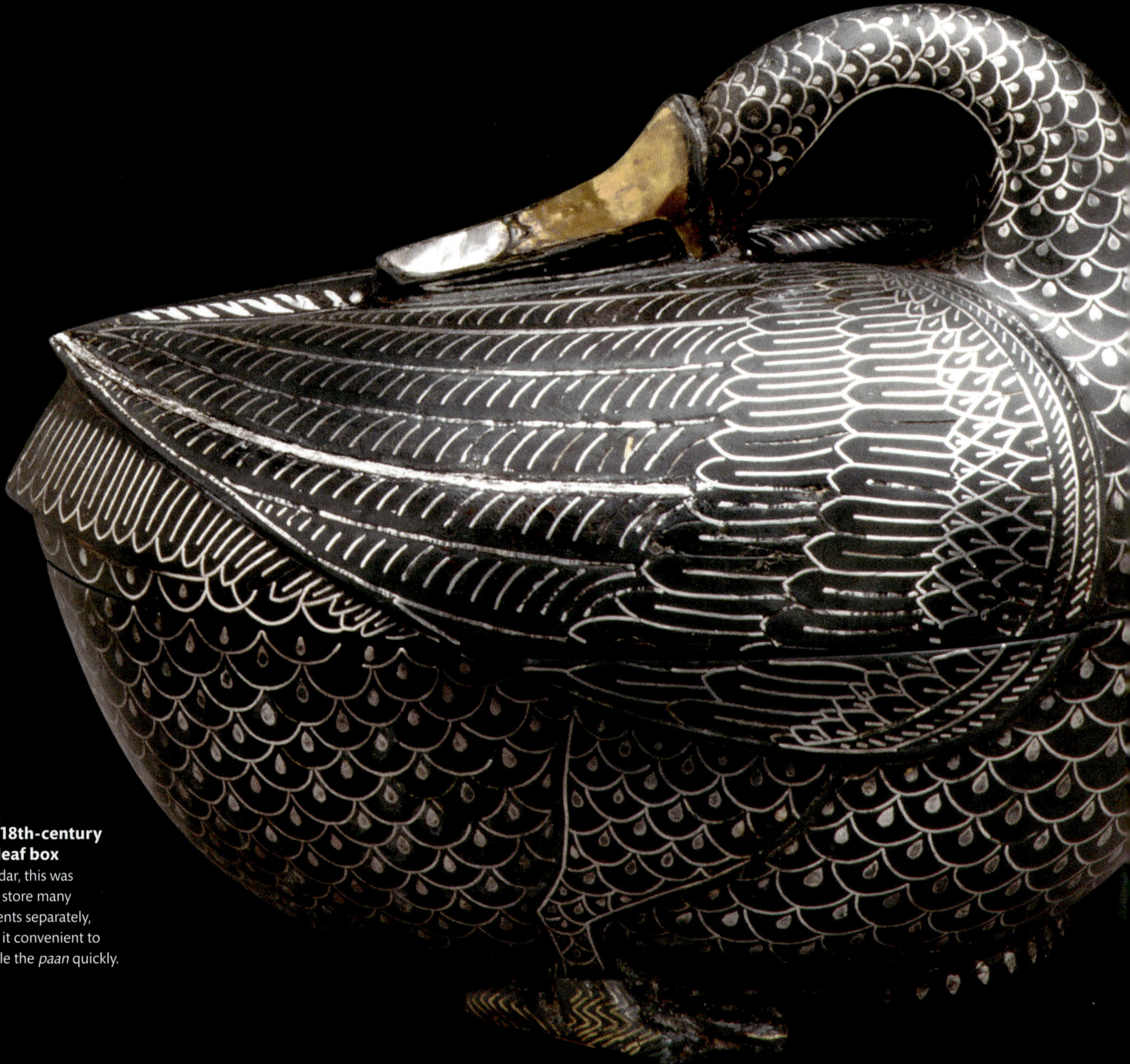

► An 18th-century betel leaf box from Bidar, this was used to store many ingredients separately, making it convenient to assemble the *paan* quickly.

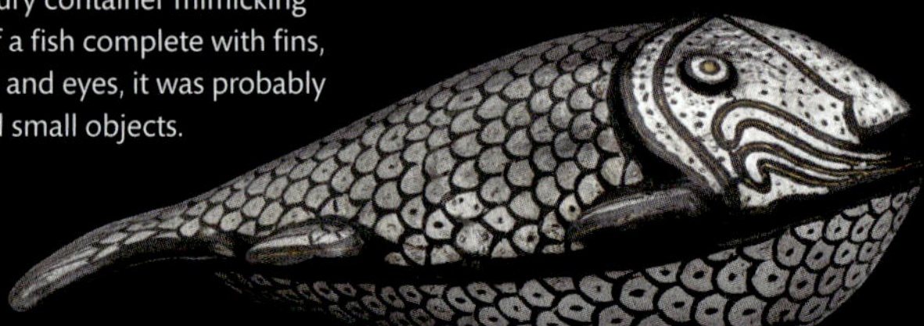

► Fish-shaped box
A 19th-century container mimicking the shape of a fish complete with fins, gills, mouth, and eyes, it was probably used to hold small objects.

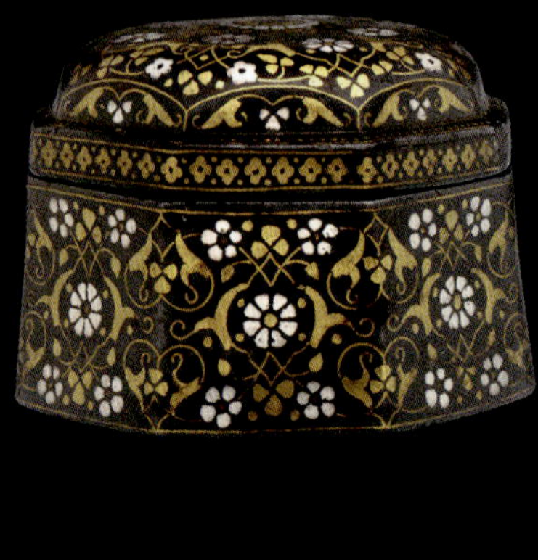

◄ Betel leaf box
An early–mid-17th-century *paandan*, this vessel with several compartments held the ingredients for making a betel quid *(paan)*.

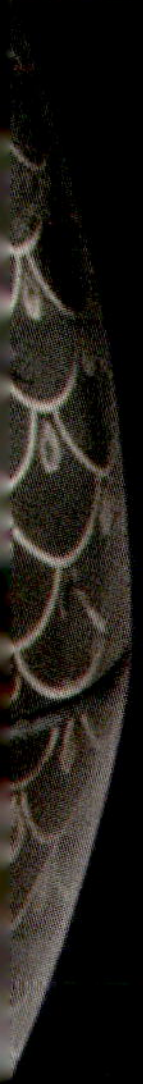

Era 17th century CE | **Medium** Zinc or copper alloy with silver | **Height** 14.3 cm (5.6 in)

BIDRIWARE

Inlaid masterpieces of the Deccan Sultanates

With its origins in Persia and its efflorescence at Bidar, in present-day Karnataka, the stunning craft of Bidri flourished into an iconic art form of the Deccan with the help of royal patronage and excellent craftsmanship in the 17th century.

In Bidri craftsmanship, metals such as silver, gold, or brass are meticulously worked into the design to adorn objects crafted from an alloy of zinc and copper. The striking Bidri box, shaped like slumbering duck (left) may have been influenced by Chinese porcelain objects featuring the same duck motif as they were quite prevalent in the subcontinent during the 18th century. It was once used to store the spices necessary for preparing *paan*, a digestive aid made of betel nut and lime powder.

A MIGRATION OF TECHNIQUES

During the Abbasid era in Persia, inlaid copper objects were a common sight in the palaces of sultans and the homes of merchants. Over time, the popularity of the technique grew, and gold and silver inlay work became widespread. It's possible that craftsmen from Persia migrated to the Deccan region during the rule of the Bahmanis and Baridis, as these dynasties were known for promoting art and learning and attracted talented individuals to their kingdoms. The skill of these artisans resulted in the Bidri craft becoming one of India's most renowned metalcrafts. These works were deeply influenced by traditional Islamic motifs of the era. The swirling silver floral designs bordered by geometric patterns and set against a black background have since become the hallmark of Islamic metalwork in India. Another school of thought suggests that the craft originated from Hindu kings of Bidar, who created items for religious rituals, and it was developed further under the Sultanates.

According to historical accounts, articles gifted to Allauddin II of Bidar during his coronation impressed him that so much that he extended an invitation to the craftsmen to establish themselves in Bidar. He bestowed the moniker of 'Bidari' or 'Bidri' upon the art form, which it continues to be known by. The craft received royal patronage, with craftsmen creating *hookah* (waterpipe), *sailabchi* (basins), *aftaba* (ewer), and *palang-pae* (cot legs) for the palace. The Asaf Jahis or Nizams of Hyderabad, too, held a great appreciation for the Bidri craft and generously supported its creation, commissioning pieces for use in their court and as gifts.

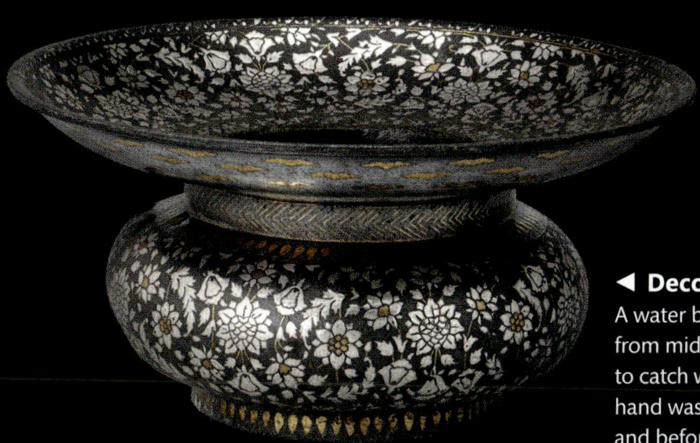

◀ **Decorated basin**
A water basin, or *sailabchi*, from mid-17th century, used to catch water poured during hand washing before prayer and before and after meals.

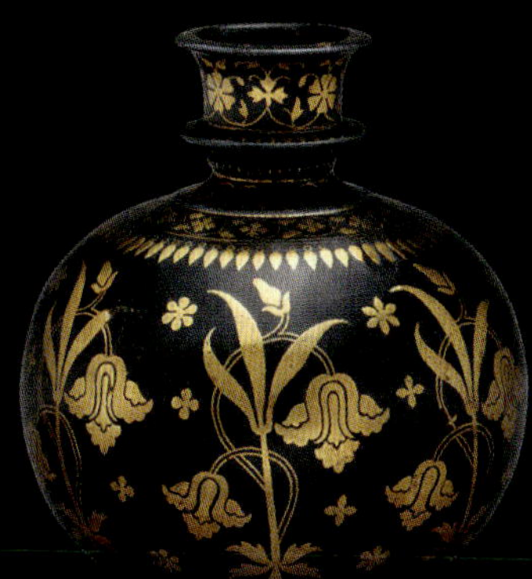

◀ **Waterpipe base**
A late 17th-century globular container used for smoking tobacco with scented water. These were made in large numbers in Bidar.

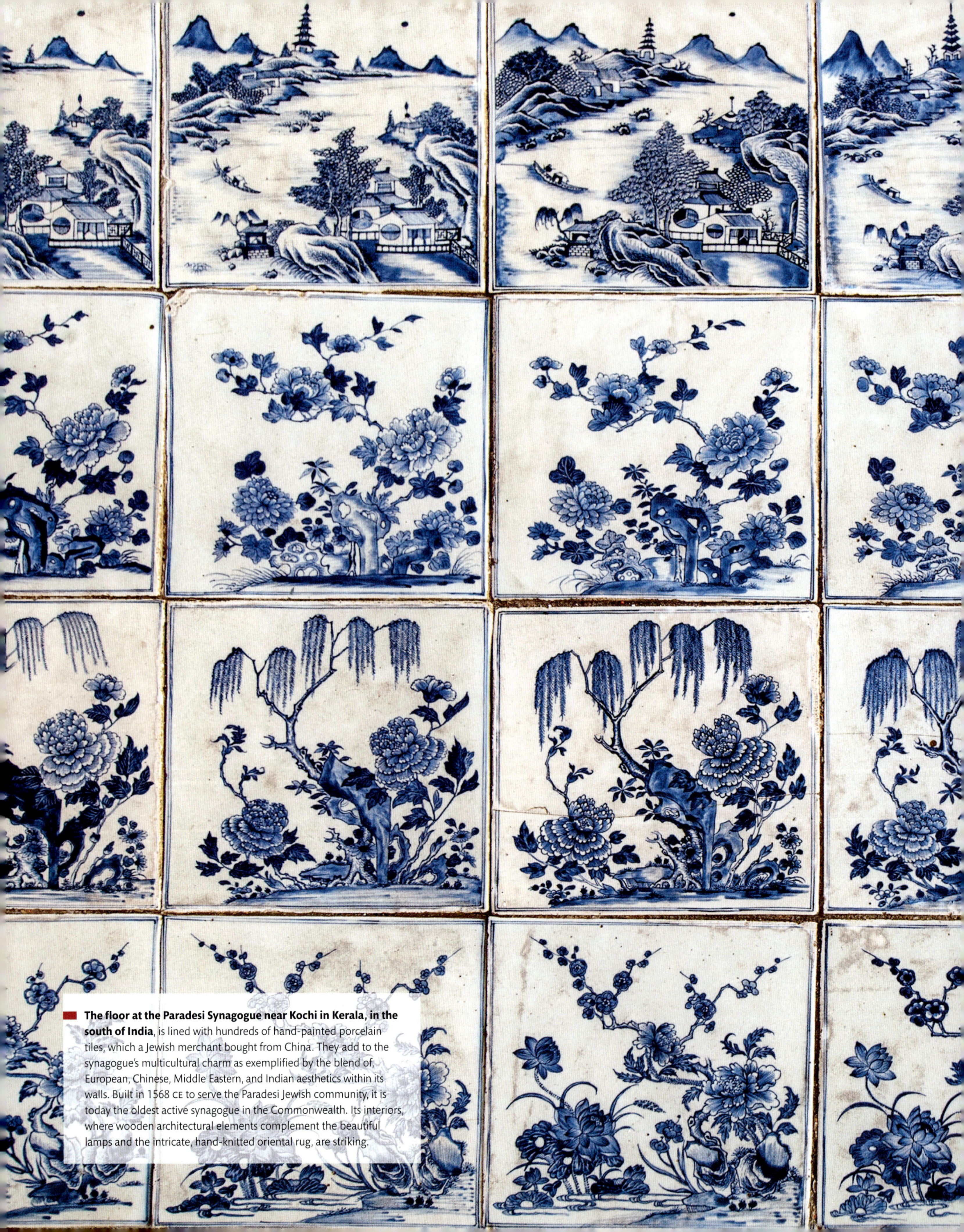

The floor at the Paradesi Synagogue near Kochi in Kerala, in the south of India, is lined with hundreds of hand-painted porcelain tiles, which a Jewish merchant bought from China. They add to the synagogue's multicultural charm as exemplified by the blend of European, Chinese, Middle Eastern, and Indian aesthetics within its walls. Built in 1568 CE to serve the Paradesi Jewish community, it is today the oldest active synagogue in the Commonwealth. Its interiors, where wooden architectural elements complement the beautiful lamps and the intricate, hand-knitted oriental rug, are striking.

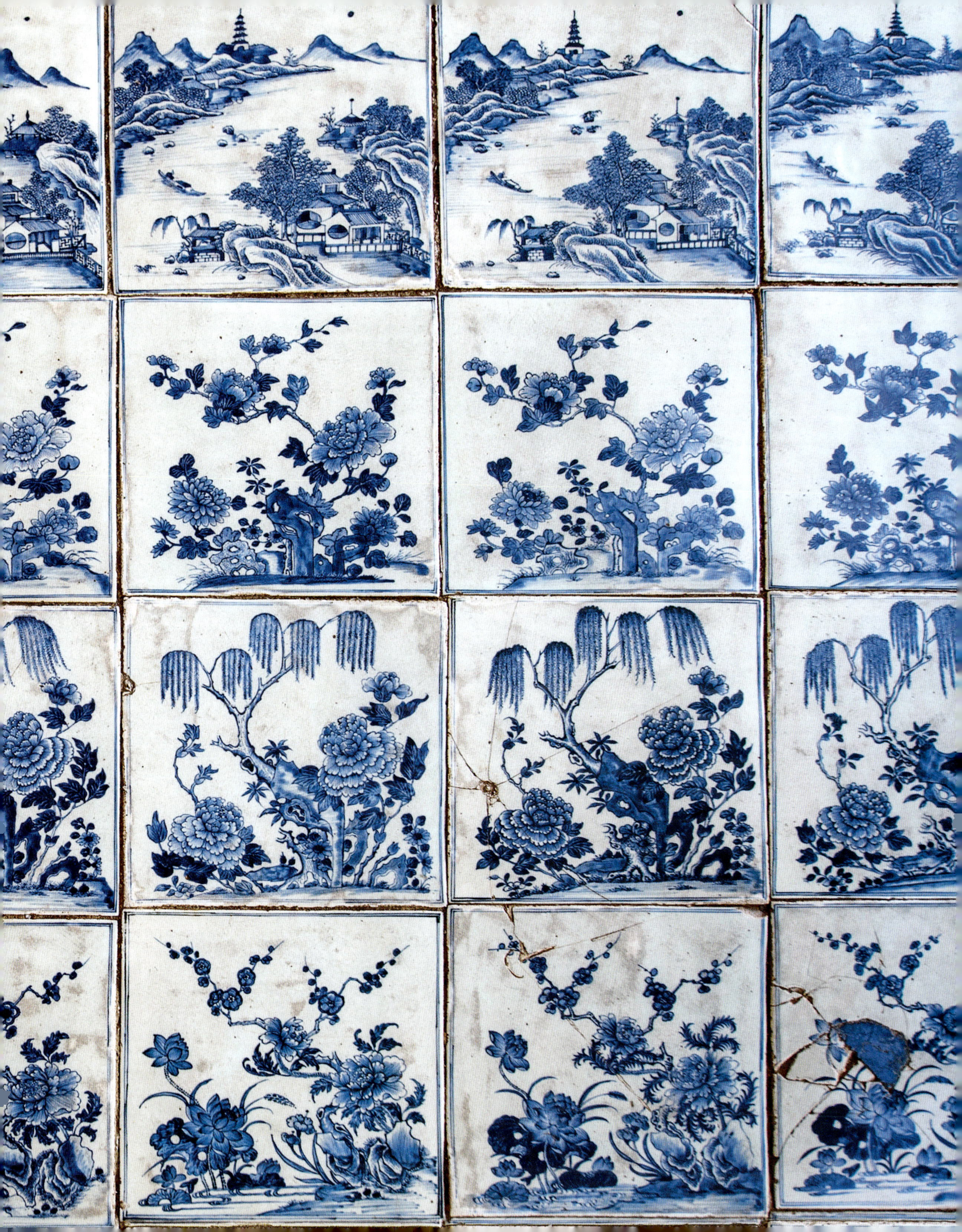

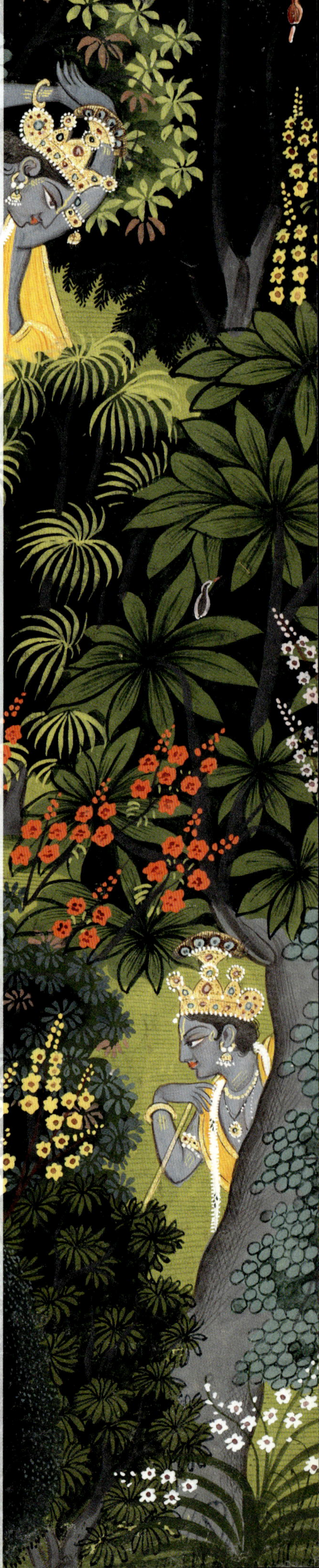

c. 1600–1800 CE

RAJPUT PAINTINGS

The miniature style of painting flourished under the patronage of Rajput kings in western and northern India, which had elements of Persian, Mughal, and European techniques, and aspects of Jain manuscripts and the central Indian Malwa painting style.

In the courts of the Rajput rulers, numerous master artists, schooled in the Mughal miniature style of painting, trained local painters to create various distinct regional styles. Many exceptional ateliers developed in Rajasthan – a style developed – in the kingdoms of Amber, Mewar, Marwar, Kishangarh, Kota, and Bundi. A distinct Rajput style of painting also emerged from smaller courts in the Rajput kingdoms located in the Himalayas, such Kangra, Guler, Basohli, Mankot, Mandi, and Scrota.

Vegetal and mineral pigment colours captured scenes from royal and everyday life, while gold and precious stones enhanced their beauty and value. Artists used extremely fine brushes to achieve hairsbreadth detail such as those on the horses' saddles and their manes.

"[W]hen they [paintings] are enlarged ... they gain in grandeur, and it would be difficult to guess that they had not been designed originally on the large scale."

– Ananda Coomaraswamy, *Rajput Painting*, 1916

DEPICTIONS OF EVERYDAY LIFE AND THE DIVINE

The paintings covered themes ranging from topographic depictions, replete with battle-ready fortifications, royal hunts, and regal equestrian portraits, to narrative scenes from the epics and the Puranas, especially the *Devi Mahatmaya*, a Hindu text translating to "Glory of the Goddess". Allegorical representations of musical ragas and seasons as well as illustrated ballads and heroic poetry were also popular.

Many paintings portray the deity Krishna and his consort Radha in romantic settings. Painters from Kota and other parts of Rajasthan often personified the court nobles as the two divine lovers. The landscape and flora resonated with human emotion, and provided a guide to understanding the prevailing mood of the painting.

► **This painting of a scene from the poem *Gita Govinda*** was made in Kangra, Himanchal Pradesh, in c. 1820–1825. It depicts a restless Krishna waiting for Radha (top right, in yellow), who is busy talking to her confidante. He is shown in different moods and points of time.

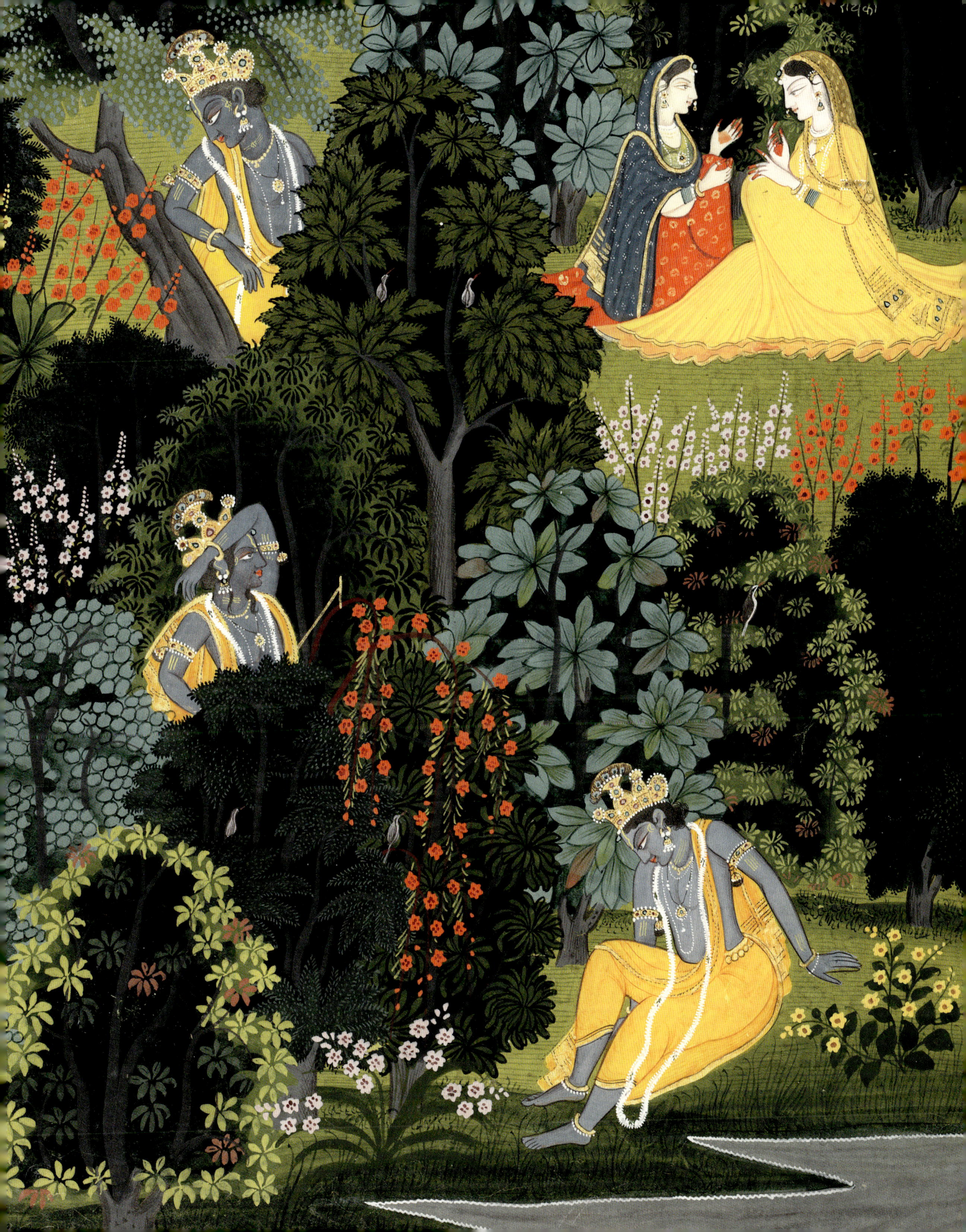

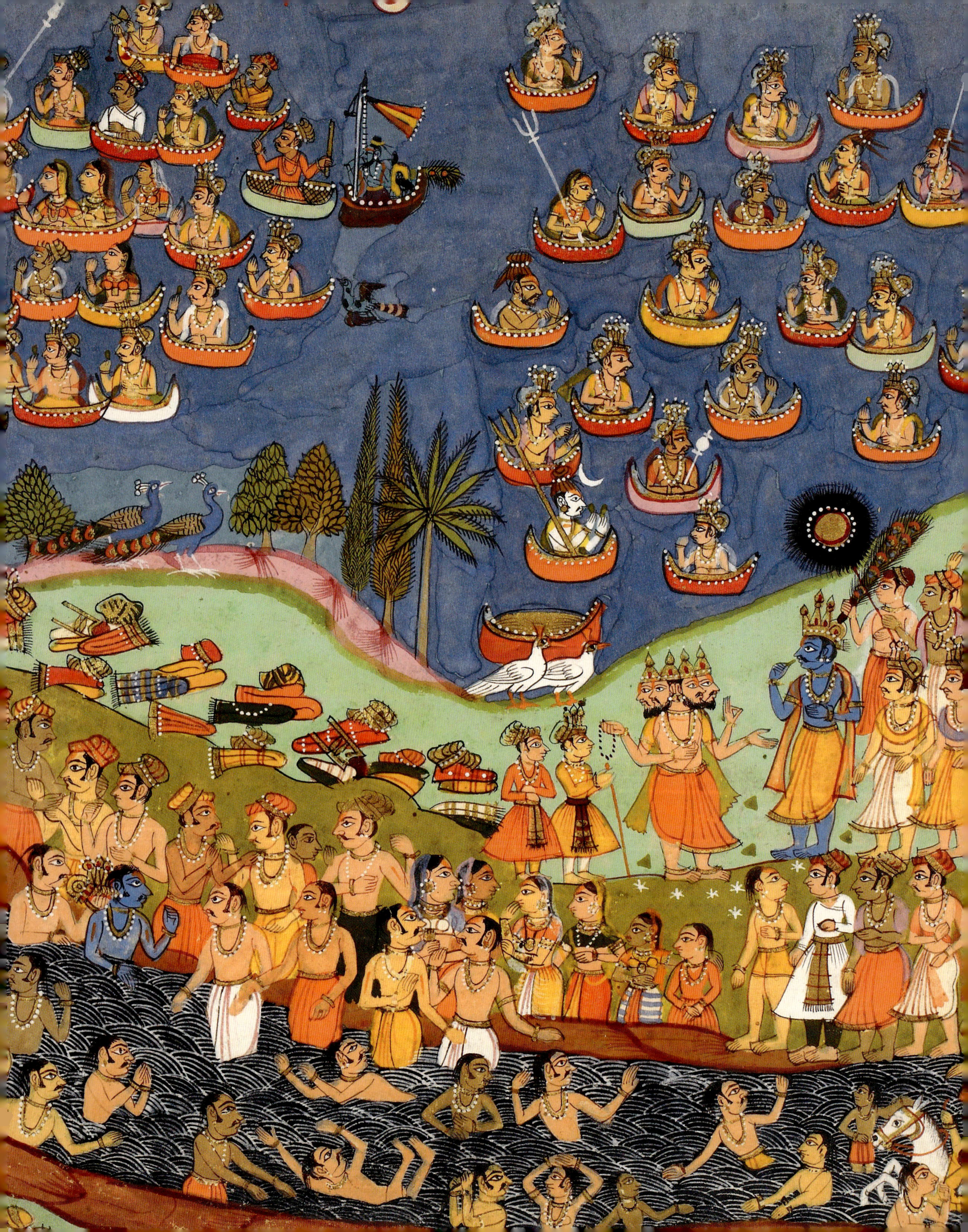

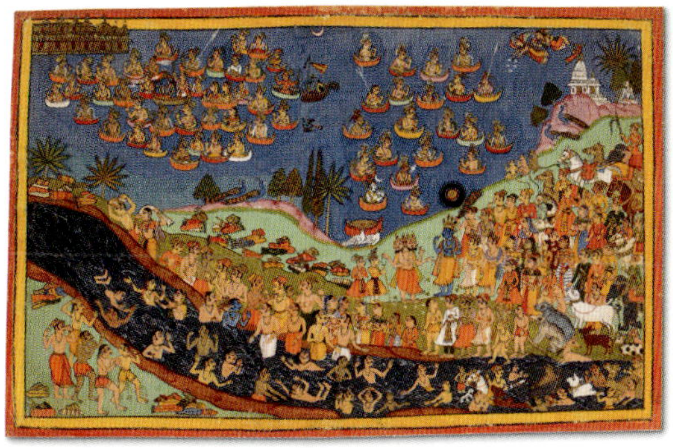

Era 17th century CE | **Medium** Watercolour on paper | **Dimension** 23 × 29 cm (9 × 10.6 in)

JAGAT SINGH'S RAMAYANA

An epic brought to life

Commissioned by Rana Jagat Singh II, the Rajput king of Mewar, this manuscript contains as many as 450 paintings and is one of the most heavily illustrated copies of the great Hindu epic Ramayana.

In 1650, a Hindu ruler from the kingdom of Mewar, in the southern part of present-day Rajasthan, Rana Jagat Singh II commissioned a manuscript of the ancient epic Ramayana (see p. 26). The narrative is about Rama, one of the most widely worshipped Hindu deities in India, and his wife Sita. Told over seven chapters, the story starts with Rama's childhood and tells of his exile, Sita's abduction, and the eventual war with the *asura* king Ravana.

AN ILLUMINATED EPIC

Rana Jagat Singh II's Ramayana is the most heavily illustrated manuscript of the epic. Created for the ruler's personal viewing, it took five years to be completed, from 1648 to 1653. Unfortunately, Rana Jagat Singh II passed away in mid-I652, and it was his son and successor Raj Singh who saw to the actual completion of this magnificent text, also known as Mewar Ramayana. The manuscript was divided into seven volumes, corresponding to the seven chapters of the epic. Featuring over 400 paintings, all but two cover the entire page. The manuscript was illustrated in a way that deviated from the Mughal style of representing every episode in the epic, but stuck to the Rajput format of simultaneous narration where many episodes were covered alongside multiple illustrations.

The paintings, made with the bright primary colours of red, yellow, and blue on thick sheets of burnished paper, feature on one side of the page while the text is on the page facing it. The manuscript was born out of the efforts and close collaboration of the scribe and painters from different communities for a Hindu patron: a single Jain scribe was responsible for all of the text in the manuscript, and at least three master artists and their respective workshops were involved in illustrating the seven volumes. Sahib Din, Jagat Singh's Muslim master artist, was responsible for creating the pages for two of its seven books.

◀ **The last painting in the** manuscript depicts the moment Rama ascends to the celestial realm as all the gods bear witness to the scene.

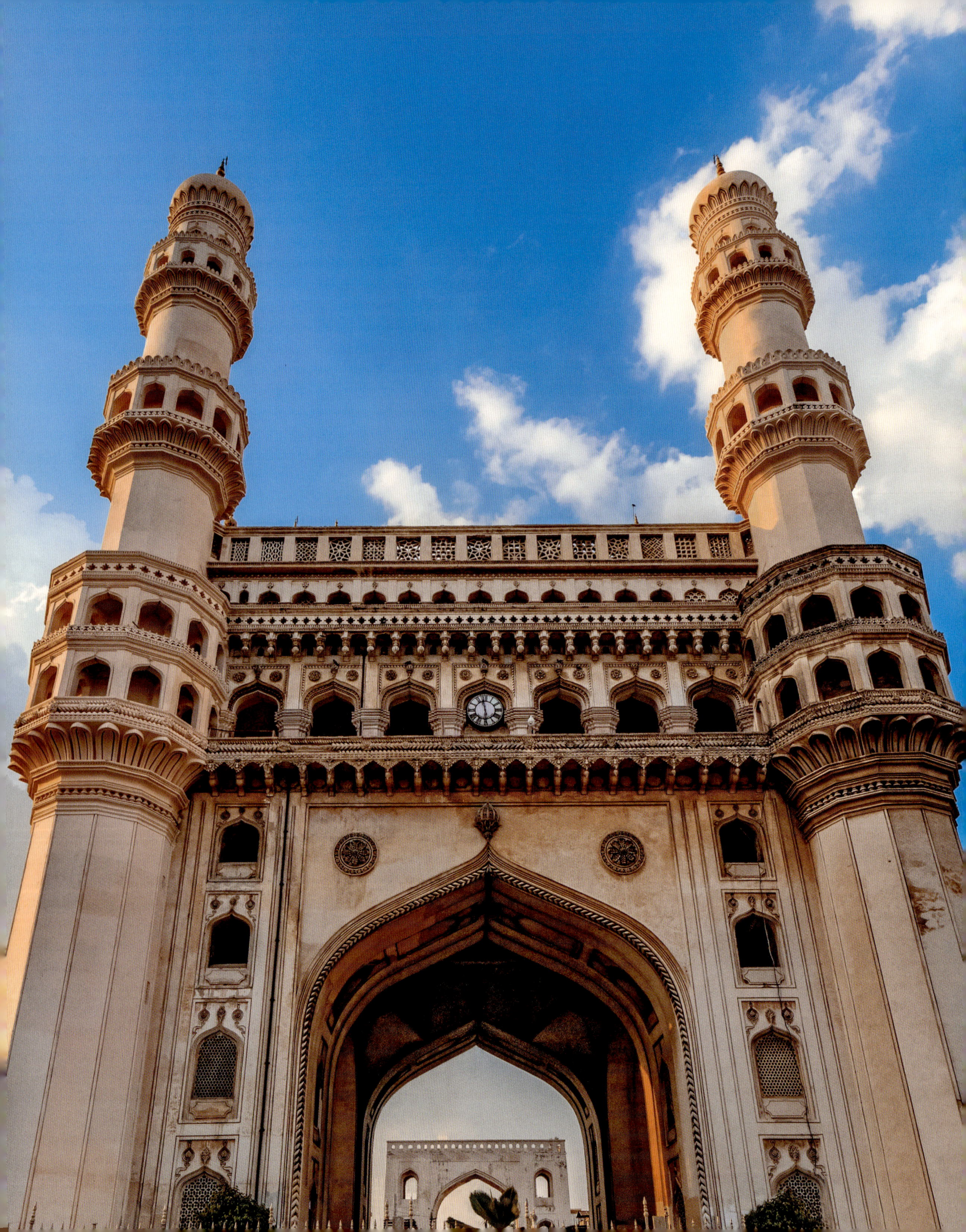

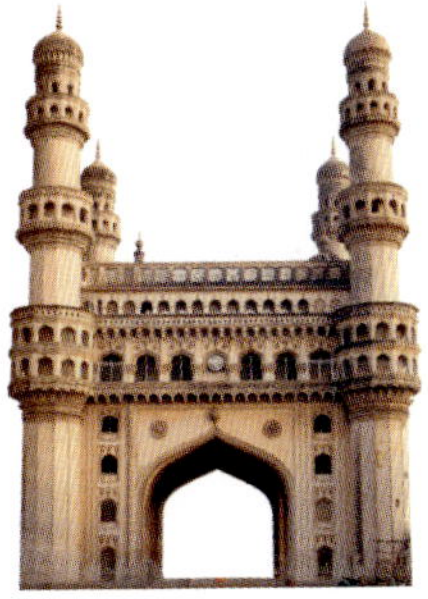

Era 16th century CE | **Medium** Limestone, mortar, granite | **Height** 48.7 m (159.7 ft)

CHARMINAR

Symbol of a dynasty set in limestone

Named after its four tall minarets, the Charminar in Hyderabad, in the southern Indian state of Telangana, is a remarkable monument of the Qutb Shahi dynasty, and stands as a key expression of the Indo-Saracenic style.

Set in the heart of the city of Hyderabad's older sections, Charminar (four towers) is the city's signature landmark. It was built in 1591 by King Muhammad Quli Qutb Shah of the Qutb Shahi dynasty, which boasted of Turkic origins and ruled the sultanate of Golkonda in the Deccan (see pp. 92–97). The structure was designed by Iranian architect Mir Momin Astrabadi and is believed to have been inspired by Shia *tazias*, a type of play that commemorates the death of Hussain, Prophet Mohammed's son-in-law, in the battle of Karbala.

The monument's four open archways each face one of the cardinal directions, while the stucco floral motifs on the ceiling and walls bear a strong Hindu influence. On the corners of the structure, a multi-sided column soars, rising above a lotus-leaf base to a minaret that reaches 48 m (160 ft) above the ground. These minarets are said to represent the first four caliphs of Islam. Each minaret has four levels with superfluous colonnaded, covered walkways around the exterior wall, and is accessed through a spiral staircase on its interior wall. Two stories rise above the main building's arches. The first housed a *madrasa* (Islamic college) during the Qutb Shahi era, and the second a small mosque, believed to be the oldest mosque of Hyderabad city. The Charminar also has 45 other prayer areas.

◄ **Grand arches frame the four** corners of the colossal monument built in Hyderabad in the south of India in 1591. Details in stucco accentuate its features.

PURPOSE OF THE MONUMENT

According to a story often told around the monument's construction states that the Charminar was built in 1591 as a symbol of gratitude for the cessation of a tragic plague that had swept through the city, afflicting thousands of people. Another theory-turned-local-folklore claims that the Charminar marks the spot where the Qutb Shahi king witnessed his eventual lover, the Hindu dancer Bhagmati, for the first time. There are multiple other theories that posit their own reasons, but the real purpose behind its construction remains a mystery, which only adds to the charm and awe that surrounds this majestic monument.

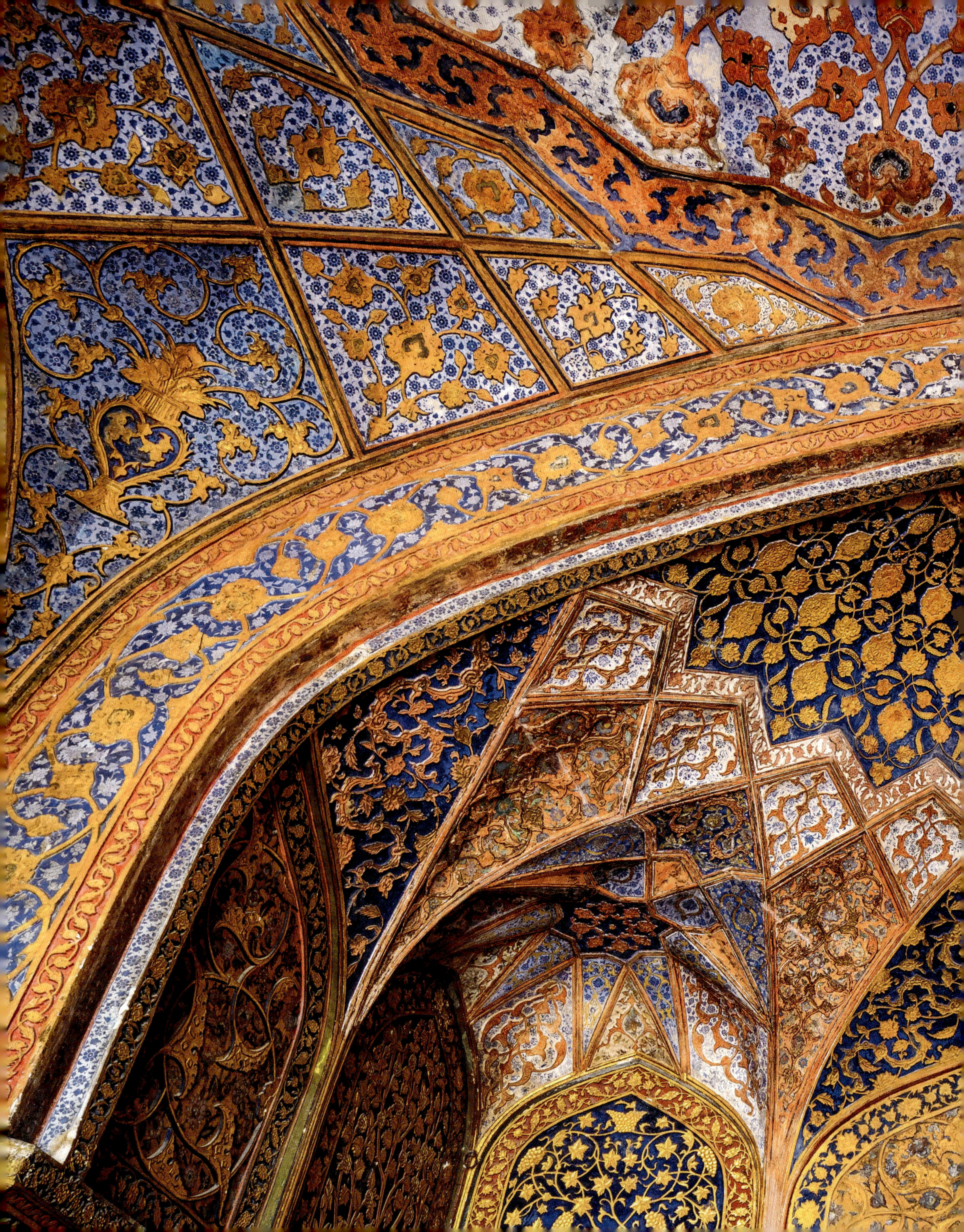

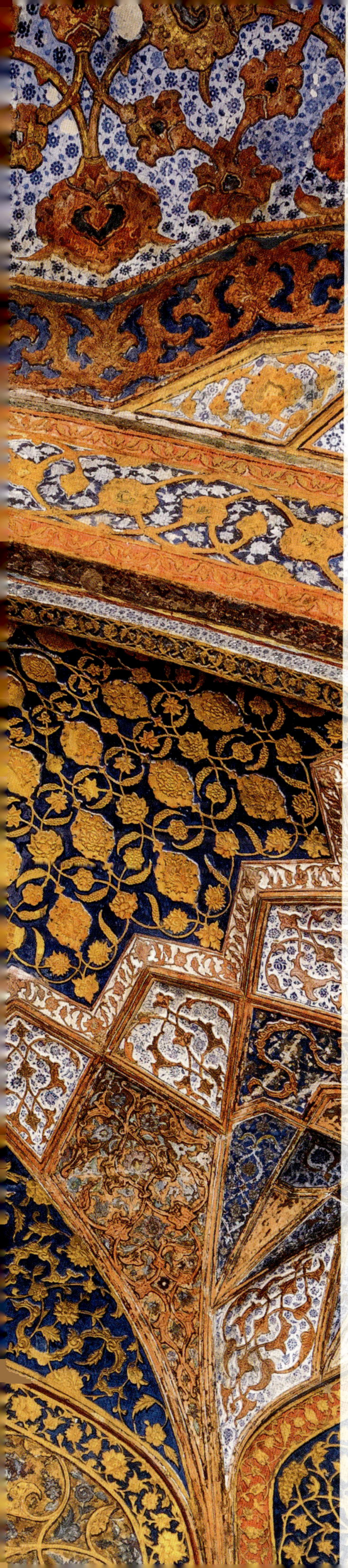

c.13th–18th centuries CE

INDO-ISLAMIC ARCHITECTURE

A unique blend of Islamic, Persian, Turkish, and Indian styles, Indo–Islamic architecture began with the Central Asian invasions of India and flourished during the time of the Delhi Sultanate and the Mughal Empire.

Beginning in the 7th and 8th centuries CE, Islamic and Central Asian influences made their way to the Indian subcontinent through the migration of Muslim merchants, traders, holy men, and conquerors. This was also characterized by the absorption of local cultural and traditional elements into Islamic practices, resulting in, among other things, the creation of an architectural style known as Indo-Islamic architecture. This was a syncretic style of structural techniques, shapes, and elements, reflecting the dynamic process of acceptance, rejection, and modification.

"[The Taj Mahal is not] a piece of architecture, as other buildings are, but the proud passions of an emperor's love wrought in living stones."

– Sir Edwin Arnold, 19th-century English poet and journalist

INFLUENCES ON THE STYLE

With the establishment of the Delhi Sultanate in the early 13th century, further and perhaps more substantial building efforts took place. The architecture of the Mamluk, Khilji, and Tughlaq dynasties (see pp. 92–97) followed, highlighted by pointed arches, domes, minarets, and ornate motifs. Teachings from the Qur'an and floral patterns are evident in the arches, while Hindu motifs such as the swastika, lotus, and bells contribute to the grandeur and beauty of the palaces. These embellishments, along with calligraphy, geometric patterns, and arabesque, give the structures a striking and unique appearance. An exceptional representation of this is the Qutub Minar (see pp. 142–143).

The tradition continued to thrive during the Mughal Empire. Emperors, particularly Shah Jahan, were patrons of art and architecture, resulting in the construction of grand and awe-inspiring monuments, palaces, forts, mosques, and tombs. Key features such symmetrical designs, bulbous domes, expansive halls, grand gateways, elegant minarets, and intricate embellishments are evident in sites such as Humanyun's Tomb (see pp. 164–165), Taj Mahal (see pp. 182–183), and Shalimar Bagh (see pp. 186–187).

◄ **Ceiling and archway at the tomb of Emperor** Akbar constructed in 1605–1613 by his son Jahangir. It is located in Sikandra in Agra, in the northern state of Uttar Pradesh.

THE EXPANSION OF AN EMPIRE

Of imperial grandeur, pageantry, and high culture

At its zenith, the Mughal Empire encompassed almost the entire Indian subcontinent. During its rule of more than three centuries, strategic conquests helped in expansion and facilitated a transformation in the arts of painting and architecture.

Zahiruddin Muhammad Babur, a descendant of Timur and Genghis Khan, came to India in search of a kingdom. Dispossessed of Fergana, his ancestral principality, he made four attempts to capture the Delhi Sultanate before defeating Ibrahim Lodhi in the First Battle of Panipat in 1526 CE. This battle, won with superior artillery (cannons were used for the first time in India), marks the beginning of Mughal rule.

One of the first autobiographies in the world, the eponymous *Baburnama*, chronicles Babur's exploits and his struggles to establish a stable kingdom. He faced threats from the Afghans in the east, and Malwa, Gujarat, and Mewar in the south. He surmounted these challenges, but died before he could stabilize his dominion.

Babur's successor, Humayun inherited a shaky kingdom threatened by the Afghans, the Rajputs, and his own brothers. Lacking Babur's military genius, he was defeated by the Afghan soldier Sher Shah Sur in the battles of Chausa and Kannauj between 1539–1540 CE. A fugitive in his own land, Humayun took refuge in the court of the Safavid Shah of Persia.

Sher Shah established his kingdom, the Suri Empire, in 1539 CE. He systematized revenue collection and introduced a coinage system that is followed even today (silver coins were called *rupiya* and copper coins were called *paisa*). Sher Shah died while besieging the fortress city of Kalinjar in 1545 CE. After him, his dynasty, riven by

1494 Babur inherits Fergana

1504–1526 Babur rules in Kabul

1526–1530 Babur wins the battle in Panipat and invades northern parts of the Indian subcontinent

1530–1540 Humayun's first reign ends with him being driven from India

1540–1545 Sher Shah Suri establishes his rule in the north

1555–1556 Humayun's reconquest and second reign in Indian subcontinent

1556–1605 Reign of Akbar

1566 Creation of new land revenue system

1571–1585 Fatehpur Sikri is chosen as the new capital

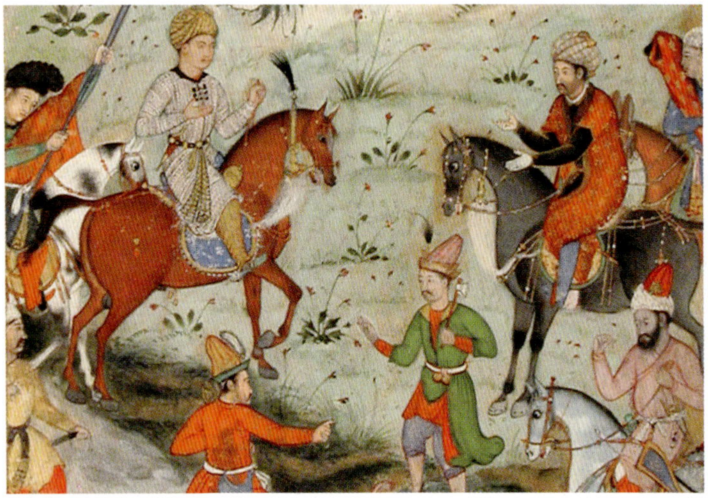

A folio from *Baburnama* depicting a meeting between Babur (left) and his cousin Ali Mirza (right), also a Timurid ruler, near Samarqand in Central Asia. The watercolour folio dates to c. 1590.

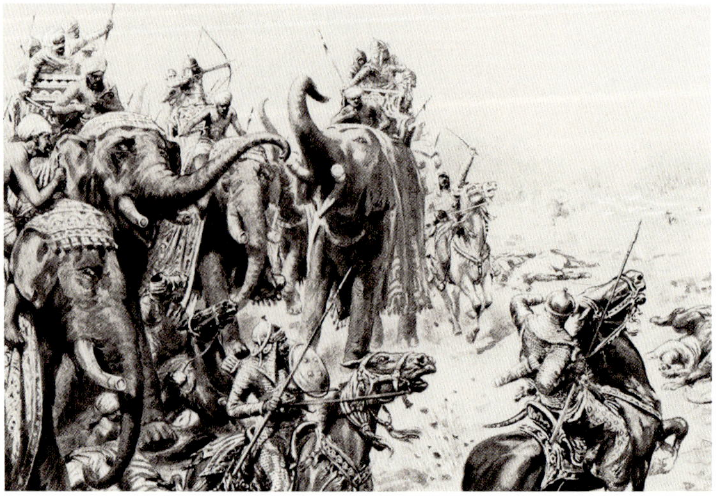

An illustration from *Hutchinson's History of the Nations*, published in 1915, depicts troops during the Battle of Panipat. This was created possibly after a painting by artist Ambrose Dudley (1867–1951).

factionalism, lasted a mere decade. Meanwhile, with the support of the Shah of Persia's forces, Humayun launched a campaign to regain his empire. He defeated Sher Shah's descendant Sikandar Shah in 1555 CE and reclaimed the throne.

CONSOLIDATION AND EXPANSION

Humayun's accidental death in 1556 CE brought his teenage son Akbar to the throne. Initially, Humayun's general Bairam Khan acted as Akbar's regent. Around this time, the Suri general Hemu captured Agra and Delhi. This led to the Second Battle of Panipat in 1556 CE between Hemu's army and Akbar's forces led by Bairam Khan. The latter's victory consolidated Mughal power, enabling Akbar to establish a strong and stable regime in the region.

Often dubbed the greatest Mughal, Akbar expanded his empire through military conquests and political alliances. His empire extended from Afghanistan to the Bay of Bengal, including Gujarat and the northern Deccan. A shrewd strategist, he ensured support from powerful Rajput clans by forging matrimonial alliances with them. He also employed Rajputs in key posts in his court. He abolished *jizya*, a tax on non-Muslims, and propounded Din-i-Ilahi, a syncretic faith that combined elements of

1571–1585 Fatehpur Sikri is chosen as the new capital

1574 Creation of the *jagirdar-mansabdar* system

1579 Circulation of a document recognizing Akbar's religious authority

1605–1627 Reign of Jahangir

1611 Rise of Nur Jahan

1628–1658 Reign of Emperor Shah Jahan

1636 Treaty of submission signed by Golkonda and Bijapur states

1638 The Taj Mahal is inaugurated

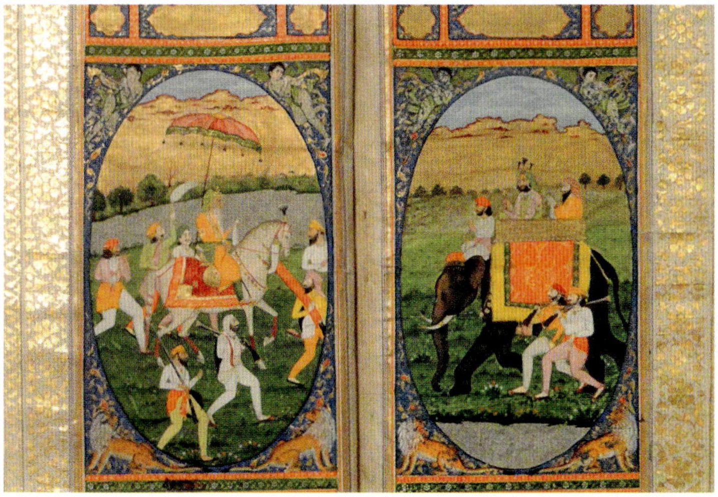

Pages from the *Ain-i-Akbari*, or the Chronicles of Akbar, completed in c. 1822 CE, possibly in Lahore, now in Pakistan. The folio is located at the Royal Ontario Museum in Canada.

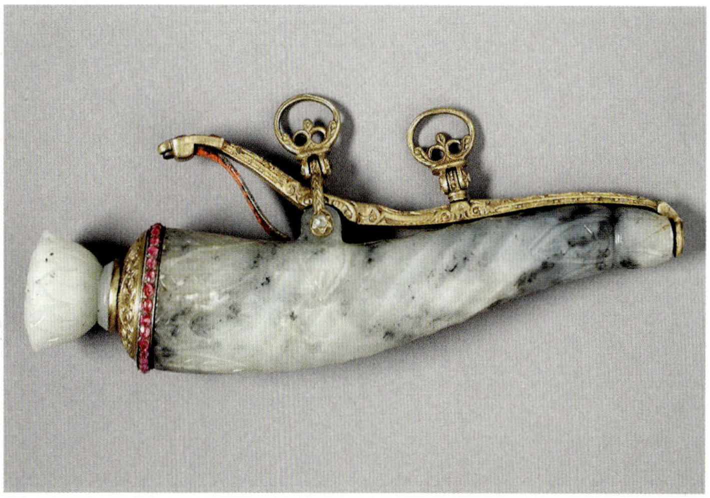

A Mughal primer flask, c. 1700–25 CE, for dispensing gunpowder. This flask is made of grey nephrite jade, and is inlaid with red spinels and clear gemstones set in gold, with gilt copper alloy fittings.

major religions. Though his tolerant religious policy was born out of pragmatism and political expediency, he was genuinely interested in learning about different religions. The nine 'gems' of his court included his trusted adviser Birbal, the legendary singer Tansen, and the chronicler Abul Fazl, whose *Akbarnama* is the chief source of information on his reign.

Akbar's son Jahangir succeeded him in 1607 CE. Jahangir continued his father's policy of conquest, forcing the Deccan rulers to accept his suzerainty. The English East India Company set up operations in India during his rule. Several records of Jahangir's reign mention his dependence on alcohol and opium, and highlight the dominance of his favourite wife Nur Jahan, who was often portrayed as the de facto emperor. She struck coins in her own name and reviewed key imperial documents. Her powerful position antagonized Jahangir's third son Shah Jahan and sparked a violent war of succession after Jahangir's death.

Shah Jahan ascended the throne in 1628 CE. He was an able military commander, noted for his successful Deccan campaigns. He annexed the deccan and created the sultanate of Ahmadnagar and made states of Bijapur and Golconda Mughal tributaries. However, his military achievements were eclipsed by his artistic and architectural legacy, which included the bejewelled Peacock Throne, and the Red Fort and Jama Masjid in Delhi. The Taj Mahal, a memorial for his beloved wife Mumtaz Mahal in Agra, and a UNESCO World Heritage Site, is the best known of his monuments.

FLASHPOINT: AN INTOLERANT REGIME

Shah Jahan's illness in 1657 CE led to a bloody war of succession among his four sons, despite him bequeathing the throne to his eldest son Dara Shikoh. Aurangzeb, his third son, emerged victorious, defeating Dara Shikoh at the Battle of Samugarh and imprisoning his father in the Agra Fort.

The last of the great Mughal emperors, Aurangzeb declared himself the Indian emperor in 1658 CE. He was beset by challenges from the Marathas in the Deccan led by Shivaji, the Jats, and the Rajputs. The Sikhs rebelled after he executed Guru Tegh Bahadur for interceding on behalf of persecuted Kashmiri pandits. Aurangzeb overcame these challenges and went on to conquer Bijapur and Golconda. During his reign, the Mughal Empire was at the height of its political and economic power, extending from Kashmir in the north to Jinji in the south, and from the Hindukush in the west to Chittagong in the east. Much of the east had been ruled by the

1639 Shahjahanabad is chosen as the new capital

1658–1666 Shah Jahan is imprisoned by Aurangzeb

1658–1707 Reign of "Alamgir" Aurangzeb

1664, 1670 The Maratha chief Shivaji captures Surat

1662–1682 Mughal-Ahom conflict increases in the east

1707–1712 Reign of Bahadur Shah

1713 Reign of Jahandar Shah

1719 Reign of Rafi-ud-Darjat

1719 Shah Jahan II ascends to the throne

1719–1748 Muhammad Shah takes over the rule

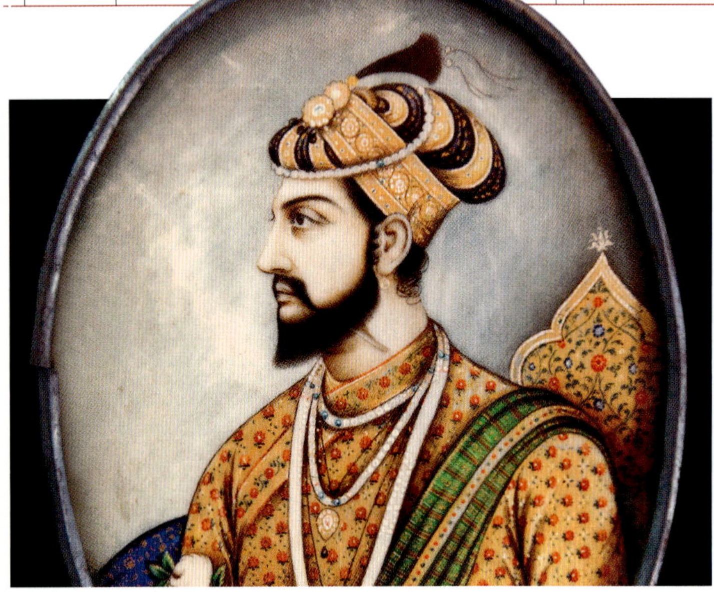

A painting of Shah Jahan, who built the Taj Mahal, a mausoleum, in Agra. Though the date is unknown, this style of miniature painting was popular in the 16th–18th centuries.

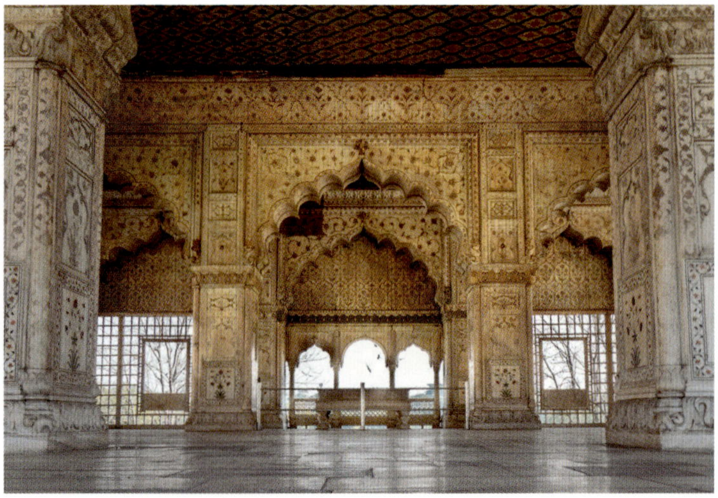

Carved details inside the Rang Mahal, a grand hall within the Red Fort complex in the capital city of Delhi, India. It was commissioned by Shah Jahan in 1638, and is today, a UNESCO World Heritage Site.

Ahoms, who attempted to drive the Mughals out of Guwahati and the surrounding region in 1667 in order to fully impose their dominance in the Brahmaputra Valley, which marked the beginning of the conflict with Aurangzeb.

However, Emperor Aurangzeb made the Mughal empire a sharia state, bound by the laws of Islam. He proscribed alcohol, singing, and dancing. As the state treasury was depleted by the previous rulers, he reimposed the *jizya* tax, which alienated most of his non-Muslim subjects. He restricted the construction of non-Muslim places of worship and destroyed several of them. Aurangzeb's death in 1707 CE marked the beginning of the end for the Mughal Empire.

THE DECLINE

The gradual disintegration of the Mughal dynasty after Aurangzeb was due to several factors: his religious policy, weak successors, the revolt of fractious nobles, the draining of the royal treasury due to endless wars, and disaffection within the Mughal army and administration. The Marathas, the Rajputs, the Jats, and the Sikhs were also a constant threat. Raids from the north-west frontiers exacerbated the situation. The Iranian conqueror Nadir Shah invaded India in 1739 CE, capturing key Mughal cities and occupying the capital city of Delhi. He looted Mughal treasures, including the Peacock Throne and the famous Koh-i-Noor diamond. After him, the Afghan ruler Ahmad Shah Abdali invaded the subcontinent seven times between 1747 CE and 1769 CE, plundering major cities. The growing economic power and military might of the European trading powers also impacted the enfeebled Mughal Empire.

THE LAST EMPEROR

Bahadur Shah Zafar was the Mughal emperor during the Revolt of 1857 CE but he was one in name only. The once-mighty Mughal Empire was now reduced to the walled city of Delhi and a few surrounding areas. Bahadur Shah preferred poetry and music to ruling. His court hosted several Urdu poets, including Mirza Ghalib and Zauq.

During the revolt, also termed as the sepoy mutiny or the first war for Indian independence by historians, rebel troops from Meerut seized Delhi and declared the reluctant emperor their leader. After the British army recaptured Delhi, he was tried for treason and exiled to Rangoon, Myanmar, where he died in 1862 CE. His death signalled the formal end of Mughal rule.

1739 Invasion of Nadir Shah

1747 Invasions by Ahmad Shah Durrani begin

1760 Battle of Panipat

1748–1754 Ahmad Shah's reign

1754–1759 Alamgir II's reign

1759–1806 Shah Alam II's reign

1803 British conquest of Delhi and establishment of its resident political agent

1806–1837 Akbar II's reign

1837–1857 Bahadur Shah II's reign

1857 Sepoy mutiny

1862 Bahadur Shah II dies in exile in Burma (now Myanmar)

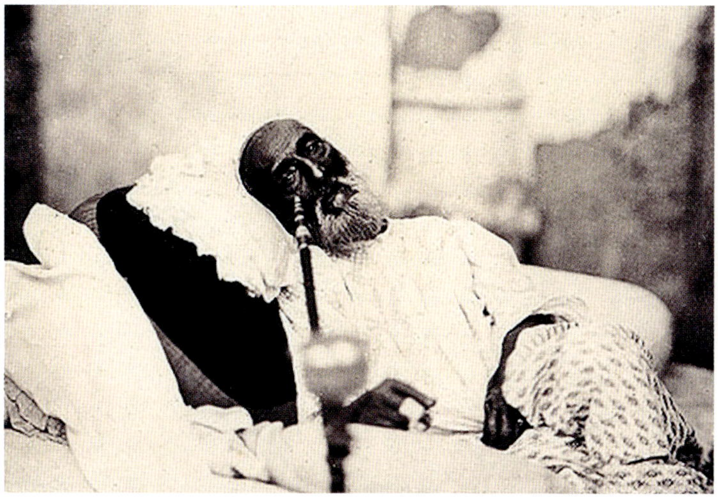

A photograph of an ageing Bahadur Shah Zafar, the last Mughal emperor to rule India before he was exiled to Rangoon in Burma (now Myanmar) by the British rulers of India.

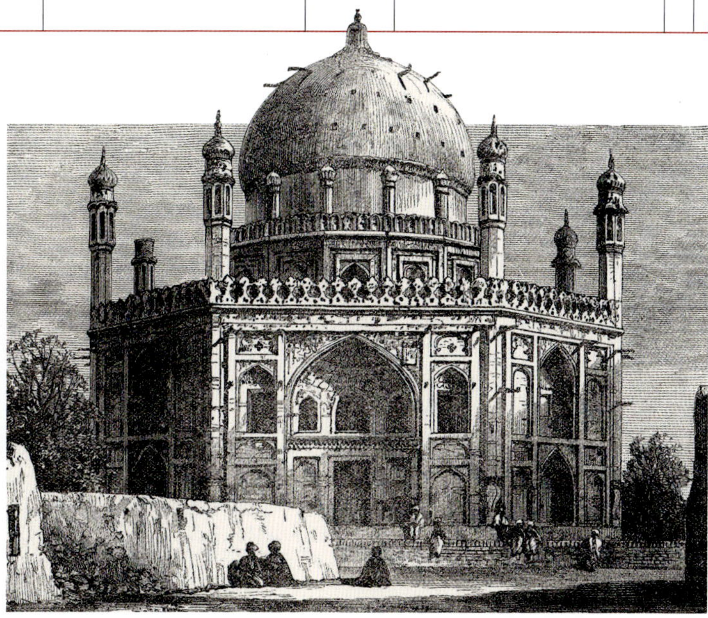

Illustration from *British Battles on Land and Sea* (James Grant) by an unknown artist depicting the tomb of Ahmad Shah Durrani in Old Kandahar, a city in Afghanistan, c. 19th century CE.

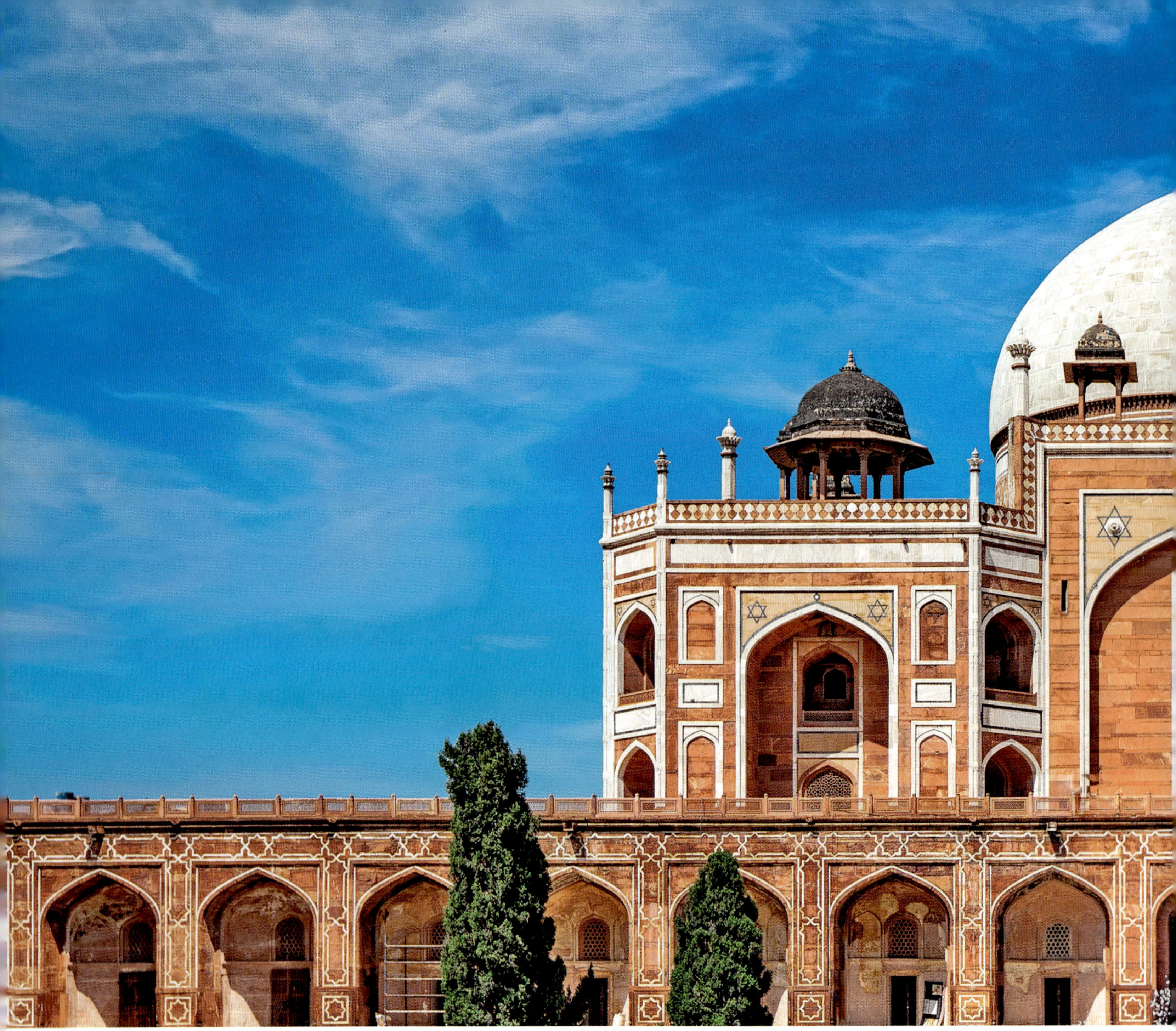

Era 1572 | **Medium** Red sandstone and marble | **Dimension** 47 × 91 m (154.1 × 298.5 ft)

HUMAYUN'S TOMB

Fountainhead of a new architectural style

As the first of the monumental dynastic mausoleums that came to be identified with the Mughal architectural style, Humayun's tomb is one of the most significant buildings in the Indian subcontinent.

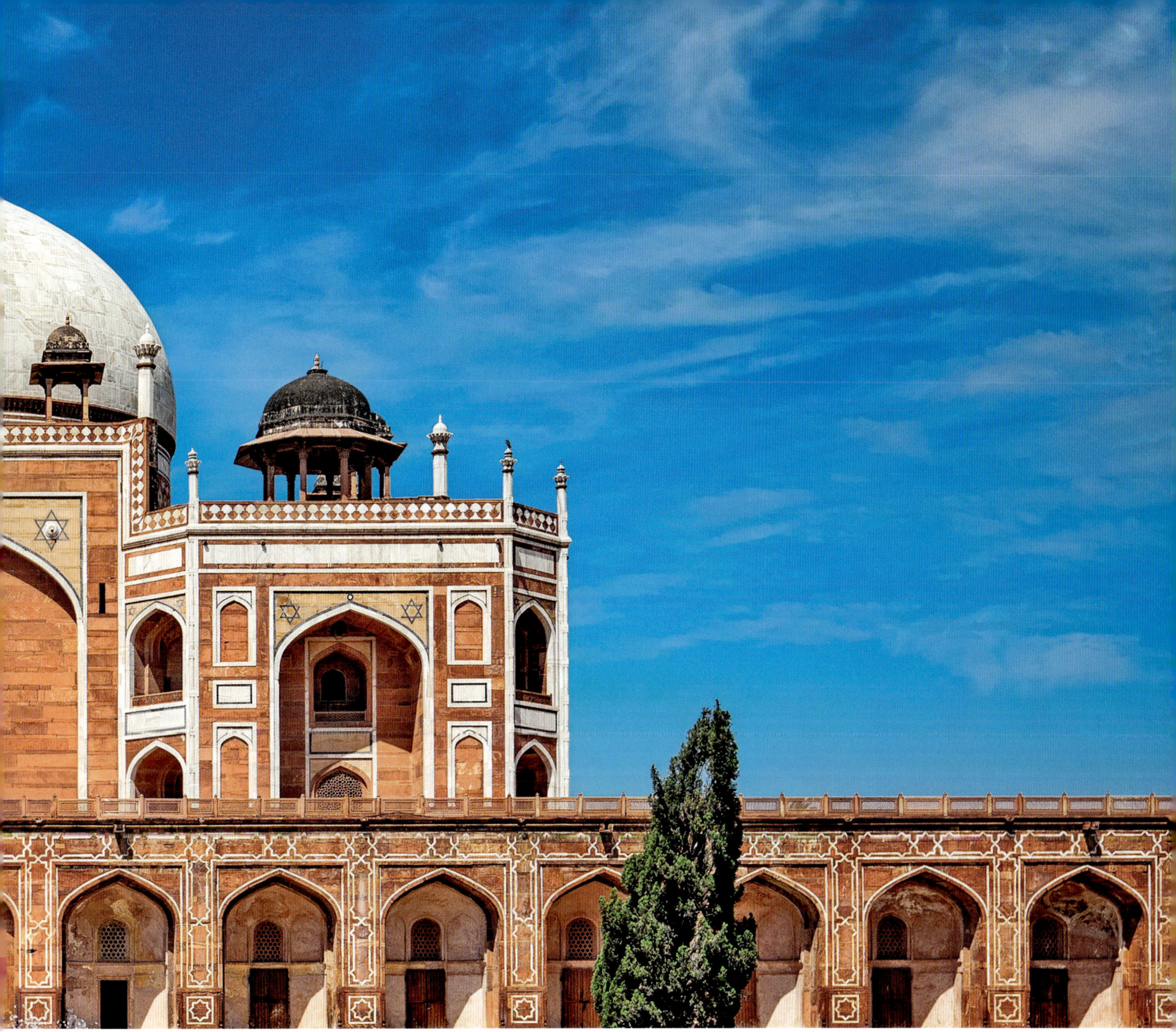

The red sandstone mausoleum sits on a high, terraced platform set within the Persian-styled *charbagh*, or four gardens, in the Indian capital of Delhi. Created by dividing the site into four parts using walkways or water channels, the plan is said to resemble the garden of paradise as described in the Qur'an. The whole is further divided into 36 smaller squares and the mausoleum situated in the four central ones reflect the perfect symmetry of the gardens. The large, double-storeyed, octagonal interior chamber is topped with a 42.5-m (139-ft) high, marble-clad double dome, also Persian in origin. The pillared structures on the four corners, however, are modelled on the *chhatris* (pavilions) typical in north Indian architecture.

A SYMBOL OF MIGHT

Said to have been commissioned in 1565 by Hamida Banu Begum, the widow of Mughal emperor Humayun, the tomb and the complex were designed by architect Mirak Mirza Ghiyas of Persia. The style of the complex, however, is a mix of Persian and Indian traditions. It was the first garden-tomb in the Indian subcontinent, bearing a resemblance to the Mughal ancestor Timur's tomb in Uzbekistan. It inspired several architectural innovations, and the Taj Mahal in Agra, in northern India, built nearly 70 years later, is the culmination of this expression. In modern times, colonial architect Edward Lutyens was so inspired by the tomb's garden layout that he recreated it when designing the Viceregal Palace – now Rashtrapati Bhavan.

Era 16th–19th centuries CE | **Medium** Ivory or cardboard | **Diameter** 7.2 cm (2.8 in)

GANJIFA

Recreational suits decked in varied styles

An exquisite insight into one of Mughal royalty's favourite pasttimes, and subsequently the populace, this ancient game of playing cards was imported from Persia in the 16th century and later emerged in different parts of the subcontinent in various forms.

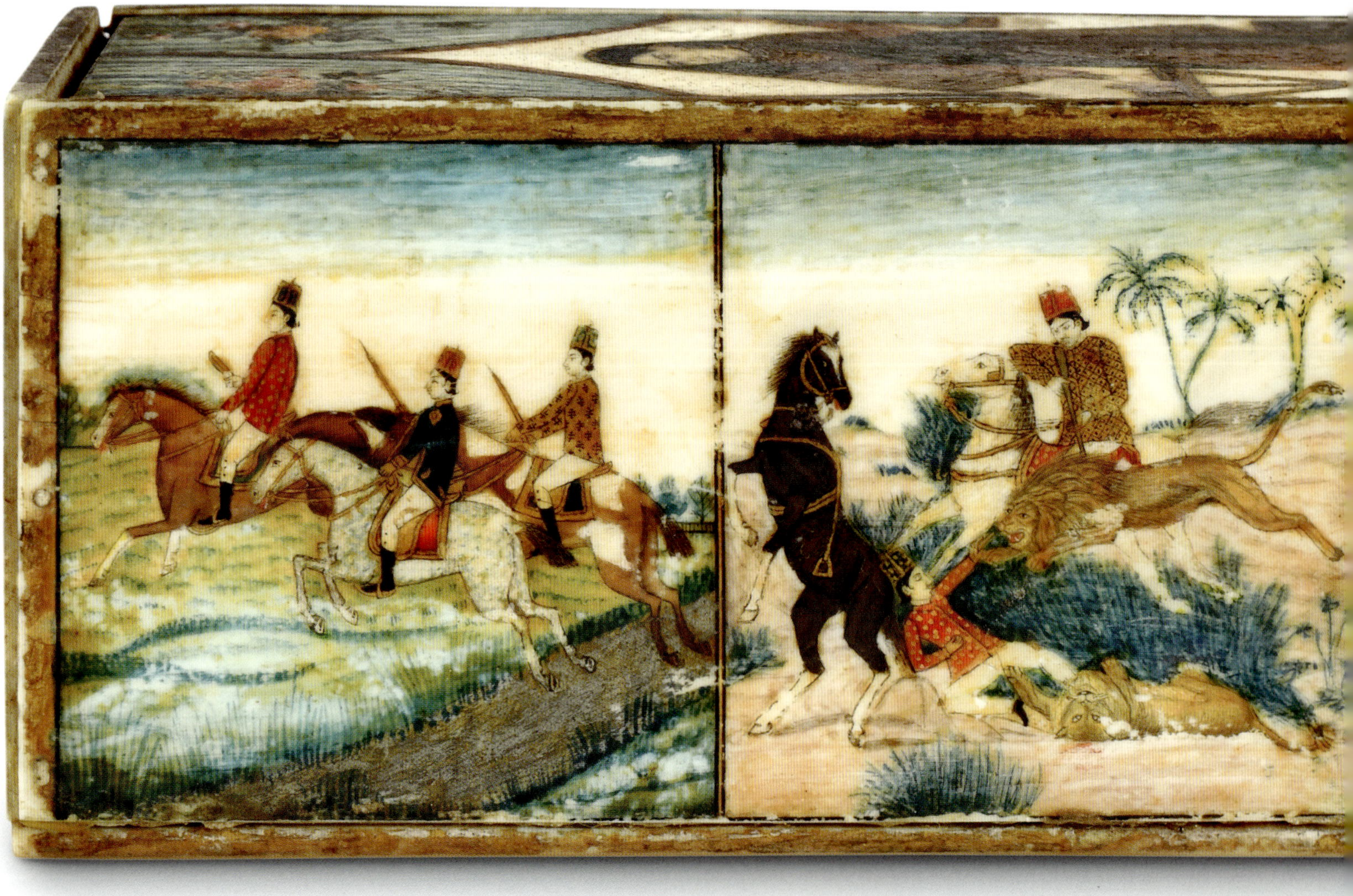

Ganjifa is a card game, Persian in origin, that became popular in India, not only at the Mughal court but with the public as well. Early mentions include Babur's memoir, *Baburnama,* which documents the gift of a *ganjifa* set to a contemporary ruler in 1527 CE. The Persian version, known as *ganjifeh*, traditionally used an eight-suited pack of 12 cards per deck. However, many variants developed in India: the *Ain-i-Akbari*, a 16th-century text about Emperor Akbar's administration, mentions the ruler playing with a 12-suited *ganjifa* deck.

THE ART OF PLAYING

The cards were mostly rectangular or circular, though the sizes varied considerably and they were crafted from all kinds of materials. Courtiers used more expensive sets of ivory and tortoise shell, while painted sets made of wood, pasteboard or palm leaf served the general public. The cards would typically be stored in a box, often also richly painted and decorated. Each suit would be a different colour. These cards, especially those belonging to royalty and nobility, were often treated as miniature paintings in their own right, as they were meticulously designed, symbolizing their high status in the gameplay. The Mughal card set had suits of swords, coins, cups, elephants, horses and even slaves. Later versions used local iconography, such as the Dashavatara Ganjifa, or 10 incarnations of Hindu deity Vishnu. Similarly, the Rashi Ganjifa used symbols from the Indian zodiac. Playing sets with Indo-European imagery became common after the 18th century. Complex *ganjifa* sets were also devised by the ruler of Mysore, Krishnaraj Wodiyar III (1794–1868). These had up to 18 suits with 16 cards each.

► These 19th-century cards, not belonging to the box set, are made of cardboard and are part of a deck themed around the 10 incarnations of the Hindu deity Vishnu.

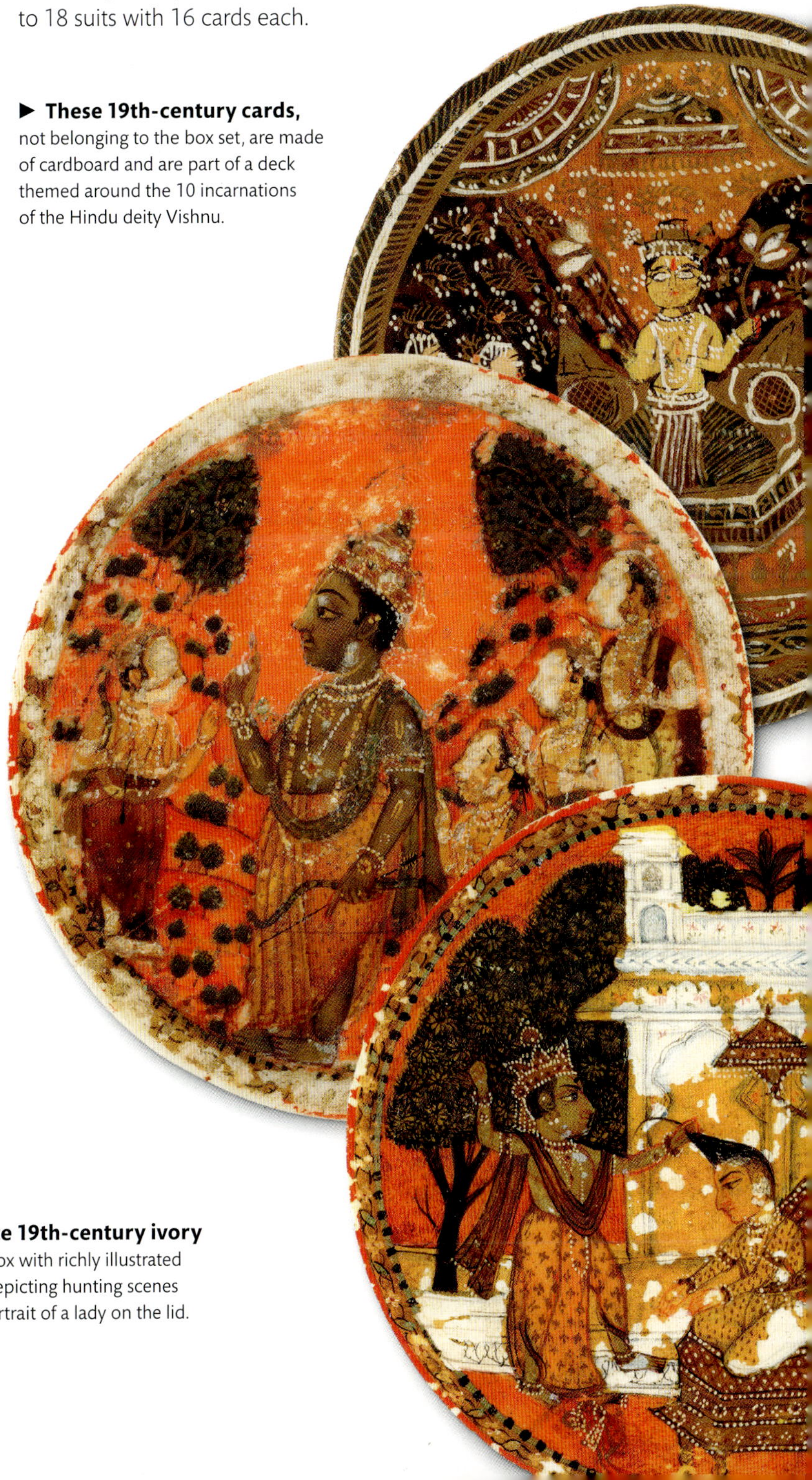

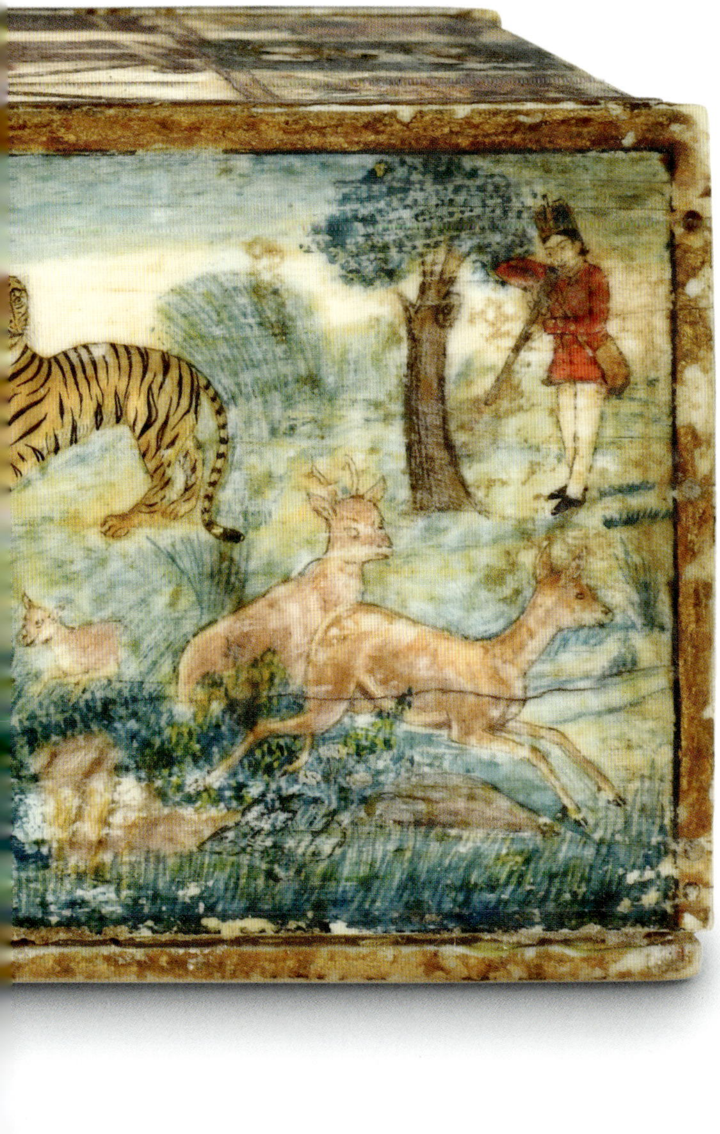

◄ A late 19th-century ivory *ganjifa* box with richly illustrated panels depicting hunting scenes and a portrait of a lady on the lid.

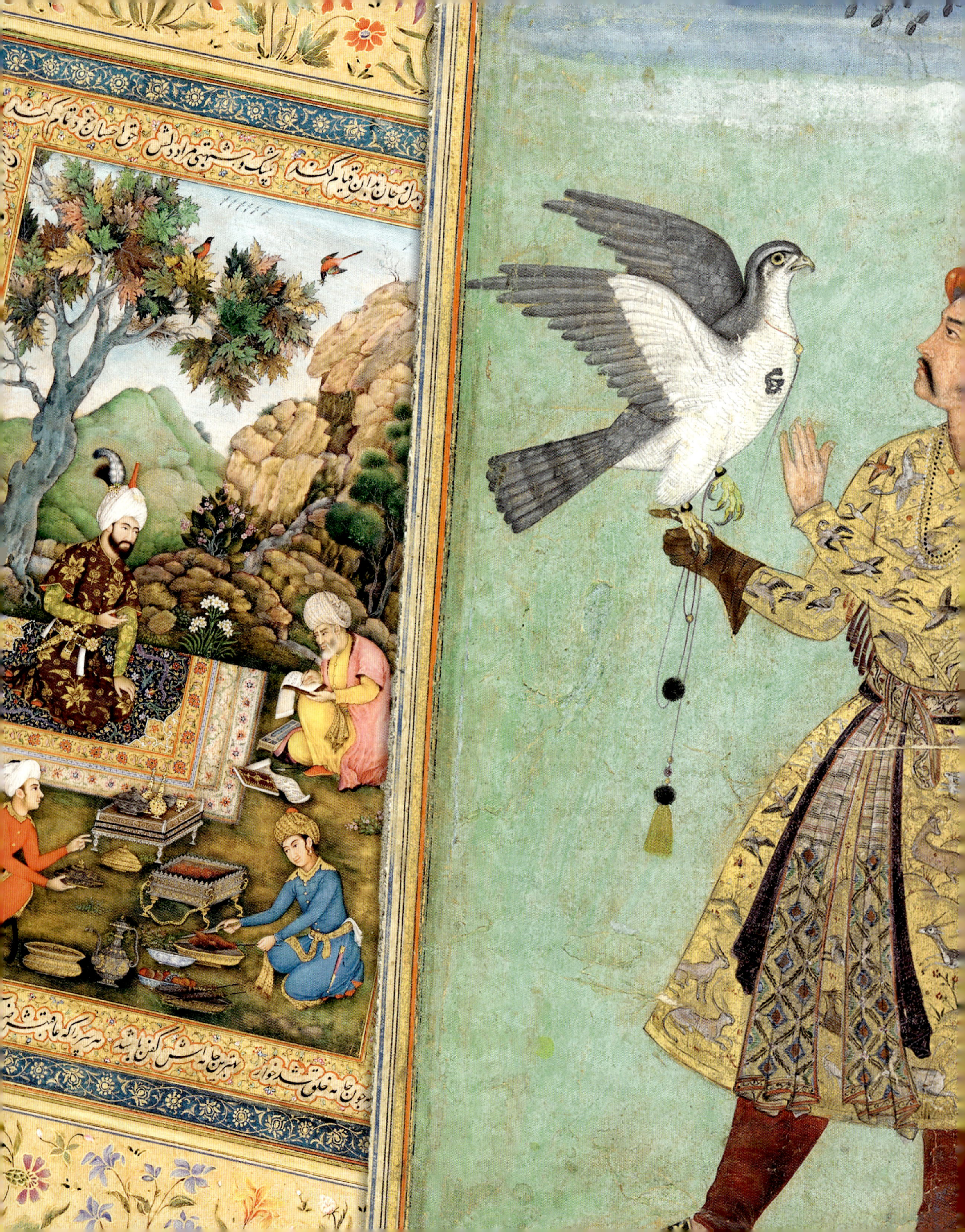

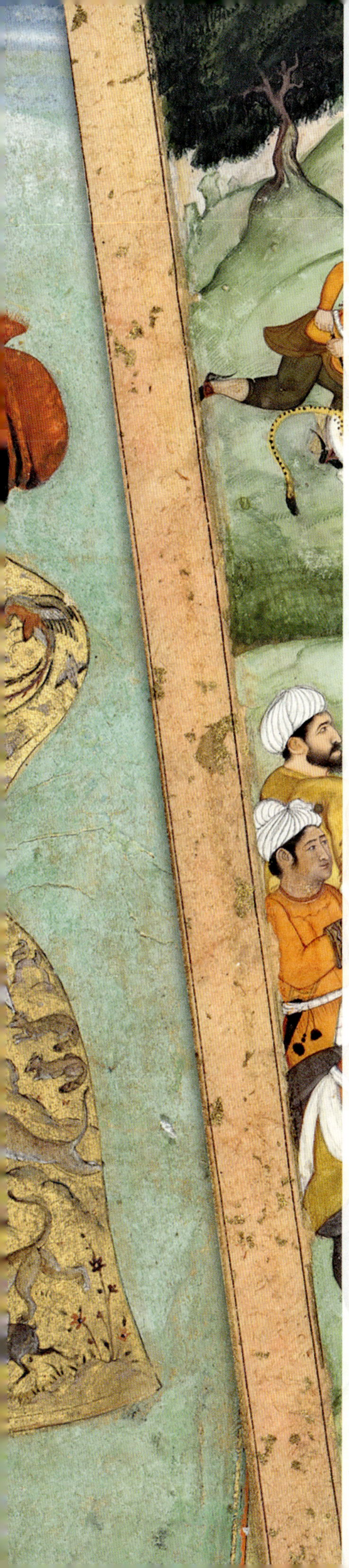

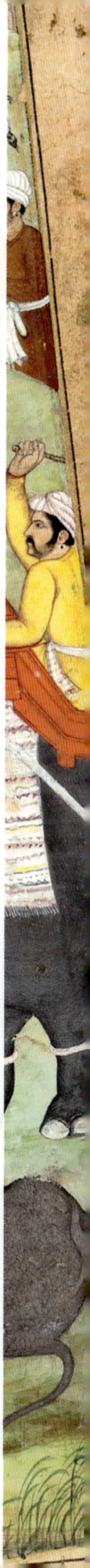

16th–18th centuries CE

MUGHAL MINIATURES

Breathtaking in their vivid imagery and exquisite detail, Mughal miniature paintings integrate the tradition of illustrated Buddhist and Jain palm leaf texts with Persian style and aesthetics.

Mughal art is characterized by delicate brushwork, burnished colours made from natural pigments, intricate borders, fine calligraphy, and strong Persian influence in style and motif. Each painting went through many processes and many hands - from preparing the paper, making the composition, tracing the drawing to colour-blocking, detailing, and burnishing. The master artist would make the final touches, using delicate, single-hair brushes. Borders with floral patterns and animals, in multicolour or gold, were prepared separately. These paintings were developed as illustrations for books or single pages for albums at imperial ateliers, the first of which was set up by Persian artists at the court of Emperor Humayun. The illustrations accompanied imperial memoirs, volumes of translated Indian epics, works on astronomy, medicine, poetry and literature, and heroic sagas. Portraits of the emperor as well as nobles at the court were also popular.

> **"Mughal art is secular, intent upon the present moment and... interested in individuality. It is not an idealization of life, but a refined... representation of a... magnificent phase of it"**
>
> – Ananda Coomaraswamy, *Rajput Painting*

THE CREATION OF A STYLE

The first major work commissioned by Emperor Akbar was the Persian saga *Hamzanama*, followed by Persian translations of Hindu epics. Among the finest miniatures are the ones found in the *Baburnama*, the autobiography of Emperor Babur, and the *Akbarnama*, the biography of Akbar. Emperor Jahangir was an avid naturalist and travelled everywhere with artists to record the landscape, flora, and fauna. Under Shah Jahan's patronage, Mughal painting showed a greater use of gold and elaborate borders. The folios of the *Padshahnama* record the finery and pomp of a prosperous imperial court in glittering detail. Some of the well-known artists of the Mughal era are Abu'l Hasan, Mir Sayyid Ali, Farukh Beg, Govardhan, Basawan, Manohar, Daswant, Bichitr and Bishandas. The artist Mansur specialized in drawing animals and birds, while Govardhan and Bishandas excelled in portraiture.

◀ **A composite of three Mughal miniatures:** Shah Tahmasp of Safavid Iran painted by court painter Farrukh Beg (far left); painting of a prince, believed to be Jahangir or Daniyal with a falcon (centre); and a folio from a *Shikarnama* showing Prince Salim on a hunt, attributed to artist Manohar (right).

Era 16th century CE | **Dimension** 32.9 × 18.7 cm (1 × 0.6 ft)

AKBARNAMA

Illustrated chronicles of an emperor's life

Much of the prevailing political, social, and cultural history of Akbar's time is revealed in this account of the emperor's court written by Abu'l-Fazl ibn Mubarak, a philosopher, scholar, and historian of the period.

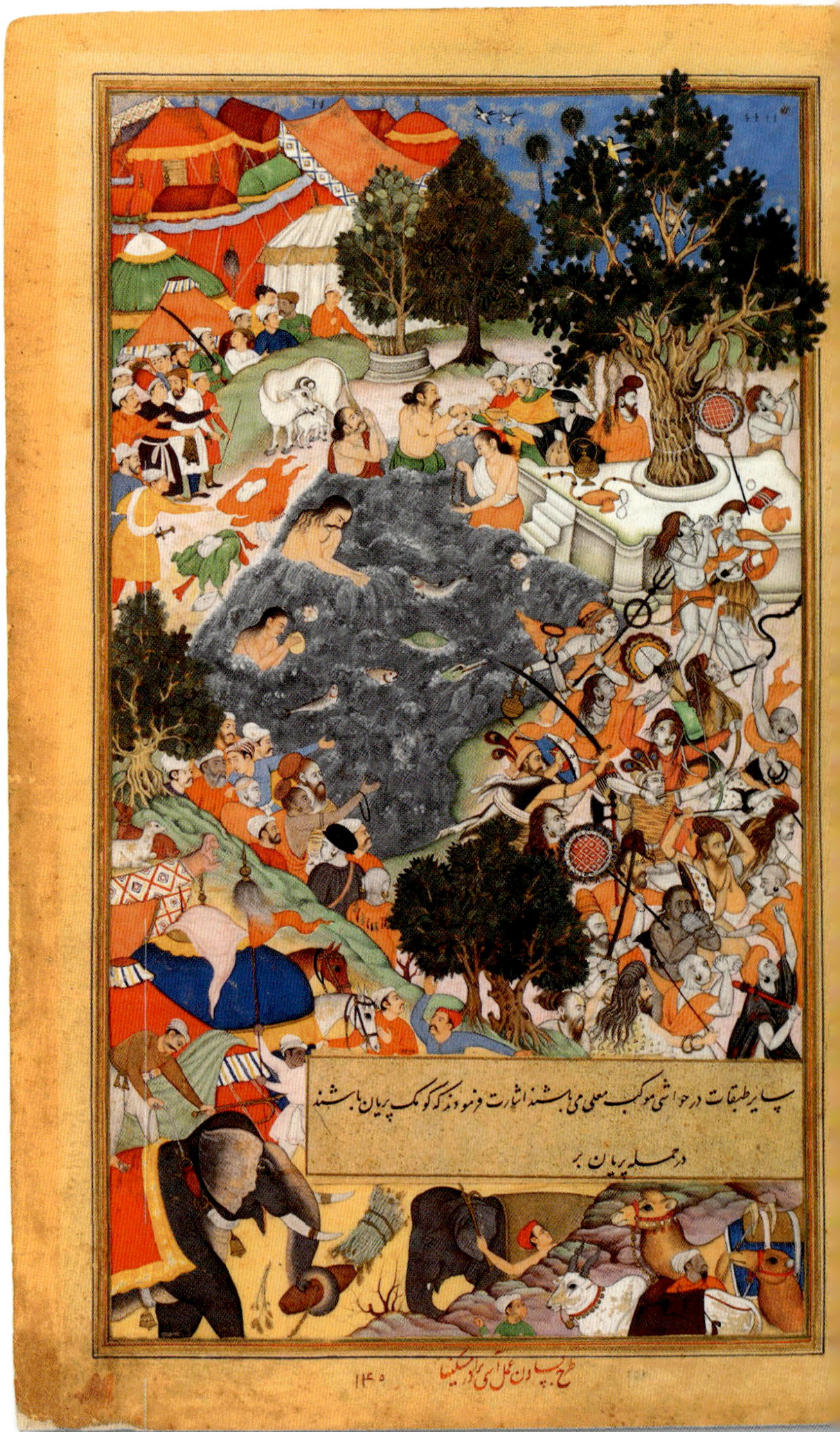

The *Akbarnama* may be a historical biography of a Mughal emperor but it offers key insights into the reign of Akbar (1556–1605), considered one of the most influential and inclusive rulers of his time. It was written in Persian by Abu'l-Fazl ibn Mubarak, one of the 'nine jewels' of his court, between 1590 and 1596.

Three volumes make up the *Akbarnama*, produced after the *Baburnama*, the biography of Babur, Akbar's grandfather and founder of the Mughal dynasty. The first two delve into the finest of details, starting with Akbar's birth, his Timurid lineage, the rule of Babur and Humayun, and later Akbar himself till 1602.

The third volume, titled *Ain-i-Akbari*, records the emperor's household, army, revenues, geography, and imperial administration. This section also contains the famous 'account of the Hindu sciences', based on a genuine desire to understand the philosophy and culture of the land. The author, Abu'l Fazl notes that intent was

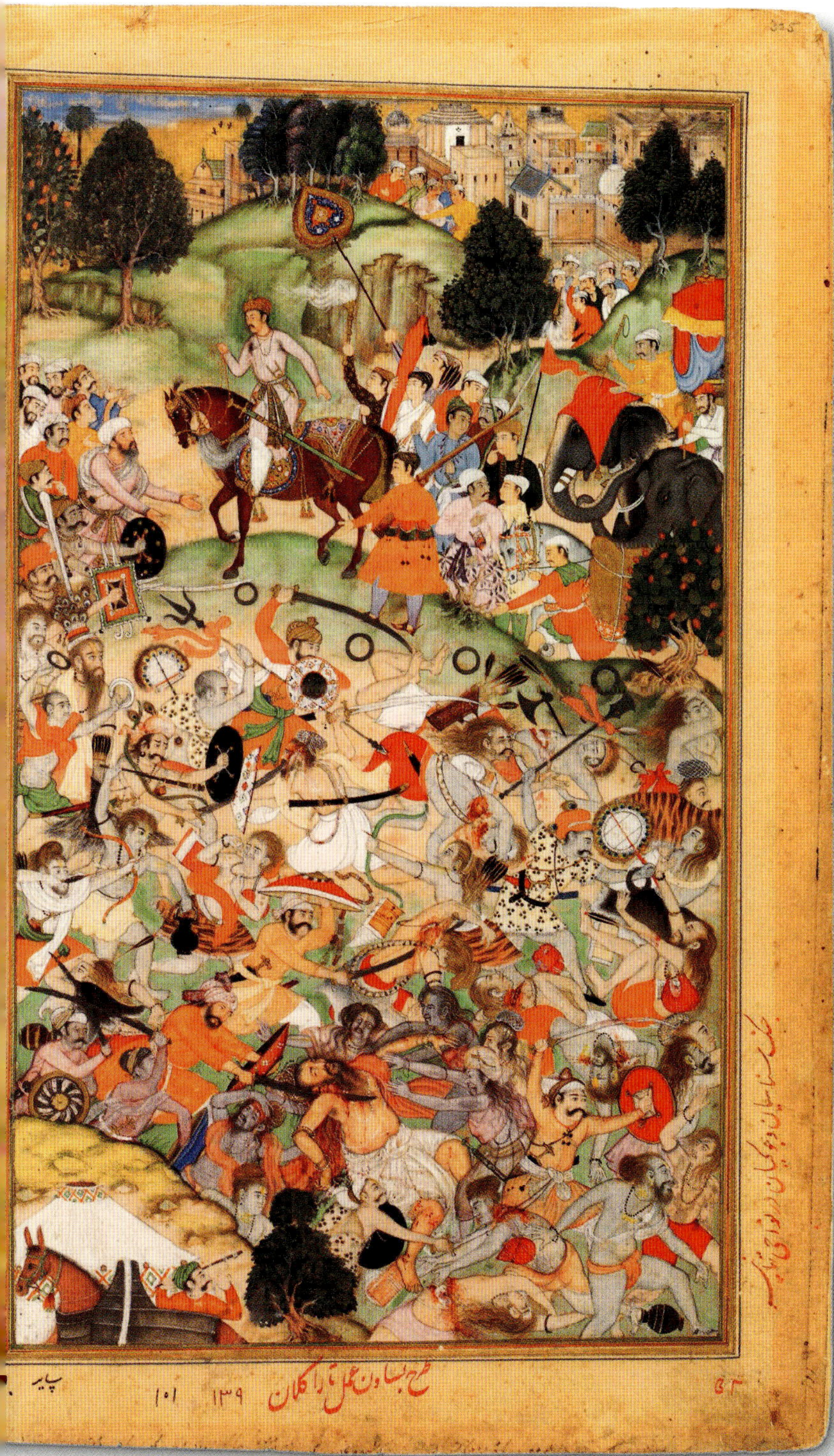

◄ A double-page composition from the *Akbarnama* showing a fight that broke out between two groups of holy men who had entered a Mughal military camp located in Thanesar in the north (in present-day Haryana). On the right, Emperor Akbar can be seen on horseback, watching the tussle.

to record "the opinions professed by the majority of the learned among the Hindus". Included in the official history, it is a sentiment that reflects the aspirations of the Emperor himself – for a syncretic culture within his empire.

ILLUSTRATED SNAPSHOTS OF THE PAST

The illustrations in the *Akbarnama* were made between 1592 and 1595 by artists under the supervision of the court artist, Abd al-Samad. Credited as one of the founders of the Mughal miniature style (see pp. 168–169), he taught Akbar painting as well. The folios within this historical text are considered authentic and realistic portrayal of the times, adorned with vibrant colours, precise details, and evocative landscapes. Indian and Persian painting traditions come to life in the illustrations. Some Western-style perspective and shading techniques can be seen in the action-filled compositions, such as the folio depicting the scuffle at Thanesar (left).

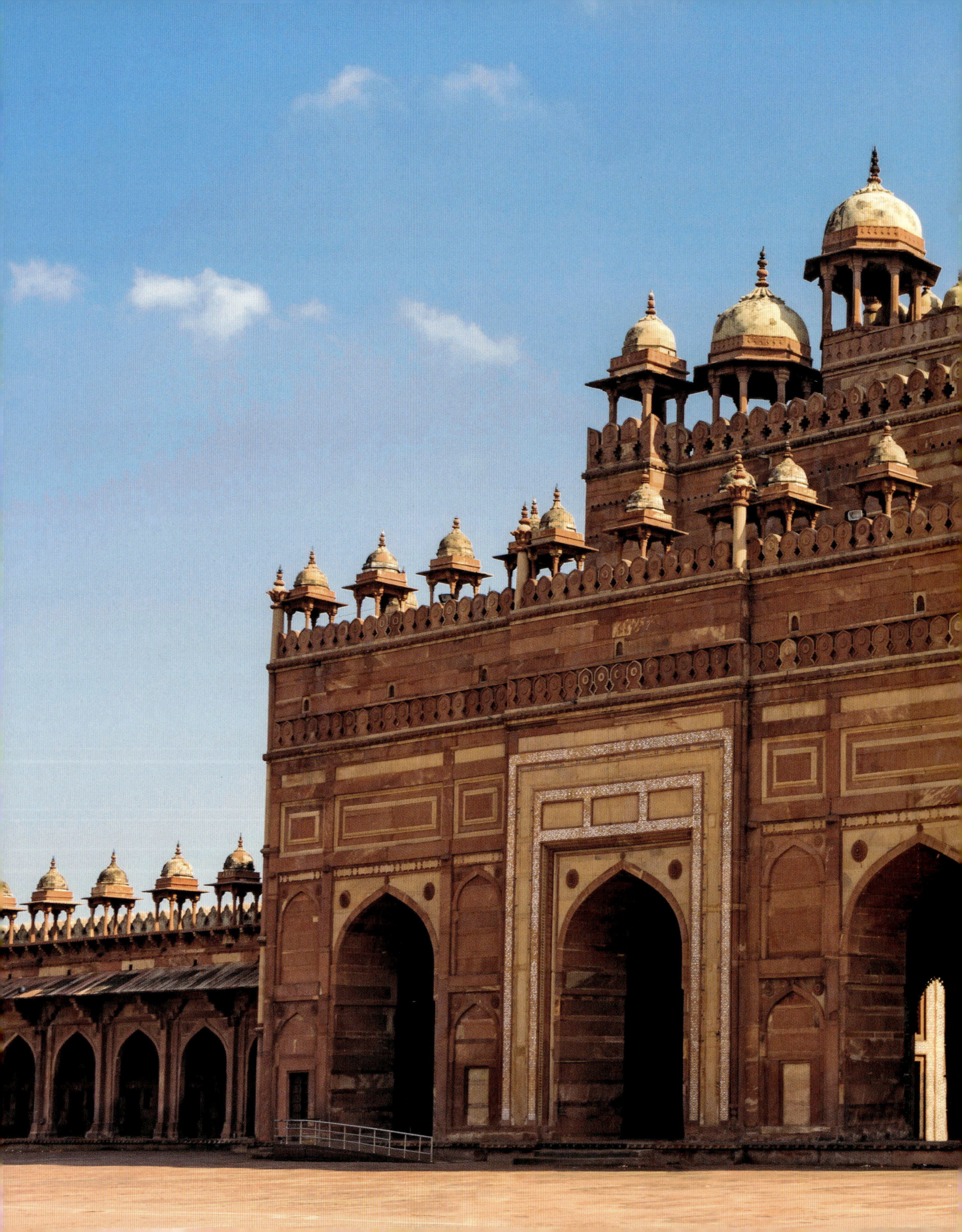

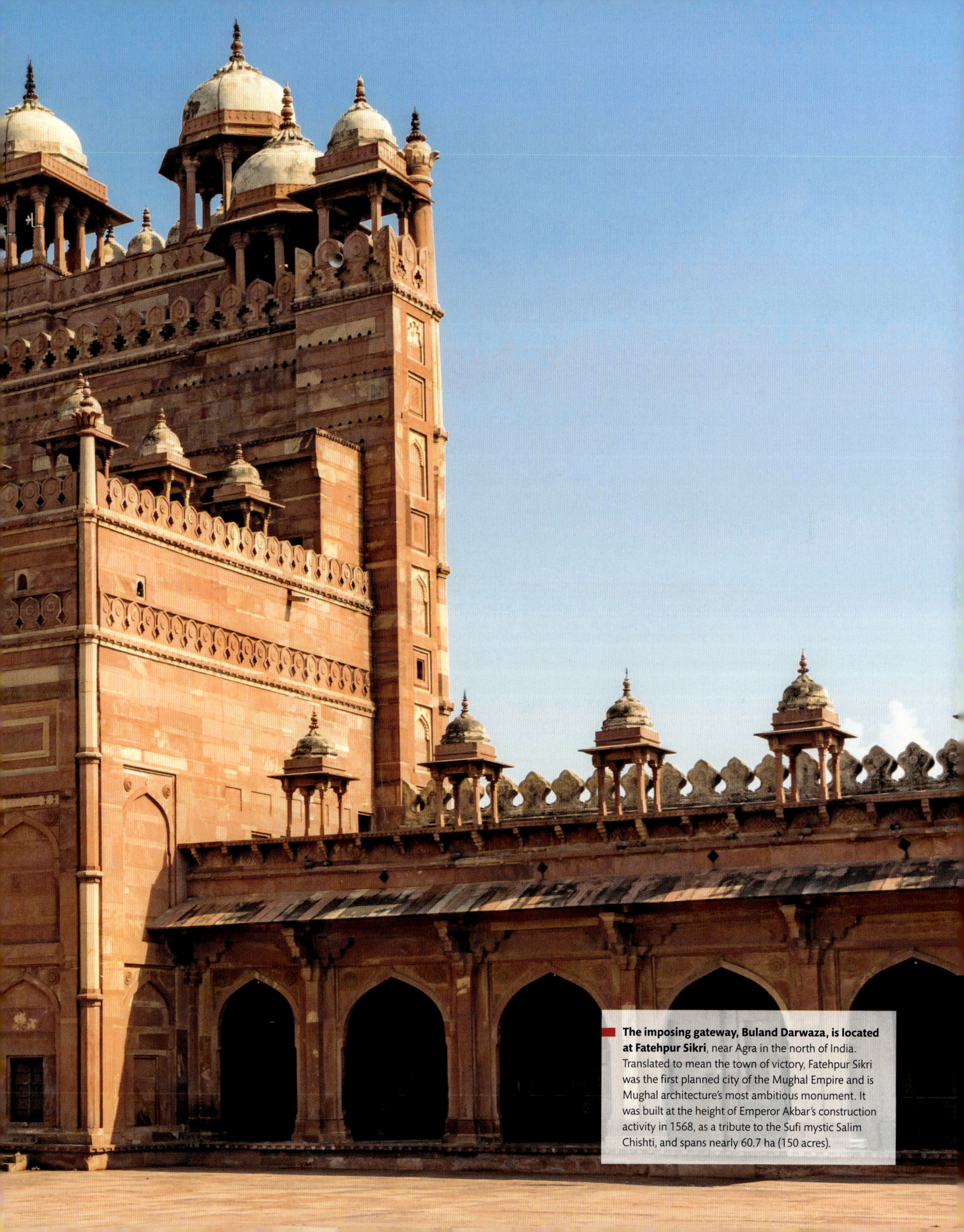

The imposing gateway, Buland Darwaza, is located at Fatehpur Sikri, near Agra in the north of India. Translated to mean the town of victory, Fatehpur Sikri was the first planned city of the Mughal Empire and is Mughal architecture's most ambitious monument. It was built at the height of Emperor Akbar's construction activity in 1568, as a tribute to the Sufi mystic Salim Chishti, and spans nearly 60.7 ha (150 acres).

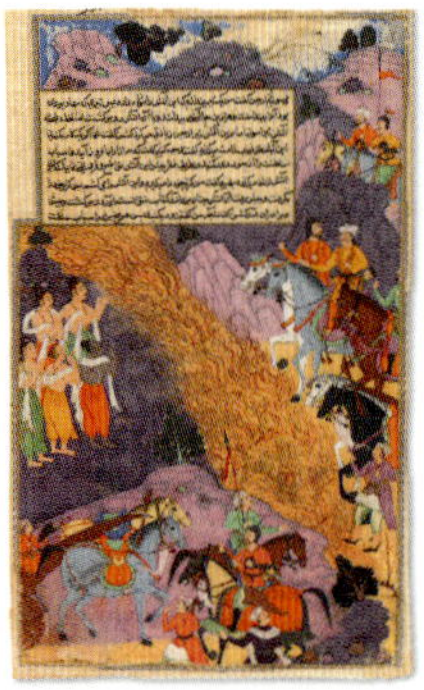

Era 1584–1588 CE | **Medium** Ink, watercolour, and gold on paper | **Height** 38.2 cm (15 in)

RAZMNAMA AND AKBAR'S RAMAYANA

A symbol of cultural unity

The Hindu epics *Mahabharata* and *Ramayana* were translated into Persian at the behest of the Mughal ruler Akbar, in the late 16th century. These iterations are representative of the emperor's interest in religious harmony in his empire.

Despite not being literate himself, Emperor Akbar had a deep love for learning. He commissioned and collected books on varied subjects, and had them read out. Akbar also hosted assemblies in his *ibadatkhana* (house of worship) at his capital in Fatehpur Sikri, located in present-day Uttar Pradesh in northern India. Hearing leaders of various faiths debate in these assemblies, Akbar realized the importance of understanding the tenets of different religions. This was the motivation for him to commission two of the most spectacular translations of the Hindu epics, Ramayana and Mahabharata, that this period has seen.

TRANSLATING THE BOOK OF WAR

The translation of the Mahabharata into the Persian *Razmnama* (The Book of War) began in 1582 CE. It was first translated from Sanskrit into Hindi and then into Persian. According to the Mughal historian Badauni, Akbar wanted to "establish exactitude in a minute manner so that nothing of the original would be lost". The first draft took 18 months to complete.

The illustrators of the atelier, skilled at following Persian masters, had no reference for this new work. Every detail of the exquisitely painted folios was thought of anew – this is what makes the *Razmnama* such a pioneering work. The elegant calligraphy was complemented by 168 full-page illustrations. There are also 13 horizontal compositions, a format not seen in Mughal manuscripts, though often used in traditional Hindu texts.

A SECOND EPIC

Gratified by the splendour of the *Razmnama*, Akbar commissioned a translation of the Ramayana. Inscribed in ornate calligraphy and embellished with 176 full-page illustrations, the Persian Ramayana was completed in 1588 CE. Around the same time, Bhakti poet Tulsidas also retold the story of Rama in *Ramcharitmanas* in Awadhi.

Copies of the two epics were made for members of the court. Though few match the delicate artistry of the original, the *Razmnama* made for Abdur Rahim Khan-i-Khanan, Akbar's trusted advisor, is held in high regard.

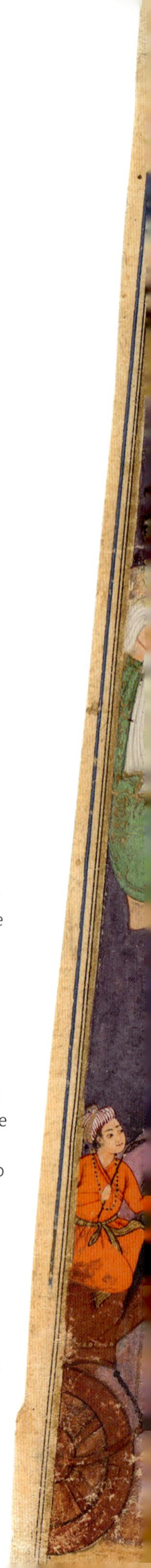

► **An illustrated folio from one of the** original copies of *Razmnama* made for Abdur Rahim, army commander to Akbar and later Jahangir, shows Asvatthama firing the Narayana weapon (cosmic fire) at the Pandavas in battle.

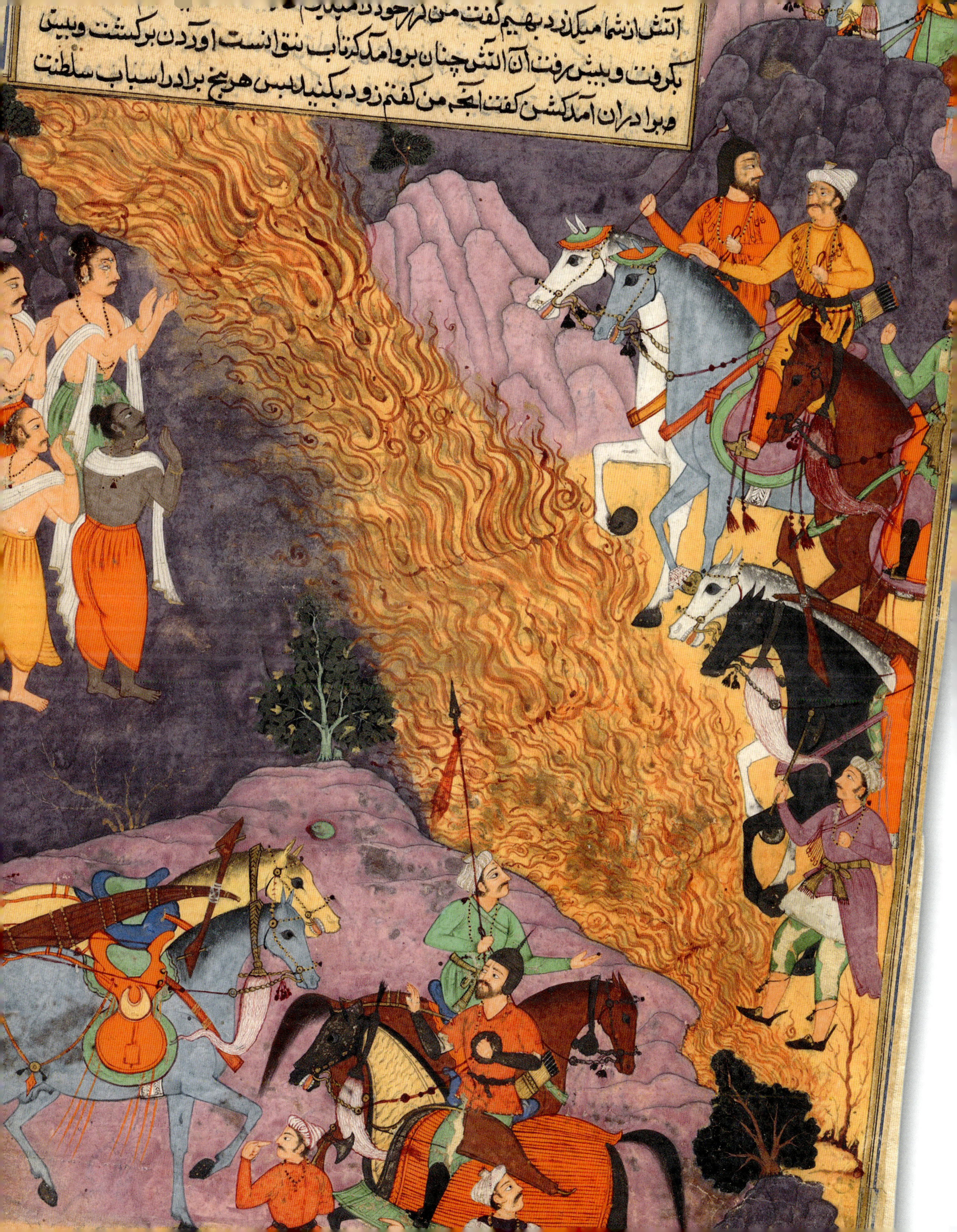
آتش از شما میگذرد بهیم گفت من
بگرفت و پیش رفت آن آتش چنان بر آمد که تاب نتوانست آوردن برگشت و پیش
و برادران آمد کشن گفت انچه من گفتم زود بکنید پس هر پنج برادر اسباب سلطنت

GEMS OF THE MUGHAL EMPIRE

The opulence of the Mughal Empire can be measured from the gem-encrusted, diamond-studded, and gilded objects, which ranged from the daily to the ceremonial. For Mughal emperors, these pieces also formed an integral part of articulating authority as they symbolized power, bolstering the legitimacy of their rule.

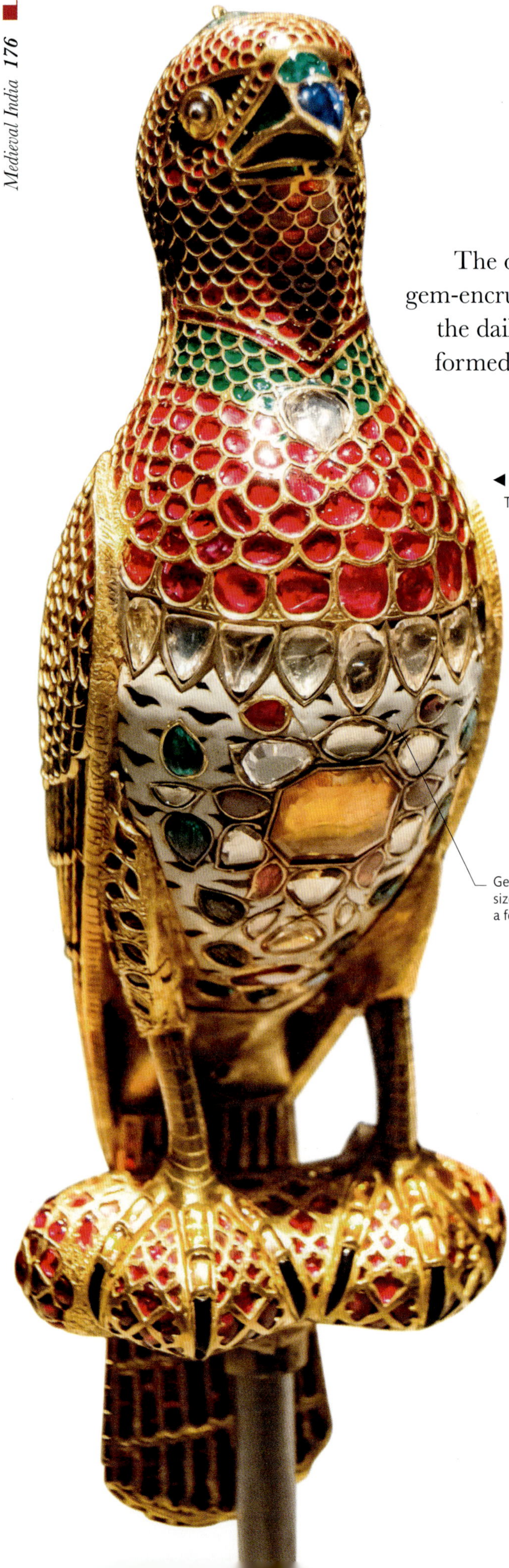

◄ Perched falcon
This exquisite golden bird, enamelled and inlaid with rubies, emeralds, diamonds, sapphires, and onyx, is believed to be a prized possession of Emperor Shah Jahan.

Gems of various sizes inlaid to give a feathered effect

▼ Shell-shaped cup
A wine cup probably used by Emperor Jahangir, such containers or servers are believed to have been the most frequently fashioned objects of jade, intended for use in the Mughal court.

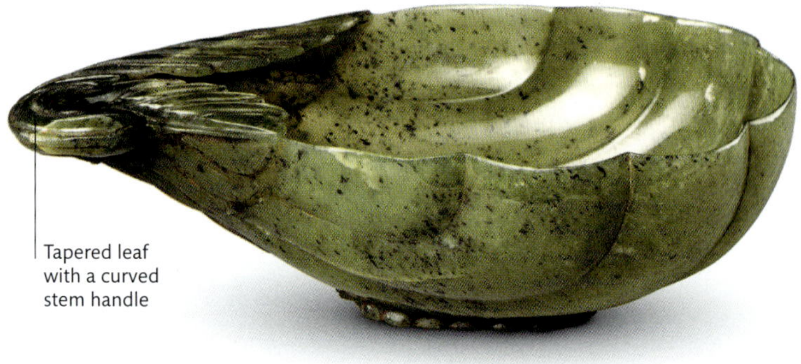

Tapered leaf with a curved stem handle

▼ Royal spectacles
Believed to have been used by Emperor Shah Jahan to soothe his tired eyes, this 17th-century pair of spectacles were made from diamonds and emeralds.

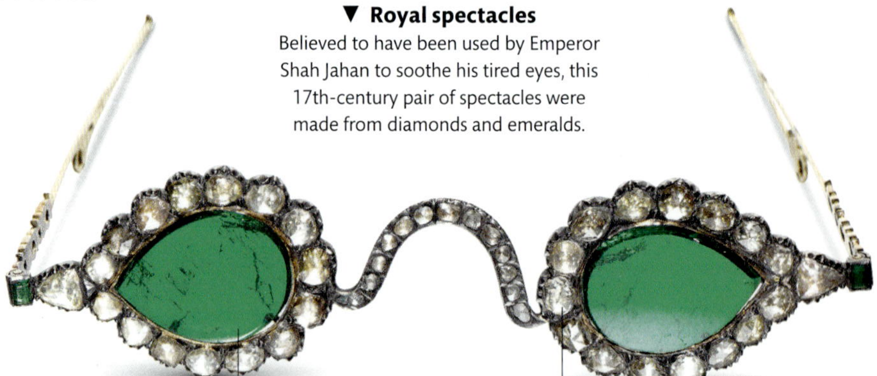

This pair of spectacles, set with green lenses, is dubbed the 'Gate of Paradise'

Diamond setting enhancing the teardrop shape of the lenses

Emeralds and **jades** were immensely popular in the **Mughal** court due to their **opacity** and **symbolic** qualities.

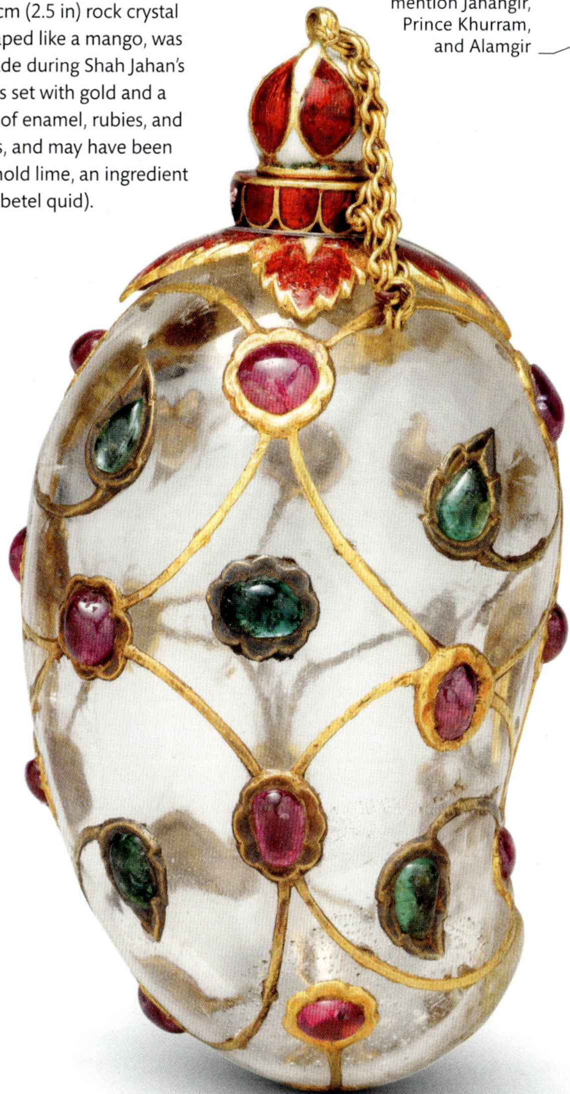

► Mango-shaped flask
This 6.5 cm (2.5 in) rock crystal flask, shaped like a mango, was likely made during Shah Jahan's reign. It is set with gold and a network of enamel, rubies, and emeralds, and may have been used to hold lime, an ingredient of *paan* (betel quid).

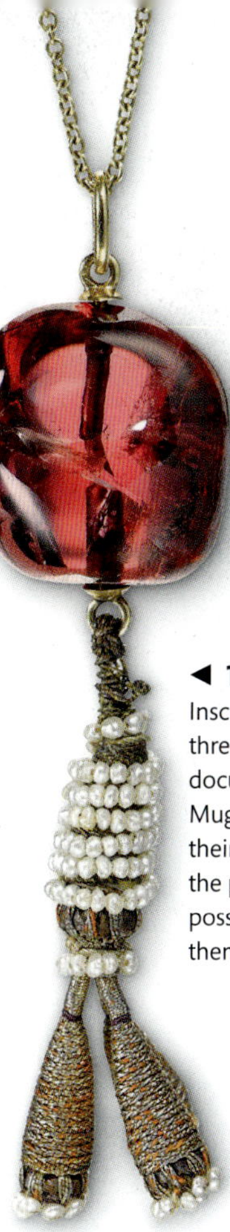

◄ 17th century spinel
Inscribed with the names of three Mughal patrons, this spinel documents the practice among Mughal emperors of inscribing their names and dates on the precious stones in their possession and of passing them on to descendants.

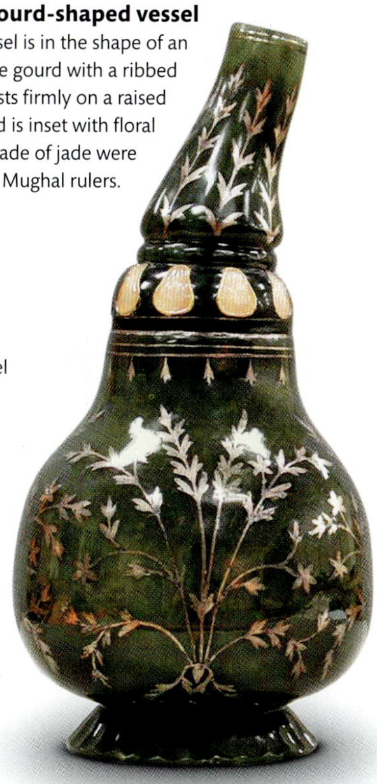

► Bottle gourd-shaped vessel
This jade vessel is in the shape of an elongated bottle gourd with a ribbed waist. The body rests firmly on a raised circular base and is inset with floral motifs. Objects made of jade were greatly prized by Mughal rulers.

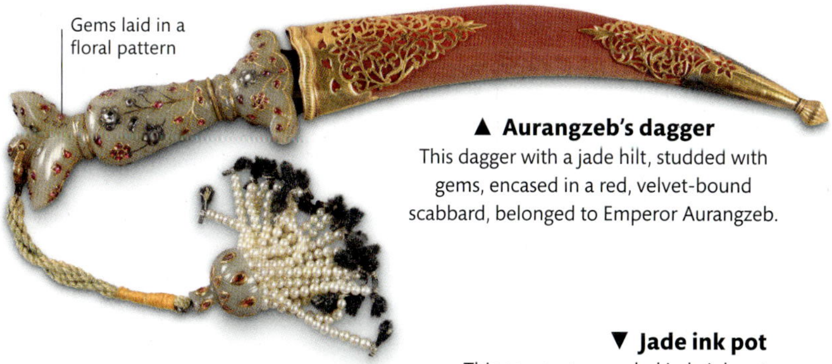

▲ Aurangzeb's dagger
This dagger with a jade hilt, studded with gems, encased in a red, velvet-bound scabbard, belonged to Emperor Aurangzeb.

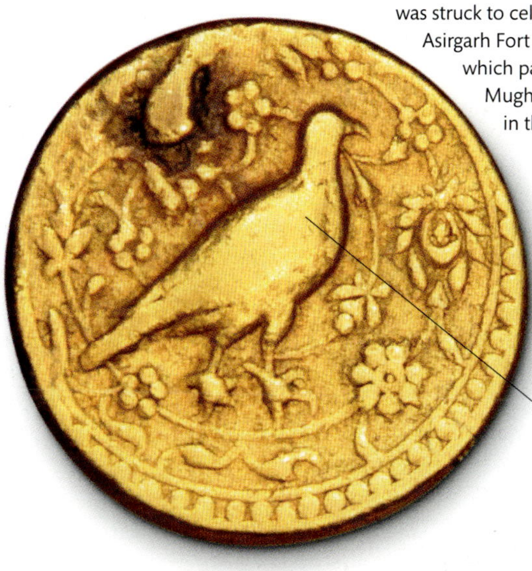

▼ Akbar's hawk coin
This gold coin from Emperor Akbar's reign was struck to celebrate the conquest of Asirgarh Fort (in Madhya Pradesh), which paved the way for the Mughals to overrun the Deccan in the early 17th century.

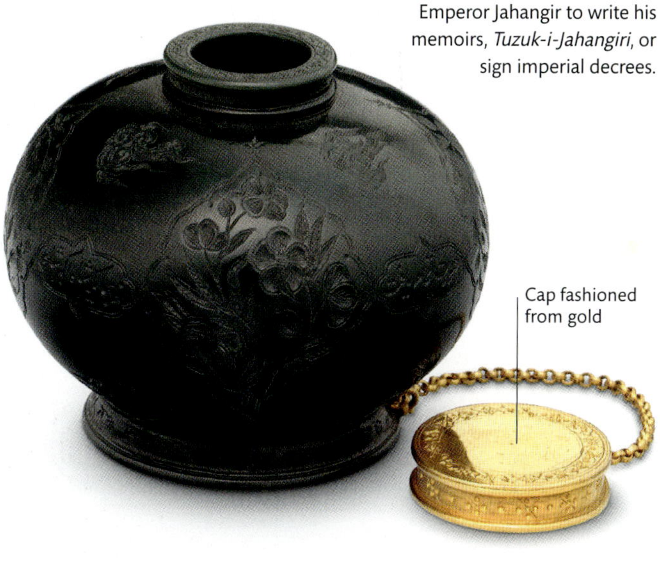

▼ Jade ink pot
This compact, rounded jade ink pot from 1618 may have been used by Emperor Jahangir to write his memoirs, *Tuzuk-i-Jahangiri*, or sign imperial decrees.

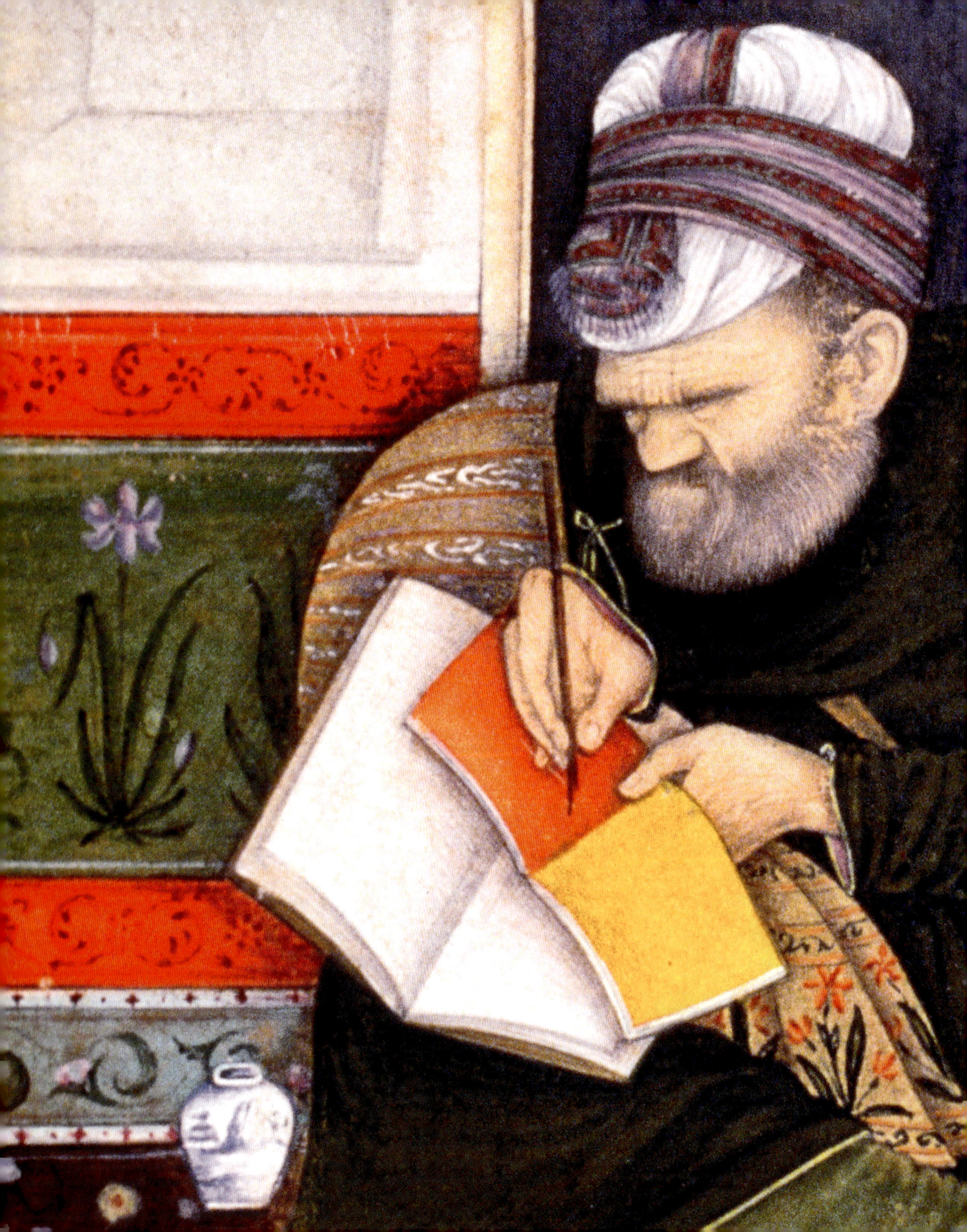

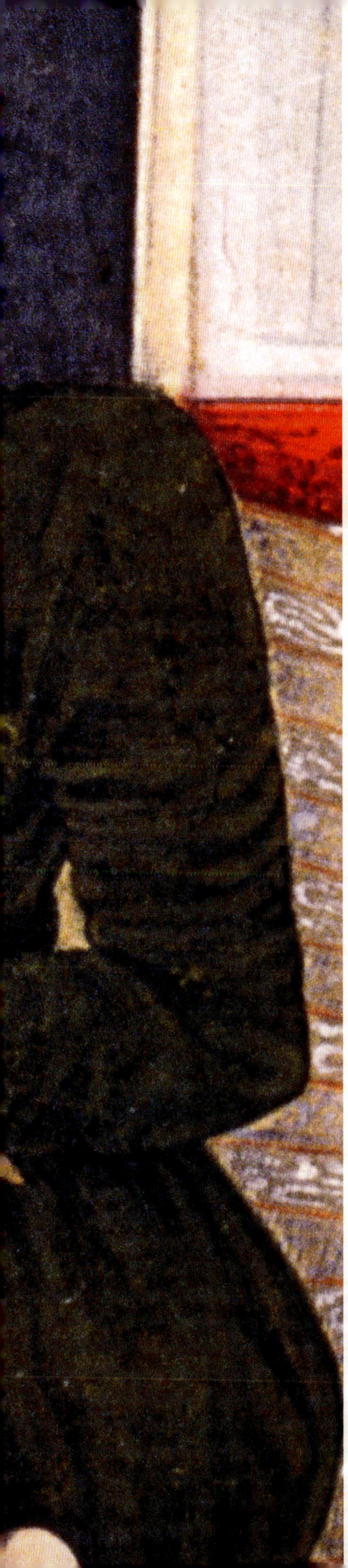

c. 16th–19th centuries CE

LITERATURE FROM THE MUGHAL PERIOD

The semblance of stability and centralized authority during the Mughal Empire encouraged creative and intellectual vigour that was reflected in the literature and arts of the time, marking a new era in the literary history of India.

Babur, the founder of the Mughal dynasty, was a learned man, familiar with Persian, Arabic, and Turki. A poet himself, he enjoyed the company of men of literature, a number of whom followed him to India. The vivid detailing of flora and fauna, in Babur's autobiography, *Baburnama,* set the tone for literary activity to follow. The life and times of each emperor were recorded in flowing detail and have since become an important resource of the period. Humayun's biography, *Humayunnama*, written by his half-sister, Gulbadan Begum, gave a rare glimpse of life in the royal harem, and it remains the only work by a Mughal noblewoman of the era. Once Humayun had established his court in Agra, the influx of Persian writers grew, and during the 16th and 17th centuries a new *sabaq hindi* or 'Indian style' of Persian literature developed. What also gained impetus was the development of *Jaban-i-Hindvi*, a mix of the Persian used in the imperial court and regional tongues. Later known as Urdu, it became the language of the common people. Works of Urdu poets from the late Mughal period, such as Meer Taqi Meer and Mirza Ghalib, continue to be influential.

"Without love, what man his goal attains? Love is desire, love its ultimate aim ..."

– "What is love?" by Meer Taqi Meer, translated by Khushwant Singh

A CONTINUED TRADITION

The golden age of literature flowered and reached its zenith during Akbar's reign and the rich outpouring of literature continued under Jahangir and Shah Jahan. Abul Fazl, Faizi, Abdur Rahim Khan-i-Khanan, and Badauni, were great literary figures of the time. The Mughal emperor's patronage extended to Persian, Sanskrit, Hindi, and works in regional languages. Akbar had the Ramayana, Mahabharata, as well as the Atharva Veda translated into Persian. His reign was recorded in the *Akbarnama* by the Persian scholar Abul Fazl, whose student, Abdul Hamid Lahori, wrote the *Padshahnama*, the official history of Shah Jahan's reign.

◄ **A c. 1625 miniature painting depicting** a Mughal calligrapher or scribe engrossed in his work. His experience is implied through physical elements, such as his grey beard and wrinkled forehead.

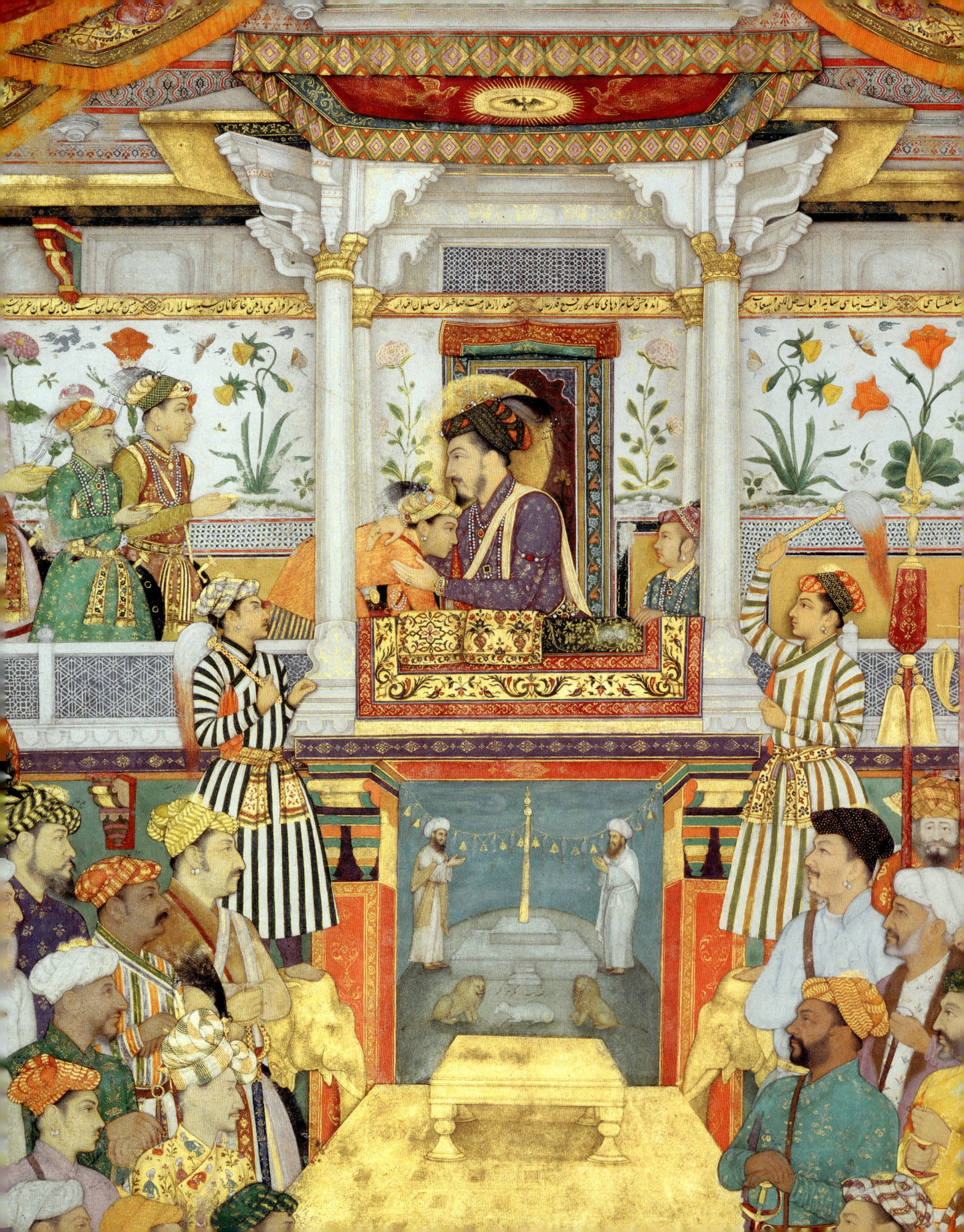

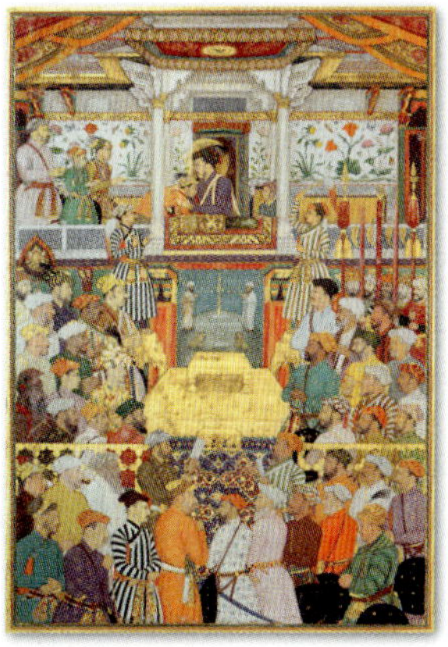

Era 17th century CE | **Medium** Watercolour on paper | **Dimension** 30.4 × 20.1 cm (11.8 × 7.8 in)

PADSHAHNAMA

Records of the reign of Shah Jahan

The *Padshahnama* or "the book of Emperors", is an official chronicle of the fifth Mughal emperor, Shah Jahan. It was the culmination of a glorious tradition of illustrating Mughal history.

Written in three volumes, the *Padshahnama* is a detailed chronological narrative of the early and middle years of Shah Jahan's reign, serving as an invaluable historical record of life at the court of the emperor. The manuscript contains several pages of text and no less than 50 illustrations, bound in leather with gold and silver embossing. It is the last illustrated history of the Mughal period, as Shah Jahan's son and successor Emperor Aurangzeb condemned historical paintings on religious grounds and consequently disbanded imperial workshops in the 17th century.

Unlike the texts of Shah Jahan's predecessors, Babur and Akbar, which were memoirs or included descriptions of what the ruler ate and drank besides courtly events, the *Padshahnama* has an objective of strictly focusing on the creation of appropriate images in an official style. This is to say that both the text and paintings remained confined to documenting official events, the ceremonial and grisly alike: royal courts, battles, and other state occasions.

The primary author, Abdul Hamid Lahori, composed the text using a blend of prose and verse in a flamboyant style, characterized by intricate allegories and metaphors. In his preface, Lahori referred to the text as "an adorned text, the description of which fills the listener's dress with jewels".

◄ **A folio, c. 1630–1650, from the** *Padshahnama* depicting Shah Jahan receiving his three older sons, Dara Shikoh, Shah Shuja, and Aurangzeb, during his accession ceremony at the Agra Fort in March 1628.

AN EMPEROR'S LEGACY

The *Padshahnama* is recognized as a grand artistic exercise by the Mughal court's atelier, serving as a testament to the height that Mughal miniature paintings achieved. The scenes are minutely executed; the descriptions of people, the architecture, and the textiles, by which they are surrounded, are depicted with convincing realism.

Several versions of the text were penned, however, the manuscript currently housed in the Royal Collection at Windsor Castle in the UK remains the only surviving, illustrated imperial volume. The *Windsor Padshahnama*, as it is now referred, is only one of three volumes that make up the complete text.

Era 17th century CE | **Medium** White marble | **Height** 73 m (240 ft)

TAJ MAHAL

A timeless eulogy to love and beauty

The apogee of the many outstanding achievements of Mughal architecture in the subcontinent, the Taj Mahal was undoubtedly a monument designed to be memorable from its very conception.

This sublime garden-tomb, an image of the Islamic garden of paradise, took 20,000 labourers around 15 years to build. It was commissioned by the Mughal emperor Shah Jahan in memory of his late wife, Mumtaz Mahal. Its perfect proportions and exquisite craftsmanship have been described as a vision, a dream, a poem, a wonder.

A WONDER OF THE WORLD

Double arcade galleries flank the majestic beauty of the main entrance. Beyond it, the long water channel that forms the central axis draws the eye to the jewelled perfection of the mausoleum. The gardens on both sides are laid out in classic Mughal landscaping as squares quartered by walkways. The overall plan follows the *charbagh* (garden of paradise) concept - in fact, a line of fine calligraphy inlaid on the entrance gate invites the faithful to enter paradise. The deviation is in the placement of the tomb on a raised plinth at the end instead of at the centre of the garden. This imparts an added depth of perspective to the impact of the building's almost ethereal beauty.

Within its square exterior, the interior of the tomb is a perfect octagon, a reference to the eight levels of paradise. At the precise centre of the dome lies Mumtaz Mahal's cenotaph, marking the true grave in the crypt below. Shah Jahan's tomb was later placed beside it. The imagery in motifs is mostly floral, in keeping with the concept of paradise on earth created by the emperor as the final resting place for his beloved wife.

1. The Taj Mahal reflected in perfect symmetry in the narrow pool. **2.** Detail from a *pietra dura*, filigree work, decoration of a floral motif, found widely in the interior of the building and laid usually in white marble. **3.** Gilded finial topping the main dome incorporates Islamic motifs, such as the crescent moon, and Hindu elements, like the bulbous water vessel. **4.** A panoramic view of the Taj Mahal, from across the bank of river Ganga. **5.** The decorated cenotaphs commemorating the emperor and his wife on the main level. **6.** Flowers and leaves elaborately inlaid in a variety of hues that enliven the white marble. **7.** Qur'anic inscriptions and colourful inlaid decoration on a section of the main entrance and dome. **8.** One of the four identical and ornamental minarets which frame the main building.

1

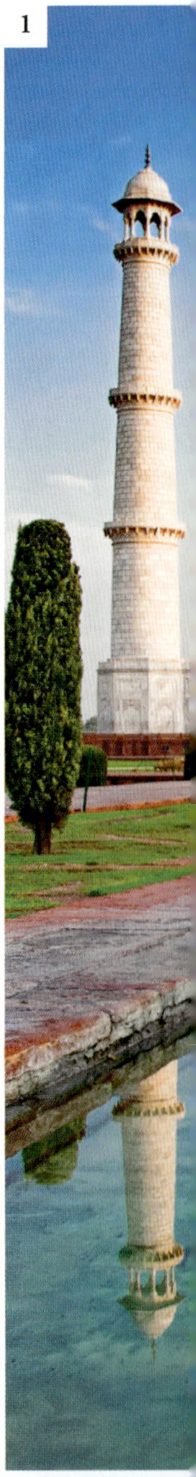

2

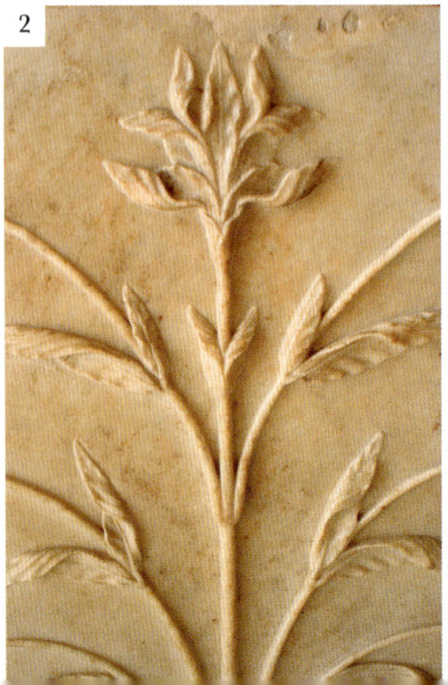

3

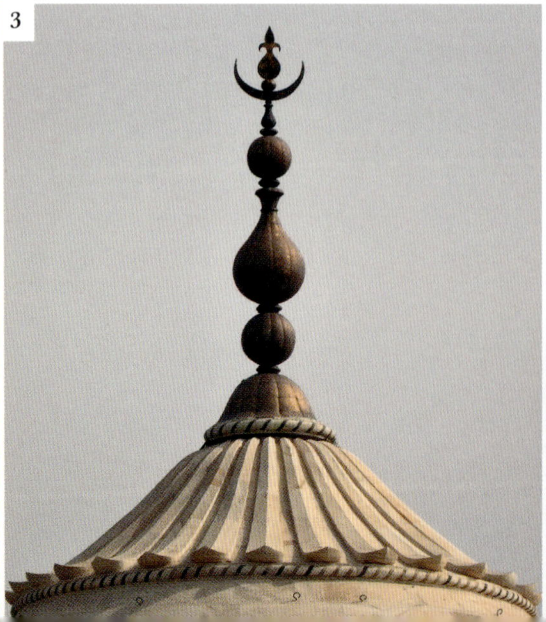

4

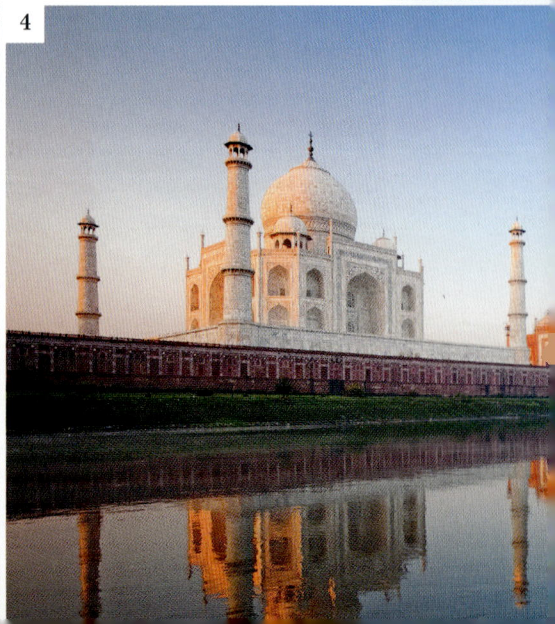

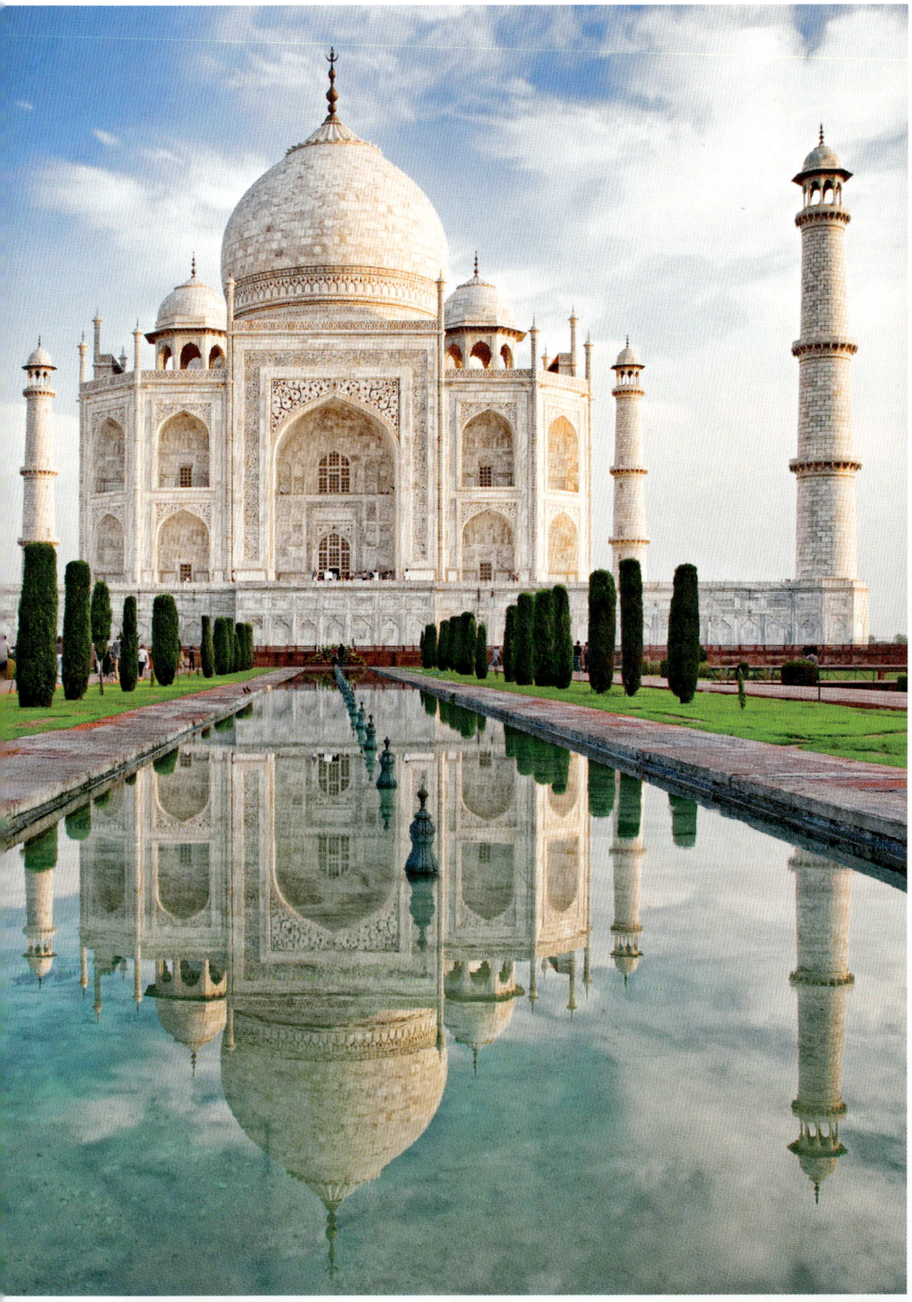

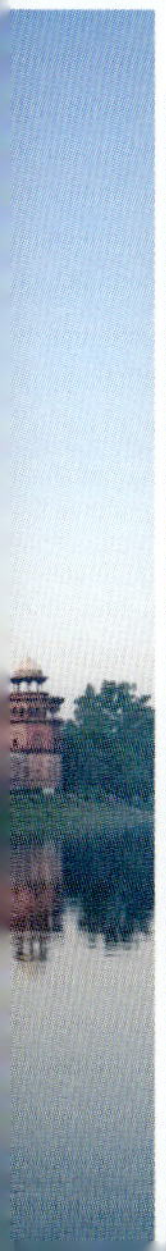

5

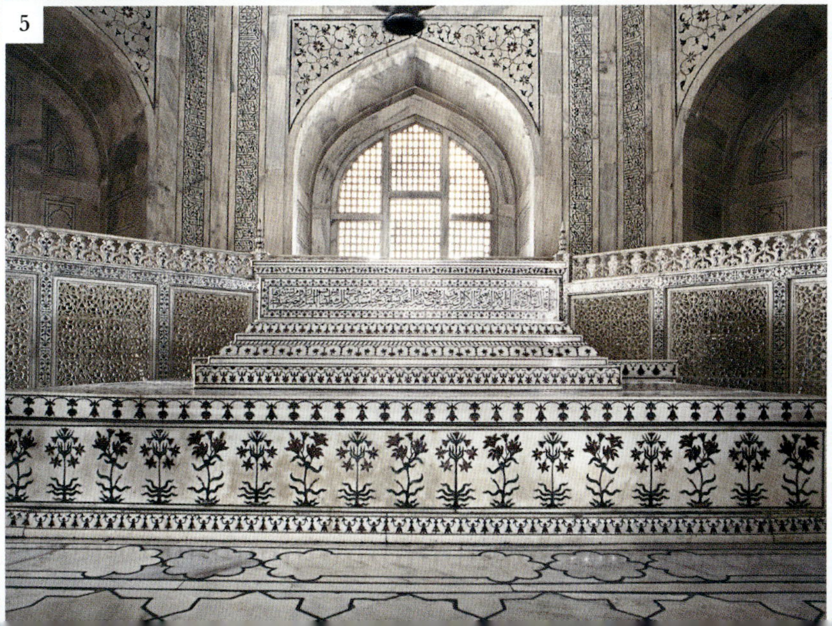

6

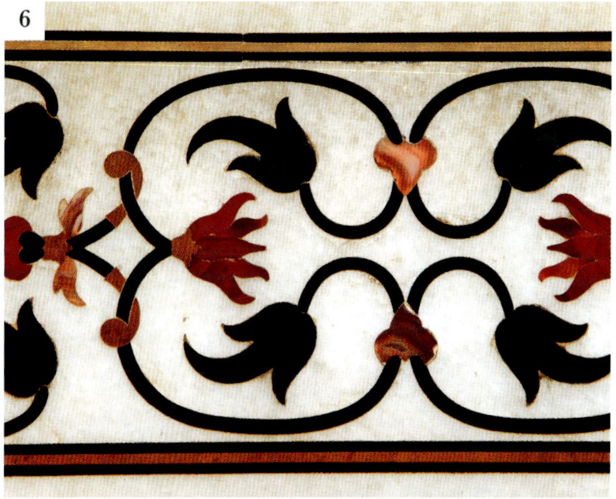

7

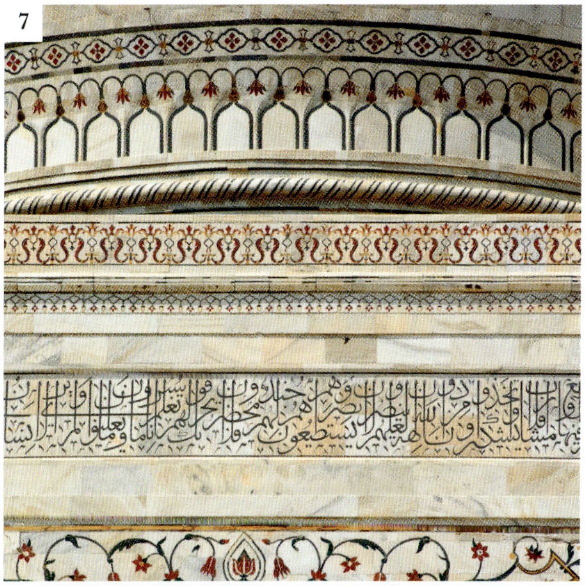

8

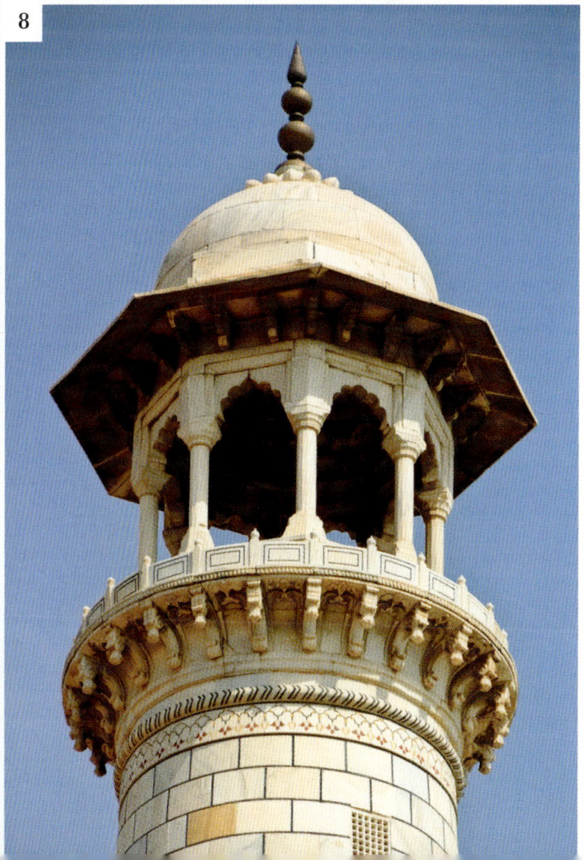

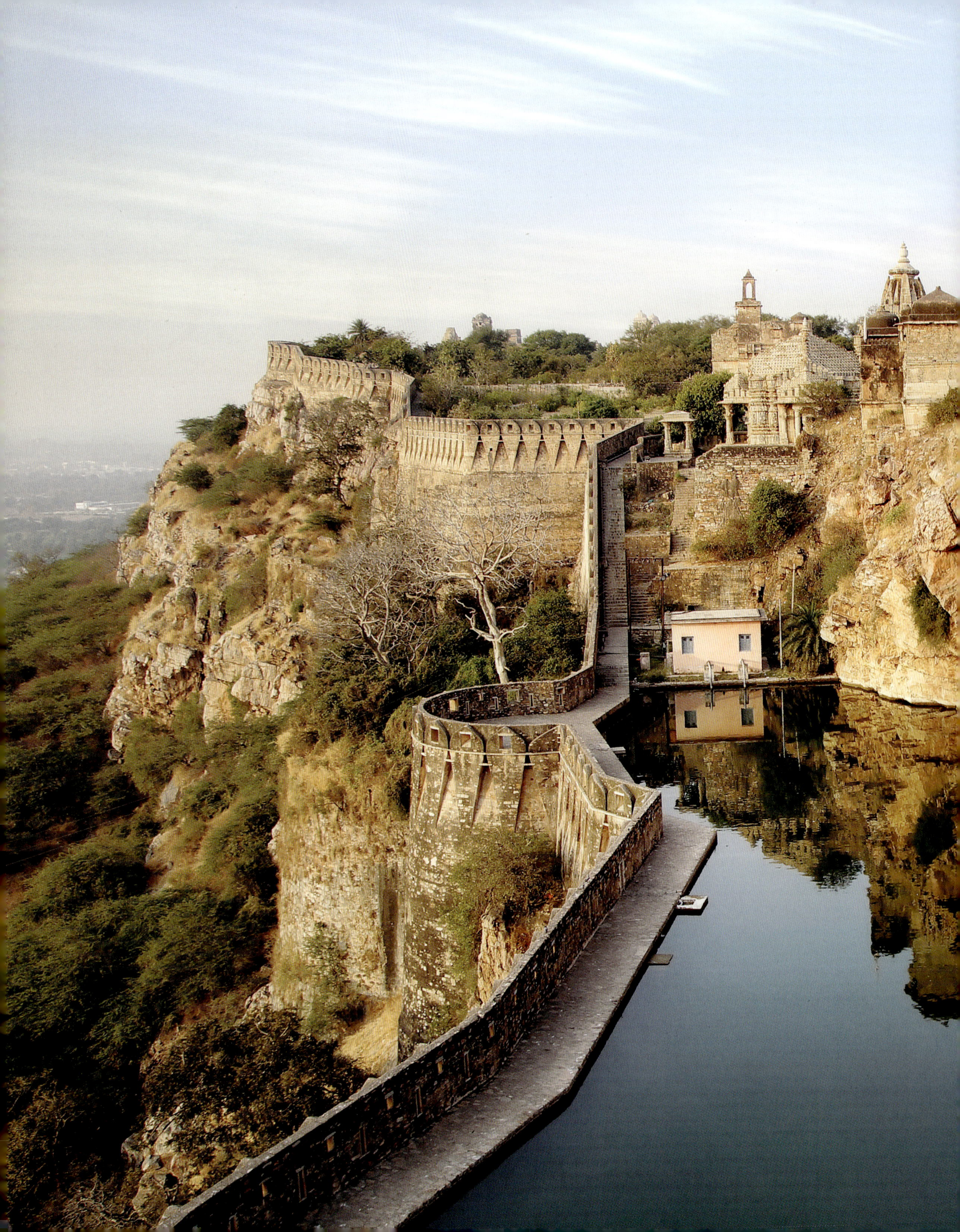

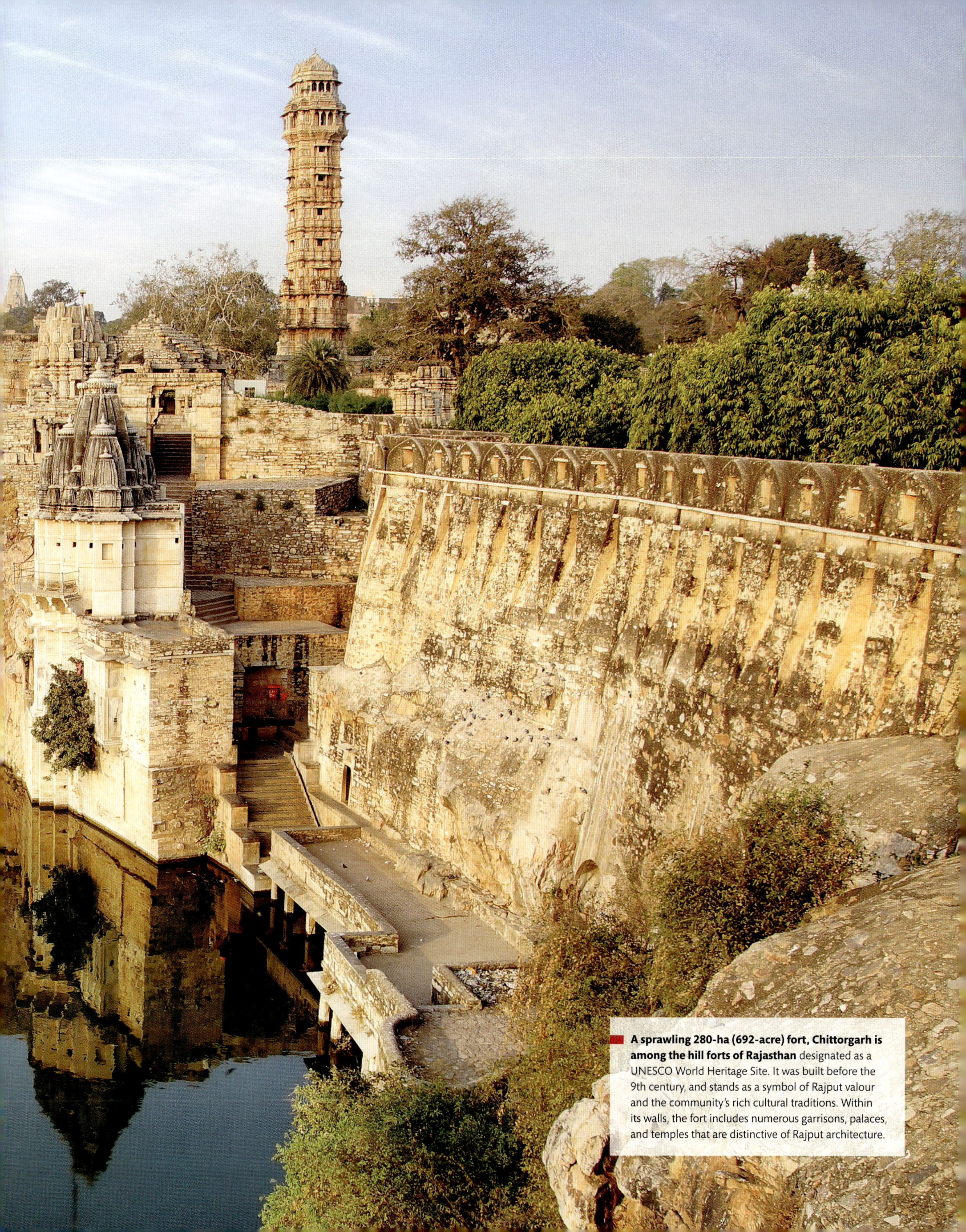

A sprawling 280-ha (692-acre) fort, Chittorgarh is among the hill forts of Rajasthan designated as a UNESCO World Heritage Site. It was built before the 9th century, and stands as a symbol of Rajput valour and the community's rich cultural traditions. Within its walls, the fort includes numerous garrisons, palaces, and temples that are distinctive of Rajput architecture.

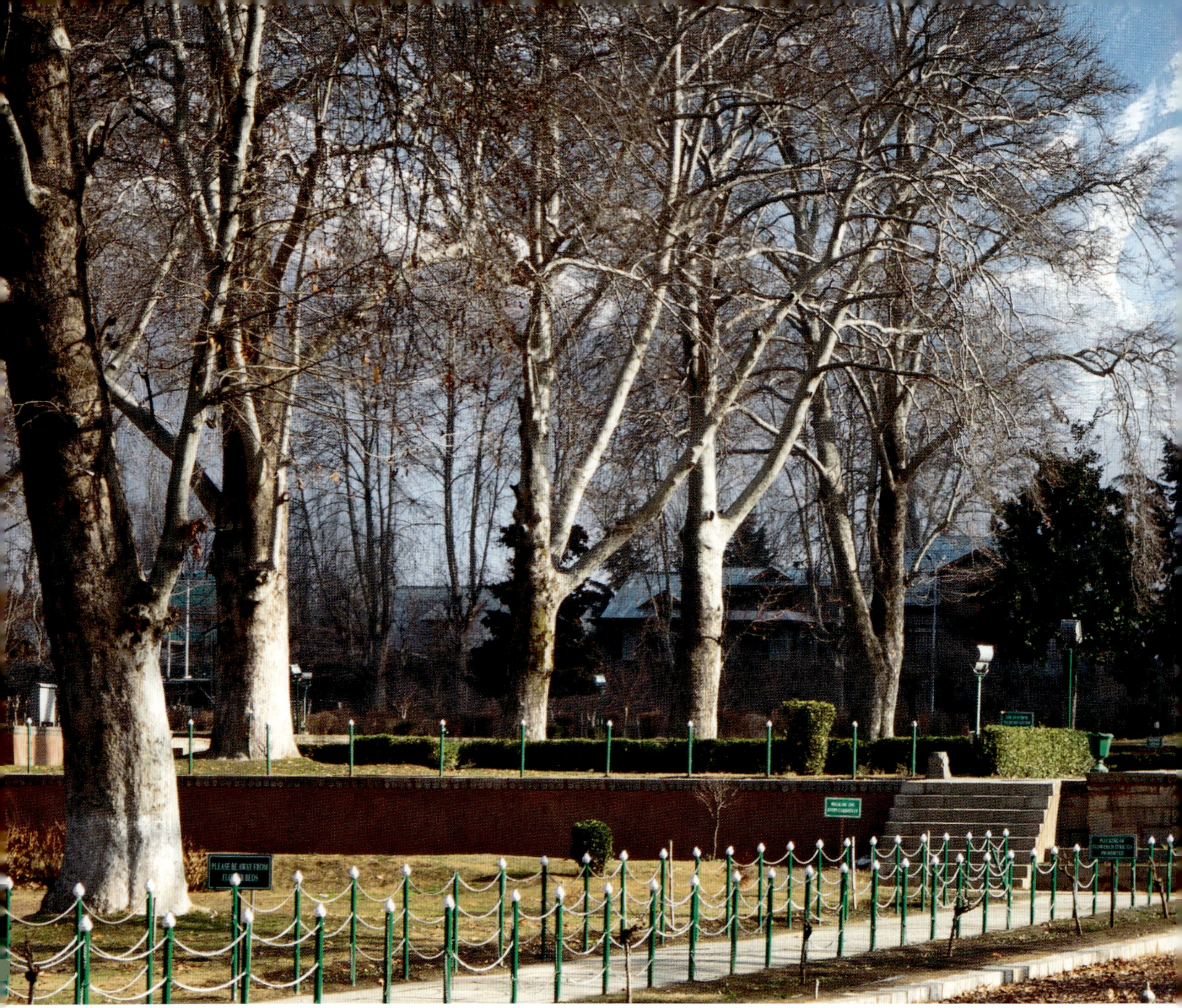

Era 17th century CE | **Area** 31 acres (12.4 ha)

SHALIMAR BAGH

A garden of paradise built for a queen

Looking out from the right bank of the Dal Lake to a breathtaking view of the valley, Shalimar Bagh, the Garden of Delight, was laid out by the Mughal emperor Jahangir for his wife Nur Jahan, and is considered the epitome of Mughal horticulture.

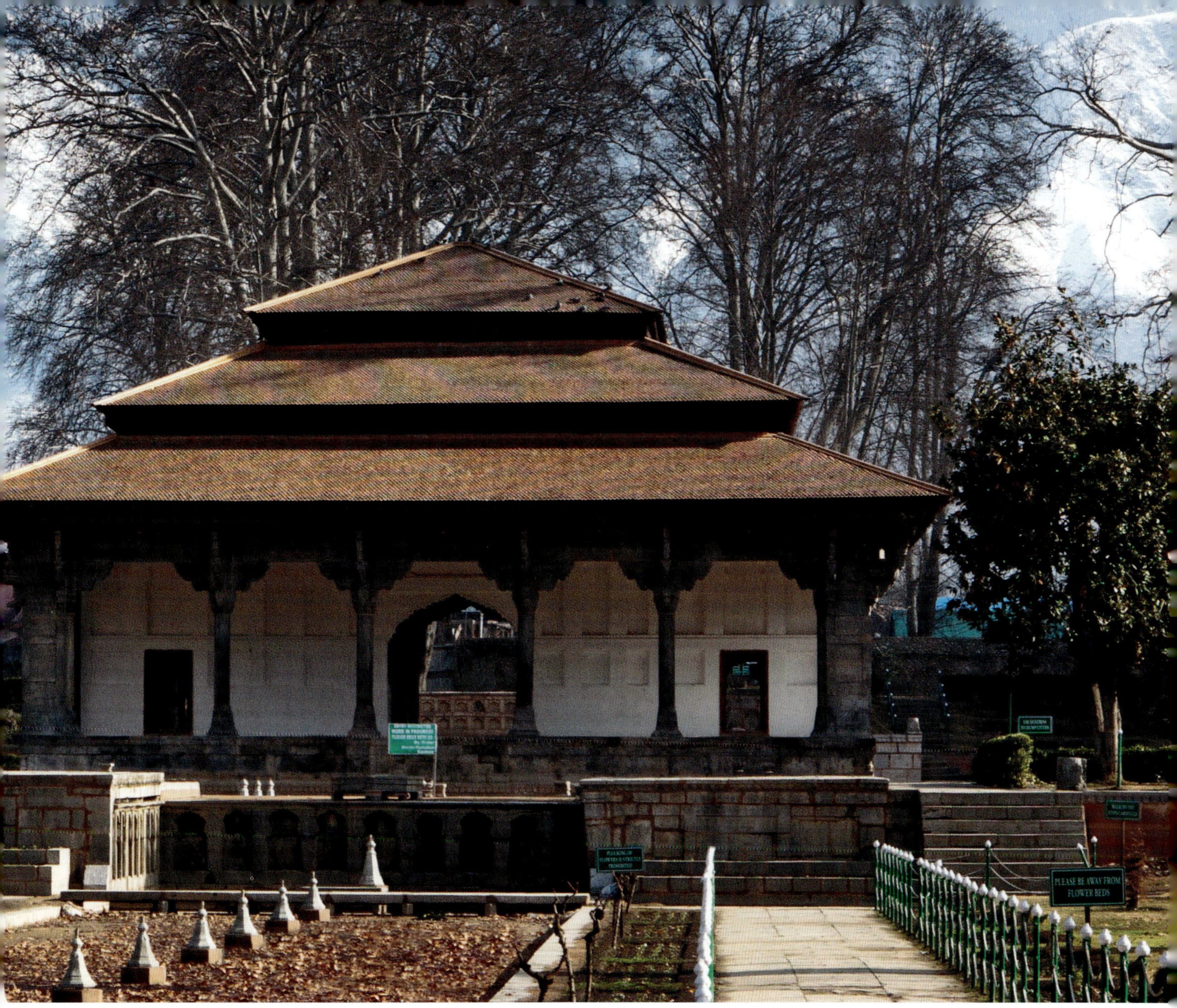

Shalimar Bagh stays true to the concept of the *charbagh* vision of a paradise garden as described in the Qur'an, with some concession to the specifics of the hilly terrain. The landscape was intended as a representation of an ideal place where humans coexisted in harmony with nature, and were thus closer to the divine. The gardens are laid out in the form of three terraces. A water channel that takes advantage of the natural spring flowing through all levels as the main axis and out into the lake via a canal, is a unique feature.

A THOUGHTFUL EXECUTION

The three terraces were functionally divided. The first, at the lowest level, was the public garden, the Diwan-e Aam (hall of public audience) with its small, black marble throne marking the transition to the next level. Accessible only to nobles and guests of the emperor, this second garden was focused around the pink pavilion of the Diwan-e Khas (hall of private audience). The third and the highest level was private – the Zenana Garden, guarded by two pavilions built in the local style. Emperor Jahangir's son, and the new emperor, Shah Jahan, added a *baradari* (pavilion) of black marble set within a fountain pool. The pink and the black pavilions are adorned with carved columns and brackets, elaborate niches and beautiful *naquashi* (a type of sculptural art) derived from the Kashmiri papier-mâché tradition on the walls and ceilings. The carefully thought-out plantation complements the *charbagh* plan with avenues of poplar and chinar trees.

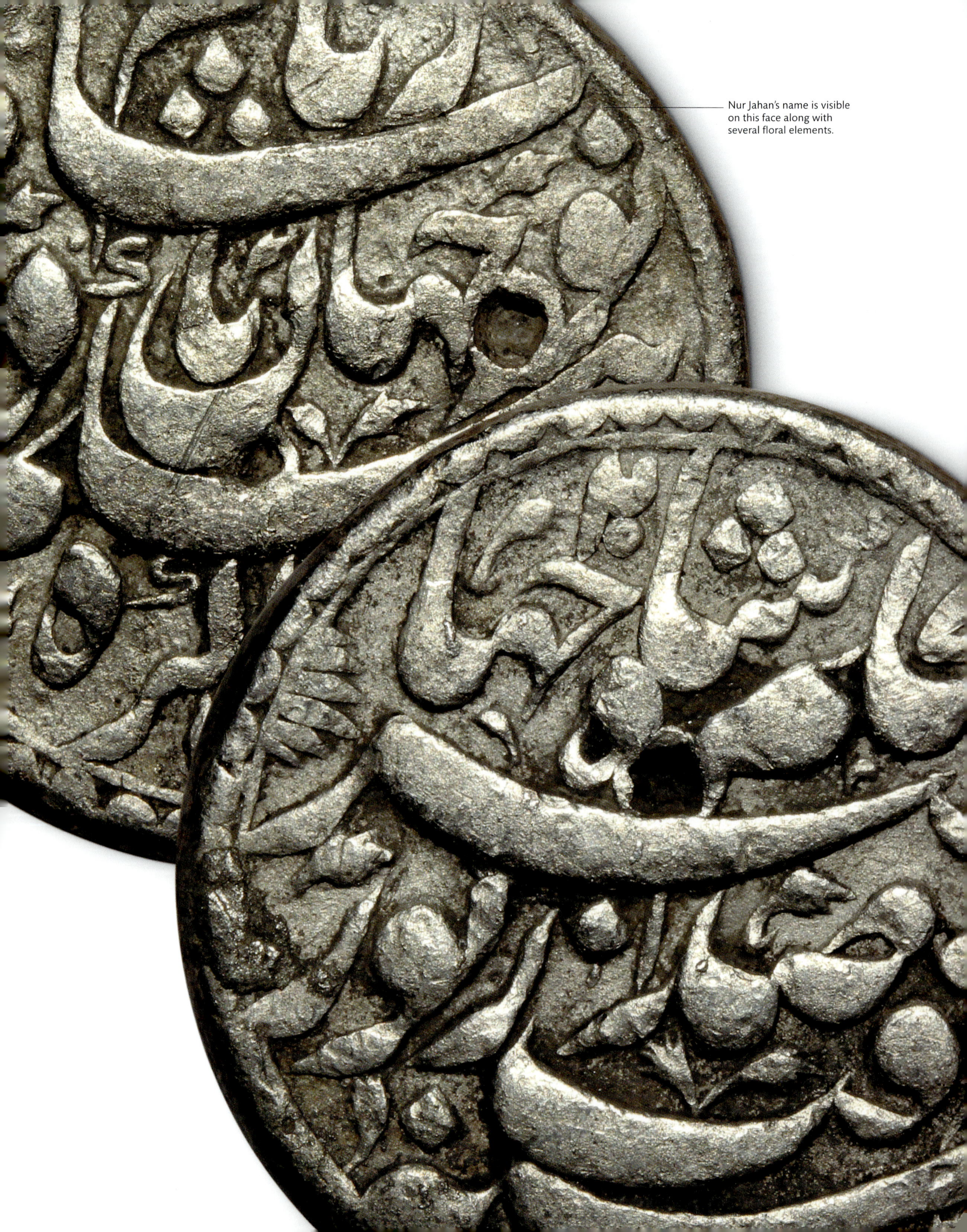

Nur Jahan's name is visible on this face along with several floral elements.

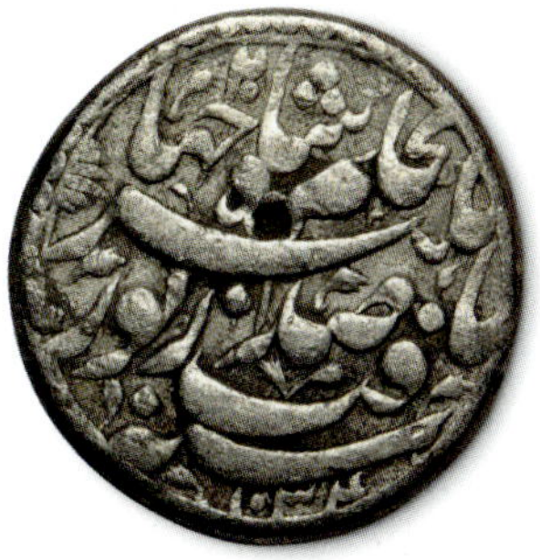

Era 16th–17th centuries CE | **Medium** Bronze (Copper alloy) | **Diameter** 68.3 cm (26.8 in)

NUR JAHAN'S COINS

Evidence of a Mughal woman's political influence

Nur Jahan, the wife of Emperor Jahangir, was one of the most influential royal women of the Mughal Empire. Rare gold and silver coins bearing her name have been found, a testimony to the unprecedented political power she wielded.

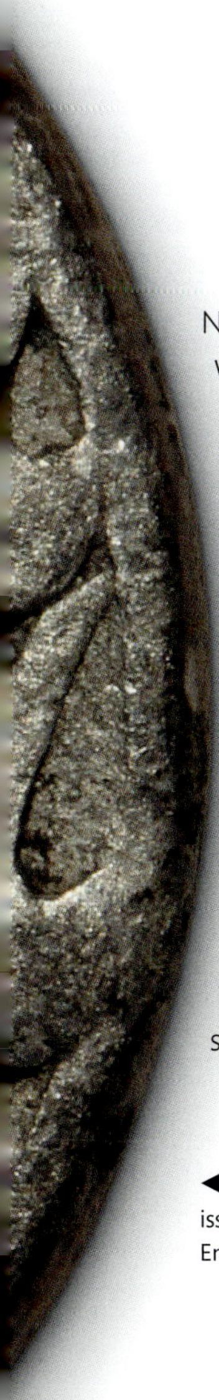

Nur Jahan, the 20th and last wife of Emperor Jahangir, was a skilled poet, hunter, diplomat, and art lover. She grew increasingly active in court politics, so much so that her name was engraved in the coinage of the time.

Nur Jahan married the Mughal emperor in 1611. As Jahangir withered, succumbing to the effects of alcohol and opium, Nur Jahan and her family members took control of governance and administration. She soon became the only woman in the Mughal dynasty to rule openly and actively. With the support of her husband, she had coins minted in her name - an unprecedented development since the honour was only reserved for the emperor. During her reign, she initiated trade with foreign merchants, managed the court's promotions and finances, held audiences in her palace, oversaw new developments in art and religion, and designed many Mughal gardens. As queen, she was able to create many architectural works with the substantial fortune she acquired through trade routes, family fortune, and money given to her by Jahangir. However, her end was as fateful as that of her coins. Her stepson and future emperor, Shah Jahan launched a rebellion against her and forced her into exile. She drew her last breath in Lahore, far away from what was once her place of glory, Agra. To further emphasize her fall from grace, upon his ascension, Shah Jahan made it a crime to possess coins that had been minted during her time in power. He ordered that they be returned to the mint to be melted, and those that were not melted were deliberately defaced to remove any references to the empress's name. Any coins that exist today are rare survivors.

◄ **Two silver rupee coins of Nur Jahan,** issued in the year 1624, bearing her's and Emperor Jahangir's name.

A NEW WAVE

Nur Jahan was the one of the only women to rise to the status of co-sovereign, in contrast to the contemporary social structures of the Mughals, where women remained confined to the private sphere. However, there were several other aristocratic Mughal ladies involved in the political, economic, cultural, and religious spheres of the Mughal Empire, serving as strong advocacy groups between the 16th and 19th centuries.

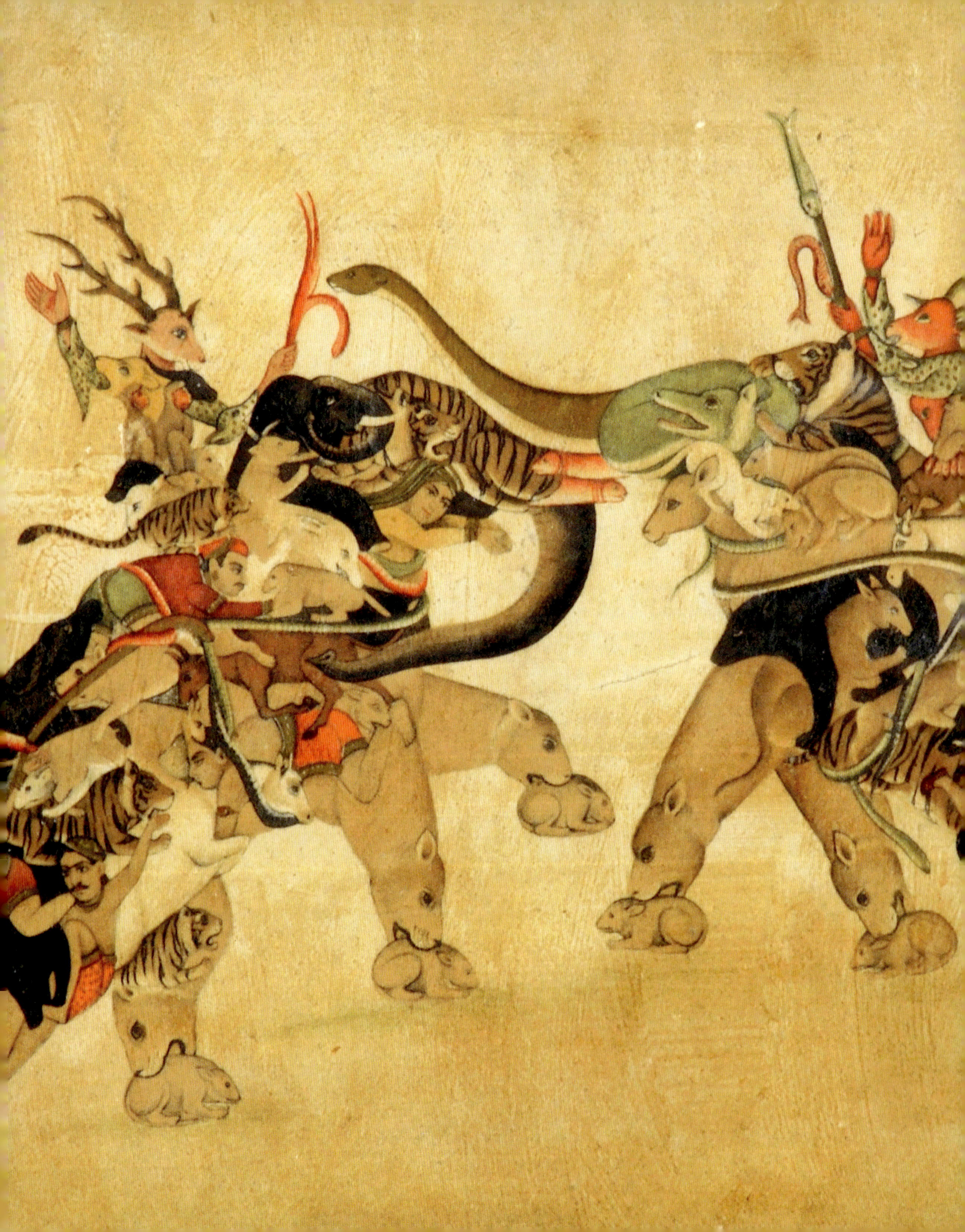

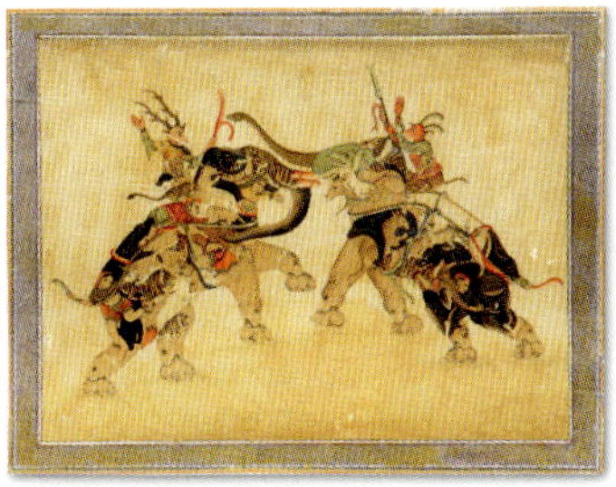

Era 16th–17th centuries CE | **Medium** Ink and gold on paper | **Dimension** 24.6 × 20.3 cm (9.6 × 8 in)

COMPOSITE PAINTING

A portrayal of the surreal and the fantastic

An animal composed of parts from other living beings – man, bird, and beast; this form of composite painting lends itself to imaginative interpretation.

There always seems to be more to the animals within the animal in these composite paintings. Some seem to battle for space, while others live in harmony. Often though, they seem to represent different aspects of human nature - some human, some beastly, gentle or even ferocious.

Two themes seem most prominent. In one, animals make up the composite animal, and in another, female figures form the composite. In both, the composite takes the form of an elephant, or *kunjar* in Sanskrit. This is perhaps why this art form gets its popular names of *pashu kunjar* (animal elephant) and *nari kunjar* (woman elephant). Other composite animals include horse, camel, lion, and tiger.

◀ **This Deccan *pashu kunjar* painting** depicts two elephants engaged in battle. They are made up of humans and animals, who form the legs, body, and tusks.

ROOTED IN REALITY

Different theories surround the inspiration for this art form. One of them lies in the idea of the cosmic cow, believed to hold within her body all the gods and goddesses. Another interpretation speaks of the symbolic portrayal of the interdependence and interconnectedness of all beings and the unification of all in the universe.

Nari kunjars usually depict the rider of the composite animal as a deity - most often Krishna - and is seen as the striving of the soul for oneness with the supreme being. Paintings of composite animals, seen from the early 16th century, are credited to Persian influence on miniature art that grew with the establishment of Mughal rule. The Deccan, Rajput, and Murshidabad schools adopted the concept, and produced some outstanding works of art. It was also adopted by the folk artists of Odisha and can be found in the traditional depictions of Patachitra style, showcasing great skill on the part of the artists.

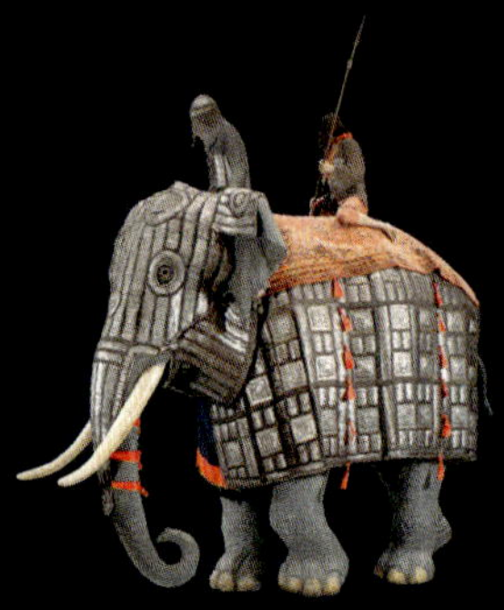

Era 16th–19th centuries CE | **Medium** Steel, brass, cotton, and leather | **Height** 3.9 m (12.7 ft)

ELEPHANT ARMOUR

Adornments for the battlefield's fiercest warriors

Asiatic battle elephants, traditionally used by the Mughal Empire, often wore these massive and elaborate metal suits of armour, embellished with intricate depictions of animals and floral motifs.

The Mughals' most-prized soldiers were the battle elephants who were often outfitted with protective armour, which ranged from full coverage to one that offered partial protection, covering just the head and the trunk. This particular armour is unique not only for having survived the ravages of time, but also for its enormous size. While parts of the armour are missing, it is believed that the full set consisted of approximately 8,439 metal plates and weighed over 160 kgs (352 lbs). A pair of 'elephant swords' complemented the armour. These would be fixed on to the war elephant's partially cut tusks. When paired with the animal's charge, it was responsible for great damage on the battlefield.

A DEADLY MOUNT

There is evidence of the long-standing practice of employing elephants in battle, with references that date as far back as the 4th century BCE. The war elephant became important during the three-centuries-long reign of the Mughals. They were an important mode of transportation in medieval India, with riders mounted either atop the animal or within a specially designed carriage known as a *howdah*. They were utilized as weapons because of their immense size and strength, and tough hides that made it difficult for conventional weapons to penetrate, making them nearly invulnerable. Elephant suits were typically crafted from a combination of plates and chain mail, scales attached to cloth, steel plates sandwiched between layers of cloth, or simply padded cloth or leather. An interesting feature of the armour was the inclusion of protective 'ears' – projections on the elephant's head designed to safeguard the rider.

▶ **This 17th–18th-century armour** has been extensively restored and displayed on an artificial elephant in the Royal Armouries Museum in Leeds, UK.

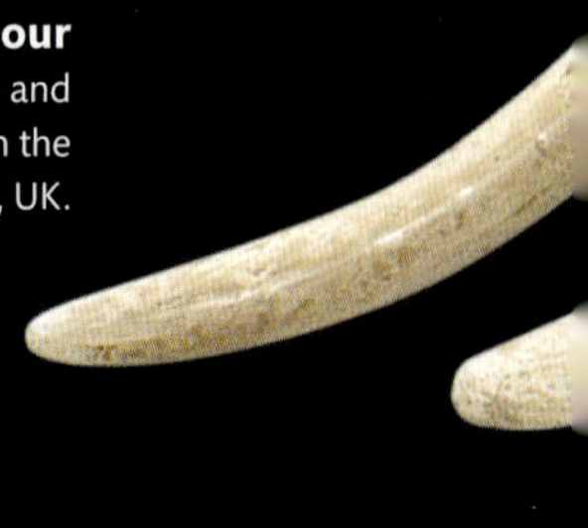

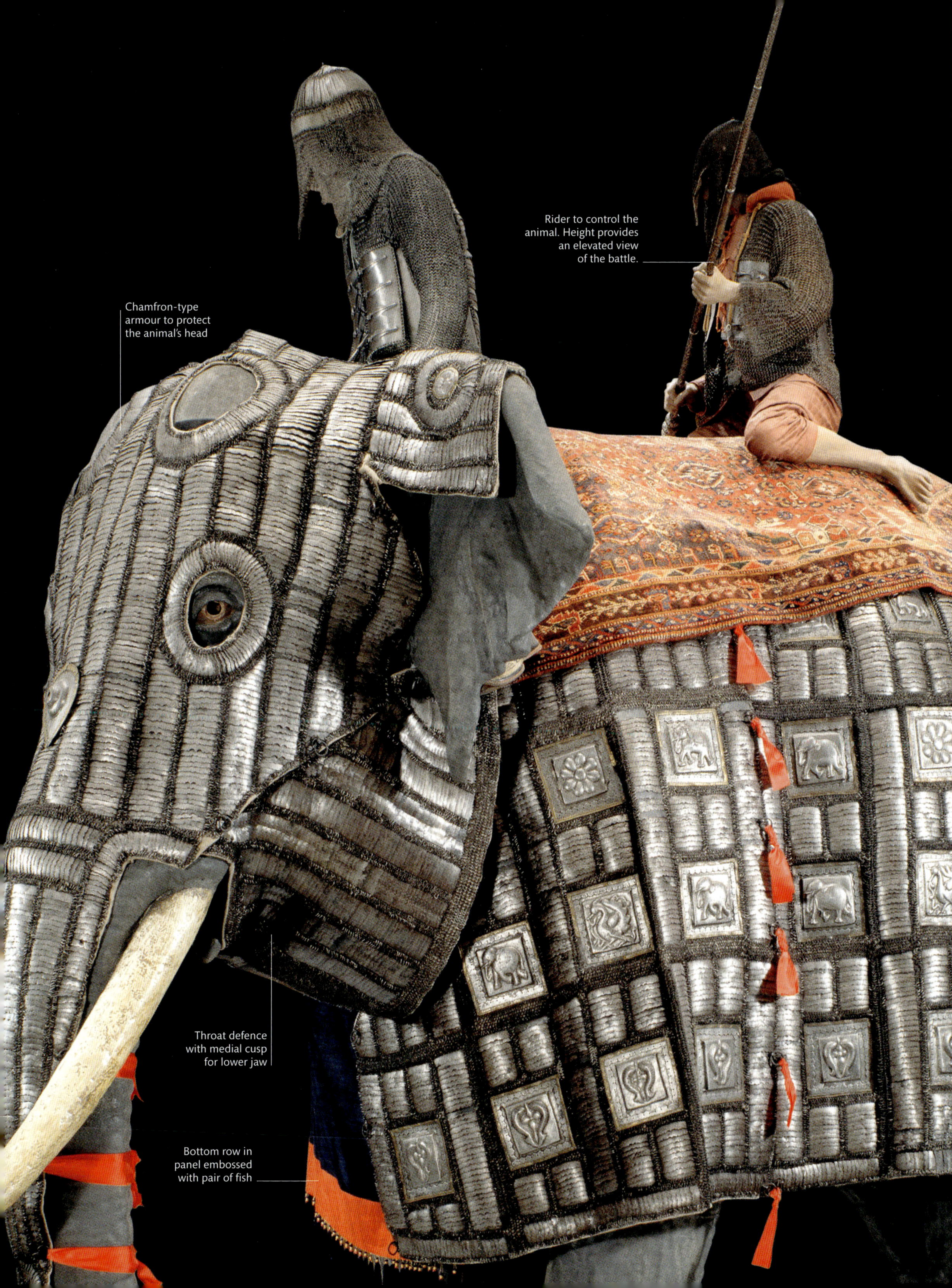
Rider to control the animal. Height provides an elevated view of the battle.
Chamfron-type armour to protect the animal's head
Throat defence with medial cusp for lower jaw
Bottom row in panel embossed with pair of fish

19th century onwards

MODERN INDIA

The decline of the Mughal Empire and the influx of Western powers led to radical transformation in India. British control over most of the subcontinent paved the way for questions of identity and freedom. These were compounded by India's long struggle for independence, which came at a great cost. During this period, the understanding of cultural wealth grew, and different sensibilities emerged within the nation. Symbolic and representative art, architecture, literature, and culture flourished, much of which can be witnessed in contemporary times as well.

HOLDING THEIR OWN

A period of continuity and change

The 18th century was a time of great flux with the decline of the Mughal Empire and the emergence of several smaller kingdoms and dynasties who fought for dominance as is chronicled in the period's literary works including poetry and paintings.

By 1761, the Mughal Empire had dwindled in influence and control and was an empire only in name. However, the Mughal emperor's symbolic position as the ruler of a large, unified land persisted since he was still considered a source of political legitimacy. Frequent changes in leadership, weak policies, and poor public perception had allowed regional kingdoms in various parts of the Indian subcontinent to declare their independence from the Mughal Empire. Three of these states, Bengal, Hyderabad, and Awadh, established by the provincial rulers of the Mughals, had never severed their ties with the centre, though they effectively maintained autonomy in local policy matters. This changed as these states rose in prominence. The shift of power from the centre has often led to the belief that this was a period of political disintegration, economic decline, warfare, and disorder. However, several historians also emphasize its vibrance, cultural richness, and economic wealth.

THE THREE SUCCESSOR STATES

Murshid Quli Khan, was appointed the governor of the Mughal *subah*, or province, of Bengal in 1717. His effective revenue administration, which rendered Bengal a consistent tax-paying surplus territory even in the days of political upheaval elsewhere

1713 Farrukh Siyar ascends the Mughal throne

1714 Hussain Ali is made viceroy of the Deccan province

1716 Execution of the Sikh warrior, Banda Singh Bahadur

1717 Farrukh Siyar allows the East India Company to trade in Bengal

1717 Murshid Quli Khan becomes the governor of Bengal

1717 Murshid Quli Khan's title as the Nawab of Bengal is recognized by the Mughals

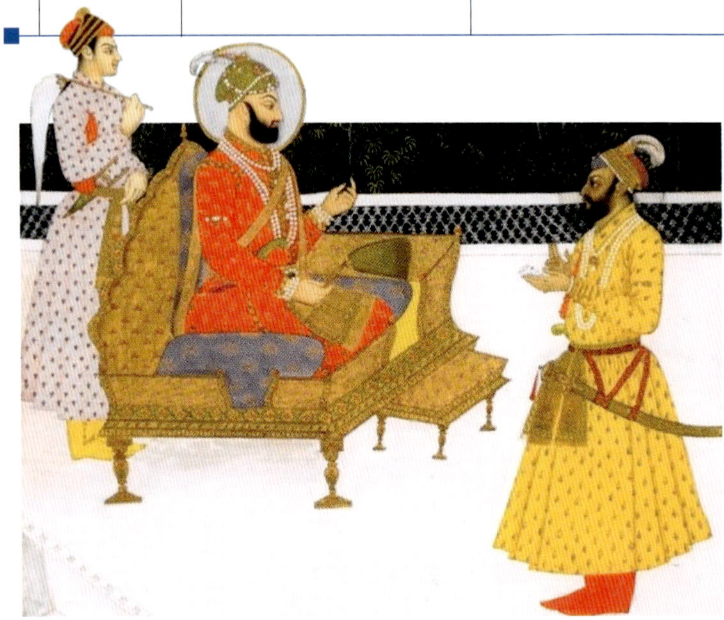

A 1717 painting depicts the Mughal emperor Farrukh Siyar receiving the new viceroy of the Deccan region, Sayyid Hussain Ali Khan Barha at his court.

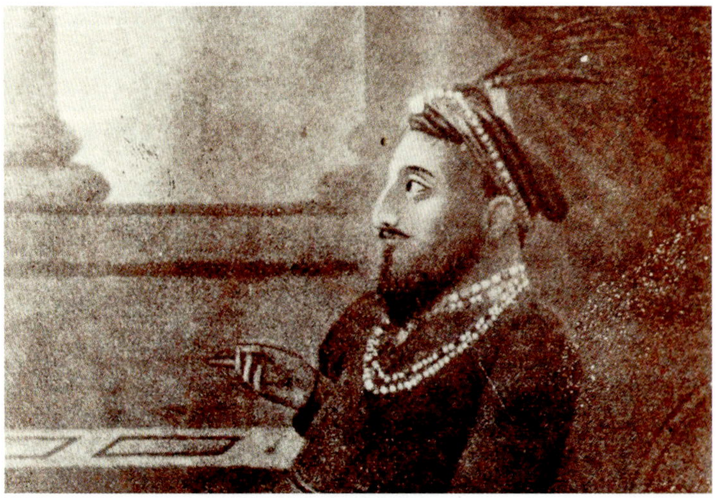

An undated portrait of Murshid Quli Khan, the governor of Bengal who established himself as the region's first nawab in 1717.

in the empire, served as the cornerstone of his dominance. It was after this that the region moved away from Mughal control and was set up as an independent state with Khan as its nawab. Different theories persist as to how he achieved the 20 per cent increase in revenue between 1700 and 1722 - it is posited that he may have been a harsh ruler, or simply that he may have levied increased taxes to the royal treasury from the locals during his time in power.

The political unrest in the 18th century, with the death of the emperor in Delhi, weakened the declining Mughal state further. This was compounded by foreign invasions, Maratha attacks on Bengal and unrest around the world. Though trade suffered at first, increased investment from the European companies – the Dutch, the French, and the English - soon led to a boom in oceanic trade in the first half of the century. Eventually, Europe undoubtedly overtook Asia as Bengal's primary export market, which had a tremendous impact on the region's textile sector.

Almost parallelly, Chin Qulich Khan, a powerful noble at the imperial court of the Mughals, was bestowed multiple titles, including the Nizam-ul-Mulk and Asaf Jah I, which alluded to his role in the governance of the Deccan region in the south-central part of the subcontinent. The former morphed into the title of the Nizam, or ruler, of Hyderabad, an autonomous

1719 Emperor Farrukh defeated and executed by the Sayyid brothers

1719 Rafi-ud-Darajat ascends the Mughal throne, with the Sayyid brothers as regents

1719 Shah Jahan II ascends the throne under the guidance of the Sayyid brothers

1719 Muhammad Shah ascends the Mughal throne and rules for 29 years

1720 Sayyid brothers defeated

1721 Kingdom of Rohilkhand established by Ali Mohammed Khan in the north

1722 Saadat Ali Khan I appointed the governor of Awadh

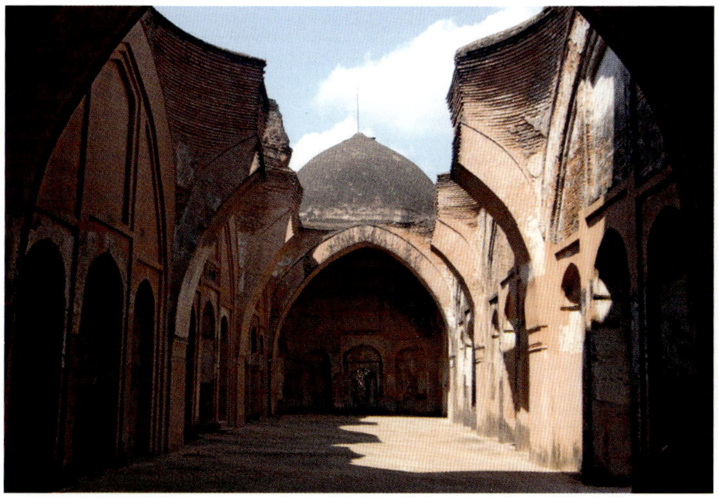

The beautiful Katra Masjid, built by the Nawab of Bengal Murshid Quli Khan in 1723 in Murshidabad, a city in present-day West Bengal. The tomb of the nawab is also located within the complex.

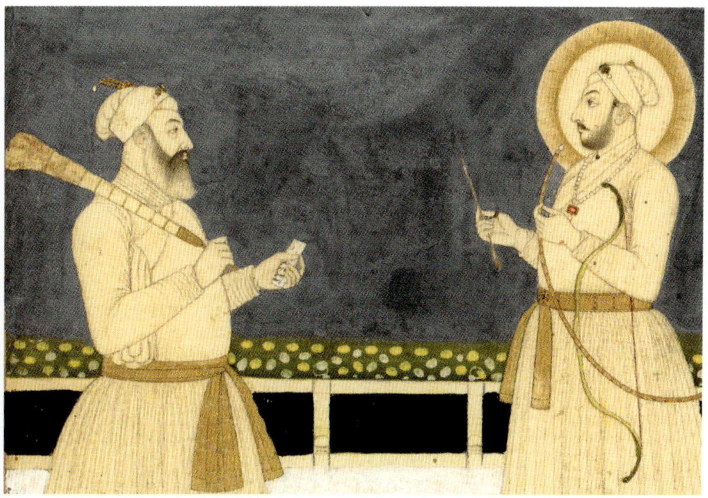

A watercolour painting, c. 1720, of Emperor Muhammad Shah with a bow and arrow, interacting with Saadat Khan, the founder of the Awadh dynasty, who is shown with a peacock feather fan over his shoulder.

kingdom that he founded in 1724, independent of Mughal control. He had been frustrated by Delhi's court politics, and the haughty assertion of power by a faction led by the Sayyid brothers, regents to the Mughal emperor. They eventually assassinated Emperor Farrukh Siyar and installed Muhammad Shah as a puppet ruler on the central throne in 1719.

The Hyderabadi administrative system under the nizam's rule sought to incorporate indigenous power structures within its territory into a 'patron-client relationship' with the central power rather than destroy all ties. By the end of the 18th century, the state of Hyderabad was characterized by a relatively new political system, with a number of new participants from different backgrounds and origins.

The third centre of regional power was Awadh, or Oudh, at first just another Mughal province. In 1722, Saadat Ali Khan I was appointed the Mughal governor of Awadh, and given the challenging task of suppressing rebellions by smaller local rulers and chiefs of the region. Deeply disappointed with the court politics of Delhi, Khan decided to establish his own base in Awadh. Towards this effort, as a first step, he appointed his son-in-law, Abul Mansur Mirza Muhammad Muqim Ali Khan, also called Safdar Jung, as his deputy. In order to establish his dynastic rule, he de-coupled the office of *diwan*, or treasurer, from all imperial control, thus giving himself autonomy over the state's plentiful resources.

STRENGTH OF THE LOCAL WARRIORS

The Mughal Empire had always interacted with different communities and, on many occasions, faced conflict with local chiefs and warriors who wished to protect their ways of life and lessen the economic burden from Mughal taxation. Chief among these were the Marathas, the Sikhs, the Jats, and the Afghan kingdoms of Farukhabad and Rohilkhand.

In the 17th century, the legendary ruler Maharaja Chhatrapati Shivaji had consolidated a small kingdom in western India in the face of fierce opposition from the neighbouring Muslim kingdom of Bijapur that was loyal to the central powers, and the pressure of the formidable Mughal army. The Marathas were immensely powerful in their region and successfully fought the Mughals on many occasions. However, dynastic factionalism and the ongoing oppression as a result of the Mughal policy of conquest in the Deccan soon weakened it, especially after Shivaji's death in 1680.

1724 Nizams set up the state of Hyderabad in the Deccan

1739 Nadir Shah attacks the Mughals in Delhi

1739 Death of Shuja-ud-din, Nawab of Bengal

1739 Sarfaraz Khan becomes Nawab of Bengal for a year

1740 Alivardi Khan takes over as Nawab of Bengal

1742 The Marathas invade Bengal

1742 French general Joseph Dupleix becomes the governor of French-occupied Pondicherry

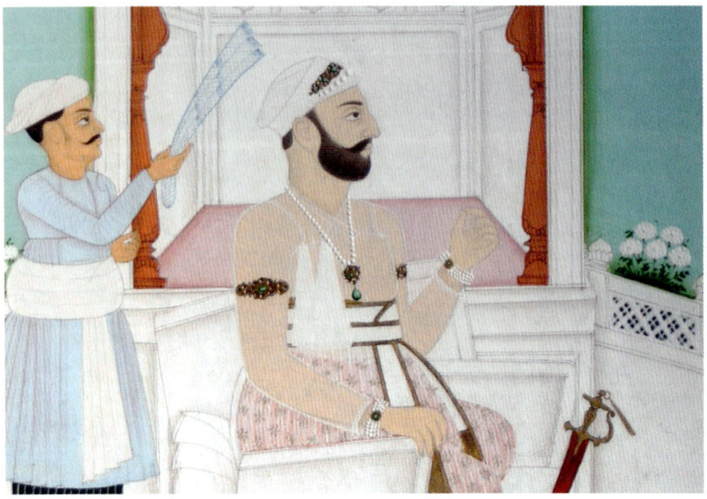

A painting of Chin Qulich Khan of the Asaf Jah dynasty, who was the Nizam-ul-Mulk, or the Nizam, meaning administrator (of the realm) of the Hyderabad state under Mughal rule.

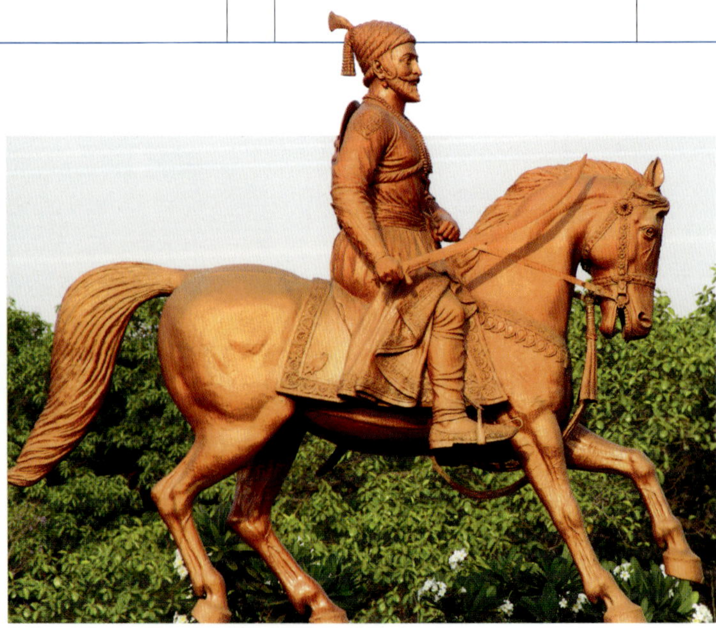

A statue of Maratha ruler Chhatrapati Shivaji Maharaj of the Bhonsle clan, riding his horse. This statue is located in the campus of the University of Pune in Maharashtra.

Local landowners took advantage of the circumstances. They occasionally sided with the Mughals, and occasionally with the Marathas. Two of Shivaji's sons, Rajaram and Shambhaji, both reigned briefly while engaging in constant combat with the Mughal army.

When Rajaram died in 1699, one of his queens, Tarabai, began to rule in the name of her infant son Shivaji II. Mughal emperor Aurangzeb's army conquered Maratha forts one after another, keeping Tarabai on the move. From late 1705, however, the tide began to turn against Aurangzeb, and when he died in 1707 after 40 years of warfare in the Deccan, the Marathas still remained a force that stood strong.

However, the Maratha state could not transform itself into an alternative to the Mughal Empire, primarily because of the way their rule was structured. The Marathas were, in essence, a confederacy where power was distributed among the *sardars*, or chiefs, such as the Bhonsles of Nagpur, in Maharashtra, Gaikwads of Baroda, in Gujarat, Holkars of Indore or Sindhias of Gwalior, both in Madhya Pradesh. These chiefs continued to recognize the emblematic role of the Mughal emperor. Their internal administration was, in effect, structured similar to the Mughals'. The one important distinction was that, unlike the Mughal system where there was an integrated civilian and military bureaucracy, the Maratha domains had a large number of civilian revenue collectors, often upper-caste Hindus, who did not go on to hold any important military positions.

A NEW POWER

In the northern parts of India in the 18th century, a community which existed alongside the Mughals in India was also growing in influence. This was the Sikh community of Punjab, a region in the Indian subcontinent's north-west parts. The first guru of the Sikhs, Guru Nanak was preaching his message of equality, spirituality, and enlightenment around the time that Babur arrived in the Indian subcontinent. This was the beginning of a faith that came to be known as Sikhism. As Nanak's message spread across the land, the religion started to draw followers. It began to take shape and acquire a definition under the guidance of the ten succeeding gurus. In 1699, Guru Gobind Singh, the tenth Sikh Guru founded the Khalsa, which established stringent community guidelines, and also militarized the Sikh populace. This marked the beginning

1744–1748 First Carnatic War between the Mughals, the French, and the British

1746 Madras is captured by the French

1747 Afghan ruler Ahmad Shah Abdali invades India

1748 Death of Hyderabad Nizam Chin Qulich Khan

1748 Death of Mughal emperor Muhammad Shah

1749 Madras passes into British hands

1949–1954 Second Carnatic War is fought

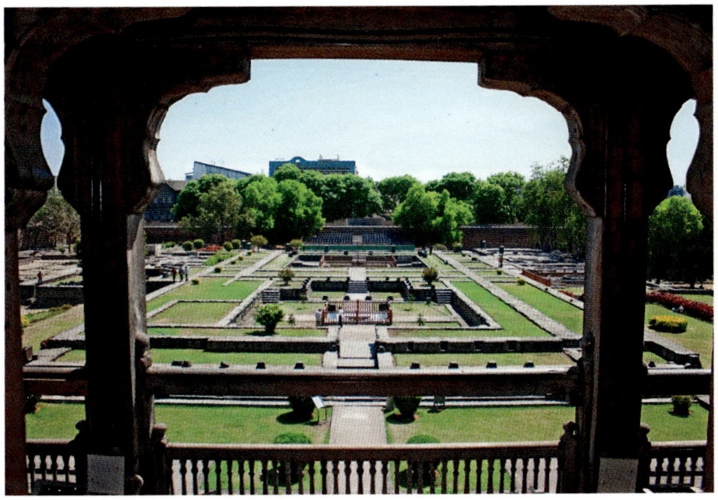

A view of the beautiful, planned garden of the Shaniwar Wada fort in Pune, Maharashtra. This fortification was the seat of the peshwas, or rulers, of the Maratha Empire until 1818.

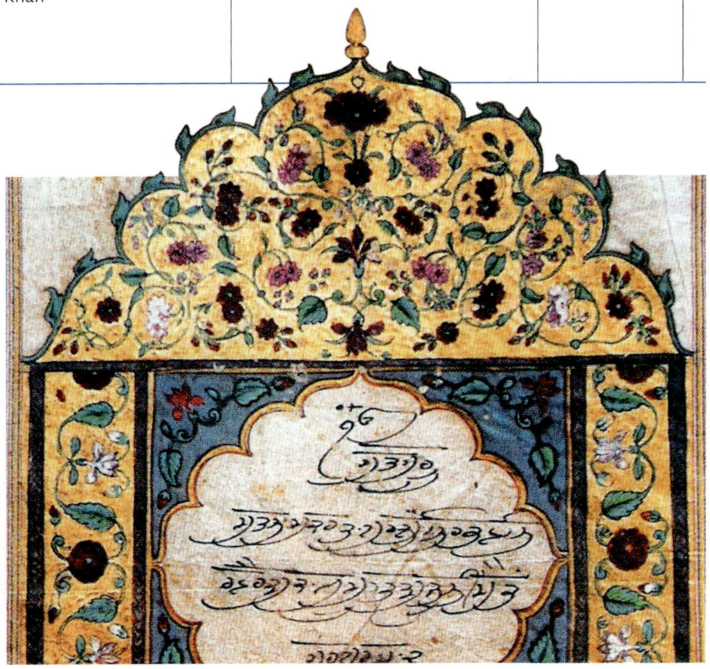

Exquisitely decorated page of the Guru Granth Sahib, the holy book and the 11th and eternal spiritual leader of the Sikh faith, as decreed by the tenth guru, Guru Gobind Singh.

of a prolonged and complex conflict between the Mughals and the Sikhs. The Sikhs had a formidable and strong army, and had successfully looted Persian invader Nadir Shah's contingents in the past.

After the death of the tenth guru, there was no subsequent human spiritual and temporal leader as Guru Gobind had placed symbolic authority upon the holy book, the Guru Granth Sahib. Instead, Banda Singh Bahadur, one of his trusted adherents, took command of the military. Under Banda Bahadur, several territories were taken back from Mughal control in the west. However, following a battle in 1715, Banda Bahadur was forced to surrender to Mughal governor, Abdus Samad Khan. He was taken to Delhi with some of his closest followers, where they were executed in March 1716.

Banda Bahadur's death did not mean the end of Sikh power in Punjab, though no one was immediately available to take up the leadership. Under committee leadership, fairly autonomous, roving bands of Sikh *misldars*, or chieftains, used the breakdown of imperial control in north India to assert their independence. Even the Afghan invader Ahmad Shah Abdali failed to conquer Punjab from the Sikhs; his governors were quickly deposed, and by September 1761, the Sikhs had established control over vast areas of the region of Punjab, from the Sutlej to the Indus rivers. After repelling the third Afghan invasion led by Abdali's successor Zaman Shah in 1798–1799, Ranjit Singh emerged as a Sikh ruler and took Lahore from the Mughals. Leading an army with improved artillery and infantry trained by European officers, he had taken control of large areas in Punjab's five doabs (the land between two streams of a river) by 1809 and established what came to be known as the Sikh Empire. Later that year, the colonial powers would recognize him as the sole sovereign ruler of Punjab in the Treaty of Amritsar.

RICHES OF THE SMALLER STATES

In tandem with the larger centres of power, various smaller states emerged in north India in the 18th century, taking advantage of the growing fissures in the Mughal Empire. A prime example of this is the Jat kingdom of Bharatpur. The Jats were an agrarian and pastoral community who lived in the Delhi–Mathura region in the north-central parts of India. Suraj Mal, the chief of the Jats from 1756 to 1763, had consolidated territories under one Jat regime, compelling the Mughal authorities to recognize him as

1751 Peace treaty between Nawab of Bengal and the Marathas

1754 Alamgir II becomes the new Mughal emperor

1756–1757 Siraj-ud-daula succeeds as Nawab of Bengal and fights the British for control over Calcutta

1757 Ahmed Shah Abdali attacks and raids Delhi and Mathura

1757 Battle of Plassey between the British and the Bengal nawab (aided by the French)

1758–1763 Third Carnatic War fought

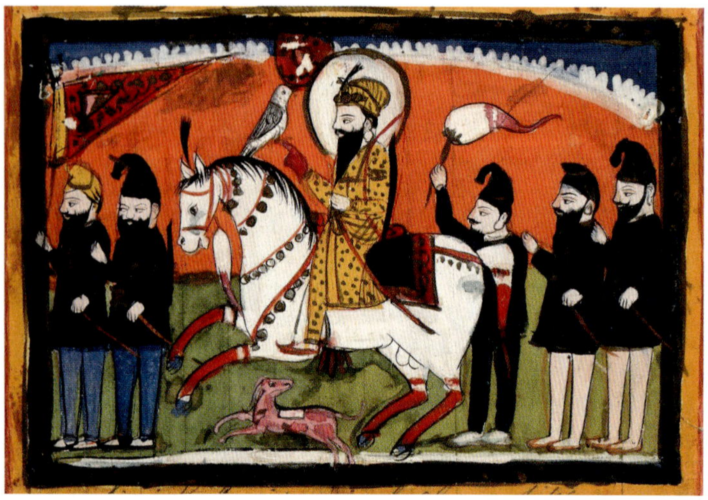

A gouache painting depicting the tenth guru of the Sikhs, Guru Gobind Singh, on horseback. His attendants accompany him with a flag and a ceremonial fly whisk.

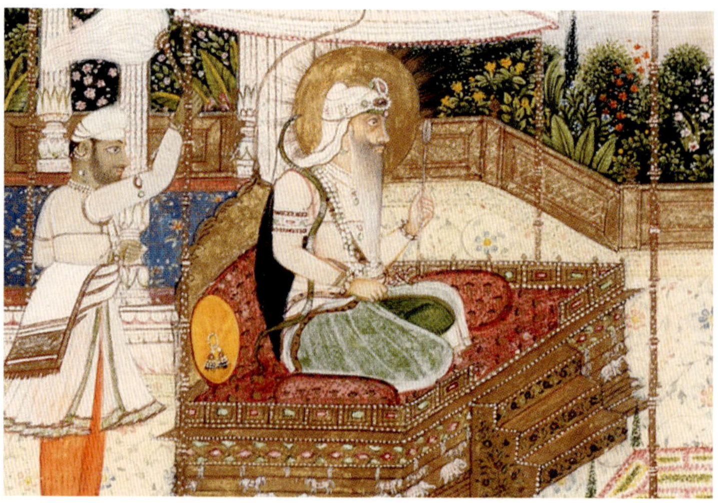

A beautiful watercolour painting, attributed to the artist Jagannath, c. 1850, portrays the first ruler of the Sikh Empire, Maharaja Ranjit Singh seated on a throne in his court at Lahore Fort.

their leader. He successfully resisted Abdali's siege and backed the Marathas in the Third Battle of Panipat. However, in terms of organization, the Jat state, despite being established with the active support of the peasants, retained its feudal character.

Following Nadir Shah's invasion, the breakdown of authority in northern India provided an opportunity for another Afghan leader, Ali Muhammad Khan, to establish the small kingdom of Rohilkhand at the foothills of the Himalayas. However, the new kingdom gained very little influence as it suffered greatly at the hands of neighbouring regional powers such as the Marathas, Jats, Awadh, and, later, the British. Another kingdom was established by Afghan ruler, Ahmad Khan Bangash, to the east of Delhi, near Farukhabad. Both Rohillas and the Bangash kingdoms aided the Afghan ruler Ahmad Shah Abdali during the Third Battle of Panipat, but their influence within the subcontinent waned rather quickly after Abdali left the Indian stage for Kabul, placing his aide, Najib ad-Dawlah, in charge of affairs in Delhi.

The principalities governed by the Rajputs in the Himalayas as well as the north-west frequently both supported and opposed the Mughals over the years, as they enjoyed considerable autonomy. Some Rajput states also maintained an alliance with the East India Company as it grew in influence, looking to them to aid them against the Marathas. Rajputs states were not the only ones to function independently of the Mughals in the 18th century. Travancore, which covers most of present-day Kerala in South India, was a dynastic region that had withstood attempts by the Dutch to gain control, as well as defeating other regional powers. They did align with the British East India Company on occasion, such as when fighting off an invasion by the kingdom of Mysore.

In the 18th century, under Haider Ali and his son Tipu Sultan, Mysore had become one of the leading centres of power, amassing territory not only from Travancore, but also the Mughals and the Marathas.

This period in history essentially stands between two clearly discernible eras, one of consolidated Mughal rule, and the other of Western colonial rule, chiefly British. The decline of the Mughals left the Indian subcontinent, with its significant amounts of resources and a lucrative region for amassing wealth, vulnerable. This, and the lack of a single, unifying power, is essentially what drew the English and other European traders and sparked a competition among them for mastery over the subcontinent.

1758 The Marathas fight the Sikhs for control over the Punjab region

1759 Emperor Alamgir II defeated by military leader Ghazi ud din

1761 Haider Ali becomes the king of Mysore

1764 The Battle of Buxar fought between the Mughal-aided Bengal and Awadh kingdoms against the British

1775–1782 The Marathas fight the British for the first time

1782 Tipu Sultan succeeds as the king of Mysore

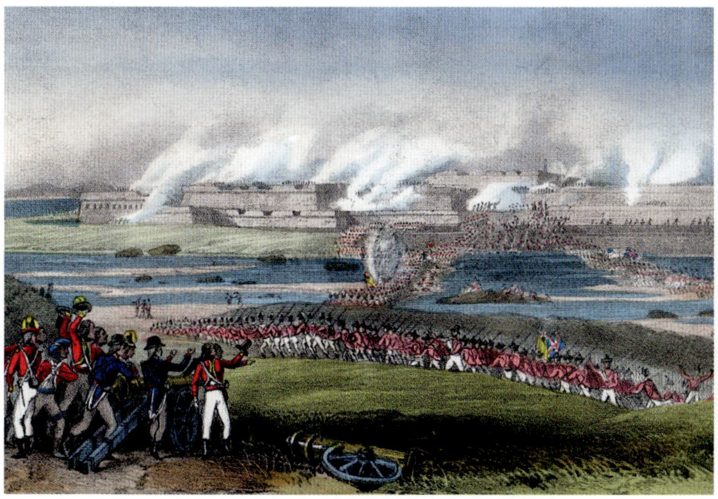

A painting showing the siege of Seringapatam in 1799, which was the final battle during the Fourth Anglo-Mysore War. It ended with the British forces taking the fortress and killing Tipu Sultan.

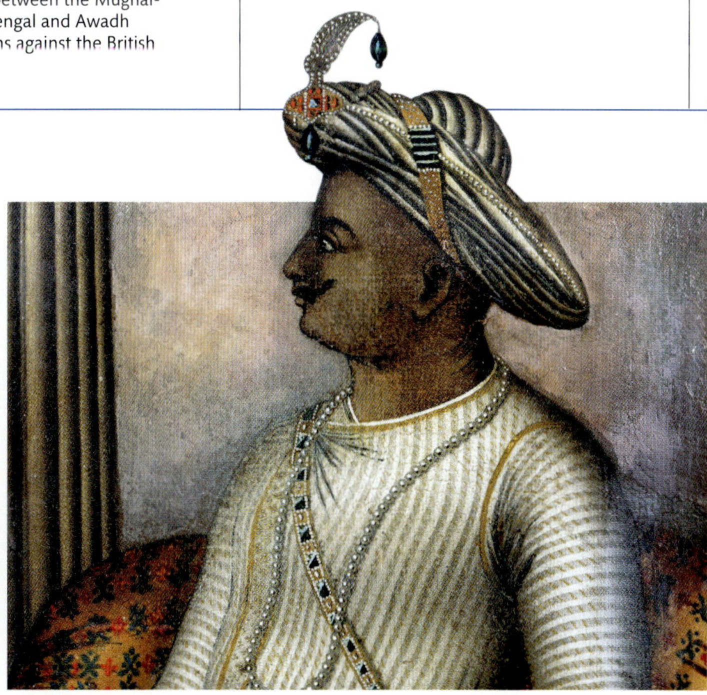

An 18th-century portrait of Tipu Sultan, the ruler of the Mysore state. He was also known as the Tiger of Mysore, and ruled the state between 1782 and 1799.

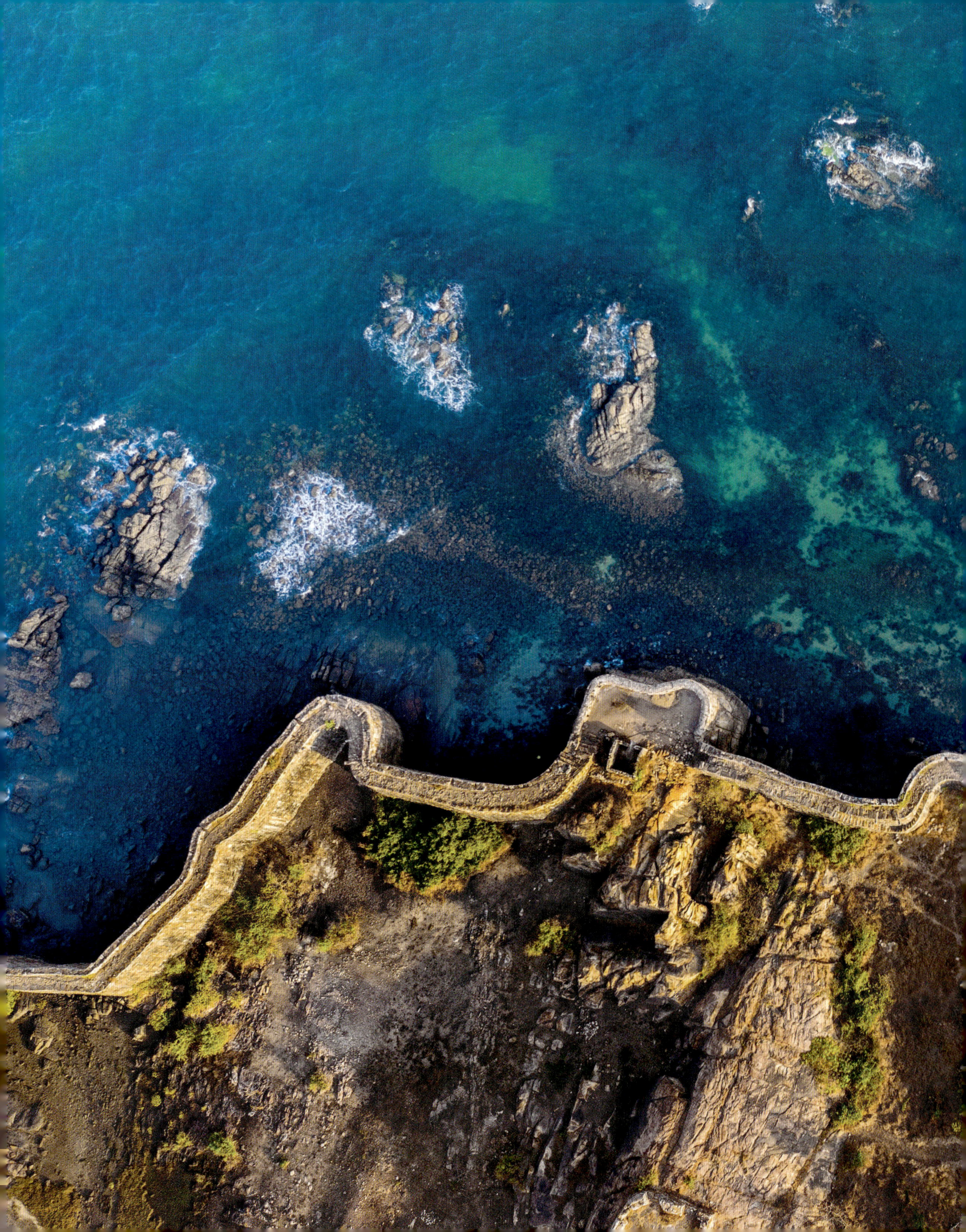

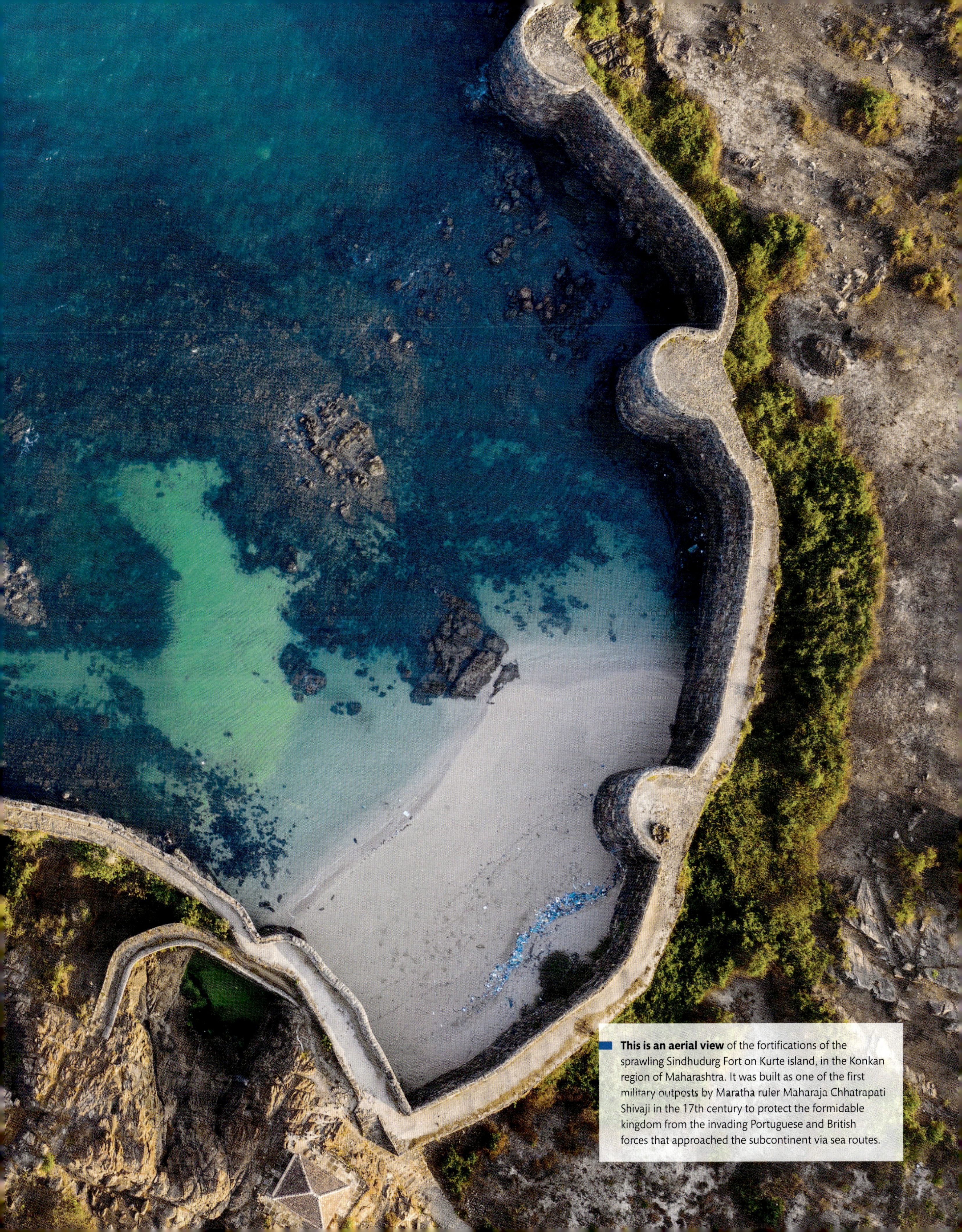

This is an aerial view of the fortifications of the sprawling Sindhudurg Fort on Kurte island, in the Konkan region of Maharashtra. It was built as one of the first military outposts by Maratha ruler Maharaja Chhatrapati Shivaji in the 17th century to protect the formidable kingdom from the invading Portuguese and British forces that approached the subcontinent via sea routes.

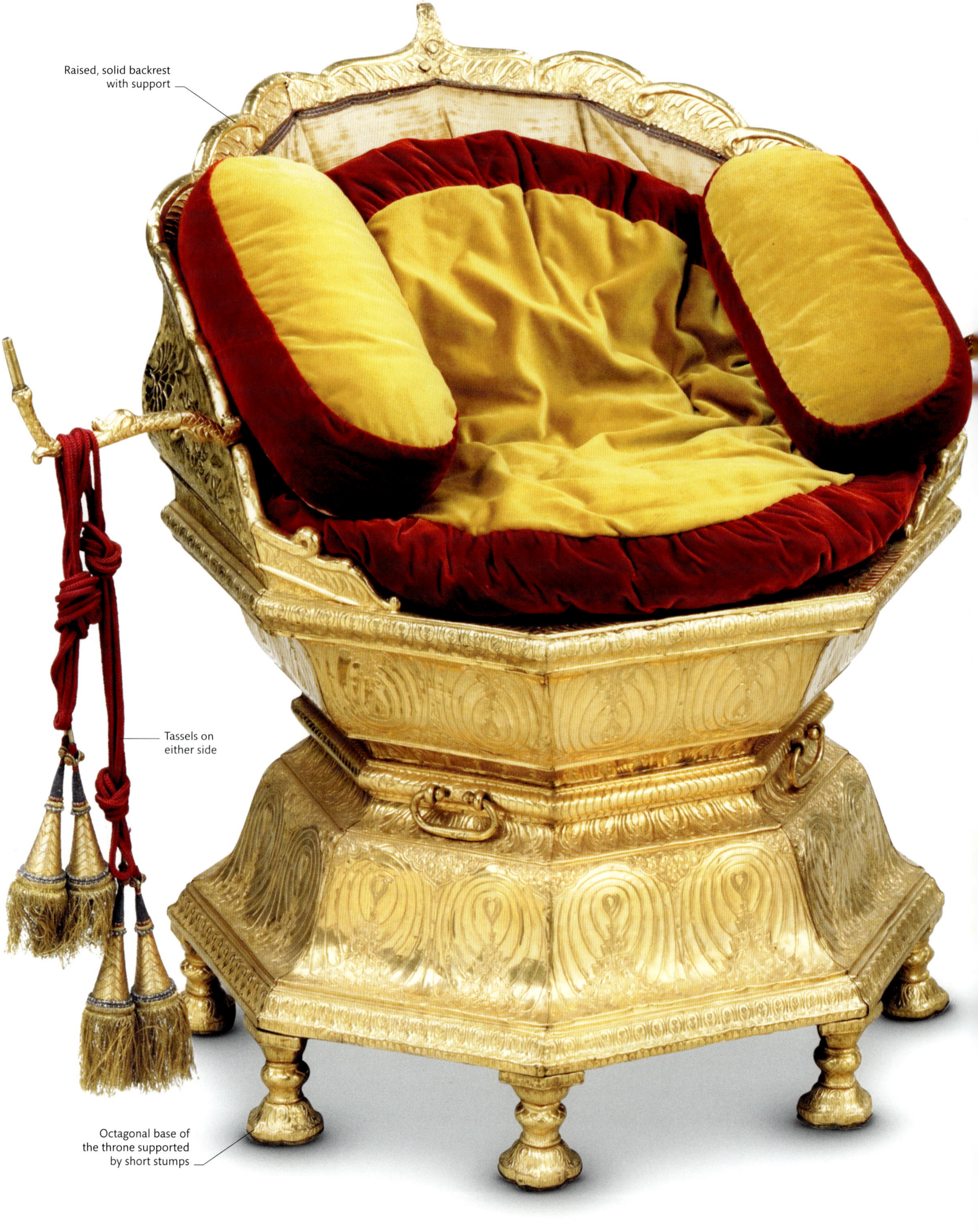
Raised, solid backrest
with support
Tassels on
either side
Octagonal base of
the throne supported
by short stumps

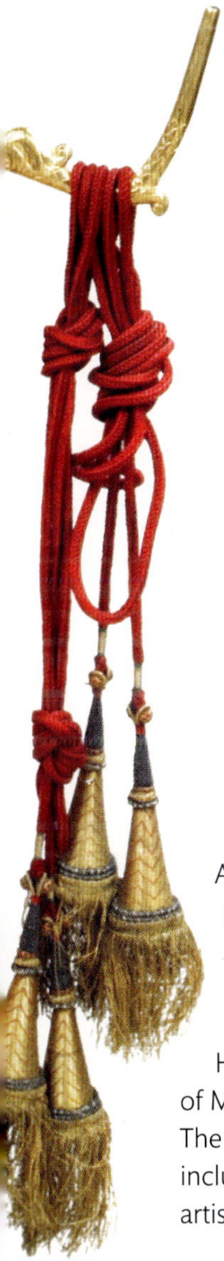

Era 19th century CE | **Medium** Gold and wood | **Height** 1 m (3 ft)

THE GOLDEN THRONE

Embodiment of royal magnificence

A ceremonial seat of state, Maharaja Ranjit Singh's golden throne is one of the greatest treasures of the Sikh Empire. It came to symbolize the undisputed power and magnificence of the kingdom.

Although not as grandiose as the thrones of the previous rulers of Lahore in present-day Pakistan, Maharaja Ranjit Singh's golden throne is a symbol of his power, wealth, and sovereignty. British accounts of the time note that the Maharaja commissioned Hafez Muhammad Multani, a goldsmith from the city of Multan, now in Pakistan, to craft the golden throne. The ruler's empire was a testament to the Sikh ideals of inclusion and equality, and the Muslim identity of the artist demonstrated its very hybrid nature.

FIT FOR GRANDEUR

The throne is not embellished with materials such as precious stones, but enveloped in thick sheets of gold. Octagonal in shape, the structure is made of wood and resin, and handles are attached at the base to aid its mobility. The seat of the throne, fitted with cushions, has a solid back with support on either side and engraved branches that once held golden orbs. The use of these materials makes it clear that the occupant was the king.

The base, uniquely shaped like a cup, has golden engravings shaped as lotus petals. In the sacred literature of the Sikhs, the gurus often employed the motif of a lotus as a symbol of purity and spirituality. The throne matched the magnificence of the maharaja's court. It was placed at the centre of the Musamman Burj pavilion, a chamber decorated with glittering glass mosaic in the Lahore Fort. The facade was aimed to impress, in particular, the European dignitaries who occasionally met the Maharaja.

In 1849, within years of Ranjit Singh's death, British forces annexed the Sikh Empire. Lahore's vast treasury, including the golden throne, was seized as spoils of war and sent to the Indian Museum in London. Interestingly, before shipping it off, Lord Dalhousie, the governor-general of India, commissioned a replica of the throne for himself, to be made in mahogany for himself – a testament to the beauty of the fabled seat of Maharaja Ranjit Singh. Today, the golden throne is on display at the Victoria and Albert Museum in London, UK.

Era 17th century CE | **Medium** Sanctum: marble, gold leaf | **Area** Sanctum: 12.25 × 12.25 sq m (40 × 40 sq ft)

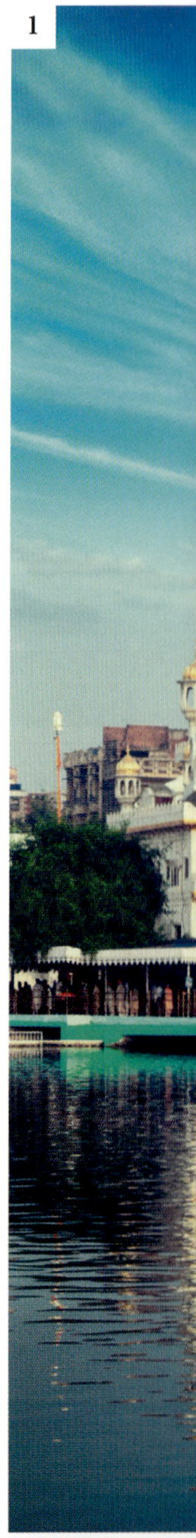

GOLDEN TEMPLE

A gilded masterpiece of Sikh faith

The Golden Temple is the primary place of worship for members of the Sikh faith. It has survived the ravages of time, including attacks by foreign invaders, and today attracts many pilgrims from around the world.

The Golden Temple is one of the most important pilgrimage sites for Sikhs. Built between the late 16th and early 17th centuries, it is the site of superb synthesis of Islamic and Hindu styles of architecture. However, it was destroyed in the late 18th century by Afghan invaders.

A RESPLENDENT SITE

The sanctum can be seen through the Darshan Deori, the arch that stands at the entrance of the complex. The main hall is situated on a small platform in the centre of the Amrit Sarovar, meaning 'pool of nectar'. While the bottom half of the structure is covered in white marble, the upper level is adorned with about 400 kg (880 lbs) of gold leaves, which were added during the restoration of the site in the reign of Maharaja Ranjit Singh, giving the temple its 'golden' moniker. Since then, the complex has undergone many refurbishments.

The complex has four entrances to welcome people from all directions, which reflects the Sikh faith's egalitarian nature, that embraces people of all faiths and backgrounds. The sanctum's ground level is home to the Guru Granth Sahib – the eternal Guru of the Sikhs – during the day, where it is placed beneath a gem-encrusted canopy for visitors to offer prayers. At night, the holy book is taken to the five-storeyed Akal Takht, which stands in white and gold opposite the causeway. The sanctum interior is decorated with gold plates, precious stones, and mirror work. A flight of stairs leads to the Sheesh Mahal, or the Hall of Mirrors, and golden domes rise above this pavilion.

1. The gold-leaf encrusted upper half and dome of the temple can be seen reflected in the Amrit Sarovar, the holy lake surrounding the sanctum. **2.** Guru Granth Sahib being recited by the *granthis*, priests, inside the sanctum. **3.** Gilded and embossed ceiling of the sanctum, decorated with jewels and defined with intricate floral and geometric patterns in vibrant colours. **4.** Worshippers queuing up at the golden arched gate, the Darshan Deori, to enter the complex. **5.** A hymn of Guru Arjan (the fifth Sikh Guru) embossed in gold on the wall of the Darshan Deori with floral motifs. **6.** The Akal Takht (Throne of the Timeless God), positioned directly in front of the sanctum, is the seat of the highest spokesman of the Sikhs.

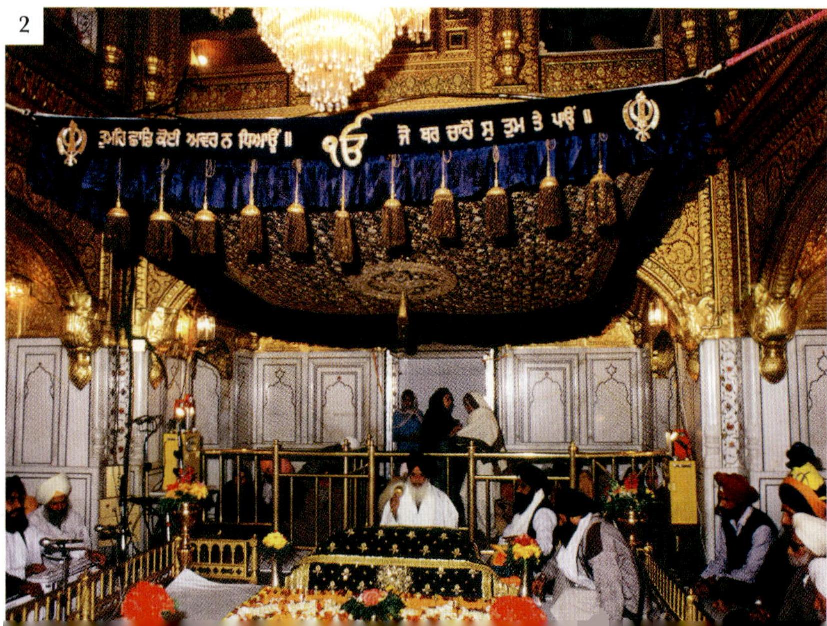

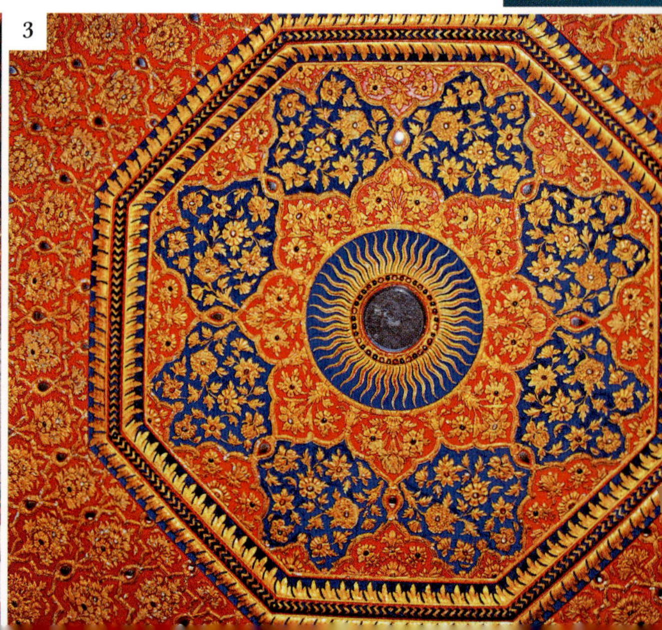

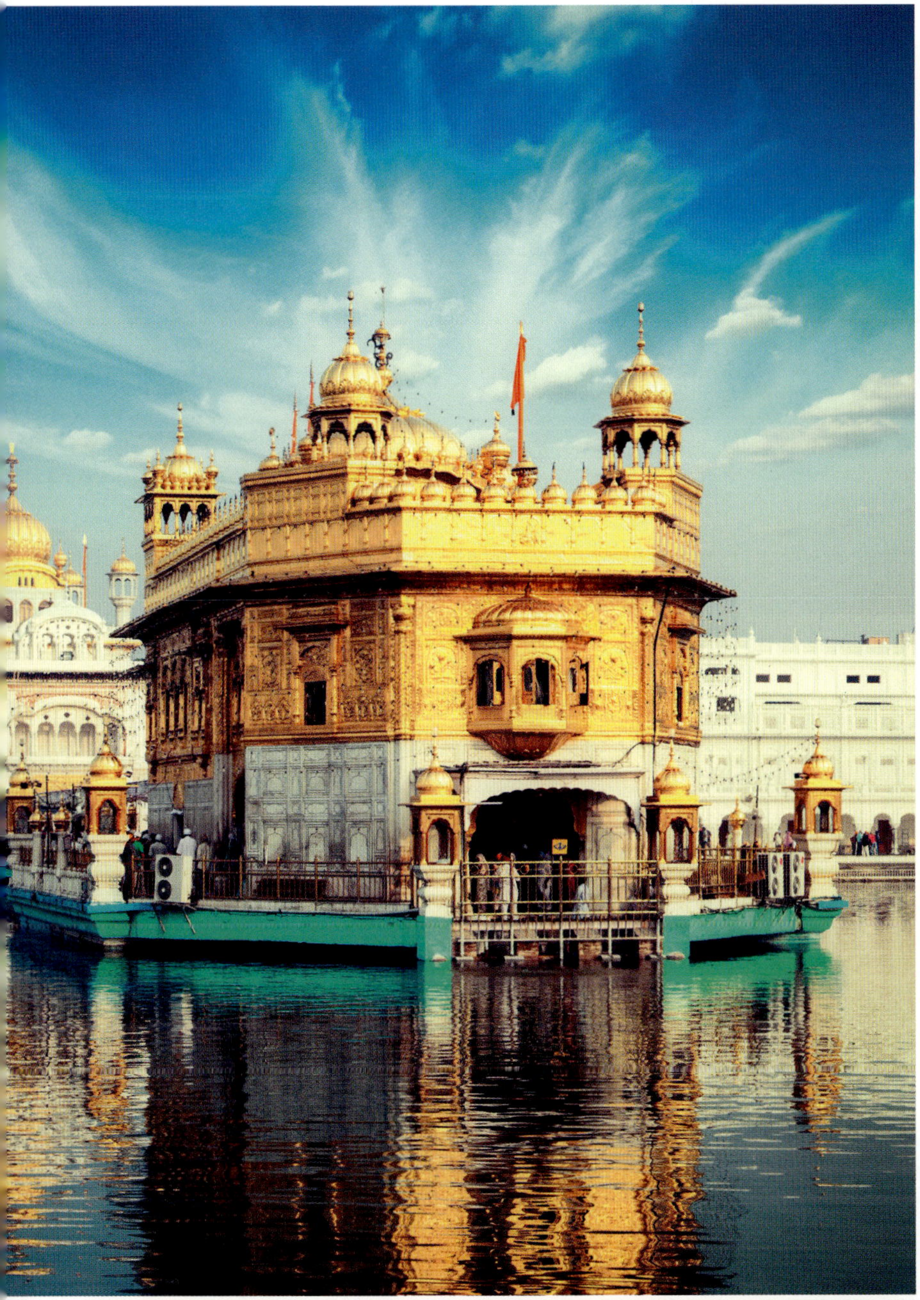

5

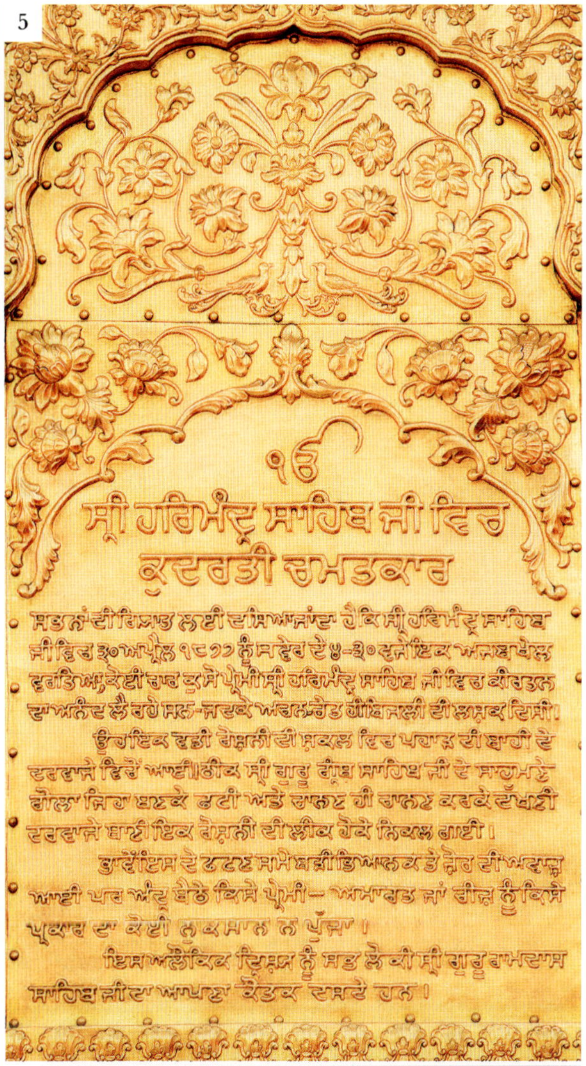

6

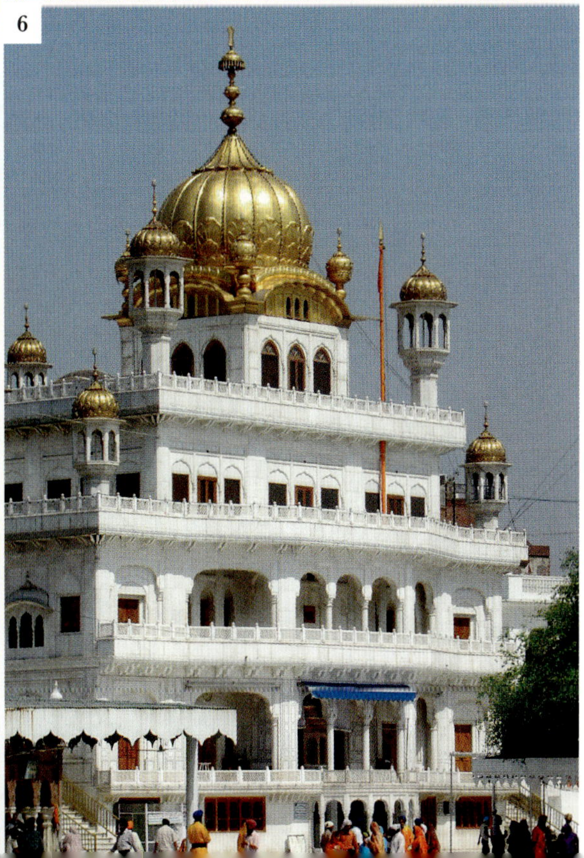

4

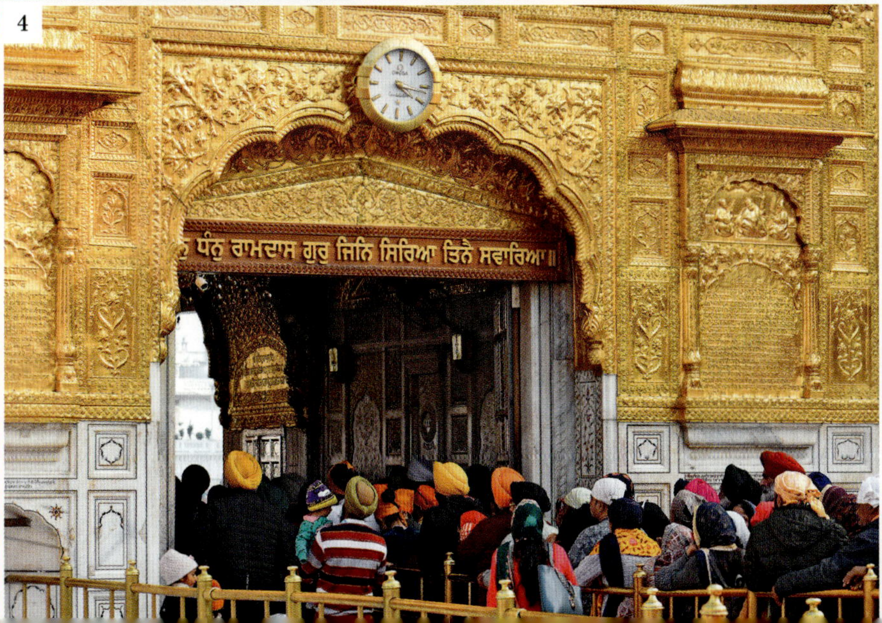

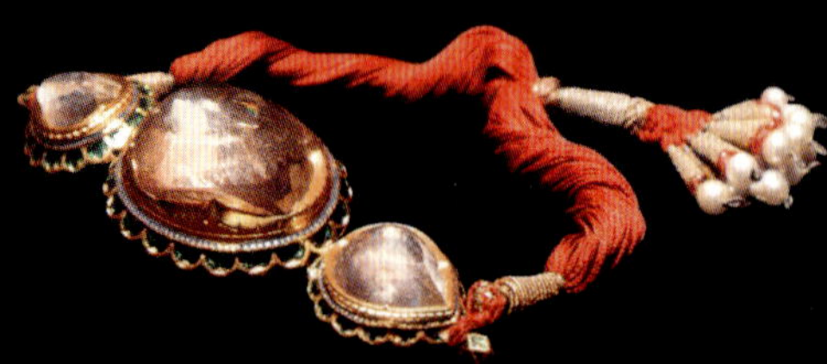

Era 1590 CE onwards | **Cut** Oval brilliant diamond | **Weight** 105.6 carats

KOH-I-NOOR

The seductive radiance of the Mountain of Light

Many a ruler once lusted after this prized diamond: it has been inherited, gifted, looted, and taken by extortion or treachery – but never bought or sold. Though it has a price, the Koh-i-Noor is priceless.

No one really knows of the exact origins of the Koh-i-Noor. The story of its birth is lost in the mists of time and this only serves to add to the mystique of this mesmerizing chunk of carbon. Some date it to 3200 BCE, while others note that it belonged to the kings of central west India who lost it to Alauddin Khilji, the ruler of the Delhi Sultanate, in 1304. The first verifiable mention of the stone is in *Baburnama*, the chronicles of Babur, the first Mughal emperor. The text notes that the Mughal acquired the diamond after he defeated Ibrahim Lodhi, the last ruler of the Delhi Sultanate. The diamond stayed with the Mughals for many years, gracing the fabled Peacock Throne (the seat of the Mughal kings) until it was looted in 1739 by Persian ruler Nadir Shah.

The stone returned to India 75 years later after Maharaja Ranjit Singh of the Sikh Empire demanded it from Shah Shuja of the Afghan Durrani dynasty. Ten years after Ranjit Singh's death, his 11-year-old son Dalip was forced to sign away his sovereignty and the Koh-i-Noor to Queen Victoria.

IN BRITISH HANDS

The earliest attested weight of the Koh-i-Noor was 186 carats. Originally, it was of a similar cut to other Mughal-era diamonds, such as the Daria-i-Noor, a tabular, free-form diamond, now located in Iran.

Unfortunately, the dull glow of the unfaceted diamond did not find approval among the glittering gemstones of the court in London. It was recut and polished, its weight reduced by almost half to 105.6 carats. Its new brilliance placed it among Queen Victoria's crown jewels and then, because of its reputation for bringing bad luck to the men who wore it, was incorporated into the queen's state crown.

▶ **In this painting by Hungarian artist** August Schoefft, Maharaja Sher Singh poses wearing the Koh-i-Noor on his arm. The artist recorded much of the Sikh Empire through his work in the 1800s.

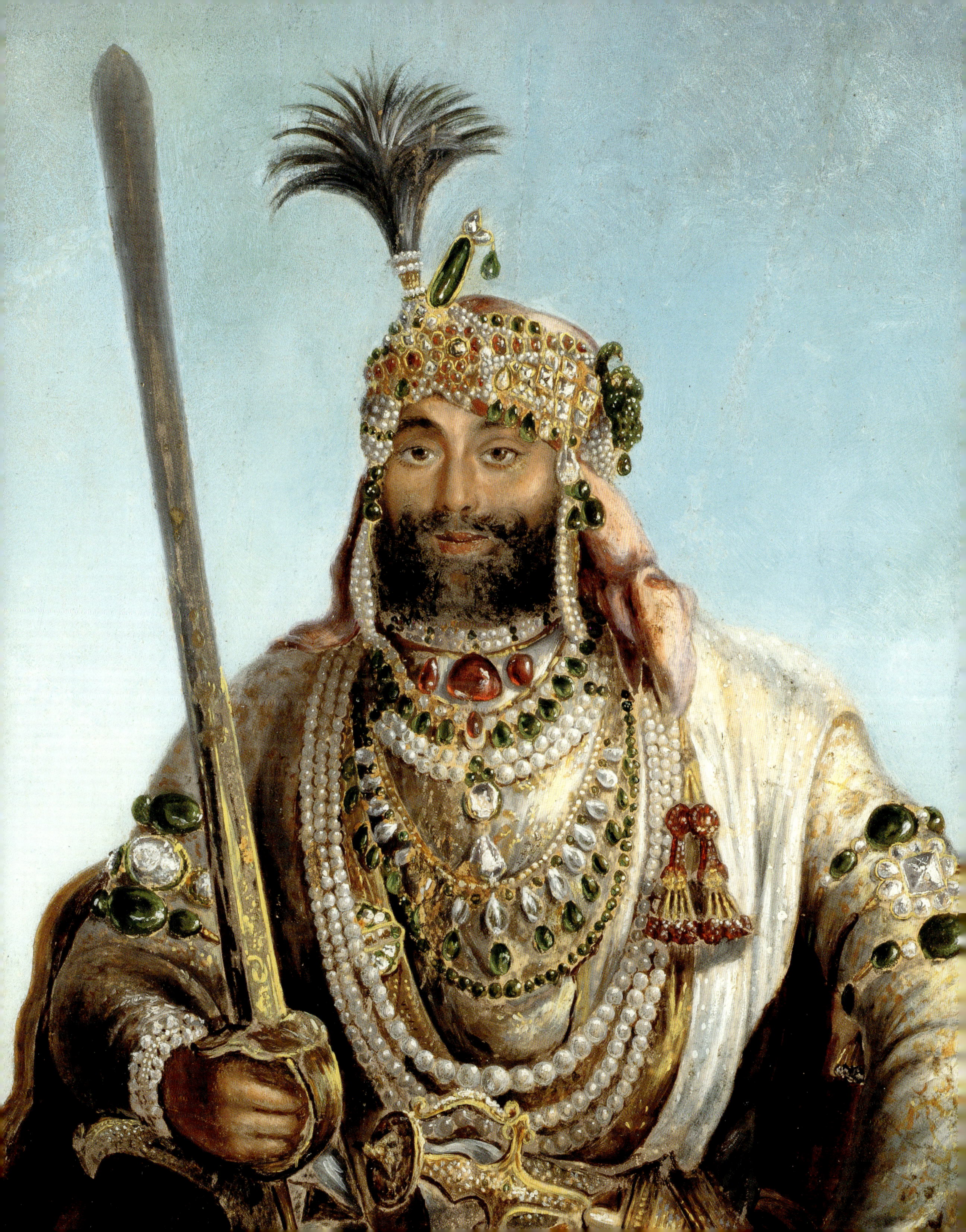

TREASURES OF THE SIKHS

Rulers have always surrounded themselves with grand accoutrements to affirm their exalted status, and members of the Sikh Empire and the princely states of Punjab were no different. An array of magnificent objects fit for Sikh kings and queens were produced by skilled artisans to reflect their dynamic and potent powers on the world's stage.

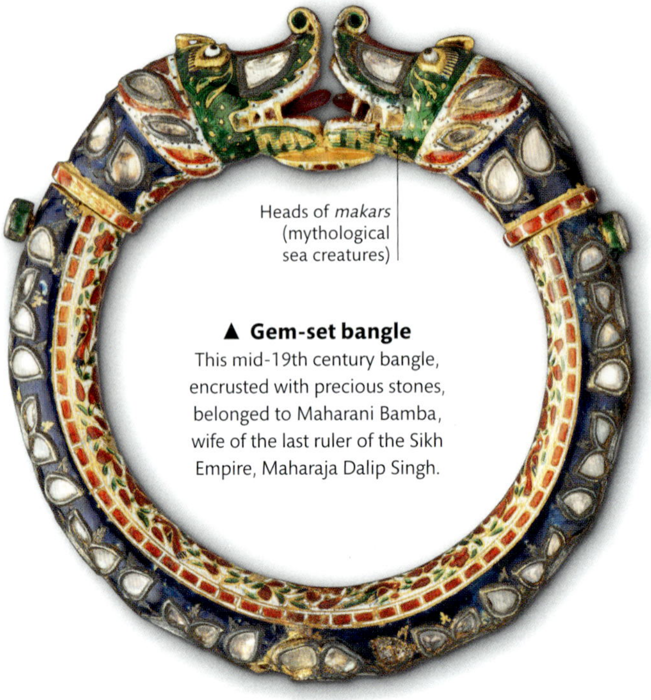

▲ Gem-set bangle
This mid-19th century bangle, encrusted with precious stones, belonged to Maharani Bamba, wife of the last ruler of the Sikh Empire, Maharaja Dalip Singh.

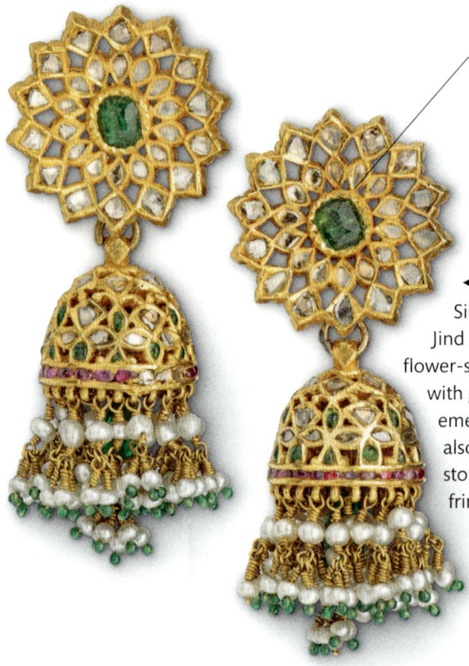

◀ Maharani's earrings
Sikh Empire regent Maharani Jind Kaur's mid-19th century, flower-shaped earrings were created with gold, diamonds, and emeralds. The dome-like drops, also studded with precious stones, have three-tiered pearl fringes and glass beads.

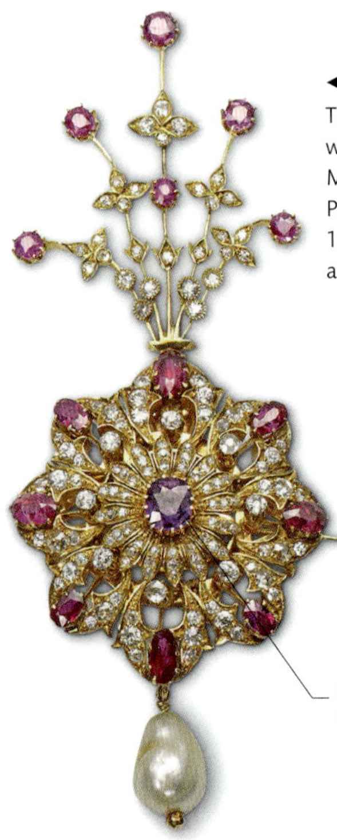

◀ Headpiece
This turban ornament *(sarpech)* was crafted around 1910 for Maharaja Bhupinder Singh of Patiala. It is encrusted with 15 rubies, 133 diamonds, and a natural pearl drop.

▼ Gold armlet
This mid-19th century gold armlet, made up of three hinged pieces, with large emeralds and diamonds, belonged to Maharani Bamba, wife of Dalip Singh, the last maharaja of the Sikh Empire.

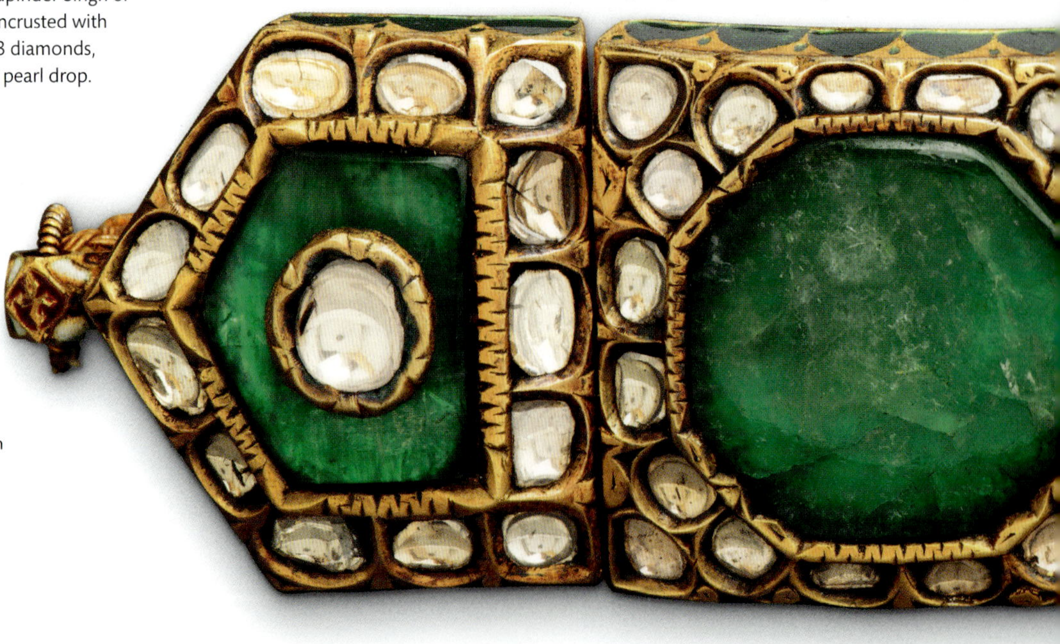

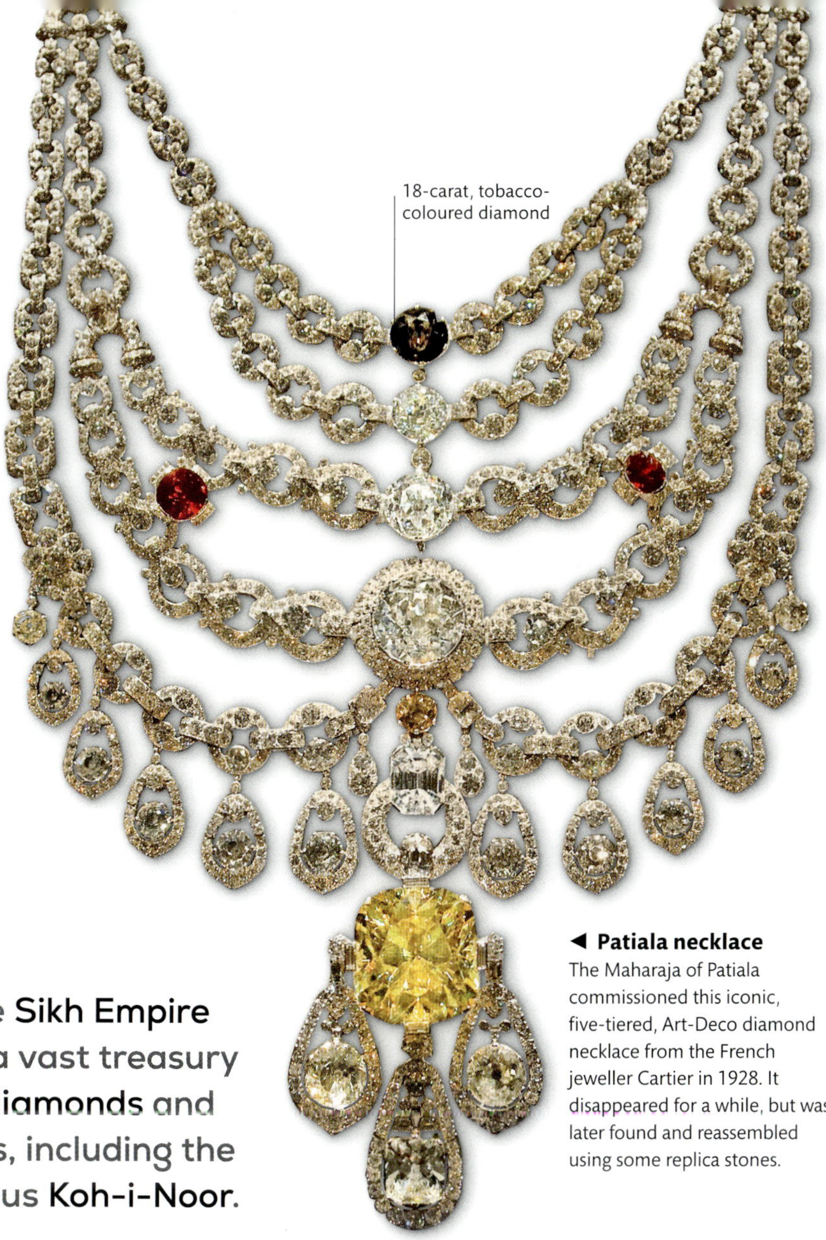

◄ **Patiala necklace**
The Maharaja of Patiala commissioned this iconic, five-tiered, Art-Deco diamond necklace from the French jeweller Cartier in 1928. It disappeared for a while, but was later found and reassembled using some replica stones.

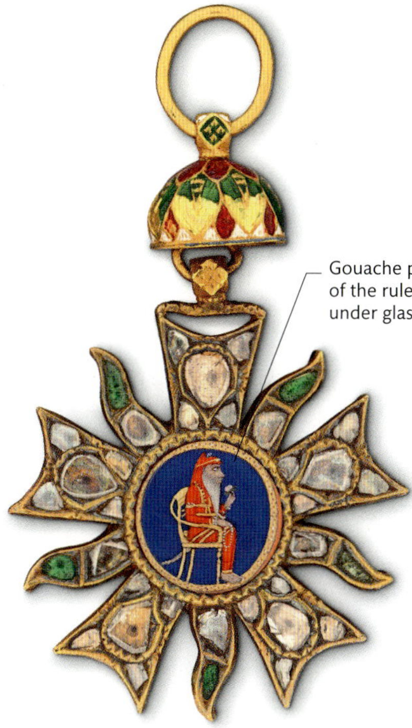

▲ **Medal of merit**
Maharaja Ranjit Singh, founder of the Sikh Empire, would award this medal of merit to those who had been of great service to the kingdom. Designed as a radiating star in gold enamel, it was set with table-cut emeralds and diamonds.

The **Sikh Empire** had a vast treasury of **diamonds** and gems, including the famous **Koh-i-Noor**.

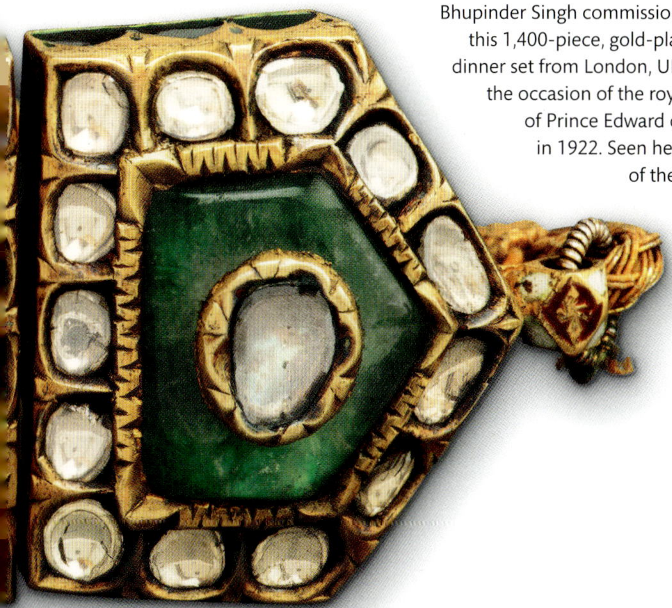

► **Dinner set**
The Maharaja of Patiala, Bhupinder Singh commissioned this 1,400-piece, gold-plated dinner set from London, UK, on the occasion of the royal visit of Prince Edward of Wales in 1922. Seen here is a part of the massive set.

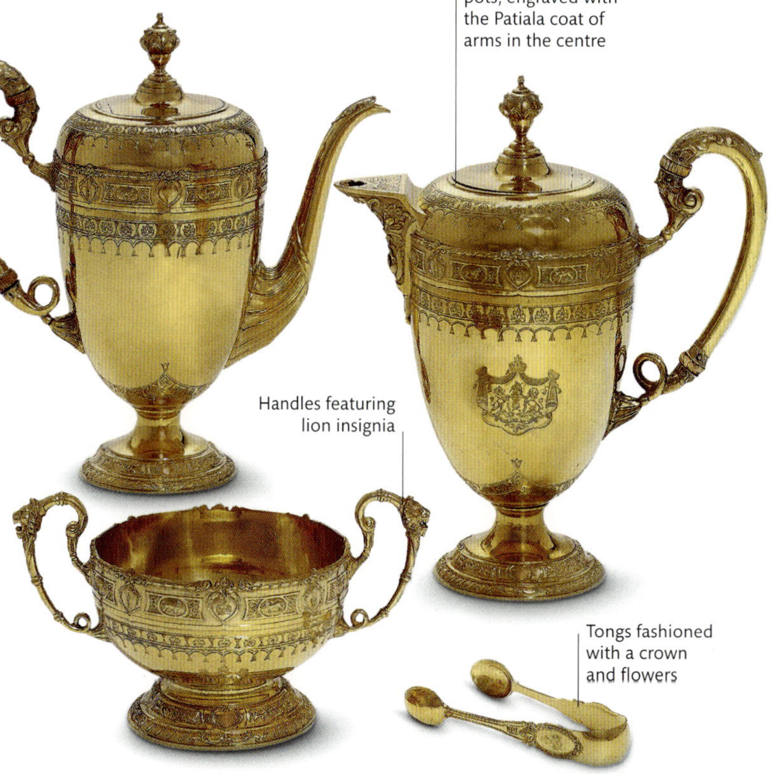

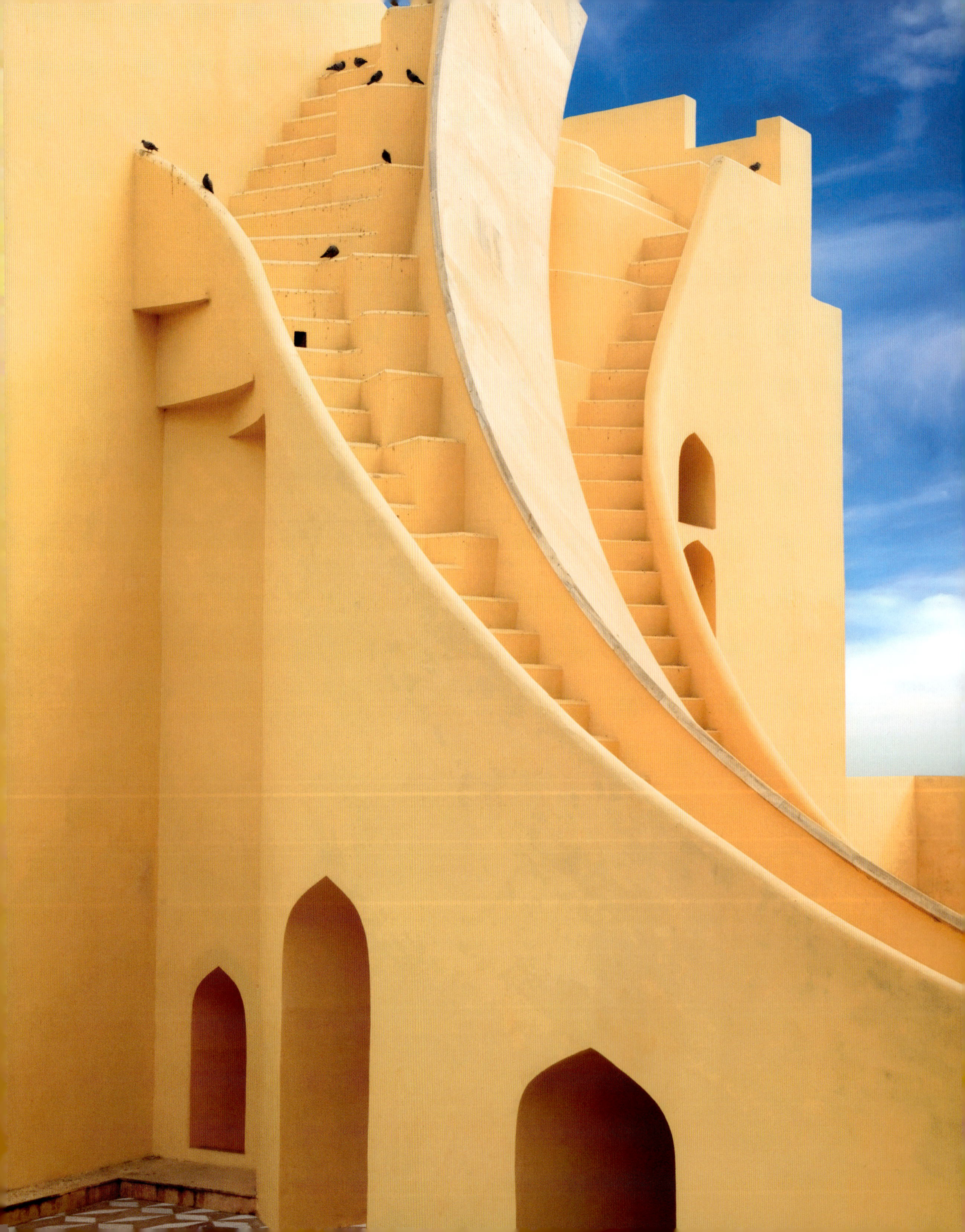

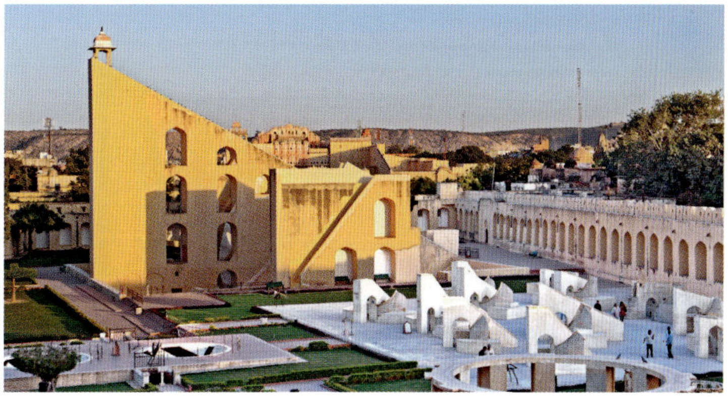

A collection of structures at the Jantar Mantar observatory in Jaipur, in the western state of Rajasthan, provide measurements of time, predict eclipses, and track locations of major stars.

Era 18th century CE | **Medium** Brick and stone | **Area** 4.6 acres (1.8 ha)

JANTAR MANTAR

A cosmic connection from the past

One among five unique brick-and-stone observatories, the Jantar Mantar in Jaipur is an expression of medieval-era scientific exploration. The astronomical monuments provide readings of the positions and movements of celestial objects.

In the early 18th century, the ruler of Amber and Jaipur in modern-day Rajasthan, Sawai Jai Singh II built five observatories in central-west India, in the towns of Delhi, Jaipur, Varanasi, Ujjain, and Mathura. Of these, the one in Jaipur is the largest and best preserved. Known as the Jantar Mantar and constructed to study the movements of celestial objects in the sky, these structures are unique among architectural monuments of astronomy and have captured the attention of people around the world. In addition to making ground-breaking developments in the field of astronomy, the observatories also represent a significant time in Indian history where the dissemination of scientific knowledge became more widespread and accessible to the general public.

◀ **The world's largest sundial**, the 22.6-m (74-ft) tall Samrat Yantra at the Jaipur observatory measures local astronomical time with a precision of 2 seconds.

TESTAMENT TO A LEADER'S MIGHT

The observatory at Jaipur resembles a giant sculptural composition, which contains a collection of some 20 massive, fixed astronomical instruments built of brick and stone – some of them are the largest ever built in their categories, including the world's largest sundial. Jai Singh was known to have a scientific inclination and kept abreast of astronomical studies from around the world. The Jaipur observatory was more than just a testament to his scientific pursuits. It was part of his larger political strategy, as he utilized architectural and ceremonial activities, along with a common thread of solar allegories, to solidify his status as a leader with celestial connections. Through these efforts, Jai Singh was able to communicate his unique vision of authority, making it comprehensible to everyone.

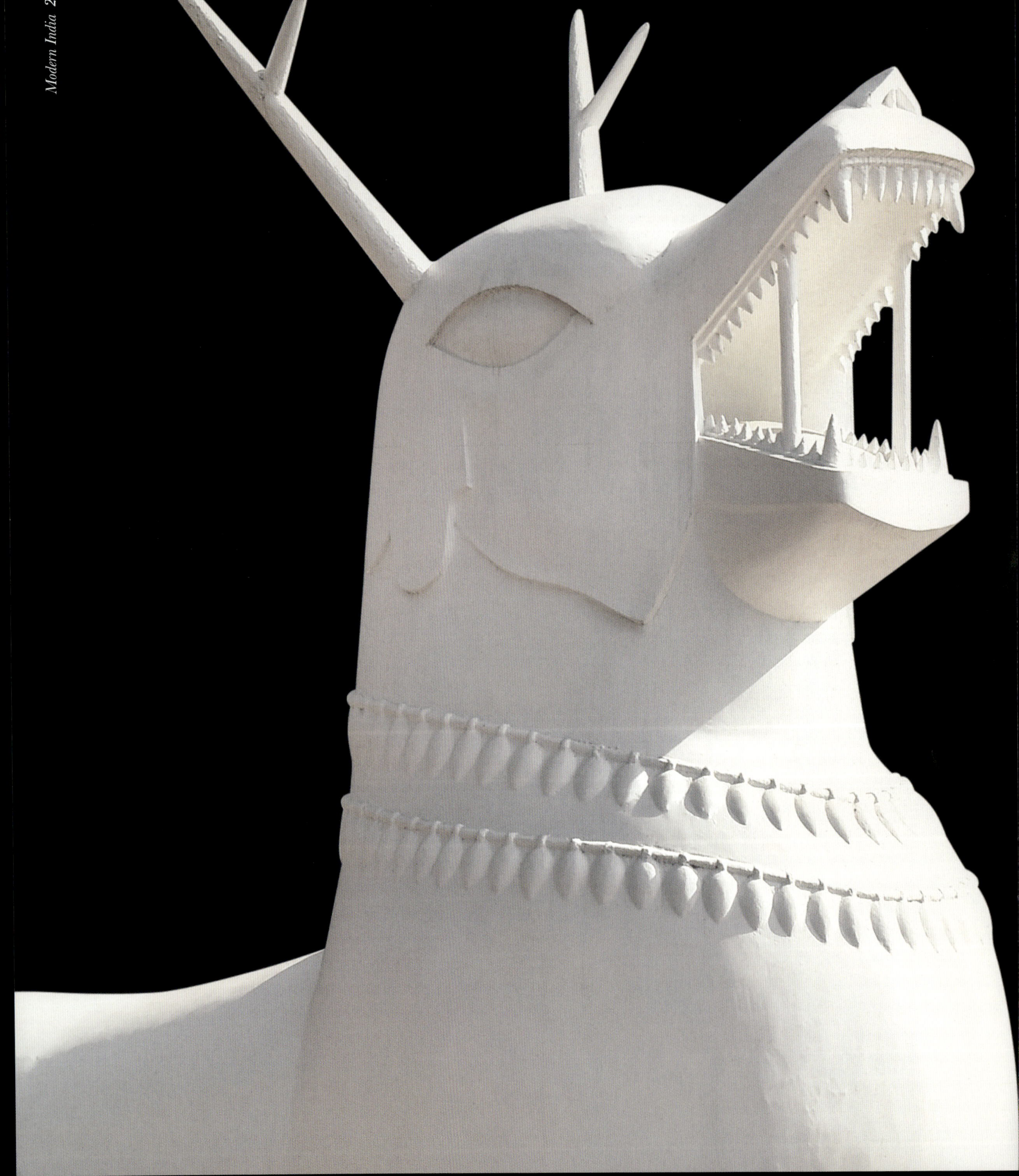

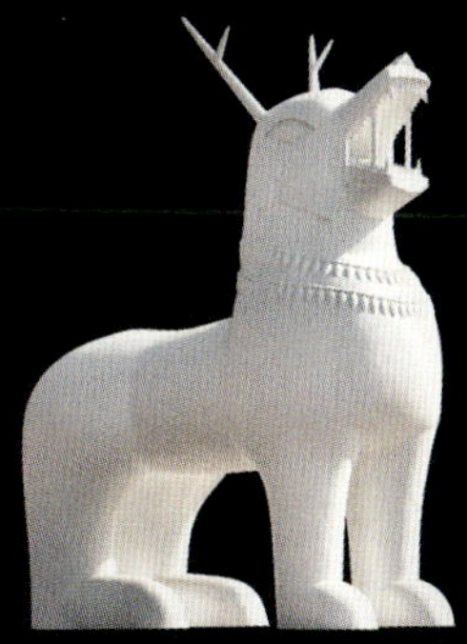

Era 19th century CE | **Medium** Brick | **Height** 5.4 m (18 ft)

KANGLA SHA

Mythical royal guardians

Fantastical lionesque beasts from Meitei mythology, Kangla Sha finds depiction in the two leogryphs that stand guard outside the Kangla Fort in Imphal, Manipur. These sculptures have been destroyed and rebuilt between the 19th and 21st centuries.

Crouched on their hind legs, tails curled towards their spines, the Kangla Sha, with their dragon heads and lion bodies, make for an awe-inspiring sight as they guard the entrance to the Kangla Fort's inner citadel or *uttara*. Their jaws are open, in a snarl, teeth bared. Their expression, it is believed in Manipur, is meant to dispel negative energy. Bifurcated horns, inspired by the brow-antlered deer, endemic to the north-eastern state, rise up from their heads, and two strings of shell-like jewels hang around their necks.

The Meiteis, and the Manipuris, call Kangla Sha Nongha or heavenly beasts, for they are the guardian deity and one of six dragons from the ancient kingdom's folklore.

◀ **According to local Manipuri** mythology and beliefs, these sacred dragon-lions are believed to protect the royal Kangla Fort, a historical palace in the state capital Imphal.

RISING FROM THE ASHES

In 1804, the Meitei king Maharaja Chourjit had a pair of leogryphs depicting the Kangla Sha built outside the Kangla Fort in Imphal. He adapted them from the grand Burmese mythical creatures known as *chinthe*, which guarded the entrance of Burma's pagodas. During the mid-18th century, Manipur had well-established connections with powerful Burmese kingdoms. However, in 1819, they invaded Manipur and razed the Kangla Fort, destroying the Kangla Sha statues with it.

The leogryphs were rebuilt in 1844 by Maharaja Narasingh of Manipur. The statues were reduced to dust a second time in 1891, when General H. Collett, a British army commander, issued an order to destroy them using cannon fire during the Anglo-Manipuri War. The leogryphs remained lost to the world until 2007, when replicas were reconstructed by the government of Manipur at their original site.

Era 1870 CE | **Dimension** 2.2 × 1.9 m (90 × 78 in)

KASHMIR MAP SHAWL

Exquisite embroidered map of a city

An amazing piece of art created on fabric, this embroidered Pashmina shawl depicting the map of Srinagar was presented to Queen Victoria by Maharaja Ranbir Singh in 1870.

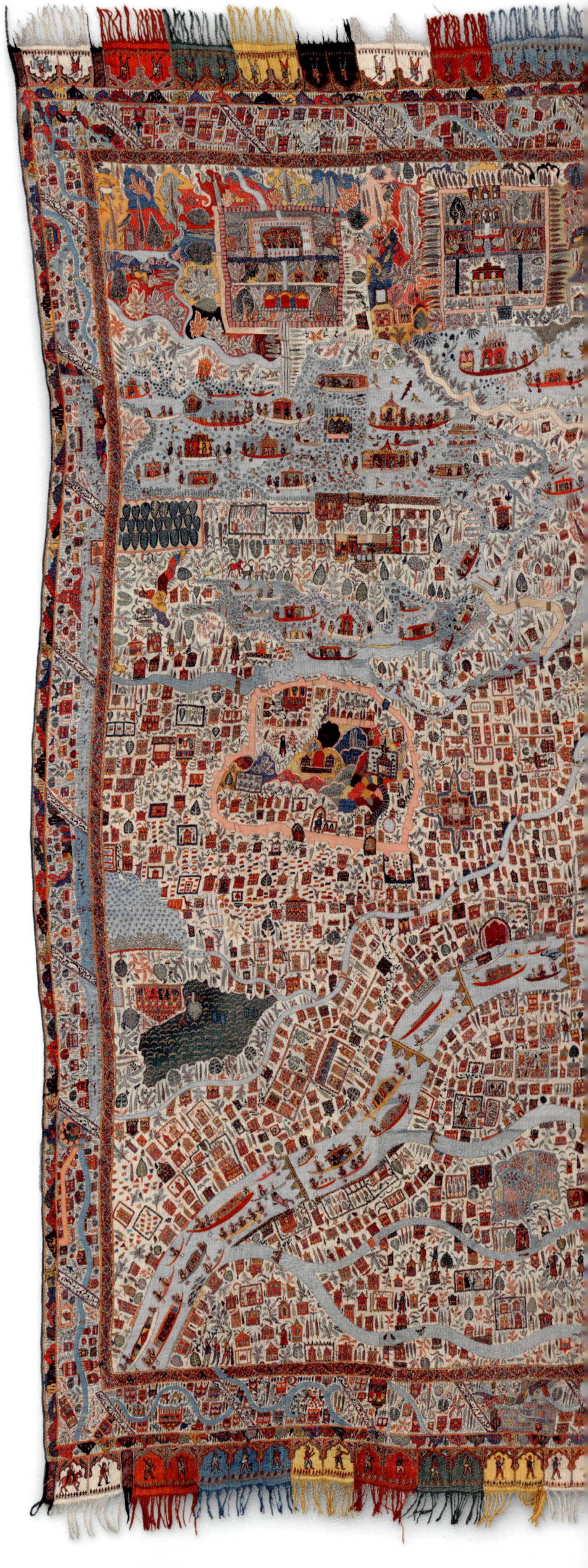

The embroidered map on the shawl is intricate. Every part of the city of Srinagar is recreated in excruciating detail, from the houses, streets, and public buildings to Dal Lake in the north-east and the boats that make their way down the river Jhelum. Even the beautiful Mughal gardens, Nishat Bagh and Shalimar Bagh, find representation, featuring the waterways that run through a series of pools and divide the gardens into four symmetrical sections known as Charbagh, a hallmark of Mughal tradition. The tiny scale of the scenes necessitated the most meticulous stitching, and the use of blue for the lake, green for the trees, and the vibrant, multicoloured rocks brought life to the map.

Though the delicate and striking work on the shawl, which took about 30 years to make, is highly admired, unfortunately, the shawl is a symbol of Maharaja Ranbir Singh's intolerant regime. The ruler is considered responsible

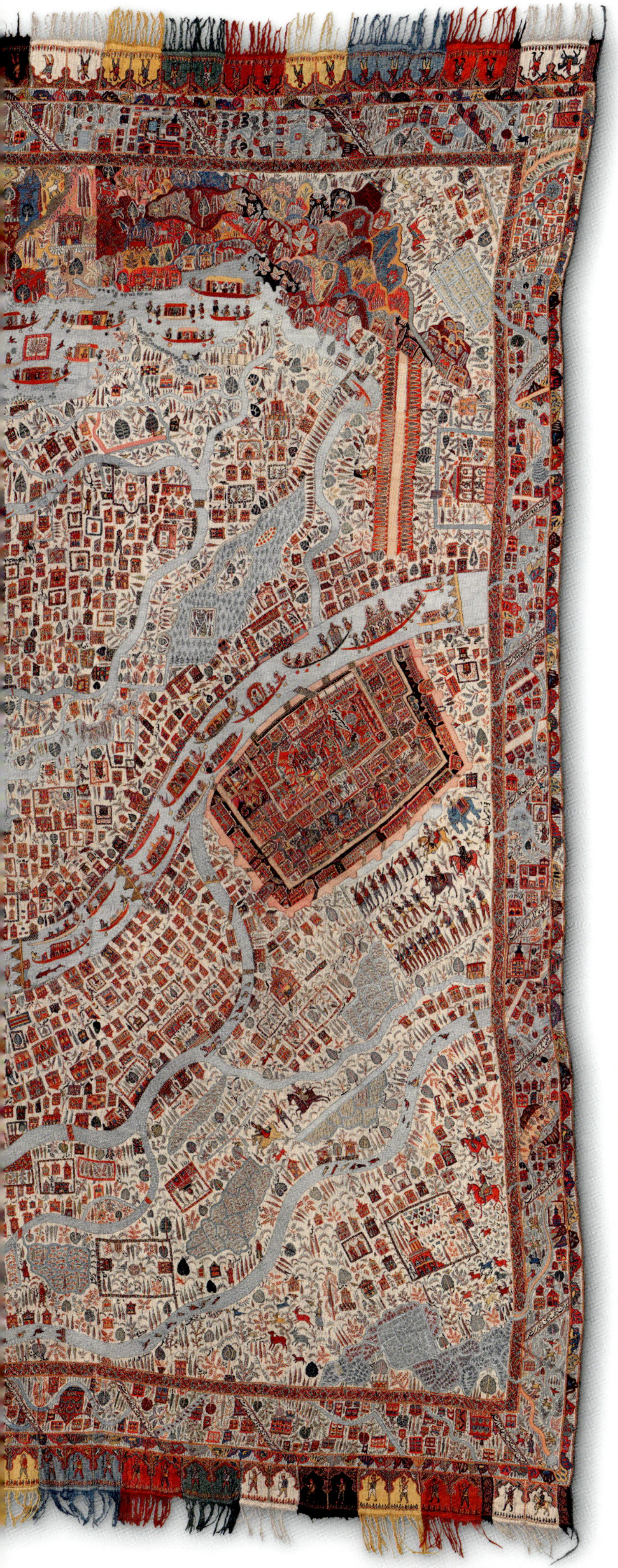

"The Kashmiris have won a great reputation as artisans, and were celebrated in the old days for their skill in art manufactures."

– Sir Walter Lawrence, a 19th-century colonial administrator working in Kashmir

◀ **This traditional Pashmina** shawl, c. 19th century CE, is made from fine goat hair and embroidered with a stylized map of Srinagar, the capital of Jammu and Kashmir. In 1970, it was acquired by the Victoria and Albert Museum in London.

for violence against the Kashmiri Muslim community, which included the makers of such shawls. In 1865, a revolt led by workers took place, calling for better working conditions for those whose talent was gaining widespread recognition. While the shawl presented to Queen Victoria ended up in a museum, many of the artisans and workers who demanded their rights were massacred.

THE PASHMINA TRADE

In 1870, only three or four specimens of map shawls were produced, all around the same time. These were souvenirs for devotees to remember their journeys and as objects of worship. Their origins can, however, be traced to 11th century CE. They were traded across North Africa, Central Asia, and Russia from the 16th century CE, and became popular in Europe from the 18th century CE onwards.

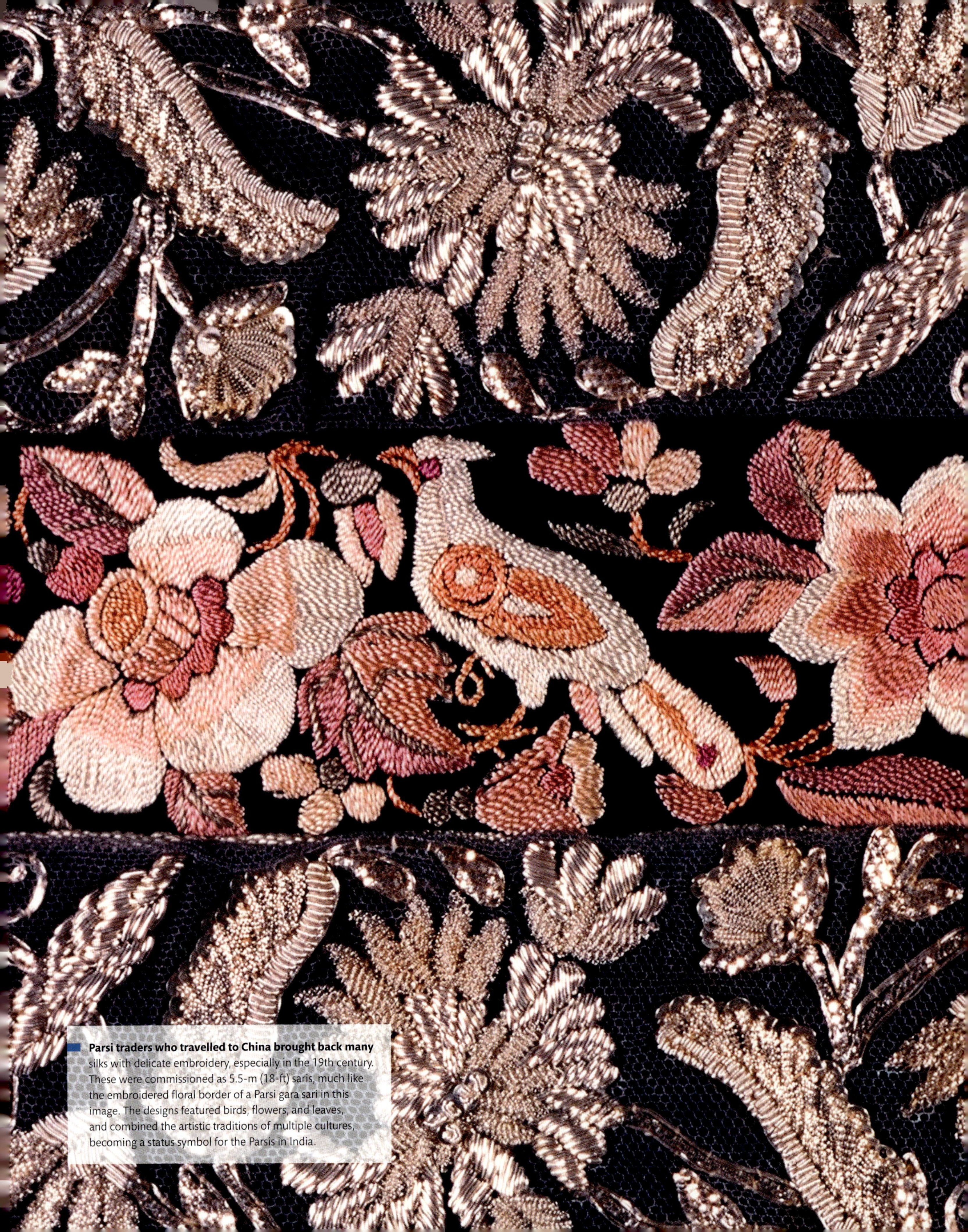

Parsi traders who travelled to China brought back many silks with delicate embroidery, especially in the 19th century. These were commissioned as 5.5-m (18-ft) saris, much like the embroidered floral border of a Parsi gara sari in this image. The designs featured birds, flowers, and leaves, and combined the artistic traditions of multiple cultures, becoming a status symbol for the Parsis in India.

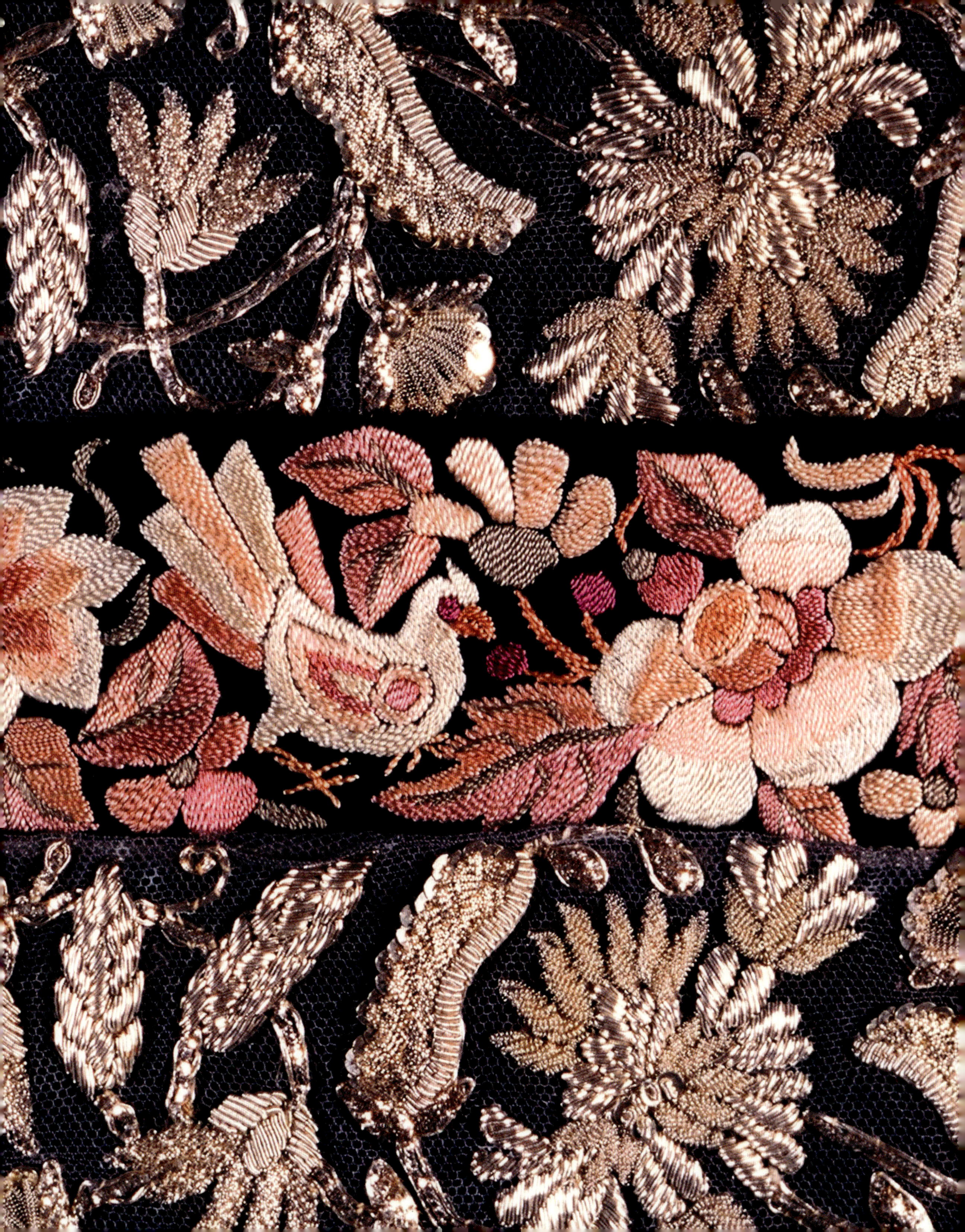

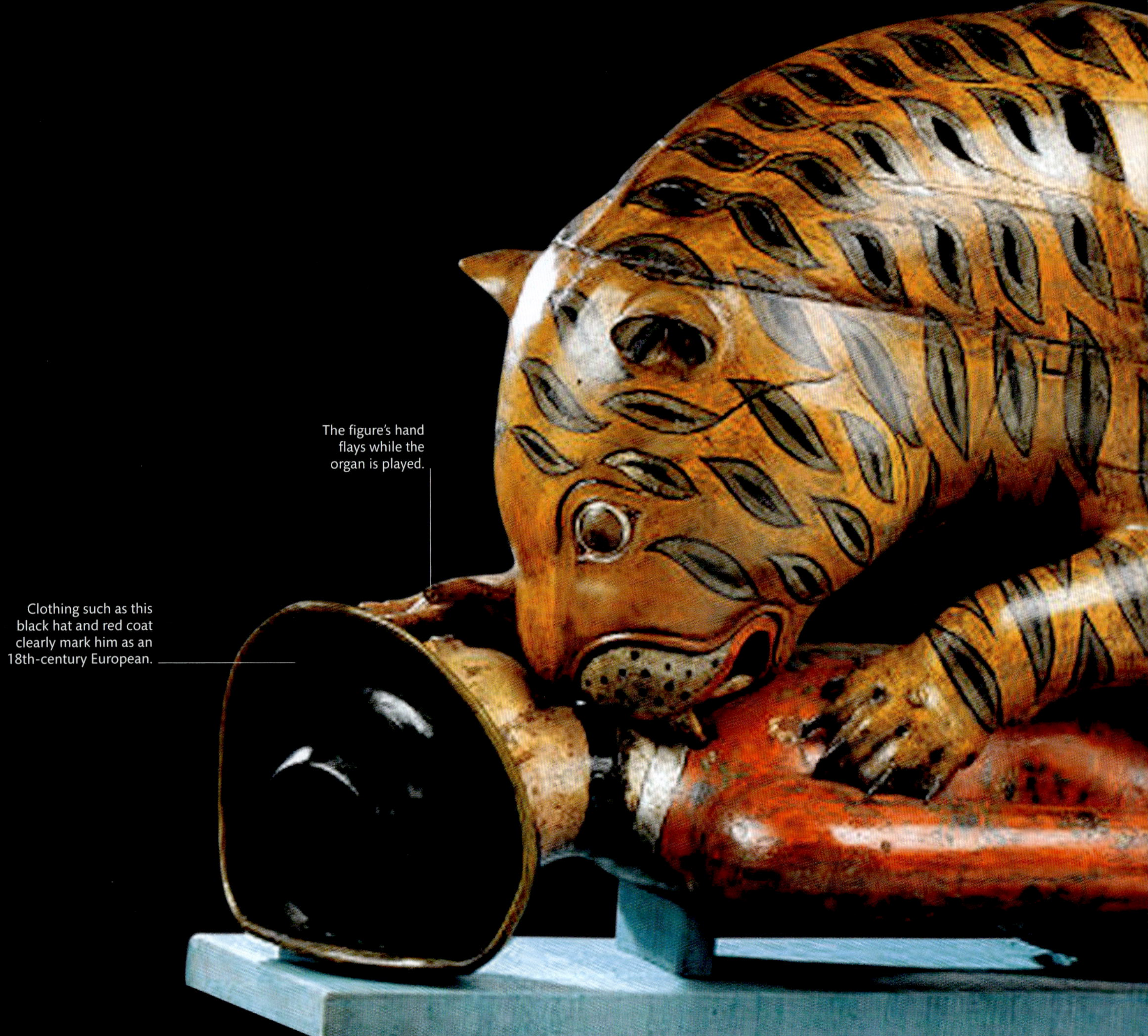

Era 18th century CE | **Medium** Wood and metal | **Height** 71 cm (28 in)

TIPU'S TIGER

A symbol of resistance and resilience

This large semi-automaton, depicting an almost life-sized tiger in the act of attacking a British man lying on his back, belonged to Tipu Sultan, the ruler of Mysore. It represents the king's defiant resistance against the English East India Company.

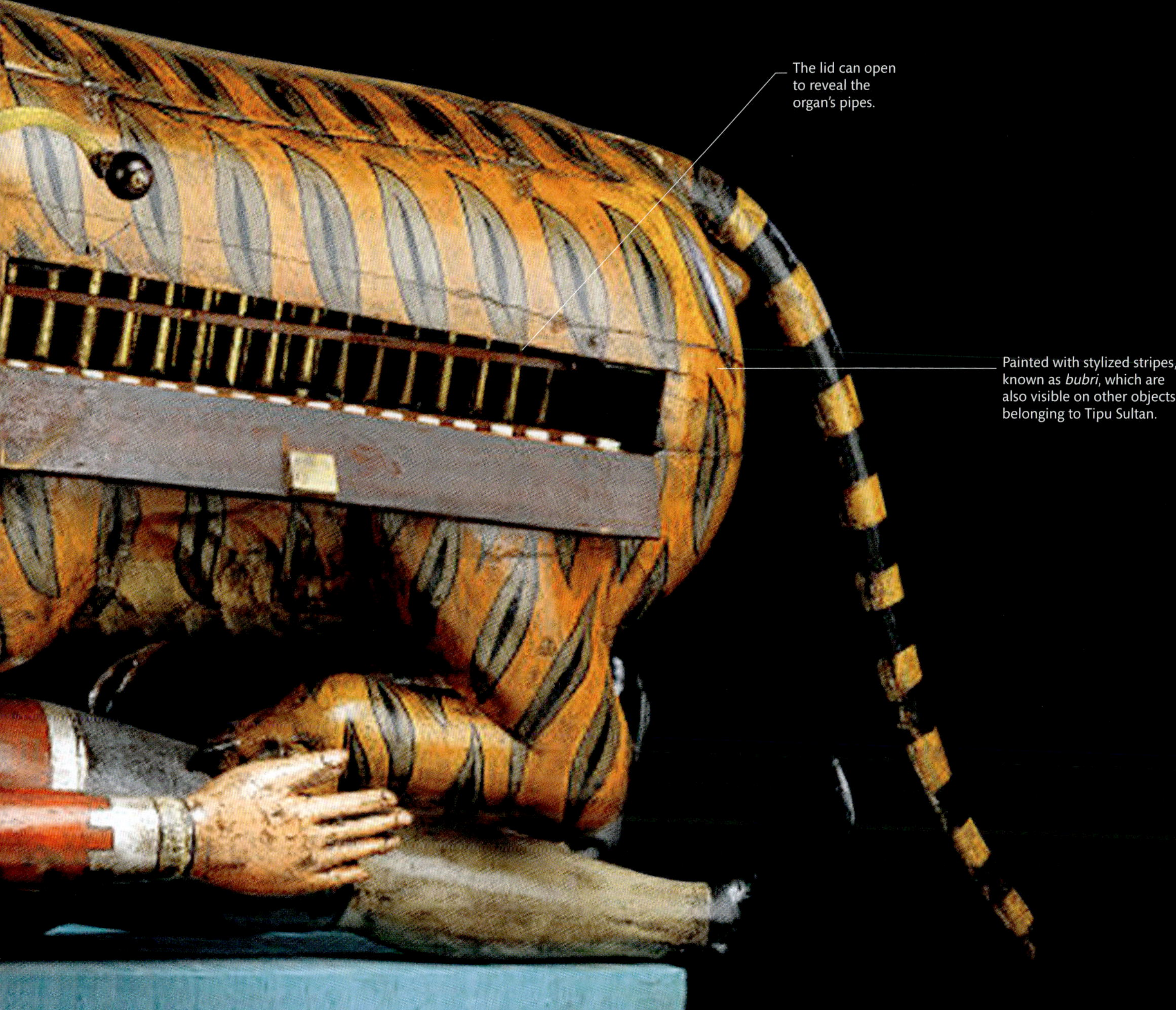

A tawny tiger, its claws extended, looms over a soldier lying stiffly on his back and sinks its teeth into the figure's neck. Concealed inside the tiger's body, behind a hinged flap, is an organ operated by the handle next to it. When the handle is turned, it produces a peculiar, unnerving sound, akin to an animal's growl as it seizes its prey. Simultaneously, the man lifts his arms up and down and emitting noises intended to imitate his dying moans. The music box is among the Tipu Sultan's many treasures, a symbol of his defiant spirit.

THE TIGER OF MYSORE

Tipu Sultan was the ruler of the kingdom of Mysore, in present-day southern India. He assumed the throne in 1782 and was known for his bravery and leadership as he defended his kingdom against the Mughals and the British, while also building new alliances. According to popular sources, he picked the tiger as his insignia after ostensibly killing one with a dagger. Tigers and related symbols appeared frequently in his possessions and anything that represented his rule. Even his throne had jewel-encrusted tiger head finials in gold, and his coinage, swords, and guns often incorporated tiger heads or stripes.

After Tipu's death following the Fourth Anglo-Mysore War in 1799, this musical box, along with other prized possessions, were taken from his palace and distributed as war booty. Objects made of precious metals and jewels were dismantled, including his golden throne. However, the wooden make of Tipu's Tiger spared it the same fate.

TIPU SULTAN'S TREASURES

The ruler of the kingdom of Mysore, Tipu Sultan was a renowned warrior, leader, and a fierce opponent of the expansionist ambitions of the East India Company. He maintained a sophisticated court that produced some extraordinary pieces of art and jewellery for his personal use, all of which were a testament to his state's sea of wealth.

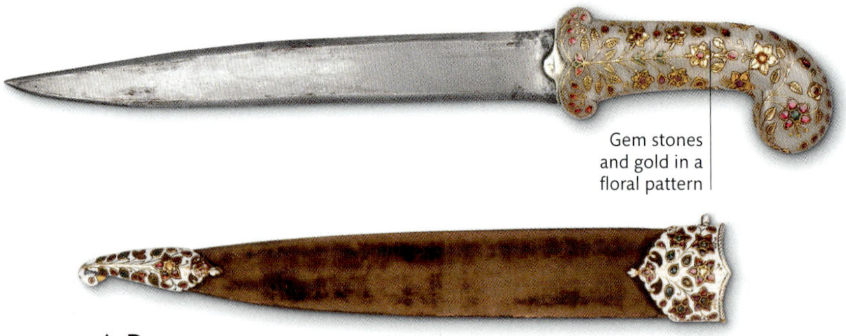

Gem stones and gold in a floral pattern

▲ Dagger
This *khanjar* (dagger) is decorated with a bejewelled jade hilt and a velvet scabbard. Tipu Sultan was often portrayed in paintings carrying such a weapon in his waistband.

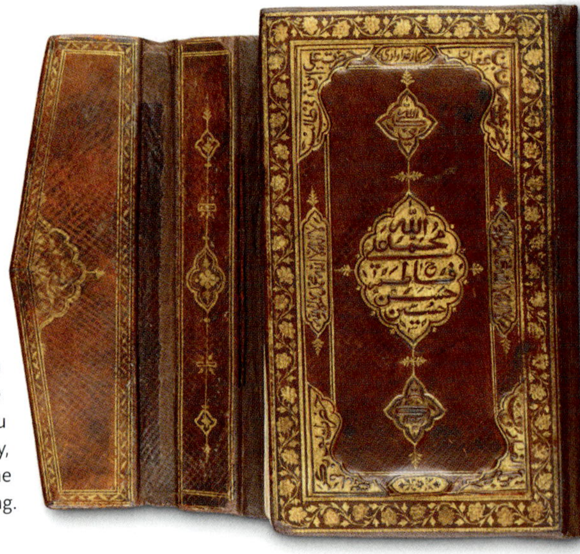

► Qur'an
This manuscript of the holy book was Tipu Sultan's personal copy, who rebound it in fine gilded binding.

Commemorative inscription proclaiming Tipu's titles

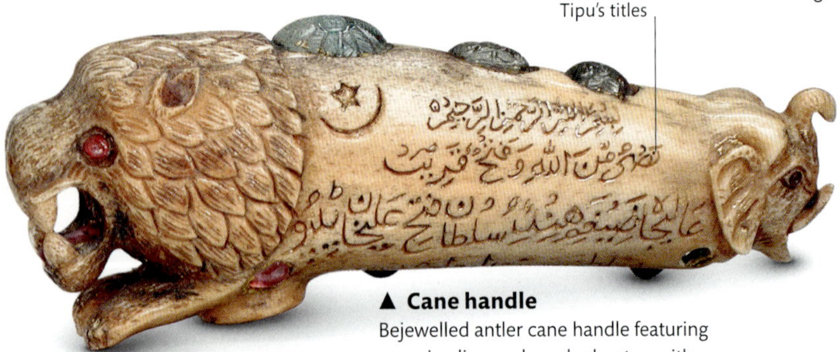

▲ Cane handle
Bejewelled antler cane handle featuring a roaring lion and an elephant on either ends. Lavish walking canes were a stylish accoutrement and status symbol.

► Belt ornament
This gem-encrusted jade piece, with a lotus motif, probably decorated the belt loop of a dagger. The accompanying note testifies its provenance.

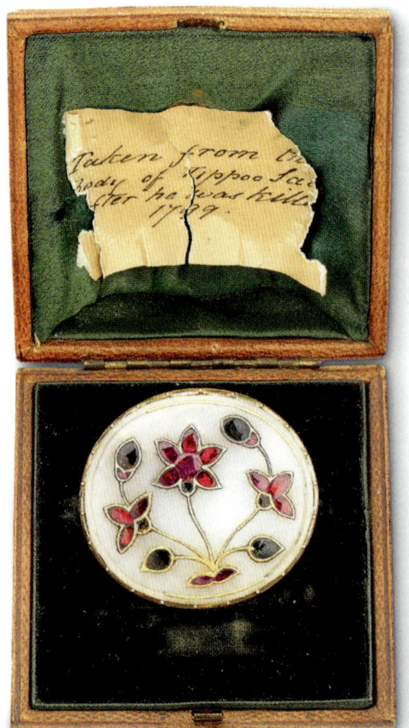

Tiger-shaped lock with priming screw

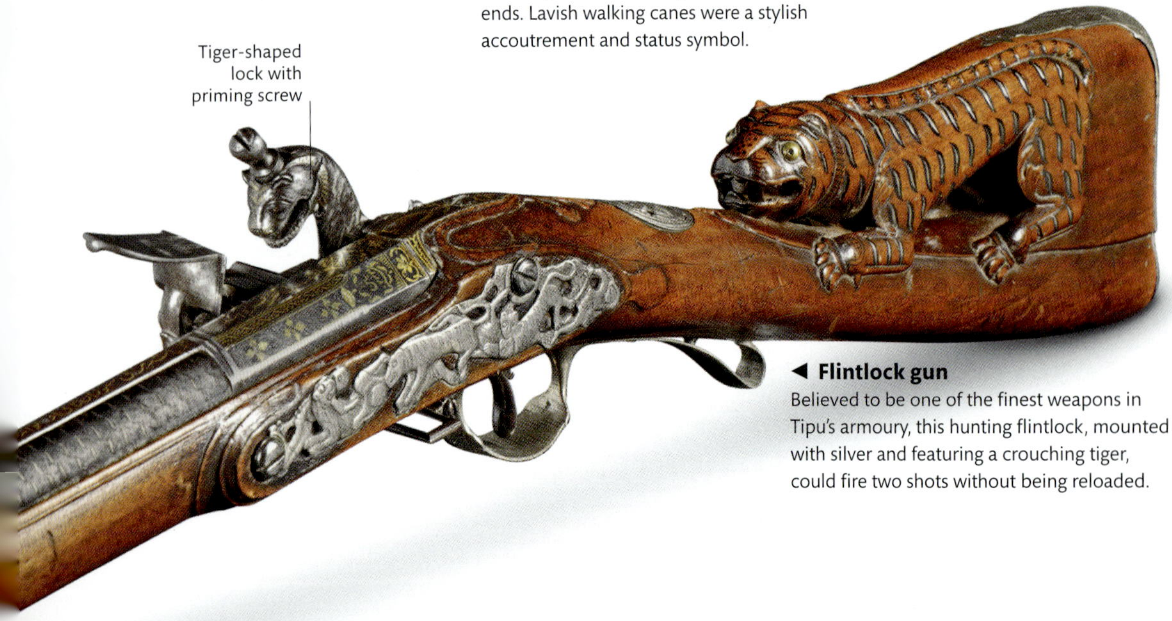

◄ Flintlock gun
Believed to be one of the finest weapons in Tipu's armoury, this hunting flintlock, mounted with silver and featuring a crouching tiger, could fire two shots without being reloaded.

Tipu Sultan adopted the symbol of a **tiger** as part of his **royal identity**, which is reflected in his courtly **objects** and **weapons**.

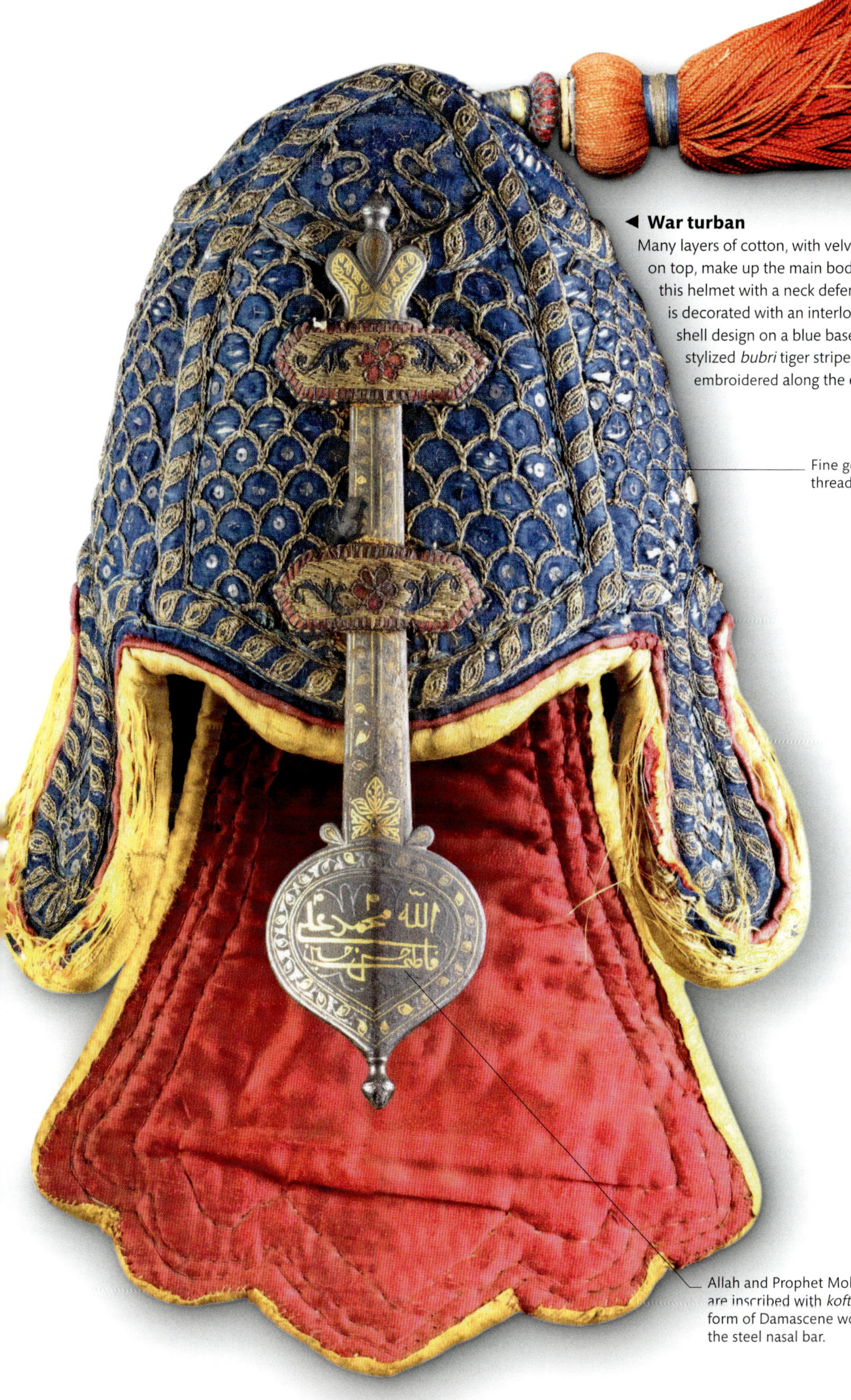

◀ **War turban**
Many layers of cotton, with velvet laid on top, make up the main body of this helmet with a neck defence. It is decorated with an interlocking shell design on a blue base and stylized *bubri* tiger stripes embroidered along the edges.

Fine gold orris thread embroidery

Allah and Prophet Mohammed are inscribed with *koftgari* (a form of Damascene work) on the steel nasal bar.

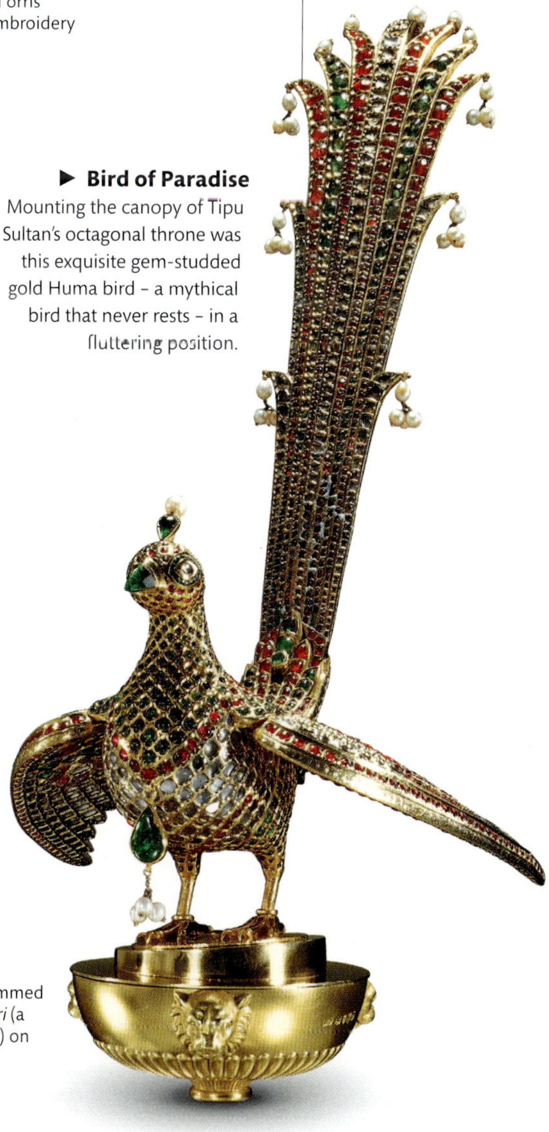

Feathers dotted with emeralds, rubies, gold, diamonds, and pearls.

▶ **Bird of Paradise**
Mounting the canopy of Tipu Sultan's octagonal throne was this exquisite gem-studded gold Huma bird – a mythical bird that never rests – in a fluttering position.

Era 19th century CE | **Medium** carved ivory | **Height** 1.61 m (5.2 ft)

IVORY THRONE

A masterpiece that forged imperial relations

This magnificent throne was the focal point of the Indian section at the 1851 Great Exhibition held in London and showcased the exceptional carving skills of Travancore artists.

The intricately carved ivory throne and footstool are masterpieces of ivory crafting. The throne features detailed elephant-ivory plaques that blend Indian and European motifs, and the conch shell from the Travancore royal family on the crest. Bedecked with gold, diamonds, emeralds, and rubies, the throne is a testament to the artistic talent of Travancore's carvers, and incorporates symbols such as lions and elephants from the southern part of India, while also incorporating heraldic symbols like unicorns that resonated with Western tastes.

The throne was presented by Maharaja Martanda Varma of Travancore to Queen Victoria as one of India's prized contributions to the Great Exhibition. The exhibition was conceived by Prince Albert in 1851 to showcase England and its colonies' industrial prowess to the world. It featured 100,000 objects contributed by over 15,000 participants. The throne's purpose was to highlight the mastery and expertise of Travancore's artisans. At the time, Travancore was widely recognized as a premier centre of ivory carving, and many rulers in the 19th century, including Maharaja Varma, were eager to advance and bolster this craft.

THRONE FIT FOR A QUEEN

Historical records consistently acknowledge the association of the throne to Queen Victoria and its status as a 'gift' from the Maharaja of Travancore, perpetuating the popular perception of the throne being a political conduit for the forging of imperial ties. However, it is interesting to note that far from being a region managed by a 'subject prince', Travancore considered itself an autonomous kingdom, lying outside of the realms of British-controlled India. The maharaja emphasizes this distinction in his letter to the queen, referring to Travancore (now in Kerala) as a small state 'neighbouring' Her Majesty's empire. Contemporaneous accounts also reveal that the throne was originally designed for the maharaja before being reassigned as a gift for the queen. These tell us about the erasure of the throne's production history, which would have taken place in 19th century England.

When Queen Victoria was proclaimed the empress of India in 1876, she selected the throne as the seat for her official portrait, which was taken at Windsor Castle.

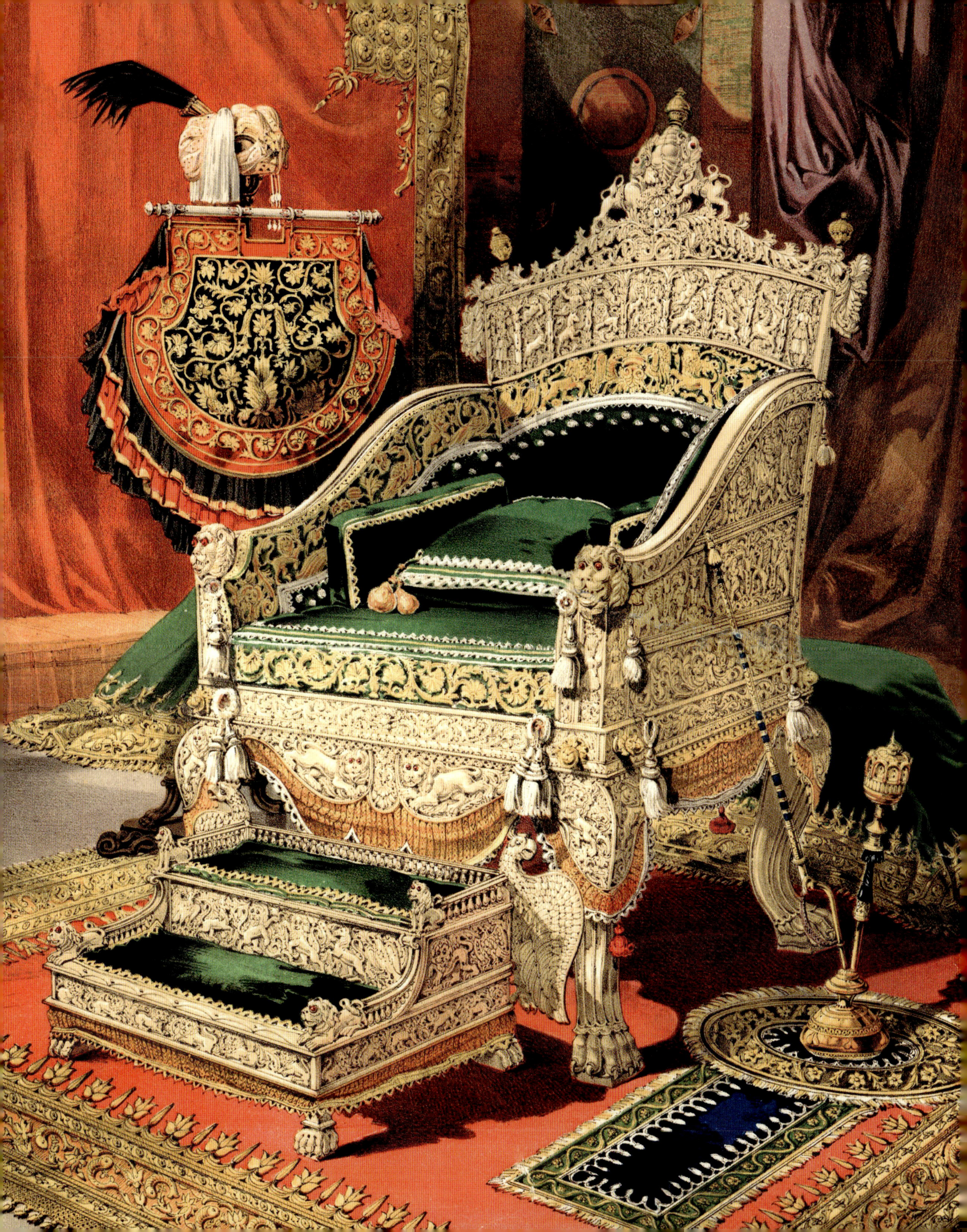

JEWELS OF THE NIZAM

One of the largest and most expensive collection of jewels comes from the treasury of the erstwhile princely state of Hyderabad in southern India. From Colombian emeralds, Sri Lankan rubies and spinels, and Kashmiri sapphires to pearls from the Gulf of Mannar and Bahrain, these jewels have graced many necklaces, ornaments, and swords.

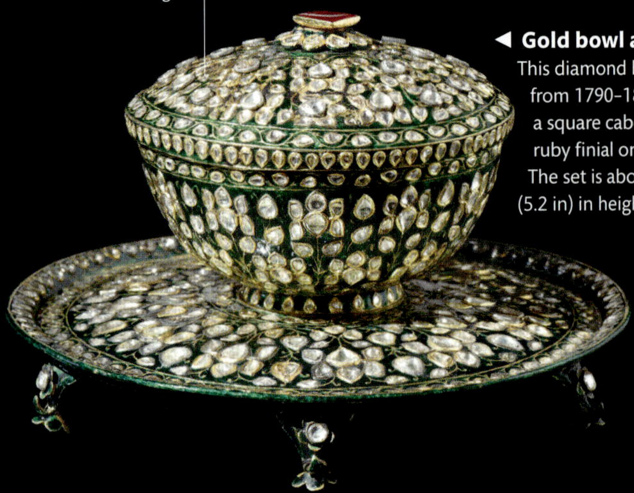

◄ **Gold bowl and stand**
This diamond bowl set, from 1790–1810, carries a square cabochon-foiled ruby finial on the top. The set is about 13.3 cm (5.2 in) in height.

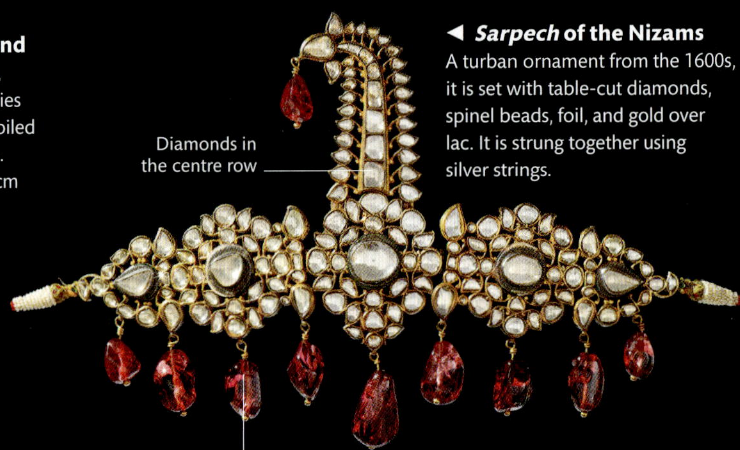

◄ ***Sarpech* of the Nizams**
A turban ornament from the 1600s, it is set with table-cut diamonds, spinel beads, foil, and gold over lac. It is strung together using silver strings.

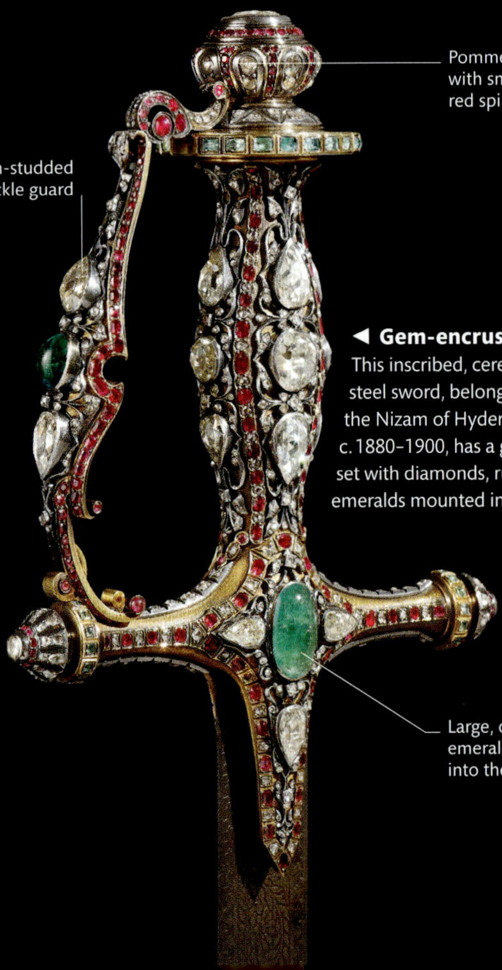

◄ **Gem-encrusted sword**
This inscribed, ceremonial steel sword, belonging to the Nizam of Hyderabad c. 1880–1900, has a gold hilt set with diamonds, rubies, and emeralds mounted in silver.

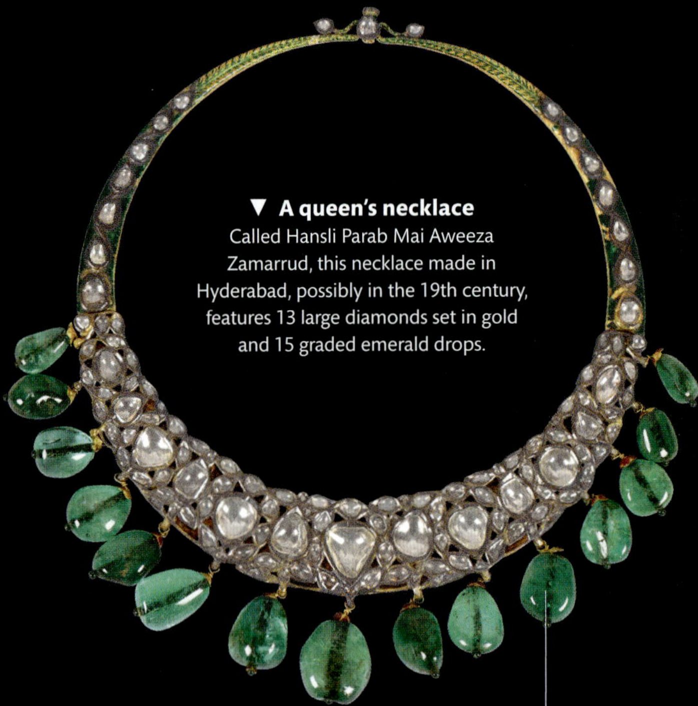

▼ **A queen's necklace**
Called Hansli Parab Mai Aweeza Zamarrud, this necklace made in Hyderabad, possibly in the 19th century, features 13 large diamonds set in gold and 15 graded emerald drops.

The last Nizam, Osman Ali Khan, amassed such wealth that he used a massive diamond, known as the Jacob, as a paperweight.

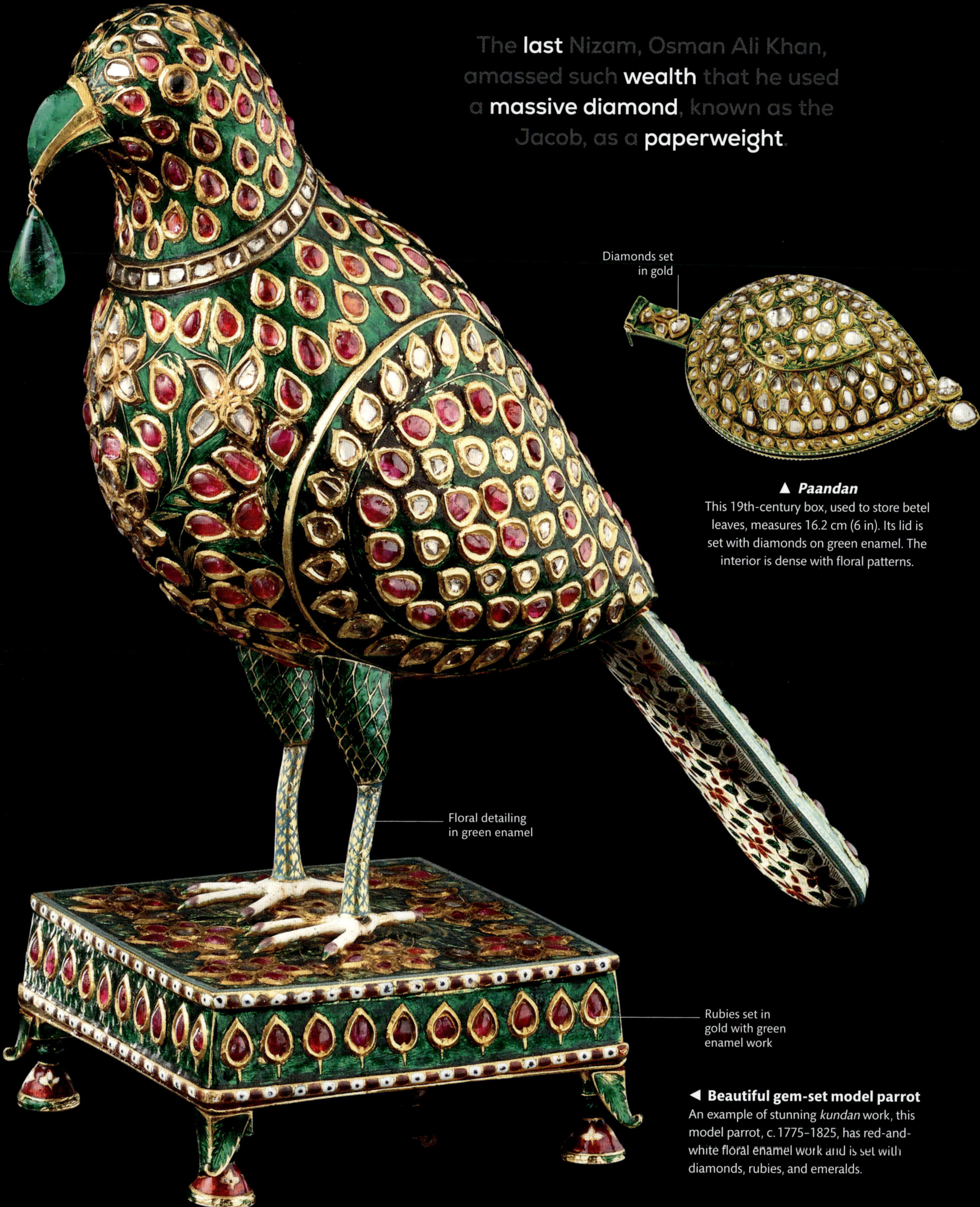

▲ *Paandan*
This 19th-century box, used to store betel leaves, measures 16.2 cm (6 in). Its lid is set with diamonds on green enamel. The interior is dense with floral patterns.

◄ Beautiful gem-set model parrot
An example of stunning *kundan* work, this model parrot, c. 1775–1825, has red-and-white floral enamel work and is set with diamonds, rubies, and emeralds.

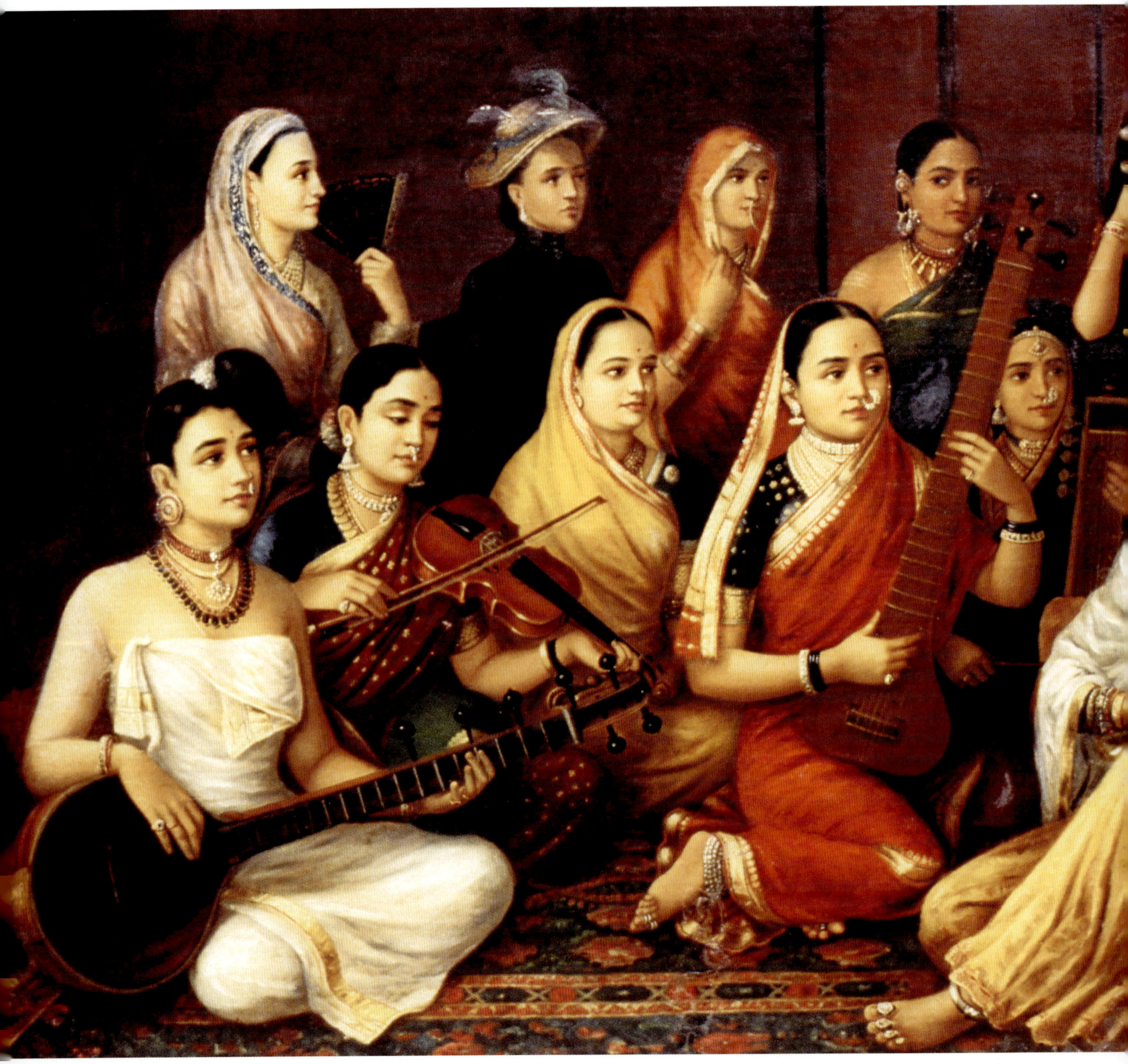

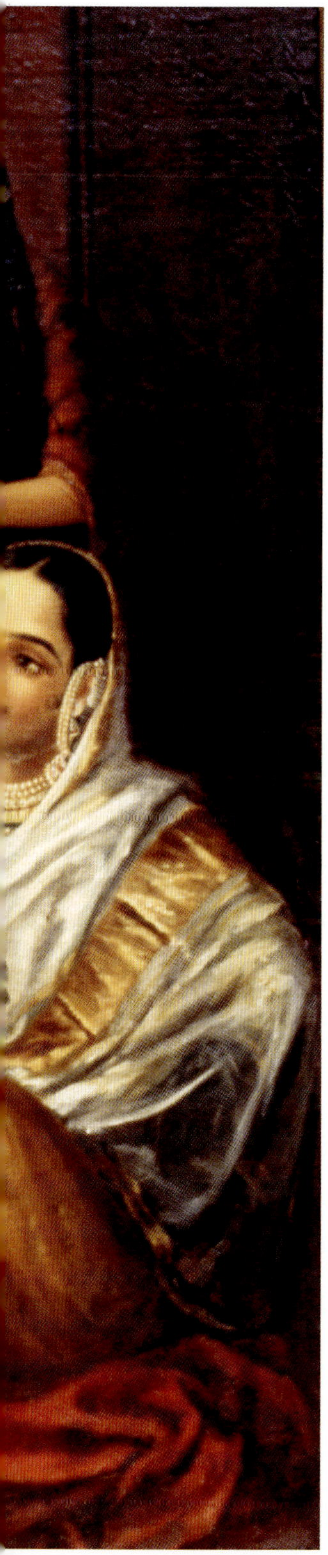

Era 19th century CE | **Medium** Oil on canvas | **Dimension** 124 × 109 cm (49 × 43 in)

GALAXY OF MUSICIANS

An allegory of a nation in transition

This gathering of Indian women with their traditional instruments, seemingly in the midst of a musical performance, gives expression to Raja Ravi Varma's view of harmonious coexistence within a country encompassing diverse identities.

Raja Ravi Varma created this painting in 1889 for Chamarajendra Wadiyar X, the Maharaja of Mysore. It depicts 11 Indian women from different social and religious backgrounds - such as a Nair woman from Kerala, an Indo-European dresser with a hat, a Muslim woman from north India, and one from Maharashtra - painted at a critical phase of the Indian freedom movement against colonial British rule. Varma conveys that though different, they all belong on a single canvas. He tried to create a sense of nationhood as imagined through the gendering of the nation as female. Varma used his art to explore the question of a national identity, which transcended regional identity, religions, and class.

The painter placed focus on one profession and on how women dressed, the differences in their clothing, jewellery, and postures. Some sit, others stand. Some hold instruments, while others seem to listen.

MASTER OF INDIAN REALISM

Raja Ravi Varma (1848-1906) was popular for having used modes of European realism and art techniques to develop features of 'Indian art', characterized by realistic portraits, rich texture, and a nuanced treatment of chiaroscuro. Varma was not only a master portrait artist for the nobility, but also a pioneer of depicting Hindu deities and scenes from Hindu mythology. Taking his art to the common man, he opened a lithographic press in 1894, making cheap copies of his paintings - specially of the mythological and religious ones. Contemporary caste hierarchies that restricted access to gods' imagery were suddenly upended as his art found a way into many Indian households. His style remained highly influential until the beginning of the 1910s when the Swadeshi ideology that sprung from the national freedom movement shunned the realisms in his iconography as foreign imports.

Era 19th–mid-20th century CE | **Dimension** 44 × 28 cm (17.5 × 11 in)

KALI OF KALIGHAT

Unique temple souvenirs

Created by traditional scroll painters as religious souvenirs at the Kalighat Temple in present-day Kolkata, West Bengal, Kalighat paintings evolved into their distinct style in the 19th century.

Brandishing a weapon in one hand, the Hindu goddess Kali bares her red tongue in glee as she holds the head of a slain demon in a second hand, while the other two are raised as if to bless her worshippers. Encapsulating the appearance of the deity worshipped inside the Kalighat Temple, this image was the main type of *pata* or *patta,* meaning scroll, produced by the *patuas* (painters) in the 19th century. Eventually, the paintings came to be named after the temple.

KALIGHAT PAINTINGS

Characterized by bright colours, bold outlines, and simple images, Kalighat paintings evolved as a unique genre of Indian painting in the 19th century. Local and visiting

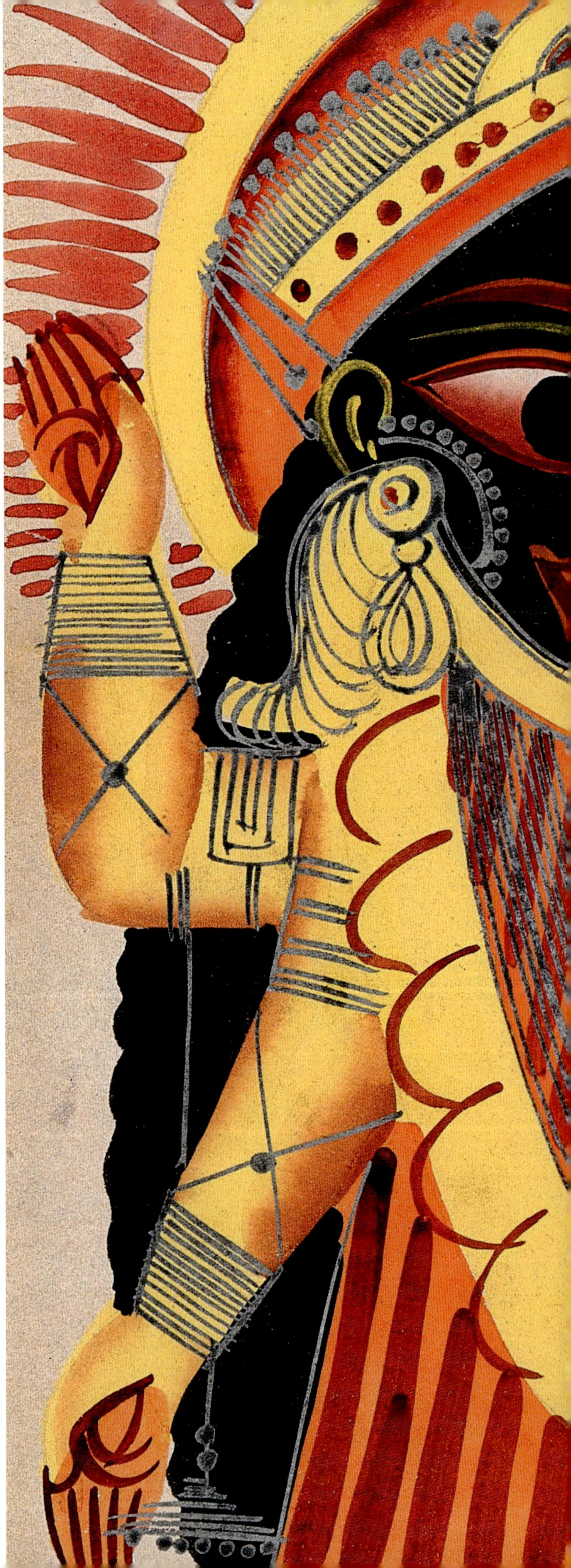

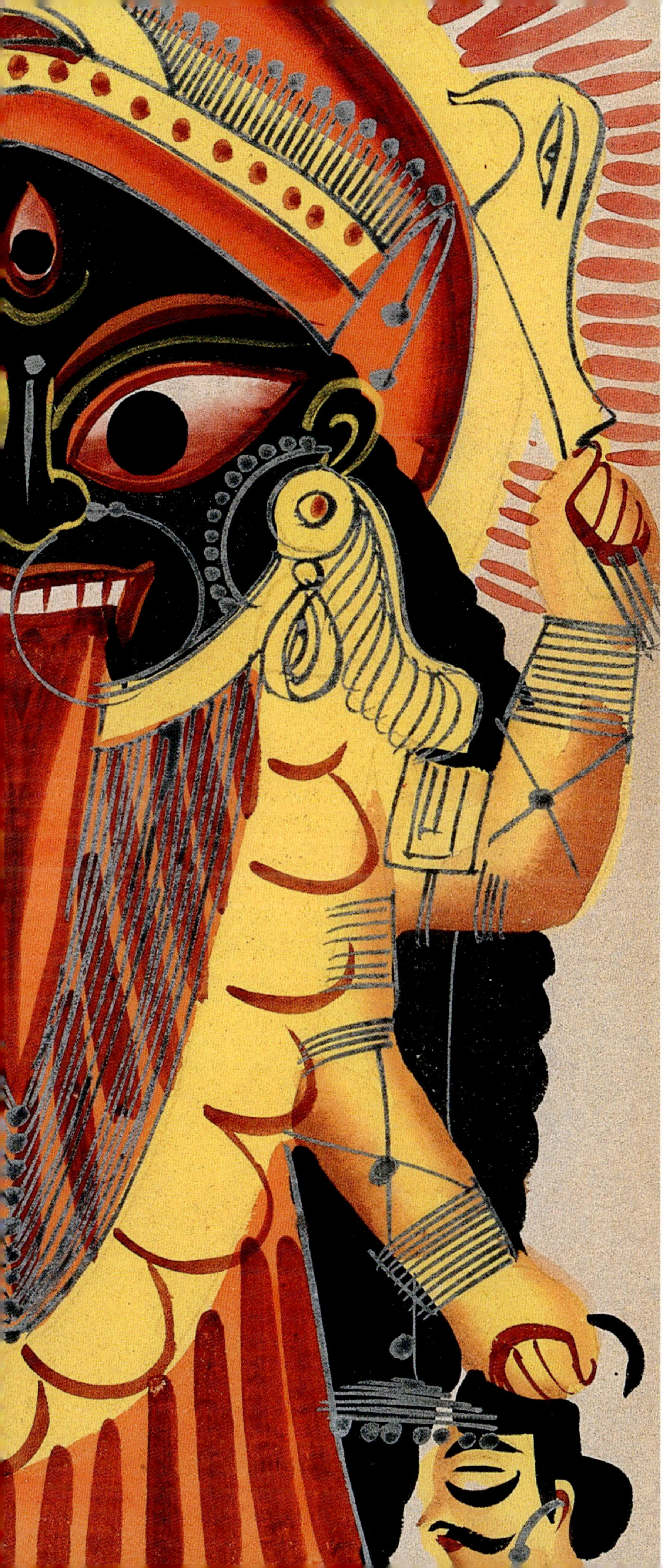

pilgrims who wished to take a sacred souvenir from the temple patronized the *patuas.* The painters were traditionally storytellers who painted elaborate scenes from epics and mythologies. However, the daily horde of pilgrims provided the perfect opportunity to the local artists to produce and sell quickly made, cheap paintings. The earlier narrative style was replaced with single pictures involving one or two figures, background detailing was abandoned, all non-essential details were removed, and basic combinations of colours were used. Starting from the depiction of gods and other mythological characters, the paintings developed in style over time to reflect a variety of religious and secular themes.

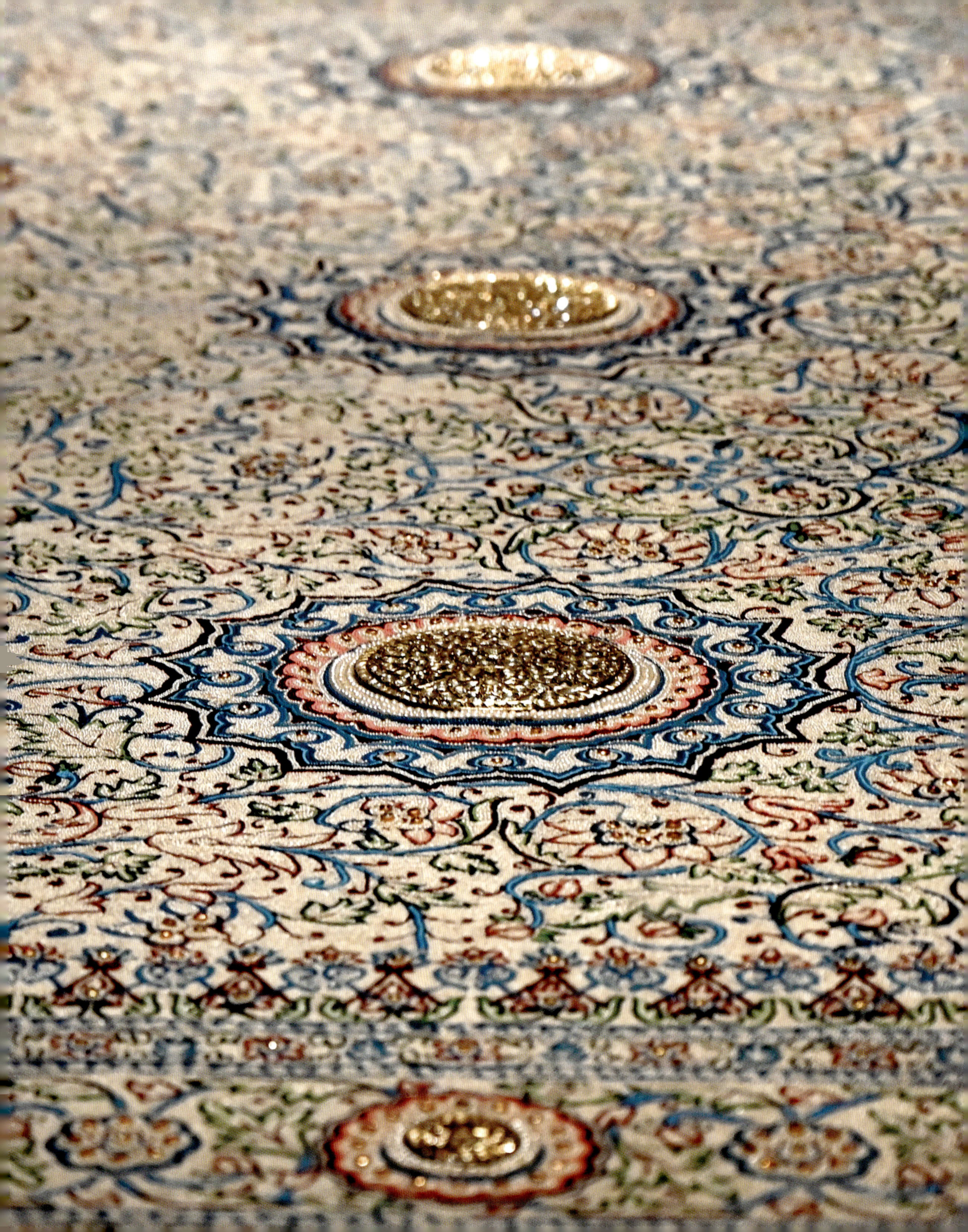

Era c. 19th century CE | **Medium** Silk and deer hide | **Dimension** 1.7 × 2.6 m (5.8 × 8.8 ft)

PEARL CARPET OF BARODA

A Hindu king's extravagant offering to Medina

Commissioned as an offering for the revered tomb of Prophet Mohammed at Medina, in Saudi Arabia, by Khande Rao Gaekwad, the Maharaja of Baroda, this pearl-studded carpet bears testimony to the grandeur of the Gaekwad dynasty.

Over 1.5 million pearls decorate the remarkable carpet, crafted in 1865 on the order of Khande Rao Gaekwad, the Maharaja of Baroda. Diamonds, sapphires, emeralds, and rubies accentuate it further, creating a breathtaking display of wealth and opulence. It is the rare freshwater Basra pearls, however, that make it an invaluable objet d'art, sourced as they were from the Gulf region and the coasts of Qatar and Bahrain. Accounts suggest that the primary motivation behind the creation of this opulent carpet was to fulfil a vow Gaekwad made to cover the tomb of the Prophet in Medina. The beauty of the pearl carpet quickly gained fame and its splendour was documented as early as 1880, most notably by George M. Birdwood, a 19th century art consultant to the Victoria and Albert Museum in London, UK, who wrote: "But the most wonderful piece of embroidery ever known was the *chaddar* or veil made by order of Kunde Rao ... When spread out in the sun it seemed suffused with a general iridescent pearly bloom, as grateful to the eyes as were the exquisite forms of its arabesques."

ARABESQUE DESIGN

The design is a nod to the Mughal style, with the intricate vine pattern forming three arches, each crowned by a grand diamond-studded roundel and a graceful palmette. The elaborate vines and profuse floral motifs are reminiscent of the 18th-century millefleur designs seen in the finely woven north Indian Pashmina shawls and rugs. It is also a vivid testimony of the thriving pearl trade that once existed between the Persian Gulf, the oldest and most prolific pearl bank in the world for over four millennia, and the Indian subcontinent.

CHANGE OF GUARD

From traders to rulers

From the late 15th to the 17th century, many European powers set out to capture India's thriving spice trade. The British soon emerged as a powerful player in the political realm and left a lasting impact on every aspect of the country, including its art and architectural styles.

Indian spices had always been popular in Europe, however, the Arabs and later the Turks had monopolized all land trade routes. This prompted the Europeans to search for alternative sea routes to the Indian subcontinent. Then, in the late 1490s, the first Europeans landed on the western coast of India. Subsequently, many European powers emerged on the scene, competing with each other for control of the lucrative spice trade. However they remained on the fringes for hundreds of years as traders, coming to dominate the subcontinent only in the 17th and early 18th centuries. Over time, as big and small empires fragmented into regional states, these traders offered military service to the rulers in exchange for land and money. The biggest benefit of such settlements was not having to pay taxes, which led to greater profits. One of the first European powers to make an impact on the politics and economy of the country were the Portuguese, who dominated the scene for about 100 years. They started in the Malabar region of the west coast and eventually fortified trading centres in Goa along the Coromandel coast, and in parts of Bengal.

By the beginning of the 17th century, other European powers followed. The Dutch East India Company set up bases in 1605 in Tamil Nadu, Bengal, and Gujarat, and sourced textiles. The French were a late entrant and only established a factory in Gujarat in 1667, followed by many other settlements, including

1498 Portuguese explorer Vasco de Gama arrives in Calicut (Kozhikode)

1510 Portuguese capture the eastern coastal region of Goa.

1600 English East India Company founded in London, UK

c. 1606 First Dutch factories set up in Masulipatnam and Petapalli, Andhra Pradesh

1613–1614 English East India Company sets up factory in Masulipatnam and trading post at Surat

1667 French establish their factories in Gujarat

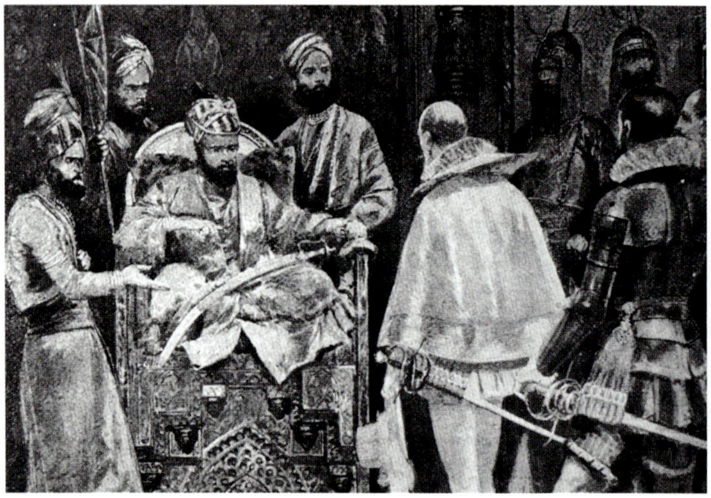

An early 20th-century illustration visualizing the Mughal Emperor Akbar receiving John Mildenhall, an ambassador of the British Queen Elizabeth I in 1599.

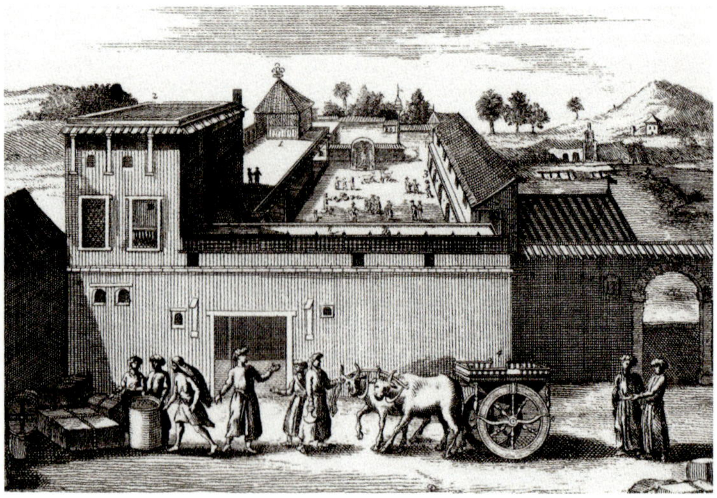

A 1738 etching on paper by Italian artist Giuseppe Filosi depicting a trading post established by the British East India Company at Surat, in modern-Gujarat, in the 17th century.

one in Pondicherry. However, none of these European powers had the overwhelming impact that the British did, as the East India Company, and later the Crown, went on to establish its rule across the Indian subcontinent.

ENGLISH EAST INDIA COMPANY

In 1600 in London, a group of British merchants and traders formed the English East India Company (EIC), which began operations under a royal charter granted by Queen Elizabeth I that gave them monopoly on trade in Asian waters. By the late 17th century, the EIC had set up more than 20 factories across India to buy goods, such as fabrics, sugar, and saltpetre. By 1668, King Charles II had granted it the rights to raise its own army, to rule territory in its own name, and to mint its own money. In the years that followed, the EIC gradually drove the French and the Dutch out of most of the Indian subcontinent, and aggressively annexed territories. In a bid to establish stronger operations in Bengal, a Mughal state and the richest province in India, Robert Clive, an employee of the Company, led its army against the Mughals in the Battle of Plassey. The defeat of the Mughals in 1757, established the British as the rulers of Bengal. This was seen as the decisive inauguration of British rule in India.

More regions were brought under their control, either through battle or through subsidiary alliances (which signed over a king's military and political power over to the British). The doctrine of lapse, which regulated succession in subordinate Indian states in the absence of a biological

1744–1763 Anglo-French wars for control of territory

1746 Madras (Chennai) sieged by the French

1751 Robert Clive captured Arcot in modern-day Tamil Nadu as French and British fight for control of South India

1757 Battle of Plassey, won by the British

1765 EIC gets rights to collect revenue in Bengal

1767 First Anglo-Mysore War

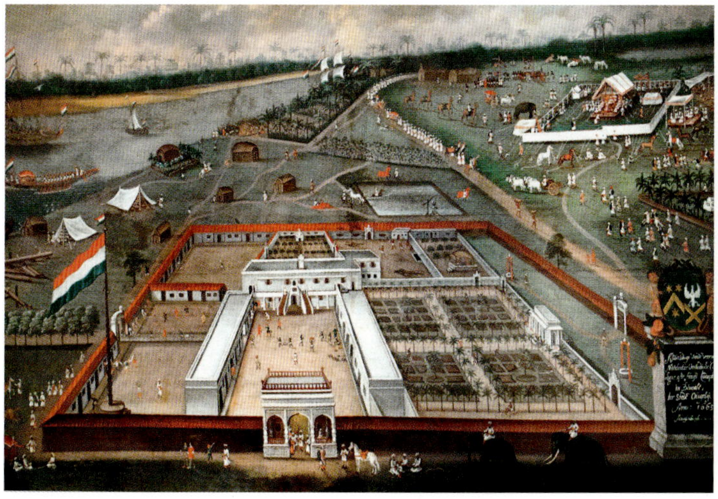

A 1655 oil painting by Hendrik van Schuylenburgh, a Dutch painter, depicts, in detail, the Dutch East India Company's trading post on the banks of river Ganges in Hooghly, West Bengal.

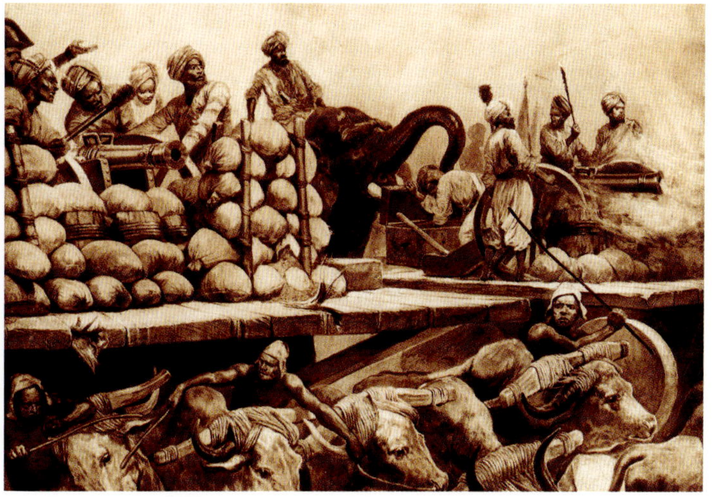

A 19th-century artist's painting of the 1757 Battle of Plassey, depicting the fight between the English East India Company and the Nawab of Bengal and his French allies.

male heir, was another tool in their arsenal. The territories under the peshwa, the states of Rajputana, Punjab, the kingdoms of Satara, Jhansi, Nagpur, Sambalpur, Jaipur, Udaipur, Surat, and Awadh all fell prey to this policy. In 1856, the EIC declared that Mughal emperor Bahadur Shah Zafar's descendants could no longer hold the title of 'emperor'.

By 1848, the EIC's territories spanned almost the entire subcontinent. There were other attempts to consolidate, by way of making administrative, economic, and social changes in the late 18th and early 19th centuries. The police and the army were reorganized, a code of law and justice was put in place based on British systems, manufacturing was increased in India, roads were built, and the railroads, postal system, and telegraph were introduced. India's first newspapers published in English, as those in Indian languages came later. The shift in policy had strong economic and social underpinnings.

The Industrial Revolution in Britain transformed India into a supplier of raw materials and made it a vast market to be exploited for the benefit of British industries and the British economy. British land revenue settlements dispossessed landholders, both big and small, foreign commerce drove artisans and weavers to ruin, and some aspects of the new the legal system were oppressive. By the early 19th century, the British had alienated many parts of Indian society, Hindus and Muslims alike, from princes and landowners, to the peasants. There was a surge in rebellions, as the period from 1763 to 1856 saw more than 40 major uprisings across the subcontinent, apart from hundreds of minor ones. The EIC's ultimate decline came in 1857 with an uprising that turned out to be a cataclysmic event in the history of the subcontinent. It has been, by turns, labelled the Sepoy Mutiny, the Revolt of 1857, and even the First War of Indian Independence, depending on who is writing the history. However, its impact is undebatable. What began as soldiers protesting against the British enveloped the peasantry and other classes over a vast expanse in north India. No single factor in itself led to the mutiny; however, the cumulative effect meant that all that was needed was a single catalyst. This came in the form of cartridges greased in animal fat for the newly introduced Enfield rifles. A move that offended the religious sensibilities of the Hindus and the Muslims.

1770 Famine in Bengal and Bihar

1772 Warren Hastings appointed as governor of Bengal

1773 EIC gets monopoly to sell opium in Bengal

1803 Second Anglo-Maratha War and the fall of Delhi

1806 Sepoy mutiny in Vellore, Tamil Nadu

1813 EIC's charter is renewed but its monopoly over Indian trade is abolished

1835 English made official language for Company work

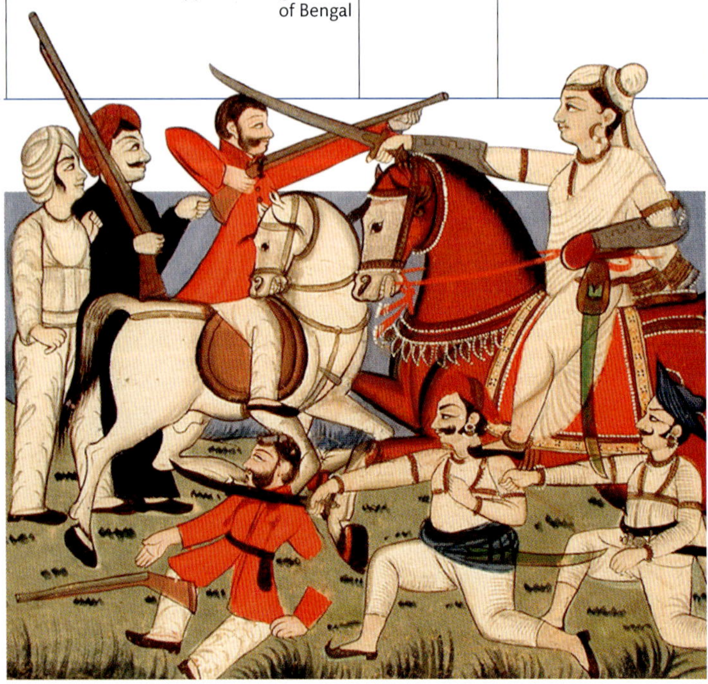

In this painting, the Rani of Jhansi, an iconic figure of resistance against the British, is depicted on horseback, killing British officers with her sword during the Revolt of 1857.

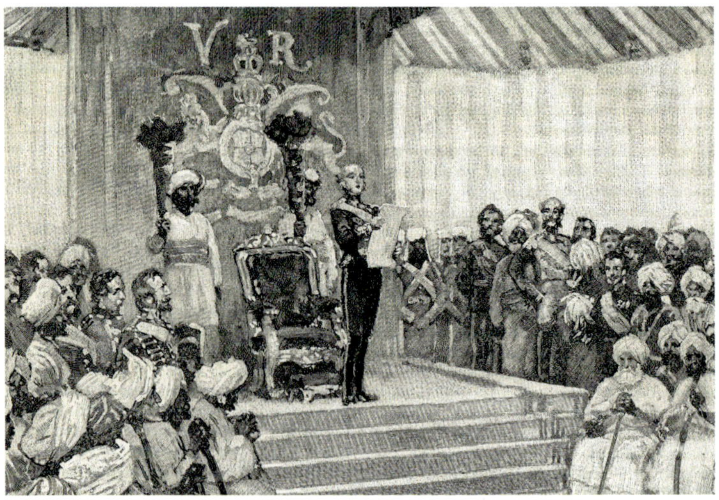

A sketch illustrating the Queen's proclamation of 1858 being read out as a group of Indian farmers, British officers, and seated princely rulers look on.

THE UPRISING OF 1857

The mutiny broke out in the Bengal troop of the army, with Mangal Pandey, a sepoy, attacking British officers in Barrackpore (in modern-day West Bengal) in March 1857. He was executed and his regiment disbanded, but the revolt had picked up pace. By April, about 85 sepoys were imprisoned in Meerut (in modern-day Uttar Pradesh) because they refused to use the Enfield cartridges. This incensed their comrades, who broke them out of prison, ransacked the nearby military station, and killed any European they could find. In the absence of leaders from their own ranks, the sepoys turned to the Indian royalty, including Mughal emperor Bahadur Shah Zafar in Delhi, Naha Saheb Peshwa in Kanpur, and Rani Lakshmibai in Jhansi.

The British administration toppled. News of these developments spread far and wide, encouraging further rebellions thousands of people across the country joined the revolt. The rebels' proclamations appealed to all sections of the population, to reject British rule, and to condemned the British for their annexations and the treaties they had violated.

THE EIC'S RESPONSE

The British were initially slow to respond, confounded by the speed and ferocity of the uprising. However, the reprisals far outweighed the excesses. Much of northern India was placed under martial law and the ordinary processes of law and trial were suspended as military officers as well as civilian Britons were given the power to punish any Indians suspected of rebellion. The British reestablished their rule; but this authority took on a different character in 1858.

A NEW GOVERNMENT

Following the uprising, the British Crown took direct control of India by issuing the Queen's Proclamation of 1858. The EIC was nationalized, its rights and responsibilities transferred to the British state, and Queen Victoria declared the sovereign. The replacement of the rule of the English East India Company did not really change much. Under the garb of new reforms and policies, the British continued the same practices. The years between the restoration of British authority and the beginning of the 20th century marked the culmination of colonial rule in India as Indian attitudes began to change and nationalist ideas began to take shape.

1843 The doctrine of lapse comes into force

1848 Lord Dalhousie becomes the governor-general of India

1853 First railway line laid between Thane and Bombay in Maharashtra

1856 Introduction of the Enfield rifle

1857 Sepoy Mutiny

1858 Queen's proclamation issued

1858 India comes under the Crown, ending East India Company's rule

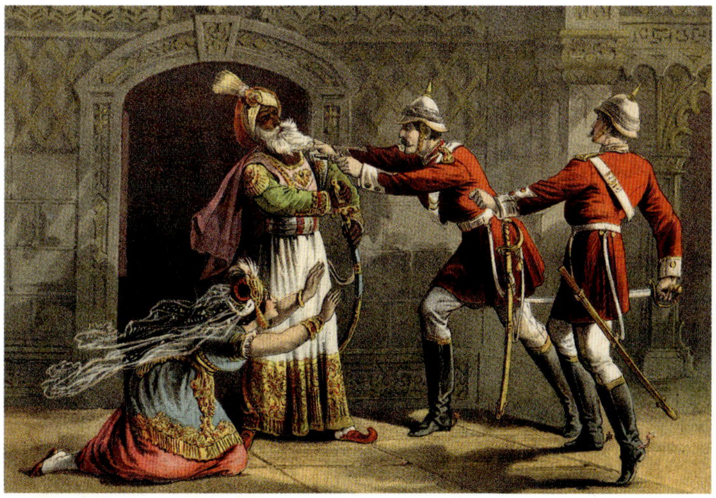

An 1878 illustration showing British officers apprehending Bahadur Shah II, the last Mughal Emperor, in the aftermath of the revolt of 1857.

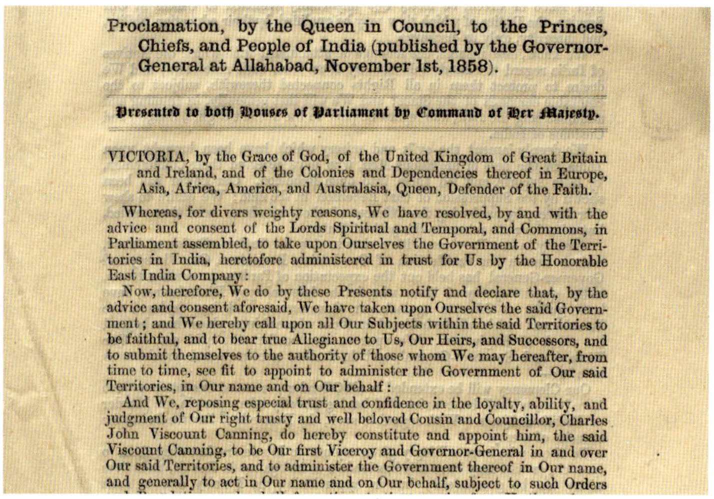

Proclamation, by the Queen in Council, to the Princes, Chiefs, and People of India (published by the Governor-General at Allahabad, November 1st, 1858).

Presented to both Houses of Parliament by Command of Her Majesty.

VICTORIA, by the Grace of God, of the United Kingdom of Great Britain and Ireland, and of the Colonies and Dependencies thereof in Europe, Asia, Africa, America, and Australasia, Queen, Defender of the Faith.

Whereas, for divers weighty reasons, We have resolved, by and with the advice and consent of the Lords Spiritual and Temporal, and Commons, in Parliament assembled, to take upon Ourselves the Government of the Territories in India, heretofore administered in trust for Us by the Honorable East India Company:

Now, therefore, We do by these Presents notify and declare that, by the advice and consent aforesaid, We have taken upon Ourselves the said Government; and We hereby call upon all Our Subjects within the said Territories to be faithful, and to bear true Allegiance to Us, Our Heirs, and Successors, and to submit themselves to the authority of those whom We may hereafter, from time to time, see fit to appoint to administer the Government of Our said Territories, in Our name and on Our behalf:

And We, reposing especial trust and confidence in the loyalty, ability, and judgment of Our right trusty and well beloved Cousin and Councillor, Charles John Viscount Canning, do hereby constitute and appoint him, the said Viscount Canning, to be Our first Viceroy and Governor-General in and over Our said Territories, and to administer the Government thereof in Our name, and generally to act in Our name and on Our behalf, subject to such Orders

This photograph depicts a printed copy of the Queen's proclamation, issued to the English East India Company in 1858.

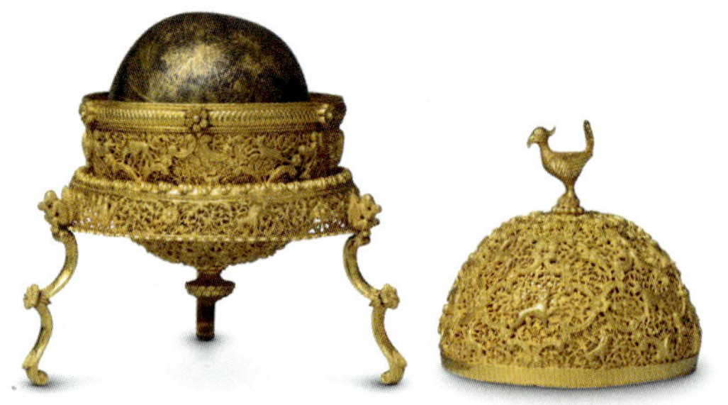

Era 17th–19th centuries CE | **Medium** Organic and inorganic materials | **Height** 6.7 cm (2.6 in)

GOA STONE

Myth, magic, and healing powers

Encased in extravagant cases of gold and silver, and exported to Europe from an obscure Jesuit monastery in the Portuguese colony of Goa in the 17th century, these stones came to be coveted by the nobles and the lay people for their medicinal properties.

Formed by a chemical reaction between bile and food matter that was not digested, these stones, known as bezoars, were taken from the stomachs of goats found in western Persia. Muscle contractions shaped them into smooth, hard, and roughly round or oval shapes. Introduced in Europe by Arabian traders in the 11th century, these stones were believed to possess healing properties and to be an antidote to arsenic and other poisons, in addition to being a cure for diseases such as leprosy, plague, measles, and even depression. For hundreds of years, slivers of the fist-sized balls were shaved off and ingested via drinks.

FABLED STONES OF POWER

The strong reputation, popularity, and consequent high monetary value made the bezoars hard to acquire. So, the mid-17th century saw a group of Portuguese Jesuit priests in the small Indian state of Goa combine a range of additional ingredients with locally obtained bezoars to manufacture artificial bezoars known as Goa stones. The makers of the Goa stones still believed in their efficacy, as the additives would have only enhanced the beneficial effects. The polished balls were made with all sorts of materials: precious stones, seed pearls, ambergris, musk, fossil shark teeth, or deer horn tips. These were weighed, ground, mixed, and prepared in an elaborate process that involved fermenting for six months, before being shaped into balls and dried. By keeping the recipes secret, the priests ensured that they were able to monopolize production and trade by late 17th century.

One of the earliest accounts of the Goa stone comes from the German botanist G.E. Rumphius, who claimed that not even a true bezoar could match the healing properties of the Goa stone. Myths surrounding the properties of the ingredients added to its mystique. Exquisitely packaged in ornately carved cases of gold and silver, they came to be sought after as status symbols as much as for their reputed healing powers.

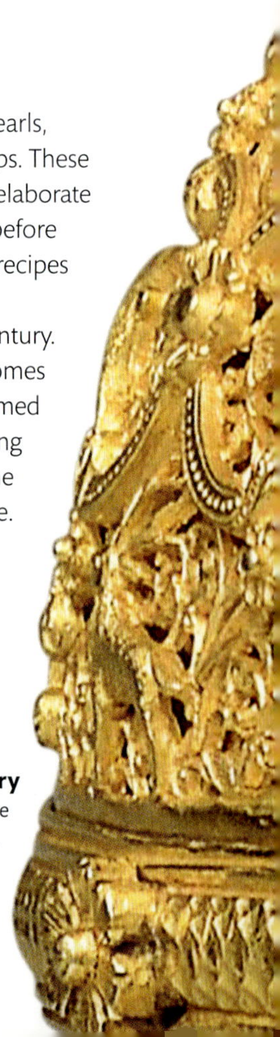

► **Invented by mid-17th century** Jesuit priests in Goa, the Goa stone was coveted for its antidotal powers, and each stone was encased in gold.

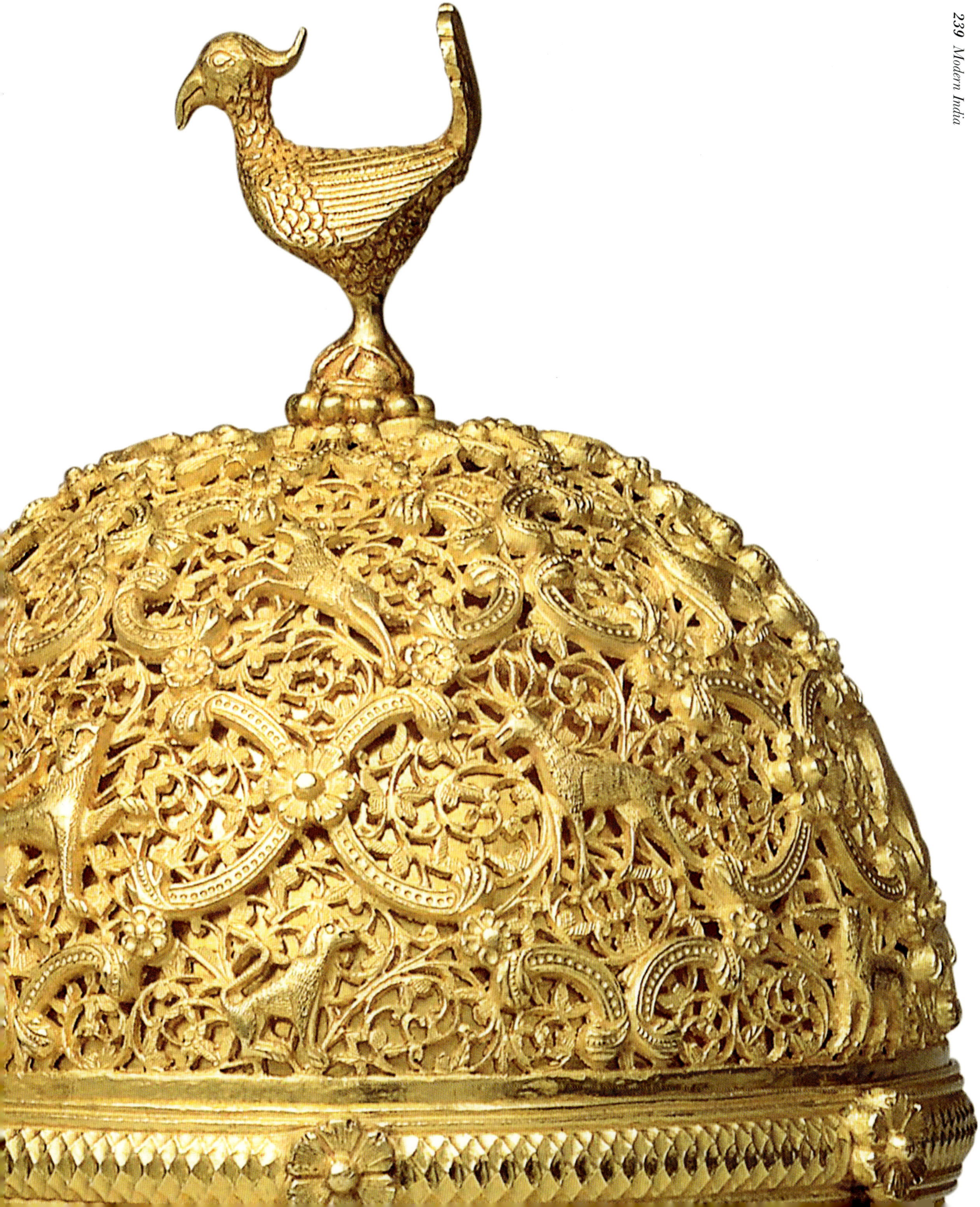

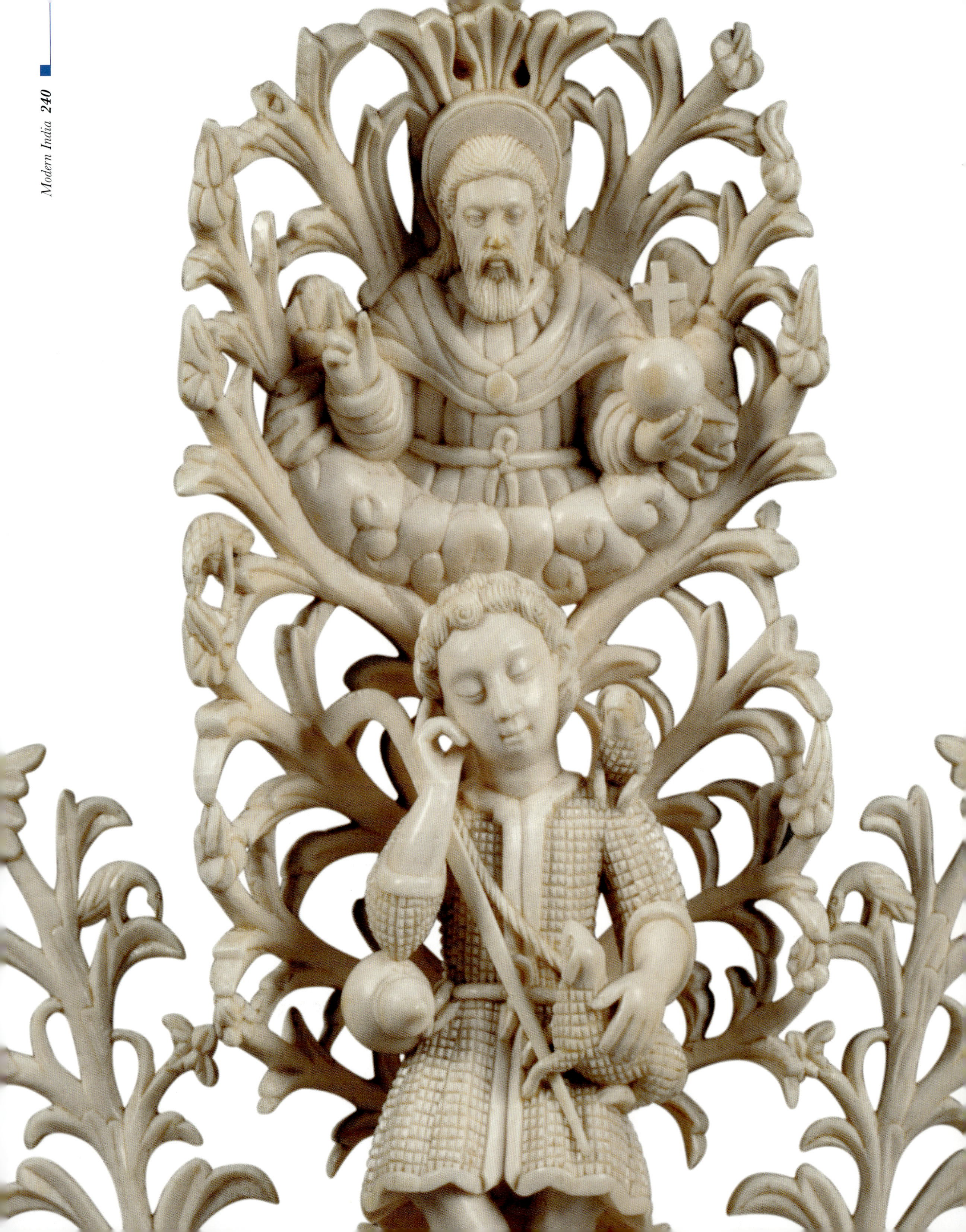

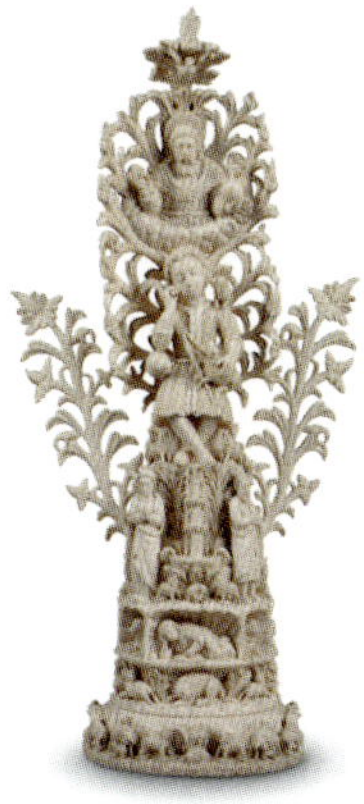

Era 17th century CE | **Medium** Ivory | **Dimension** 43 × 15 cm (16.9 × 5.9 in)

MOUNT OF GOOD SHEPHERD

Goan art born out of Portuguese evangelism

The iconography of the Mount of the Good Shepherd is a fusion of figures from Christian mythology with elements and poses reminiscent of temple carvings of the Indian subcontinent. They were introduced to Goa by Portuguese evangelists.

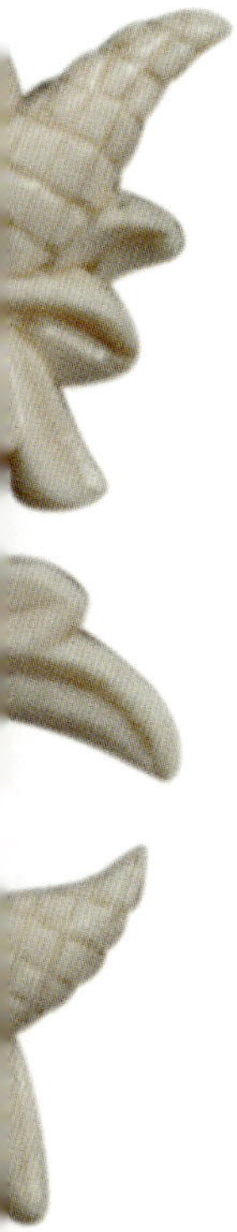

This intricately carved ivory image of the youthful Jesus, known as the Menino Jesus Bom Pastor, portrays him as the good shepherd. This particular representation of Jesus as a child with crossed legs in a peaceful slumber, atop a three-tiered hill symbolizing the mountain of life, is a distinctively Portuguese-Goan interpretation. Three branches with leaves fan out from the back. On one is a relief of God as his father holding an orb in his left hand. Above this branch is a dove. Various animals are carved into the base. That depiction of Jesus as a child is reminiscent of the Hindu deity Krishna, while his tranquil expression mirrors images of the Buddha.

ART AND THE SPREAD OF CHRISTIANITY

Goa was conquered by Alfonso de Albuquerque during the reign of Manuel I of Portugal in the early 1500s. The primary motivation behind Portugal's interest in India was trade domination, but Christian settlers and missionaries also sought to convert the local population to Christianity. To aid in these evangelical efforts, religious images in ivory were commissioned. From the 16th century onwards, the four main Christian missionary orders – Augustinians, Dominicans, Jesuits, and Franciscans – erected churches and carried out conversions. Indian iconography also made its way into the carvings, with the Mount of the Good Shepherd serving as the most notable example of this fusion. Much of the ivory used is believed to have been sourced from Mozambique in East Africa.

Numerous carvings from India, such as this one, were also directly imported to Europe, particularly to Spain and Portugal. They became the treasured possessions of churches, monasteries, and went to even aristocratic collections. Some of these pieces were also sent to Spanish and Portuguese territories such as Mexico and the Philippines. These intricately crafted ivory sculptures now serve as a rare reminder of India's rich and diverse cultural legacy, as well as a vivid illustration of Portugal's maritime and mercantile prowess during its heyday as a major seafaring and trading nation.

◀ **This Goan ivory carving, c. 1650, of a young** Jesus, also features images of Saint Joseph and Mary Magdalene. The latter is shown to be reading a book.

Era 16th century CE | **Medium** Laterite stone | **Height** 61 ft (18.5 m)

BASILICA DE BOM JESUS

A gem of the Roman Catholic world

This church, designated as a UNESCO World Heritage Site, is dedicated to the Infant Jesus and houses the remains of St Francis Xavier in Goa. In 1946, Pope Pius XII gave it the status of minor basilica, the first church in South Asia to receive the honour.

Commissioned by the Jesuits in 1594 under the guidance of Fr Alexander de Castro, the grand Basilica de Bom Jesus is a baroque structure that blends Corinthian, Doric, Ionic and composite styles in its magnificent three-tiered façade. It was completed in 1605 and consecrated in 1609. The church is revered by Roman Catholics all over the world as it houses the remains of Goa's patron saint, Francis Xavier, who came to the Indian subcontinent in 1542.

A GRAND CHURCH

One of the standout features of the basilica is its façade. It features a central rectangular pediment adorned with intricate carvings. This church is unique in Old Goa as it is the only one that does not have plaster on the exterior. Inside, the basilica is laid out simply beneath a wooden ceiling. The gilded altar takes pride of place with St Ignatius Loyola, a 17th century Spanish saint, protecting the figure of the Infant Jesus. He gazes above his head at the gilded sun, above which is a representation of the Holy Trinity. The main altar is flanked by the altars of Our Lady of Hope (Virgin Mary) and St Michael the Archangel. To the right is the marble-and-jasper tomb of St Francis Xavier. It has four bronze plaques depicting scenes from the saint's life, and the silver reliquary containing the sacred relics is surmounted by a cross with two angels. The adjoining two-storeyed Professed House of the Jesuits (1589), predating the basilica, was used as the priests' quarters until it was damaged by a fire in 1633.

1. The grand and impressive exterior of Basilica de Bom Jesus, the only church in Goa with a distinctive red laterite façade. **2.** Exquisitely carved wooden door leading to the sacristy. **3.** A basalt stone tablet carved into the top central exterior panel, with the Jesuit motto, *Iesus Hominum Salvator* - or Jesus, Saviour of Men in Latin. **4.** The tomb of St Francis Xavier, built with influences of Italian and Indian styles. **5.** A cross placed on a pedestal outside the church. **6.** The massive gilt altarpiece featuring statues of St Ignatius of Loyola, accompanied by the Infant Jesus and cherubs crafted by artisans in the local style. **7.** Ornate gilded statue of Mary with the Infant Jesus on the right side of the main altar.

1
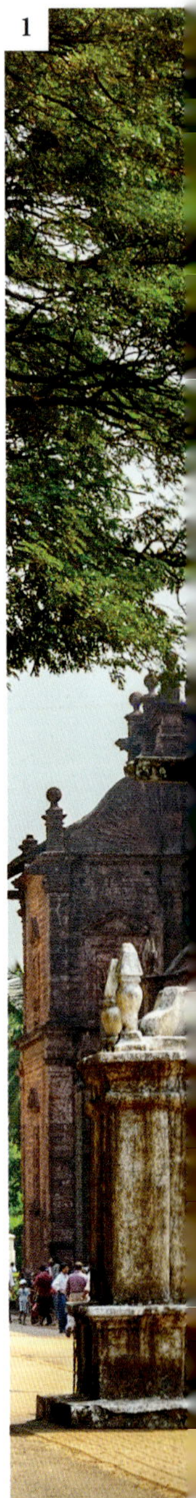

2
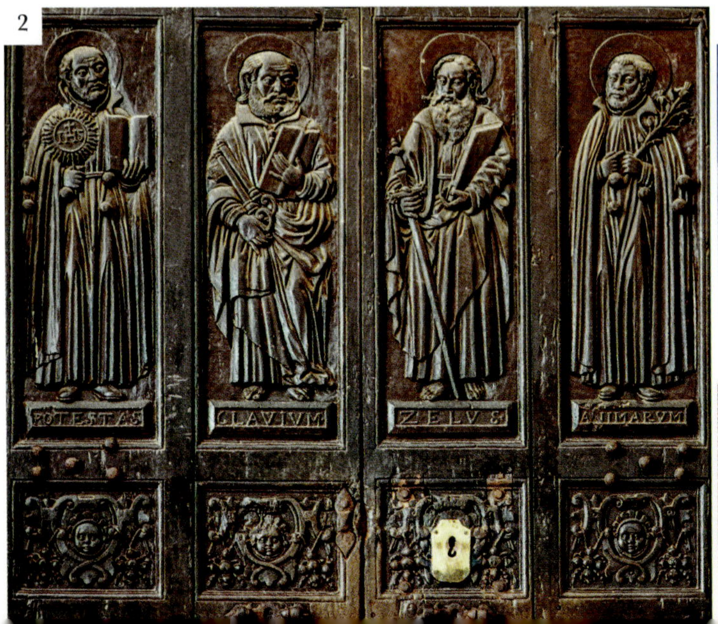

3
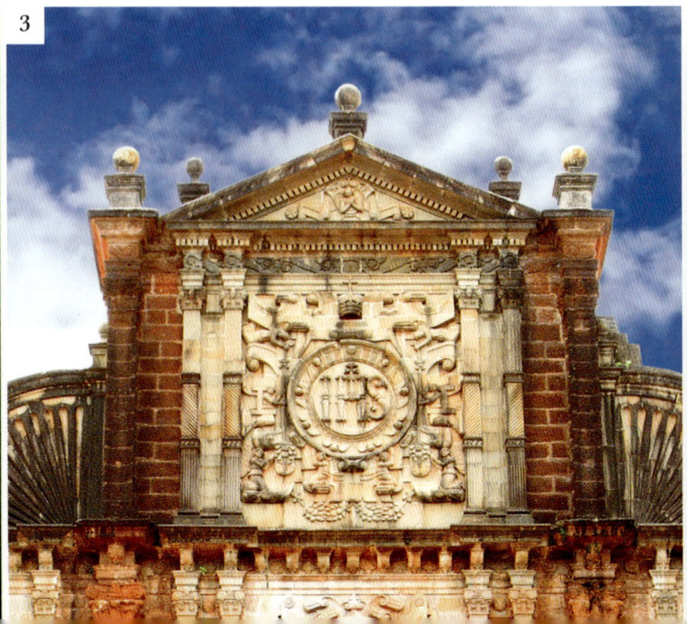

4
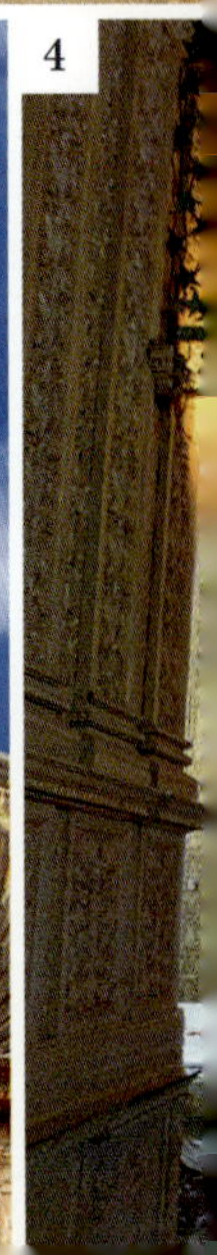

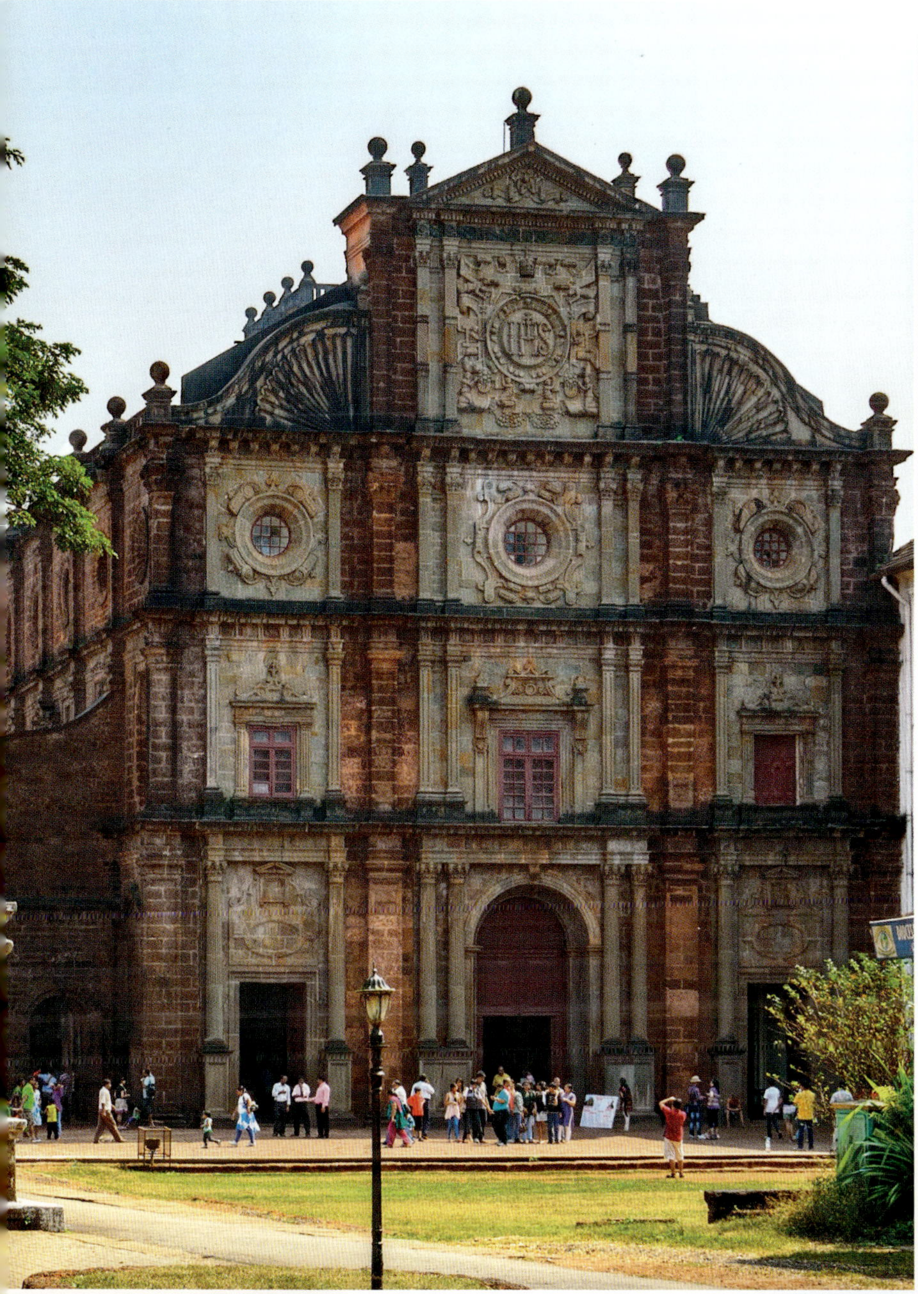

6

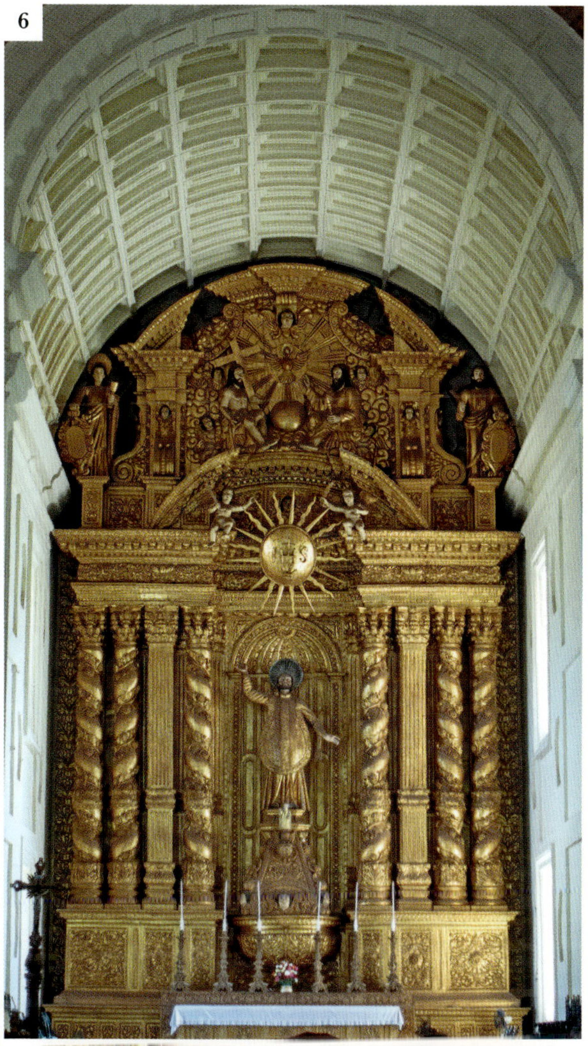

7

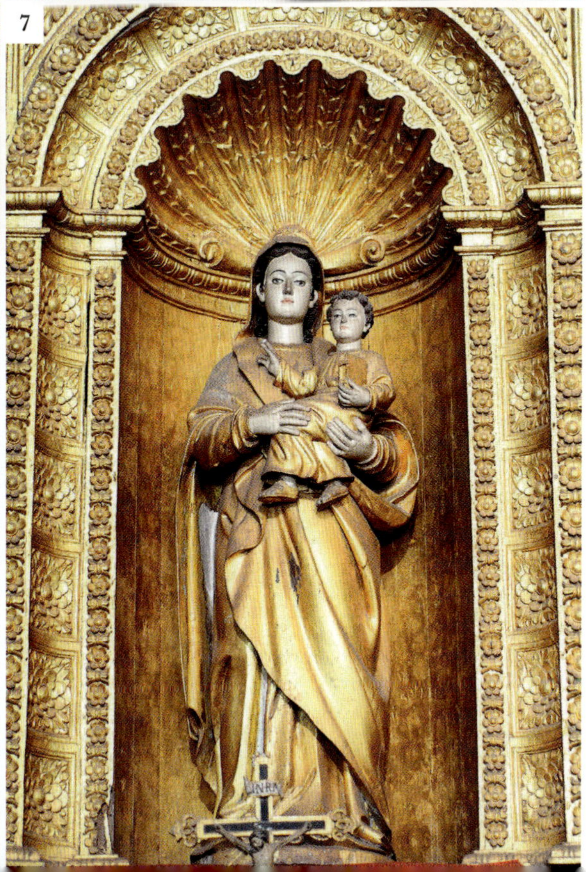

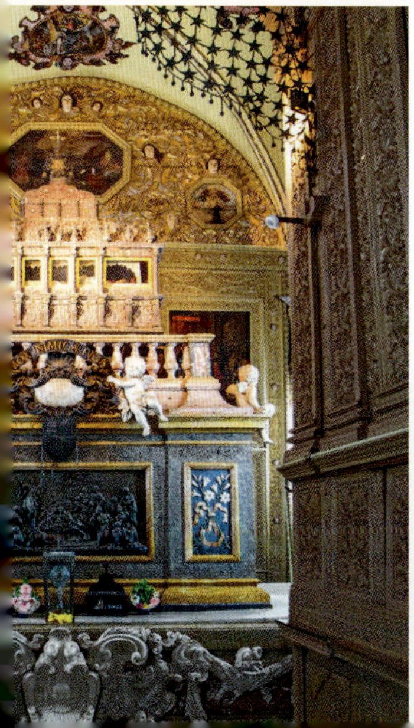

5

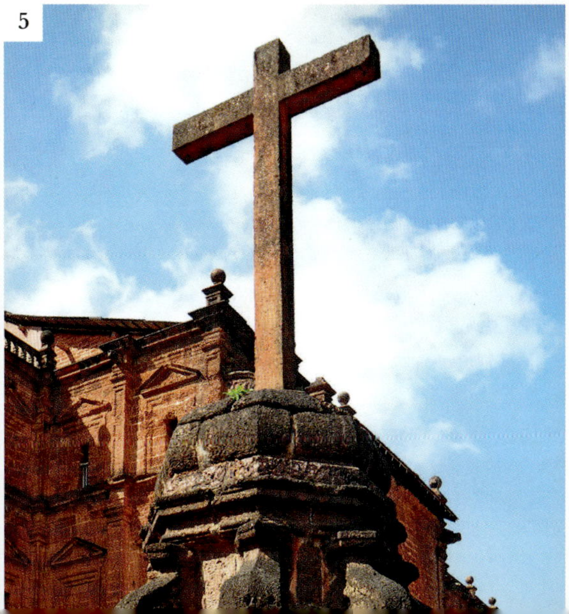

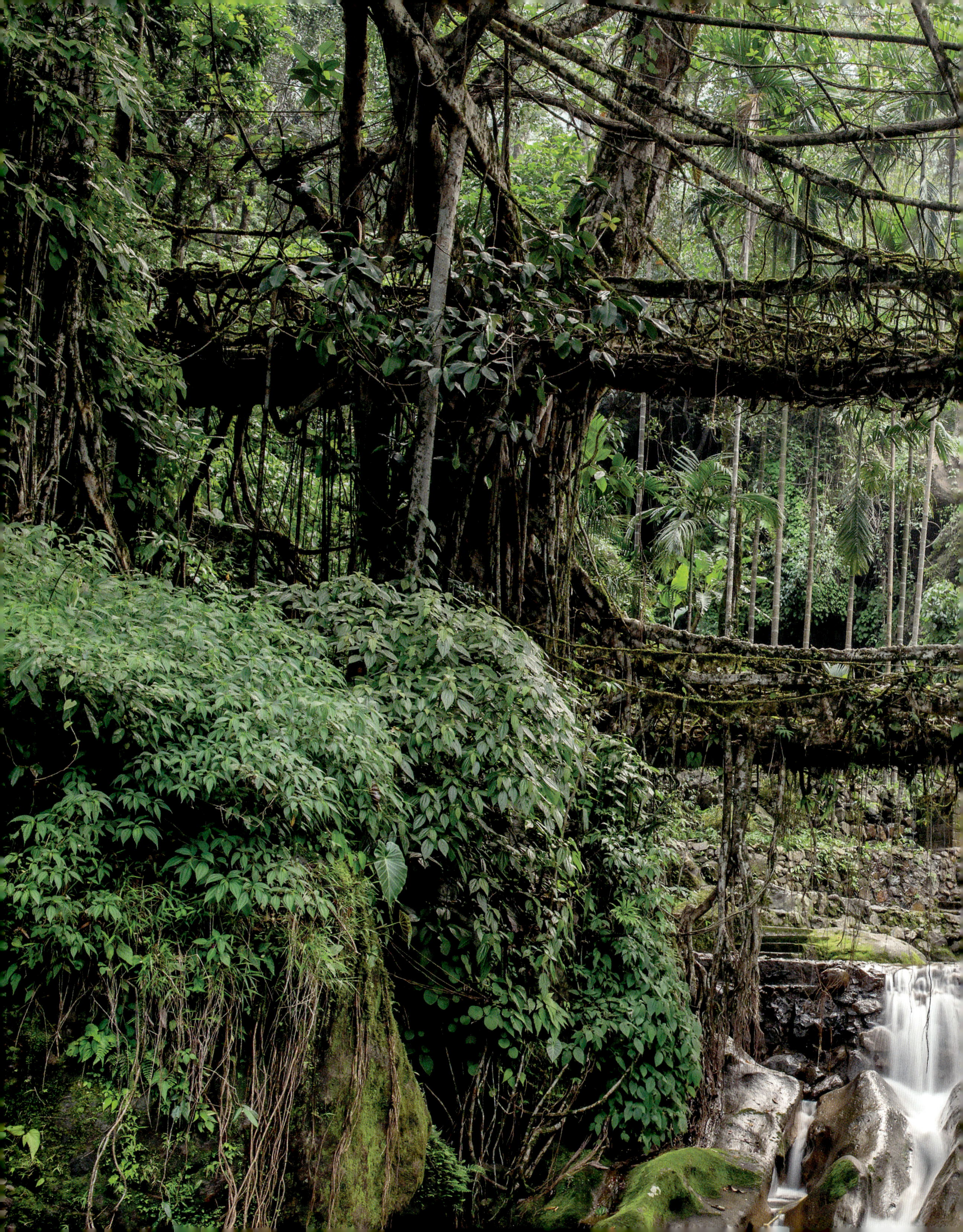

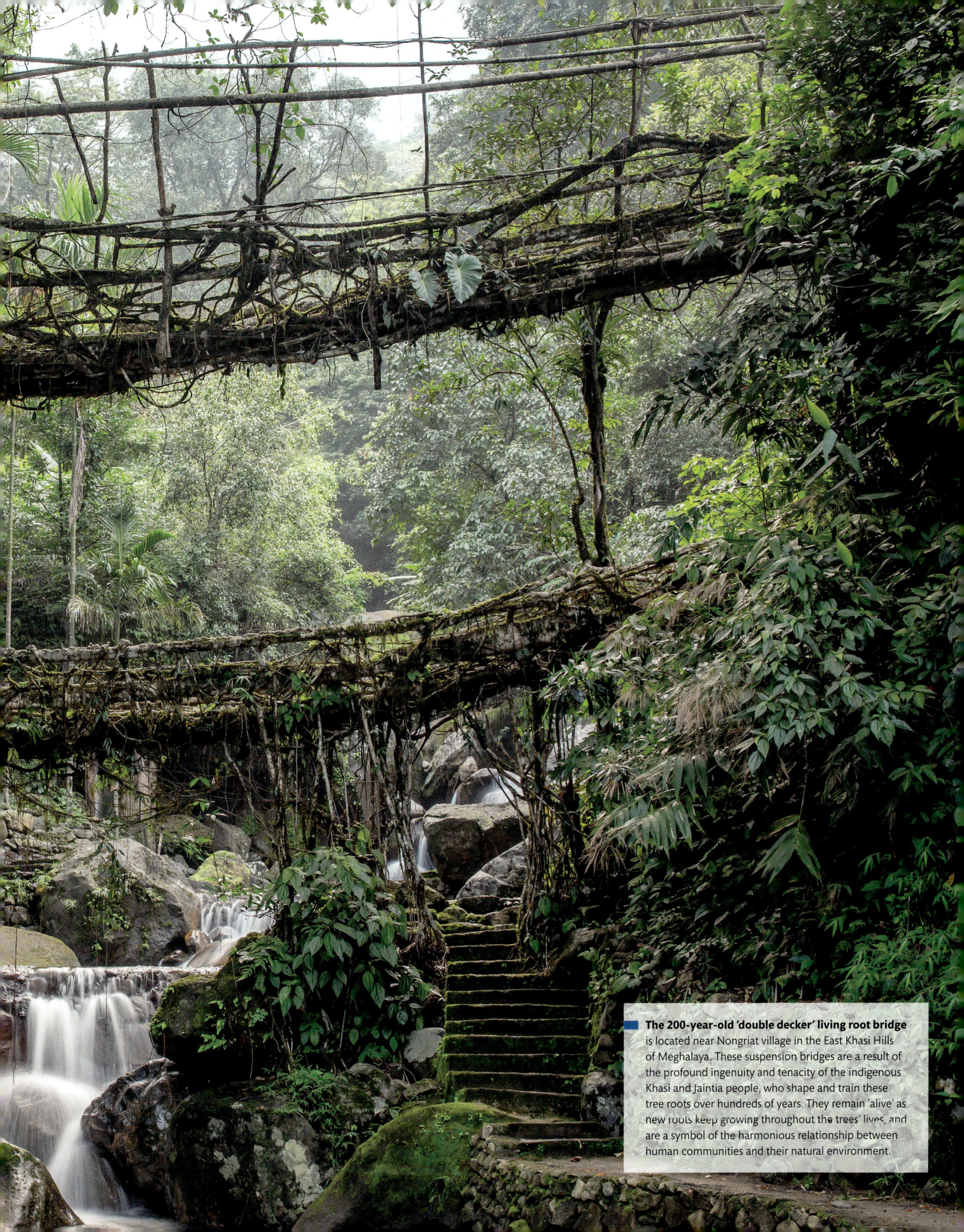

The 200-year-old 'double decker' living root bridge is located near Nongriat village in the East Khasi Hills of Meghalaya. These suspension bridges are a result of the profound ingenuity and tenacity of the indigenous Khasi and Jaintia people, who shape and train these tree roots over hundreds of years. They remain 'alive' as new roots keep growing throughout the trees' lives, and are a symbol of the harmonious relationship between human communities and their natural environment.

COMPANY PAINTINGS

During the 18th and 19th centuries, with the expansion of British influence in India, patrons from the East India Company commissioned Indian artists to document varieties of everyday life in the country. Highlights of the resulting body of work were striking illustrations that display a unique fusion of Indo-European art.

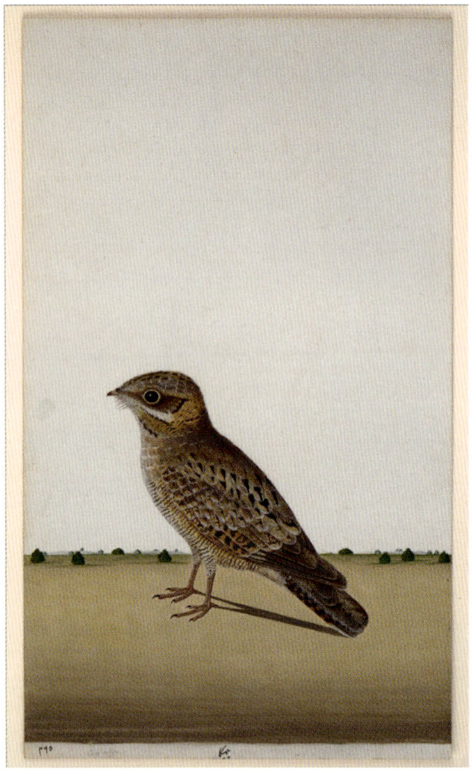

▲ **Painted in watercolour** on paper, this is a late 18th-century painting of an Indian nightjar. Botany and animal life was one of the most popular topics commissioned by British observers studying wild species. Sparing backdrops were a common feature.

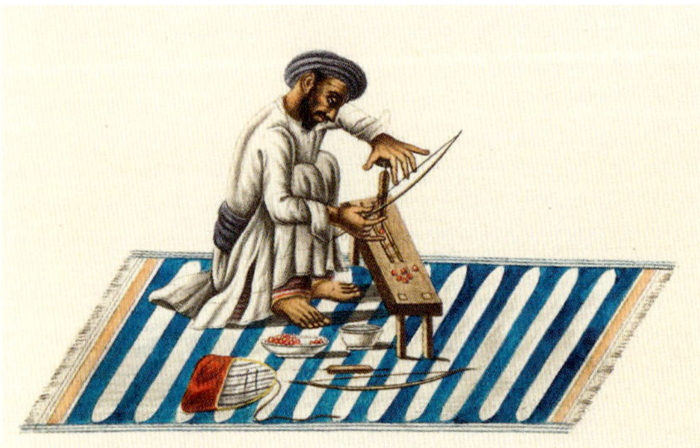

▲ **This early 18th-century painting,** is a study of a lapidary cutting precious stones with a bow-drill. Company paintings also documented different occupations that existed at the time.

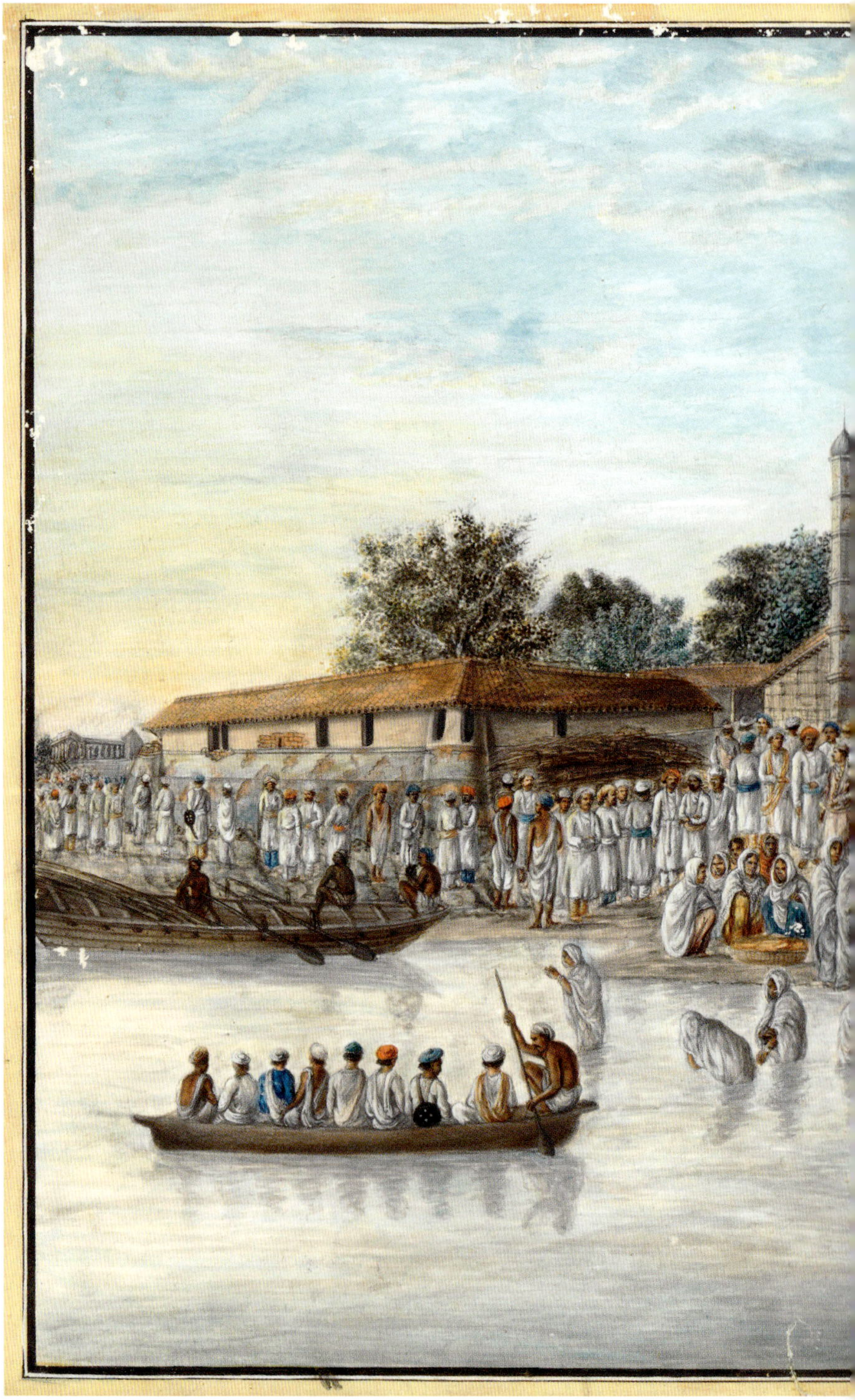

Commonly depicted subjects included flora and fauna, monuments, festivals, occupations, and costumes of the subcontinent.

▼ **This late 18th-century painting of** Chhat Puja, a significant religious festival of Bihar, is believed to be one of the earliest examples of Company School paintings made in Patna. It captures women making offerings to the sun god.

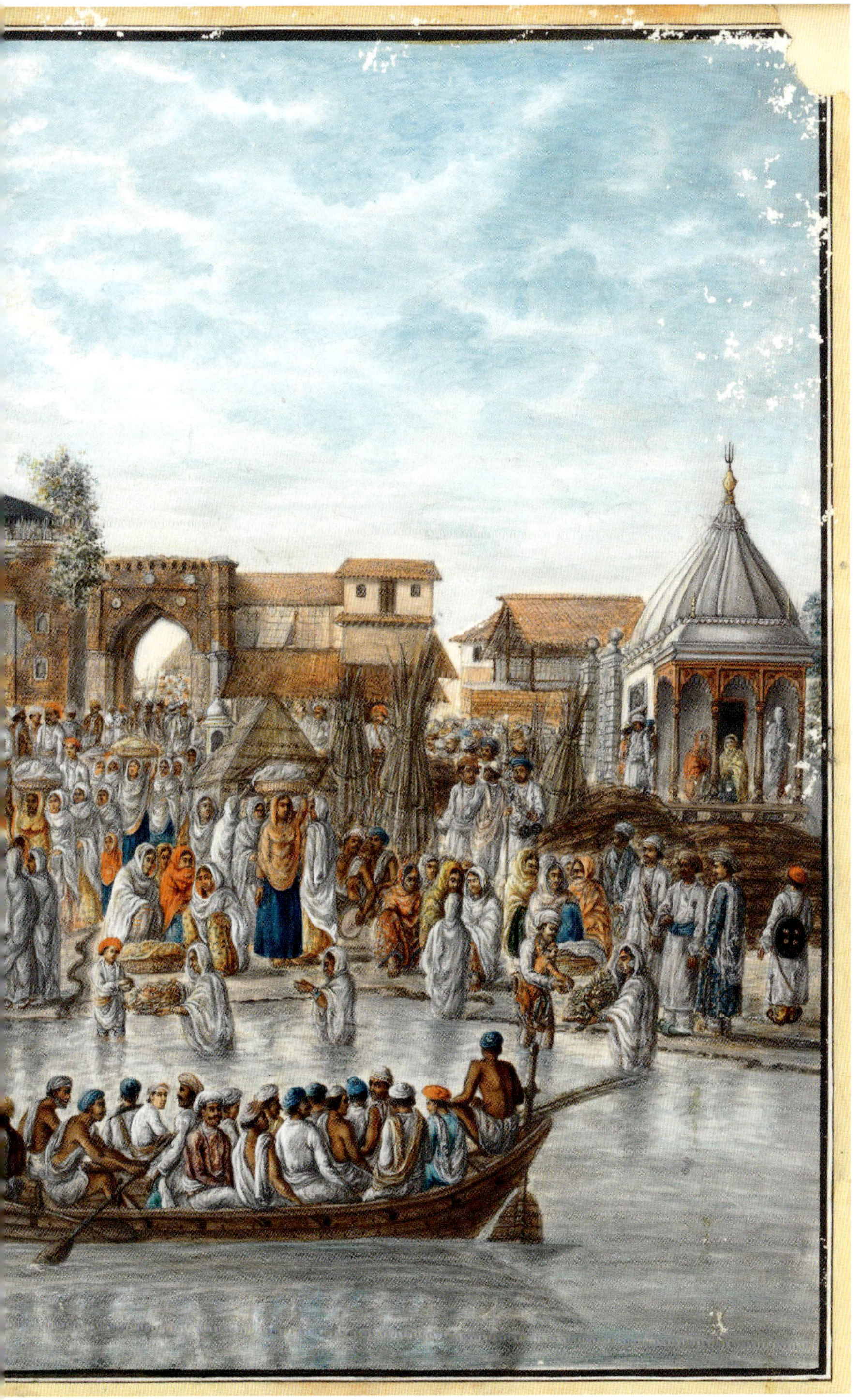

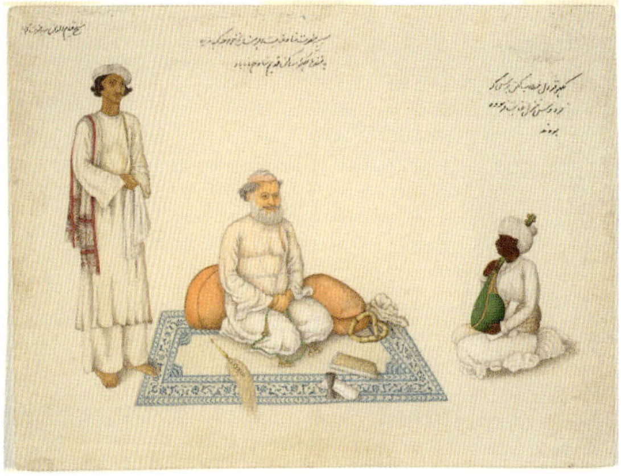

▲ **A page from an album of** paintings documenting the people of Delhi, this early 19th-century artwork depicts a nobleman with his musician and his attendant. It is captioned in the Urdu language, which many British officials had learnt.

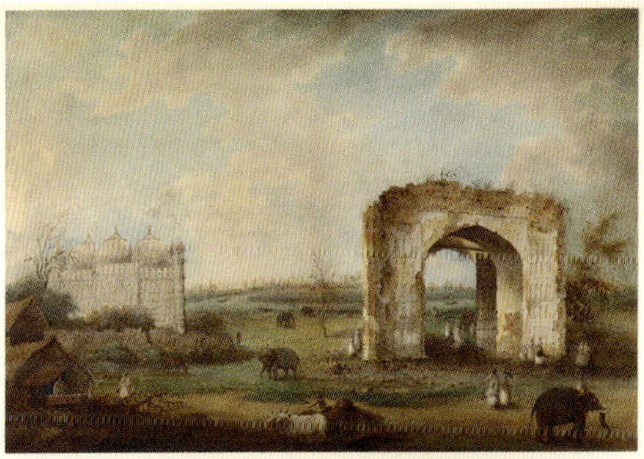

▲ ***The View of a Mosque and a Gateway at Motijhil*** is an early 19th-century painting illustrating a palace complex in Bengal. It manipulates perspective for greater effect.

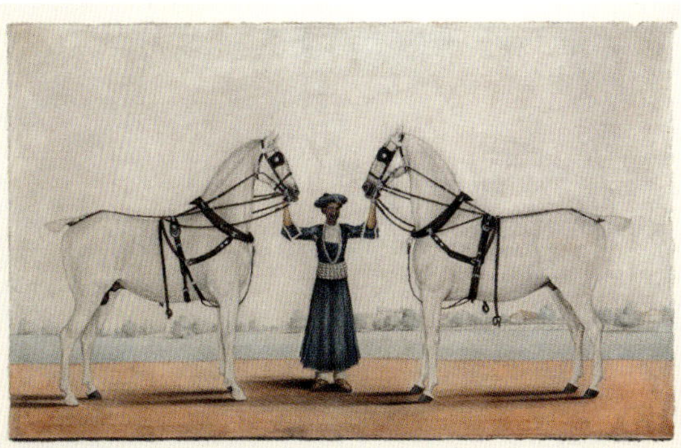

▲ **Depicting naturalism,** the artist has painted a syce, or groom, holding two almost identical horses in this late 19th-century painting.

c. 500 BCE onwards

YOGA

Even though yoga emerged in India in c. 500 BCE, leading practitioners in the 19th century refined its metaphysics and techniques into the popular form that is widely recognized around the world today.

The understanding and practices of yoga have changed over the centuries. Textual evidence, including the *Upanishads* and Patanjali's *Yoga Sutras*, takes us to its origins in north India, between the 5th and 3rd centuries BCE. By the 7th century CE, the core concepts, practices, and vocabulary of almost every yoga system were established, though variations and expansions continued. Prior to the 19th century CE, when Europeans began to learn of its philosophical depth, most Western writers described the yogis they encountered as degenerates, vagrants, and beggars. However, the translation of the Bhagavad Gita into English as *The Song Celestial* in 1885 underlined its essential spirituality. Yoga came to be defined as a means to attain realization and union with God: *karma*, *bhakti*, and *gyana* were the three ways of yoga.

"Yoga, however, took on new meanings in the late colonial period, becoming a mental, physical, and ethical discipline."

– Suzanne Newcombe, *Oxford Research Encyclopedia of Religion*, 2017

A NEW WAVE

The revival of yoga as a physical discipline leading to spiritual awakening can be traced to the establishment of the Brahmo Samaj by Raja Ram Mohan Roy in 1828. The Brahmo Samaj was reformist, looking to revive the Hindu identity, aligned with Western cultural ideals and values. Among the traditions that its progressive members re-articulated was yoga, with Swami Vivekananda as its leading exponent. He referred to the ancient *Yoga Sutras* to present yoga as an aspect of Hindu philosophy that was universal. To the three ways of yoga, he added *rajayoga* – the realization of divinity through control of the mind. Yoga as it is commonly practised today – in India and the Western world – derives from raja yoga. In the 1920s and '30s, yogis such as T. Krishnamacharya and Swami Sivananda attempted to make yoga more accessible, introducing hatha yoga – a preliminary practice to raja yoga as explained in the 15th-century *Hatha Yaga Pradipika* by Swami Swatmarama. Hatha yoga is the practice of physical disciplines to achieve harmony and balance in mind, body, and spirit, before moving on to the much more difficult task of mastering the mind.

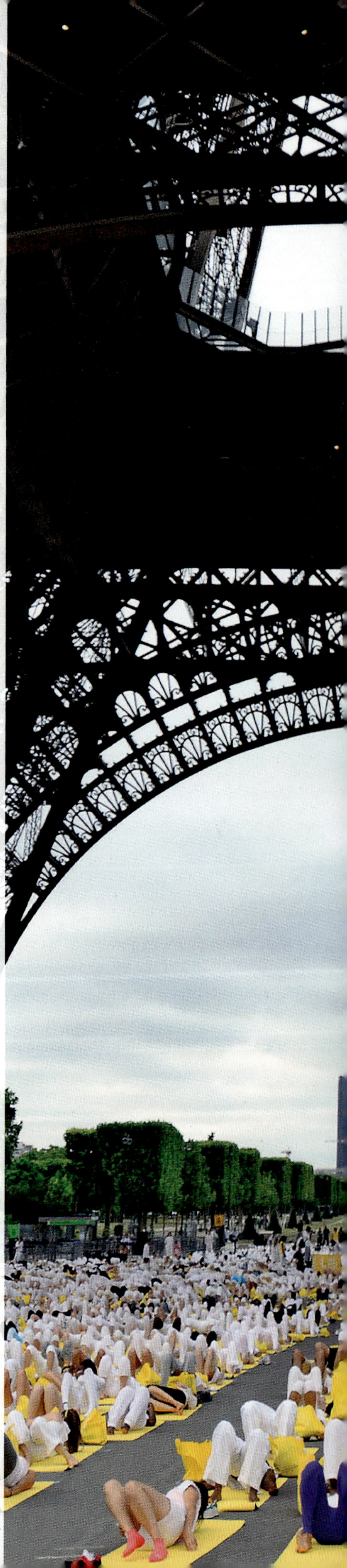

► **Yoga has gained popularity across the world** as is evident from the International Yoga Day, which takes place annually in June. This photograph depicts participants celebrating the day at the iconic Eiffel Tower in Paris, France, in 2015.

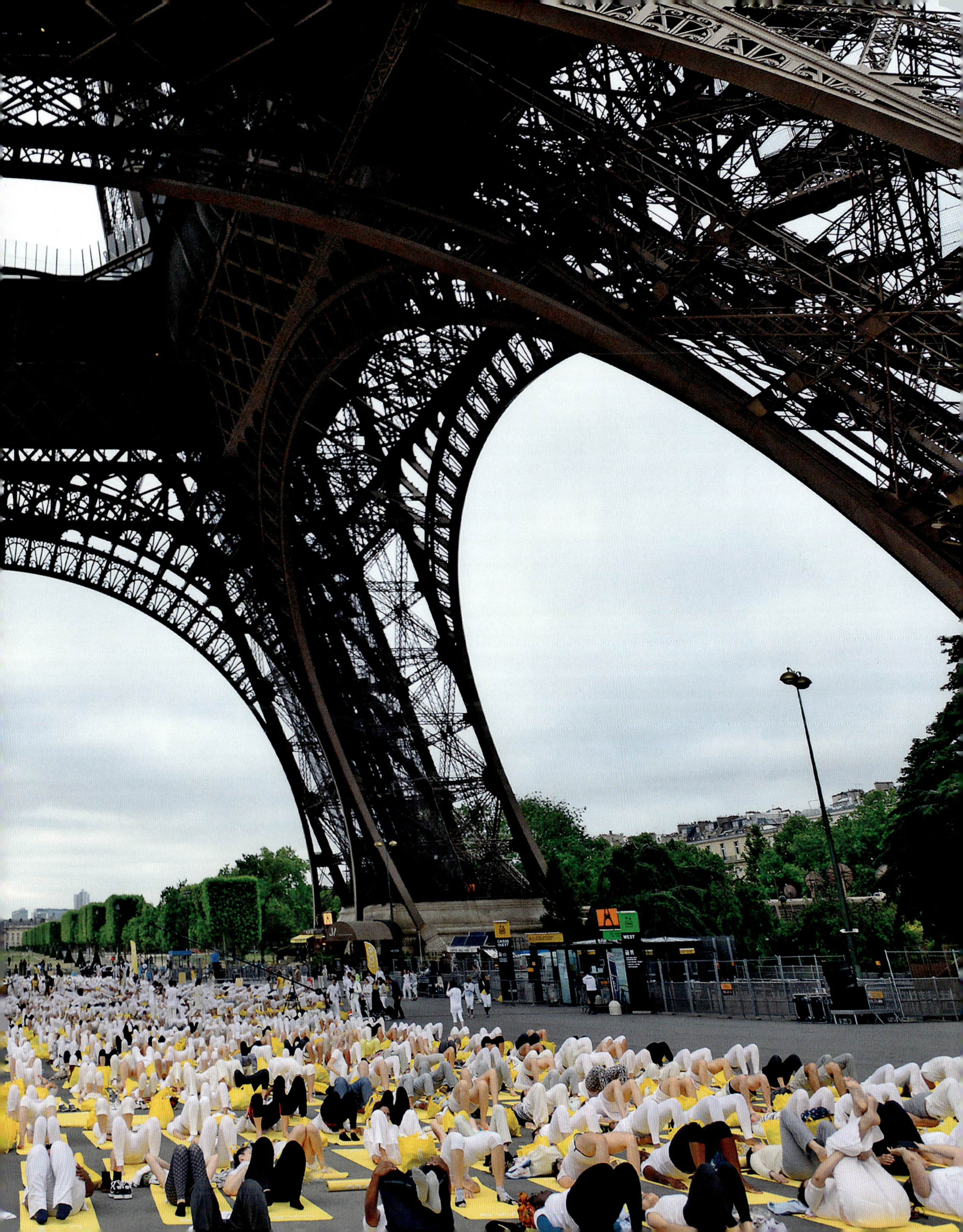

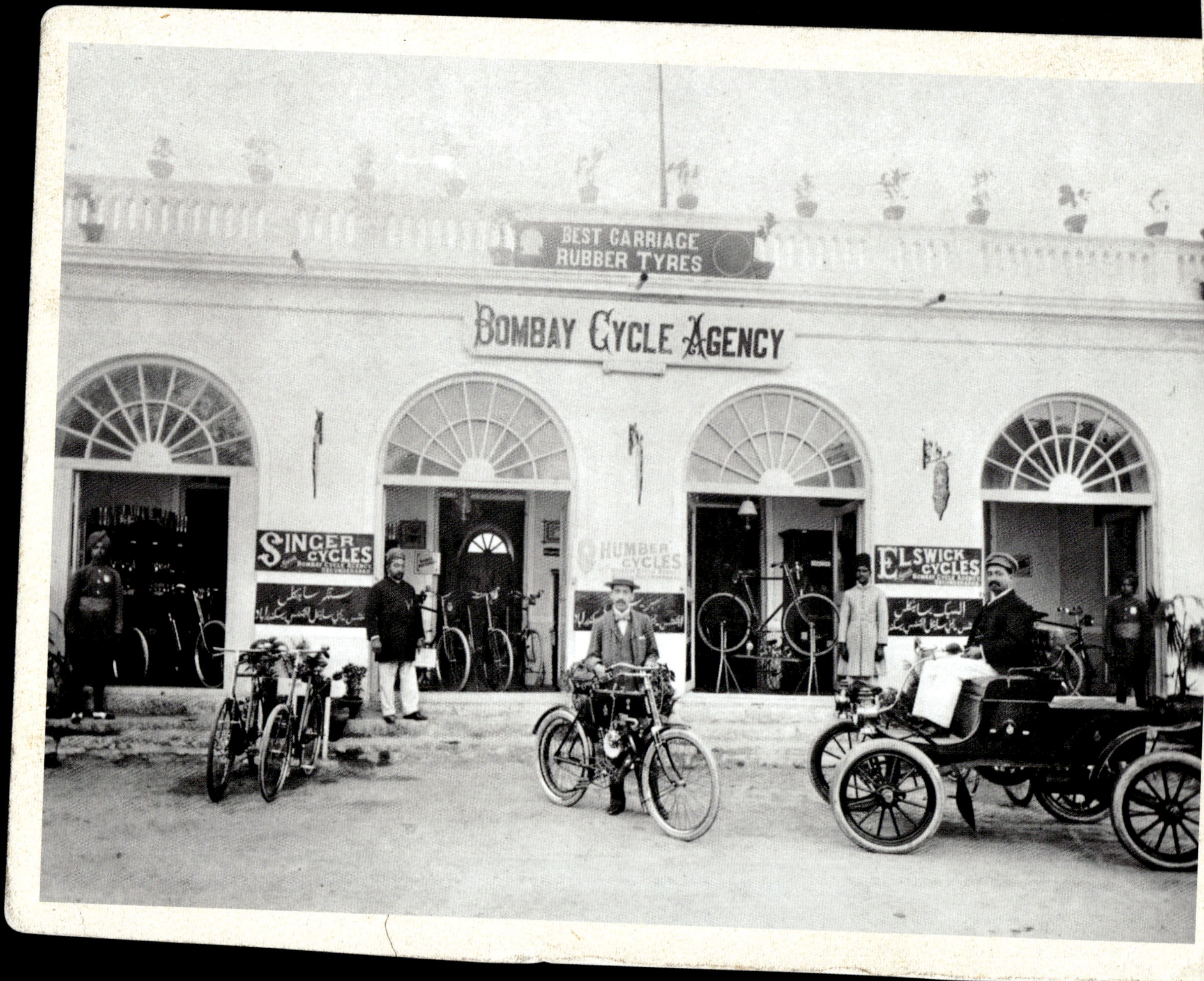

Era 19th–20th centuries CE

LALA DEEN DAYAL'S PHOTOGRAPHS

Capturing moments in time

The history of photography in India is inextricably linked to the country's eventful transition from colonial rule to independence. Indian photographers such as Lala Deen Dayal emerged on the scene within the context of colonial control.

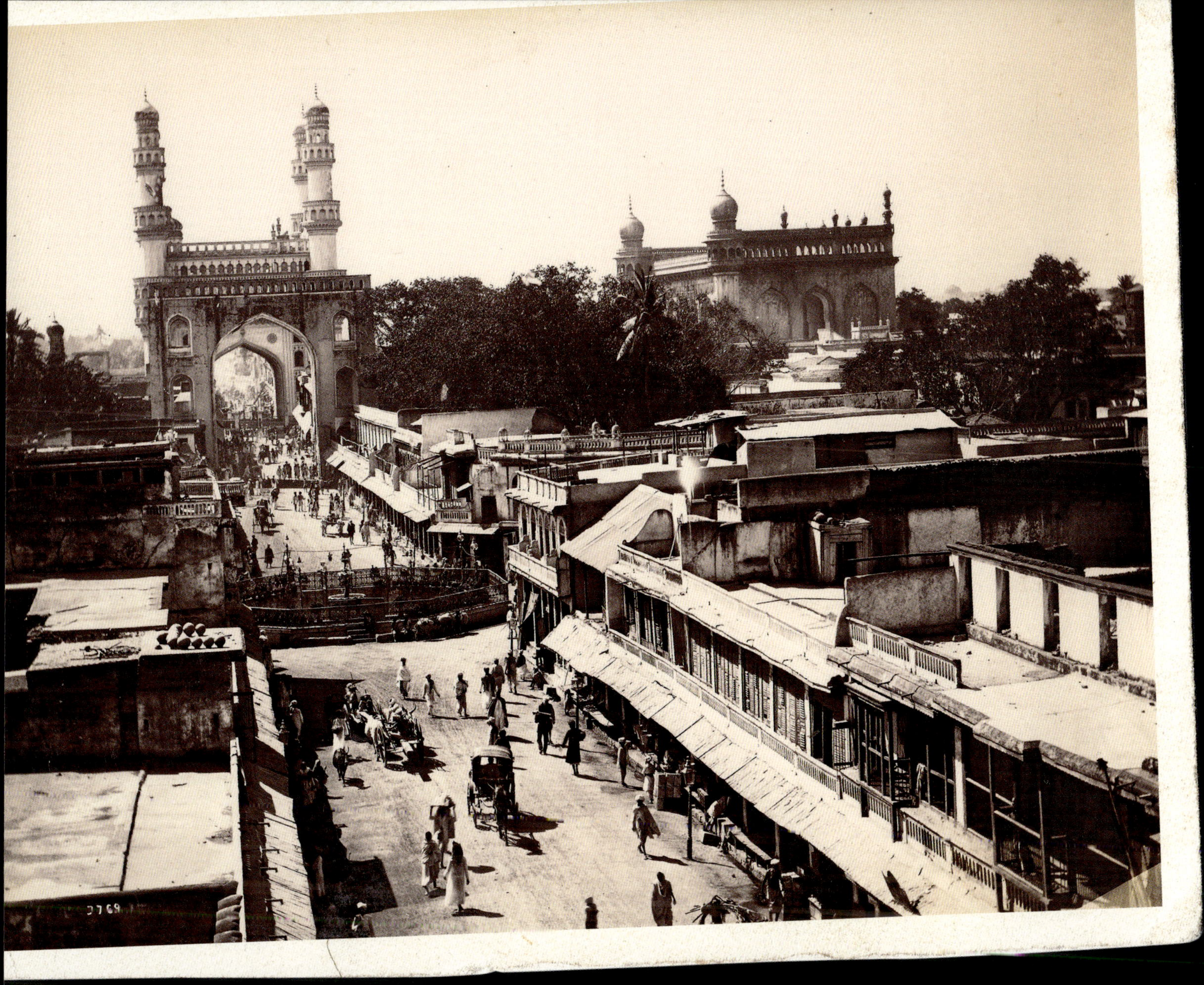

In the late 19th century, Indian photographers produced depictions of India that both aligned with and diverged from the norms of European photography. Lala Deen Dayal, one of the most notable names in Indian photography, had an extensive portfolio, from landscapes and monuments to royal visits and portraits of elite households. He set up studios around the country and was also named the court photographer to the sixth Nizam of Hyderabad in 1885.

CAMERA AS THE THIRD EYE

On 19 August 1839, a pioneering technique known as the Daguerreotype process was unveiled at the French Academy of Sciences in Paris. Within months, the *Bombay Times* in India devoted three articles to the arrival of a new camera. Impressively, by 1840, Calcutta-based Thacker & Company had already begun importing the Daguerreotype camera.

In its early days, photography was a luxury reserved for monarchs and the affluent due to its cost. The British used it as a tool of imperialism, documenting terrain, population, and events, like the portrayal of 1857 revolt by Felice Beato. Photo studios cropped up in British presidencies, transmitting 'exotic' images and fuelling curiosity about the 'orient'.

By the 1920s, photography had become more accessible to the public. Photojournalism and press photography also took root. A prominent figure was Homai Vyarawalla, India's first female photojournalist. By the 1930s, when she started working for the press, film had replaced heavy cameras and glass plates, making photography a more accessible pursuit. Other prominent photojournalists, such as Kulwant Roy and Sunil Janah, left a lasting impact by documenting critical moments in India's political history leading up to and following independence.

▲ Two photographs by Indian photographer Lala Deen Dayal. One from 1904 depicting the Bombay Cycle Agency (left), and the other a gelatine silver print of Pineapple Street in Hyderabad from 1844 (right).

19th century CE *onwards*

INDIAN RAILWAYS

There's little doubt that railways had a significant impact on the Indian landscape. They were introduced to the subcontinent to serve British economic interests as well as their perceived role as drivers of modernization.

The birth of the Indian railways was a direct result of the establishment of colonial rule, and the railways operated primarily on two grounds: military (for expansion and consolidation), and economic (for accruing financial gains). They were first conceived by the East India Company with the belief that they would be beneficial, as claimed by Governor General Lord Hardinge, "to the commerce, government and military control of the country". The very first railway line in India ran 32–38 km (20–24 miles) between Bombay and Thane. It was completed and opened in April 1853. A flurry of expansion followed and by 1900, more than 38,624 km (24,000 miles) of track had been laid. This enormous project was financed entirely by private British investment capital. Efforts were made to link different parts of the country, from the hills of Darjeeling in the east to the North-West Frontier Province.

"Everywhere, in every direction, the wanderer comes up against rail-road track, meandering about like a colossal centipede. Yet there is romance and legend, too, amidst the dust and smoke."

–John W. Mitchell, *The Wheels of Ind*, 1934

LINKING A NATION

By the time of the freedom struggle, the railways had become more than a tool for colonialism, they had become a medium for resistance as well. They helped in the successful implementation of various independence movements and brought people together – Mohandas Karamchand Gandhi used trains and railway stations to spread his ideas. Post independence in 1947, the Partition saw the division not just of the lands, but the railway systems as well. A massive rebuilding exercise began with the realization that the railways were perhaps the best way to connect a country as vast as India. Today, too, modernization and technological innovation drive the railways, as the intricate network of lines are still what best links every corner of the country.

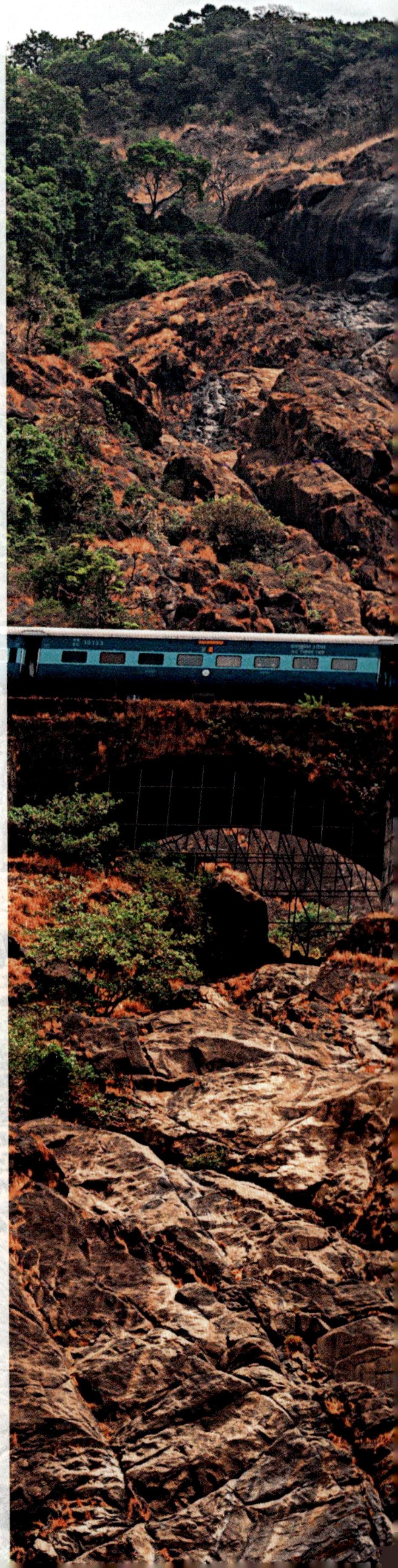

► **A train over a bridge passing along the** Dudhsagar Falls (literally, Sea of Milk), one of the tallest waterfalls in India. It is located on the Belgavi–Vasco Da Gama rail route of the Konkan Railway.

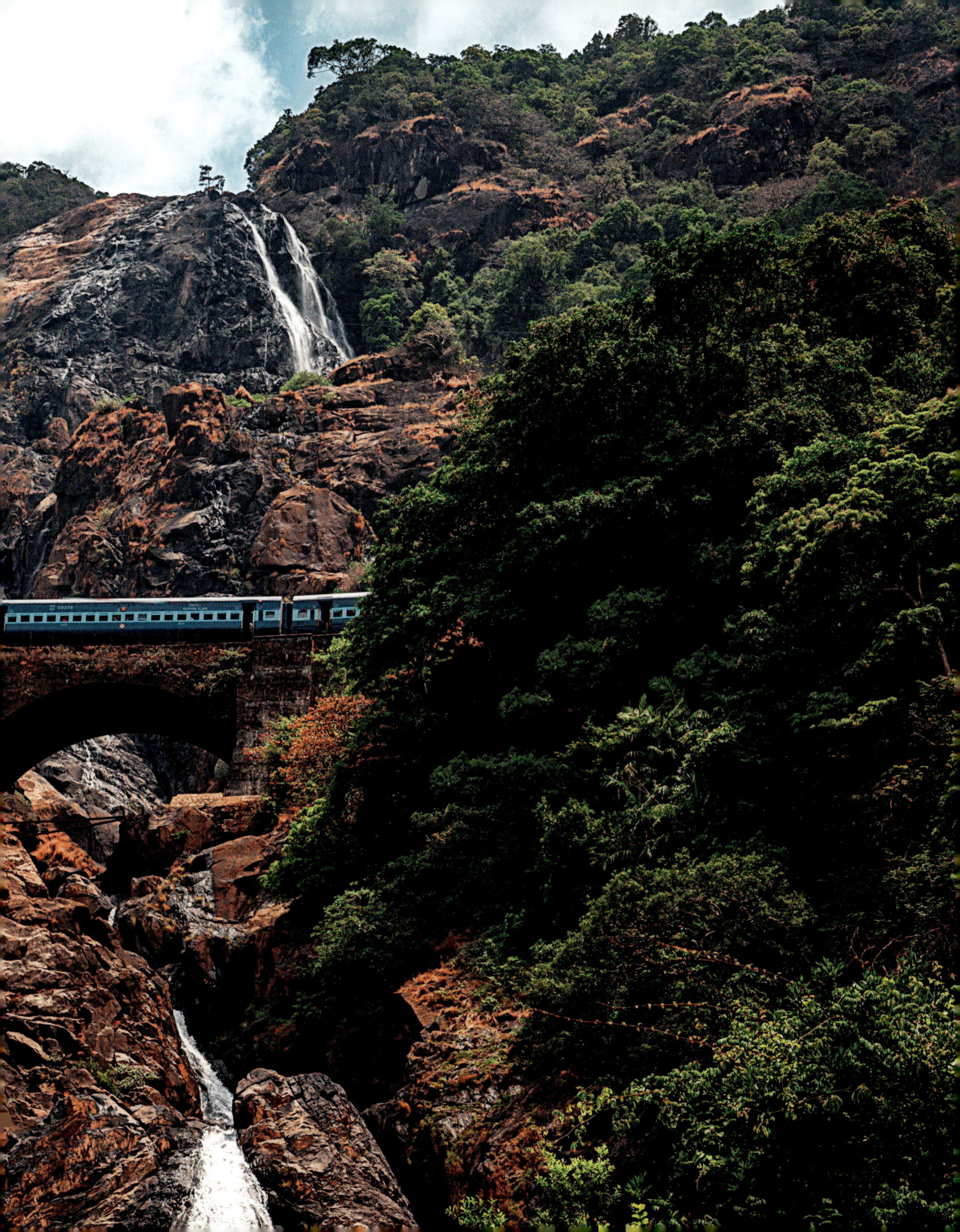

Era 19th century CE | Medium Bronze (Copper alloy) | Height 68.3 cm (26.8 in)

FAIRY QUEEN

A record-holding national treasure

The world's oldest working steam locomotive, the *Fairy Queen* was built in 1855 by Kitson, Thompson and Hewitson, a British locomotive manufacturing company. It was supplied to the East Indian Railway (EIR) and began work in 1885.

During the mid-19th century, at the height of the Industrial Revolution, steam locomotives captured the imagination of the whole world. In India, the earliest steam locomotives were introduced in the 1850s. They were a ubiquitous feature of the local landscape for over a century and a half, arousing both fear and curiosity.

The *Fairy Queen* came into operation as Loco No. 22 in August 1885. It later came to be known as the EIR 22, before getting the name it is known by in 1895. This 1.7-m-long engine first hauled mail trains on the Howrah–Raneegunge line in Bengal. There are records of it being used to haul trains of troops, from Howrah to Raneegunge, deployed to quell uprisings during the Revolt of 1857. It was later dispatched to line construction duty in Bihar. Withdrawn from service after 1909, it was plinthed in Howrah till 1943. In 1977, it was displayed at the National Rail Museum (NRM), New Delhi.

REHAUL AND LATER USE

The 26-tonne engine was revived and completely overhauled in 1996 in the Perambur workshop of the Southern Railway. Several modifications were made to bring it back to life. Its driving wheels were relaxed, small compressors were put in to make it into an independently working air-braked unit, and a majority of its brass tubes were replaced with more modern fixtures. In July 1997, the *Fairy Queen* re-entered service as a part of a semi-regular heritage train - the *Fairy Express* - between Delhi and Alwar in Rajasthan. In July 2004, while parked at NRM, vandals stole a few of its parts - two brass handles and four copper pipes. This 'queen' was withdrawn from service in 2011 because of its special operational requirements - it needed specially made parts to keep the engine up and running. In 2017, it was reintroduced into service as a part of the 'steam express' programme of tourist trains.

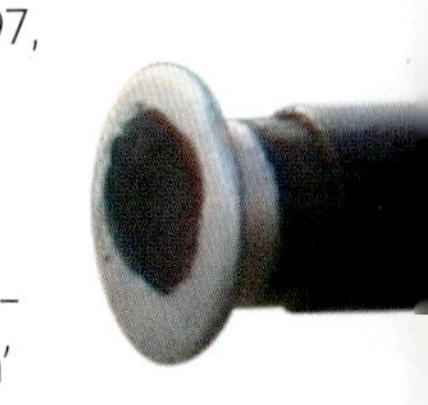

► **The *Fairy Queen*** was listed in the Guinness World Records as the world's oldest working locomotive in 1998.

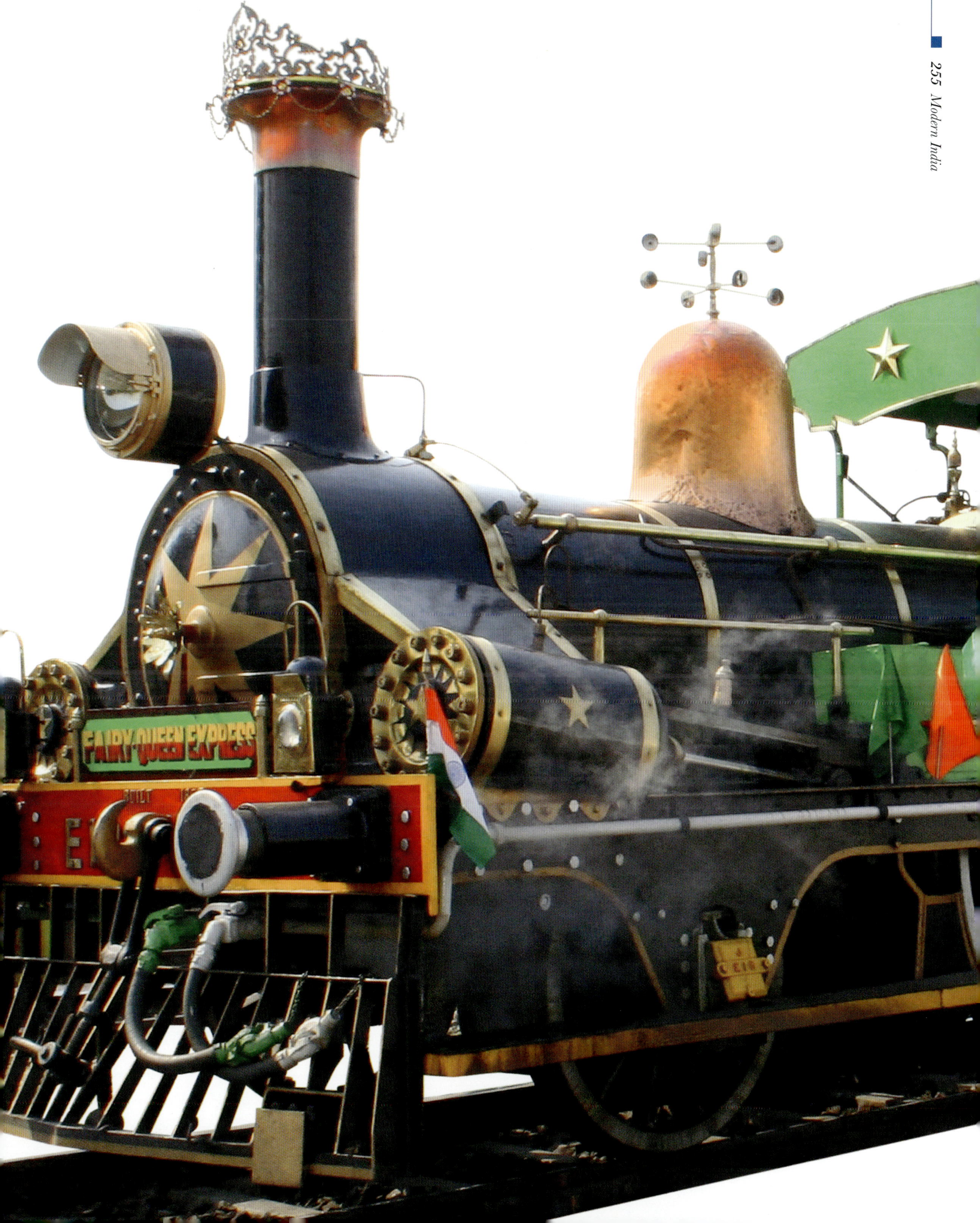
FAIRY QUEEN EXPRESS

Era 19th century CE

HILL RAILWAYS

Connecting treacherous terrain and providing resplendent views

The Himalayan hills were a favoured retreat for the British owing to cool temperatures, and the Revolt of 1857 helped realize their military importance. Extensive rail construction soon followed. Today, mountain railway systems are unique for the connectivity they provide and the views they offer.

Hill towns such as Darjeeling, Ootacamund (Ooty), Simla, Soobathoo (Subathu), Dalhousie, and Almora served as seasonal residences for the viceroys of India and other senior government officials. However, the arduous and expensive journey to these places excluded everyone but the rich. Building railway lines to the hill capitals was, therefore, imperative, not just for the British morale, but also to retain their hold over India. Initially, this undertaking was viewed by the British as an unprofitable venture that required high investment. This perception changed when three remarkable hill railway systems were built across the country.

THE THREE JEWELS

The first of these was the Darjeeling Himalayan Railway (DHR), which opened in 1881. It grew famous for its complicated loops and reversing stations. Its highest point, at around 2,300 m (7545 ft), is Ghoom (or Ghum), also one of the highest railway stations in the world. The Kalka-Shimla Railway (KSR), one of the most surveyed lines at the time, opened for use in 1903. Its bridges and tunnels, including the 1.14-km (0.7 miles) long Barog Tunnel, set it apart from others. The Nilgiri Mountain Railway (NMR) followed in 1908, with its rack system and X class steam locomotives.

The Darjeeling, Kalka-Shimla, and Nilgiri railways are part of the UNESCO World Heritage list. They are still operational, and are living examples of the engineering enterprise of the late 19th and early 20th centuries.

1. The Batasia Loop or the double spiral on the Darjeeling Himalayan Railway is considered one of the most remarkable engineering feats of its time. **2.** The Kalka-Shimla Railway passes over 102 bridges on its way to the hill station of Shimla. **3.** The Nilgiri Mountain Railway connects the town of Ooty (Udhagamandalam) to Coonoor (Kunnur) and Mettupalayam across the Nilgiri mountain range in the southern state of Tamil Nadu. **4.** The Kangra Valley Railway (1927) was once a narrow gauge line that carried heavy machinery; today it runs from Pathankot in Punjab to Joginder Nagar in Kangra in present-day Himachal Pradesh. **5.** The Neral-Matheran train (1907) in present-day Maharashtra was a line that was conceived, funded, and built by an Indian.

1

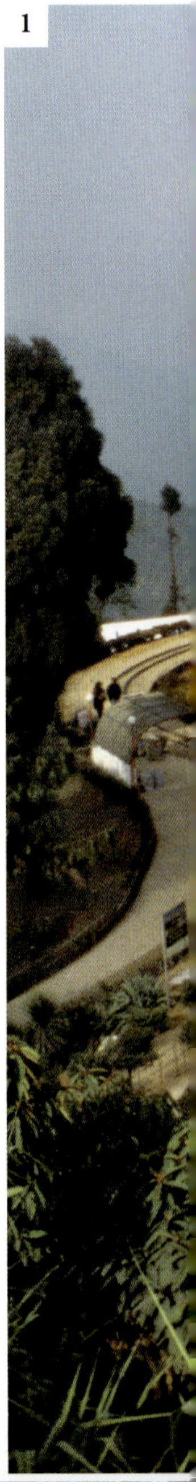

2

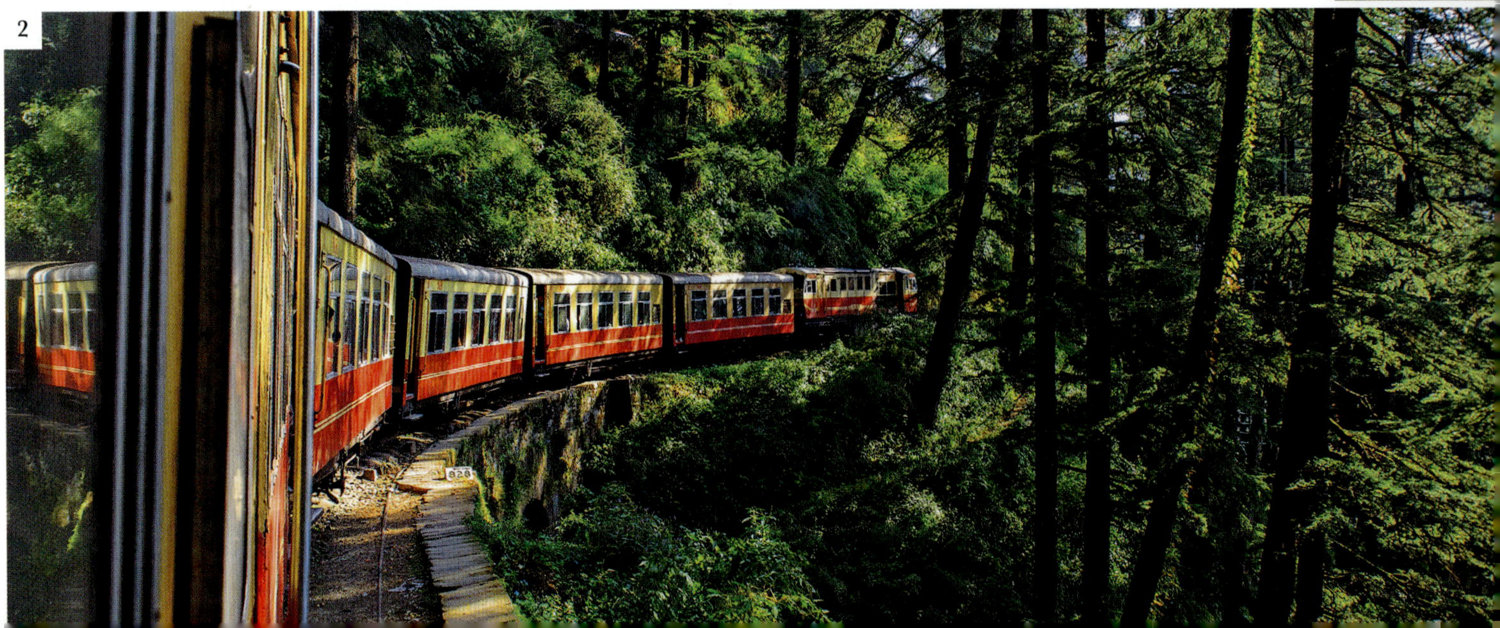

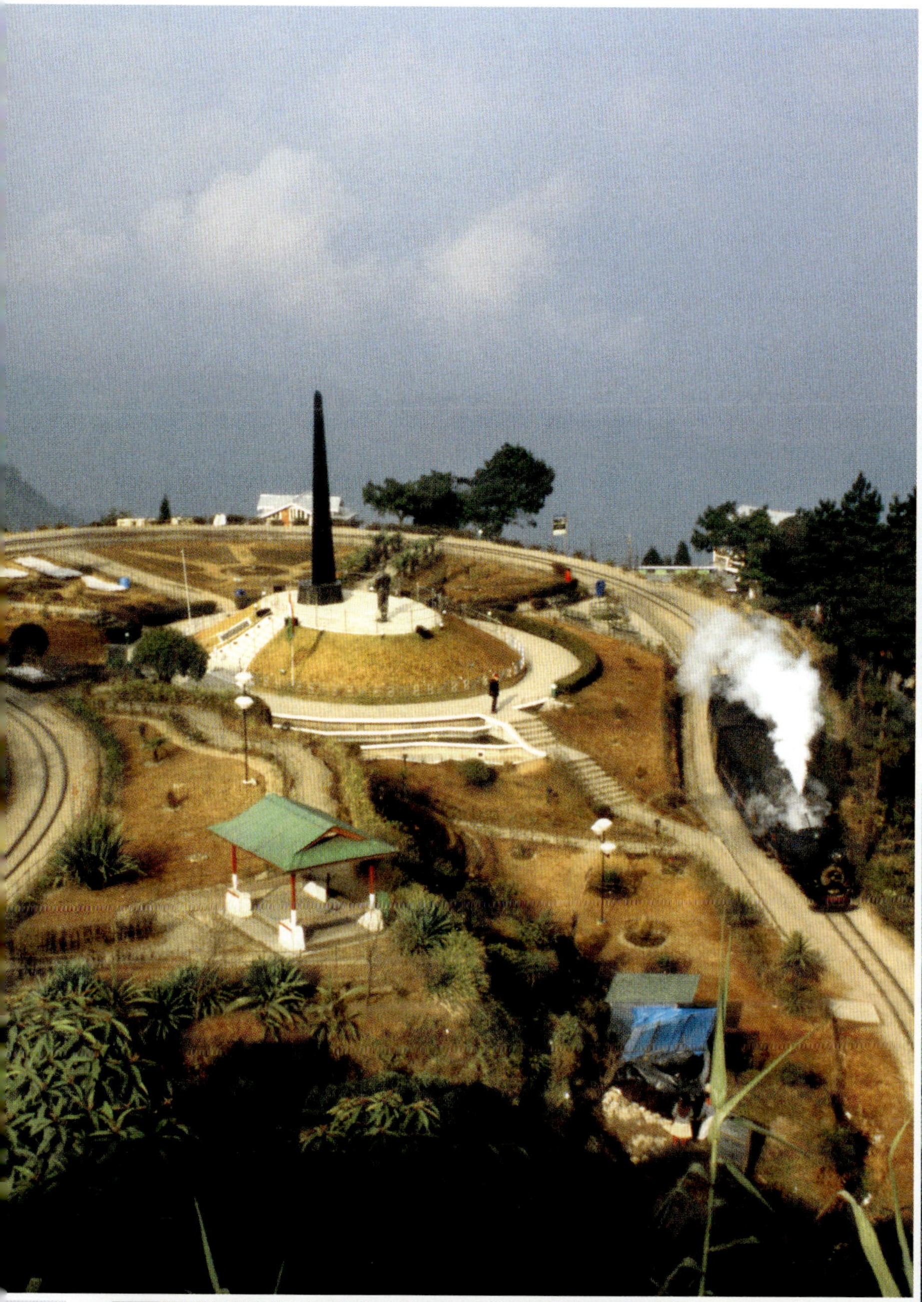

4

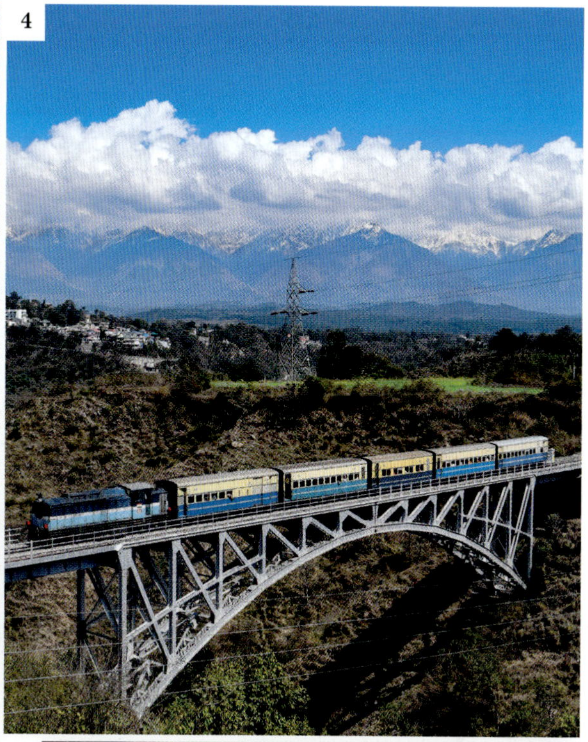

5

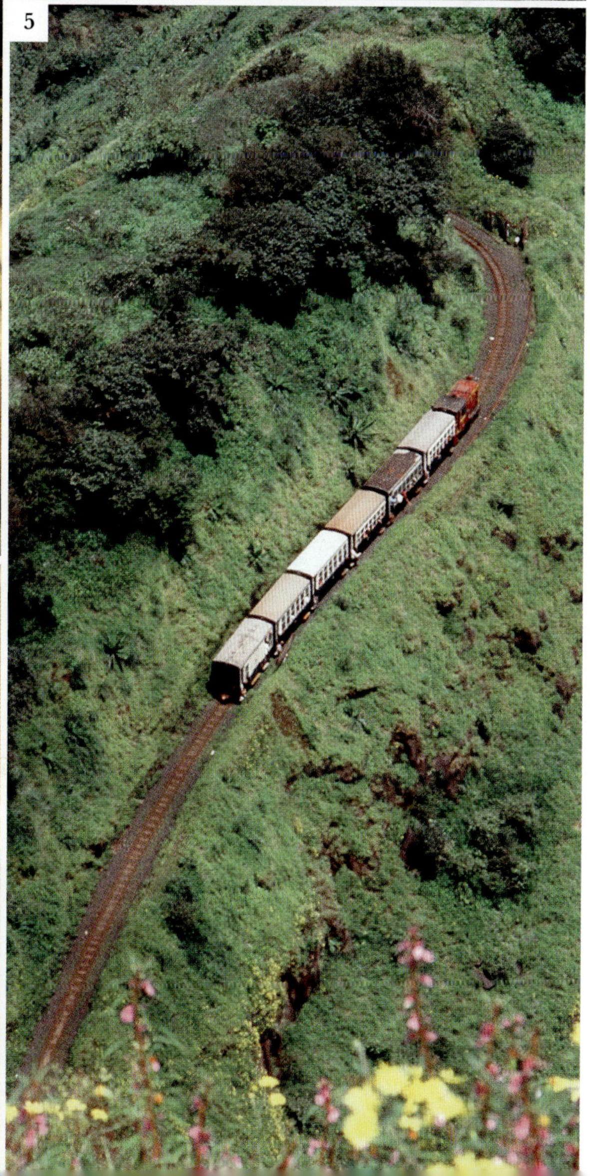

3

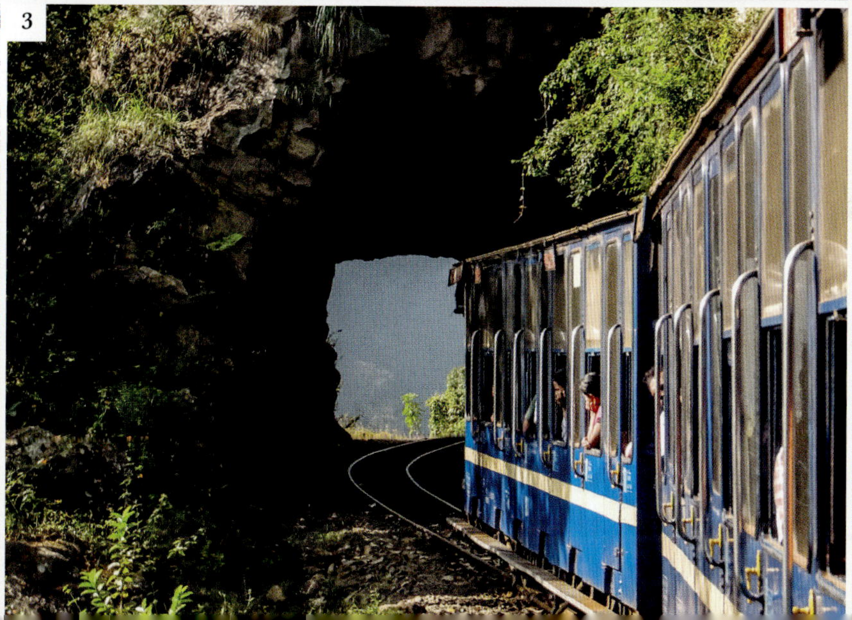

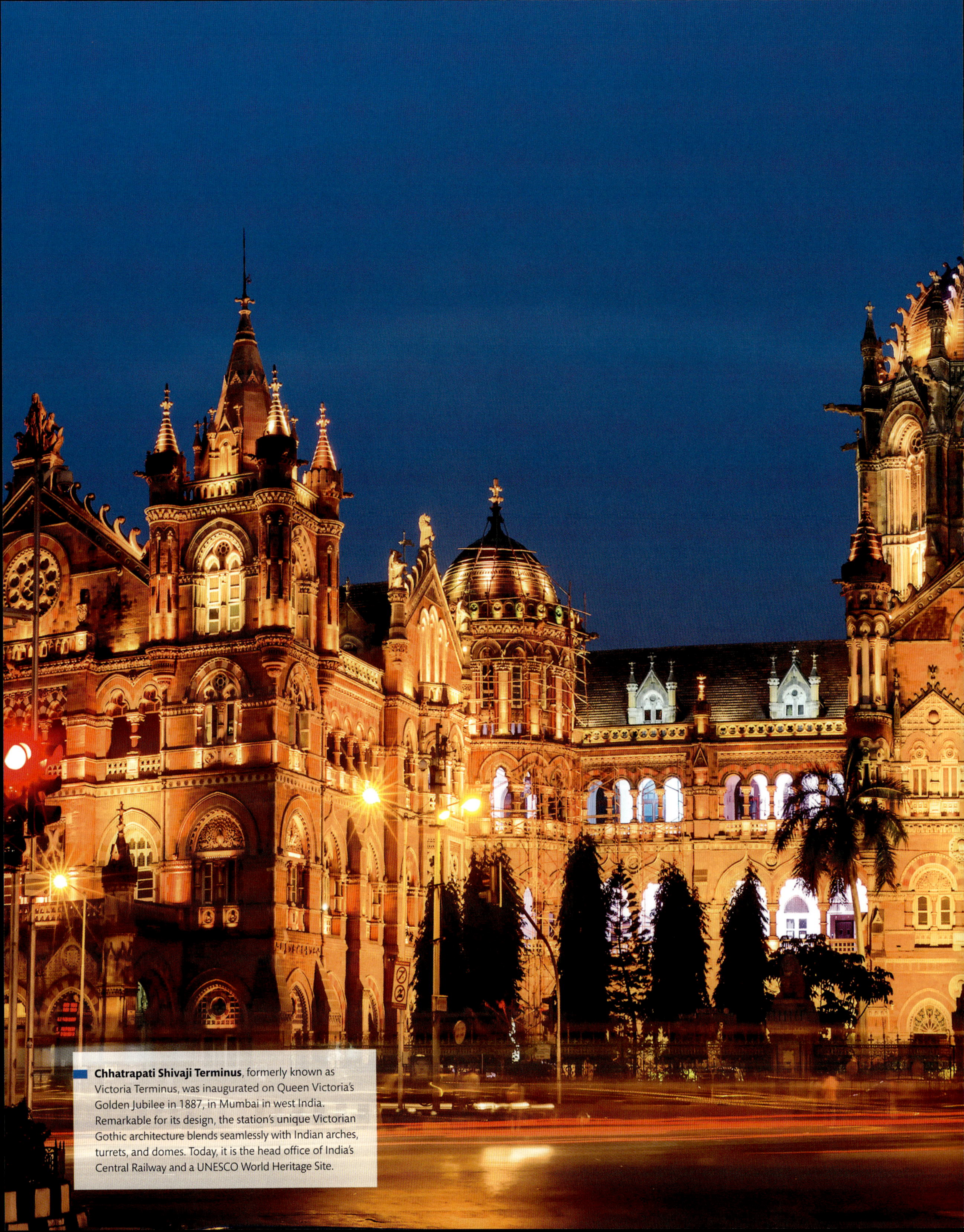

Chhatrapati Shivaji Terminus, formerly known as Victoria Terminus, was inaugurated on Queen Victoria's Golden Jubilee in 1887, in Mumbai in west India. Remarkable for its design, the station's unique Victorian Gothic architecture blends seamlessly with Indian arches, turrets, and domes. Today, it is the head office of India's Central Railway and a UNESCO World Heritage Site.

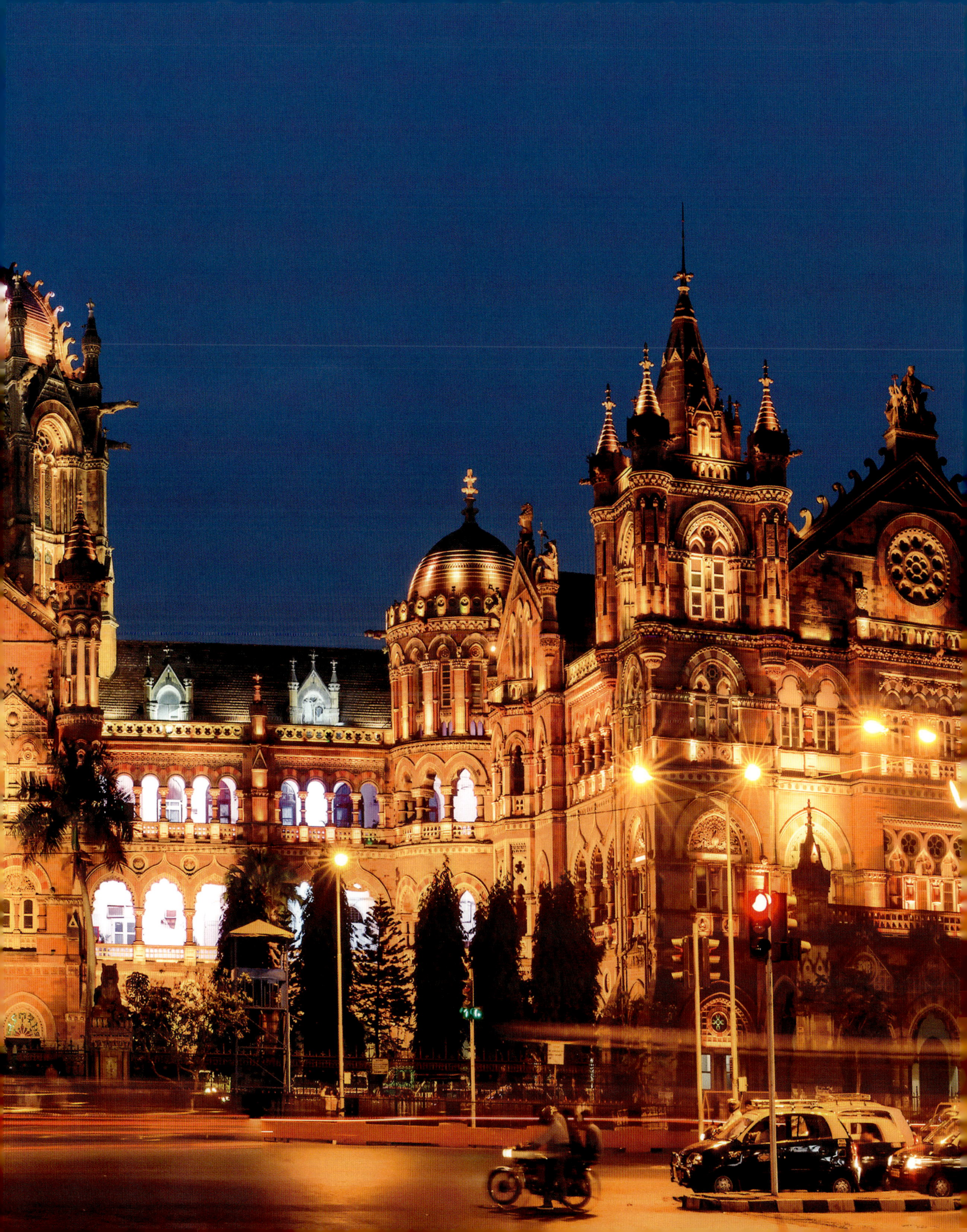

TRYST WITH DESTINY

India's long road to freedom

Though the idea of nationalism emerged under the weight of colonial rule, it drew upon patterns of social relations, attachment to land, and loyalties to shape and form the freedom movement. Literature, paintings, and other arts reflected the shifting realities of a new nation.

"Long years ago we made a tryst with destiny, and now the time comes when we shall redeem our pledge, not wholly or in full measure, but very substantially. At the stroke of the midnight hour, when the world sleeps, India will awake to life and freedom. A moment comes, which comes but rarely in history, when we step out from the old to new, when an age ends, and when the soul of a nation, long suppressed, finds utterance," said Jawaharlal Nehru, independent India's first prime minister, as he made his now-iconic speech in Parliament, in Delhi, on 14 August 1947. He reflected on the extensive struggle for freedom that the people of India had fought for.

In fact, the national movement was not a linear narrative. It was informed by the changes in circumstances and often saw regional powers accede to the colonial rulers, as well as oppose them. This continued until 1857, when Indian soldiers employed by the British revolted. This rebellion, known as the 1857 Revolt, led to the end of the East India Company rule, as the British government took over the governance of India.

The echoes of 1857 led to a quest for freedom in the following decades. Though it assumed a non-violent, constitutional tone, its objective was to attain representative government and the admission of Indians to higher civil and military services. The issue of inclusion

1857 Indian soldiers in the British army revolt

1858 East India Company is disestablished

1858 Queen Victoria's government takes over administrative control of India

1885 Formation of the Indian National Congress (INC)

1905 Partition of Bengal

1905–1911 Swadeshi Movement begins

1906 Congress calls for self-rule

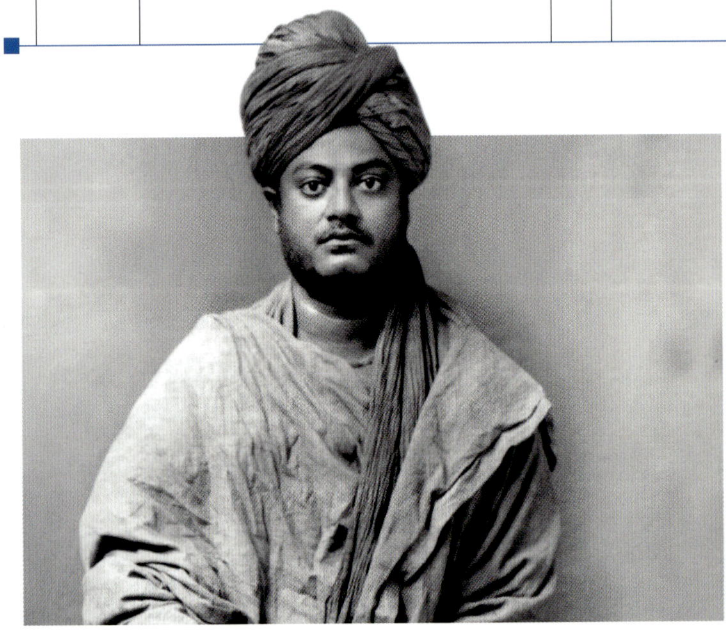

Portrait of the young Swami Vivekananda, a Hindu philosopher and religious teacher who brought about interfaith awareness, and raised Hinduism to the status of a major world religion.

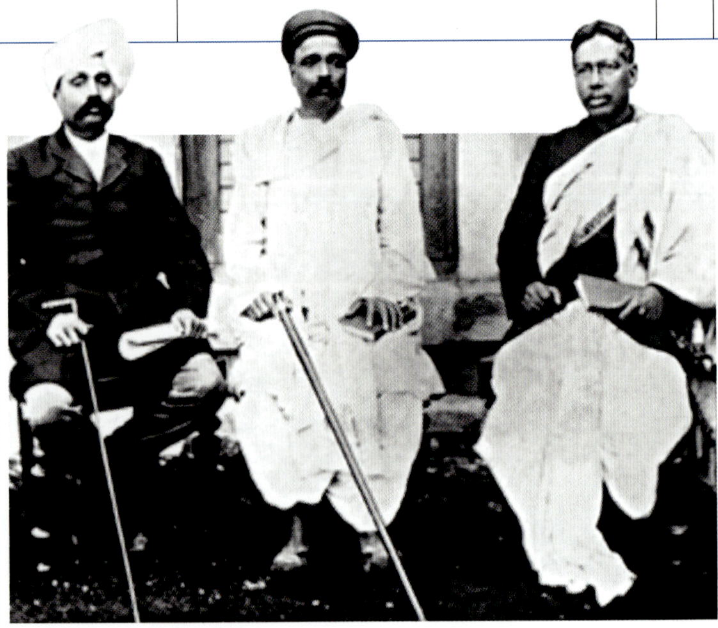

Photograph of Bal Gangadhar Tilak, Lala Lajpat Rai, and Bipin Chandra Pal, three prominent figures of the early Indian Independence movement.

of Indians into the Indian Civil Service ignited a need for a national political organization. In 1885, this gap was filled by the Indian National Congress (INC). Though not radical in its programme, INC in its early days represented the 'moderate' phase of nationalism. The politicians did not envision a separation from the British Empire, but aspired for limited self-governance within the framework.

THE RISE OF REVOLUTIONARIES

By the end of the 19th century, the failure of moderate politics became apparent and an alternative emerged from within the Congress circle. This new trend came to be known as 'extremist'. The Swadeshi movement in Bengal (1905–1911) is perhaps the best expression of this during the period, which began as an agitation against the partition of Bengal in 1905, a territorial reorganization of the region into East Bengal and West Bengal, which Governor-General Lord Curzon had crafted as a method for suppressing political opposition in the province.

A wave of radical revolutionaries emerged in the late 19th and early 20th centuries. This was predicated on multiple external and internal factors that left their imprint on the minds of young people. The most important factor was religious revival in the late 19th century. Multiple events

1906 Mahatma Gandhi coins the term *satyagraha* for the non-violence movement in South Africa.

1907 Congress split into moderates and extremists at its Surat session

1907 Lala Lajpat Rai is deported to Mandalay in Burma after riots in Punjab

1908 Bal Gangadhar Tilak sentenced to six years imprisonment for sedition

1909 Morley-Minto Reforms or the Indian Council Act of 1909 announced

1909 All-India Muslim League (AIML) established

1911 Capital of India shifted from Calcutta to Delhi

1912 Bomb thrown at Lord Hardinge in Chandini Chowk, Delhi by Rashbehari Bose and Sachindra Nath Sanyal.

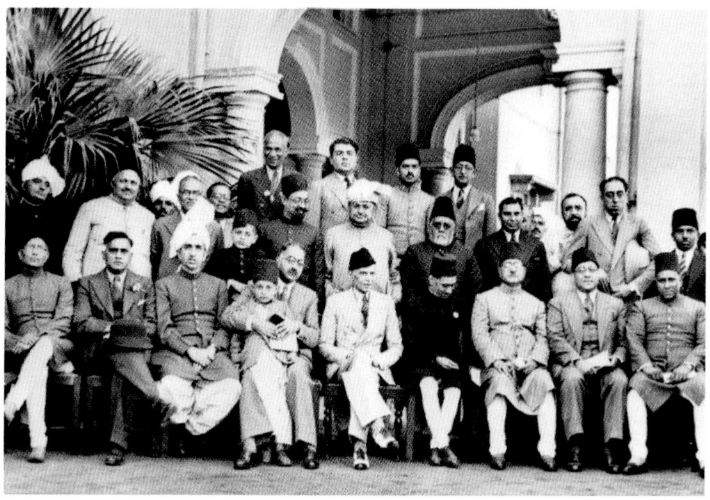

A historic photograph from 1940 of the prominent leaders of the All-India Muslim League, following a dinner party. Seated in the centre, in a light-coloured suit and dark cap, is Mohammad Ali Jinnah.

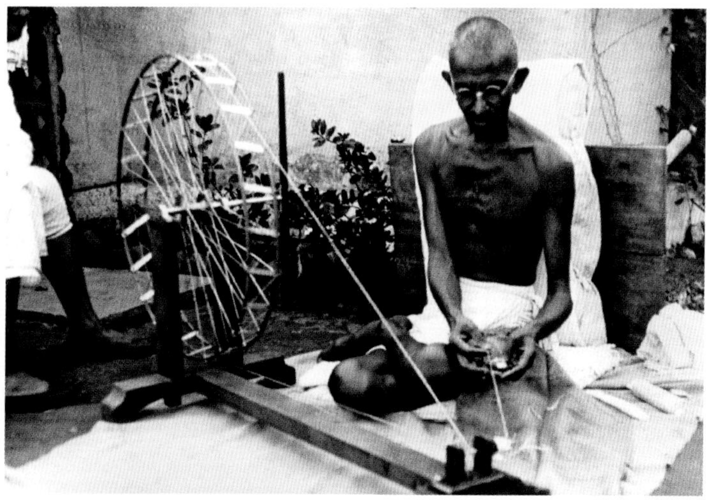

Mohandas Karamchand Gandhi with his spinning wheel, or *charkha*, with which he spun cloth, possibly at Sabarmati Ashram in Ahmedabad (in western India)

around the world also had a profound impact, such as the American War of Independence, the Irish struggle for freedom, the unification of Italy and the contribution of nationalists Garibaldi and Mazzini, the Japanese victory over Russia, and the revolution against the Tsarist regime in Russia.

In India, the two centres of revolution emerged from Maharashtra in the west and Bengal in the east. While Bal Gangadhar Tilak and Veer Savarkar conceptualized and led the struggle in Maharashtra, Bankim Chandra, Aurobindo Ghosh, and Swami Vivekananda roused the masses in Bengal.

There were, however, some groups who contested the politics of the Indian National Congress. One of those went on to create the All-India Muslim League (AIML) in 1906, which, many years later, became pivotal to the partition of the country.

The Indian Councils Act of 1909, or the Morley–Minto Reforms (named after the Secretary of State, Lord Morley and the Viceroy, the Earl of Minto), came as a 'compromise' after the suppression of *swadeshi* activists. It provided limited self-government, and as a consequence, satisfied none of the political groups. Amongst all the reforms in British India, this was the most short-lived. It had to be completely revamped within 10 years.

THE INDIA OF GANDHI

Mohandas Karamchand Gandhi's involvement in the independence movement began with the 1909 publication of what would become his most famous political tract, *Hind Swaraj* (Indian Home Rule), which he wrote while in South Africa. A more pronounced expression of *swaraj*, or home rule, came in following his return to India in 1915, which saw his rise to power, and the first major mass mobilizations against British rule. The culmination of these was the Non-Cooperation Movement (1920–1922). In four short years, he became the face of the INC and reinvented, reorganized, and gave a new agenda to the political organization. However, the Non-Cooperation Movement came to a rather controversial end after the outbreak of violence at Chauri Chaura (in present-day Uttar Pradesh), where policemen who had fired upon protesters were chased into a police station, which was then set on fire, leaving 23 dead. The movement as Gandhi had envisioned lost its cause.

After the withdrawal of the Non-Cooperation Movement, the INC was not prepared to launch another public movement. Gandhi distanced himself from direct politics and focused on social reform, such as the campaign against untouchability; the promotion of the

1913 Ghadar Party formed in San Francisco, USA to overthrow British rule in India

1914 World War I takes place; Indian soldiers fight for the British

1916 Gandhi returns to India and sets up Sabarmati Ashram in Gujarat

1917 Farmers in Champaran, Bihar join Gandhi in a protest

1919 Jallianwala Bagh Massacre occurs

1920 Non-Cooperation Movement begins

1929 Civil Disobedience Movement begins

1930 Gandhi leads the salt march to Dandi

1935 Government of India Act, passed by the British, gives India political rights at the provincial level

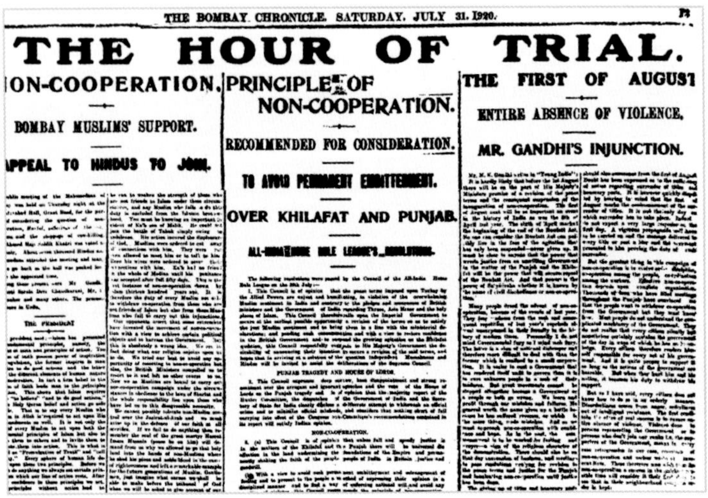

THE BOMBAY CHRONICLE. SATURDAY, JULY 31. 1920.

THE HOUR OF TRIAL.

NON-COOPERATION.

BOMBAY MUSLIMS' SUPPORT.

PRINCIPLE OF NON-COOPERATION.

RECOMMENDED FOR CONSIDERATION.

OVER KHILAFAT AND PUNJAB.

THE FIRST OF AUGUST

ENTIRE ABSENCE OF VIOLENCE.

MR. GANDHI'S INJUNCTION.

A 1920 newspaper article from *The Bombay Chronicle* detailing the start of the Gandhi-led Non-cooperation movement which aimed at persuading the British to grant self-governance to Indians.

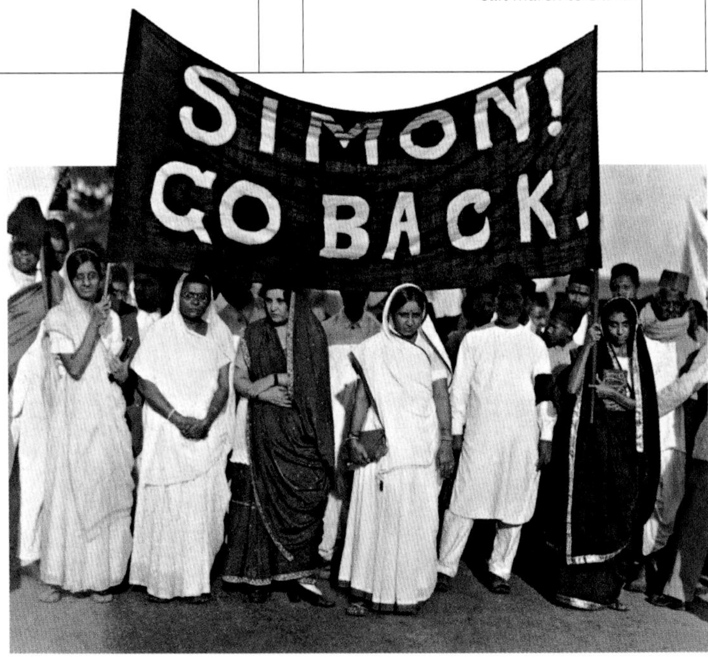

Protestors in Poona (present-day Pune) in Maharashtra march against the Simon Commission in 1928 opposing the lack of Indian representation within the commission which aimed to devise further reforms.

charkha, or spinning wheel, as a tool for self-help; and the construction of Sabarmati Ashram in Ahmedabad, Gujarat, in the west. He launched the Civil Disobedience Movement in 1930 in response to the law that made it illegal for anyone to make salt except the government which then controlled its distribution. It began on 12 March 1930, with a march from the Sabramati Ashram to Dandi on the west coast of the Arabian Sea. The movement continued, and was later withdrawn through the Gandhi-Irwin Pact of 5 March 1931, which, among other things, also removed the salt tax.

Amid the chaos and uncertainty, a few years later, the Government of India Act of 1935 came into effect. It replaced the dyarchy of the 1919 Reforms with 'responsible' self-government in all the departments. The Act, most importantly, gave separate electorates to the Muslims and reserved seats for the Scheduled Castes (a new term for the most oppressed and resource-poor social classes) in the provincial and central legislatures.

Over the decades, other theatres of the struggle kept the momentum going as well, whether it was in the east, led by Surya Sen, the Ghadar revolutionaries internationally, Subhash Chandra Bose's Azad Hind Fauj across the region, or the Hindustan Socialist Republican Association (HSRA).

NEW BEGINNINGS

Independence was not achieved as a result of the actions of one group. The struggle was always a multi-class movement of the populace. There were different ways of imagining the nation and these multiple imaginations had one thing in common: freedom.

India attained independence in the shadow of war and bloodshed. On 14 August 1947, the country was partitioned into India, and the new nation of Pakistan. Mohammad Ali Jinnah of the Muslim League was appointed first Governor-General of the Dominion of Pakistan. An extravagant ritual and ceremony was planned for the transfer of power from Britain to India. The constituent assembly met at midnight of 14 August, and free India's "tryst with destiny" began. For millions, the movement had achieved its resounding end.

However, the country remained in a sense of flux as the horrors of Partition unveiled themselves. Millions were displaced from their homes, and droves of people migrated across the border, all this against the backdrop of two nations finding their feet.

India inherited the unitary central apparatus of British India, as well as the civil bureaucracy, the military, and the police. In the years that followed, the nation faced many challenges on its long road to becoming a secular, socialist, republic.

1940 Lahore session of the Muslim League passes the Pakistan Resolution

1942 Quit India Movement, which calls for complete freedom from British rule, begins

1943 Subhash Chandra Bose takes charge of the Azad Hind Fauj

1947 Partition and the formation of Pakistan

1947 Indian Independence Act is passed and British rule ends

1948 Mahatma Gandhi is assassinated

1950 India becomes a republic as the Constitution comes into effect

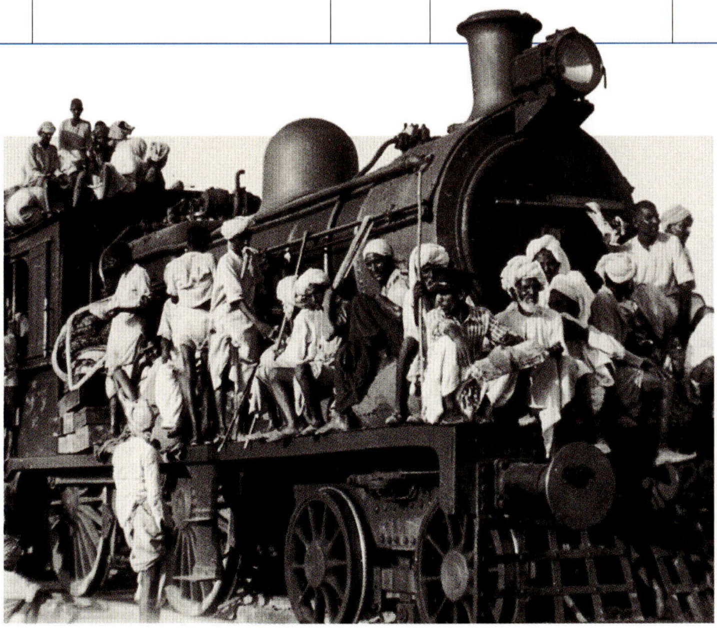

Refugees, by means of a train, flee the violence that erupted following the Partition of the country into India and Pakistan, leaving behind their homes and belongings.

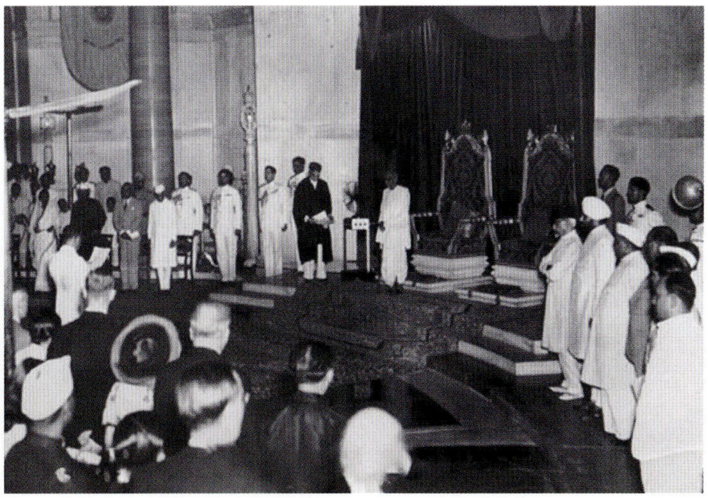

Prime Minister Jawaharlal Nehru prepares to give his famous speech, "A Tryst with Destiny", on the eve of Independence at Parliament in Independent India, in 1947.

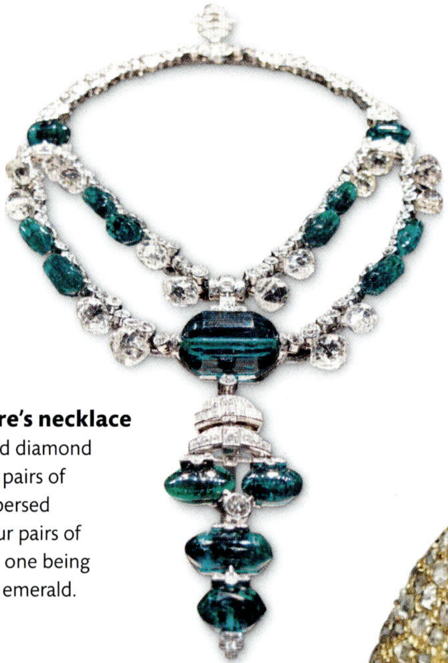

► Maharaja of Indore's necklace
This large double-stranded diamond necklace consists of eight pairs of sizeable diamonds interspersed with smaller ones, and four pairs of emeralds, with the largest one being a 45-carat, barrel-shaped emerald.

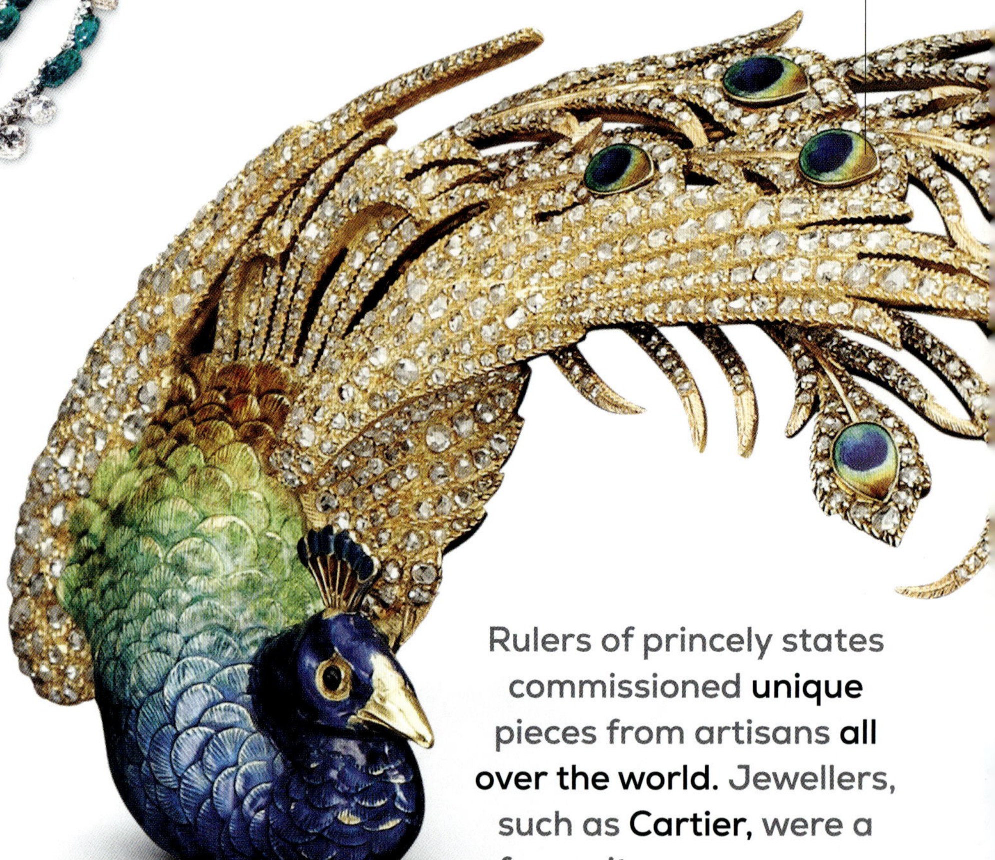

► Peacock accessory
Made by the French jewellery house Mellerio dits Meller in 1905, this charming aigrette, or ornament, in the shape of a peacock is fabricated in vibrant enamel and set with rose-cut diamonds. Maharaja Jagatjit Singh of Kapurthala wore this as a *sarpech* and his wife Anita Delgado, formerly a Spanish dancer and singer, often used it as a hair pin.

Rulers of princely states commissioned **unique** pieces from artisans **all over the world.** Jewellers, such as **Cartier**, were a favourite among many royal households for creating **ornaments** that they could display and pass on to their kin as **heirlooms**.

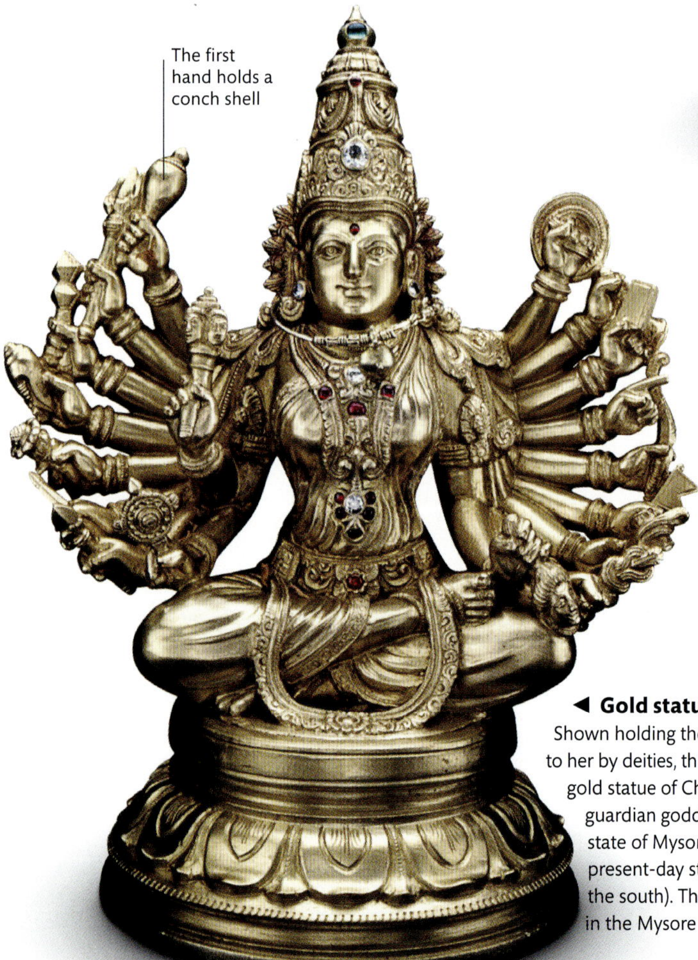

◄ Gold statue
Shown holding the weapons gifted to her by deities, this is a 40-cm (16-in) gold statue of Chamunda, the guardian goddess of the erstwhile state of Mysore (now a city in the present-day state of Karnataka in the south). The statue is now in the Mysore Palace.

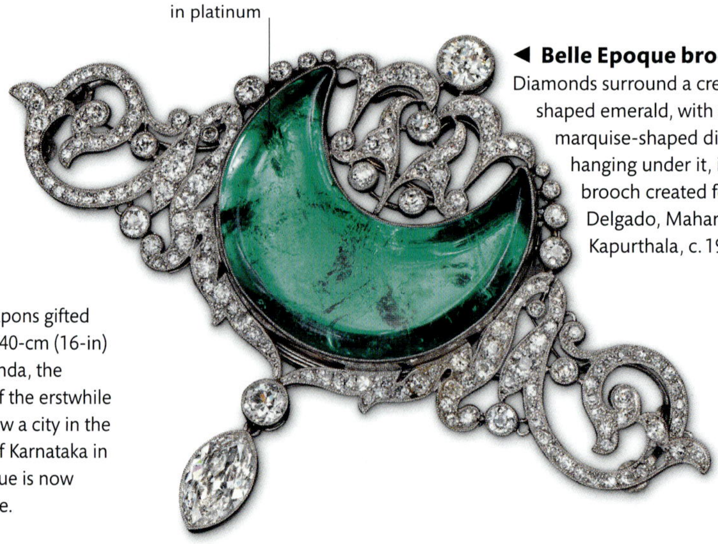

◄ Belle Epoque brooch
Diamonds surround a crescent-shaped emerald, with a marquise-shaped diamond hanging under it, in this brooch created for Anita Delgado, Maharani of Kapurthala, c. 1910.

JEWELS OF THE ROYALS

At the time of Independence, there were 565 princely states in India, which had nominal sovereignty during the British rule, though their ruling dynasties often pre-dated the colonial power. Royal states, such as Mysore, Indore, and Kapurthala, were patrons of art, and commissioned jewellers to create stunning pieces that reflected and added to their prestige.

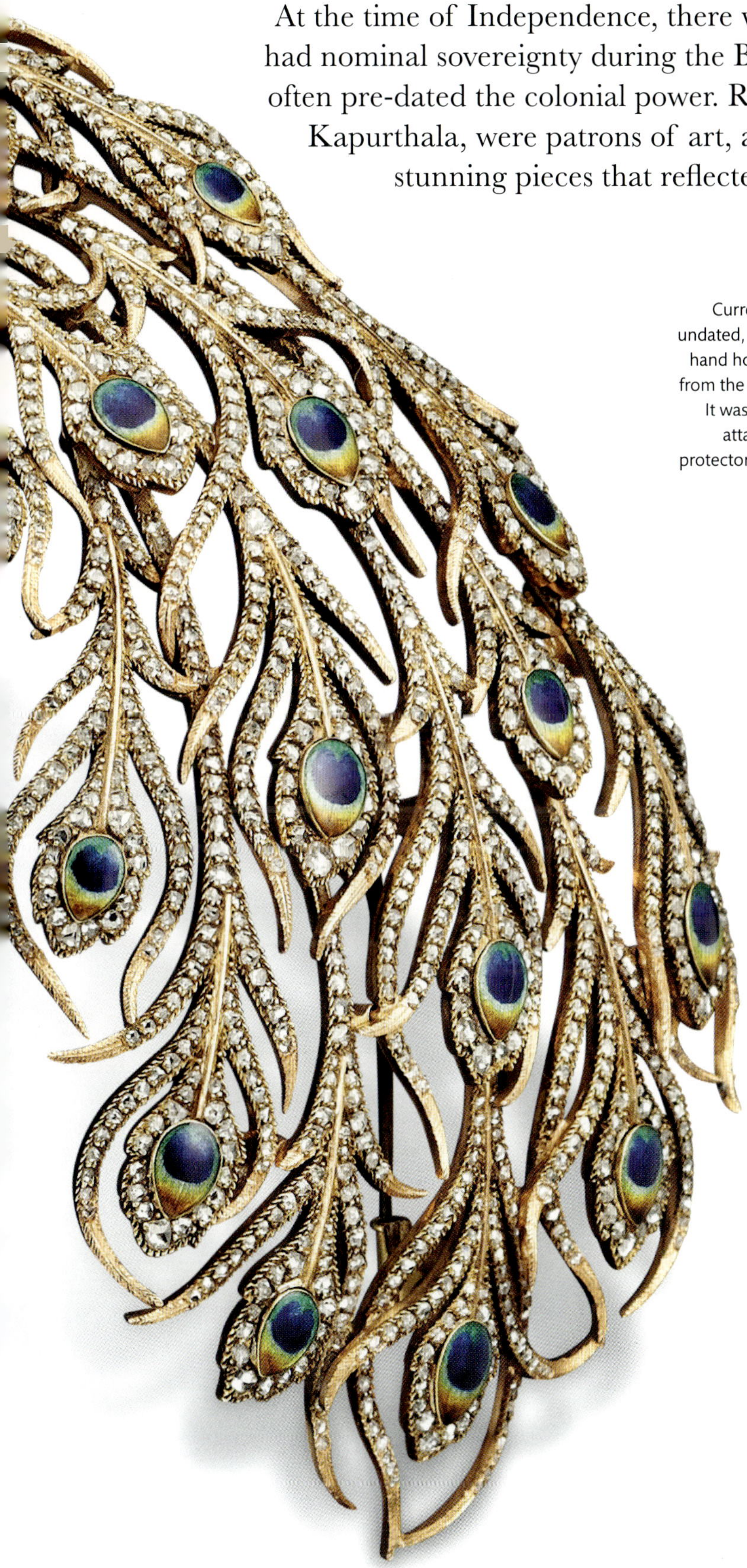

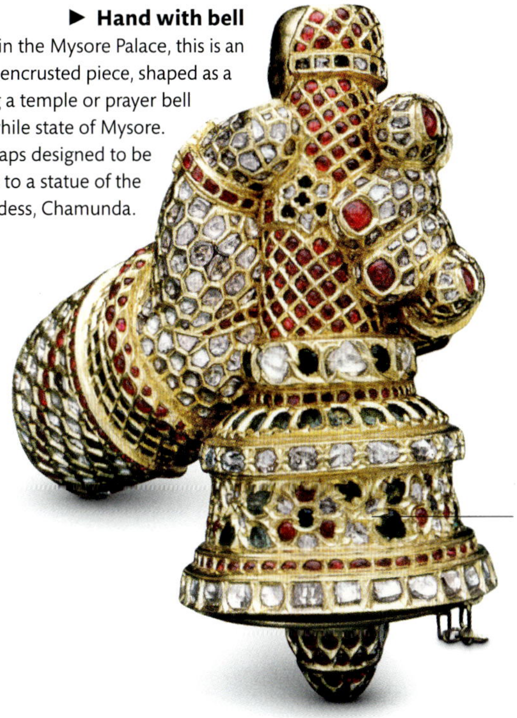

► Hand with bell
Currently in the Mysore Palace, this is an undated, gem-encrusted piece, shaped as a hand holding a temple or prayer bell from the erstwhile state of Mysore. It was perhaps designed to be attached to a statue of the protector-goddess, Chamunda.

Diamonds, rubies, and emeralds set in gold interspersed in a floral pattern

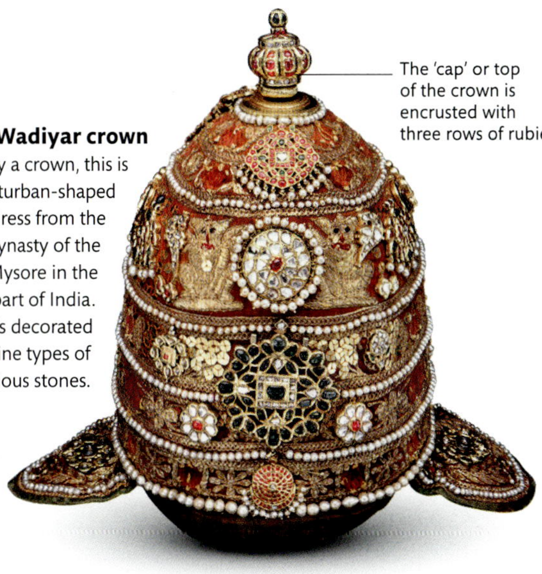

► Wadiyar crown
Most likely a crown, this is an undated, turban-shaped headdress from the Wadiyar dynasty of the state of Mysore in the southern part of India. The crown is decorated with nine types of precious stones.

The 'cap' or top of the crown is encrusted with three rows of rubies

19th–20th centuries CE

ART AT THE TURN OF THE CENTURY

The introduction of the individual artist was a significant result of British presence in India. Until then, art had been a hereditary occupation, largely within the purview of ateliers.

As European artists arrived in India in search of exotic subjects, they brought with them a new realism in painting style that came to be known as the Company School (see pp. 246–247). The first influence of this school on Indian artists is evident in the work of Raja Ravi Varma (see pp. 228–229). He adopted a neo-classical approach with which to interpret Indian culture. Works such as *Damayanti and Her Friend* and *Sita Bhumi Pravesh* pioneered a new movement in Indian art. In the 1850s, art academies were set up in Madras, Calcutta, and Bombay presidencies. While education in the fine arts catered to European styles and perspectives, the academies promoted and popularized art as a profession, beyond just the skill of an artisan.

"What is Art? It is the response of man's creative soul to the call of the Real."

– Rabindranath Tagore, 19th-century poet, writer, social reformer, and painter

NATIONALISM IN ART

The changing political scenario of the late 19th century and the rejection of British supremacy brought nationalism into individual artistic expression. In Calcutta, Abanindranath Tagore and the Bengal School of Art particularly influenced this trend. The use of indigenous material and incorporation of traditional styles from Ajanta and miniature paintings (see pp. 168–169) established a modern Indian aesthetic, the iconic representation of which is Abanindranath Tagore's *Bharat Mata*. The founding of the Visva-Bharati by Rabindranath Tagore at Santiniketan in 1921, at first a movement and later a university, also signalled a return to Indian roots. Gaganendranath Tagore, Asit Kumar Haldar, Nandalal Bose, Jamini Roy, and Ramkinkar Baij took forward the idea of Indian modernism in art. Amrita Sher-Gil (see pp. 268–269), however, laid no claim to nationalist art. She was drawn to her Indian heritage as she searched for authenticity in which to root her modernism. The shift in theme from nation to individual began around the 1940s when artists, such as Francis Newton Souza, Tyeb Mehta, Manjit Bawa, and M.F. Hussain, assimilated the modernist idiom. They are representative of the progressive movement in India.

► **An evocative painting by celebrated 20th-century artist** Abanindranath Tagore, titled *Journey's End* (1913), depicts a worn-out camel, which critics believe was an allegory for India under British rule.

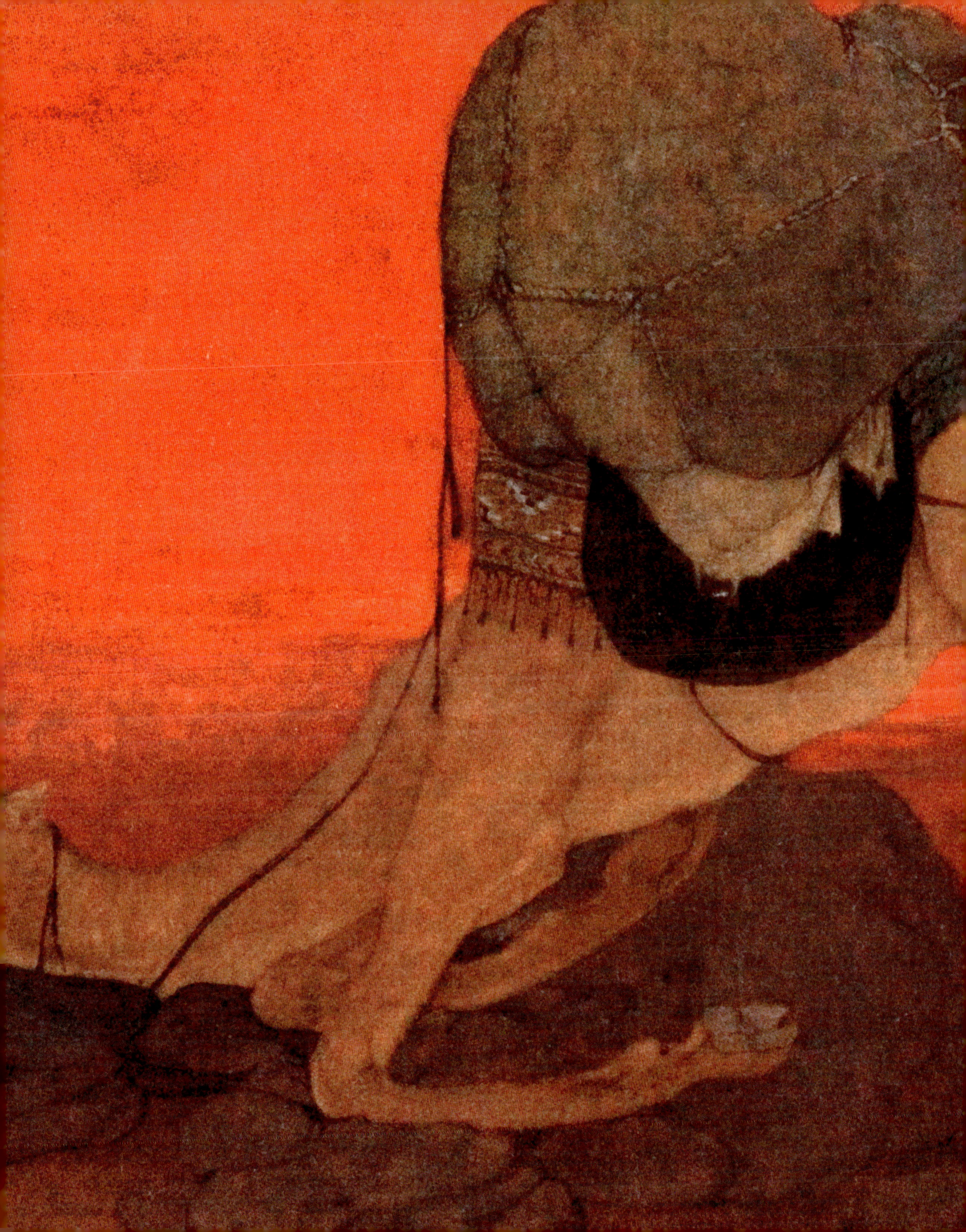

Era 20th century CE | **Medium** Oil on canvas | **Dimension** 73.5 × 99.5 cm (28.9 × 39.1 in)

THREE GIRLS

Portraits of resilience, patience, and the human spirit

Also known as *Group of Three Girls*, this evocative painting by the Hungarian–Indian painter Amrita Sher-Gil shows three young women seated together. Though simple in its essence, it speaks of the artist's mastery over technique and colour.

Three beautiful, seated figures, feminine and demure, wait for something with an air of defeated resignation. This painting, titled *Three Girls*, was Amrita Sher-Gil's first canvas following her return from Europe. In 1937, *Three Girls* won the artist a gold medal from the Bombay Art Society, a non-profit organization formed in 1888 that held an annual art exhibition in the city. Her paintings from the early 1930s carried a post-Impressionist influence and included many self-portraits. *Three Girls* marks a change in Sher-Gil's visual language and showcases her brilliant use of colour, especially red, which became even more distinct in her later work.

PORTRAIT OF A PAINTER

Early in her life, Sher-Gil spent time engaging in the study of art, particularly in Paris and Italy, including at the prestigious Ecole des Beaux-Arts, and won membership to the exclusive Paris Grande Salon. However, in her own words, she "was haunted by an intense longing to return to India, feeling in some strange, inexplicable way that there lay my destiny as a painter." She married her Hungarian cousin, a doctor, and lived with him in Gorakhpur, a city in the Indian state of Uttar Pradesh, where she painted some of her most influential paintings that have inspired generations of Indian artists.

Today, Sher-Gil is recognized as a pioneering artist of Indian modern art; her impact on the art movement in India is perhaps as impressive as that of Abanindranath Tagore and Nandalal Bose, pioneers of the Bengal School of painting. Though she died at the age of 28, her oeuvre of 172 works includes self portraits, figures, and nudes, and some still life. She is, perhaps, best known for her haunting portrayal of Indian people in which she captures emotions and everyday life. Her paintings of groups particularly reflect the influence of south Indian art, Ajanta cave paintings, Pahari and Mughal miniatures, and also the Bengal School. Her use of colour and her style resonate with the aesthetic traditions of the East and the West.

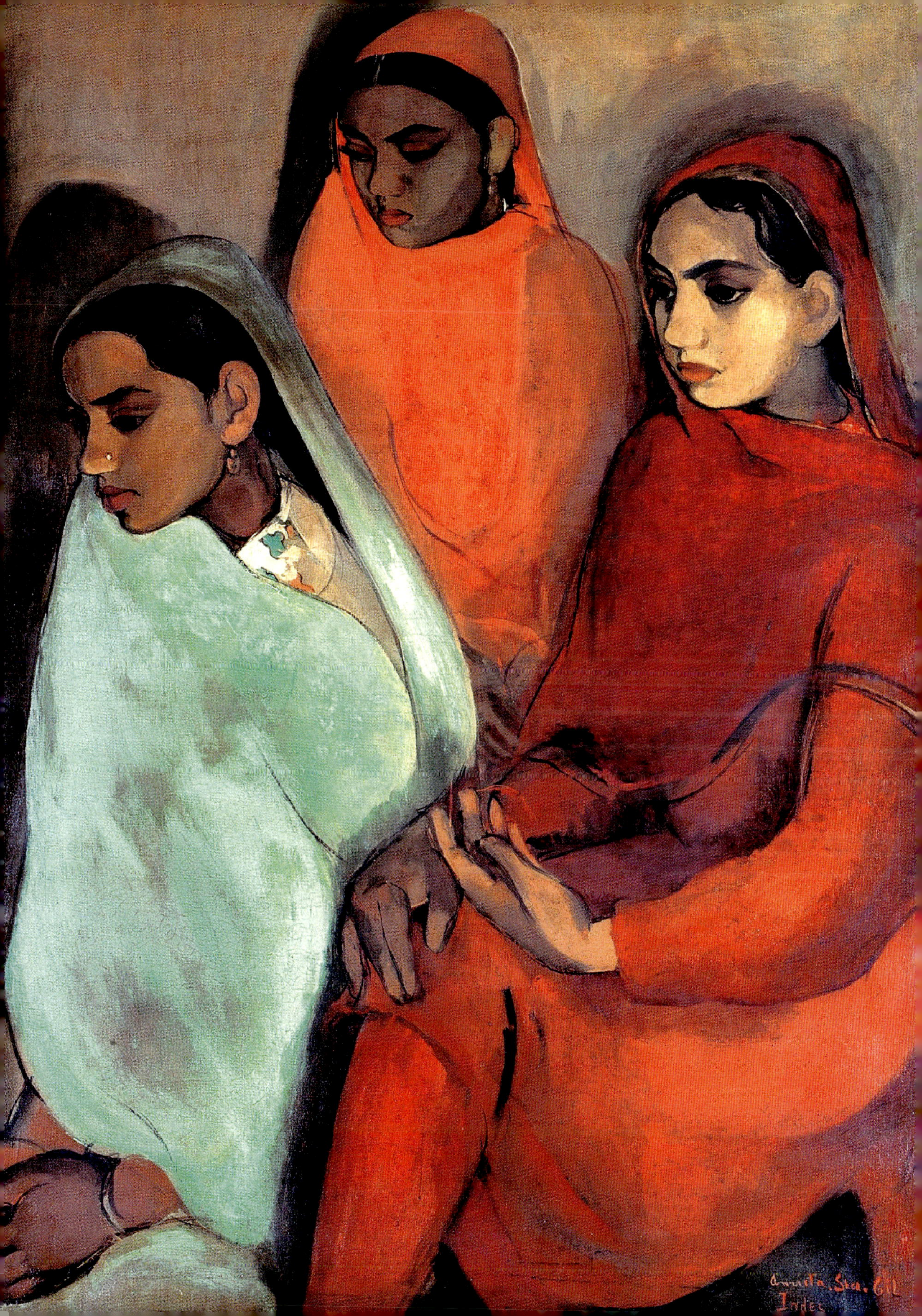

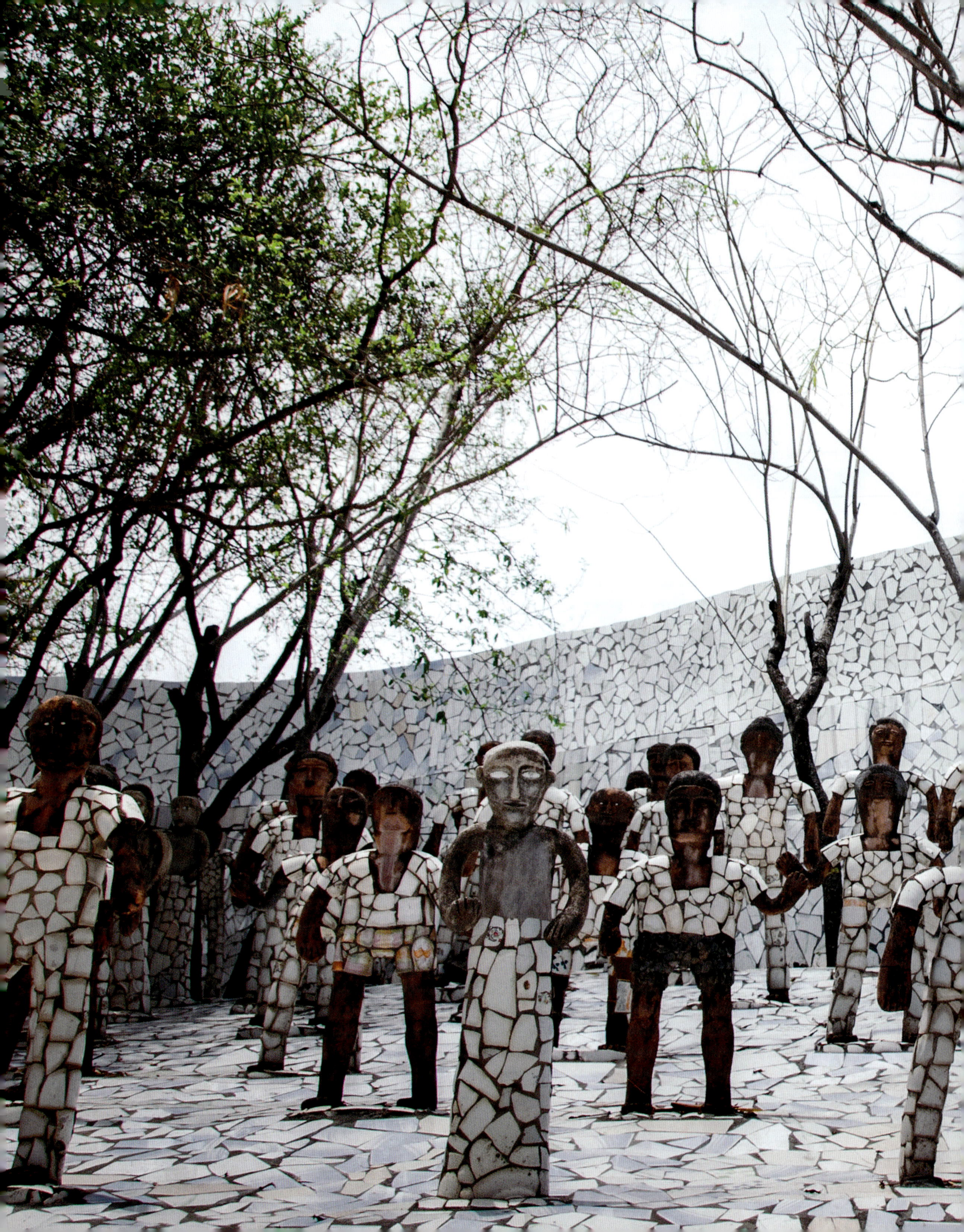

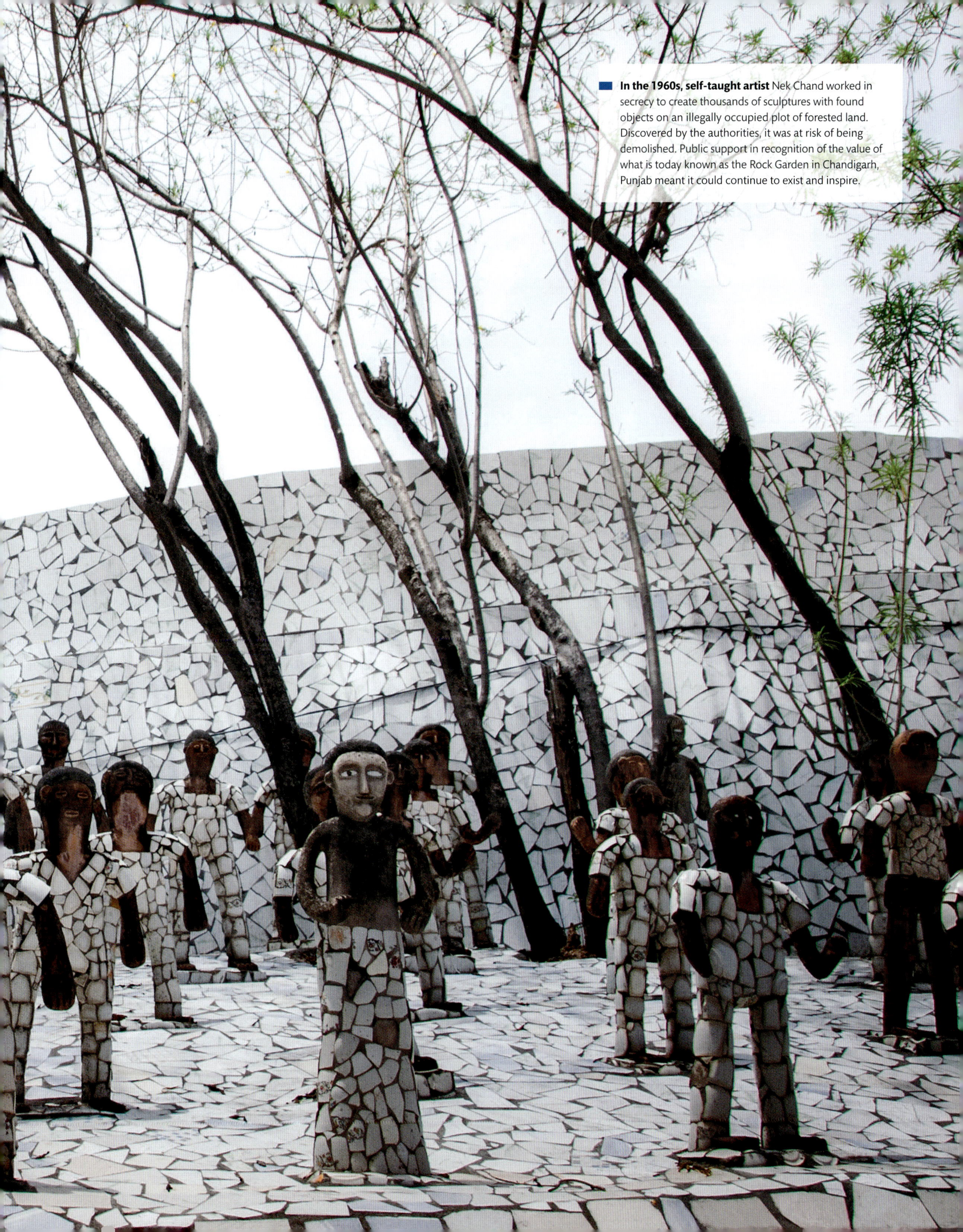

In the 1960s, self-taught artist Nek Chand worked in secrecy to create thousands of sculptures with found objects on an illegally occupied plot of forested land. Discovered by the authorities, it was at risk of being demolished. Public support in recognition of the value of what is today known as the Rock Garden in Chandigarh, Punjab meant it could continue to exist and inspire.

TEXTILES OF INDIA

Dyed, printed, painted, embroidered, or woven with threads of gold and silver, the textiles of India attest to the enduring creative genius of the country's craftspeople from different regions and communities of the Indian subcontinent.

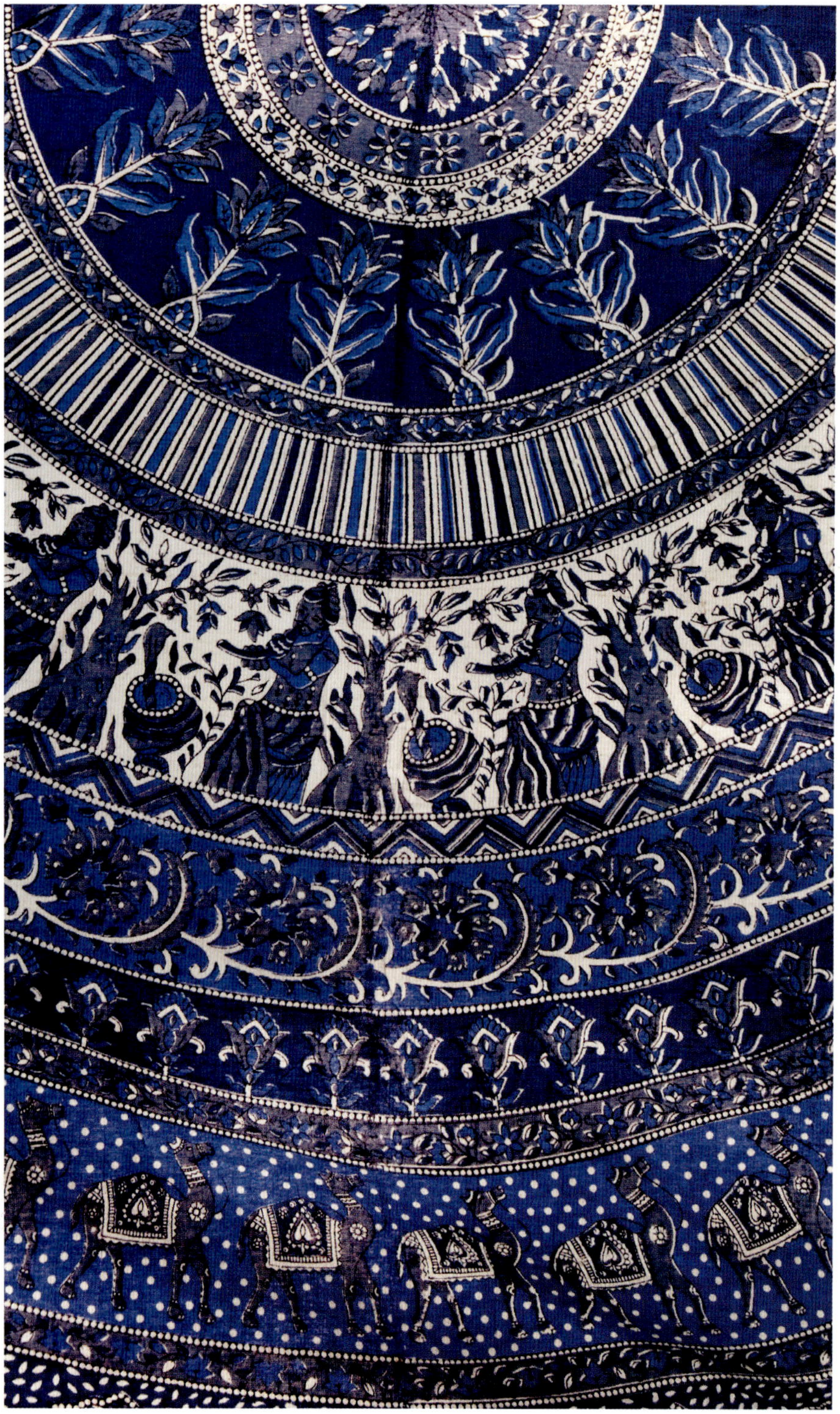

◀ **The defining blue of Indigo** fabrics comes from a natural dye derived from the leaves of the plant *Indigofera tinctoria*. Its use in dyeing fabric can be traced back to the Harappan culture.

Ever since 2500 BCE, countries across the **world** have **sourced** the finest **muslin**, the most luxurious **silks**, and the softest **wool** from India.

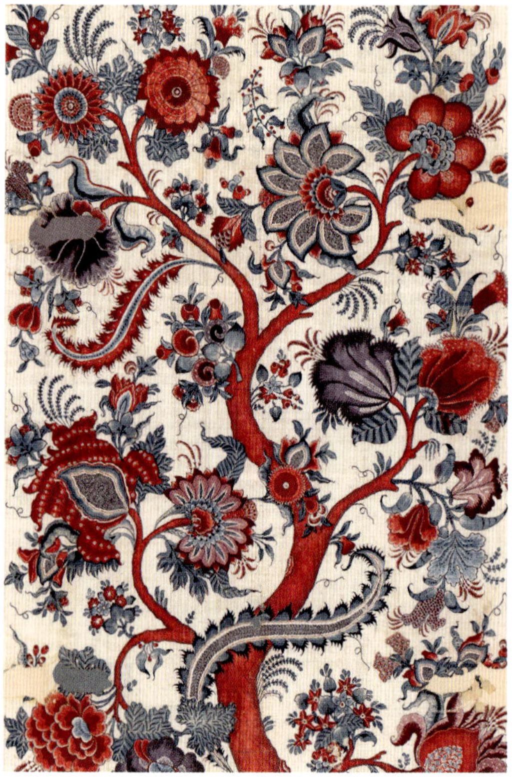

▲ **The chintz** was a luxurious cotton textile, block-printed or painted in exotic designs, and exported to the royal courts of Europe in the 16th and 17th centuries, initially as furnishing.

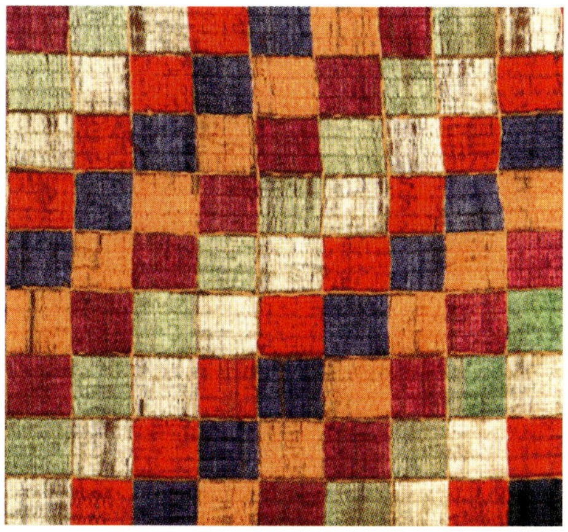

▲ **Traditional hand-embroidered shawls** and scarves made by the women of Punjab for their own use on significant events of their life, Phulkari patterns are usually geometric and executed with colourful silk threads on a heavy cotton base.

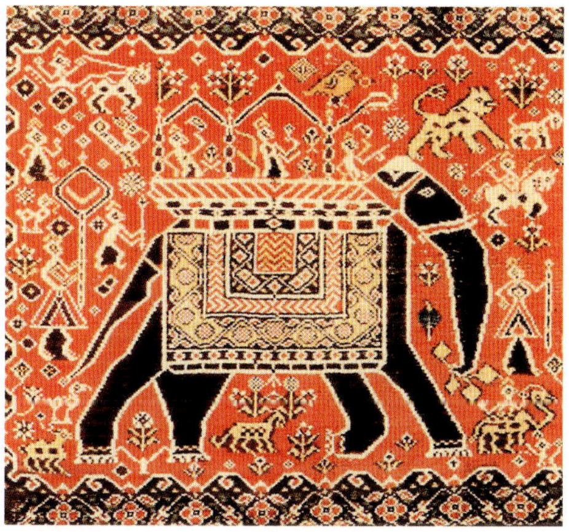

▲ **Ikat, a dyeing technique, is produced** on fabrics by tying the yarn into a desired pattern and resist-dyeing it. The designs can be seen only after the fabric is woven.

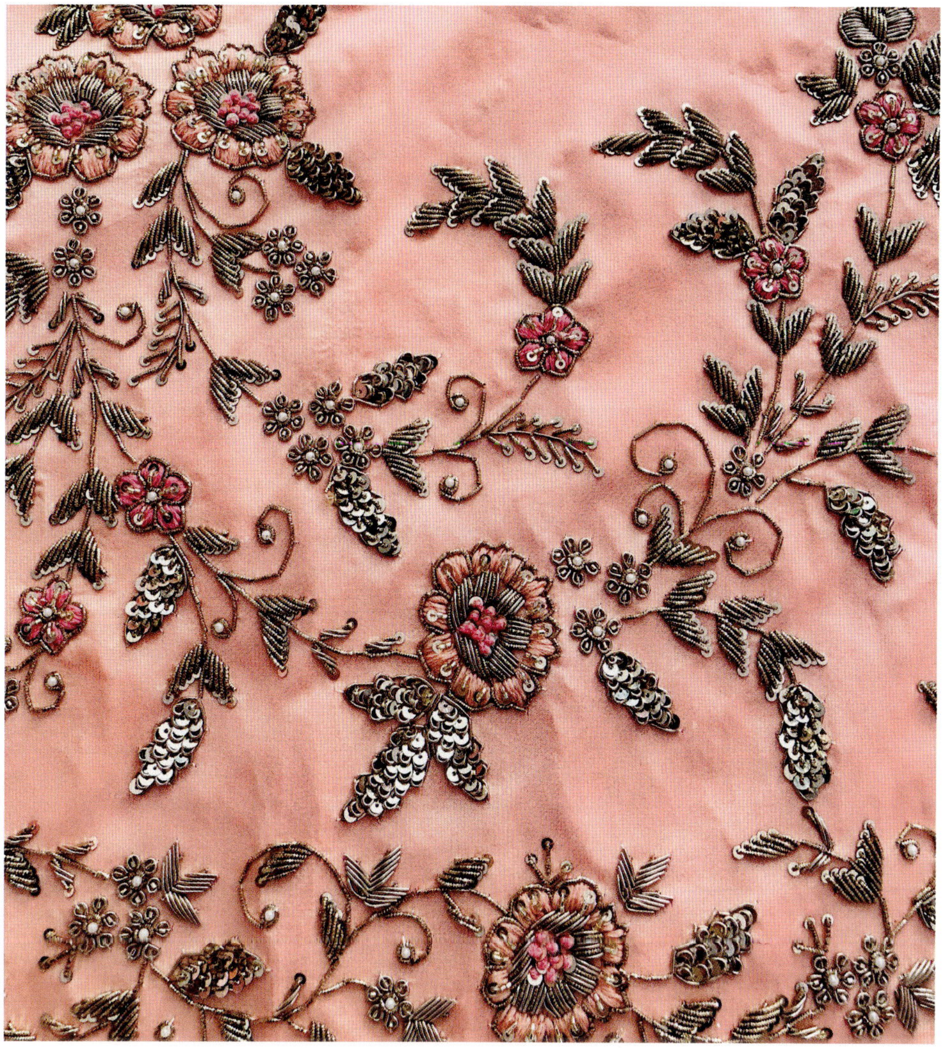

▲ **Zardozi is the art of embroidery on silk with threads** of fine gold and silver. It also incorporates pearls and precious stones at times. Brought to India by the Mughals, Zardozi textiles were an integral part of the magnificence of royal courts.

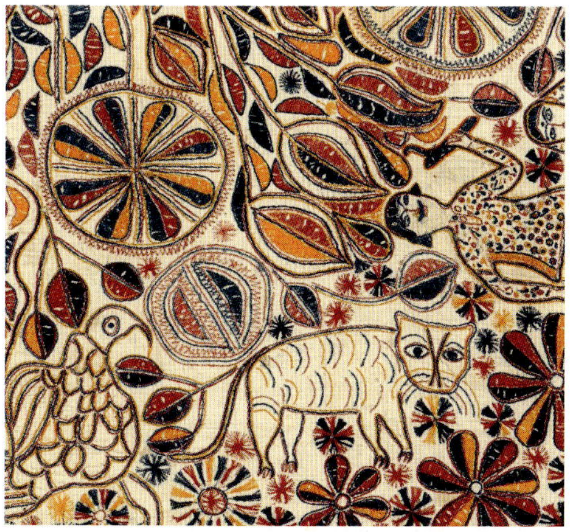

▲ **Kantha** refers to both the embroidery style of running stitch as well as the finished textile. Traditionally, discarded fabrics were layered with running stitches to make quilts and bed covers.

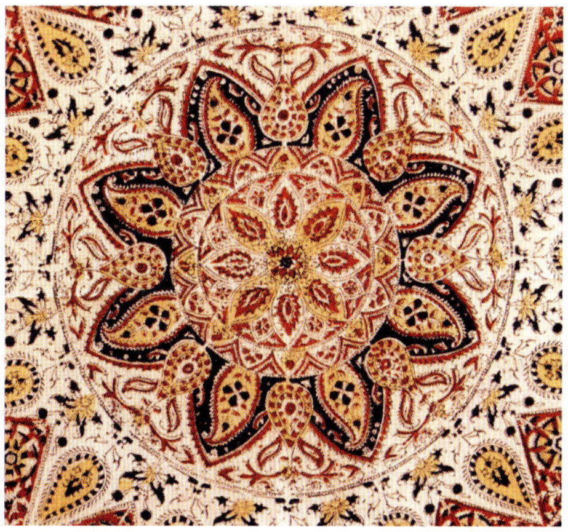

▲ **The Kalamkari is an intricate style of** hand-painting fabrics with natural colours and dyes, which emerged from the ancient art of painted scrolls that narrated mythological stories.

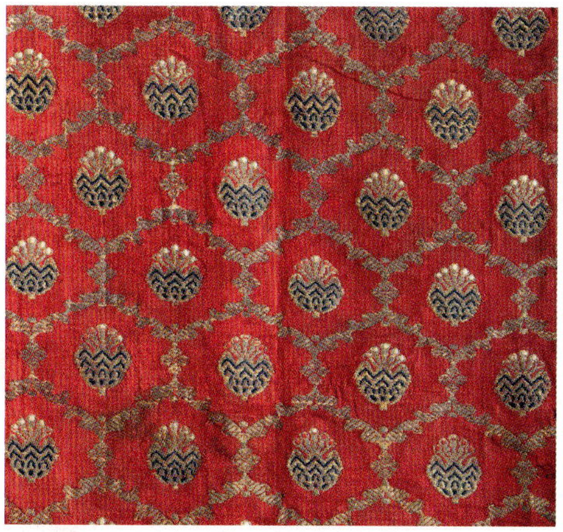

▲ **Brocade is a heavy silk fabric with** patterns or motifs woven with gold, silver, or silk thread, usually in contrasting colours. Varanasi brocades are renowned the world over.

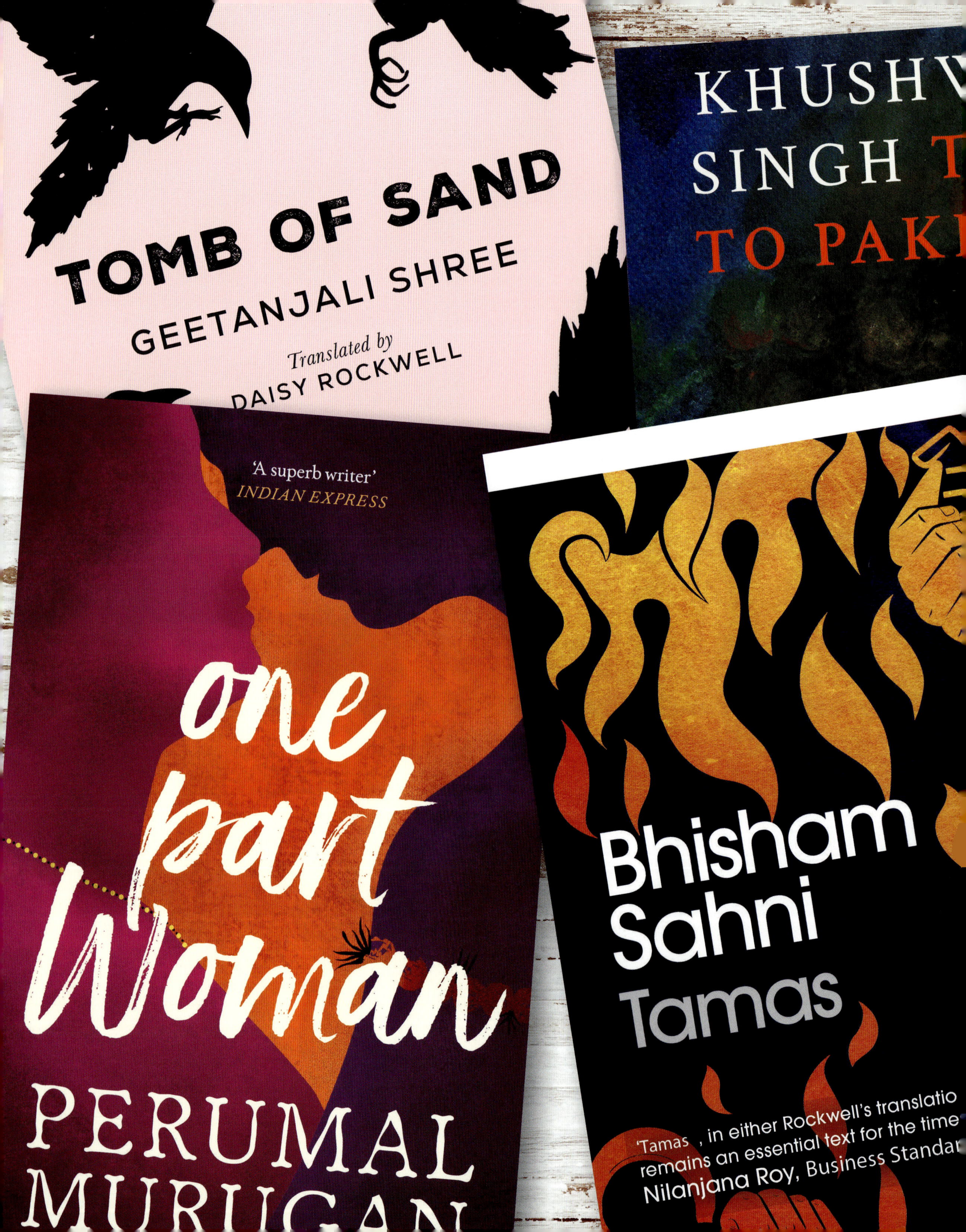
TOMB OF SAND
GEETANJALI SHREE
Translated by
DAISY ROCKWELL
SINGH
'A superb writer'
INDIAN EXPRESS
one part Woman
PERUMAL
Bhisham
Sahni
Tamas

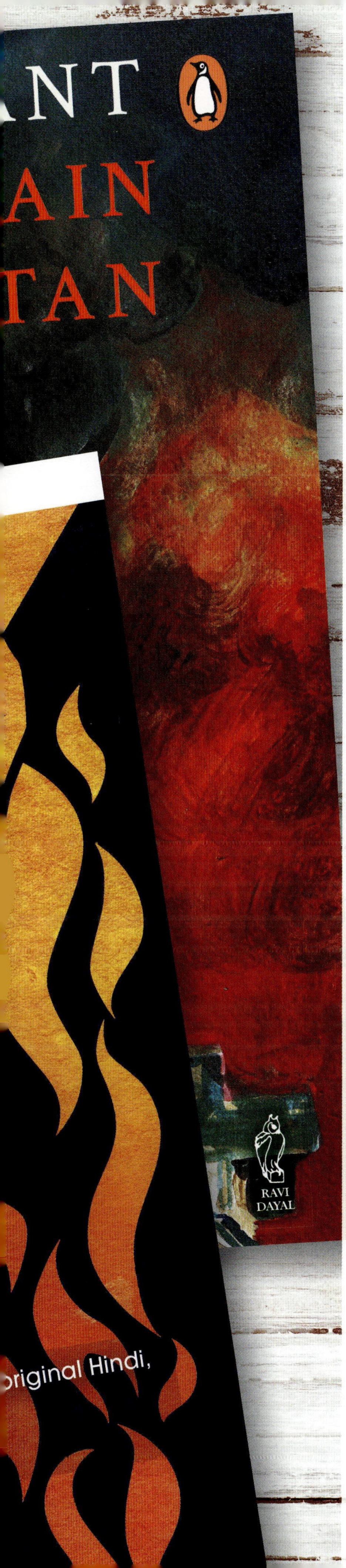

c. 20th century CE *onwards*

LITERARY VOICES

From writings about social inequalities and the Partition to stories and plays that chronicle the experience of being Indian, literature has been a seminal part of the Indian cultural milieu.

A shift towards realism and an expanding canon of literary genres emerged in the 20th century. Short stories, in particular, became increasingly popular. Works such as Munshi Premchand's *Godaan* (Hindi), Rabindranath Tagore's *Nastanirh* (Bengali), and Mulk Raj Anand's *Lajwanti* (Urdu) tackled subjects such as people's struggles, poverty, and women in society. The emergence of the anti-imperialistic Progressive Writers' Movement of India drew attention to social inequalities. The Partition of India in 1947 left a profound impact on the subcontinent's literature. Through books such as *Pinjar* and *Train to Pakistan*, Punjabi and Hindi writer Amrita Pritam and English novelist Khushwant Singh spearheaded the genre of Partition literature, addressing themes of displacement and loss, and the search for identity.

"I write for only one sake: to present a human truth, or to show a new angle of looking at common things."

– Munshi Premchand, "Sahitya ka Uddeshya" (The Aim of Literature) speech at the first meeting of the India Progressive Writers' Association, 1936

Theatre flourished as plays, such as Badal Sircar's *Evam Indrajit* (Bengali), Vijay Tendulkar's *Shantata! Court Chalu Aahe* (Marathi), and Mahasweta Devi's *Hajar Churashir Maa* (Bengali), brought attention to marginalized voices. This was aided by movements like Indian People's Theatre Association and the Nautanki tradition. Later plays, such as Girish Karnad's *Tughlaq* (Kannada), drew from mythology and history to highlight prevalent issues. Indian poets, meanwhile, explored the themes of identity, ethos, and the challenges of modernity. This can be seen in Nissim Ezekiel's "Goodbye Party for Miss Pushpa TS" (English) and A.K. Ramanujan's "Prayers To Lord Murugan".

GLOBAL THEMES IN LITERARY WORKS

Writing in English came to the fore in the 1950s and '60s, with writers such as R.K. Narayan who, in *Malgudi Days*, examined the Indian experience. A new form of 'modern epic' poetry emerged in the 1980s with C.N. Reddy's "Viswambhara", which looked at free will and redemption, and later the novel in verse, *The Golden Gate*, by Vikram Seth. In the 1980s and '90s, literary works such as Amitav Ghosh's *The Shadow Lines* and Arundhati Roy's *The God of Small Things* focused on post-colonial identity, and more recently, the translated novels, *One Part Woman* by Perumal Murugan, and *Tomb of Sand* by Geetanjali Shree looked at relationships.

◄ **Popular Indian books, *Train to Pakistan* (Khushwant Singh, 1956),** *Tamas* (Bhisham Sahni, 1974), *One Part Woman* (Perumal Murugan, translated 2013), and *Tomb of Sand* (Geetanjali Shree, translated 2022).

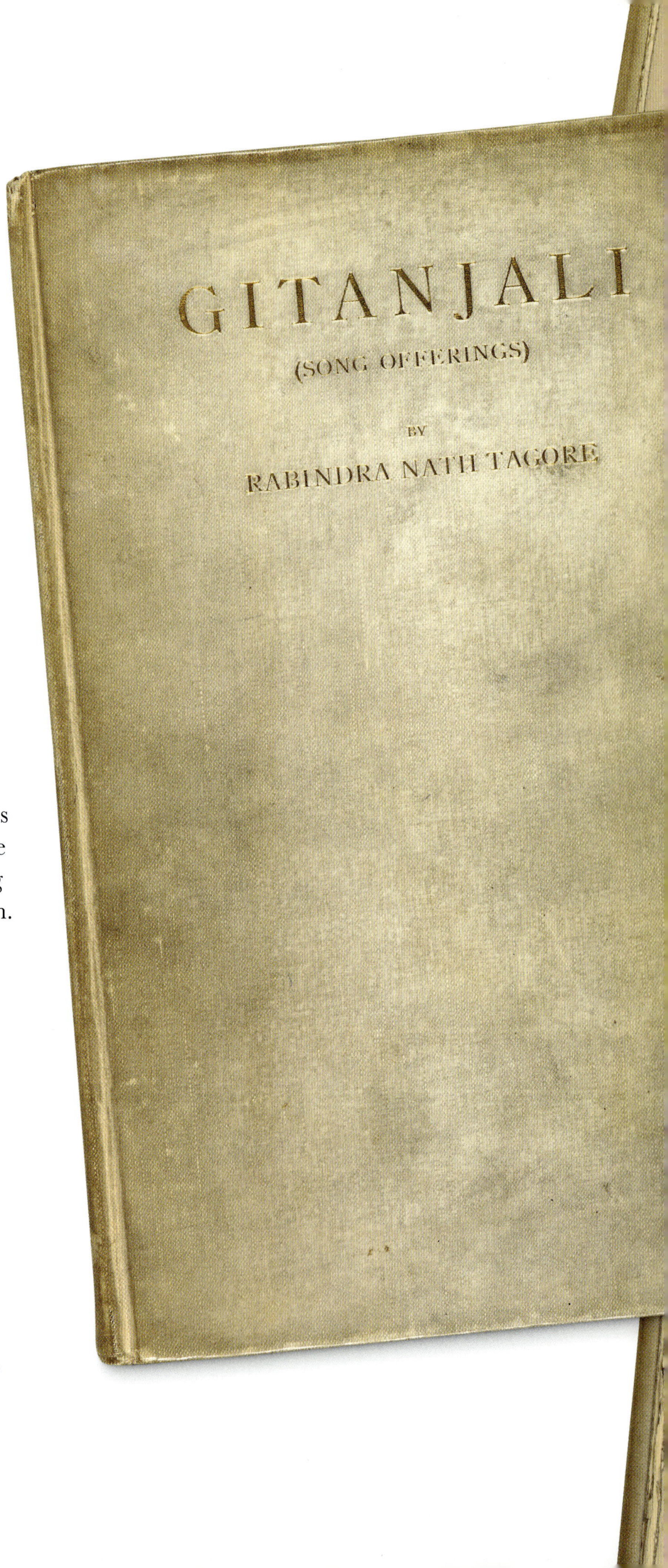

Era 20th century CE | **Page extent** 64 pages

GITANJALI

A Nobel song offering

Rabindranath Tagore's magnum opus, *Gitanjali* is a collection of devotional poems whose lyricism and spirituality won him the Nobel Prize for Literature in 1913, making him the first Asian to achieve this distinction.

Translated as *Song Offerings*, *Gitanjali* expresses the poet's intense longing to connect with God, as he perceives the presence of the divine in the natural world and within himself through words, imagery, and symbols. Rabindranath Tagore drew inspiration from the *Upanishads*, the Bhagavad Gita, the songs of the Bauls (the Bhakti itinerant singers of Bengal), and the ideals of the Brahmo Samaj, a reformist religious movement.

The metaphysical musings of *Gitanjali* emerged from an existential crisis Rabindranath Tagore faced between 1902 and 1907, when he witnessed the deaths of his wife and two of his children. He poured his grief into these poems, which were published in Bengali in 1910. Hoping to secure an English publisher, Tagore brought the self-translated manuscript to England, but left it in the London Underground. Luckily, it was found and eventually published in 1912. Conveying the peace of the soul in harmony with nature, the poems struck a chord with European readers, especially the Irish symbolist poet

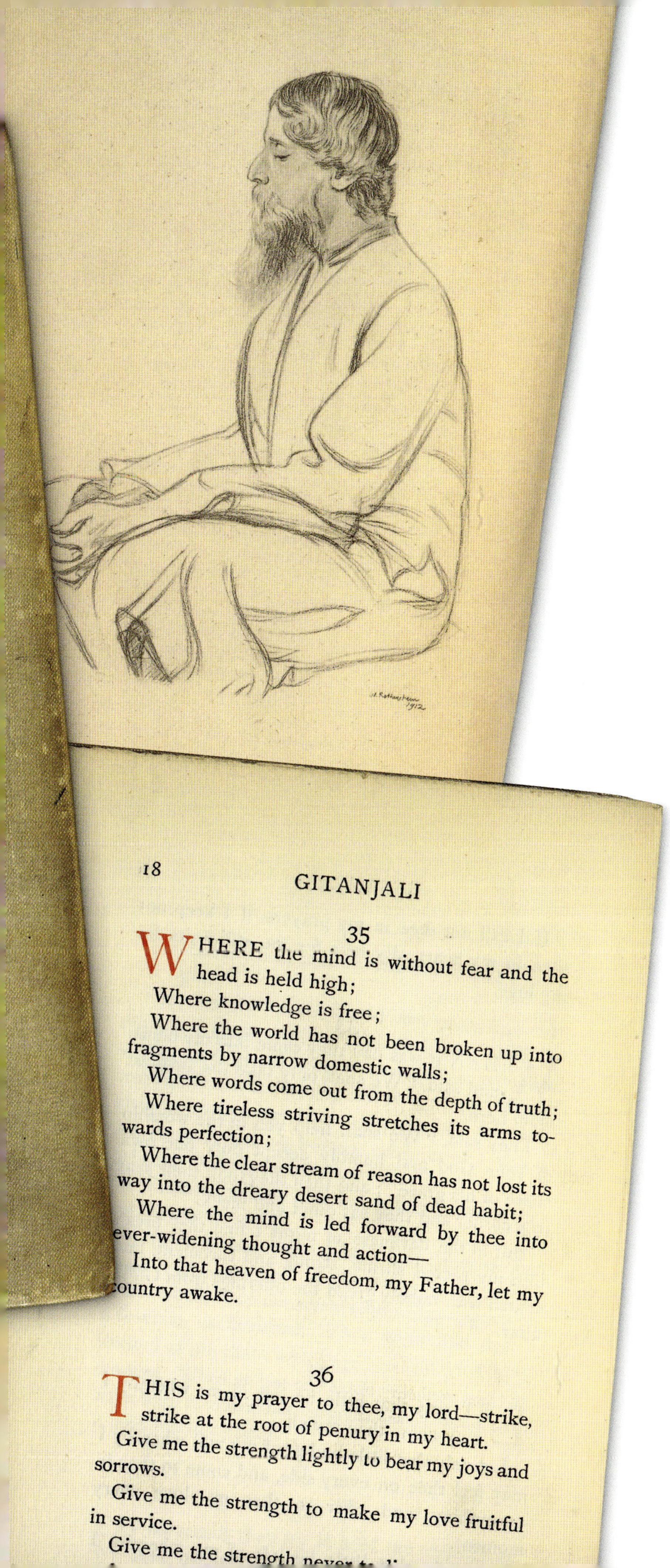

"Thou hast made me endless, such is thy pleasure. This frail vessel thou emptiest again and again, and fillest it ever with fresh life."

– Opening lines of *Gitanjali*, translated by Rabindranath Tagore

◀ **The book cover of the** 1912 English edition, including folios of translations by Tagore and a portrait of the author by English painter, W. Rothenstein.

W.B. Yeats, who used allusive imagery and symbolic structures in his work. In his introduction to *Gitanjali's* English edition, Yeats confessed to being deeply moved by the innocence and simplicity of the poems. He also introduced Tagore to the American modernist poet Ezra Pound. Enraptured, Pound compared Tagore to Italian poet Dante Alighieri in an article, which is widely believed to have led to his nomination for the Nobel prize.

THE GIANT

A polymath, Rabindranath Tagore was an accomplished musician and artist, an eclectic philosopher, as well as a passionate political activist. *Gitanjali* was written during the period of British imperialism, when India was in political and social turmoil. His anti-colonialist sentiments and his longing for a free India find expression in *Gitanjali* in the oft-quoted lines from his poem, "Where the Mind is Without Fear": Into that heaven of freedom, my Father, let my country awake.

c. 16th century CE onwards

INDO-SARACENIC ARCHITECTURE

The Europeans brought with them the art and architecture of their cultures. As they adjusted to the demands of the landscape, styles that incorporated elements from different cultures emerged, setting the stage for statements in stone, brick, and mortar.

The Portuguese, the French, the Dutch and the British all left their mark in Indian architecture. Portuguese baroque and classical influence are best seen in Goa in Fort Aguada itself and the magnificent cathedrals and churches such as the Se Cathedral. Bolgatty Palace in Kochi still showcases the Dutch presence, while narrow street fronts opening into courtyards, shuttered windows, gables, arches, and sloping roofs continue to distinguish the French from the Indian quarter in Pondicherry and Chandernagor.

"Architecture is a three-legged stool: climate, technology, and culture."

– Charles Correa, prominent 20th-century Indian architect and urban planner

A LASTING COLONIAL INFLUENCE

The British East India Company's interests were protected by the grey granite walls of Fort St George, Chennai, established in 1644. It was the British buildings of the 19th–20th centuries that expressed an imperial vision. Calcutta, the capital of the British in India from 1772–1911, was designed to match the grandeur of any capital in Europe.

Victoria Memorial, built to honour the Empress of India from 1876–1901 is the largest monument to a monarch anywhere in the world. The structure had barely been completed when King George V, Emperor of India, announced the transfer of the capital to a city to be built as New Delhi. The architectural style that evolved in its construction took forward the late 19th-century Indo-Saracenic adaptations of Gothic revivalism in the arts and crafts traditions of India. A hybridization of Indian (mostly Mughal) and European stylistic elements, it served to integrate the empire with the cultural history of the subcontinent.

The heart of the new capital, and the apogee of the Indo-Saracenic style, was the Viceroy's House, which today, as Rashrapati Bhawan, houses the President of India, on the top of Raisina Hill. Remarkable in its rooted monumentality, it is a marker of continuing architectural statements that are innovative but remain true to their contexts.

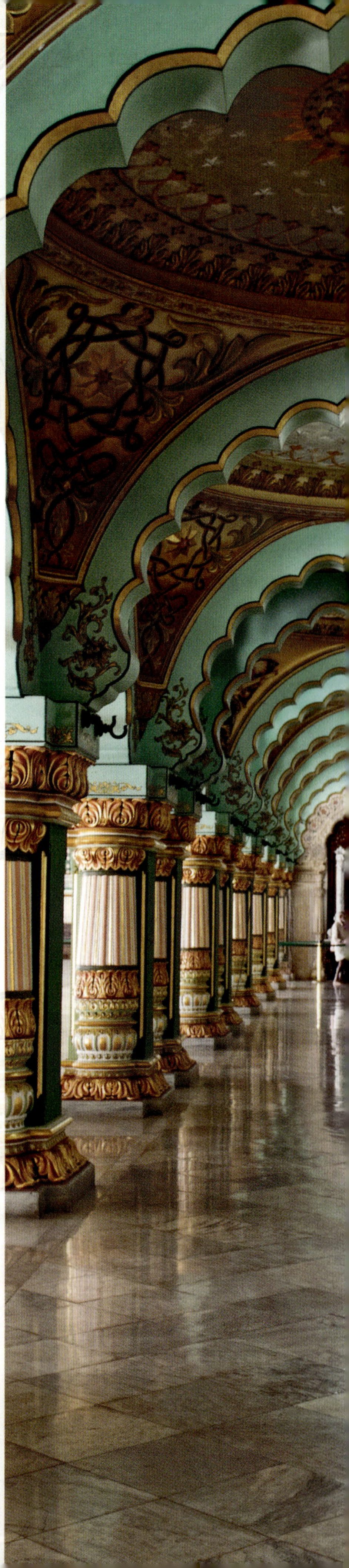

► **Beautifully painted and intricate** columns and arches at the Indo-Saracenic Mysore Palace in Karnataka in southern India.

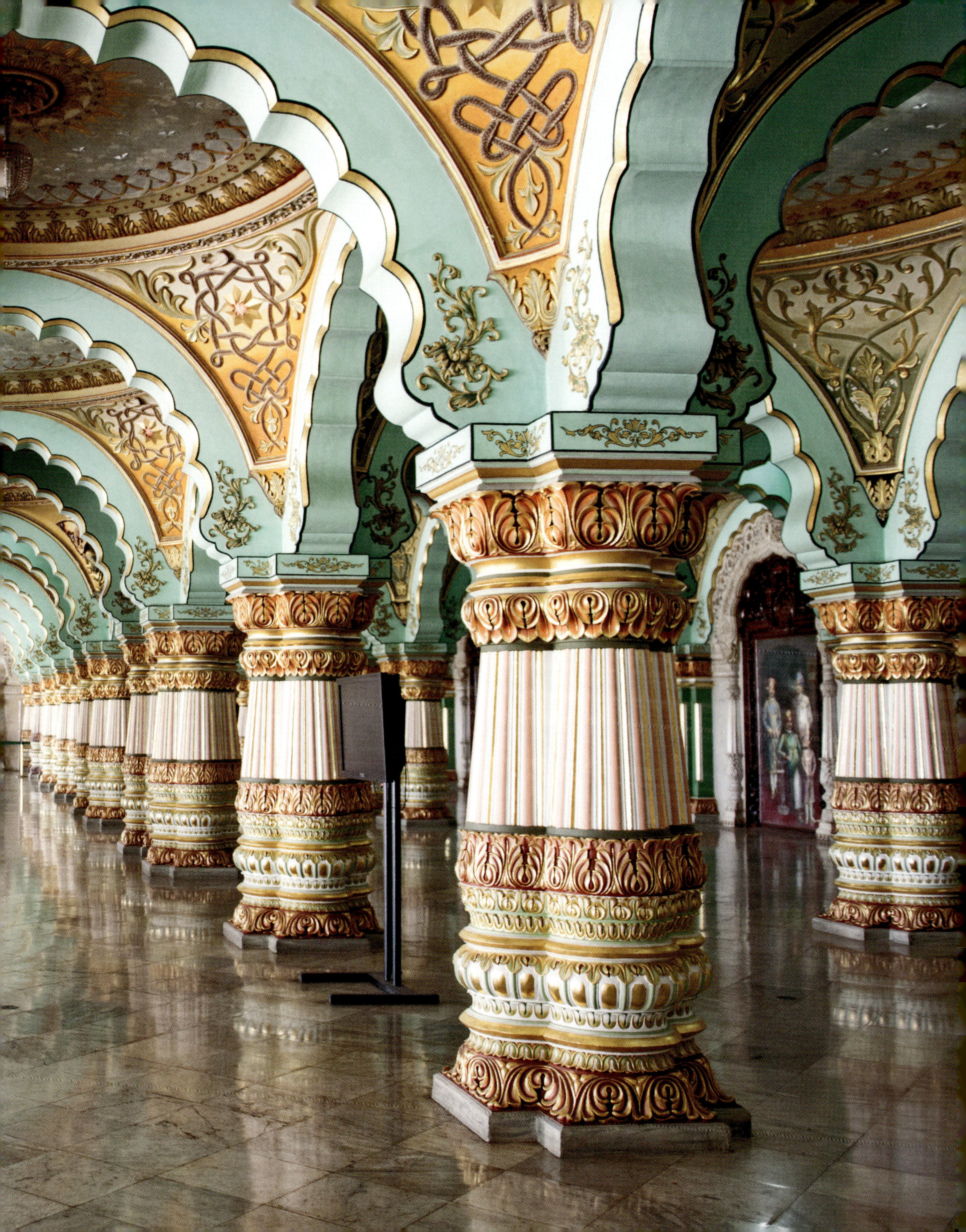

INDIAN FOLK ART

These vibrant art forms are intrinsic to the tribal and folk cultures and traditions of the country. Originally painted and still seen on entrances, floors, and walls of homes and temples, many have made the transition to paper and canvas as marketable, decorative art, making them a veritable treasure trove of visual expression.

Indian folk art has **over 500 forms**, each with **unique materials** and **techniques**, depicting **culture**, history, and mythology.

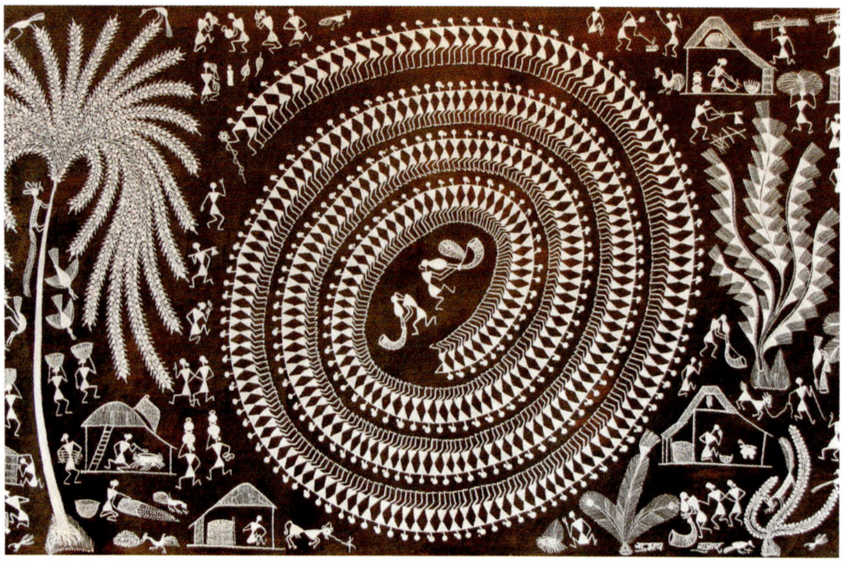

▲ **Traditionally painted on mud walls** of the homes of the Warli tribe of Maharashtra, the Warli art form closely resembles the prehistoric cave paintings of central India. Some studies trace the roots of this style back to 2500 to 3000 BCE.

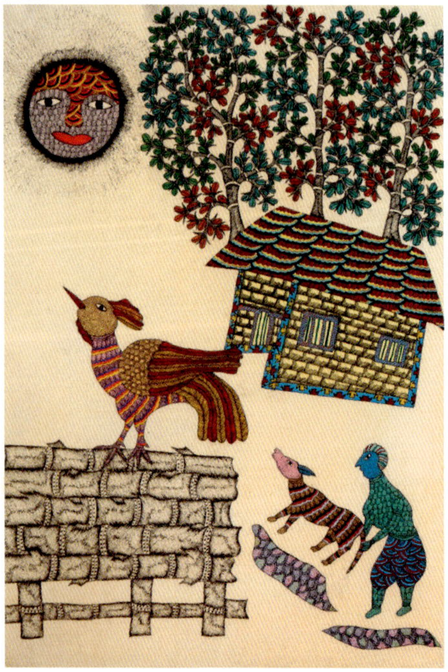

▲ **Gond art,** the work of the Gond people from central India, makes use of lines to depict motifs from the natural world.

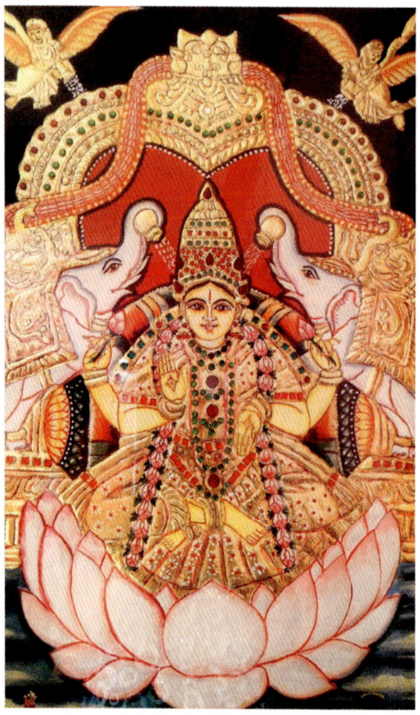

▲ **Tanjore paintings**, originating in the 16th century, are unique for the use of gold leaf, gems, and glass pieces in its portrayal of deities.

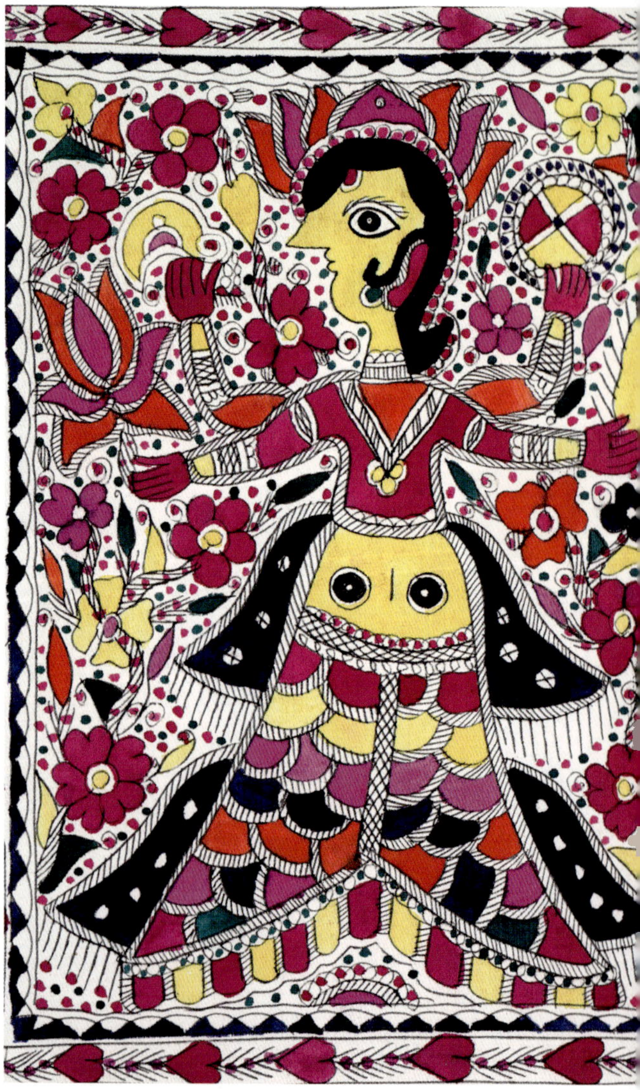

▲ **Madhubani paintings** originated in Bihar. They are characterized by geometric designs and line work in vibrant colours depicting nature, mythology, and daily life.

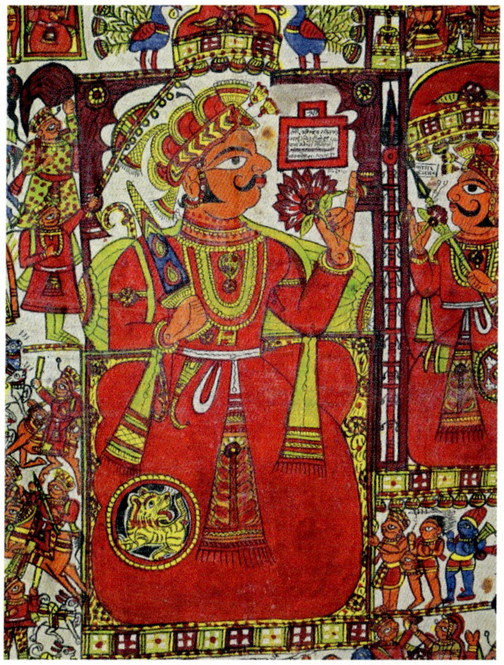

◄ **Phad scrolls** are used by *bhopas* (traditional priest-singers of Rajasthan) to narrate the legends of Devnarayan (a reincarnation of the Hindu deity Vishnu) and Pabuji (a local hero). For more than 700 years, a family from Bhilwara in the state were the sole creators of these.

► **Cloth-based** scroll paintings originating from the eastern Indian states of Odisha and West Bengal, the Pattachitra paintings are based on Hindu mythology, commonly depicting Lord Jagannatha of Puri.

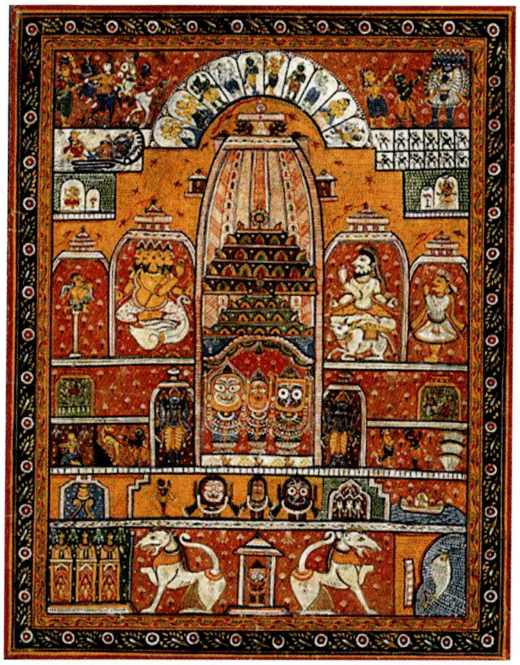

▼ **Kerala murals** date back to the 8th century, though most existing ones are from the 14th century. The Mattancherry Palace in Ernakulam district has extensive murals highlighting the characteristic use of five colours: red, yellow, green, black, and white, the last being the colour of the wall itself.

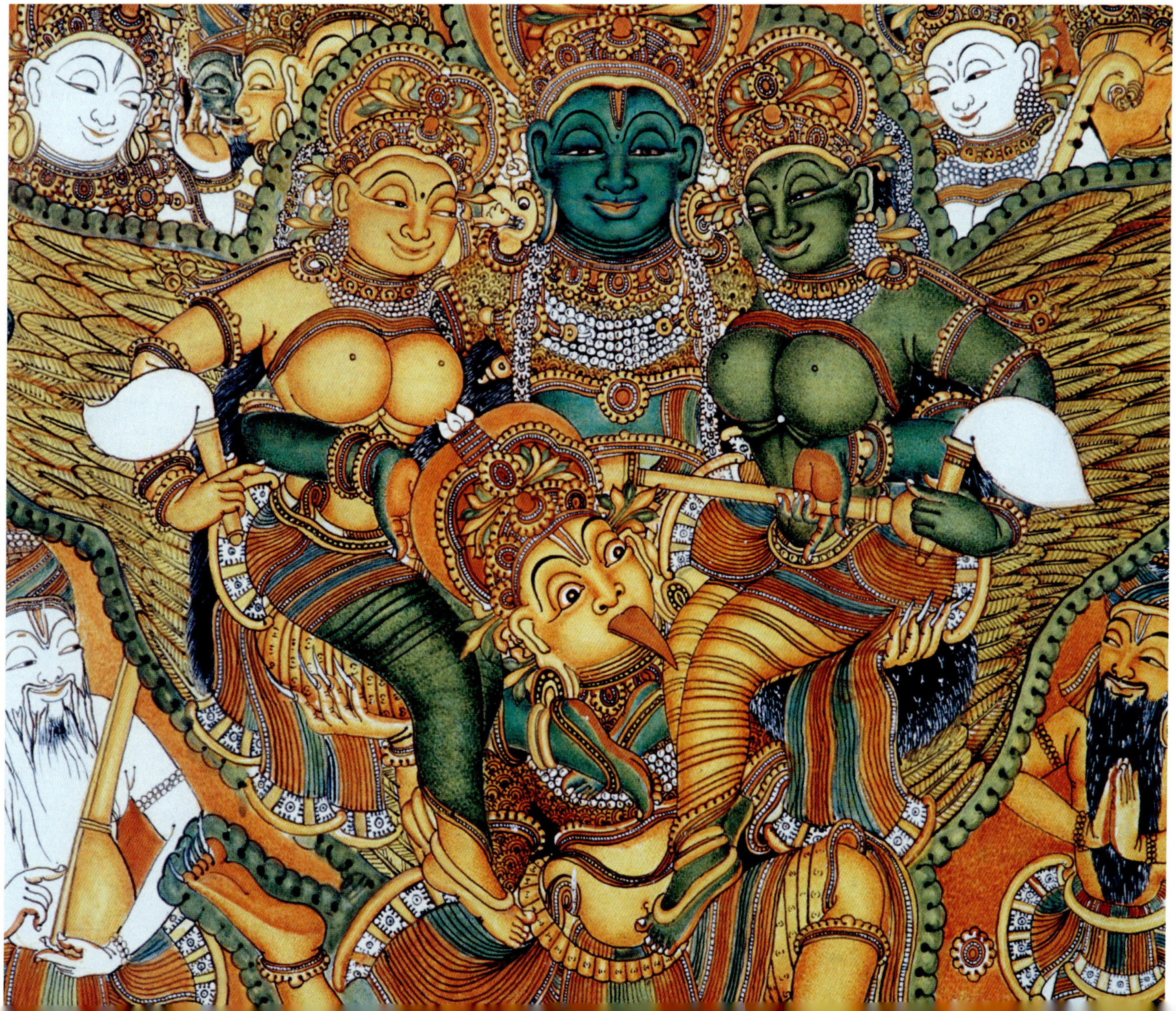

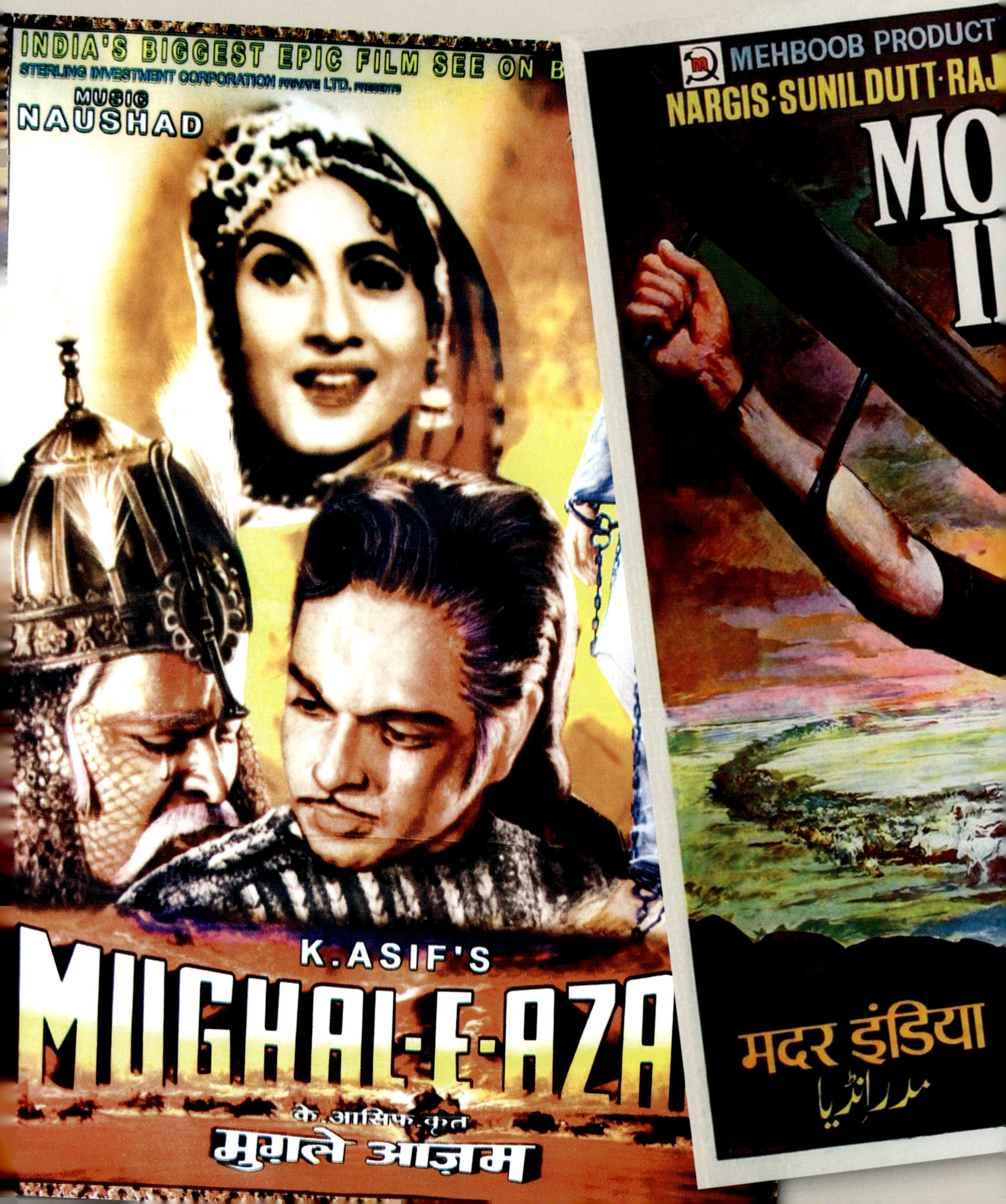
INDIA'S BIGGEST EPIC FILM SEE ON B
STERLING INVESTMENT CORPORATION PRIVATE LTD. PRESENTS
MUSIC
NAUSHAD
K.ASIF'S
MUGHAL-E-AZA
के.आसिफ कृत
मुग़ले आज़म
MEHBOOB PRODUCT
NARGIS·SUNIL DUTT·RAJ
MO
I
मदर इंडिया
مدر انڈیا

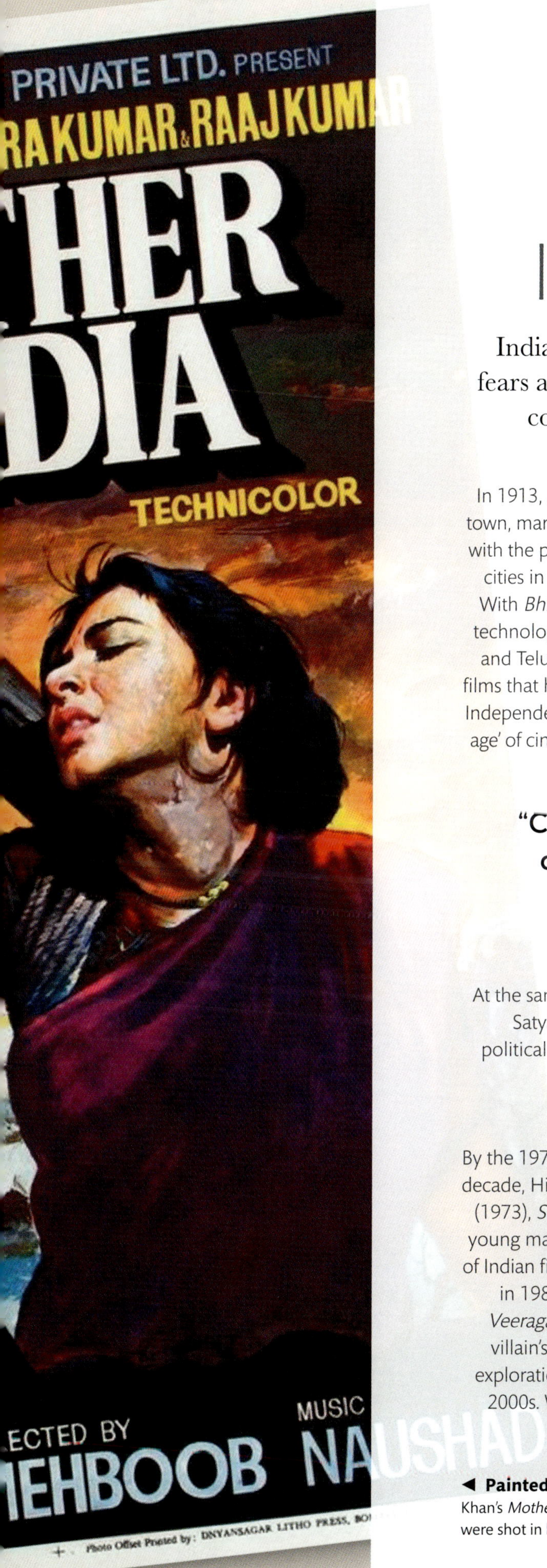

20th century onwards

INDIAN CINEMA

Indian cinema is an incredible medium for expressing the fears and passions of the nation. The songs, stars, and stories come together to produce a unique film experience.

In 1913, *Raja Harishchandra*, a silent film, was screened in Bombay, a western port town, marking the birth of the Indian film industry. The next few decades were replete with the production of silent films not just from Mumbai, as it is now known, but also cities in the south. The first film from Madras or Chennai was *Keechaka Vadham*. With *Bhishma Pratighna* in 1921, Telugu films joined the fray. The advent of audio technology led to the first sound films in 1931: *Alam Ara* (Hindi) and *Kalidas* (Tamil and Telugu). Over the next few decades, studios such as Bombay Talkies made hit films that highlighted social issues, such as *Achhut Kannya* (1936). This continued after Independence, as films helped forge a new national identity. This was called the 'golden age' of cinema, and saw actors such as M.G. Ramachandran, Sathyan, Prem Nazir, Raj Kapoor, Dilip Kumar, Nargis, and Madhubala become 'stars'.

"Cinema's characteristic forte is its ability to capture and communicate the intimacies of the human mind."

– Satyajit Ray, prolific 20th-century Indian filmmaker

At the same time, in West Bengal, a 'parallel cinema' movement began with director Satyajit Ray's 1955 film *Pather Panchali*. These films referenced the socio-political climate of the times, as exemplified by K.A. Abbas's *Dharti Ke Lal* (1946), which was based on the Bengal famine of 1943.

A PERSEVERING MEDIUM TO TELL STORIES

By the 1970s, India had overtaken USA as the world's biggest film producer, and in this decade, Hindi cinema was defined by vivid colours and glamour. Films such as *Zanjeer* (1973), *Sholay* (1975), and *Deewar* (1975) ushered in a new protagonist, the 'angry young man', portrayed by Amitabh Bachchan, one the most widely recognized icons of Indian film. Rajinikanth's *Padayappa* was the first Tamil film to be released worldwide in 1989, to great success. Another pioneering production was *Oru Vadakkan Veeragatha* (1989), which inverted Malayalam folklore to tell the story from the villain's point of view. Each decade brought with it new themes, whether it is an exploration of familial relationships in the 1990s, or the experimental cinema of the 2000s. What they all have in common is that no one remains untouched by the magic of Indian films.

◀ **Painted posters of two Hindi-language films,** Mehboob Khan's *Mother India* (1957), and K. Asif's *Mughal-e-Azam* (1960). Both were shot in black-and-white and later colourized.

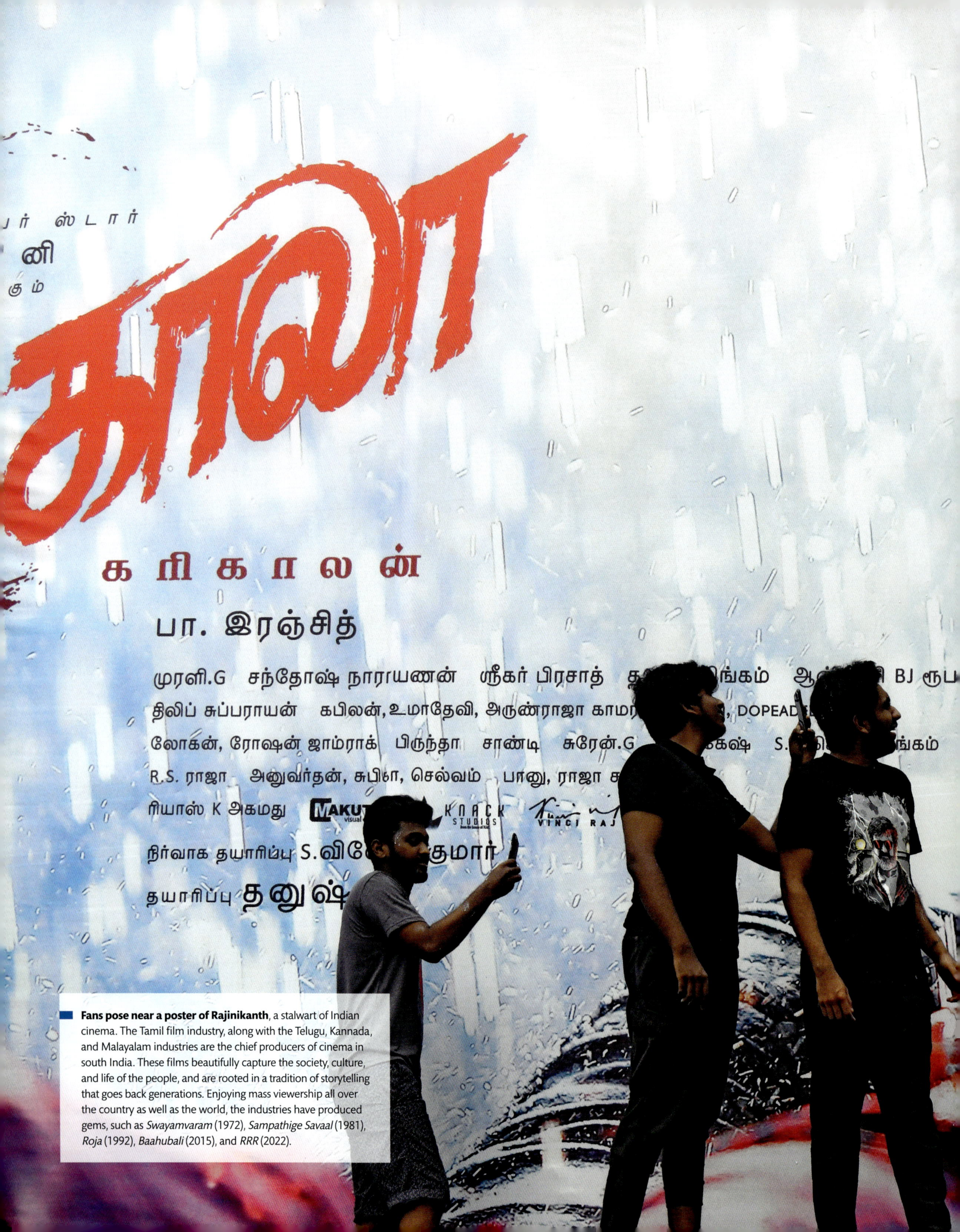

Fans pose near a poster of Rajinikanth, a stalwart of Indian cinema. The Tamil film industry, along with the Telugu, Kannada, and Malayalam industries are the chief producers of cinema in south India. These films beautifully capture the society, culture, and life of the people, and are rooted in a tradition of storytelling that goes back generations. Enjoying mass viewership all over the country as well as the world, the industries have produced gems, such as *Swayamvaram* (1972), *Sampathige Savaal* (1981), *Roja* (1992), *Baahubali* (2015), and *RRR* (2022).

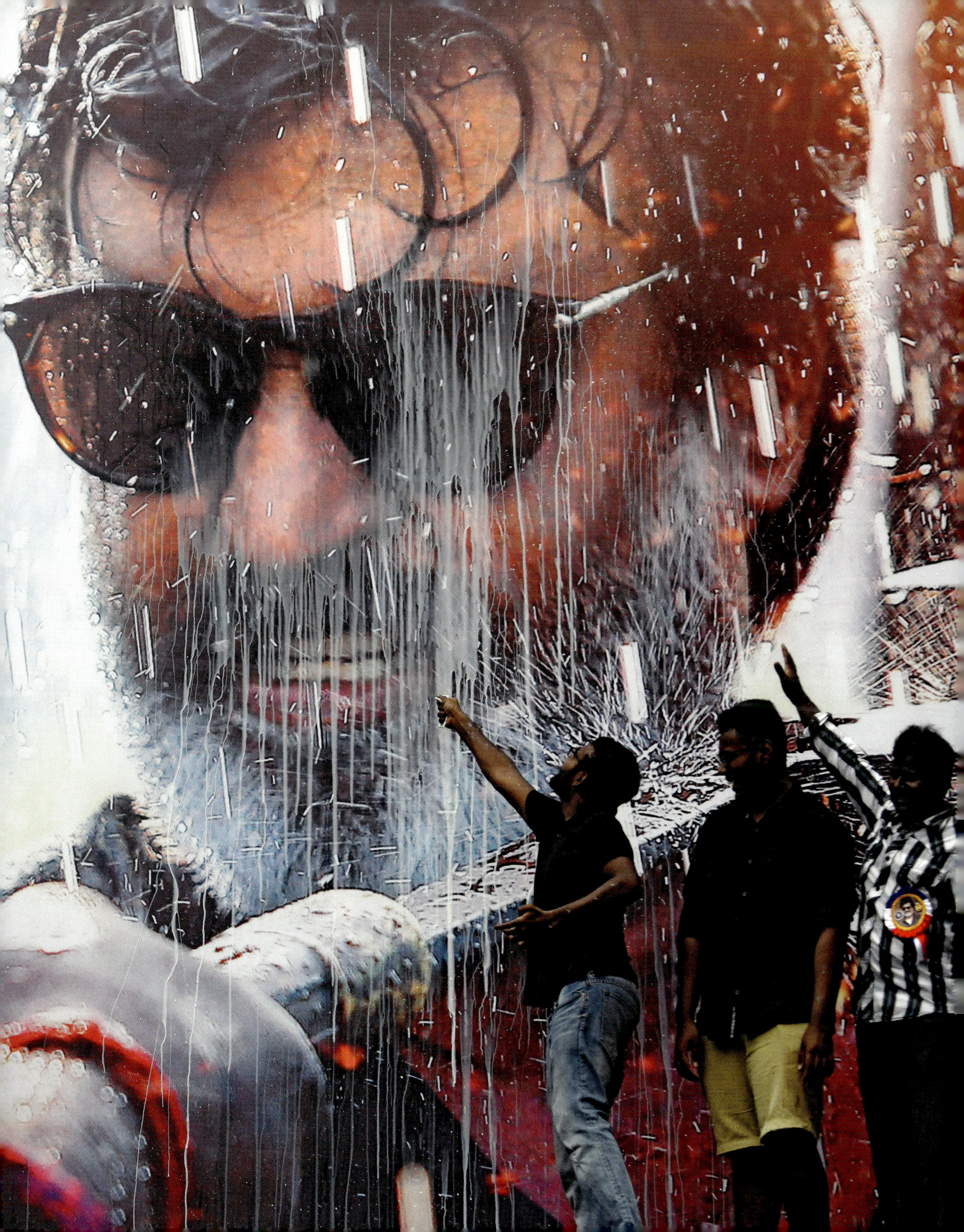

GLOSSARY

APSARA In Hinduism, water nymphs are young women of great grace and beauty who reside in heaven, in the court of the king of gods, Indra. They are excellent dancers and are often the companions of celestial musicians.

AQUEDUCT Bridge built on arches with stone channels to supply water. Aqueducts source water from distant water bodies and carry it across difficult landscapes.

BCE Before the Common Era. The years before 1 CE. This abbreviation has largely replaced BC (Before Christ).

BODHISATTVAS Highly enlightened Mahayana Buddhist beings who delay *nirvana* so that they can devote themselves to the service of others. Bodhisattvas can be both female and male.

BRITISH COLONIZATION The Indian subcontinent was under rule of the East India Company from around 1757, after the Battle of Plassey, until 1857, when the Sepoy Mutiny took place. Thereafter, the British Crown took over the region's rule, which lasted until 1947. The region administered by the British was collectively known as British India, and it included kingdoms governed by local rulers under British paramountcy.

CASTE SYSTEM The traditional Hindu system of grouping people as "higher" or "lower" in the social order as per the nature of their work. This includes Brahmins (priests), Kshatriyas (warriors), Vaishyas (merchants), and Shudras (peasants).

CE Common Era. The years from 1 CE to the present day. The abbreviation has largely replaced AD (Anno Domini, which is Latin for "in the year of the Lord").

CONTRAPPOSTO A curving, asymmetrical representation of the human figure in modes of art, where the shoulders, hips, and legs are arranged in different planes.

COROMANDEL COAST South-eastern coastal region of the Indian subcontinent, bound by the Utkal Plains to the north, the Bay of Bengal to the east, the Kaveri delta to the south, and the Eastern Ghats to the west.

DALIT Derived from the Hindi term "dalan", meaning oppressed. It refers to someone outside of the caste system. Legally the term is used for members of Scheduled Castes as defined by the Constitution of India.

DASHAVATAR The 10 primary avatars of Vishnu, a principal Hindu god. He is believed to descend to earth, in moments of great need, in the form of an avatar to restore cosmic order.

DECCAN Derived from the Sanskrit word "daksina", which means south. Refers to the southern Indian peninsula, south of the River Narmada.

DHARMA Hindu scriptures describe dharma as a way of life that follows the path of righteousness. The objective of dharma is the attainment of *moksha* or ultimate liberation.

DIGAMBARAS One of the two major schools of Jainism. A Sanskrit term, it translates to sky-clad, which refers to the monks' practice of staying in the nude. They differ from the other sect in their understanding of Jain scriptures and the tirthankara Mahavira's life.

DRAVIDIAN People residing in South Asia, specifically in the southern part of the Indian subcontinent. They are the indigenous population of the land, and speak the Dravidian languages, Tamil, Kannada, Telugu, and Tulu.

GANGA As a goddess, Ganga is the personification of the sacred river, which is said to have descended from the abode of Brahma the creator. To break the impact of the water, Shiva trapped it in his hair, mitigating its flow down the Himalayas as small streams. As a tangible aspect of cosmic energy, bringing life, the Ganga is both pure and purifying.

GURU A spiritual guide, who reveals the meanings and potential of life, and shows the path to self-realization. It is also used for a learned teacher or expert in a particular field of knowledge. In Sikhism, it is used for Guru Nanak and his successors.

GURU DAKSHINA The traditional transaction that ended the period of learning with a guru. It was a donation made to the guru, which was regarded as a symbolic payment for knowledge imparted. Usually a gift of land or cows, it could also be in the form of a task performed for the guru.

GURUKUL Traditional system of schooling where students lived in proximity to the guru to learn from and help in chores and upkeep of the residence. Traditionally, students would go and live with the guru for the period of education, to both learn and perform service. This interaction facilitated an understanding of both the spirit and substance of the knowledge being imparted.

HINDU TRINITY OF GODS Also called the *Trimurti*, this refers to the three forms of divinity in Hinduism, where three cosmic functions are personified. These are Brahma the creator, Vishnu the preserver, and Shiva the destroyer.

INDIAN SUBCONTINENT Historical and physiographic region in South Asia, consisting of the countries of India, Pakistan, Bangladesh,

Nepal, and Bhutan. Before Independence in 1947, India was made up of many kingdoms, which acceded to the union as its states, or formed separate countries.

INDIAN UNION OF STATES India is a union of states, with the President as its constitutional head. There are 28 states and 8 union territories in the country. In the states, the Governor, as the representative of the President, is the head. Union Territories are administered by the President through an Administrator. Unlike a state, a union territory is partly ruled by the Central government.

INDUSTRIAL REVOLUTION In the 18th and 19th centuries, in Britain, followed by other western countries, the change in social and economic organization resulting from the replacement of hand tools by machine and power tools and the development of large-scale industrial production.

JIZYA A tax imposed on non-Muslims to ensure freedom to practise their own religion in a Muslim state.

KARMA In Hinduism and Buddhism, karma is the belief that a person's life and belongings are the effects of the actions of their past lives.

MUDRAS Symbolic hand gestures made by deities. Derived from the Sanskrit word, *mud* that means joy and *ra* that means produce. As a result, mudras mean gestures that produce joy and happiness. Many of the goddesses in their iconography are seen showing these. The most popular ones are the boon-giving and the fear-not *mudras*.

MYA Million Years Ago. In scientific terms, this abbreviation is commonly used to show the length of time before the present.

MYSTIC MOVEMENTS The Bhakti movement in Hinduism sought to bring religious reforms to all strata of society through the method of devotion to achieve salvation, while Sufism in Islam is a mystic practice characterized by a focus on Islamic spirituality, ritualism, asceticism and esotericism.

NAWAB A title given to Muslim princes or large landowners. For example, the Nawab of Arcot, a town in present-day Tamil Nadu.

NIZAM A title given to the ruler of Hyderabad from 1724 to 1948

PREHISTORY The time before the development of civilizations and before the invention of writing.

PRINCELY STATES Territories ruled by princes during the British rule in India.

PURANAS Sanskrit literature describing Hindu legends, gods, and saints in an encyclopedic manner.

SATYAGRAHA A Hindi term, meaning force of truth. Gandhi adopted the term to refer to a form of peaceful civil disobedience that relies upon moral force to fight against injustice.

SHAKTI In Hinduism, Shakti is the divine power or energy worshipped in the form of the female consort of Shiva, or another god.

SUTRAS Ancient and medieval texts from Hinduism and Buddhism. The sutras preserve important teachings of their respective faiths and guide a follower who is adherent on the path devoid of ignorance and entrapment in the endless cycle of rebirth and death towards spiritual liberation.

SHVETAMBARAS One of the two major schools in Jainism. A Sanskrit term, it means clad in white. It refers to the practice of the monks wearing white clothes, setting them apart from the Digambaras. They differ from the other sect in their understanding of Jain scriptures and the tirthankara Mahavira's life.

TIRTHANKARA A spiritual teacher in Jainism. Twenty-four tirthankaras are revered as founders of Jainism.

UPANISHADS Sanskrit texts that outline the fundamental beliefs of Vedic religion.

VEDAS The oldest Hindu scriptures, they are four in number. The *Rigveda* and the *Samaveda* are a collection of hymns, the *Yajurveda* contains instructions for rituals and the *Atharvaveda* is replete with spells.

WESTERN GHATS A mountain range that stretches from the west coast of the Indian peninsula across Tamil Nadu, Kerala, Karnataka, Goa, and Gujarat.

YA Years Ago. In scientific terms, this abbreviation is commonly combined with prefixes for thousand, million, or billion, to show the length of time before the present.

YAKSHAS/YAKSHIS
Power and benevolent forest-spirits, who are believed to be the guardians of treasures and are very fond of riddles. They are often seen paired together in a lot of Jain iconography in temples.

YOGINIS
Incarnations of the goddess Parvati, and practitioners of yoga. They are worshipped in Yogini temples across the Indian subcontinent.

INDEX

F

G

H

I

J

K

SELECTED BIBLIOGRAPHY

BOOKS

Apte, *D.G. Universities in Ancient India*. Life Span Publishers and Distributors, 2015.

Bandyopadhyaya Sekhara. *From Plassey to Partition and after: A History of Modern India*. Orient BlackSwan Private Limited, 2017.

Banerjee-Dube, Ishita. *A History of Modern India*. Cambridge University Press, 2015.

Basham, A.L. *The Wonder That Was India: Vol. I A Survey of the History and Culture of the Indian Sub-Continent before the Coming of the Muslims*. Picador, 2004.

Blurton, T. Richard. *Hindu Art*. British Museum Press, 2007.

Chandra, Bipan; Mukherjee, Aditya; and Mukherjee, Mridula. *India since Independence*. Penguin Random House India, 2017.

Chandra, S. *History of Medieval India: 800-1700*. Orient BlackSwan, 2020.

Chitgopekar, Nilima. *Shakti: An Exploration of the Divine*. DK Publishing India, 2022.

Cohn, Bernard S. *Colonialism and Its Forms of Knowledge the British in India*. Princeton University Press, 2006.

Craven, R.C. *A Concise History of Indian Art*. Thames and Hudson, 1976.

Dalal, Roshen. *The Puffin History of India*. Vol I & II. Puffin Books, 2014.

Devji, Faisal. *The Impossible Indian Gandhi and the Temptation of Violence*. Harvard University Press, 2012.

Dhar, Parul Pandya. *Indian Art History: Changing Perspectives*. D.K. Printworld and National Museum Institute, 2011.

Findly, Ellison Banks. *Nur Jahan, Empress of Mughal India*. Oxford University Press, 1993.

Fisher, Michael Herbert. *A Short History of the Mughal Empire*. Bloomsbury Academic, 2020.

Great Monuments of India. DK Publishing, 2009.

Guha, Ramachandra. *India after Gandhi: The History of the World's Largest Democracy*. Picador, 2023.

Guha-Thakurta, Tapati. *Monuments, Objects, Histories: Institutions of Art in Colonial and Postcolonial India*. Columbia University Press, 2004.

Garodia Gupta, Archana and Garodia, Shruti. *The History of India for Children*. Vol I & II. Hachette India, 2018.

Harle, J. C. *The Art and Architecture of the Indian Subcontinent*. Yale University Press, 1994.

Howland, Douglas; Lillehoj, Elizabeth; and Mayer, Maximilian. *Art and Sovereignty in Global Politics*. Palgrave Macmillan US, 2018.

Kaegi, Adolf and Arrowsmith, Robert. *The Rigveda: The Oldest Literature of the Indians*. Ginn & Co, 1886.

Keay, John. *India Discovered: The Recovery of a Lost Civilization*. HarperCollins, 2001.

Keay, John. *India: A History*. William Collins, 2002.

Kenoyer, Jonathan M.; Frenez, Dennys; Jamison, Gregg M.; Law, Randall William; Vidale, Massimo; and Meadow, Richard H. *Walking with the Unicorn: Social Organization and Material Culture in Ancient South Asia*. Archaeopress Publishing Ltd, 2018.

Ketakara, Sandhya, and Rao, Anil M. *The History of Indian Art*. Jyotsna Prakashan, 2016.

Kosambi, Damodar Dharmanand. *An Introduction to the Study of Indian History*. Sage Publications India Private Limited, 2016.

Kosambi Damodar Dharmanand. *The Culture and Civilisation of Ancient India in Historical Outline*. Routledge and Kegan Paul, 1965.

Kumar, Sunil. *The Emergence of the Delhi Sultanate, 1192–1286*. Permanent Black, 2017.

Kunz, George Frederick and Charles Hugh Stevenson. *The Book of the Pearl*. The Century Co., 1908.

Martin, Lerner and Johnson, Peter. *The Flame and the Lotus: Indian and Southeast Asian Art from the Kronos Collections*. Metropolitan Museum of Art, 1984.

Mirza, Mohammad Wahid. *The Life and Works of Amir Khusrau*. Idarah-i Adabiyat-i Delli, 1935.

Murphy, Chuck. *A Concise History of Indian Art*. Thames & Hudson, 1976.

Bala Krishnan, Usha R. and Ramamrutham, Bharath. *Jewels of the Nizams*. Government of India & India Book House Mumbai, 2001.

Rowland, Benjamin Jr. *Gandhara Sculpture from Pakistan Museums*. The Asia Society, 1960.

Sanyal, Sanjeev. *Revolutionaries: The Other Story of How India Won Its Freedom*. HarperCollins India, 2023.

Sharma, Ram Sharan. *India's Ancient Past*. Oxford University Press, 2008.

Singh, Upinder. *A History of Ancient and Early Medieval India: From the Stone Age to the 12th Century*. Pearson India, 2019.

Stein, Burton and Arnold, David. *A History of India*. Wiley-Blackwell, 2010.

Thapar, Romila. *The Penguin History of Early India: From the Origins to AD 1300*. Penguin Books India, 2003.

Tharoor, Shashi. *An Era of Darkness: The British Empire in India*. Aleph, 2016.

Timelines from Indian History. DK Publishing India, 2021.

Titley, Norah M. *The Ni'matnama Manuscript of the Sultans of Mandu: The Sultan's Book of Delights*. Taylor & Francis Ltd., 2012.

Welch, Stuart Cary. *India, Art and Culture 1300-1900*. The Metropolitan Museum of Art, 1985

WEBSITES, PERIODICALS, AND JOURNALS

Academy, MAP. EIA editors. https://mapacademy.io.

Anderson, Dr. Jocelyn. "Tipu's Tiger." Smarthistory, 2023. https://smarthistory.org/tipus-tiger.

Anglo Sikh Wars. https://www.anglosikhwars.com.

Basu, Chandreyi. "The heavily ornamented female figure from Pompeii." in Il Fascino Dell'Oriente Nelle Collezioni E Nei Musei D'Italia, edited by Beatrice Palma Venetucci, pp.59–63. 2010.

"The Boy Jesus as the Good Shepherd in Carved Ivory." Michael Backman Ltd, May 2018. https://www.michaelbackmanltd.com/object/the-boy-jesus-as-the-good-shepherd-in-carved-ivory.

"Charting the Ethical Landscape: Tagore's Vision of Nation in 'Where the Mind Is without Fear'." The Wire. https://thewire.in/culture/rabindranath-tagore-nation-gitanjali.

Dehejia, Vidya. "The Treatment of Narrative in Jagat Singh's 'Ramayana': A Preliminary Study." Artibus Asiae 56, no. 3/4, 303. 1996. https://doi.org/10.2307/3250121.

"Digitally Reunifying the Mewar Ramayana Manuscript". https://www.bl.uk/onlinegallery/whatson/exhibitions/ramayana/pdf/mewar_ramayana_project.pdf.

Dokras, Dr. Uday. "Past and Present of the Ancient University of Nalanda." INAC, January 2022. https://www.academia.edu/77326073/Past_and_Present_of_the_Ancient_University_of_Nalanda.

Encyclopædia Britannica. http://www.britannica.com

"Gandhara, the Ancient Kingdom That Gave World Its First Buddha Sculptures." ThePrint, November 2022. https://theprint.in/pageturner/excerpt/gandhara-the-ancient-kingdom-that-gave-world-its-first-buddha-sculptures/1226137.

"Hampi: Return to a Forgotten Empire." Open The Magazine, May 2017. https://openthemagazine.com/essay/hampi-return-to-a-forgotten-empire.

"Illuminating India: Starring the Oldest Recorded Origins of 'Zero', the Bakhshali Manuscript." Science Museum Blog, September 2017. https://blog.sciencemuseum.org.uk/illuminating-india-starring-oldest-recorded-origins-zero-bakhshali-manuscript.

"India - Throne and Footstool." Royal Collection Trust. https://www.rct.uk/collection/1561/throne-and-footstool.

"Indian Culture." http://www.indianculture.gov.in.

Indian Heritage. http://www.indian-heritage.org.

"Indian Textiles." The Burlington Magazine. https://www.burlington.org.uk/archive/exhibition-review/indian-textiles.

"Jantar Mantar: Architecture, Astronomy, and Solar Kingship in Princely India." Cornell Journal of Architecture. https://cornelljournalofarchitecture.cornell.edu/article/jantar-mantar-architecture-astronomy-and-solar-kingship-in-princely-india/.

Kumari, Krittika. "The Photographic Journey of India." February 2023. https://map-india.org/the-photographic-journey-of-india.

Lamba, Bikram. "Martand Temple in Kashmir: Its Grandeur Survives, and so Do Its Controversies." WordPress, September 2022. https://www.academia.edu/86414577/Martand_Temple_in_Kashmir_Its_grandeur_survives_and_so_do_its_controversies.

"Last Breath for India's Steamers." Los Angeles Times. July 1994. https://www.latimes.com/archives/la-xpm-1994-07-21-mn-18324-story.html.

MANAS. http://www.southasia.ucla.edu.

Mantena, Karuna. "Another Realism: The Politics of Gandhian Nonviolence." American Political Science Review 106, no. 2 (2012): 455–70. https://doi.org/10.1017/s000305541200010x.

Metropolitan Museum of Art, The. https://www.metmuseum.org.

Mishra, Tanvi. "Contemporary Indian Photography: A Long Read on Indian Photography." https://dutchculture.nl/sites/default/files/atoms/files/DutchCulture_Long%20Read_Spreads.pdf.

Mishra, Patit Paban. "Royal Women in the Mughal Empire." World History Encyclopedia. October 2022. https://www.worldhistory.org/article/2098/royal-women-in-the-mughal-empire.

Mohd, Shaib. "Tracing the History, Heritage and Scenic Beauties of Martand and Chatbal Destinations in Twin Parganas of Mattan And Kuthar." International Journal of Scientific and Research Publications Volume 7, no. Issue 7. 2017.

Museum, Victoria and Albert. "Kalpasutra: Unknown". https://collections.vam.ac.uk/item/O140370/kalpasutra-manuscript-page-unknown.

Museum, Victoria and Albert. "The Mount of the Good Shepherd." https://collections.vam.ac.uk/item/O151876/the-mount-of-the-good-group-unknown.

"Nalanda University: An Ancient Indian Ivy-League Institution." TheCollector, November 2021. https://www.thecollector.com/nalanda-university-history.

New World Encyclopedia. http://www.newworldencyclopedia.org.

"On Display Here, Wanted by India." The Independent Digital News and Media, May 2010. https://www.independent.co.uk/news/uk/home-news/on-display-here-wanted-by-india-1988002.html#gallery.

"The 'Padshahnama' ('Book of Emperors') of Abd Al-Hamid Lahori." Royal Collection Trust. https://www.rct.uk/collection/themes/exhibitions/splendours-of-the-subcontinent-four-centuries-of-south-asian-paintings/the-padshahnama-book-of-emperors-of-abd-al-hamid-lahori.

Raj, Ankita; Johari, Ayushi; Phukan, Paran; and Menon, Rakhi. "Chronicles Of Bidri", https://issuu.com/ankita_raj/docs/final_doc.

Ramanan, R. (2007). A Sacred Grove. India International Centre Quarterly, 34 (3/4), pp.274–279. http://www.jstor.org/stable/23006347.

Rcarney. Architecture of Cities, October 2022. http://www.architectureofcities.com.

"The Romance of Steam." IRFCA, Indian Steam Railway Society Article. https://www.irfca.org/articles/isrs/isrs2-romance.html.

Saha, Poulomi. "Singing Bengal into a Nation: Tagore the Colonial Cosmopolitan: Semantic Scholar." Journal of Modern Literature, January 1970. https://doi.org/10.2979/jmodelite.36.2.1.

San Diego Museum of Art. https://collection.sdmart.org

"Scents and Sensuality." The Economist Newspaper. https://www.economist.com/1843/2017/01/04/scents-and-sensuality.

Sengupta, Arputharani. "Tantric Gudimallam Shiva Linga and Vayu Linga," https://www.academia.edu/es/73180494/Tantric_Gudimallam_Shiva_Linga_and_Vayu_Linga.

Sharma, Kamayani. "The History of the Mysterious Lajja Gauri Found around India." Scroll.in. July 2022. https://scroll.in/magazine/1028346/the-history-of-the-mysterious-lajja-gauri-found-around-india.

Sharma, Pandit Vishnu. "Wisdom of the Ages." Tales of Panchatantra. http://www.talesofpanchatantra.com.

Smithsonian Magazine. http://www.smithsonianmag.com.

UNESCO World Heritage Centre. https://whc.unesco.org.

Victoria and Albert Museum. http://www.vam.ac.uk.

World History Encyclopedia. http://www.worldhistory.org.

ACKNOWLEDGMENTS

PUBLISHER'S NOTE:
Treasures of India attempts to tell an inclusive story of India, from prehistoric to contemporary times. The publisher is cognizant that the structure of the book poses certain limitations that have influenced the selection of objects and themes. This book does not aim to be a comprehensive cultural history of India, given the country's incredible breadth and diversity. However, the team behind the book has tried to represent the cultural heritage of its peoples through an objective lens, without bias, in any form, as far as possible. This book uses the contemporary names of cities and countries, such as India, Pakistan, and Afghanistan, to indicate regions within the Indian subcontinent in the contemporary context.

Every effort has been made to acknowledge the individuals, organizations, and companies that have helped with this book and to trace copyright holders. DK apologizes in advance for any inadvertent omissions of acknowledgment. In such a case, DK will be pleased to add the appropriate acknowledgment in subsequent editions of the book.

The publisher would like to thank the following for their assistance in the preparation of this book:

Ranjana Sengupta for her invaluable support and guidance as the consultant while we conceptualized and executed the book; **Arushi Mathur** and **Madhavi Singh** for researching and writing the book; **Ankita Vinayak** for researching and writing the introductions on 10–13, 34–37, 54–57, 92–97, 160–163, 196–201, 234–237, and 260–263; **Glenda Fernandes**, **Suchismita Banerjee**, and **Maitreyi Pandey** for editorial support; and **Suchismita Ukil** for proofreading.

Parts of the contents on pages 24–25 were previously published in *Shakti: An Exploration of the Divine Feminine*, DK, 2021.

The publisher would like to thank the following for their kind permission to reproduce their photographs:

(Key: a-above; b-below/bottom; c-centre; f-far; l-left; r-right; t-top)

1 The Metropolitan Museum of Art: Rogers Fund, 2004 (cb). **2-3 © Photo courtesy Sothebys, 2023:** Sothebys London, 27 October 2021, lot 213. **4-5 Los Angeles County Museum of Art:** Nasli and Alice Heeramaneck Collection. **6 The Metropolitan Museum of Art:** Gift of R. H. Ellsworth Ltd., in honor of Susan Dillon, 1987 (tl); Purchase, Florence and Herbert Irving Gift, 1997 (tc); Gift of Florence and Herbert Irving, 2015 (tr). **7 Los Angeles County Museum of Art:** Gift of Mr. and Mrs. Julian Ganz, Jr. (tc). **The Metropolitan Museum of Art:** Purchase, Mrs. Charles Wrightsman Gift, 1993 (tr); Rogers Fund, 2004 (tl). **10 Alamy Stock Photo:** Artokoloro (br); World History Archive (bl). **11 Alamy Stock Photo:** Rob Francis (bl). **Dreamstime.com**: Suronin (br). **12 The Metropolitan Museum of Art:** Gift of Jonathan and Jeannette Rosen, 2015 (bl). **National Museum, New Delhi:** (br). **13 Alamy Stock Photo:** IndiaPicture / V. Muthuraman (br). **The Metropolitan Museum of Art:** Samuel Eilenberg Collection, Bequest of Samuel Eilenberg, 1998 (bl). **14 Dreamstime.com:** Sheetal Saini (tc). **15 Dreamstime.com:** Sheetal Saini. **16-17 Getty Images:** Yawar Nazir. **18 The Cleveland Museum Of Art:** Purchase from the J. H. Wade Fund (tl, cr). **19 National Museum, New Delhi:** (bc). **20 Alamy Stock Photo:** Angelo Hornak (tc). **21 Alamy Stock Photo:** Angelo Hornak. **22-23 Getty Images:** Angelo Hornak / Corbis. **26 Getty Images:** Dea Picture Library. **28-29 Los Angeles County Museum of Art:** Nasli and Alice Heeramaneck Collection. **31 The Metropolitan Museum of Art:** Samuel Eilenberg Collection, Bequest of Samuel Eilenberg, 1998. **32-33 Alamy Stock Photo:** Hemis. **34 Alamy Stock Photo:** ephotocorp / Asad Shaikh (bl); The History Collection (br). **35 Alamy Stock Photo:** Dinodia Photos RM (br); Robert Kawka (bl). **36 123RF.com:** lakshmiprasad Sindhnur (bl). **Alamy Stock Photo:** Dinodia Photos RM (br). **37 Dreamstime.com:** Efaah0 (br); Thamizhazhagan Nallaiyan (bl). **38-39 The Cleveland Museum Of Art:** Gift of Sri B. D. Dwivedi. **39 The Cleveland Museum Of Art:** Gift of Sri B. D. Dwivedi (tc). **40-41 Getty Images:** Holger Leue / The Image Bank Unreleased. **42-43 Getty Images:** Insights / Universal Images Group. **44-45 The Cleveland Museum Of Art:** Gift of Dr. Norman Zaworski. **46 Dreamstime.com:** Fabio Lamanna (br). **46-47 Dreamstime.com:** Saiko3p (t). **48-49 Alamy Stock Photo:** Dinodia Photos (c). **48 Alamy Stock Photo:** Dinodia Photos (tc). **50 Getty Images:** DEA / G. Nimatallah / De Agostini. **51 Getty Images:** DEA / G. Nimatallah / De Agostini (tc). **52 © The Trustees of the British Museum. All rights reserved. 53 © The Trustees of the British Museum. All rights reserved:** (tl). **54 The Cleveland Museum Of Art:** Gift of Mr. and Mrs. Severance A. Millikin (bl). **The Metropolitan Museum of Art:** Purchase, Friends of Asian Art Gifts, 2002 (br). **55 Alamy Stock Photo:** Classic Image (br); The History Collection (bl). **56 The Metropolitan Museum of Art:** Gift of Evelyn Kossak, The Kronos Collections, 1986 (bl); Gift of Christian Humann, 1977 (br). **57 Alamy Stock Photo:** Dinodia Photos RM (br). **The Metropolitan Museum of Art:** Purchase, Florence and Herbert Irving Gift, 1991 (bl). **58-59 The Metropolitan Museum of Art:** Gift of Jeffrey B. Soref, in honor of Martin Lerner, 1988 (All 4 Views). **60-61 Alamy Stock Photo:** Heritage Image Partnership Ltd (c). **60 Alamy Stock Photo:** Heritage Image Partnership Ltd (tc). **62-63 The Metropolitan Museum of Art:** Gift of John and Evelyn Kossak, The Kronos Collections, 1981. **62 The Metropolitan Museum of Art:** Gift of John and Evelyn Kossak, The Kronos Collections, 1981 (tc). **64 The Cleveland Museum Of Art:** Gift of Morris and Eleanor Everett in memory of Flora Morris Everett 1972.43 (tc). **65 The Cleveland Museum Of Art:** Gift of Morris and Eleanor Everett in memory of Flora Morris Everett 1972.43. **66 Alamy Stock Photo:** agefotostock (l, tc). **67 Getty Images:** DEA / A. De Gregorio (r). **68 Birmingham Museums Trust licensed under CC0. 69 Birmingham Museums Trust licensed under CC0:** (tc). **70 Alamy Stock Photo:** Dinendra Haria. **72-73 Getty Images:** Abhisek Saha /

SOPA Images / LightRocket. **74-75 Alamy Stock Photo:** Zoonar GmbH. **74 Alamy Stock Photo:** Zoonar GmbH (tc). **76 Alamy Stock Photo:** Jon Arnold Images Ltd. **77 Alamy Stock Photo:** Jon Arnold Images Ltd (tl). **78 Getty Images / iStock:** Mongkolchon Akesin. **80 National Crafts Museum & Hastkala Academy.:** Venkat Raman Singh Shyam. **82 Dreamstime.com:** Mukulbanerjee (bl). **82-83 Dreamstime.com:** Mukulbanerjee (c); Yakthai (b); Saiko3p (t). **83 Dreamstime.com:** Anil Dave (bl); Yakthai (tc); Zzvet (tr). **Getty Images:** Corbis / Christophe Boisvieux (br). **85 akg-images:** Roland and Sabrina Michaud. **86-87 Alamy Stock Photo:** agefotostock. **88-89 American Institute of Indian Studies. 89 American Institute of Indian Studies:** (tc). **92 Alamy Stock Photo:** Classic Image (bl). **Dreamstime.com:** Zzvet (br). **93 Alamy Stock Photo:** Karlmarx Rajangam (br). **Getty Images:** Hulton Archive / Culture Club (bl). **94 Alamy Stock Photo:** Classic Image (br). **The Metropolitan Museum of Art:** Purchase, Lita Annenberg Hazen Charitable Trust Gift, in honor of Cynthia Hazen and Leon B. Polsky, 1982 (bl). **95 The Art Institute of Chicago:** Purchased with funds provided by the Joseph and Helen Regenstein Foundation (bl). **Dreamstime.com:** Swapan Banik (br). **96 Alamy Stock Photo:** Classic Image (bl); The Picture Art Collection (br). **97 Alamy Stock Photo:** Wirestock, Inc. (br). **Dreamstime.com:** Byheaven87 (bl). **98-99 Alamy Stock Photo:** Paramvir Singh. **98 Alamy Stock Photo:** Paramvir Singh (tc). **100 Dreamstime.com:** Leonid Andronov (bl); Aliaksandr Mazurkevich (bc). **100-101 Dreamstime.com:** Leonid Andronov (t); Saiko3p (c, b). **101 Dreamstime.com:** Sanga Park (cr); Saiko3p (c); Prashant Vaidya (br). **102 Dreamstime.com:** Aliaksandr Mazurkevich. **103 Dreamstime.com:** Aleksandra Lande (tc). **104-105 123RF.com:** Dmitry Rukhlenko. **106-107 Dreamstime.com:** Naresh Sharma. **108 Alamy Stock Photo:** ephotocorp. **109 Alamy Stock Photo:** ephotocorp (tc). **110 Dreamstime.com:** Praveen Indramohan. **111 Dreamstime.com:** Lalam Mandavkar (tc). **112-113 The Metropolitan Museum of Art:** Gift of R. H. Ellsworth Ltd., in honor of Susan Dillon, 1987. **112 The Metropolitan Museum of Art:** Gift of R. H. Ellsworth Ltd., in honor of Susan Dillon, 1987 (tc). **114-115 Getty Images / iStock:** draco-zlat. **116-117 Alamy Stock Photo:** Dinodia Photos. **118 Getty Images:** ePhotocorp (bl). **118-119 123RF.com:** realityimages (b). **Alamy Stock Photo:** dbtravel (t). **119 Dreamstime.com:** Ajijchan (br); Alisali (tr); Elilarionova (bc). **120-121 V&A Images / Victoria and Albert Museum, London:** Purchased from Mr A. Churchill, 1923.. **122-123 The Metropolitan Museum of Art:** Purchase, Lila Acheson Wallace Gift, 2001 (t). **123 The Metropolitan Museum of Art:** Purchase, Lila Acheson Wallace Gift, 2001 (b). **124 Getty Images:** Amith Nag Photography / Moment. **125 Dreamstime.com:** Kattiya Loukobkul (tc). **126 Getty Images:** Godong / Universal Images Group. **127 Alamy Stock Photo:** B Christopher (br); Historic Images (cr). **Getty Images:** B P S Walia / IndiaPictures / Universal Images Group (tr). **128 Dreamstime.com:** Max5128 (bc). **Shutterstock.com:** Sun_Shine (bl). **128-129 Dreamstime.com:** Konstantin Litvinov (b); Saiko3p (t). **129 Dreamstime.com:** Max5128 (br); Saiko3p (crb). **Getty Images:** Stone / Anders Blomqvist (tr). **130-131 The Metropolitan Museum of Art:** Gift of Florence and Herbert Irving, 2015. **131 The Metropolitan Museum of Art:** Gift of Florence and Herbert Irving, 2015 (tc). **132 Dreamstime.com:** Bgopal (bl). **132-133 Dreamstime.com:** Milosk50 (b); Jeremy Richards (t). **133 Dreamstime.com:** Aapthamithra (tr); Anil Dave (br); Jeremy Richards (bl). **134-135 Alamy Stock Photo:** Dinodia Photos. **136-137 The Metropolitan Museum of Art:** Gift of Alexander Smith Cochran, 1913. **137 The Metropolitan Museum of Art:** Gift of Alexander Smith Cochran, 1913 (tc). **138 Dreamstime.com:** Zoom-zoom (Background). **Getty Images:** Photosindia Collection. **139 Alamy Stock Photo:** Art World (tc). **140 Alamy Stock Photo:** Album / British Library`. **141 Alamy Stock Photo:** Album / British Library`. **142 Dreamstime.com:** Lazar Adrian Catalin (bl). **142-143 Dreamstime.com:** Faper9 (b); Anurag Jha (t). **143 Dreamstime.com:** Leonid Andronov (bc); Kattiya Loukobkul (tr); Beat Germann (cr); Dmitry Rukhlenko (br). **144-145 Wellcome Collection:** The Chandnee Chouk or market place, Delhi. Coloured lithograph by W. Gauci after Thomas Colman Dibdin after Bacon, 1840./https://creativecommons.org/publicdomain/mark/1.0. **146 Dreamstime.com:** Byheaven87 (tc). **147 Getty Images / iStock:** sonatali. **148 The Metropolitan Museum of Art:** Gift of Robert W. and Lockwood De Forest, 1919 (bl); Purchase, Florence and Herbert Irving Gift, 1997 (t); Louis E. and Theresa S. Seley Purchase Fund for Islamic Art and Rogers Fund, 1996 (bc). **149 The Cleveland Museum Of Art:** Severance and Greta Millikin Purchase Fund (bl). **The Metropolitan Museum of Art:** Louis E. and Theresa S. Seley Purchase Fund for Islamic Art and Rogers Fund, 1984 (br). **150-151 Alamy Stock Photo:** imageBROKER. **152-153 The Cleveland Museum Of Art:** Bequest of Mrs. Severance A. Millikin. **154 Alamy Stock Photo:** Album / British Library. **155 Alamy Stock Photo:** Album / British Library (tc). **156 Shutterstock.com:** prudhvichowdary. **157 Dreamstime.com:** Gansham Ramchandani (tc). **158-159 Getty Images / iStock:** R.M. Nunes. **160 Alamy Stock Photo:** Classic Image (br). **The Metropolitan Museum of Art:** Louis V. Bell Fund, 1967 (bl). **161 Alamy Stock Photo:** Historic Images (bl). **Los Angeles County Museum of Art:** Nasli and Alice Heeramaneck Collection, Museum Associates Purchase (br). **162 Alamy Stock Photo:** dbtravel (bl). **Dreamstime.com:** Virender Singh (br). **163 Alamy Stock Photo:** Archivah (bl); history_docu_photo (br). **164-165 Dreamstime.com:** Dmitry Rukhlenko. **166-167 National Museum, New Delhi. 167 Los Angeles County Museum of Art:** Gift of Mr. and Mrs. Julian Ganz, Jr. (cr, cb, br). **168 Alamy Stock Photo:** Universal Art Archive (l). **168-169 Los Angeles County Museum of Art:** From the Nasli and Alice Heeramaneck Collection (c). **169 Los Angeles County Museum of Art:** Purchased with funds provided by The Ahmanson Foundation (r). **170-171 Alamy Stock Photo:** The Picture Art Collection. **172-173 Alamy Stock Photo:** John Rees. **174 The Metropolitan Museum of Art:** Rogers Fund, 1955 (tc). **175 The Metropolitan Museum of Art:** Rogers Fund, 1955. **176 Alamy Stock Photo:** Mark Andrews (l). **The Metropolitan Museum of Art:** Gift of Florence and Herbert Irving, 2015 (cr). **© Photo courtesy Sothebys, 2023:** Sothebys London, 27 October 2021, lot 213 (crb). **177 The Metropolitan Museum of Art:** Bequest of Joseph H. Durkee, 1898 (bl); Gift of Heber R. Bishop, 1902 (tr); Purchase, Mrs. Charles Wrightsman Gift, 1993 (tl); The Sylmaris Collection, Gift of George Coe Graves, 1929 (br). **© Photo courtesy Sothebys, 2023:** Sothebys London, 26 April 2017, lot 191 (tc). **177**

Courtesy of Salar Jung Museum: (crb). **178-179 Alamy Stock Photo:** ephotocorp. **180 Getty Images:** Fine Art Images / Heritage Images. **181 Getty Images:** Fine Art Images / Heritage Images (tc). **182 Dreamstime.com:** Konstantin Litvinov (bc); Leslie Mcginnis (bl). **182-183 Dreamstime.com:** Elenatur (t); Pius Lee (b). **183 Dreamstime.com:** Boonsom (cr, br); Rene Drouyer (tr). **184-185 Dreamstime.com:** Plotnikov. **186-187 Alamy Stock Photo:** Neil McAllister. **188-189 Sarmaya Foundation. 190-191 Courtesy of Salar Jung Museum. 192 Alamy Stock Photo:** Royal Armouries Museum (tc). **193 Alamy Stock Photo:** Royal Armouries Museum. **196 Alamy Stock Photo:** Signal Photos (bl); The Reading Room (br). **197 Alamy Stock Photo:** Album / British Library (br); Dinodia Photos RM (bl). **198 Alamy Stock Photo:** CPA Media Pte Ltd / Pictures From History (bl). **Dreamstime.com:** EPhotocorp (br). **199 Alamy Stock Photo:** Historic Collection (br). **Dreamstime.com:** Aleksandar Todorovic (bl). **200 Los Angeles County Museum of Art:** Gift of Jane Greenough Green in memory of Thomas Pelton Green (br). **Wellcome Collection:** Page 53: Guru Gobind Singh on horseback with his falcon and attendants. Gouache drawing. (bl). **201 Getty Images:** DeAgostini / DEA Picture Library (br); Hulton Archive / Print Collector (bl). **202-203 Alamy Stock Photo:** MovingMaratha. **204 V&A Images / Victoria and Albert Museum, London:** Hafiz Muhammad Multani (maker). **206 Alamy Stock Photo:** Art Directors & TRIP / ArkReligion.com (bl). **206-207 Alamy Stock Photo:** Dinodia Photos RM (b). **Dreamstime.com:** Dmitry Rukhlenko (t). **207 Alamy Stock Photo:** Photosindia.com (tr). **Dreamstime.com:** Singhramana (bc); Westhimal (br). **208 Alamy Stock Photo:** Tom Hanley (ca). **209 Toor Collection. 210 Getty Images:** VCG Wilson / Fine Art / Corbis (bl). **Toor Collection:** (cla, cra). **210-211 Toor Collection:** (b). **211 Bridgeman Images:** Christie's Images (br). **Getty Images:** Marco Secchi (tl). **Toor Collection:** (cra). **212 Dreamstime.com:** Plotnikov. **213 Dreamstime.com:** Meinzahn (tc). **214-215 Shutterstock.com:** Chingtham Thanil Singh. **216-217 V&A Images / Victoria and Albert Museum, London:** Gift of Mrs Estelle Fuller through The Art Fund. **218-219 Alamy Stock Photo:** Dinodia Photos. **220-221 Alamy Stock Photo:** CPA Media Pte Ltd. **222 Bridgeman Images:** British Library (cra); National Army Museum (cla). **Los Angeles County Museum of Art:** Purchased with funds provided by the Southern Asian Art Council, The Summit Foundation, and the South and Southeast Asian Acquisition Fund (clb). **Shutterstock.com:** Bonhams / Bournemouth News (bl, br). **223 Alamy Stock Photo:** CPA Media Pte Ltd / Pictures From History (l). **Bridgeman Images:** Royal Collection Trust / © His Majesty King Charles III, 2023 (br). **225 Getty Images:** Hulton Archive / Stringer. **226 Bridgeman Images:** Christie's Images (bl, cla, cra). **National Museum, New Delhi:** (br). **227 Bridgeman Images:** Christie's Images (l, cra). **228-229 Getty Images:** Dinodia Photo. **230-231 Wellcome Collection:** Kali holding a demon's head./https://creativecommons.org/publicdomain/mark/1.0. **232 Getty Images:** Rubina A. Khan. **234 Getty Images:** Universal History Archive / Universal Images Group (bl, br). **235 Alamy Stock Photo:** Peter Horree (bl); Lakeview Images (br). **236 Alamy Stock Photo:** Art Collection 2 (bl); Historical Images Archive (br). **237 Alamy Stock Photo:** Album / British Library (br). **Getty Images:** Paul Popper / Popperfoto (bl). **238 The Metropolitan Museum of Art:** Rogers Fund, 2004. **239 The Metropolitan Museum of Art:** Rogers Fund, 2004. **240 V&A Images / Victoria and Albert Museum, London:** Given by Dr W.L. Hildburgh in 1949. **241 V&A Images / Victoria and Albert Museum, London:** Given by Dr W.L. Hildburgh in 1949 (tc). **242 Dreamstime.com:** Anil Dave (bl); Dr Ajay Kumar Singh (br). **242-243 Alamy Stock Photo:** dbtravel (b). **Dreamstime.com:** Nataliia Sokolovska (t). **243 Alamy Stock Photo:** Dinodia Photos RM (br). **Dreamstime.com:** Efaah0 (bc); Nike Sh (tr). **244-245 Dreamstime.com:** Aliaksandr Mazurkevich. **246 Alamy Stock Photo:** Ashmolean Museum of Art and Archaeology / Heritage Images (bl). **The Metropolitan Museum of Art:** Louis E. and Theresa S. Seley Purchase Fund for Islamic Art, 2004 (cl). **246-247 Alamy Stock Photo:** Emin Yavuz. **247 The Art Institute of Chicago:** Samuel M. Nickerson Fund (tr). **The Metropolitan Museum of Art:** Cynthia Hazen Polsky and Leon B. Polsky Fund, 2002 (cr); Louis E. and Theresa S. Seley Purchase Fund for Islamic Art and Rogers Fund, 1994 (br). **248-249 Getty Images:** Frederic Stevens. **250 Alamy Stock Photo:** photo-fox. **251 Alamy Stock Photo:** Artokoloro. **252-253 Alamy Stock Photo:** victoria chaikova. **255 Getty Images:** Ramesh Lalwani / Moment. **256 Dreamstime.com:** Biplab Roy Chowdhury (b). **256-257 Getty Images:** Bhaswaran Bhattacharya / IndiaPictures / Universal Images Group (t). **257 Alamy Stock Photo:** Dinodia Photos RM (br). **Dreamstime.com:** Denisvostrikov (bc). **Shutterstock.com:** Scoping Owl (tr). **258-259 Dreamstime.com:** Aliaksandr Mazurkevich. **260 Alamy Stock Photo:** History and Art Collection (bl); Matteo Omied (br). **261 Alamy Stock Photo:** History and Art Collection (bl); Scherl / Sddeutsche Zeitung Photo (br). **262 Alamy Stock Photo:** Dinodia Photos RM (bl); Scherl / Sddeutsche Zeitung Photo (br). **263 Alamy Stock Photo:** UtCon Collection (br). **Getty Images:** Daily Herald Archive / National Science & Media Museum / SSPL (bl). **264 Alamy Stock Photo:** Vidura Luis Barrios (tc). **Bridgeman Images:** Christie's Images (br); Granger (bl). **264-265 Bridgeman Images:** Christie's Images. **265 Bridgeman Images:** Granger (br). **Shutterstock.com:** Granger (cr). **266-267 Alamy Stock Photo:** Niday Picture Library. **269 Alamy Stock Photo:** IanDagnall Computing. **270-271 Alamy Stock Photo:** Travel / Nek Chand Foundation. **272 Alamy Stock Photo:** Keren Su / China Span (l). **The Metropolitan Museum of Art:** Purchase, Fernando Family Trust Gift, in honor of Dr. Quintus and Mrs. Wimala Fernando, 2010 (r). **273 Alamy Stock Photo:** Bottle Brush / Balan Madhavan (bc); Azhar Khan / Stockimo (tr). **The Cleveland Museum Of Art:** Gift of Mr. and Mrs. Walter Upson (tl); Gift of The Textile Art Alliance (cl); Gift of The Textile Arts Club (bl); Purchase from the J. H. Wade Fund (br). **274 Penguin Random House:** Design: Ahlawat Gunjan / Illustration: Shruti Mahajan (tr); Design: Ahlawat Gunjan (tl); Design: Ahlawat Gunjan / Illustration: Harshad Marathe (bl); Cover illustration by Studio Kohl (br). **274-275 Dreamstime.com:** Ezthaiphoto. **276 Bridgeman Images:** British Library (r). **277 Bridgeman Images:** British Library (tl, bl). **278-279 Dreamstime.com:** Diego Calvi. **280 Alamy Stock Photo:** Indiascapes (bl); Yogesh More (cla). **The Cleveland Museum Of Art:** Gift of Pamela Elizabeth Ward in loving memory of her parents, William E. and Evelyn Svec Ward (br). **Dreamstime.com:** Sathies Kumar (bc). **281 Alamy Stock Photo:** Medium Format Collection / Balan Madhavan (b); Yogesh More (tl); The History Collection (tr). **282 Alamy Stock Photo:** Matteo Omied / Shaukat Khan, Mehboob Studios (r); Dinodia Photos / Shapoorji & Pallonji Group, Deepesh Salgia, Vidhya Binoy (l). **284-285 Getty Images:** Arun Sankar / AFP.

Endpaper images: *Front and Back:* **Alamy Stock Photo:** Zvonimir Atleti.